ILLUSTRATED DICTIONARY OF BUILDING

ILLUSTRATED DICTIONARY OF
BUILDING

Paul Marsh Dip. Arch., RIBA

Construction Press London and New York

Construction Press
an imprint of:
Longman Group Limited
Longman House, Burnt Mill, Harlow
Essex CM20 2JE, England
Associated companies throughout the world

A division of Longman Group Limited, London

Published in the United States of America
by Longman Inc., New York

First published 1982
Reprinted 1984, 1985

British Library Cataloguing in Publication Data
Marsh, Paul H.
Illustrated dictionary of building.
1. Construction industries – Dictionaries
I. Title
338.4'769 HD9715.A2
ISBN 0–86095–848–5

Library of Congress Cataloguing in Publication Data

Marsh, Paul Hugh
Illustrated dictionary of building.

1. Building – Dictionaries. I. Title.
TH9.M32 690'.03'21 81-12522
ISBN 0-86095-848-5 AACR2

Produced by Longman Singapore Publishers (Pte) Ltd.
Printed in Singapore.

PREFACE

Because building is essentially a conservative industry its present-day terminology is still a curious mixture of words derived from the traditional building crafts (and which therefore are often subject to regional variations) and scientific terms introduced as building has moved towards its greater contemporary sophistication.

In assembling a dictionary such as this, the major problem has been one of selection. What should be omitted? What should be included? Which old-fashioned words can be safely left out? Which regional terms are still sufficiently well-known to warrant inclusion? Such judgements have, of necessity, to be subjective; and there are grey areas where decisions are very difficult.

The aim, however, has been to produce a practical reference work which is reasonably comprehensive, while remaining still of manageable size and with relevance to what goes on on a building site today. It does not include archaic terms which have ceased to be commonly used on the site or in the architect's office; it equally omits the too-highly specialized scientific expressions which may, on rare occasions, appear in treatises on building research.

The hope is that the dictionary will be a useful book for any one involved in the business of building, from the architect to the site foreman, from the building or architectural student to the quantity surveyor or his secretary.

Entries are listed alphabetically using the 'letter-by-letter' method – thus, for example: airborne noise; air bottle; air brick; . . . air-conditioning; . . . high-build paint; high-lighting; high pressure mercury vapour lamp. Cross-references to other entries are indicated by the use of **bold** type within the definition. Illustrations appear as near as possible to the corresponding entry; numerical references on them relate to the alternatives given within the definition.

Paul Marsh
February 1982

A

abatement The amount by which timber is reduced in size by the action of working it, by sawing or planing, to achieve the wrought size.

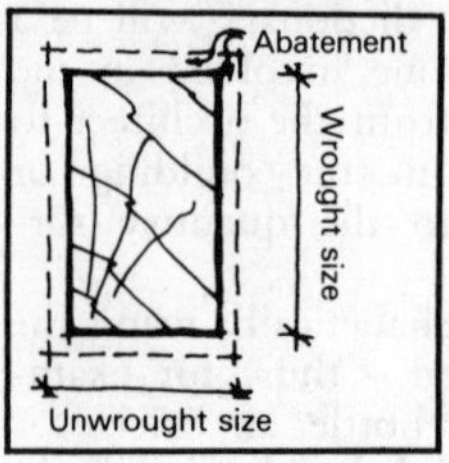

abrasion resistance The property of a material or finish which gives it a resistance to that wear which is caused by friction.

abrasive A hard material, usually in the form of powder, grit or small stones, used to shape, clean or smooth the surface of a material, or to sharpen tools. Artificial abrasives include **carborundum** and powdered glass; natural abrasives include emery, quartz or flint sand. An abrasive is most effective when it is only slightly harder than the surface being treated. Masonry and brick are often abraded by using a piece of similar material.

abrasive blasting Subjecting a material to a jet of air under pressure, charged with sand, grit or other abrasive particles in order to clean the surface of the material (as in the case of metals) or to remove the top layer of the surface (as in the case of concrete, in order to expose the aggregate).

abrasive tool A tool such as a file, a rasp or a sandpaper block, used to abrade a material.

ABS See **acrylonitrile butadiene styrene**.

absolute pressure Pressure measured from absolute zero, *ie* from a complete vacuum. It equals the algebraic sum of the atmospheric pressure and the gauge pressure.

absolute viscosity The resistance to flow, being measured as the tangential force on the unit area of either of two parallel planes, at unit distance apart and having the space between filled with the fluid in question, caused by one of those planes moving at unit velocity in its own plane relative to the other. The unit of measurement is the poise, or centipoise (0.01 poise).

absorbency The capacity of a substance to take in liquid by chemical or molecular action. cf. **absorption**.

absorptance The ratio of the energy (light or heat) absorbed by a surface to that which is incident upon the surface. cf. **absorptivity**.

absorption The act of a solid or a liquid taking in radiation, or of a solid taking in liquid, resulting in: (a) the reduction in intensity of the radiation passing through the matter; (b) the dampening of sound waves passing through the matter; (c) the retention of liquid absorbed by the matter (expressed as a percentage increase in weight of the (originally) dry material after immersion for a stated period).

absorption factor A percentage factor which expresses how much light is absorbed by a substance (*eg* 10% of the light which falls on the substance is absorbed).

absorption rate See **absorptivity**.

absorptivity Of solar radiation, the ratio of the thermal radiation absorbed by a surface to that which is incident upon the surface. cf. **absorptance**.

abstracting The act of collecting together the various related activities involved in a contract preparatory to drawing up a **Bill of Quantities**.

abut To adjoin or meet. cf. **butt**.

abutment 1. The meeting end to end; that place of junction. 2. The pier, wall, etc. of an arch which resists the thrust or lateral pressure (cf. **arch**) or bridge. 3. The junction of an inclined roof surface and a wall rising above it.

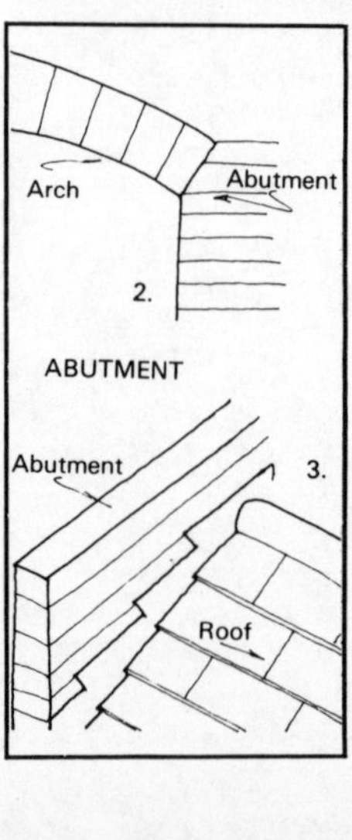

abutment cheek The surface which receives the thrust from the shoulder of a tenon. cf. **mortise**.

abutment piece (USA) A **sill** or **sole plate**.

abutting tenon Two tenons abutting each other end on in one mortise, which they enter from opposite sides.

accelerated test A test devised to simulate the long-term effects of ageing or wear, etc. on a material in a shorter period of time.

accelerator 1. A chemical, such as calcium chloride ($CaCl_2$), used in small quantities to speed up the setting and hardening of cement in a mortar or concrete mix. cf. **additive, admixture**. 2. An inorganic salt added to anhydrous calcium sulphate to produce a wall plaster. 3. In the case of **adhesives** and **sealants**, a **hardener** or catalyst which, when mixed with **synthetic resin**, increases the rate of hardening. It can be mixed with the adhesive or sealant, or applied separately to one side of the joint whilst the resin is applied to the other side, action then taking place when the two are brought together under pressure. 4. A pump for inducing the flow of water through a wet **central heating** system; particularly in **small-, mini-**, or **micro-bore** systems.

access eye An opening in a drain to allow the pipe to be rodded (hence its alternative name of **rodding eye**). It is usually positioned at a change of direction of the drain and is closed by a plate bolted into position.

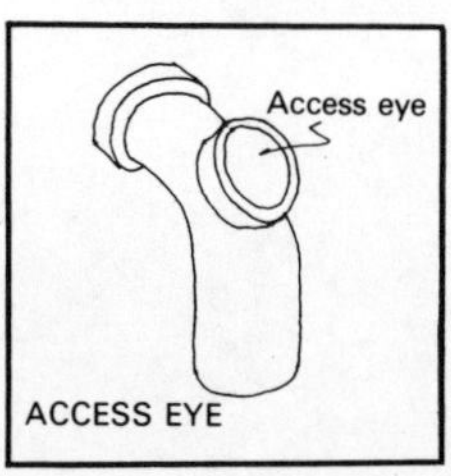

access gully A **gully** in a drainage system which has a removable access plate to allow inspection of the drain and rodding.

access plate A plate bolted to the side of a tank or in similar locations on a hot-water system, or internal drainage system, which allows inspection and remedial action in the case of the system becoming blocked. Similar plates are used on some external drainage fittings, such as **inspection eyes** and **access gullies.**

acetal resin A thermoplastic material derived from the polymerization of formaldehyde as sole or principal monomer.

acid-proof brick Salt-glazed fire bricks, or vitrified bricks containing a high percentage of true clay.

acid resistant paint A paint designed to be resistant to attack by strong acids, such as sulphuric acid. The term is of little value unless linked to a standard of performance.

acid treatment 1. The removal of the **laitance** and cement face on a concrete element, by means of acid, to expose the aggregate. 2. The etching of glass, by means of acid, to form a patterned or obscured surface.

acoustic clip A clip, incorporating a sound absorbent pad, which is built into a suspended concrete floor slab and used to hold the battens supporting timber flooring (cf. **floor clip**); particularly used on a **separating floor** between flats.

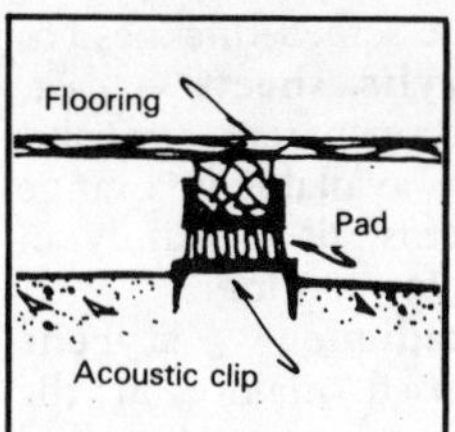

acoustic construction A structure which reduces sound levels at source and is used to impede the passage of **airborne noise** and **impact sound transmission** by means of its surfaces, its **discontinuous construction** or its density.

acoustic fibre board A low density **fibre board** which has a low reflectancy of sound waves. Its absorption of sound is sometimes improved by means of perforations, which penetrate only the outer layers of the material on the face side.

acoustic plaster A special plaster with a porous and usually textured surface which absorbs a high proportion of the sound incident upon it.

acoustic reduction factor See **sound reduction factor**.

acoustic tile A tile made of highly sound-absorbent material, often with a perforated or heavily textured surface, used particularly on ceilings and in suspended ceiling systems and occasionally on walls, to reduce the reverberation in a room; usually manufactured from fibre board, mineral board or cork.

acoustic transmission factor See **sound transmission coefficient**.

acoustics The science of sound, particularly its transmission within buildings.

acrylate copolymer A rapidly drying paint coating for interior or exterior use depending on the added pigments. It is resistant to alkalis and can be applied to damp surfaces without danger of breakdown. It cannot, however, withstand **efflorescence**.

acrylic/PVC alloy A synthesis of acrylic and PVC plastic to combine the impact resistance of PVC with the weathering and transparency properties of acrylic. It is used to produce shatter-proof glazing.

acrylics A group of plastics, the best known member of which is Perspex. They are used in various forms including: (a) **acrylic emulsion mixes** – these are added to sand/cement screed mixes in a proportion of 10–20% of the cement weight to provide greater adhesion of the screed to the subfloor and greater resilience and resistance to cracking, allowing the screed thickness to be reduced; (b) **acrylic sheets** – cast, flat or corrugated, transparent, translucent, or opaque sheets available in a range of colours and patterns; used mainly in the transparent form for roofing.

acrylonitrile butadiene styrene (ABS) A plastic used mainly in the form of pipes in chemical, pharmaceutical and food installations where good impact resistance (even at temperatures as low as −40 °C) and non-toxicity are required. It is also used extensively for domestic cold water services and waste systems, but is not suitable for persistent high temperature applications, such as domestic hot water or central heating systems.

action In mechanics, a term used to describe the effect of forces or loads. A force acting in opposition to another force is referred to as a reaction. When the reaction equals the force a condition of equilibrium is said to exist.

activated sludge Aerated sewage used in the purification of untreated sewage.

activator A substance added in small quantities to another to promote activity; for instance, the addition of silver or copper to zinc sulphate in paints promotes luminescence.

activity An action, operation or process consuming time and possibly other resources. It is represented on programme networks either by an arrow or a node. cf. **activity-on-arrow network**, **activity-on-node network**.

activity-on-arrow network A visual representation of a group of inter-related activities in which the activities are represented by arrows, the length of the arrow not necessarily being related to the duration of the activity. cf. **activity-on-node network**.

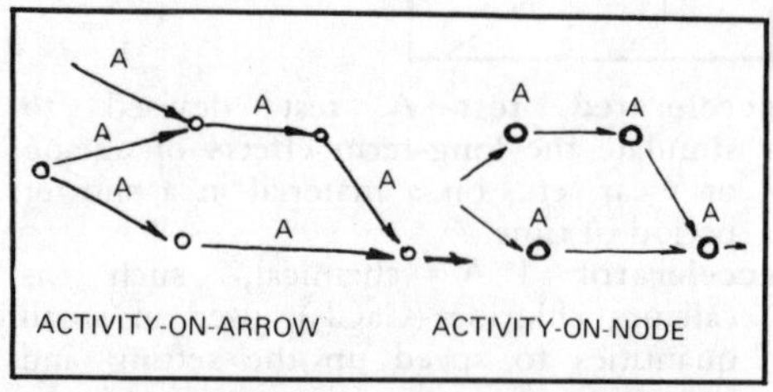

activity-on-node network A visual representation of a group of inter-related activities in which the nodes of the network represent the activities. cf. **activity-on-arrow network**.

activity sampling A method of determining the frequency of a particular activity or delay. The technique depends on making a large number of observations over a given period of time of a worker or a group of workers, machines or processes, and recording precisely what is happening at the instant of observation. From an analysis of the recordings a statistical assessment can be made of the frequency of particular happenings.

actual capacity 1. In plumbing, the capacity of a cistern up to the water line. 2. The volume of the contents of a completely filled tank or cylinder.

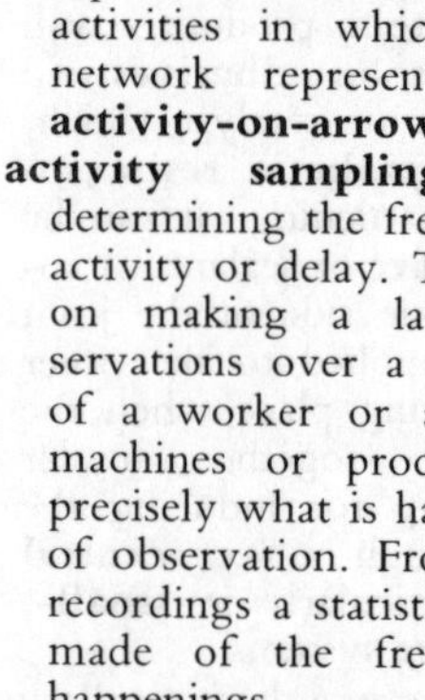

adaptation period The time taken for the eye to adjust from one set of lighting conditions to another.

adaptor 1. An electrical accessory used to make contact between the terminals of a socket outlet or a lampholder and terminals of a different size or type on a piece of electrical equipment, or to connect two or more pieces of equipment to one electricity supply point. 2. A fitting used in making a joint between a steel tube and a copper pipe, or between a steel tube and a plastic pipe.

additive In concrete or plaster, a chemical added in a small quantity to the binder to alter the properties of the mix or the pattern of hardening. cf. **admixture**.

addling A defect in rendering when the render coat falls off the wall due either to a lack of adhesion with the structure, or to the use of a weak undercoat in combination with a strong finishing coat.

adherend That which is adhered. A component which is connected to one or more other components by the use of an adhesive.

adhesion 1. The state in which two surfaces are held together by interfacial forces as opposed to mechanical keys. This can be produced by the use of a glue or mortar, depending on the adherends. cf. **bond**. 2. The attachment between a film of paint or varnish and the ground on which it has been placed.

adhesive A substance capable of maintaining a surface bond between two or more components of similar or dissimilar materials.

adhesive seal A seal, made by the use of a non-setting compound applied either by hand or gun, to prevent the penetration of air or water into a building at the junction between adjoining units in the outer shell – often referred to as a **mastic seal**.

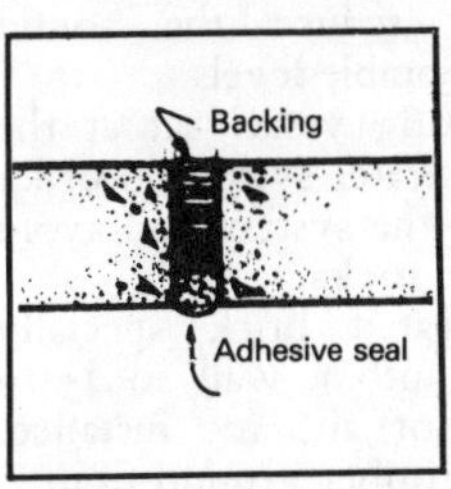

adjunct spring A spring door closer in which the spring is housed in a metal cylinder, pivoted to a plate fixed to the door frame. The cylinder is fitted with a small roller which runs on a metal plate fixed on the surface of the door.

admittance A measure of the ability of a construction to admit heat, expressed in the same units as **thermal transmittance** (W/m^2 °C)

admixture A chemical added in a small quantity to a concrete, mortar or plaster mix to change its properties or pattern of hardening. cf. **accelerator**, **additive**, **plasticizer**, **air-entraining agent**.

adobe Unburnt, sunbaked blocks about 100 × 450 × 300 mm, containing reinforcement in the form of chopped straw. They are still used in parts of Central America, Australia and some areas of the Middle East. They are noted for their excellent thermal insulation characteristics.

adze-eye hammer A claw hammer.

aerated concrete (**autoclaved aerated concrete**) A lightweight concrete without coarse **aggregate**, consisting of cement, lime and sand, with the addition of a small quantity of aluminium powder which causes a chemical reaction, releasing bubbles of hydrogen (later replaced by air) and producing a cellular consistency. Subsequent autoclaving results in the formation of tri-calcium silicate crystals. The concrete is of low strength but good thermal insulating properties. It is easily cut with a saw and is nailable. There are many grades of aerated concrete, some of which are unsuitable for use below ground level. Water absorption may impair its thermal performance.

aerobic bacteria In sewage treatment, the bacteria present in the filter bed, which require air to survive. The **filter bed** usually succeeds settlement tanks in which anaerobic bacteria have commenced the breakdown of the sewage. cf. **anaerobic bacteria**.

A-frame A structural frame based on two inclined members which meet at their heads, their feet being restrained from moving apart by a horizontal tie member at some position up the incline.

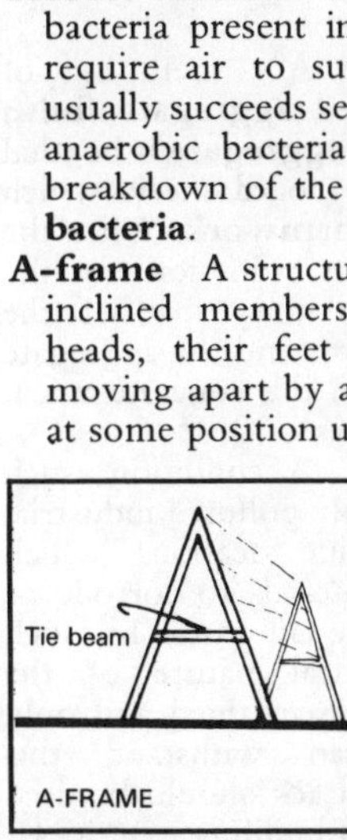

after-flush The small quantity of water that remains in the cistern when a w.c. pan is flushed and which subsequently trickles down to remake the seal.

age hardening One of the changes in the properties of certain materials, that occurs over a period of time; such as the increase in hardness and in tensile strength and the reduction in ductility after the solution treatment and quenching of most heat-treatable alloys – which is substantially complete in four or five days. Often referred to as natural ageing when it takes place at normal temperatures. cf. **artificial ageing**.

aggregate The broken stone, slag, gravel or sand which forms the substantial part of concrete, plaster, mortar, asphalt and tarmacadam. **Coarse aggregate** used for concrete will be retained by a screen with 5 mm square holes, while **fine aggregate** (or sand) will pass through.

aggregate finish See **exposed aggregate finish**.

aggregate plywood **Plywood** coated with an epoxy resin into which mineral chippings of various colours and sizes are bonded to provide an external decorative finish; used for external walls, infill panels, fascias etc.

AGGREGATE PLYWOOD

aggregate transfer A method of obtaining an **exposed aggregate finish** to concrete. Selected **aggregate** is bonded to plywood or fibre board sheets which are used to line the **formwork**. When the concrete has set, its adhesion to the aggregate is greater than that of the aggregate to the board, and the aggregate remains embedded in the concrete when the formwork is struck.

aggressive condition A condition, such as that found in heavily polluted industrial atmospheres or marine locations, which encourages some materials to corrode or otherwise deteriorate in use. In such locations the chemical nature of the pollution should be ascertained and only materials which can withstand this particular chemical attack should be used in the construction of building exteriors.

Agrément Board An independent body set up in 1966 under Government sanction to test and assess innovative building materials and techniques submitted to it by manufacturers on a voluntary basis. Suitability for a particular purpose is indicated by the award of an **Agrément Certificate**. The Agrément Board restricts its activities to new materials and techniques, or new uses for existing ones. It has close working associations with the **British Standards Institution** (**BSI**) and the **Building Research Establishment** (**BRE**) but is independent of both. It is a member of the European Union for Agrément, thus achieving a measure of acceptability abroad for certified products.

Agrément Certificate A certificate issued by the **Agrément Board** for a new building product or technique which has been found, after test, to be satisfactory for a particular purpose. Each certificate is the outcome of an independent assessment of the finished quality of a product, its method of manufacture and its performance in particular applications, following a programme of appropriate tests.

agricultural drain A drain composed of unsocketed, unglazed earthenware pipes laid end to end without any jointing material; used to drain the subsoil.

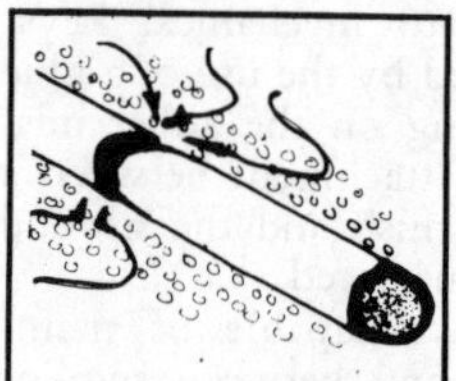
AGRICULTURAL DRAIN

airborne noise Sound having its source as sound waves in the air, as opposed to **impact noise** which is structure-borne; to prevent the passage of such sound from one room or property to another, the separating structure has to be sufficiently well insulated to reduce the sound transmission to acceptable levels.

air bottle A collecting vessel set at the high point of a hot water system in order to collect any air in the system and avoid the formation of **air locks**.

air brick A perforated brick specially made for building into a wall so as to allow the passage of air, for instance, below a suspended timber ground floor.

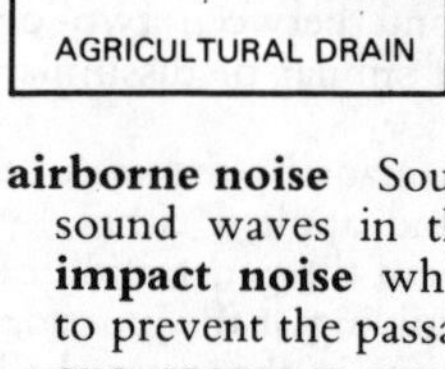
AIR BRICK

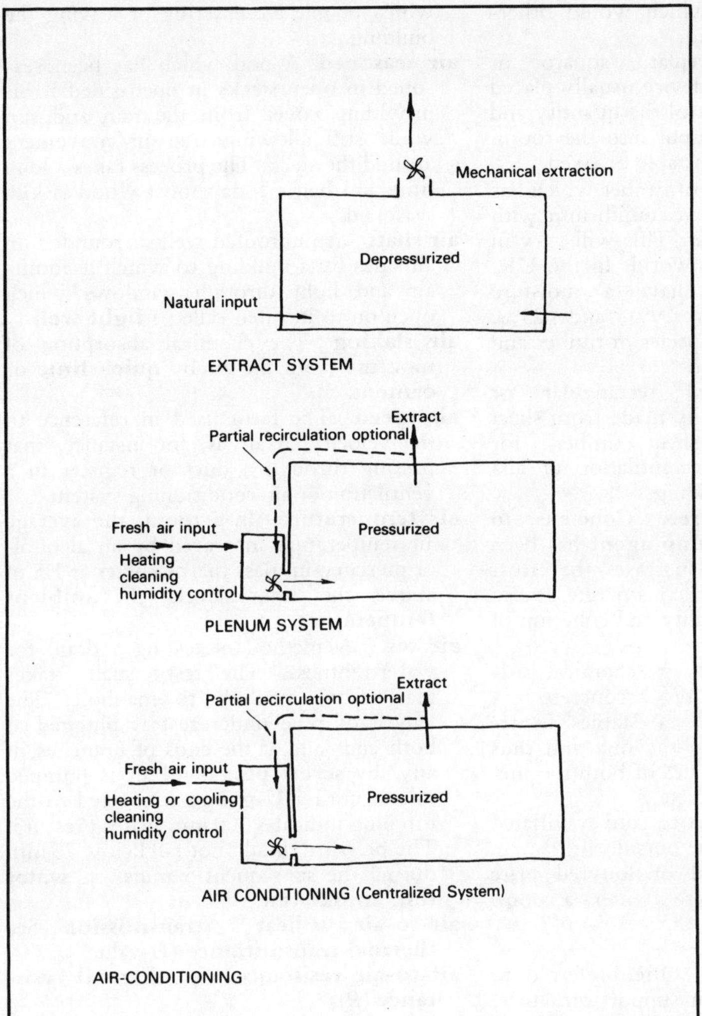

air brush A small **spray gun** used for painting.

air change A quantity of air equal to the volume of a room, which periodically has to be supplied to that room in order to keep it adequately ventilated. The number of air changes that will be required per hour will depend on the nature and location of the room and on its occupancy.

air cock A key-operated valve which allows trapped air to escape from hot-water fittings, such as radiators, in the event of an **air lock**.

air-conditioning The production and maintenance of an internal environment in which the temperature and the freshness, cleanliness and humidity of the air is fully controlled. It differs from some systems of **mechanical ventilation** in that the air which is introduced into the building can, if necessary, be cooled as well as heated. The system can consist of either a centralized system with a central plant and distribution ducting, or a series of unit air-conditioners, one or more serving each room. cf. **ventilation**.

air-cooled slag A dense **blast furnace slag** which can be used in road construction or as an aggregate in concrete.

air curtain A forceful downward current of warm air produced by a motorized fan unit designed to be positioned over large permanently open entrances, as in department stores and loading bays, to dissipate the cold air which would otherwise enter the building.

air diffuser A circular, square or rectangular terminal device usually placed in the ceiling, to control the quantity and direction of the air input into the room. Diffusers may be adjustable or fixed.

air-dry A description of timber which has a **moisture content** in equilibrium with that of the ambient air. This will vary in different parts of the world. In the UK, air-dry timber can have a moisture content of between 19% and 23%, depending upon the species of timber and the prevailing weather.

air-duct An enclosed rectangular or circular passage, usually made from sheet metal, plastic or sheet timber, for conveying air in the ventilation or air-conditioning of a building.

air entrained concrete Concrete to which an **air entraining agent** has been added, usually to increase the frost resistance of the hardened concrete. It also improves the workability and cohesion of the mix.

air entraining agent A chemical **admixture** introduced into a concrete mix in order to produce a stable dispersion of air bubbles in the mix and thus change the characteristics of both the mix and the resultant concrete.

air flue A vertical duct to convey vitiated air from a room to the outside air.

air grating A slotted or louvred plate over an **air-duct** where it enters a room. cf. **register**.

air gun A **spray gun**.

air-inflated structure Often referred to as an air house or air-support structure, this may be any one of three types of structure: (a) A single-skin inflatable structure with semi-circular cross section, maintained in an erect position by an internal air pressure created by fans, and entered through an air-lock; (b) A double-wall unit in which stiffness is given to the structure by air pressure between the inner and outer walls; (c) A single-skin structure supported on a series of tubes which are inflated through a Schrader-type valve.

air inlet A valve with a mica flap to allow fresh air into a drainage system without letting foul air escape; now rarely used.

air lock 1. The stoppage of the flow of water in a hot water system due to the presence of a bubble of air trapped in it. 2. (USA) **weather strip**. 3. A system of double doors to avoid the loss of pressure in an **air-inflated structure** whilst people are entering or leaving the building.

air seasoned Wood which has been seasoned in open stacks in open-sided barns providing cover from the rain and sun while still allowing free air movement around the stack. The process takes a long time and hence today most wood is kiln seasoned.

air shaft An unroofed well surrounded on all sides by a building to which it admits air and light through windows which open on to it; often called a **light well**.

air slaking The chemical absorption of moisture from the air by **quick lime** or **cement**.

air speed The term used in reference to the velocity of air as, for instance, that passing through a duct or register in a ventilation or air-conditioning system.

air temperature In a room, the average air temperature measured by an alcohol- or mercury-in-glass thermometer at 1.5 m above the floor level. cf. **ambient temperature.**

air test A method of testing a drain for watertightness. The test usually takes place from manhole to manhole. The length of pipe under test is plugged at both ends and at the ends of branches, if any, by **screw plugs** and air is pumped into it until a **U-gauge** connected to the top plug indicates 100 mm water pressure. The pressure should not fall below 75 mm during the subsequent 5 mins. cf. **water test**, **smoke test**.

air-to-air heat transmission See **thermal transmittance** (*U*-value).

air-to-air resistance See **thermal resistance** (*R*).

air washer A chamber in an **air-conditioning** system in which air is cleaned by being passed through water sprays or over wet plates which remove dust and smells.

alarm call point The position at which a device is installed for the manual operation of an electrical alarm system (usually a fire alarm system).

alarm control and indicating equipment A combination of fire alarm control equipment and fire alarm indicating equipment.

alignment Arrangement in a straight line.

alkali A chemical, such as potash, soda or lime, which neutralizes acids. Small quantities increase the fusibility of fire-clays.

alkaline hardness The presence of dissolved salts (calcium or magnesium) in water, causing so-called 'hardness'. The formation of scale is the result of the precipitation of these salts in a water system where the water is heated to a temperature below atmospheric boiling point (such as low pressure hot water heating systems, or domestic hot-water supply systems). It can be removed by treatment with hydrated lime (calcium hydroxide). The salts also react with soap, preventing it from lathering easily.

alkali resistance A property required of those materials which come into contact with alkalis, and particularly of paint applied to new concrete, brickwork or plaster, the lime in which can break down the oil in the paintwork (cf. **saponification**). An alkali resistant primer should be used to protect subsequent coats of paint. Many synthetic resins have alkali resistance.

alkyd A synthetic resin used as a **binder** for **emulsion paint**.

alkyd moulding material A material suitable for moulding, based on a thermosetting unsaturated polymeric ester, normally an alkyd resin or a polyester. The term **alkyd** has a different meaning in the paint industry.

alkyd resin A synthetic resin made by the condensation of polyhydric alcohol, such as glycerol or pentaerythritol, with a polybasic acid, such as phthalic acid. This is used in paint manufacture.

alkyd resin paint A pigmented solution of an alkyd resin, modified by combination with a vegetable oil or fatty acid.

alligator wrench A **pipe wrench** with serrated jaws.

all-in aggregate Aggregate for concrete making which contains all sizes of **aggregate**, from the maximum nominal size specified downwards (*ie* from **coarse aggregate** to **fine aggregate**).

allowable bearing pressure The maximum allowable load at the base of a foundation which will not produce a settlement movement that is likely to distress the superstructure and cause cracking. It is a function of the properties of the site subsoil and the capacity of the superstructure to accept settlement.

allowable load The maximum load which may be applied with safety to a structural member, taking into account the strength of the member, the strength of its bearing surface (or the material of construction of such bearing surface) and a factor of safety. In the case of a pile, the allowable load would be the load which could be safely applied after allowing for the pile's ultimate bearing capacity, negative friction, pile spacing and the bearing capacity of the subsoil.

alloy A mixture of two or more metals to achieve desirable properties, *eg* bronze is an alloy of copper and tin. Sometimes a non-metal is introduced.

altazimuth A surveying instrument based on a telescope and used for measuring altitudes and **azimuths**.

alternating current (ac) Electrical current which flows first in one direction, then in the opposite direction (*ie* positive to negative, then negative to positive) in regular cyclic curves, increasing and decreasing in flow on either side of zero. cf. **direct current**.

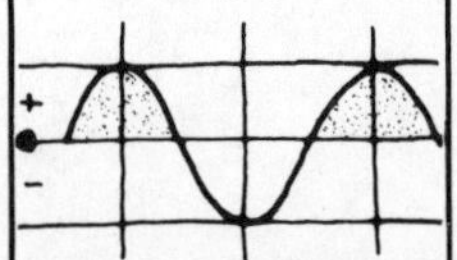

ALTERNATING CURRENT

alum A mineral salt used to control the setting of plaster.

alumina Oxide of aluminium; found, for instance, as the chief constituent of all clays.

aluminium (alloy) Aluminium to which other elements have been added in small amounts to improve the properties of the pure metal for specific building uses. (Pure aluminium is not used in building). All aluminium alloys are light weight, and fall into two categories – cast and wrought alloys – each category containing both non-heat-treatable and heat-treatable alloys. Some additives are: manganese and magnesium – to increase the strength while still retaining the corrosion resistance of the pure metal; silicon – to increase the strength and improve the casting properties while reducing the corrosion resistance; copper – to increase the strength while considerably reducing the corrosion resistance; zinc – to increase the strength significantly.

aluminium foil Aluminium sheet that is thinner than 0.15 mm and which reflects both light and heat rays. Hence it is used, often backed by **Kraft paper**, in thermal insulating constructions. Because of its resistance to the passage of water vapour it is often used as a **vapour barrier**, bonded to the back of plasterboard sheets.

aluminium paint Paint made from aluminium powder. Used chiefly on metalwork – it protects steel against corrosion; it can also be used wherever a paint of particular durability is required. It can be used on asbestos cement.

ambient temperature The prevailing temperature of the air surrounding an enclosure or surrounding a person or object. cf. **air temperature**.

Ambrosia Beetle A tunnelling beetle living in logs or live trees (usually when the wood is damaged or unhealthy) and belonging to the families Platypodidae and Scolytidae. Its tunnels are about 3 mm in diameter.

American bond Brick walling (known in the UK as **English garden wall bond**) in which all courses are **stretchers**, except the fifth, sixth or seventh course, which is a **header** course. Also known as common bond in the USA.

AMERICAN BOND

aminoplastic resin See **amino resin**.

amino resin A synthetic resin of the thermosetting type made from the reaction of urea, thiourea, melamine or allied compounds usually with formaldehyde. It is usually cured by stoving and is often blended with other resins to make paint for metal articles. It can be cured chemically at air temperature.

ammeter An instrument for measuring the force of an electric current.

ampere A unit of electrical current. One ampere (A) is that current which would produce a force equal to 2×10^{-7} N/m between two straight parallel conductors of infinite length and negligible circular cross section, placed 1 m apart in a vacuum.

amplitude The maximum extent of vibration or oscillation from a position of equilibrium. In the case of sound, the maximum vibration of a particle; in the case of electric current, the maximum

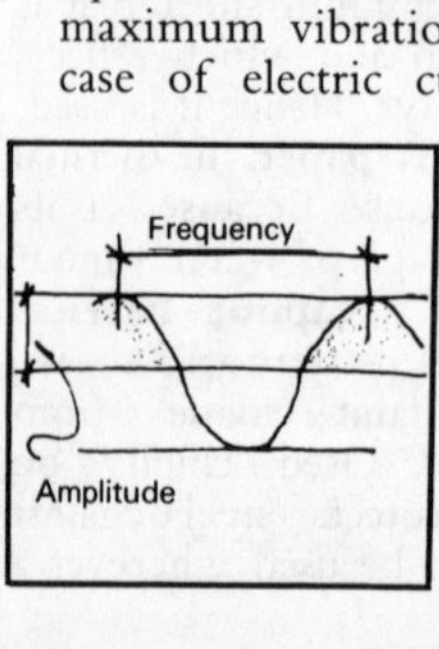

departure from the average of **alternating current (AC)**.

amyl acetate A solvent with a strong pear-like smell, used in cellulose laquers, bronzing fluids and metallic paints.

anaerobic bacteria In sewage treatment the bacteria which, because they require no air to survive, exist in the settlement tank and commence the breaking down of the raw sewage. cf. **aerobic bacteria**.

anaglyptic wallpaper An embossed wall-covering made from a heavy-weight paper.

anchor 1. Any means whereby a fixing is obtained into a masonry mass or base, to support or hold down other elements of structure; **plugs**, **anchor bolts** or **chemical anchors** are included in the definition. 2. In carpentry, the metal straps which hold down roof trusses, frames etc. to supporting walls.

anchorage fixing A fixing which is achieved by means of a device passing through the minor component of an assembly and anchoring into, without completely piercing, the base component. **Plugs, anchor bolts, chemical anchors**, etc. give this type of fixing.

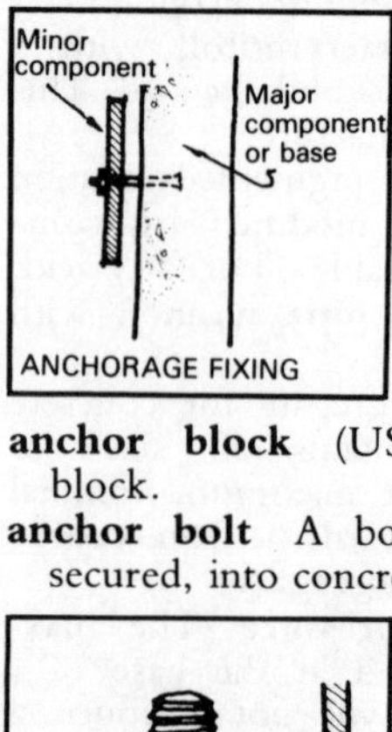

ANCHORAGE FIXING

anchor block (USA) A wood fixing block.

anchor bolt A bolt cast, or otherwise secured, into concrete flooring, a concrete

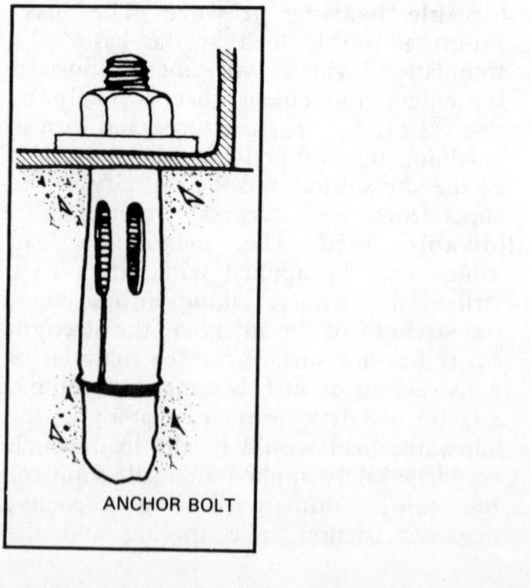
ANCHOR BOLT

foundation or mass walling to hold down, or otherwise secure, a structural part of the building.

anchor plate 1. A perforated metal plate used as a tile in heavy industrial applications, bedded in the concrete floor or screed. The plate is usually about 300 mm square and made of 10 g steel, with lugs on the underside which project down into the concrete. 2. Plates or washers used in connection with an **anchor bolt**.

ancient light A window that has had continuous access to light for at least 20 years and is consequently legally entitled to the continuance of that light, unobstructed by other buildings or structures.

angle bead On external angles of plastered walls, a protective metal strip, or plasterer's permanent **screed**. In the past such angles were carried out as a **hard plaster** rounded corner. A round timber moulding was also used, sometimes enriched and called an angle staff.

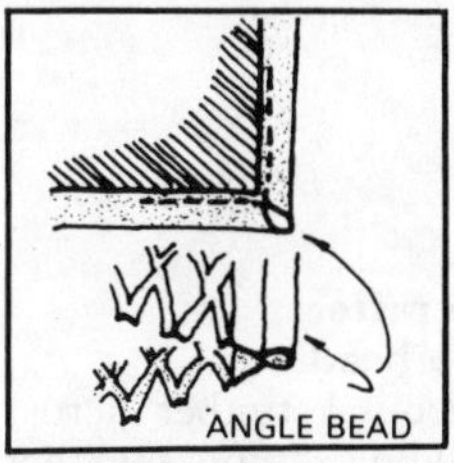

ANGLE BEAD

angle block A small timber block, often in the form of a right-angled triangular prism, glued and pinned into the corner of a frame to stiffen it; particularly used in staircase construction to stop creaking.

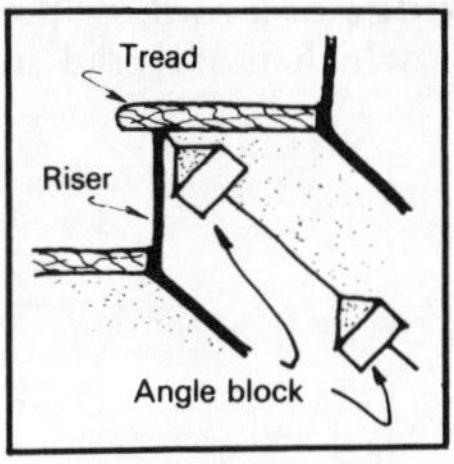

angle board In carpentry a board used as a gauge when planing a piece of timber to a particular angle.

angle brace A tie member fixed across an angle in a frame to make it more rigid. cf. **diagonal brace**.

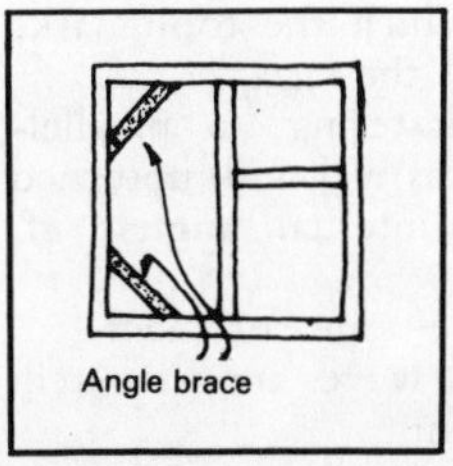

angle bracket An L-shaped bracket, usually projecting from a wall and often used to support a shelf. cf. **angle iron** 2., **gallows bracket**.

angle closer A brick so cut that it may be used to complete the bond at the corner of a wall and continue the bond on the adjacent wall surface.

angle corbel A **corbel plate** bent at right angles to form a ledge on which a heavy building component can be seated. Angle corbels can be gusseted at each end to give greater strength.

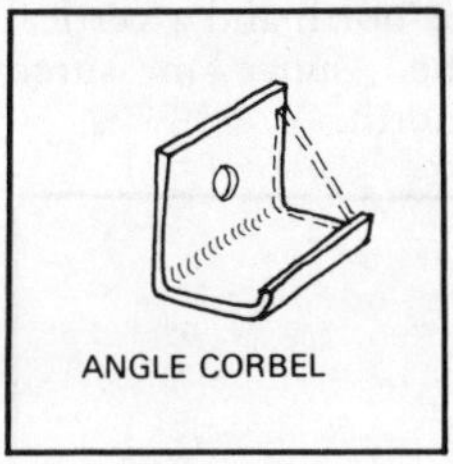

ANGLE CORBEL

angle-drafted margin At the corner of a building, a **drafted margin** which returns around the corner of a **quoin** stone to show drafting on both wall faces.

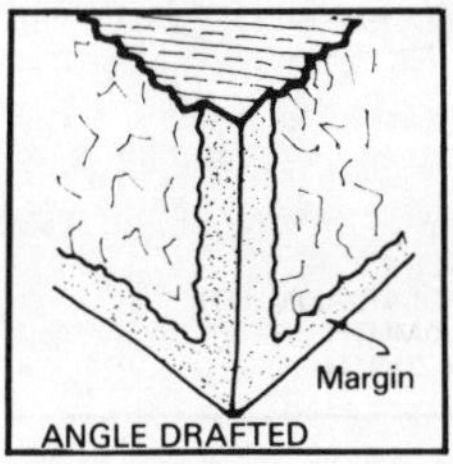

ANGLE DRAFTED

angle float A plasterer's tool for finishing internal corners. cf. **angle trowel**.

angle gauge A template used in setting out work on a building site and in checking angles.

angle iron 1. A standard rolled steel member with an L-shaped cross-section. It may have either equal or unequal legs. 2. An angle bracket, which need not be right-angled, used to reinforce the joint between two timbers meeting at an angle.

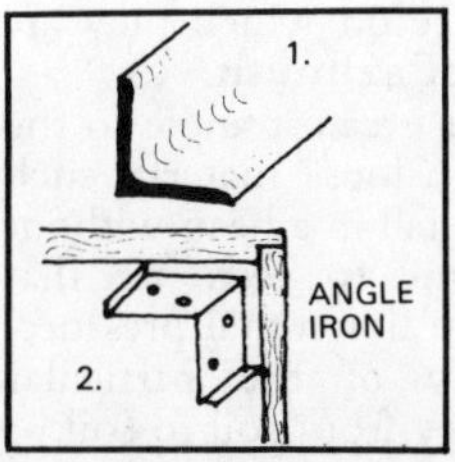

ANGLE IRON

angle joint In carpentry, a joint between two pieces of timber meeting at an angle, as opposed to a **lengthening joint** where they meet end to end.

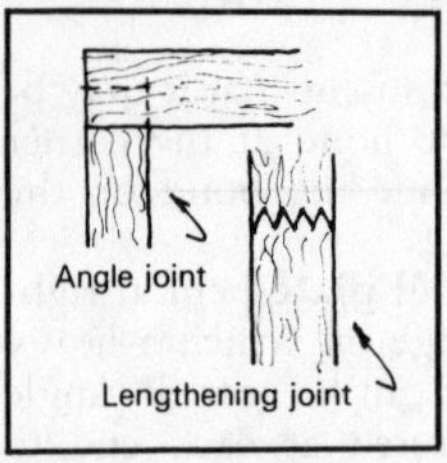

angle of azimuth From a given point, the angle between the north and a vertical plane through the sun, measured clockwise from the north.

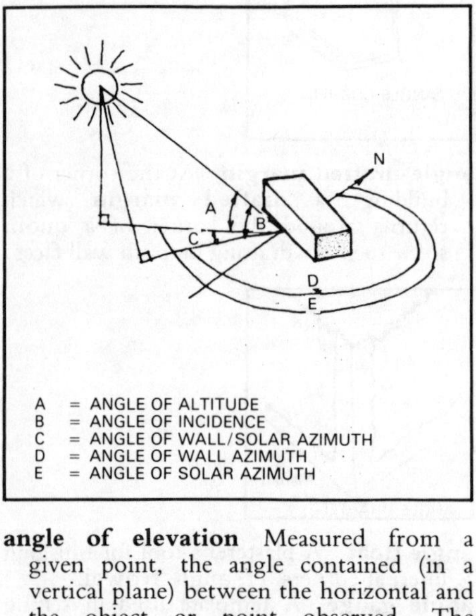

A = ANGLE OF ALTITUDE
B = ANGLE OF INCIDENCE
C = ANGLE OF WALL/SOLAR AZIMUTH
D = ANGLE OF WALL AZIMUTH
E = ANGLE OF SOLAR AZIMUTH

angle of elevation Measured from a given point, the angle contained (in a vertical plane) between the horizontal and the object or point observed. The measurement is used in surveying, and also in reference to the sun to indicate its elevation above the horizon – and therefore the angle of its rays – in relation to a particular building face or window.

angle of friction See **angle of repose**.

angle of incidence The angle at which the sun's rays strike a surface, being the angle contained by those rays and a line normal to the surface on which they are incident. cf. **angle of azimuth**.

angle of repose The greatest angle to the horizontal at which a loose material such as soil, if allowed to fall in a heap without hindrance, will come to rest. At that angle it will exert no horizontal pressure. This is a property of the particular material and will vary from soil to soil.

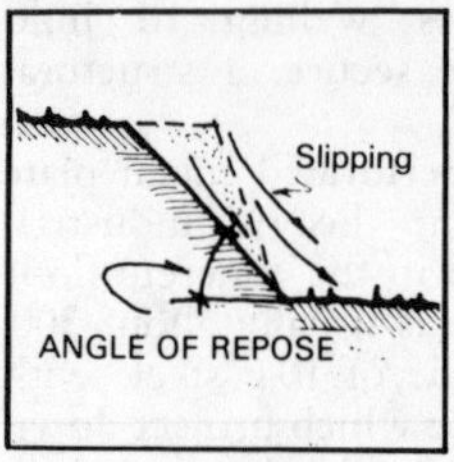

ANGLE OF REPOSE

angle of saw-tooth The angle between the opposing edges (the face and the back) of a **saw-tooth**; usually between 40° and 70°.

angle of wall-solar azimuth The angle between a line perpendicular to a wall and the sun's azimuth. cf. **angle of azimuth**.

angle pier A pier at the meeting of two walls, constructed on the external angle.

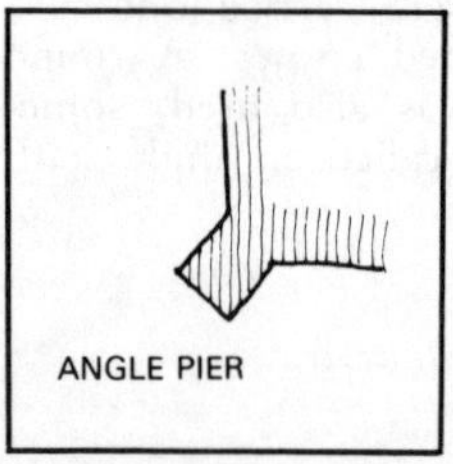

ANGLE PIER

angle rafter See **hip rafter**.

angle staff See **angle bead**.

angle tie 1. A horizontal timber across the corner of a building, tying together the **wall plates** and, where a **dragon beam** is used, also carrying one end of that beam. Sometimes referred to as a dragon tie. 2. An **angle brace**.

angle tile A plain tile shaped to an angle to cover the **hip** or **ridge** of a roof, or the corner of a building which is covered in **tile hanging**.

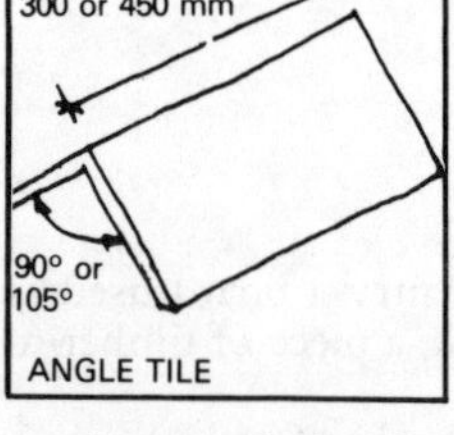

ANGLE TILE

angle tooled (Scotland) The dressed finish of stone in which the tool marks run diagonally across the face.

angle trowel In plastering, a parallel-sided, square-ended trowel with upturned edges for shaping internal angles. cf. **angle float**.

Ångström (Å) The measurement of length in which light waves are measured; 1 Å = 1/10,000,000 mm.

angular hip tile See **angle tile**.
angular ridge tile See **angle tile**.
anhydrite Calcium sulphate ($CaSO_4$) in anhydrous form, which occurs as a natural mineral or may be produced by a chemical process. Anhydrite plaster (sometimes called hardwall plaster) is made from this mineral by mixing with **accelerators**. It is different from **anhydrous gypsum plaster**.
anhydrous Free from water; a term used to describe certain **gypsum plasters** which do not react quickly with water and to which an **accelerator** is added.
anhydrous gypsum plaster ($CaSO_4$) A type of gypsum plaster used as a finishing coat; generally harder than hemihydrate plaster, but less quick to harden. Sometimes it exhibits a double set (an early stiffening followed by a more gradual hardening). **Keene's cement** is a special form of anhydrous plaster. cf. **anhydrite**.
animal glue A strong glue, but one having no resistance to water; manufactured from bones, sinews, skins and hides of animals and prepared by soaking the material for several hours and then heating but not boiling it.
anneal To toughen glass or metal by softening it by heat at a temperature sufficient to cause recrystallization and then cooling it slowly.
annual ring One of the rings seen when the bole of a tree is cut across, each ring indicating one year's growth of the tree. The lighter section of the ring indicates spring growth and the darker section summer growth. The width of a ring gives an indication of the type of weather experienced during that growth year. cf. **cambium.**
annular bit See **hole saw**.
annular nail A nail whose shaft has a series of projecting rings making its withdrawal, once driven home into a fibrous material like timber, more difficult than that of an ordinary nail.
anode The electrode through which direct current enters an **electrolyte** and at which negative ions are discharged, positive ions are formed or other oxidizing reactions occur.
anodic coating A protective, decorative or functional coating of one metal by another using electrolysis.
anodizing A specialized electrochemical process which builds up a natural (but artificially augmented) protective oxide film on the aluminium. This provides increased protection to the metal and the

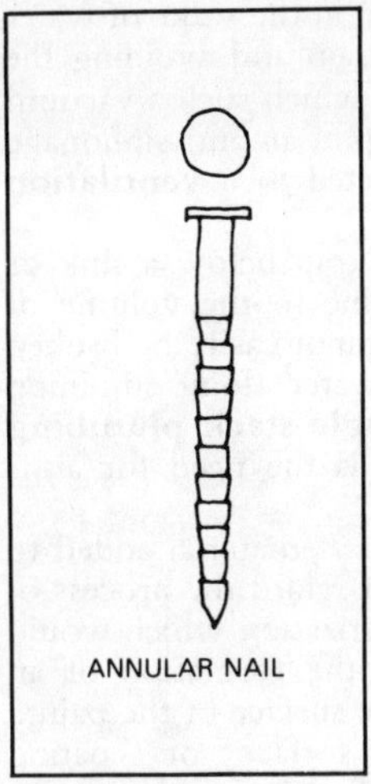
ANNULAR NAIL

film is chemically stable and relatively hard. The treated surface can be dyed.
anti-actinic glass See **heat-absorbing glass**.
anti-condensation paint A paint designed to minimize the effects of condensation in conditions of intermittent humidity. It usually has a matt, textured and absorbent surface and frequently contains a heat insulating filler.
anti-corrosive paint A paint containing corrosion-inhibiting pigments which deter the corrosion of metal surfaces to which the paint is applied.
antimony oxide (Sb_2O_3) A dense white pigment used in paints; also called antimony white.
anti-siphonage pipe An air pipe in a plumbing system which admits air downstream of a water seal in a w.c., sink or washbasin, thus preventing the

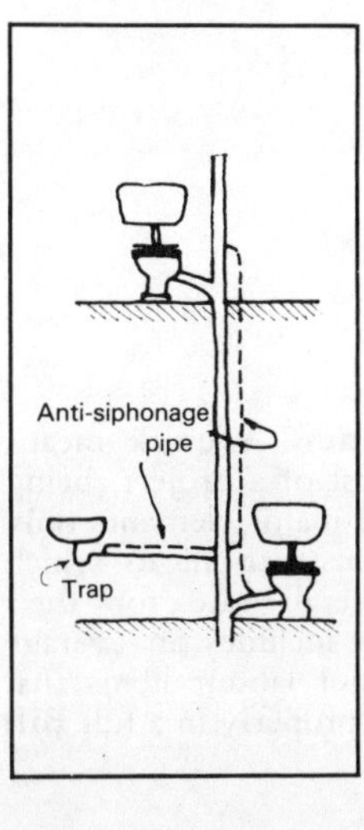

creation of a vacuum in the wake of water flushed down the drain and avoiding the breakage of the seal which such a vacuum could cause. The top of an anti-siphonage pipe may be connected to a **ventilation pipe**.

anti-siphon trap A trap below a sink or washbasin which, due to the volume of water in the seal, cannot easily be broken by the passage of water along adjoining pipes. Its use in **single-stack plumbing systems** often avoids the need for anti-siphonage pipes.

anti-skinning agent A material added to a paint to prevent or retard the process of oxidation or polymerization which would otherwise result in the formation of an insoluble skin on the surface of the paint.

anti-slip finish A surface or coating which, because of its roughness or abrasive character, discourages slipping; materials with an anti-slip finish are often applied to stair **treads** and **nosings**.

anti-splash device 1. A device fitted to the nozzle of a water tap to discourage the discharging water from splashing. 2. Of a floor channel, a block channel in which the curve of the cross-section of the waterway is more than half of a circle, thereby discouraging liquid from spilling over its edges. 3. A **rainwater shoe**.

anti-vibration mounting A device, usually positioned below a piece of machinery, which will absorb or dampen the machine's vibrations, due to the resilience of the material(s) of which it is made.

apex stone The crowning stone of a gable (where it is often called a saddle stone) or a dome or vault. The **keystone** of an arch. cf. **arch**.

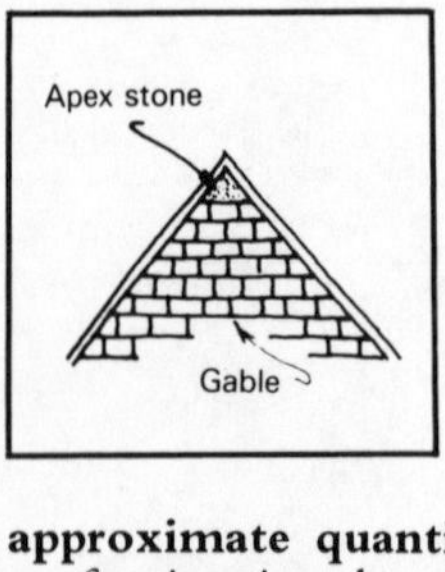

approximate quantities A quick means of estimating the cost of a project, being the quantities of the major elements only of the proposed construction, to which are applied an overall rate for their construction, which includes an average cost for all the minor labour items that would be measured properly in a full **Bill of Quantities**.

apron eaves piece A piece of sheet material usually metal, plastic or asbestos-based, used to provide a watertight edge to the base of an inclined roof and to direct rainwater into the eaves gutter.

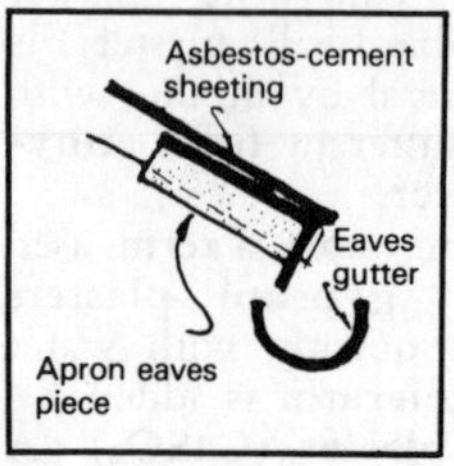

apron flashing A one-piece flashing, usually of metal or plastic or asbestos-based sheet material, used where a vertical surface penetrates an inclined roof. cf. **soaker, stepped flashing**.

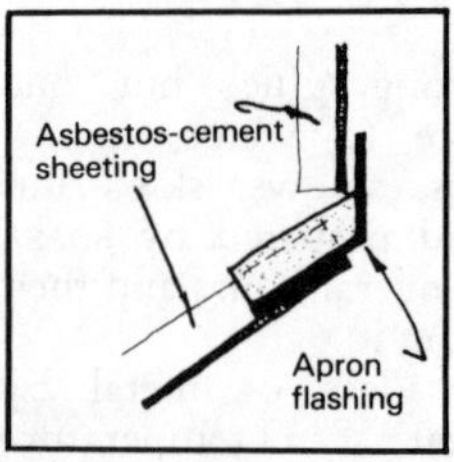

apron wall (USA) A spandrel in a multi-storey building, between the window head on one floor and the window sill on the floor above.

arbitration A method whereby disputes which arise during the course of a building contract can be settled without resorting to action in the courts. Most **forms of contract** stipulate that disputes should be so handled and often define the methods to be employed. Both sides in the dispute argue their case before an independent arbitrator, who is sometimes named in the contract.

arcade 1. A series of arches on the same plane, open or closed, or columns or pilasters. 2. A walkway which is arched over. 3. Any covered pedestrian way with shops on one or both sides.

arch An arrangement of wedge-shaped stones or bricks supporting each other while spanning an opening. The lines of thrust are maintained within the structure, thereby avoiding tension in the masonry or brickwork. Lateral thrust is supported by the **abutments**. Arches today are often formed monolithically in reinforced concrete, but the principles are broadly similar.

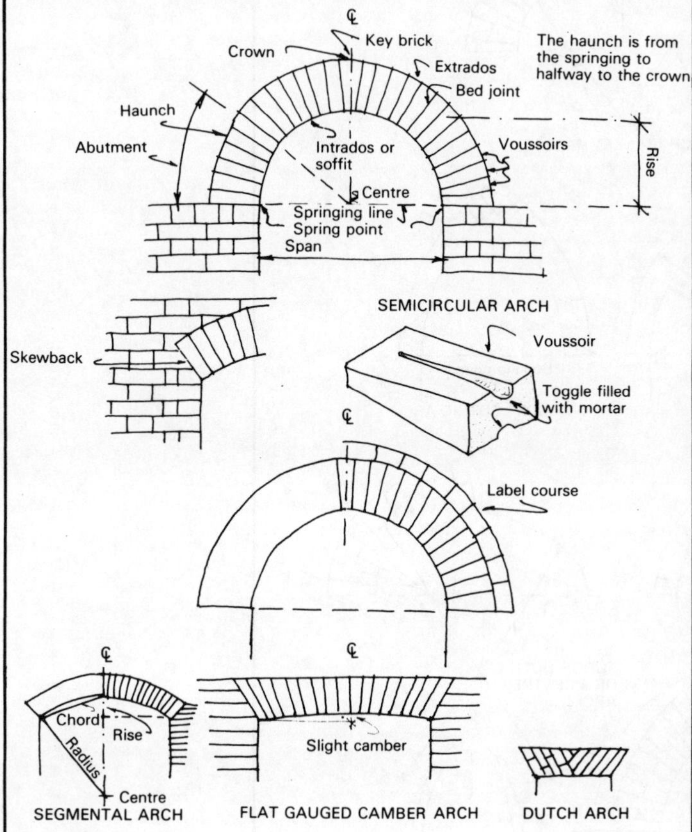

ARCH

arch-brick or voussoir A wedge-shaped brick, usually shaped by rubbing or cutting, and used to construct arches, wells or culverts. Sometimes it is specially made, when it is called a **culvert brick**.

architectural ironmongery Items of ironmongery such as **door furniture** and **window furniture** and such accessories as hat and coat hooks, door stops etc. They need not be made of ferrous metal.

architrave A trim, often of wood, fixed on **grounds** so as to cover the joint between a door or window frame and the adjoining wall finish.

architrave block (or plinth block, or skirting block). A flat-topped block at the foot of an **architrave** which is slightly wider and deeper than the

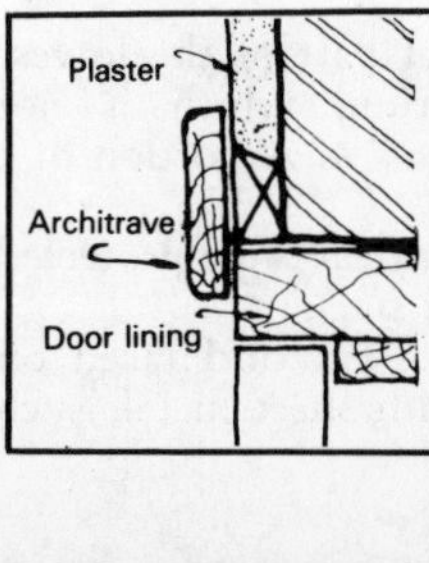

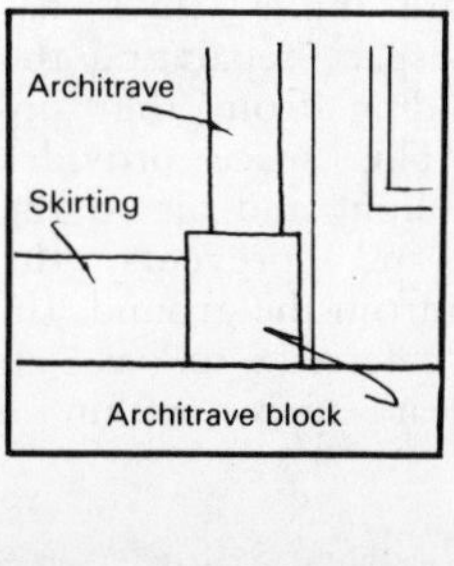

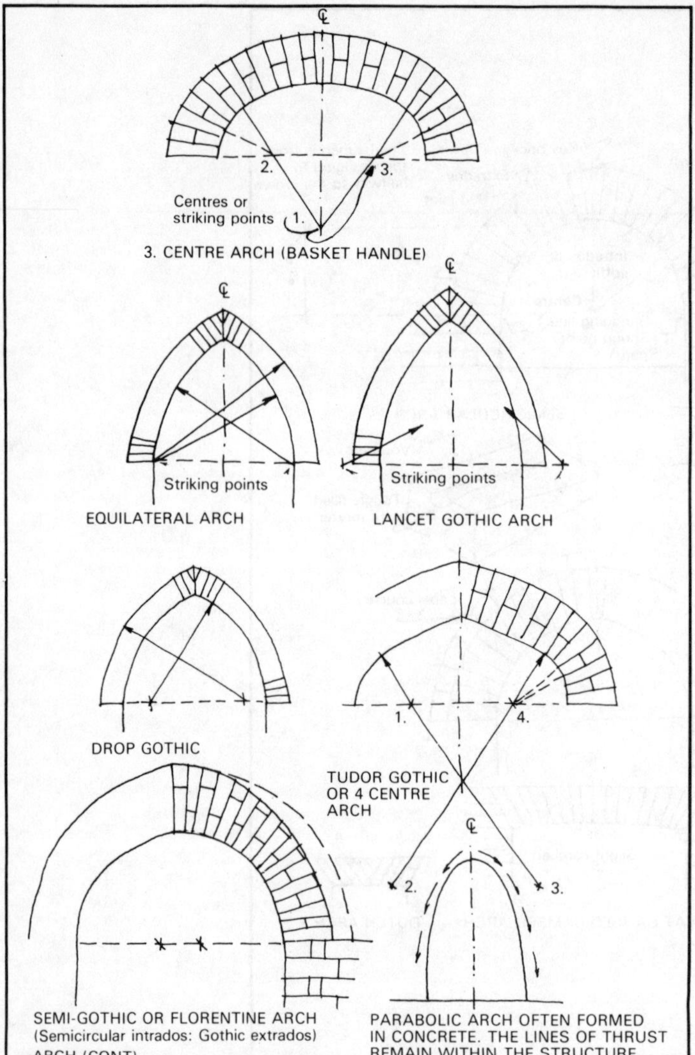

ARCH (CONT)

skirting (board) and against which both the architrave and skirting stop.

arch-stone See **voussoir**.

arcuated Built of arches, rather than of **beams** and **lintels**.

arc welding A method of fusing together metal by means of an electric arc.

area 1. The superficial extent of an internal or external space or a surface expressed in square units (m^2, ha, etc.). 2. A sunken space separating the basement of a building from the surrounding ground. This space provides a means of getting light and air to the basement rooms and prevents the penetration of damp from the ground. (In the USA it is referred to as an areaway). 3. A clear space within a

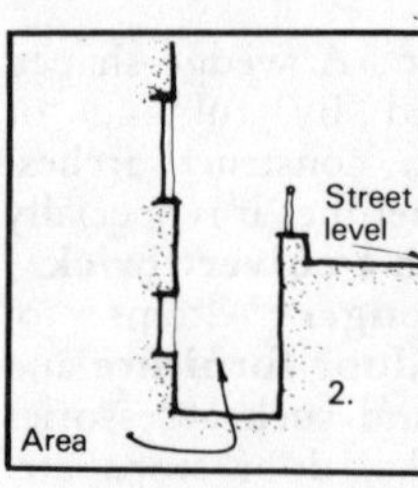

building, such as that part of the lowest floor of an auditorium which is not underneath a balcony. 4. A portion of a surface.

armoured cable Electrical cable protected by a binding of sheet steel.

armoured plywood **Plywood** faced on one or both sides with sheet metal, such as galvanized steel, aluminium or copper.

armour-plate glass Clear **plate** (or **float**) **glass** that has been subjected to heating and sudden cooling, which results in increased mechanical strength and greater resistance to impact and large, sudden temperature variations. When broken, it disintegrates into relatively harmless particles. It should not be cut or worked and is supplied in specific finished sizes.

arris 1. A sharp edge, as of a building material or component. 2. The upper edge of an asphalt skirting.

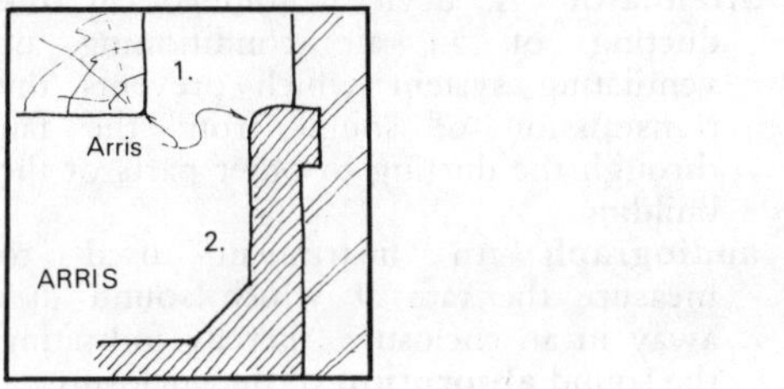

arris fillet A **tilting fillet**.

arris tile An **angle tile**.

arris-wise 1. A term referring to the laying of bricks or tiles diagonally. 2. A term referring to the cutting of materials diagonally.

artificial ageing The encouraging of increased hardness and tensile properties of a material by means of higher than normal room or atmospheric temperatures. cf. **age hardening**.

artificial marble A simulated marble made from **gypsum plaster.** cf. **scagliola.**

artificial stone See **reconstructed stone**.

asbestine An **extender**; talc.

asbestos An incombustible mineral with thin, tough fibres. It is used extensively in building, usually in combination with other materials, to take advantage of its fire resistant and thermal insulating properties. Because of the danger of inhaling asbestos dust, its manufacture, working and use are subject to severe safety regulations. cf. **asbestos cement** and **asbestos cement insulation board**.

asbestos based bitumen felt Roofing felt, containing at least 80% asbestos fibre and no more than 20% organic material, saturated in bitumen. It is preferable to felts based on organic fibres as it is more resistant to decay and is less likely to distort on becoming wet. cf. **bitumen felt**.

asbestos cement A combination of cement and asbestos fibre used to manufacture such products as corrugated or flat sheets for low-cost roofing and wall cladding, which are particularly suited to industrial and agricultural buildings; also rainwater goods, flue pipes and accessories. The material is incombustible, but has poor thermal insulation properties.

asbestos cement insulation board A range of sheets with varying proportions of asbestos fibre in their manufacture. The more fully compressed wall boards are incombustible, but have poor thermal insulation properties. The less heavily compressed sheets are softer, but have better thermal insulation and fire resistance. These are used to provide fire resistant linings to steel structural members and to line ducts etc.

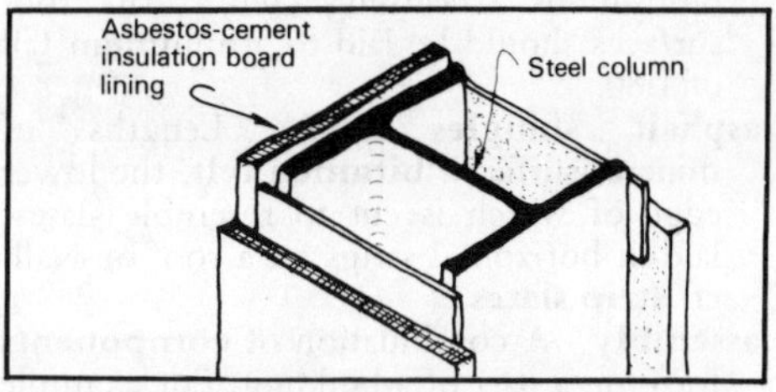

asbestos-diatomaceous earth A mixture of asbestos fibre, diatomaceous earth and a **binder** from which insulating and fire resistant blocks and boards can be manufactured.

asbestos plaster A pipe insulation made from **asbestos-diatomaceous earth**.

asbestos rope An asbestos-based material used as packing in pipe joints.

asbestos sheeting See **asbestos cement**.

as-cast finish A term applied to concrete which is left without any surface treatment after the striking of the formwork.

ash dump (USA) A container beneath an open fire grate into which the ashes fall and which is removed through an access hatch either on the outside of the building or in a basement.

ashlar 1. Well wrought and finely dressed squared building stone, laid in courses with joints down to 3 mm thick. The face may be plain or **vermiculated** or may have **drafted margins**. 2. (USA) Walling in burnt clay blocks larger than bricks; equivalent to **terra cotta** walling in the UK.

ashlar brick (USA) A brick that has been worked to resemble a stone.

ashlering Short studs to cut off the acute internal angle made where a pitched roof meets the floor in attic rooms. The studs are usually covered with plasterboard.

Asiatic closet See **squatting closet**.

asphalt Natural asphalt is a mixture of about 10% bitumen with inert mineral matter and is believed to be the residue after the evaporation and oxidation of petroleum from outcropping strata. Asphalt is defined as to origin (**rock asphalt** or **lake asphalt**) or type (**mastic asphalt** or **compressed rock asphalt surfacing**).

asphaltic cement Bitumen or lake asphalt, or blends of these with one another or with flux oil, having adhesive qualities and being suitable for the manufacture of **mastic asphalt**.

asphalt roofing A roof covering, usually to flat roofs, consisting of two layers (each 10 mm thick) of mastic asphalt on a bituminous sheathing felt. All roof surfaces should be laid to a minimum fall of 1:80.

asphalt shingles (USA) Lengths of mineral-surfaced **bitumen felt**, the lower edge of which is cut to resemble slates, laid in horizontal strips on a roof or wall. cf. **strip slates**.

assembly A combination of **components** forming a part of a building. For example a **wall panel** which is made up of a number of components becomes known as an assembly.

assembly drawing A drawing showing in detail the construction of a building and the junctions between its elements, between element and component and between component and component. Metric scales used are 1:20 (50 mm to 1 m), 1:10 (100 mm to 1 m) and 1:5 (200 mm to 1 m).

atomization The process used in the operation of a **spray gun**, by which fluid (**paint**, **lacquer** or **varnish**) is broken up by compressed air into very fine drops before ejection.

attached pier A vertical projection from a wall face which is fully bonded to the wall and represents a thickening of the wall at that point. It provides additional stiffness and is often positioned where a beam bears upon the wall to give extra **bearing** area.

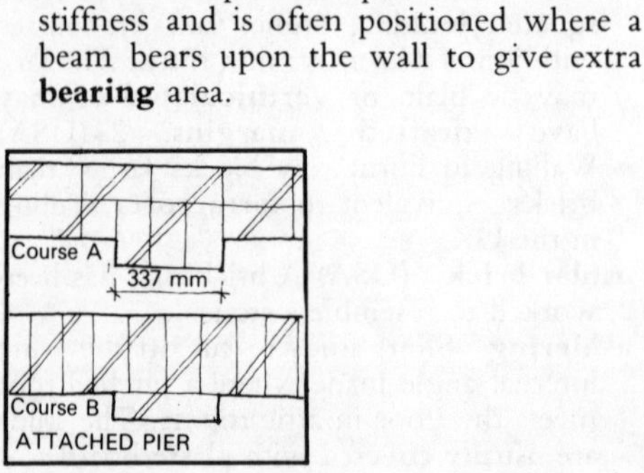

attendance The assistance given by the general contractor's operatives to a subcontractor to enable him to execute his work satisfactorily. It is priced by the general contractor in his estimate. The nature of the assistance can vary from the use by the subcontractor of hoists or ladders, and help in off-loading the subcontractor's materials and equipment, to the cutting of holes and chases.

attenuation Transmission loss other than that due to spread, for instance the transmission loss of sound passing through a wall.

attenuator A device mounted in the ducting of an air conditioning or ventilating system which prevents the transmission of sound from the fan through the ducting to other parts of the building.

audiograph An instrument used to measure the rate at which sound dies away in an enclosure, thereby indicating the sound **absorption** of the enclosure.

auger A tool shaped like a cork screw, used for drilling holes by hand without the use of a **brace**.

auger bit An **auger** shaped **bit** for use with a **brace**.

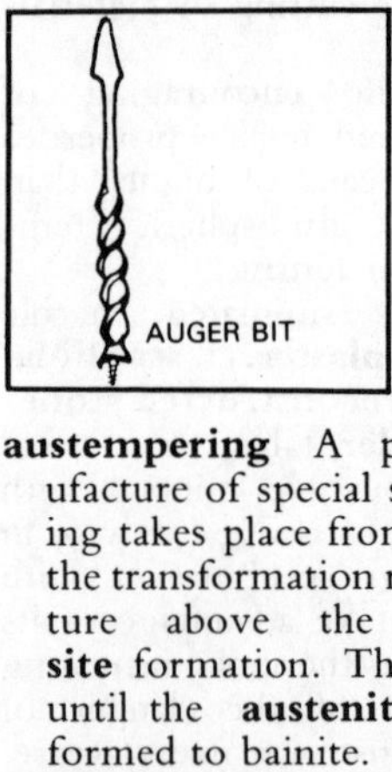

austempering A process in the manufacture of special steel in which quenching takes place from a temperature above the transformation range to some temperature above the limit of **martensite** formation. This temperature is held until the **austenite** is completely transformed to bainite.

austenite The solid solution of carbon and/or alloying elements in gamma iron.

austenitic steel Steel which, owing to the presence of high percentages of certain alloying elements, such as manganese and nickel, retains austenite at atmospheric temperatures. Most austenitic steels are non-magnetic.

autoclave A pressure vessel used in the sterilization of hospital equipment at high temperatures, or the manufacture of certain building products, such as **sand-lime bricks** and some **aerated concrete** blocks.

automatic flushing cistern A **flushing cistern** which is supplied by a continuous, controlled flow of water and which is arranged to flush automatically when the water level in the cistern reaches a particular height.

automatic valve A gas control on an instantaneous water heater operated by the pressure difference created by water flow through a venturi throat or an orifice. A term also used of motorized valves.

awl A carpentry tool for marking or scribing wood or piercing thin sheet materials, having a steel point and a wooden handle parallel to the shaft. cf. **gimlet**.

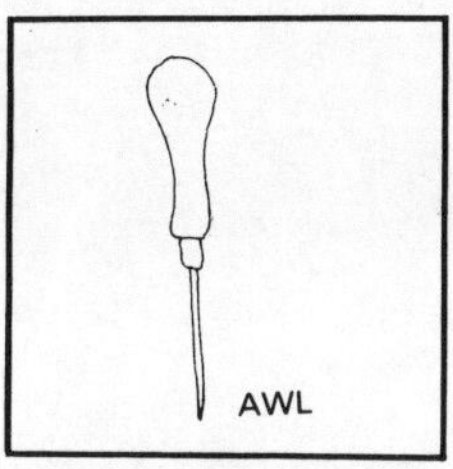

awning blind An external blind, usually of canvas on a framework, which is fixed over a window to provide shade. The most usual types either retract into a **blind box** or hinge up on four or five bonnet frames on each side.

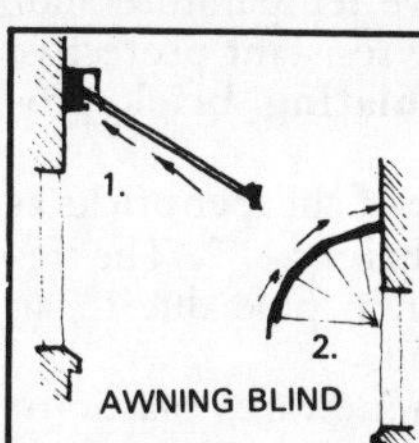

awning window A window similar to a **top-hung window**, but hinged by means of hinged stays fixed to the **jamb** frames, so that on opening the window drops and slides outwards at the same time and does not swing from the **top rail**.

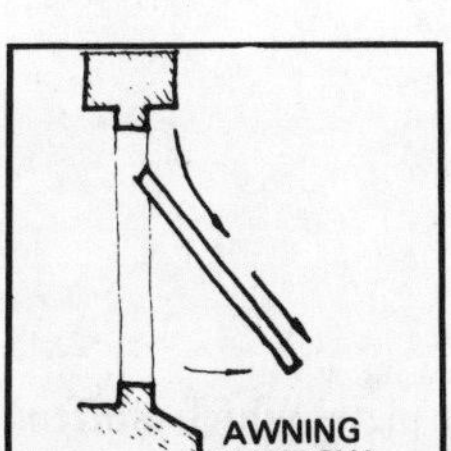

axe 1. A tool for cutting down and trimming trees, and later for rough dressing the timber 2. A **bricklayer's hammer**.

axed The description of a stone surface which has been treated by **bush hammering**.

axed arch A brick arch in which the bricks are roughly cut into a wedge shape by means of a bricklayer's hammer. cf. **gauged arch.**

axed brick A brick cut with a bricklayer's hammer rather than being given **rubbed finish**. The joints in this case are rather wider than when the bricks have been rubbed.

axed work A stone face showing the axe marks.

axial load A load or force acting on a structural member in such a way that the line of force passes through its **centre of gravity**.

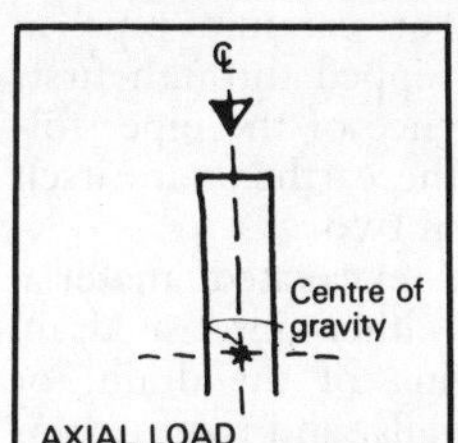

axis An imaginary line through the **centre of gravity** of an object so that the object is symmetrical about the line.

axle pulley The wheel in a **sash window** which is set into the head of the lining and over which the counterweight cords pass.

azimuth The angle between north and a vertical plane through an object or celestial body, measured from north in a clockwise direction.

B

BA thread British Association thread style; a system of metric threads confined to small sizes and having a thread angle of 47½°; used mainly in conjunction with electrical equipment, instruments, etc.

back boiler A metal vessel containing water, fitted behind an open fire or stove. The water thus heated provides a domestic hot water supply and, in some cases, a limited amount of space heating.

back drop A connection to a manhole in which the branch is at a higher level than the main drain, into which it discharges by way of a vertical pipe (hence back drop manhole). The purpose of a back drop is to avoid unnecessary excavation for the branch drain or excessive fall on that drain.

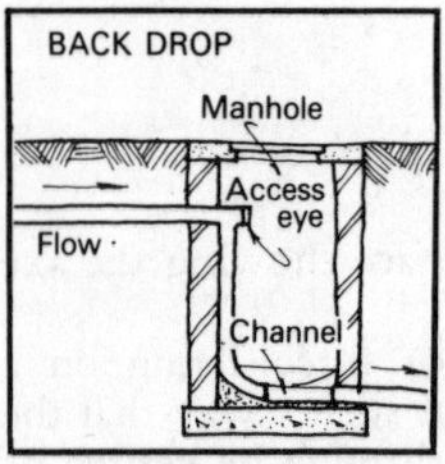

back edging The technique of cutting a glazed earthenware or ceramic pipe in which the glaze is chipped through first, round the circumference of the pipe, followed by chipping the earthenware itself until the pipe is cut in two.

back filling 1. The excavated material which is returned either into a drain trench after the laying of the drain, or around foundation walls, and rammed into place. Also the action of placing back filling. 2. (USA) Brick **backing**.

back-flap The back leaf of a **boxing shutter** which is not seen when the shutter is folded away.

back-flap hinge A door hinge, similar to a wide **butt hinge**, used face-fixed to a thin door and its frame. It is used only when the door is too thin to take a butt hinge.

back flow The flow of liquid in a pipe in the opposite direction to the expected flow, as in the **backing up** of sewage in a drain due to overload or an obstruction in the drain, or contrary flow in a plumbing installation.

back form A piece of **formwork** for a concrete surface which will be unseen in the finished structure.

back gauge The distance between the centre line of a bolt or rivet hole and the back edge of an angle **cleat** which it is fixing.

background heating A heating system used to provide a level of warmth lower than that needed for full thermal comfort, and which will need topping up by some other heat source.

back gutter A gutter formed at the back (or higher side) of a chimney or other projection through a pitched roof; usually lined with metal.

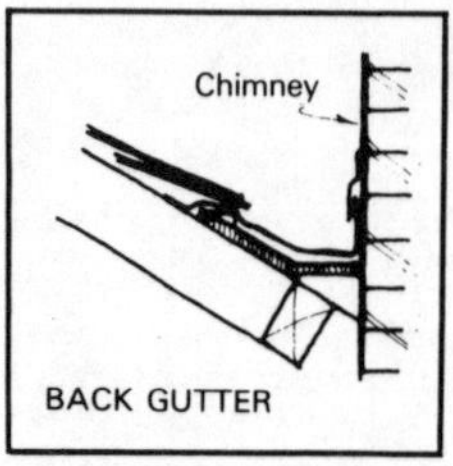

backing Common brickwork behind a **facing brick** facade.

backing coat A coat of plaster other than the finishing or **setting** coat; sometimes referred to as the **render coat**.

backing insulation An insulating material shielded from excessive temperature and/or abrasion by a more resistant protective material, such as **insulating brick** protected by **fire brick**.

backing up 1. The use of cheaper bricks as **backing** to **facing bricks**. 2. The reversal of flow in a drain pipe due to an obstruction or overload.

back-inlet gully A stoneware, plastic or cast iron **gully** having a horizontal or vertical inlet for rainwater or waste arranged so that the liquid is received above water level in the gully but below the grating or seal cover.

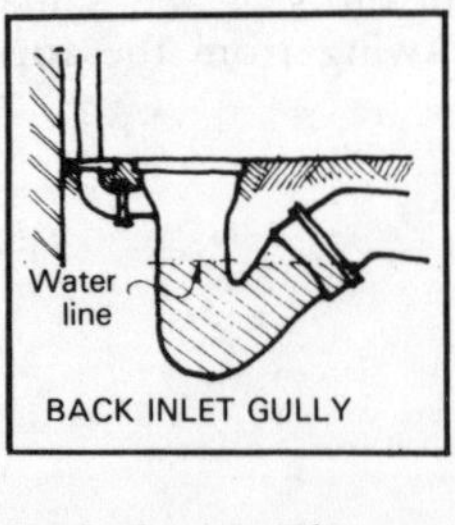

back iron The steel plate which stiffens the **cutting iron** of a **plane**.

back lining See **sash window**.
back lintel A lintel supporting the **backing** of a wall but not seen on the façade.
back mortaring (USA) See **pargeting**.
back nut A flanged hexagonal nut used for securing the waste fitting to the outlet position of a sanitary fitting.
back plastering (USA) Rendering to an area which is not visible.
back prop A raking strut used to transfer the weight of timbering to the ground in deep trenches; usually placed below every second or third frame.
back putty That portion of the glazing compound which remains between the glass and the back of the **rebate** after the glass has been pushed into position in the bedding putty.

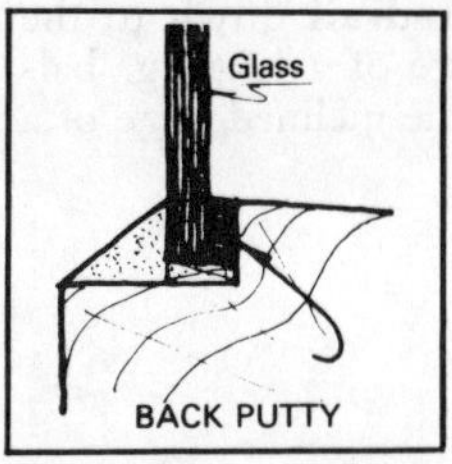

back saw A carpenter's saw, such as a **tenon** or **dovetail saw**, with a fold of steel or other metal along its back.
back shore See **raking shore**.
back sight A sighting taken in surveying immediately after the instrument has been moved. The reading is taken back to the previous sighting position before the instrument was moved.
back siphonage **Backflow** caused by siphonage of a liquid from an appliance or storage vessel into the pipe feeding it.
back up (USA) See **backing**.
back vent (USA) A **fresh-air inlet**.
bacteria beds **Filter beds** used in the treatment of sewage.
badger 1. A large wooden rebate plane similar to a **jack plane** but with the cutting iron flush with the sides of the plane. 2. A tool used to clean out the jointing mortar and other debris from inside a drain after it has been laid.
baffle 1. A reflecting structure used to modify or restrict the distribution of sound. 2. A flexible, pre-formed section designed to be fitted into the grooves between adjacent **wall panels** to minimize direct entry of rain into a **drained joint**. 3. A board or plate used to prevent a fluid from flowing in the direction it would normally follow and to direct it into the desired path.
bag plug (bag stopper) An inflatable bag used as a stopper in testing a length of drain.
bagging Making good the pinholes which appear in cement surfaces due to trapped air.
bain-marie An item of equipment used in commercial kitchens. It consists of a vessel of hot water within which another vessel containing food is placed to keep hot or to cook slowly.
baked brick An under-burned brick such as a **rubber** brick or a **fire brick**.
baked plaster A plaster (such as Keene's) which is slow setting but gives a very hard surface; produced by gypsum being calcined at very high temperatures.
bakelite One of the earliest plastics, produced in 1916 by Dr Baekeland. It is a synthetic thermo-setting resin made from phenol and formaldehyde with fillers, and it is infusible; used particularly in the manufacture of electrical fittings.
baking (USA) See **stoving**.
balanced construction A construction in which the forces induced by changes in moisture content in the components of the construction will not cause warping. This is achieved by matching any pair of veneers or layers on either side of the centre line in both species and thickness and in the direction of their grain. It is found in plywood in which the plies are symmetrical about the central ply, and are of the same species and thickness, produced by the same method of cutting and placed in the same grain direction.
balanced flue appliance A room-sealed appliance which draws its combustion air from a point adjacent to the point at which the combustion products are discharged, the inlet and outlet being so disposed that the air movements are substantially balanced.
balanced sash See **sash window**.
balanced step See **dancing step**.
balance weight One of the pair of weights used to balance the sashes of a vertical **sash window**. The pair of weights for the lower sash should be slightly lighter than the sash; the pair of weights for the upper sash slightly heavier.
balcony A platform projecting from the wall of a building and surrounded by a balustrade or railing.
bales catch A type of **ball catch**.
bale tack A **lead tack**.
balk See **baulk**.
ballast 1. Unscreened gravel consisting of sand, grit and stones of less than **boulder**

size. 2. An electrical term loosely synonymous with **choke**.

ball bearing A hardened steel ball used in combination with others in bearings to lessen the friction.

ball catch A spring-loaded door catch which comprises a small ball, projecting from a mortise in the leading edge of the door, which engages in a hole in a striking plate set within the rebate of the door frame.

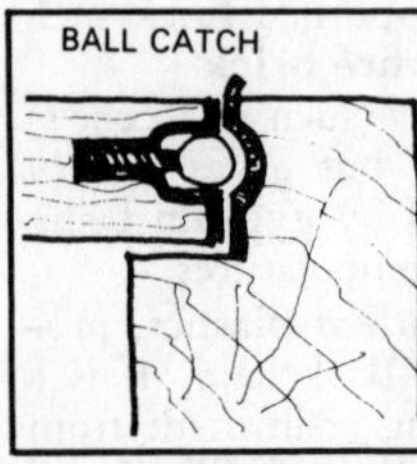

ball cock See **ball valve**.

balloon frame A type of timber framed house construction which originated in North America in the nineteenth century, in which the **studs** run from the foundation wall (or floor slab) to the **wall plate** and to these the first floor joists are side-fixed. cf. **platform frame**.

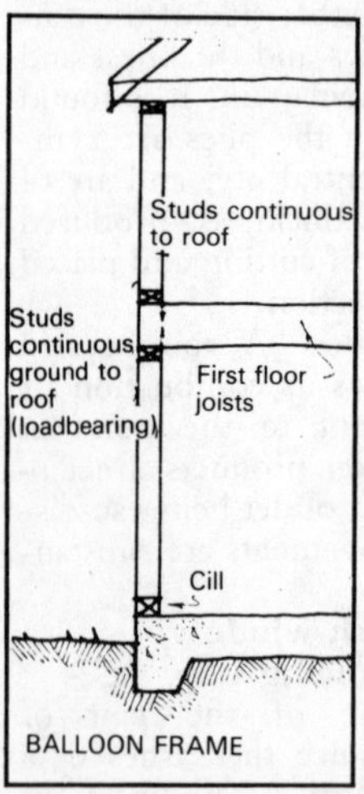

ball-peen hammer An engineer's **hammer** with a hemispherical **peen**.

ball valve A valve on the supply pipe of an open-topped water tank or a w.c. cistern, which is on the surface of the water. A float is fixed on the end of a rod which is hinged to the body of the valve.

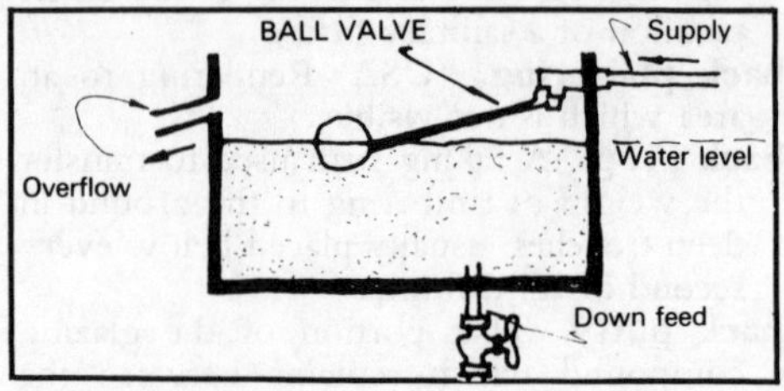

baluster A post or pillar in a balustrade, also called a **banister**.

balustrade A collective description of the infilling from the **handrail** down to the floor level at the edge of a landing, balcony, bridge, or to the inclined edge of a stair or ramp.

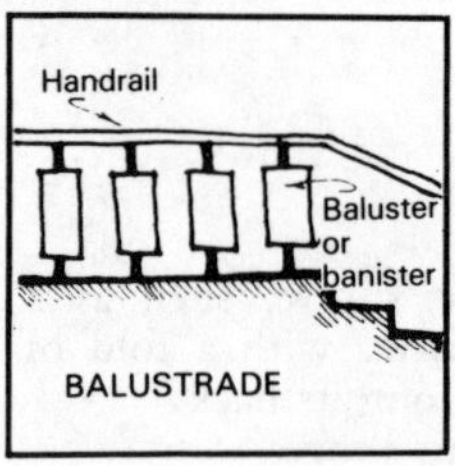

band-and-gudgeon (or band-and-hook) hinge A gate hinge of heavy wrought iron, consisting of a long strap bent into a circle at one end and rotating on a vertical pin (or gudgeon). Strictly the gudgeon should be fixed to brickwork or masonry. With any other fixing the hinge is more accurately described as a band-and-hook hinge.

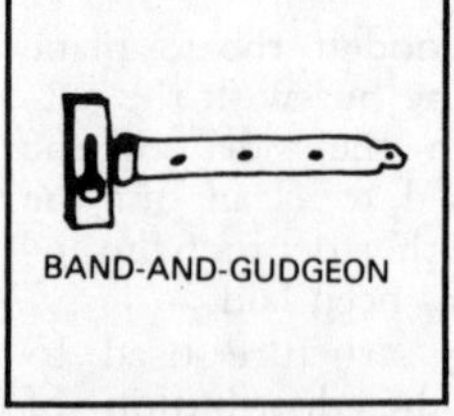

banding See **lipping**.

band saw A mechanical saw for cutting intricate shapes. It consists of an endless steel band with teeth on one edge. There is also a log band saw for use in cutting logs into square sawn timber.

banister See **baluster**.

banker A small board or platform on which concrete, mortar or plaster is mixed by hand; usually three sides have an upstanding edge.

bar A round, rectangular or polygonal solid section of metal which is supplied in straight lengths, of not less than 6 mm in diameter or minimum dimension, *eg* the elements of steel reinforcement in reinforced concrete work.

bar-bending machine A machine, operated mechanically or by hand, which will bend reinforcing bars to any required shape for use in reinforced concrete.

bar (or bar line) chart A chart on which activities in a programme of work are represented by lines drawn to a common scale and showing the sequence and duration of operations.

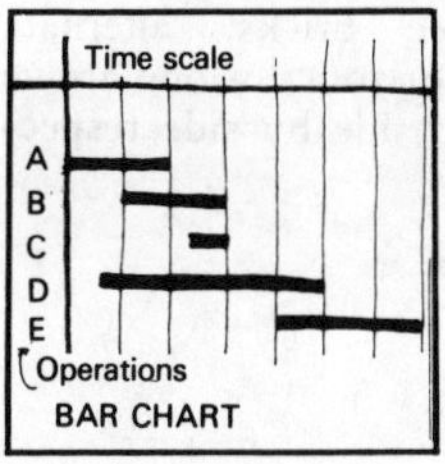

bare A term signifying slightly smaller than the stated dimension.

barefaced tenon A **tenon** having only one shoulder.

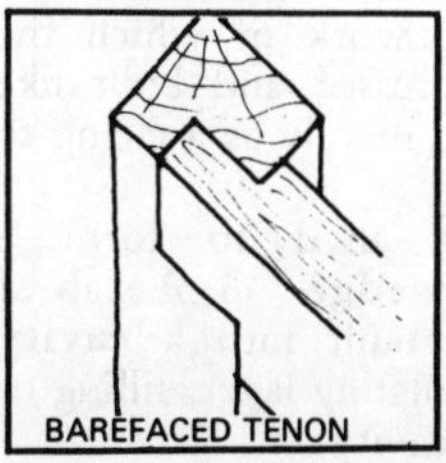

barge board A board inclined at the pitch of a sloping roof surface and covering the end of the roof timbers at the gable. It is usually placed outside the line of the **gable** wall so that the roof covering oversails the wall and protects it. Also known as a **verge board** or **gable board**.

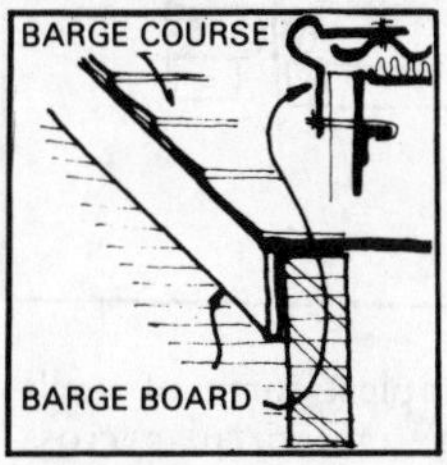

barge couple The pair of rafters on a **duo-pitched** roof that complete the roof structure at the **gable** and overhang the gable wall.

barge (or verge) course 1. The tiles or slates next to the **gable**, which slightly oversail it. 2. A brick coping to the **gable** wall – often brick on edge with a tile **creasing** – slightly overhanging the wall.

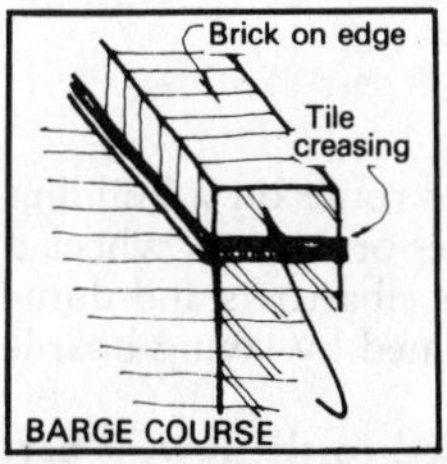

barium concrete Concrete containing a high proportion of barium compounds. It is used as a protective material against radiation.

barium plaster A plaster containing barytes aggregate with **gypsum plaster** as a **binder**. It is used for lining hospital X-ray rooms, etc. as a protection against radiation.

bark beetle One of a group of small beetles belonging to the family *Scolytidae* which, in the adult and larval stages, bores in the bark, or between the bark and the wood, of live trees, fallen trees and logs.

bark pocket Bark which has been partly or wholly enclosed by the growth of the tree. The bark is usually in a flute or pocket, or associated with a knot. Resin or gum may sometimes be present in the pocket.

barrel That portion of a pipe throughout which the internal diameter and cross-section remain uniform.

barrel bolt A hand-operated door fastening comprising a metal rod which is moved within a slotted cylindrical guide.

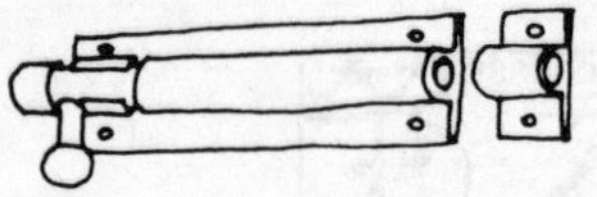
BARREL BOLT

barrel vault The simplest form of vaulting, usually with a semi-circular cross-section; nowadays usually constructed of concrete or as a plywood **shell construction**, or a light metal triodetic framework.

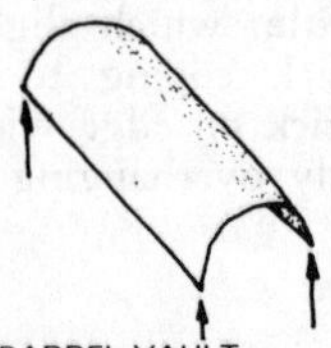
BARREL VAULT

barrow run A traffic route on a building site for the passage of minor wheeled vehicles, such as wheelbarrows and dumper trucks; often formed by laying boards on the ground.

base 1. A term applied to the lowest part of any vertical structural member such as a wall, column, pier etc. 2. The major of two components between which a fixing is made, usually by **anchorage fixing** in the major component, such as a concrete slab to which a steel **base plate** is connected by **rag bolts**. 3. The **ground** which receives a finish, such as plaster or paint. 4. A concentrated dispersion of pigments in a paint medium which, in order to form a usable paint, requires to be diluted with more of the same medium or with another liquid.

base course The lowest visible part of a masonry wall, sometimes projecting beyond the general wall face. cf. **plinth**.

base exchange A process for softening water on a domestic scale involving the passing of water through a mineral reagent called **zeolite**, which removes those salts which make the water hard. The zeolite is periodically rejuvenated and the salts removed by flushing with a salt solution.

base moulding The **moulding** at the top of a **plinth** which often acts as a weathering to the increased thickness of the plinth and forms a functional and aesthetically pleasing junction between the two wall faces.

base plate A steel plate, usually at the foot of a steel stanchion or under a piece of heavy equipment, which is used to spread the load on the concrete foundation or floor slab and hold down the superimposed structure or equipment.

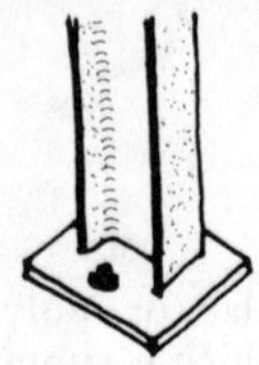
BASE PLATE

basic space In dimensional co-ordination, the space (bounded by **reference planes**) which is assigned to receive a building **component** or **assembly**, including, where appropriate, allowance for **joints** and **tolerances**.

basket grate A loose iron framework on legs within which the fire is contained in an open fireplace.

basket handle arch See **arch**.

basket weave or diaper bond Ornamental brickwork involving square groupings of three bricks, alternate groups being laid horizontally one above the other or on end side by side respectively.

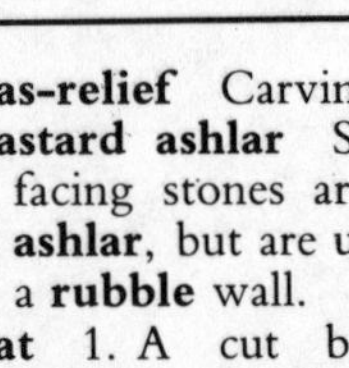
BASKET WEAVE

bas-relief Carving in low relief.

bastard ashlar Stonework in which the facing stones are dressed and built like **ashlar**, but are used merely as a facing to a **rubble** wall.

bat 1. A cut brick used to form a **bond**. 2. A **lead wedge**. 3. A slab of insulating material built into a **cavity wall** to form an insulating layer, filling or partially filling the cavity.

batch 1. The quantity of concrete, mortar or plaster mixed in one operation in a **batch mixer**. 2. A given quantity of a mixture of materials prepared for delivery to a furnace or some other production area or machine. 3. A quantity of material of the same specification and size produced or processed at one time, or presented for test at one time.

batch box A measuring device used to control the quantity of **coarse aggregate** and sand in a concrete mix. Often the box has no bottom, being placed on the mixing platform or **banker** and filled and then removed. In this way the full batch box is never lifted.

batching plant Mechanical equipment for measuring, either by weight or by volume, the quantities of different ingredients required to make up each complete charge of a mixer.

batch mixer A mixer in which materials are added, mixed and discharged one **batch** at a time.

batted surface See **batting**.

batten 1. A piece of square sawn softwood 50 to 100 mm thick × 125 to 200 mm wide. 2. A piece of 50 × 25 mm softwood to which **tiles, slates** or **weather-boarding** are fixed.

batten board A **coreboard** whose core strips are less than 75 mm wide, glued between outer **veneers** (usually of plywood) whose major grain direction is at right angles to the grain of the core strips. cf. **blockboard**.

batten (or ledged) door A simple door made up of vertical boards fixed (often with **nails**) to two or more horizontal **ledges** at the back. Diagonal bracing may sometimes be included between the ledges, but the door has no surrounding frame. cf. **framed, ledged and braced door**.

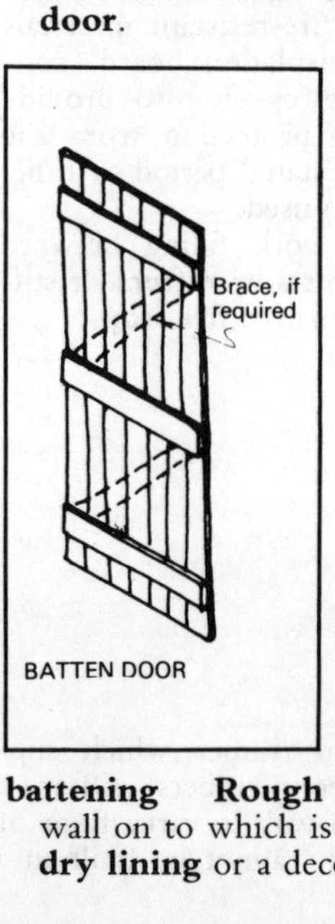

BATTEN DOOR

battening **Rough grounds** fixed to a wall on to which is fixed a finish such as **dry lining** or a decorative sheet material.

batter The inclination of a surface from the vertical, as in the face of a **retaining wall**.

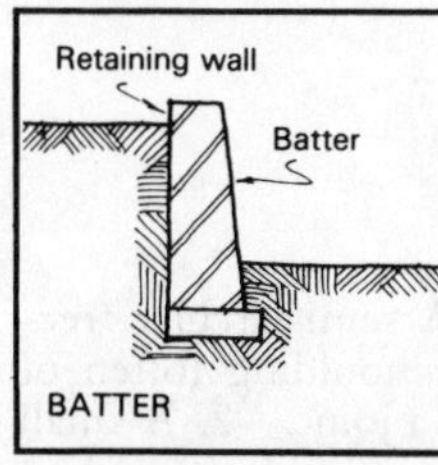

BATTER

batterboard (USA) A **profile**.

batter brace (USA) A **diagonal brace** usually in a **truss**.

batter peg One of a group of pegs driven into the ground to set out the limits of an earth slope.

batting The surface of a stone treated with a regular pattern of vertical or angled chisel marks cut into the face with a **batting tool**. The chisel marking is to the full height of the stone face and spacing varies between 2.5 and 3.5 mm. Vertical chisel marking is often referred to as tooling.

batting tool A mallet head mason's chisel for surfacing stone. Its blade is about 100 mm wide.

baulk A sawn or hewn softwood timber of approximately square section greater than 100 × 112 mm.

bay 1. One of several uniform divisions of a building, often representing the spaces between the columns of a framed structure. 2. An area of concrete floor (or floor, wall or roof finish) laid or placed at one time.

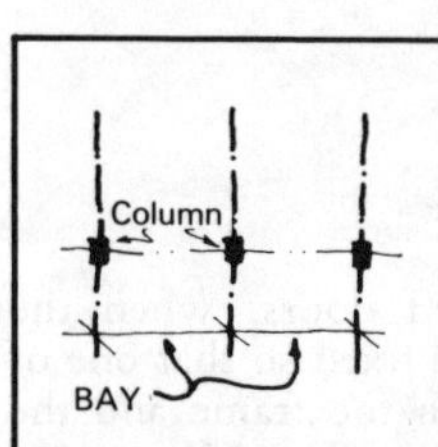

bayonet cap On a lamp, a cap with small pins on its shell which engage in slots in the lampholder.

bay window A window which projects beyond the line of the general wall surface, usually with angled side lights or side lights normal to the wall, and a sill wall which is built up from a foundation (unlike an **oriel window** that is carried on **corbels**).

bead or beading 1. A semi-circular, rectangular or quadrant moulding (often of timber) used to mask a joint. 2. A small rectangular or convex moulding used to retain a sheet of glass in a window frame. cf. **bead glazing**. 3. In zinc and copper roofing, the edge of a sheet at an eaves, or the edge of a flashing bent into a tubular shape or through 180° to stiffen the edge of the sheet. 4. An accumulation of paint at the lower edge of a painted area due to excessive flow. cf. **deep bead**.

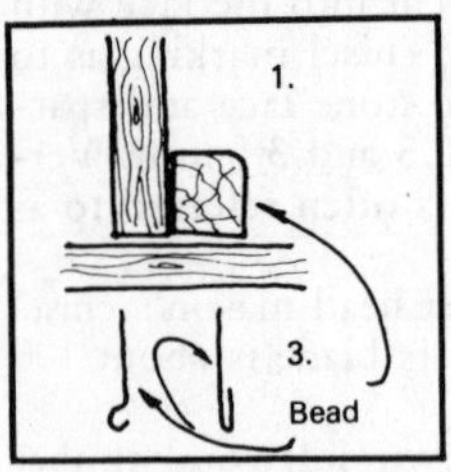

bead and quirk A **bead** separated by a narrow groove or **quirk** from the rest of the surface which it decorates.

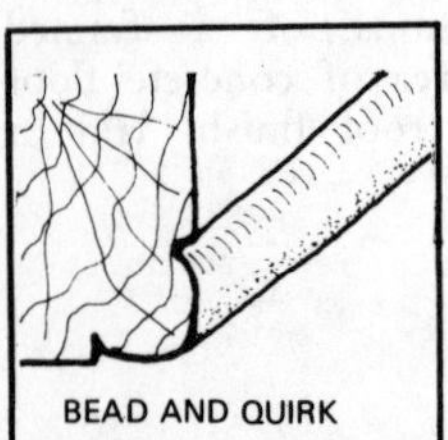

bead butt In panelled doors, when the panel is a thick board fixed so that one of its faces is flush with the frame and the other is recessed without **mouldings**. On the flush side there may be a moulding or

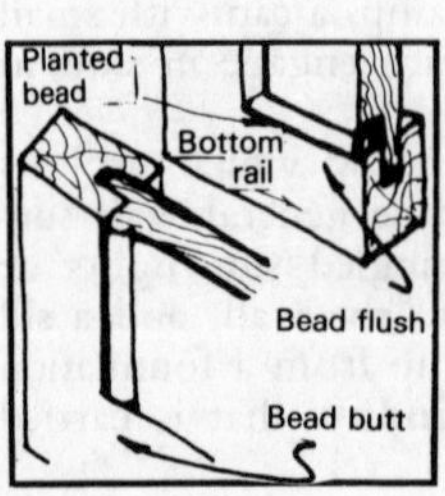

bead cut into the panel, but only in the direction of the grain (*ie* adjacent to the **stiles** and **muntins** of the door). The bead thus butts against the rails and the resulting appearance is known as bead butt.

bead flush Work as in **bead butt**, but with the panels beaded all round, the horizontal beads across the grain being **planted**.

bead glazing Glazing in which the glass is held in position by a wooden or metal **bead**.

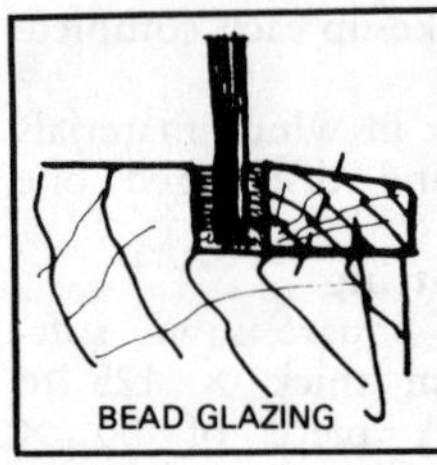

beading See **bead**.

beading tool or bead plane A joiner's **plane** used to form the shape of a **bead** on a section of wood, or for cutting grooves to receive beads.

beam A structural member set horizontally between two supports, carrying the load of the floor or roof above and any **point loads** set on it by the structure. A beam could be a steel **RSJ,** a **reinforced concrete** beam, a light metal **lattice beam (girder),** a solid timber beam or a **laminated beam.**

beam casing The lining or encasement of a steel beam with fire-resistant materials (asbestos cement insulation board, concrete, sprayed asbestos etc.) to provide that member with protection from the effects of fire for a stated period of time; also the materials so used.

beam filling Brickwork filling between **floor** or **ceiling joists** or **rafters**. It stiffens the joists and forms a **fire stop**.

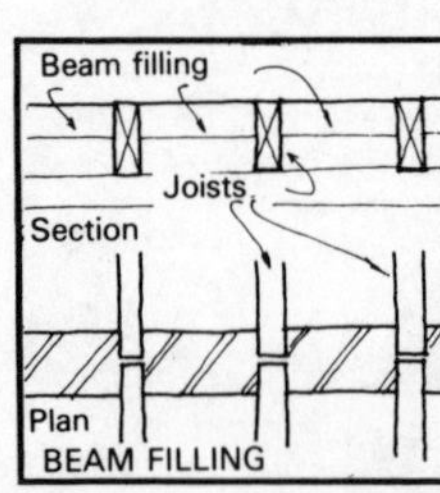

bearer A horizontal timber which supports other timber members. Often a bearer is fixed to a wall to carry floor or ceiling joists which cannot be built into the wall, or to a beam to carry floor panels between the beams.

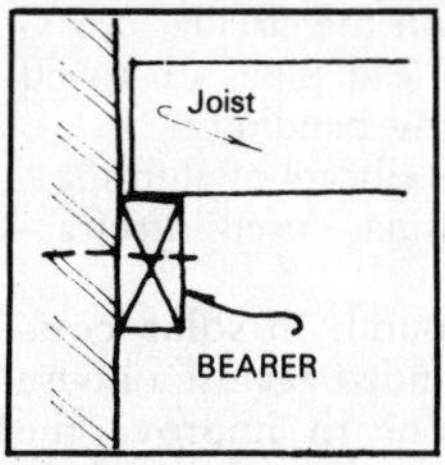

bearing 1. The interface between beam and support. 2. The resistance of a rivet to crushing. 3. The mechanism supporting a rotating shaft. 4. In surveying, the angle (measured in a horizontal plane) between a survey line and a given reference point or direction.
bearing area The area of interface over which bearing stress exists (*eg* the area of the subsoil under a building's foundation).
bearing capacity The safe load per unit area which the ground under a foundation or other structural base can carry.
bearing plate A plate in a wall which is placed under a beam to spread its load over an area of the wall which is sufficient to avoid local crushing.
bearing stress The compressive stress which exists at the interface between two structural members where the force exerted by one member on the other tends to crush the material of which the members are made.
bed The under surface of a brick, stone, slate or tile as laid, or the mortar or **bedding** in contact with this surface.
bedding The layer of material (or the act of placing a component on a layer of material) which provides some degree of continuous support, *eg* mortar under a brick, concrete under a drain, or **glazing compound** in a glazing rebate behind and underneath the glass.
bed dowel A dowel in the centre of the bed of a stone.

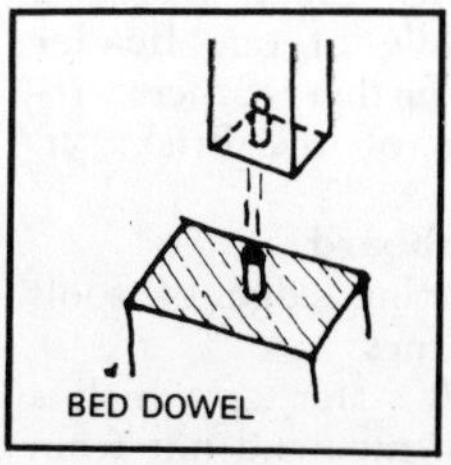

bed joint The horizontal joint in brickwork or stonework and the joint between **voussoirs** of an **arch.**
beeswax The wax which is used in wax stains and polishes for wood, and is produced by the honey-bee.
beetle 1. A heavy wooden **maul** or **mallet** used in paving. 2. An insect which causes damage to timber. cf. **bark beetle, death-watch beetle, pinhole borer, powder post beetle** and **woodworm**.
bel(B) A measure of the intensity of sound equal to 10 decibels (dB).
Belfast sink A deep-sided stoneware sink.

Belfast truss A wooden **truss** made up of small timber members with a curved upper **chord** and a horizontal **tie** or **string**, braced together by diagonal members. Both the upper chord and the string are usually made up of two parallel timbers with the braces fitted between.

bell-and-spigot joint (USA) See **spigot-and-socket joint**.
bell cast The shaping of the lower edge of an external **rendering** to shed rainwater.

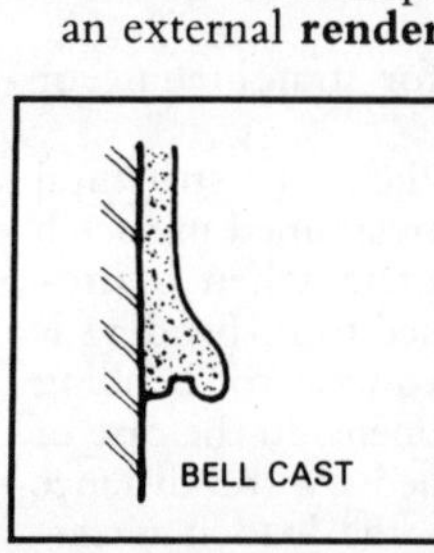

bell cistern A **flushing cistern** with a siphonic action activated by the movement of a bell in the cistern.
belly See **bow**.
belt course A **string course.**
belt rail A **lock rail.**
belt stress The horizontal stress in a dome.

bench holdfast A cramp for holding wood on a bench while it is being worked.

benching A steeply sloping surface constructed of concrete on each side of a **channel** in a **manhole** to stop the accumulation of solids and encourage complete drainage.

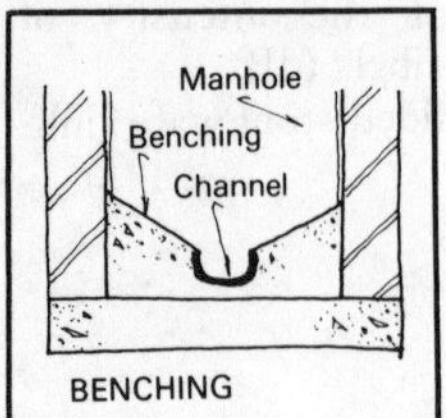

BENCHING

bench mark A surveyor's fixed point of reference for use in **levelling**, the **reduced level** of the point – in relation to some **datum** – being known. cf. **Ordinance Bench Mark**.

bench plane A plane, such as a **jack plane**, **smoothing plane** or **try plane**, which is used mainly on a bench.

bench sander A fixed sanding machine of the disc, belt or reciprocating pad type. All use a strong glass paper or cloth.

bench stop An adjustable wooden or metal stop projecting through a work bench to hold wood being planed on the bench.

bend A curved length of pipe, tubing or conduit. A 90° bend is a quarter bend and a 45° bend is an eighth bend.

bend allowance The allowance that must be made in the original length of a flat component to ensure that when it is bent it will be the required length. It will vary with the radius of the proposed bend, the angle contained and the thickness of the component.

bending iron A tool for straightening or expanding lead pipe.

bending moment When a structural component is fixed or restrained in such a way that it cannot rotate when a **moment of force** is applied to it, bending is induced. This is referred to as the bending moment of that component. In the case of a beam it is conditioned by the distance the beam is spanning, the load it is carrying and the degree of restraint of the beam ends. This bending moment, if equilibrium is to be maintained, must be equalled by the **moment of resistance** of the beam – a property of its size, shape and material of construction.

bending schedule A list of lengths, sizes, bending dimensions and identification marks of the reinforcing bars required for a project.

bending spring A length of spiral steel spring used to maintain the circular cross-section of copper or lead pipes up to 50 mm in diameter during bending.

bentonite Anhydrous silicate of alumina – 60% silica, 20% alumina – used in refractory materials.

berm 1. An earth mound. In **solar construction**, earth mounded against a house wall or over the roof to improve the building's thermal performance. 2. In civil engineering, a horizontal ledge on the side of an embankment to strengthen it and intercept falling earth.

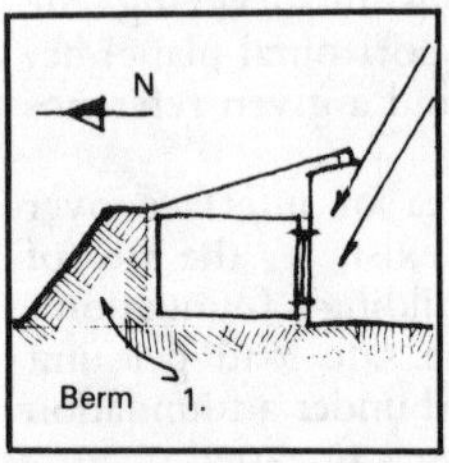

best hand-picked lime The best quality lime – large lumps of quick lime chosen for their size and containing no ash.

best reed Best thatching reed.

bevel 1. An angle formed at the meeting of two surfaces, which is not a right angle. cf. **chamfer**. 2. An adjustable tool that can be set to any angle; used in setting out angles.

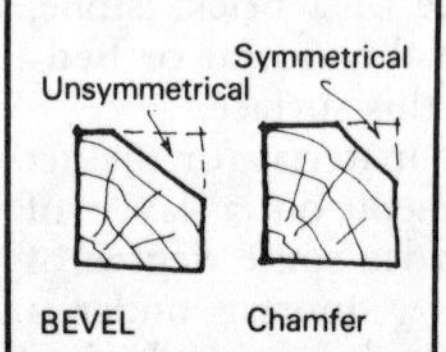

BEVEL

bevel halving A **halved joint** with a slight bevel to prevent the two pieces from pulling apart.

bevelled closer A brick cut in a vertical plane from the middle of one **header** face to one of the further corners, removing one quarter of the brick. cf. **bond**.

bevel siding See **clapboard.**

bezel The sloped cutting edge of tools such as chisels and planes.

bib tap or bibcock A water tap which is fed from a horizontal pipe and not from below as is usual in washbasins and baths. It is sometimes used over **Belfast sinks** or **bucket sinks** and for filling cisterns.

bid A tender.
bidet A vitreous china low level basin adapted for sitting upon and fitted with a **mixing valve**. It is used for washing the excretary organs. The older douche type of fitting is now not often used because of the danger of **back-siphonage**.
billet A piece of wood with three sides sawn and the fourth left round.
billing The act of writing out a **Bill of Quantities**.
Bill of Quantities A complete list of the materials and labour operations necessary to construct a building or civil engineering project, together with a measurement of the quantities of materials and work involved. This document forms the basis of the contractor's **tender** and each item is priced by the contractor by inserting a **rate** against each item and multiplying it by the quantity. These **extended prices** are then added together to arrive at the full tender. A fully **priced bill** constitutes the contractor's offer to undertake the work at that price and forms the basis for assessing the cost effect of any **variation order** made during the course of the work.
binder 1. A material used to bind together a mixture of other materials, such as cement (**concrete** or **mortar**), tar (**tarmacadam**), bitumen, gypsum plaster and lime. 2. A wooden or steel beam spanning an opening and carrying the **common joists**. 3. In paint, that non-volatile part of the **medium** which retains the pigment in a coherent **film**, such as **linseed oil**, some other drying oil, a **size** or a **resin**.
binding rafter See **purlin**.
birdseye A decorative **figure** or feature in the grain of a wood (particularly in maple) caused by an irregularity in the growth of the tree, resulting in parallel depressions in the **annual rings**. These produce a series of small circular patterns in the grain when the wood is cut in a direction parallel to the annual rings.
birdsmouth joint A re-entrant angle or notch cut into the end of a **rafter** (or similar timber member) to fit over a **wall plate** or other cross member.

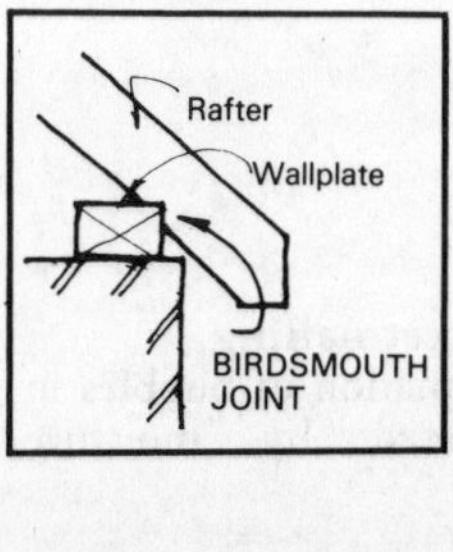

biscuiting The second burning of glazed bricks after the glaze has been applied.
bit 1. An interchangeable drilling point connected to a **brace** or **drill**. 2. The working head of a **soldering iron**.
bit gauge or bit stop A device temporarily fixed to a **bit** to avoid drilling too deep a hole.
bitumen A viscous liquid or a solid consisting of hydrocarbons and derivatives soluble in carbon disulphide. Non-volatile, it softens slowly with heat. It may be obtained by refining from petroleum, but is also found naturally.
bitumen emulsion A dispersion of **bitumen** in water, often containing inert **fillers**.
bitumen felt A damp-proof membrane which is used as a **roof cladding or covering**, **damp proof course**, gutter lining etc. and is made by saturating a felt in bitumen. Felts used including fibre felts, **asbestos based bitumen felts** (containing 80% asbestos and 20% organic fibre) and **glass fibre** felts. There are various finishes available including: (a) saturated, in which there is no bituminous coating on the felt and therefore no surface dressing is required; (b) self-finished, in which the felt is coated with oxidized bitumen and surfaced on each side with finely divided talc; (c) coated and sanded, in which the felt is coated with oxidized bitumen and surfaced on each side with fine sand; (d) mineral surfaced, in which the felt is coated as above and surfaced on one side with mineral granules instead of sand.
bitumen impregnated fibreboard **Fibre board** impregnated with **bitumen** during or after manufacture to improve its resistance to moisture, having a density not exceeding 400 kg per m^3 and a mean thermal conductivity not exceeding 0.065 W/m °C.
bitumen macadam Coated macadam in which the **binder** is wholly or substantially **bitumen**.
bituminized fibre pipe See **pitch fibre pipe**.
bituminous paint A paint, usually of a dark colour, containing a high proportion of **bitumen**.
bituminous plastic Plastic made from natural **bitumen**.
black bolt A cheap unfinished mild steel bolt used in structural steel fabrication. It has a comparatively wider range of size tolerances than a **precision bolt** and is used where high structural performance is not required.

blackheart An abnormal black or dark brown discoloration which may occur in the **heartwood** of certain timbers; not necessarily associated with decay.

black Japan A black varnish frequently applied to the ironmongery intended for cheap joinery work. It is subsequently stoved. cf. **japanning**.

black knot An adherent **knot** of a colour in distinct contrast to that of the surrounding wood.

blackout blind An opaque internal blind running in channels at each window jamb and intended to exclude all daylight.

blaes Clays mined from a considerable depth; also partly calcined clays and shales from collieries, used in brick making and, in Scotland, as **hardcore**.

blank A piece of timber cut to a specific size and shape, from which an article is to be made.

blanket or quilt An insulating material (fibre glass or mineral wool) formed into a strip, sometimes lined on each face with paper, and used to insulate roof spaces, the cavities of prefabricated **wall panels** and those between lightweight **cladding** systems and the internal lining.

blank wall A wall without a window or door opening.

blast cleaning The cleaning and roughening of a surface by the use of natural grit or artificial grit or fine shot (usually steel) which is projected on to the surface either by compressed air or by mechanical means.

blast finishing The process of removing **flush** from mouldings and/or dulling their surfaces by causing media such as steel balls or plastic pellets, etc. to impinge against them.

blast-furnace slag Slag from iron smelting, used as an aggregate in the making of concrete. cf. **foamed slag**.

bleaching The fading of colour in paintwork as a result of alkaline or acid attack.

bleeder tile (USA) A drain pipe built through the retaining wall of a basement of lead water in the soil outside the wall to a drain within the building.

bleeding 1. The penetration of glue fixing a **veneer** through the veneer to the surface. 2. The passage of a colour or **vehicle** through a covering material or finish; usually prevented by a **sealer**.

blender A round paint brush, originally of badger hair, used to blend colours and remove the marks of coarser brushes in a paint coat.

blind A sheet of fabric or a thin, metal, slatted screen which is lowered over a window either internally or externally to give privacy or to control the effects of external sunlight and solar radiation. cf. **roller blind**, **solar control blind** and **Venetian blind**.

blind box The boxing above a window into which a **roller blind** or an **awning blind** retracts.

blind fastener A fixing device which is capable of making a connection between two or more elements of an assembly where there is access to one side only of the assembly.

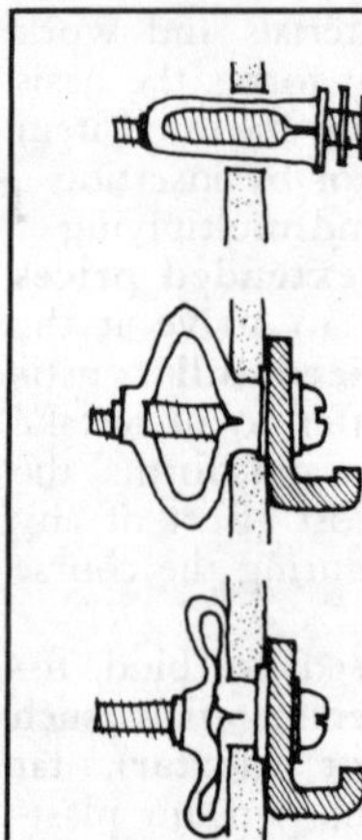

BLIND FASTENER

blind floor (USA) A **sub-floor**.

blind header A half brick that is not visible on the face of a wall.

blind hinge A concealed hinge.

blind hole A drilling that does not pass through the material drilled.

blinding A dressing of fine gravel or sand used to fill the interstices of a **hardcore** bed before pouring concrete.

blind mortise A **mortise** that does not pass completely through the timber into which it is cut. It is formed to receive a **stub tenon**.

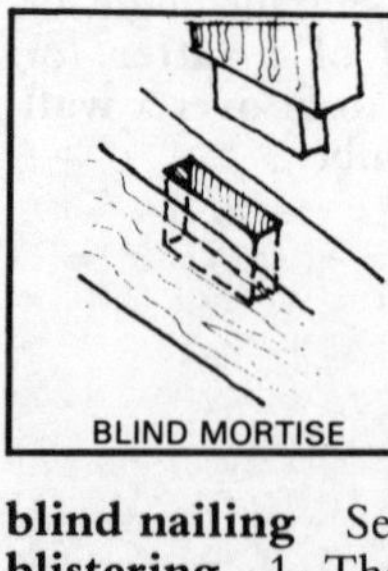

BLIND MORTISE

blind nailing See **secret nailing**.

blistering 1. The formation of bubbles in a paint film caused by moisture vaporization behind the film. 2. In plasterwork, bubbling occurring as a result of lime **slaking** taking place after completion of the work.

blob foundation A series of isolated, shallow foundation bases.

block 1. In masonry, a building element, usually larger than a brick, which may be hollow, cellular or solid, and is often made from concrete of various formulations or from clay; laid to bond in mortar. cf. **blockwork**. 2. A triangular piece of timber used in the angle between two pieces of wood which are joined together, to reinforce and stiffen the joint (as between the **tread** and the **riser** in a timber stair). cf. **angle block**. 3. A term used for many types of preformed building element, such as a **glass block**, **hollow clay tile**, **hardwood floor block**.

blockboard A **coreboard** made up of a core of **laminae** less than 25 mm wide with outer facings of plywood sheets whose major grain direction lies at right angles to the core grain.

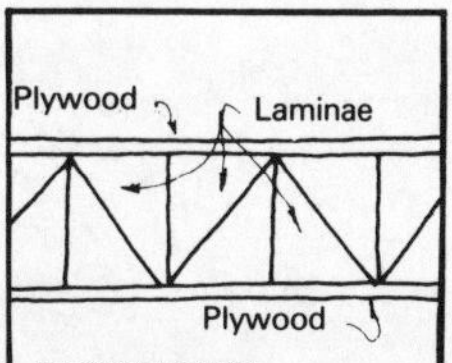

BLOCKBOARD

block bonding The practice of bonding several **courses** of brickwork of one wall into a number of courses in another wall (*ie* every individual course is not individually bonded). Block bonding is often used when bonding new brickwork to existing brickwork, particularly if the two sets of brickwork do not course similarly.

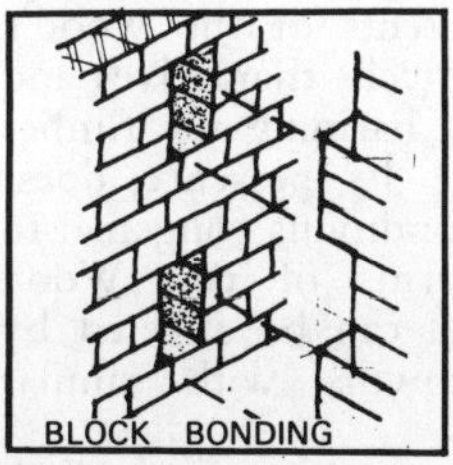
BLOCK BONDING

block channel A semi-circular channel formed in a rectangular base. cf. **anti-splash device** (2).

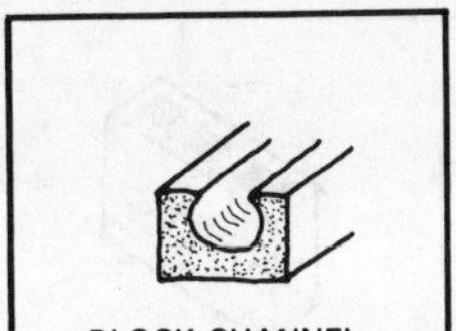
BLOCK CHANNEL

block plan A small-scale, outline plan of a building, usually showing the building's relationship to its site and to neighbouring properties, roads and footpaths but showing no internal details of the building.

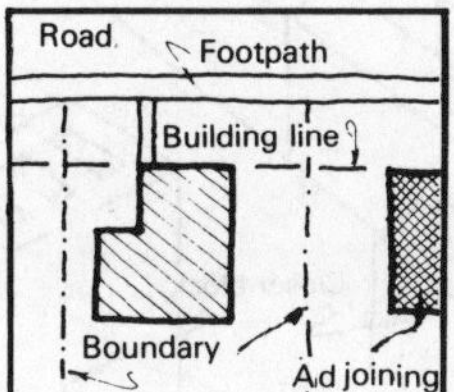

BLOCK PLAN

block plane A small metal **plane** up to 100 mm long for cutting end grain.

block quoin A decorative brick **quoin** made up of slightly projecting or different coloured bricks, each block consisting of, say, three courses in height and alternate quoins being usually one or one-and-a-half bricks long.

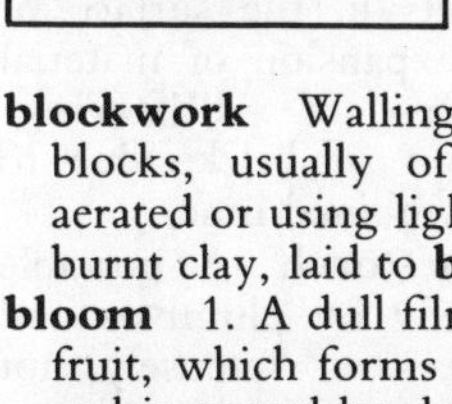
BLOCK QUOINS

blockwork Walling built of building blocks, usually of concrete (sometimes aerated or using lightweight aggregate) or burnt clay, laid to **bond** and in a **mortar**.

bloom 1. A dull film, like the bloom on a fruit, which forms on a gloss paint finish and is caused by defective composition of the paint or improper application, (*eg* during humid conditions. 2. A slight discoloration of the surface of a steel mould. 3. A surface film caused by weathering. 4. A surface film of sulphites and sulphates formed during the annealing process.

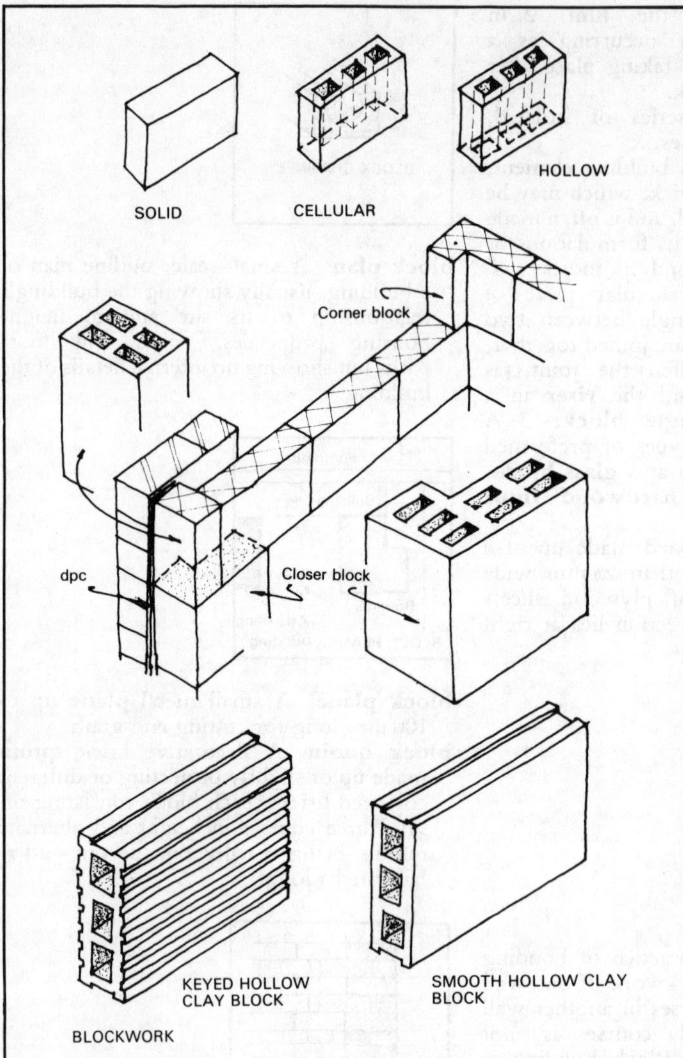

blowing 1. Small pits in the surface of plaster due to the expansion of material below the surface. cf. **blistering**. 2. The disintegration of bricks due to the presence of uncombined lime.

blow lamp or blow torch A portable apparatus used chiefly by plumbers and painters. It produces an intensely hot flame which is used for melting solder or lead or **burning off** paint.

blown joint A joint in lead pipework in which one pipe is heated and opened to receive the other pipe which is rasped to fit. The joint is then finished with solder.

blub 1. The hole in a plaster cast caused by an air bubble. 2. (USA) **blistering**.

blue brick See **Staffordshire blues**.

blue stain or sap stain A blue fungal discoloration of a **sapwood**, the fungi feeding on the contents of the wood's cells and not on the cells themselves and thus not signicantly harming the timber or its performance. Its presence does, however, indicate conditions congenial to other damaging forms of rot. Wood other than sapwood can be affected by similar mould growths with similar characteristics.

blushing A milky opalescence which forms in a **lacquer** due to the presence of moisture or a lack of compatibility in the paint.

board 1. In softwood, square sawn timber under 50 mm thick and 100 mm or more wide. 2. In hardwood, square sawn or unedged timber 50 mm or less thick and of a width varying with the grade of the timber and the country of origin. 3. A manufactured rigid or semi-rigid sheet, such as **laminboard**, wood **chipboard** or other **particle board,** or **hardboard.**

board and batten Timber **cladding** with alternate thick and thin boards in which the thick boards are grooved to receive the thin boards, giving a recessed effect externally.

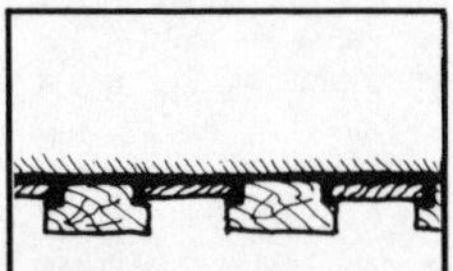

BOARD AND BATTEN

boarding Closely laid **boards** over **rafters**, **joists** or **studs** to provide a surface on which to fix tile or slate **battens**, insulation, or **cladding** or to provide a floor. cf. **weather-boarding**.

boarding joist A common **joist**.

board lath 1. A **gypsum lath/plank**. 2. (USA) Wood **laths**.

boasted ashlar A rough finished **ashlar** produced by a **boaster**.

boaster A mason's chisel, 38–75 mm wide, which is struck by a **mallet** and used to dress stone. Also referred to as a **bolster**

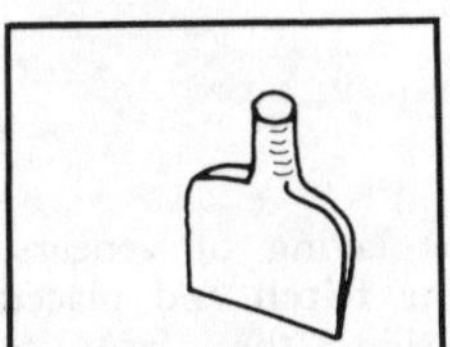

BOASTER (BOLSTER)

boasting The dressing of stone with parallel, oblique or vertical strokes from a **boaster**. The strokes are usually uneven and do not extend across the complete face of the stone.

bobtail truss A **roof truss** in which the inclined rafters are of the same pitch, but of a different length, resulting in the vertical surfaces of the building being of a different height on opposing sides if the ground is level.

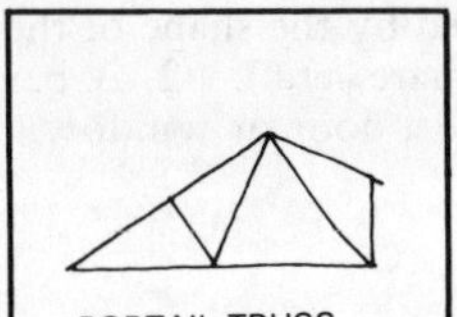

BOBTAIL TRUSS

body 1. The apparent viscosity of a paint or varnish film. 2. The build and/or solidity of a paint or varnish film. 3. The major part of a valve. 4. A blend of raw materials, after they have been mixed and are ready for making into refractory products. 5. To increase the viscosity of drying oils by heat treatment.

bodying in The early stages of French polishing before spiriting off, comprising staining, filling and first polishing.

boiled oil Linseed oil used in paint manufacture, which has been heated to about 260 °C but *not* boiled (in spite of its name). Boiled oil encourages quicker drying in a paint.

boiler Equipment used for heating water, by means of solid fuel, gas, oil or electricity, for use as domestic hot water or for central heating.

bole The trunk of a tree.

bolection mould A rebated wooden **moulding** surrounding an inset panel (as in a **panel door**), the surface of the moulding standing proud of the frame surrounding the panel.

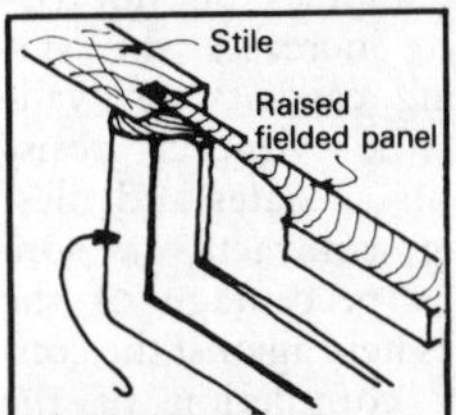

BOLECTION MOULD

bollard A short strong post placed to provide a warning of a hazard, or to preserve pedestrian areas from the intrusion of vehicular traffic.

Bolomey's curves Graphical curves showing the proportion and grading of aggregate for concrete of low permeability.

bolster 1. A timber **capping** to a post or pile to give a larger bearing area. 2. A bricklayer's or mason's cutting chisel. cf. **boaster**.

bolt 1. A strong metal **through-fixing** device with a cylindrical shank which has a head and a threaded end to receive a

nut; usually described by the shape of the head (hexagonal, square, etc.). 2. A bar or pin used to secure a door or window.

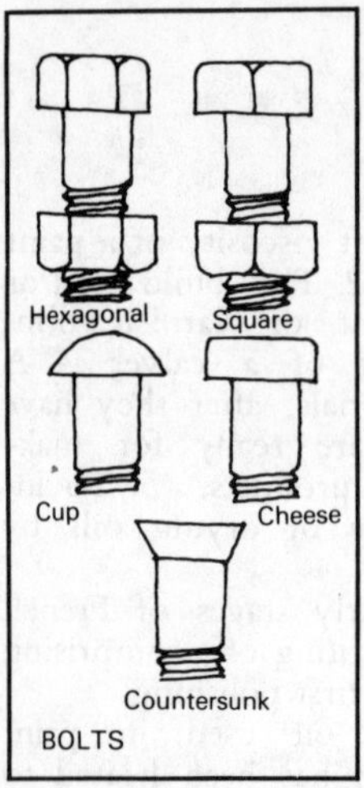

BOLTS

bolting iron A narrow **chisel** used to cut mortises for drawer locks.

bolt sleeve A cylindrical or other shaped form through which a **bolt** passes so as to separate the bolt from the surrounding concrete.

bond 1. The mechanical adhesion between two materials resulting from the use of a **glue**, **adhesive** or **bonding agent**; also called the interface strength. 2. The method of laying bricks, blocks, slates and tiles so that their vertical joints in succeeding courses do not coincide. This practice increases the stability and loadbearing capacity of walling elements and the weather resistance of such elements as slates and tiles. 3. In some building contracts, a sum of money (usually a percentage of the contract sum) which is held against the contractor's satisfactory completion of the works.

bond course A course of **headers** particularly in English garden wall bond. cf. **bond**.

bonding agent 1. A substance incorporated in a coating composition in order to improve its adhesion to a **substrate**, or to a previously applied coat. 2. A material normally applied to a smooth surface to improve adhesion.

bonding compound In **bitumen felt** roofing an oxidized bitumen applied hot to bond together the layers of felt and to bond the lower layer to the **substrate**.

bonding conductor A safety device involving an earthing wire connecting the metal frame of an item of electrical apparatus to earth.

bonding plaster A low-expansion retarded hemihydrate plaster which will adhere to low-suction surfaces like dense concrete.

bond stone A long stone laid through the wall in solid construction. In thick walls the bond stone does not usually penetrate completely through the wall, but bond stones penetrate from alternate sides of the wall to approximately two-thirds of the wall thickness.

BOND STONE

bond stress The shear stress on the surface of reinforcement resulting from the interaction between the steel and the concrete at their interface whereby relative displacement is restrained.

bonnet 1. A wire balloon-shaped grating inserted into a vent pipe to prevent the access of birds. 2. A roof over a bay window.

bonnet tile A **hip** tile flared like a sun bonnet.

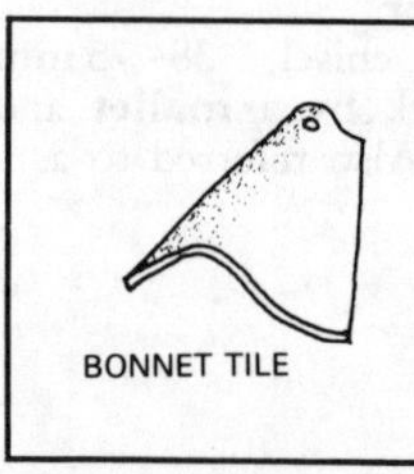
BONNET TILE

book matching The laying of veneers, sliced from the same **flitch** and placed side-by-side, reversing the face of alternate veneers to produce a mirrored grain pattern.

boot lintel A concrete lintel with a projection at the foot of its front face

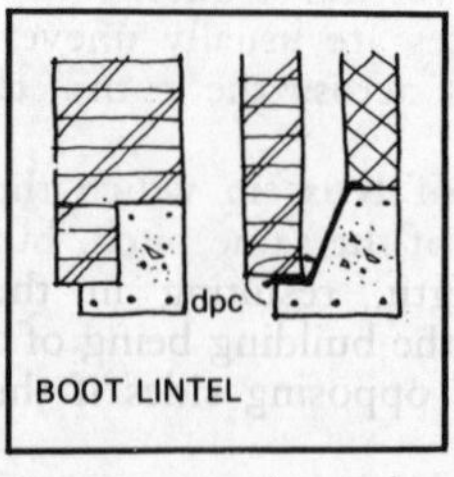

BOOT LINTEL

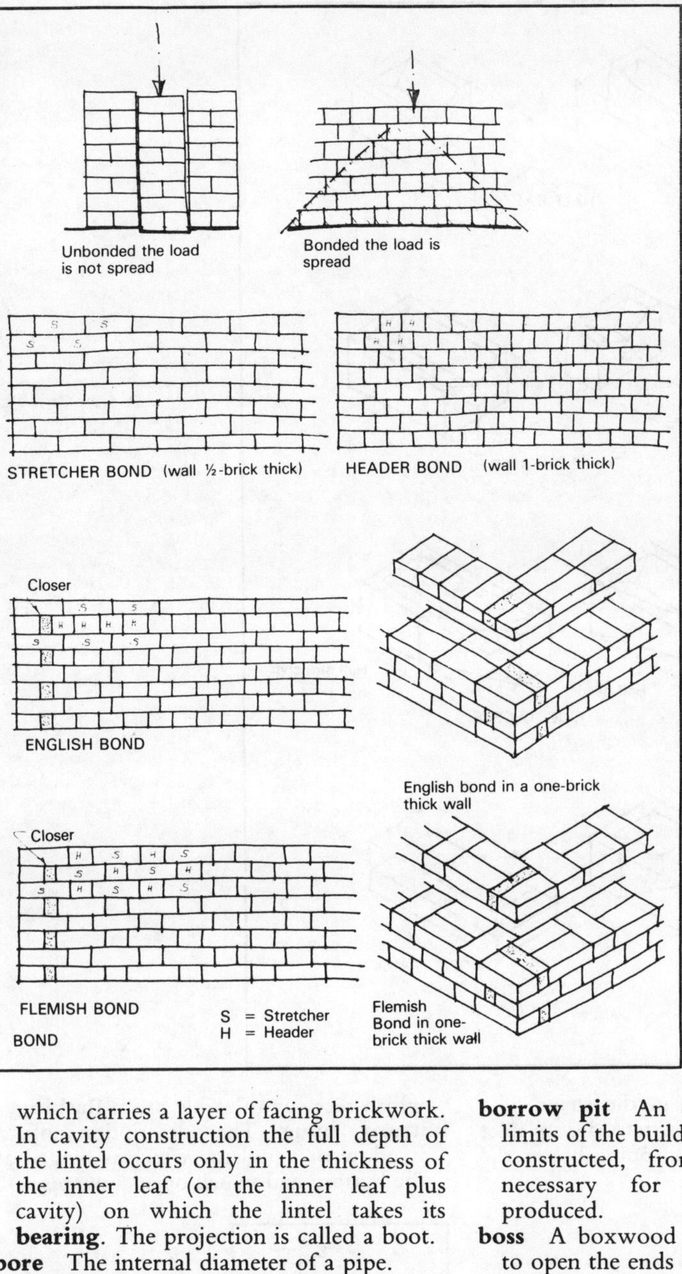

BOND

which carries a layer of facing brickwork. In cavity construction the full depth of the lintel occurs only in the thickness of the inner leaf (or the inner leaf plus cavity) on which the lintel takes its **bearing**. The projection is called a boot.

bore The internal diameter of a pipe.

bored pile A pile made by filling with fresh concrete a hole made in the ground with an earth **auger**.

bore hole A hole made in the ground to determine the nature of the subsoil at various levels and also its bearing capacity; often referred to as a trial hole.

borrowed light A window in an internal **partition** for the purpose of distributing natural light from one room or area to another.

borrow pit An excavation, outside the limits of the building works or road being constructed, from which the material necessary for the construction is produced.

boss A boxwood cone used by plumbers to open the ends of lead pipes.

bossage Roughly dressed **ashlars** laid projecting from a wall and finish-dressed in position.

bossing The shaping of a sheet of metal to fit a roof or other surface, using boxwood shapes and a mallet.

bossing stick A boxwood shaper for shaping sheet metal linings.

bottle-nose drip A rounded edge to a drip on a sheet metal roof.

bottle trap A trap on a **waste pipe** below

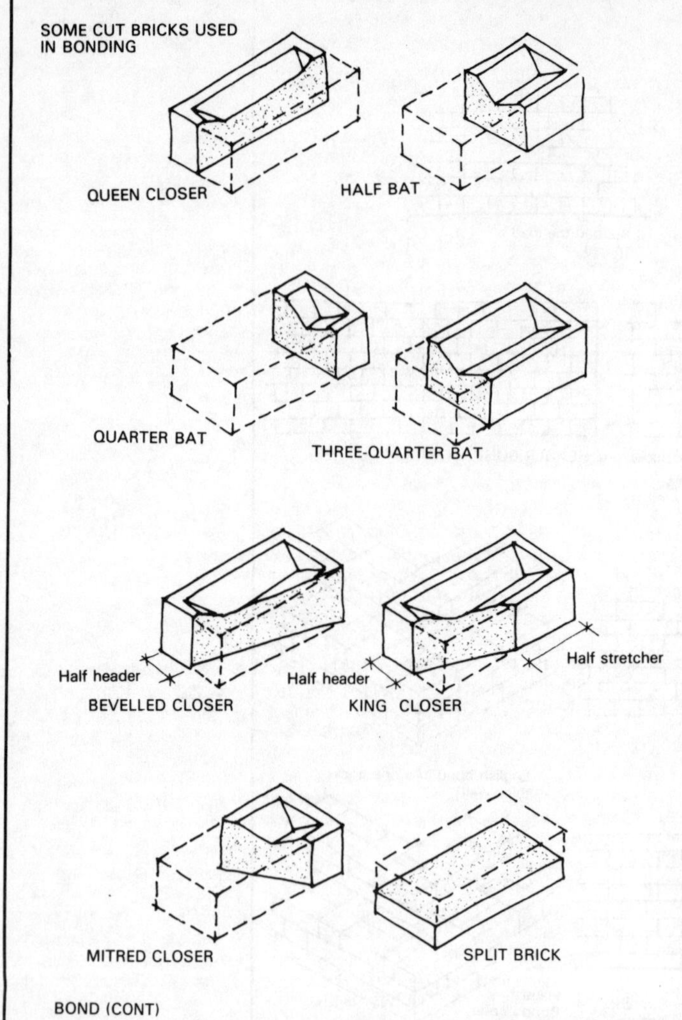

BOND (CONT)

a **sink** or **washbasin** in the shape of a bottle with an outlet in its side, its inlet being a vertical pipe dropping below the water level in the trap.

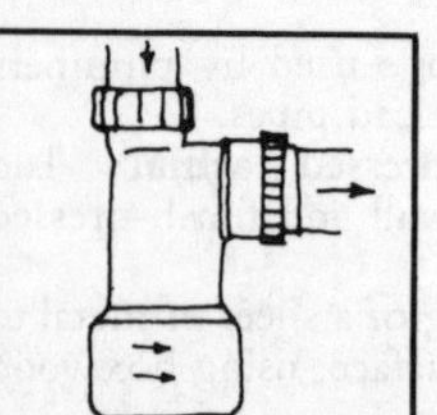
BOTTLE TRAP

bottom glazing flashing In corrugated asbestos cement and metal roofing, an accessory used below **patent glazing** which receives a flexible metal **flashing**.

bottom hung The description of a window or ventilator which is hinged at the bottom and which opens inwards.

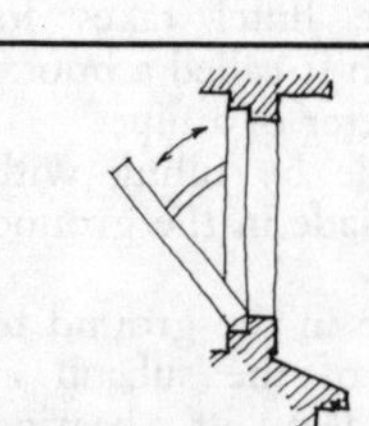
BOTTOM HUNG

bottom rail The horizontal bottom member of a door, casement or lower sash.

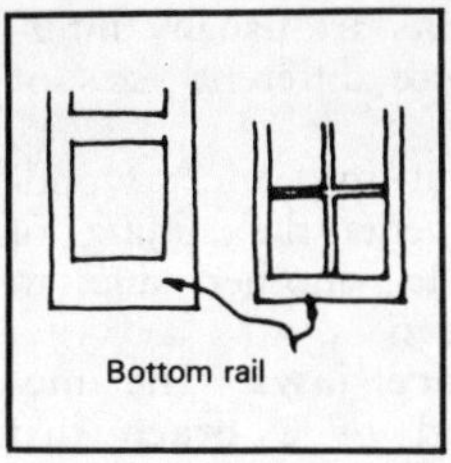

bottom shore That member of an arrangement of raking shores which is nearest the wall face. cf. **raking shore**.

boucherie process A gravity treatment by which a water-borne preservative is applied to the butt end of freshly cut, unbarked timber (chiefly poles).

boulder A rounded or sub-angular stone or piece of rock, the lower limit of size being 200 mm.

boulder clay Stony clay.

boule A log sawn through-and-through into **boards** and or **planks** and packed in the original form of the log.

boundary condition In dimensional co-ordination, the dimensional relationship of the boundary of a **zone** or **basic space** to an adjacent **reference plane**. A zero boundary condition exists when the boundary of the zone is coincident with the reference plane; a positive boundary condition when the zone extends past the reference plane; and a negative boundary condition when the zone stops short of the reference plane.

boundary wall gutter A gutter on the edge of a pitched roof having a flat sole, one upright side and one angled side to suit the slope of the adjacent sloping roof.

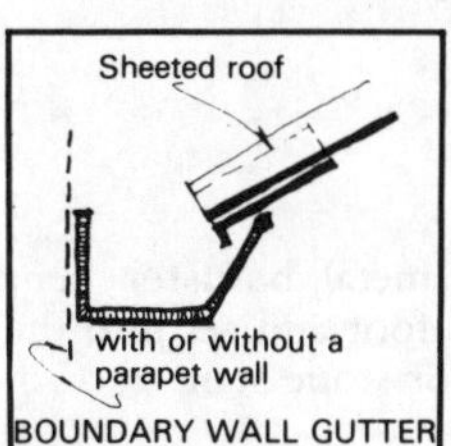

bow A bending or warping distortion of a structure or component.

bow saw A saw for cutting circular work.

Bow's notation A system of lettering the spaces between the forces acting at a point; in graphical problems in mechanics, whereby the force polygon can be similarly lettered.

bowstring roof truss See **Belfast truss**.

bow window A **bow window** which is curved on plan.

box beam See **box girder**.

box cornice A built-up hollow **cornice** made up of timber elements.

boxed eaves Projecting eaves with a closed **soffit** and **fascia** (**board**).

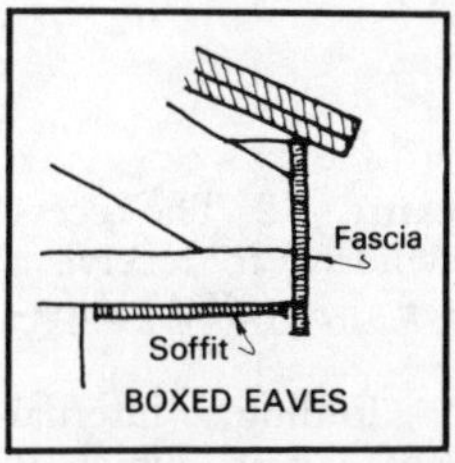

boxed frame See **cased frame**.

boxed heart Timber sawn in such a way that the centre 100 m square is cut out. This is done with some **hardwoods** which have poor **heartwood**.

boxed mullion A hollow **mullion** in a **sash window** frame, which contains counterweights for the sashes.

boxed tenon A **tenon** in the form of a right angle; used on corner posts.

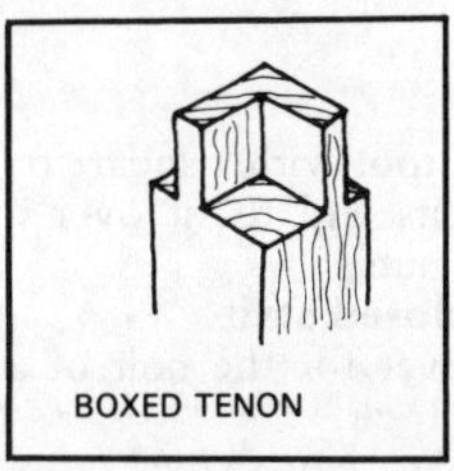

box girder In structural steelwork, a built-up **plate girder** with a double **web**. In lighter construction a **box beam** is often made up of timber **chords** with **stressed skin panels** of plywood on either side.

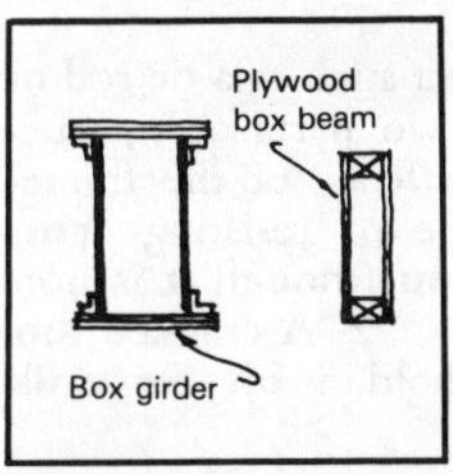

box gutter A gutter of rectangular cross-section, usually made up in timber with a lining of **flexible metal**, **asphalt** or **bitumen felt**. Box gutters can be pre-formed in asbestos cement or metal. They are used between two parallel pitched roofs and behind parapets (or **parapet walls**).

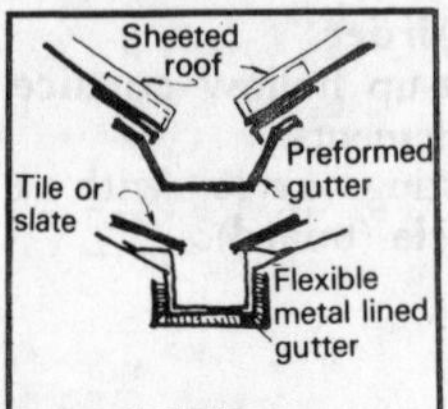

BOX GUTTER

boxing 1. A **cased frame**. 2. The recess in the **reveal** of a window to receive a folded **boxing shutter**. 3. (USA) **sheathing**.

boxing shutter A folding internal shutter, usually one of a pair, which is stored in a recess in the **reveal** of the window opening, in the thickness of the wall.

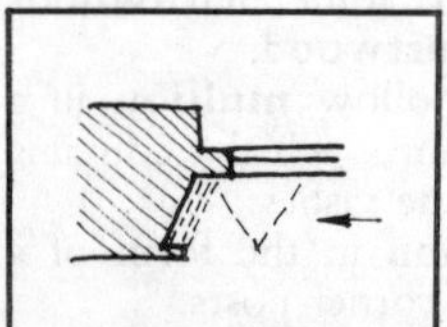
BOXING SHUTTER

box key A T-shaped tool with a square or polygonal recess in its end to fit over a **nut**; used to tighten nuts.

box stair (USA) A **closed stair**.

box staple The receiver for the bolt of a **dead lock** or a **rim lock**.

boxwood bobbin An egg-shaped tool drilled to take a strong thread and used to true bends in lead pipes.

boxwood dresser A hardwood (often not boxwood) tool for straightening lead sheet and pipe.

boxwood tampin A hardwood (often not boxwood) tool for enlarging the end of a lead pipe.

brace 1. A component such as a tie rod or timber connecting two parts of a structure. It acts as a stiffener of the framework and is capable of resisting **tension** and **compression** (though it is normally under tension). 2. A cranked tool which is used to hold a **bit** for drilling in wood. The bits are usually interchangeable to produce different sizes of hole.

BRACE

brace block In a built-up beam, a wooden **key** which prevents the sliding of one part relative to another due to horizontal **shear stress**.

brace chuck or brace jaws The mechanism at the end of a **brace** that clamps the **bit** in place.

braced frame Timber framing in which the edge posts of each frame pass from ground floor to roof. Into these, **binders** are framed which carry the intermediate floor joists. The studs between the edge posts carry no floor load. cf. **balloon frame**.

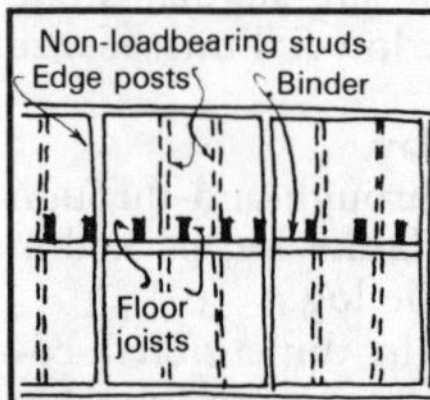

BRACED FRAME

bracket 1. A projecting support (solid, or with an inclined **brace**) for either a horizontal member such as a shelf, or a structural member. cf. **corbel**. 2. A rough support for wide treads of a timber stair, nailed to the **carriage**. cf. **stair**. cf. **angle bracket** and **gallows bracket**.

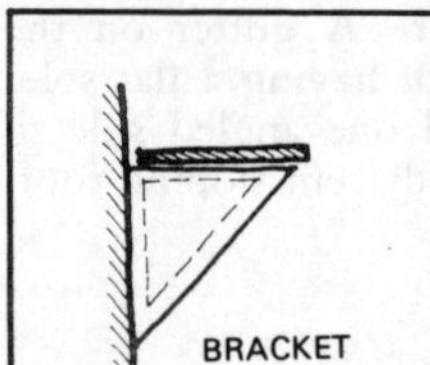
BRACKET

bracket baluster A metal **baluster** bent at right angles at its foot and set into the side of the concrete or stone stair.

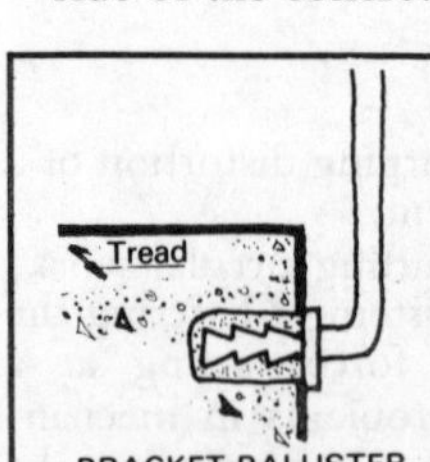

BRACKET BALUSTER

bracketed cornice A plaster **cornice** supported on brackets from the wall or ceiling.

bracketed stair A cut string stair with ornamental brackets under the projecting return **nosings**. cf. **stair**.

bracket scaffold A light scaffold hung from the wall face rather than being built up from the ground. A **grappler** is firmly driven into the wall and a right-angled steel bracket is hung from this. The **scaffold boards** span between brackets.

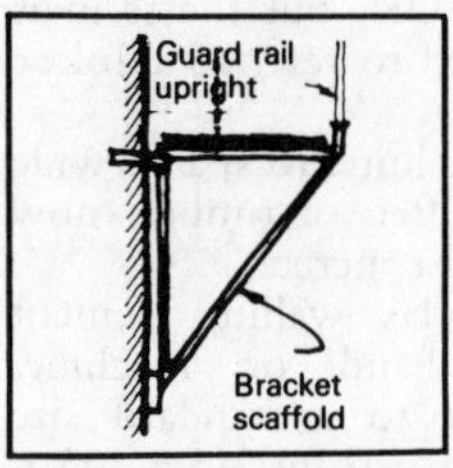

brad A cut nail of constant thickness but tapering width, with a head projecting on one side only, used for fixing floor boards.

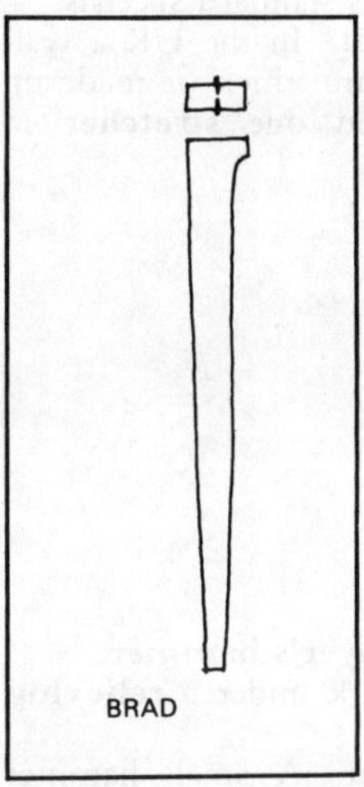
BRAD

bradawl A small hand tool with a chisel point, having its handle on the same axis as the shaft of the tool; used for making holes in wood for the insertion of nails and screws. cf. **gimlet**.

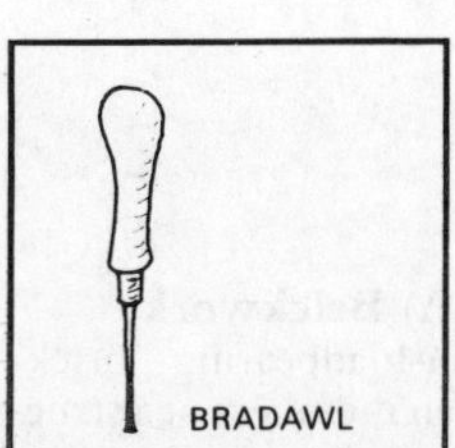
BRADAWL

BR adhesive An adhesive or glue that is 'boil resistant'. It has good weather resistance, except for prolonged exposure, will withstand cold water for many years and is resistant to micro-organisms. A typical member of this category is **melamine formaldehyde** adhesive.

brad setter (USA) A **nail punch**.

branch A subsidiary pipe providing an inlet to a main pipe **run**.

branch bend The channel bend built into the **invert** of a manhole which introduces the **effluent** from a branch drain into the main drain in the direction of flow.

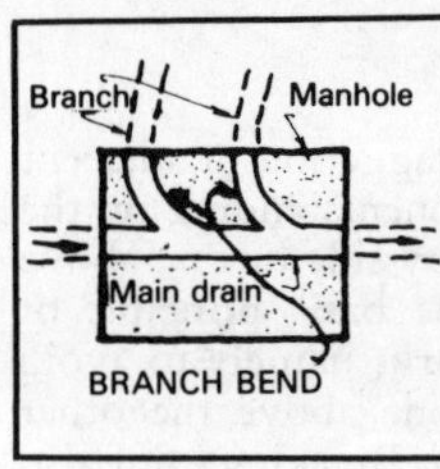

BRANCH BEND

branch fitting A fitting used to connect one or more branch pipes or channels to a main pipe or channel.

branch knot In timber, two or more knots branching from one centre.

brandering The nailing of a **lath** to the underside of a wide floor joist (usually over 75 mm wide), to which plaster laths are subsequently nailed. This allows the plaster to acquire a better **key** under the joist than if the plaster laths were fixed directly to the joist.

brash or brashy 1. Small pieces of disintegrated rock. 2. Timber which breaks on impact with little or no splintering.

brass An alloy containing zinc and more than 50% copper, which tarnishes on exposure to the atmosphere.

braze welding The joining of metals using a technique similar to **fusion welding** and a filler metal with a lower melting point than the parent metal, but neither using capillary action (as in **brazing**) nor intentionally melting the parent metal.

brazier A receptacle for a portable open fire.

brazing The joining together of two pieces of red hot metal (brass, copper, steel or cast iron in any combination) with a film of copper-zinc alloy (hard **solder**), using a flux such as borax. Any method of heating the metal can be used. The alloy is referred to as the **filler** metal and its melting point is usually above

500 °C, but always below the melting temperature of the parent metal. cf. **braze welding**.

brazing alloy The **filler** metal used in **brazing**.

break A change in direction of a wall or an interruption in its plane.

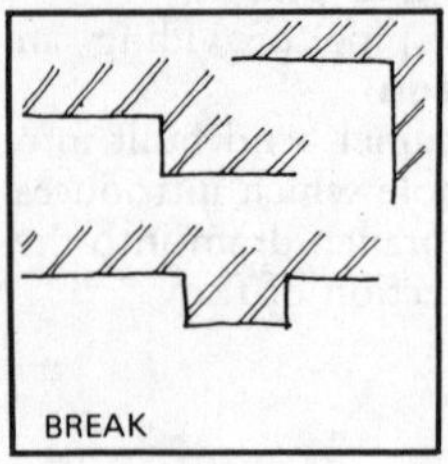

breaking joint The staggering of adjacent joints to avoid components ending on the same line either side by side or one above the other. This is the basic principle of **bonding** in **brickwork**, namely to avoid perpends occurring one above the other on succeeding courses. Breaking joint also occurs in **veneer** ends, reinforcement in concrete slabs and boarding etc.

breaking stress The amount of force necessary to overcome the resistance of a material to fracture.

breaking weight or breaking load The amount of load necessary to cause a beam or frame-member of a structure to fracture.

break iron 1. A **back iron** 2. A **dressing iron**.

breast 1. A projection into a room, containing a fireplace and its flue or flues. 2. (Scotland) The **riser** of a **stair**. 3. A **sill** wall.

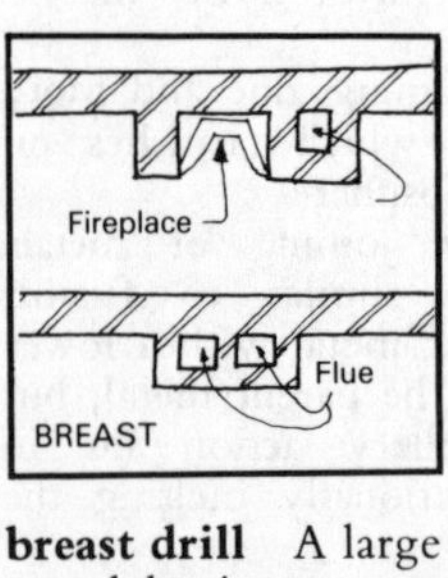

breast drill A large drill operated by hand and having an upward extension with a cross bar which rests against the operator's chest when drilling so that his weight can increase the drilling speed.

breasting Levelling the points of saw teeth prior to sharpening.

breast lining The panelling below a window sill.

breast wall A low wall, approximately breast high, used to retain earth.

breather paper A **building paper** which is moisture resistant and water repellant, but is permeable to water vapour; often used as an additional weatherproofing layer behind lightweight **cladding** where it is necessary to allow internal moisture (residual in the structure, or from internal humidity) to escape.

breeze block A **building block** made from coke breeze. These blocks are no longer made in the UK, but the term is often incorrectly used to refer to **clinker blocks**.

bressummer A large lintel to span a wide opening; formerly often of timber, now of steel or reinforced concrete.

brick A kiln-burnt clay walling element manufactured by hand or machine, pressed or wire-cut to a standard size which, in the UK, is usually 215 × 103 × 65 mm, although other sizes are available, *eg* **modular bricks**. Other materials and methods of manufacture are used to produce concrete and calcium-silicate (sand-lime) bricks. A range of special bricks is produced as standard specials.

brick-and-a-half wall In the UK a wall approximately 304 mm thick (*ie* made up of one **header** and one **stretcher** in thickness).

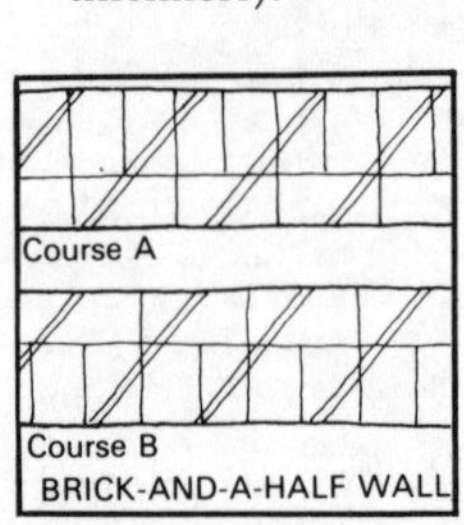

brick axe A **bricklayer's hammer**.

brick core Brickwork under a **relieving arch**.

bricklayer's hammer A small hammer with a sharp **cross peen**.

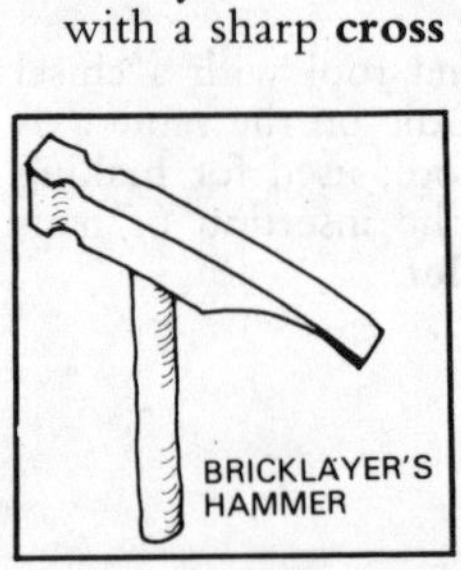

brick masonry (USA) **Brickwork**.

brick nogging Non-loadbearing brickwork infilling between members of a structural framework.

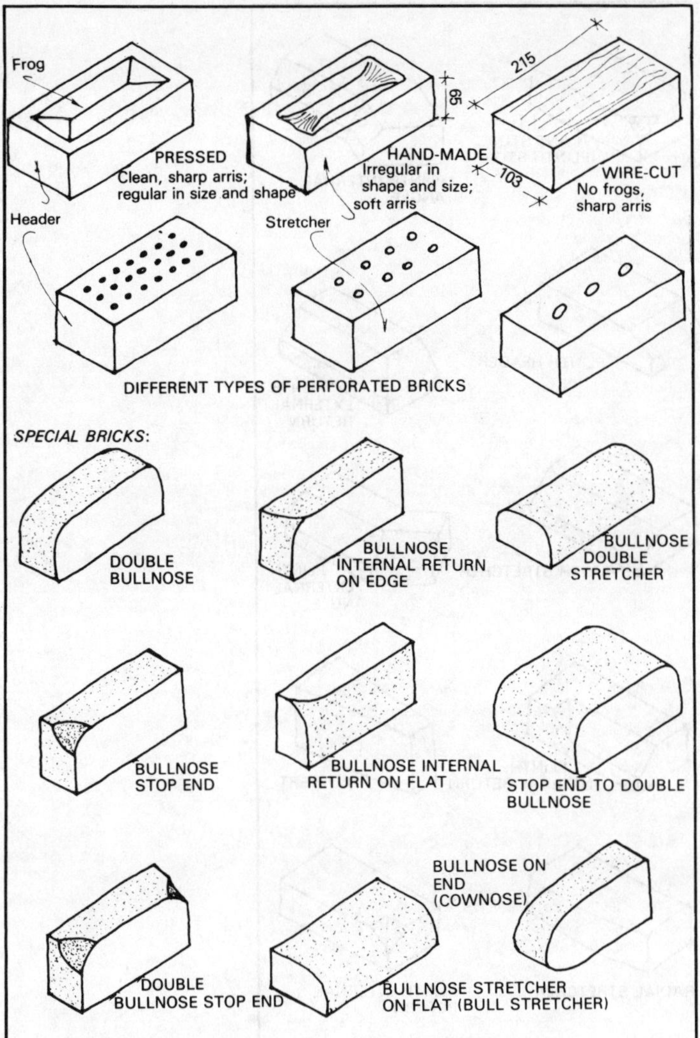

BRICK

brick-on-edge sill or coping A sill or coping made of bricks laid on edge and presenting a **header** face to the wall surface.

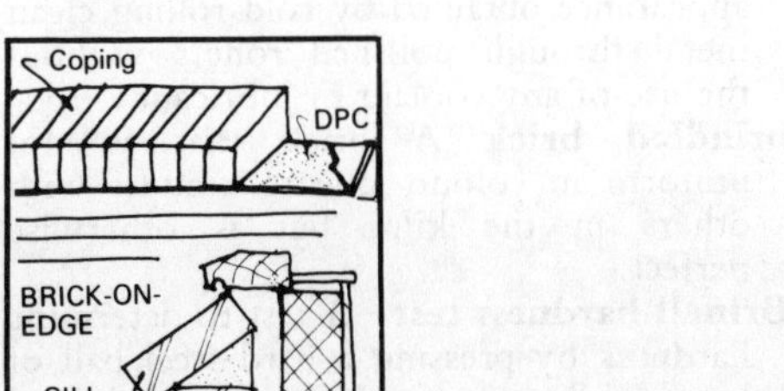

brick set (USA) A **bolster** for cutting bricks.

brick trimmer A **trimmer arch** made of brick.

brick trowel A large bricklayer's trowel with a blade about 275 mm long; used for spreading **mortar**.

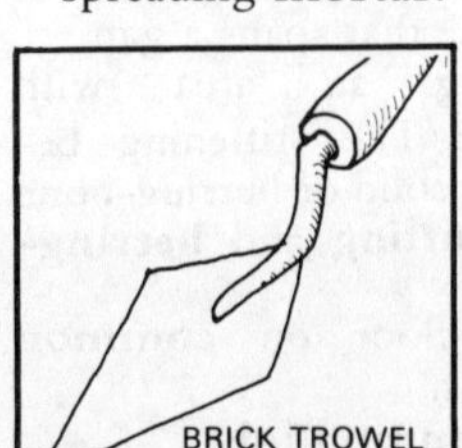

brick veneer An external skin of brickwork, usually one half a brick thick,

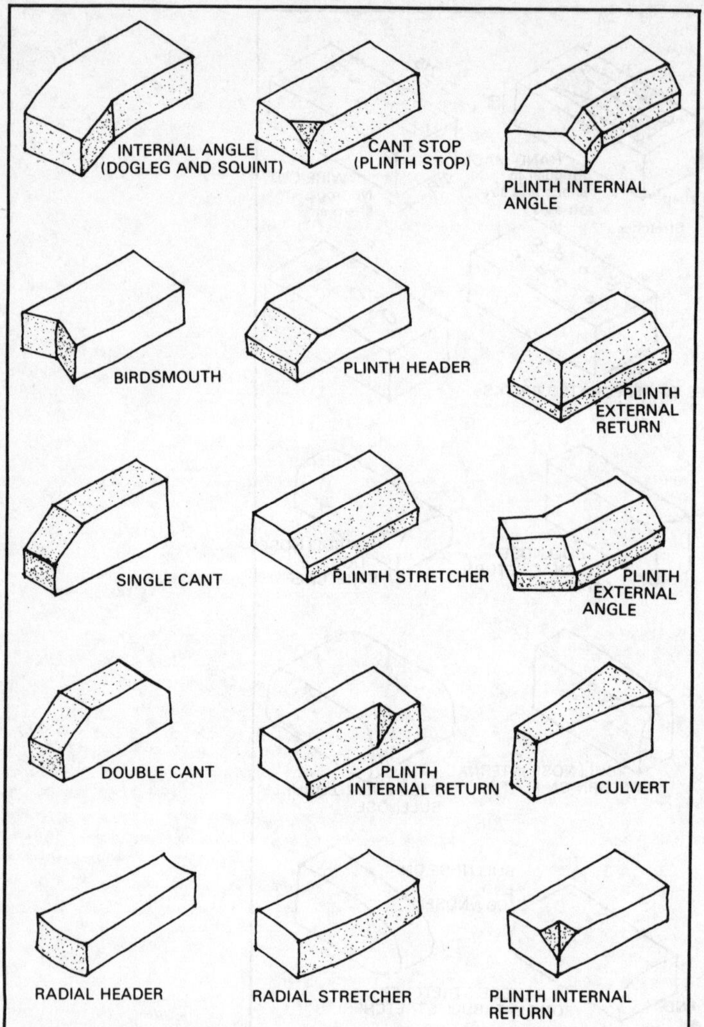

BRICK (CONT)

which serves no structural purpose but faces a framed structure, often of timber.

brickwork Walling built of bricks, laid to **bond** and in a mortar.

bridge board A **cut string**.

bridge stone A stone that spans a gap.

bridging 1. Spanning an area with **common joists** 2. The stiffening between joists in either solid or herring-bone form. cf. **solid strutting** and **herring-bone strutting**.

bridging floor A floor on **common joists** without beams.

bridging joist A **common joist**.

bridging piece A bearer between or across **common joists,** to carry a partition.

bridle (Scotland) A **trimmer joist**.

bright Of timber, free from discoloration.

bright rolled finish The burnished appearance obtained by cold rolling clean metal through polished rollers without the use of any coolant or lubricant.

brindled brick A brick that is not uniform in colour, due to contact with others in the kiln, but is otherwise perfect.

Brinell hardness test A test to determine hardness by pressing a hard steel ball of known diameter under a standard load into the surface of the material being tested and measuring the diameter of the indentation produced. The Brinell

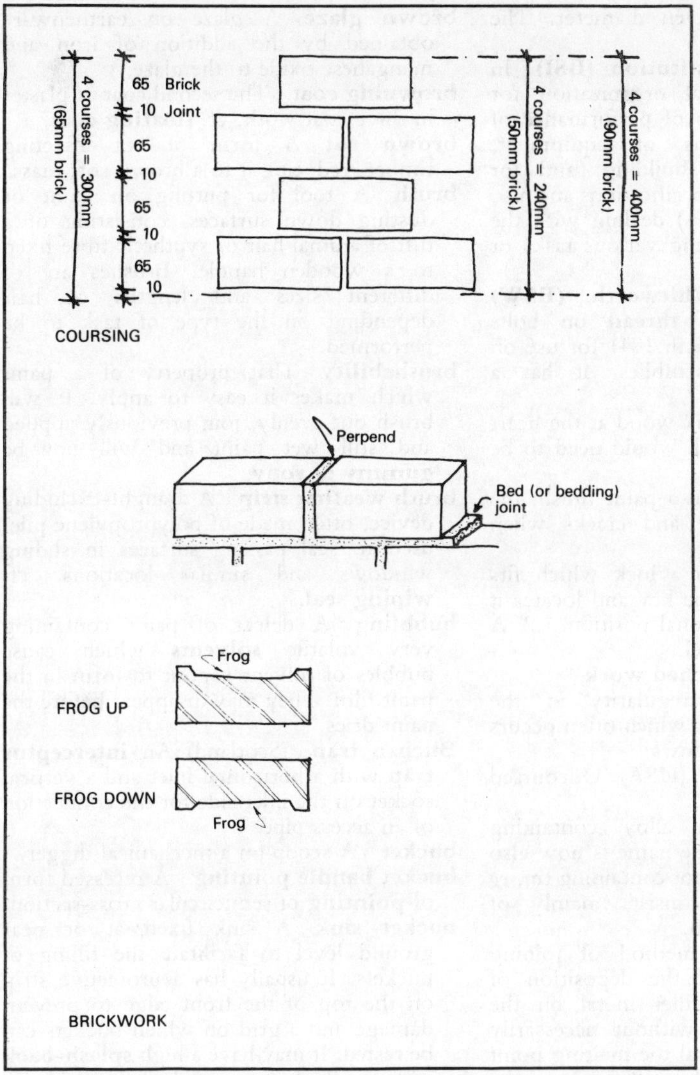

hardness number equals the load in kgs divided by the spherical area of the impression in mm^2.

brise-soleil A louvred screen set horizontally or vertically to shield the face of a building (and particularly its windows) from the direct rays of the sun.

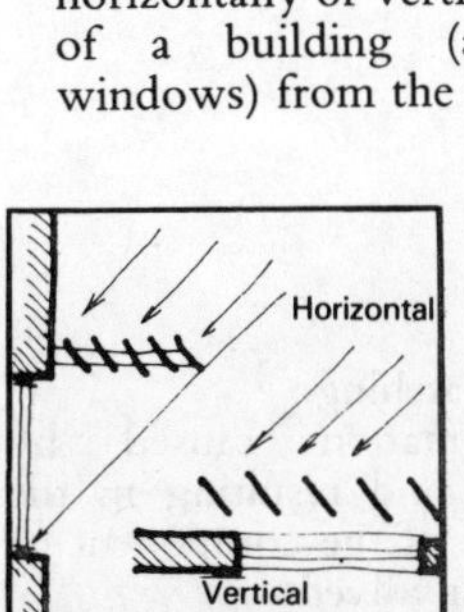

bristle brush A paint **brush** made of hair, now largely replaced by brushes made with synthetic fibres.

British Associated thread See **BA thread**.

British screw gauge A currently accepted method of sizing wood screws in the UK, based on the numbers from 0 to 20.

British Standard (BS) A document produced by the **British Standards Institution** setting out acceptable standards of performance for various items, including building materials; comparable with the W German DIN.

British Standard fine (BSF) thread A style of **thread** on bolts based on the British Standard Whitworth thread but of finer pitch for a given diameter. The thread angle is 55°.

British Standards Institution (BSI) In the UK the national organization for establishing standards of performance of materials and items of equipment, including those for building, and for publishing standard specifications and also codes of practice (CPs) dealing with the methods of undertaking various tasks or design operations.

British Standard Whitworth (BSW) thread A style of **thread** on bolts introduced in the UK in 1841 for use on heavy structural assemblies. It has a thread angle of 55°.

brittle heart The weak wood at the heart of some timber which would need to be **boxed**.

brittleness A defect in a paint finish; the paint is not flexible and cracks when stretched.

broach 1. The pin in a lock which fits inside the barrel of the key and locates it in the correct operational position. 2. A mason's pointed **chisel**.

broached work **Punched work**.

broken bond An irregularity in the bonding of brickwork which often occurs in piers between windows.

broken-range ashlar (USA) Uncoursed rubble.

bronze Primarily an alloy containing copper and tin, but the name is now also used for other alloys not containing tin, *eg* aluminium bronze consists mainly of copper and aluminium.

bronze welding A method of joining metals by means of the deposition of molten copper-rich filler metal on the parts to be joined, without necessarily fusing them. In general the melting point of the filler metal is above 850 °C and the method does not depend on **capilliarity**. It is not really welding and bronze is not necessarily used.

bronzing The application of a chemical finish to copper or copper alloys by immersion to alter the colour of their surfaces. (This must not be confused with the electro-deposition of bronze.)

brooming 1. Scratching a **floating coat** of plaster to form a **key** for the **setting coat**. 2. The bruising of a pile head by the pile driver.

brotch A **spar** in thatching.

brought to course In walling similar to uncoursed **rubble** the masonry is brought to course roughly at intervals varying in frequency with the locality, but often coinciding with the depth of the **quoins**.

brown glaze A glaze on earthenware obtained by the addition of iron and manganese oxide to the glaze.

browning coat The second coat of plaster in three coat work. cf. **floating coat**.

brown rot A form of rot affecting timber, reducing it to a brown soft mass.

brush A tool for putting on paint or dusting down surfaces, consisting of a tuft of animal hair or synthetic fibre fixed to a wooden handle. Brushes are of different sizes and lengths of hair depending on the type of task to be performed.

brushability That property of a paint which makes it easy to apply. It will brush out evenly, join previously applied and still wet paint and will not be **gummy** or **ropy**.

brush weather strip A draught-excluding device, often made of polypropylene pile, used to seal passing surfaces in sliding windows and similar locations. cf. **wiping seal**.

bubbling A defect of paint containing very volatile **solvents** which cause bubbles of solvent vapour to form in the paint film. They may disappear before the paint dries.

Buchan trap (Scotland) An **interceptor trap** with a horizontal inlet and a vertical socket on the inlet side for the connection of an access pipe.

bucket A scoop on a mechanical digger.

bucket handle pointing A recessed form of **pointing** of semicircular cross-section.

bucket sink A sink fixed at or near ground level to facilitate the filling of buckets. It usually has a protective strip on the top of the front edge to prevent damage and a grid on which buckets can be rested. It may have a high **splash-back** and usually has a grated **waste** with no plug and chain.

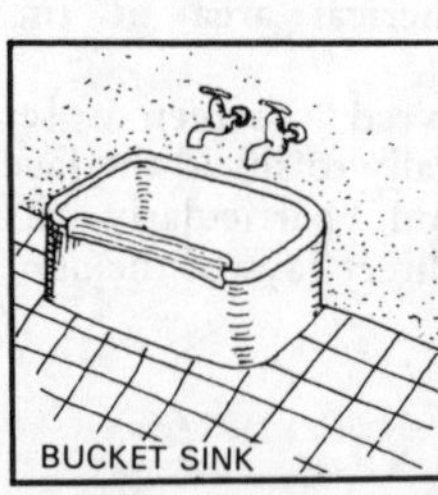

buckle A **spar** in thatching.

buckling A deformation caused by compressive forces and resulting in the bending out of line of the component or structural member involved.

budger A painter's graining tool.

buff To polish with a small degree of abrasion with buffing wheels, as in polishing **terrazzo**.

builder's level 1. A **dumpy level**. 2. A **spirit level** set in a **straight edge**.

building block See **block**.

building board A manufactured sheet material used to face framework or construct fittings; made from wood veneers (**plywood**) or laminations (**blockboard**) or fibres (**chipboard**), plaster (**plasterboard**), asbestos cement (**asbestos wall board, asbestos insulation board**) or other mineral (non-asbestos wall board).

building code A regulation controlling the methods and materials to be used in the construction of a building, equivalent in the UK to the Building Regulations.

building component See **component**.

building element See **element**.

building in Fixing a component to a brick, block or masonry wall by bedding on mortar and surrounding it with elements of the walling material; components so fixed include **wall ties**, **air bricks, joist hangers**, etc.

building line 1. A line within a building site, usually established by the Local Authority, in front of which no building can be constructed. The object is to set building frontages back from the roadway. 2. The line of the external face of a building.

building module 1. A repetitive section of a building marked either by bays of the structural frame, the size of a wall panel, etc. 2. A prefabricated section of a building.

building paper A heavy, partially waterproof paper, consisting of a fibre-reinforced bitumen core between sheets of brown paper; used as a **sheathing** to framed walls under the **cladding**, as a separating layer between materials of differing thermal and moisture movements or under next-to-earth concrete slabs to avoid loss of the cement into the base. cf. **breather paper**.

Building Regulations The **building codes** of the British Isles, comprising the Building Regulations for England and Wales, the Building Standards (Scotland) Regulations and the Building Regulations for Northern Ireland.

Building Research Establishment (BRE) A government-financed building research organization in the UK, under the control of the Department of the Environment, whose main establishments are at Garston (Watford), Boreham Wood, Princes Risborough and East Kilbride.

building sealant A joint sealant applied by hand, gun, knife or trowel, or in strip form or by pouring. It is used to maintain a seal between the sides of a joint which is subject to some degree of movement.

building system A method of building, sometimes called **industrialized building**, which conforms to a dimensional discipline and employs a limited range of components and the techniques of **prefabrication**. The aim of a building system is to provide a method of reducing the amount of time spent on the site and the amount of site labour used, and of achieving a weather-tight shell as quickly as possible to allow the finishing trades to commence work earlier. The effect of this, it is argued, should reduce the all-up cost of the building. This, however, is achieved only when the quantities of repeat components are so large as to reduce their unit cost. There are in the UK both commercially sponsored systems and Local Authority sponsored systems.

built-in See **building in**.

built-up roofing Two or more layers of **bitumen felt** used as a roof finish, mainly to flat roofs. Layers are laid to **break joint** and are bedded in bitumen.

bulk density The weight per unit volume of a material, generally expressed in kg per m^3.

bulkhead The sloping top to a staircase to allow headroom, often associated with a raised floor above at that position, for instance in a bulkhead cupboard.

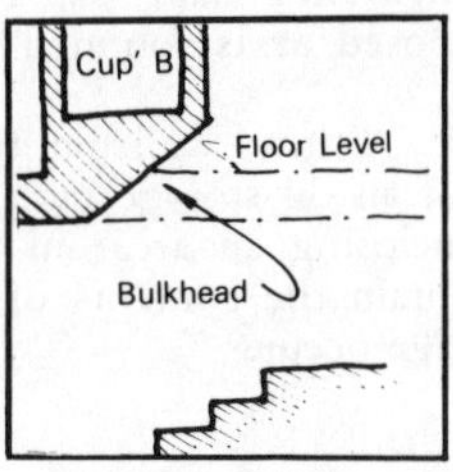

bulkhead fitting A light fitting, often used externally, mounted directly on to a wall face or a ceiling soffit; usually a heavy duty fitting.

bulking The difference in volume of a given mass of sand or other fine material in moist and dry conditions, expressed as a percentage of the volume in dry conditions. The extent of bulking will depend on the thickness of the film of water surrounding each particle (the moisture content) and the particle size.

bulldog clip A **floor clip**.

bulldog plate A **timber connector**.

bullet catch A **ball catch**.

bullhead tee (USA) A tee-shaped pipe in which the **branch** connection is longer than the **run**.

bull-nose 1. The rounded **arris** of a brick or tile or other component. 2. A small metal plane used to form rebates.

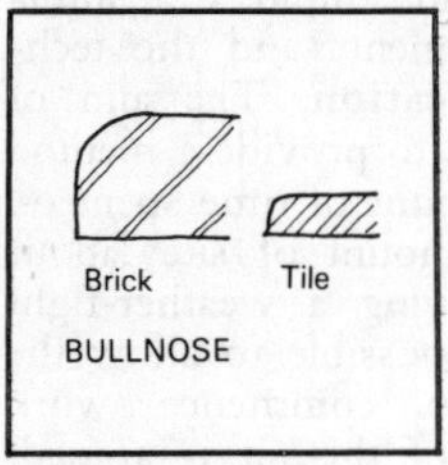

bull-nose step A step at the bottom of a flight with one or both ends rounded on plan. cf. **stair**.

bull-nose winder A **winder** in a **quarter space** of the stair with the **riser** rounded near the strings to throw the junction clear of the corner and achieve a stronger construction.

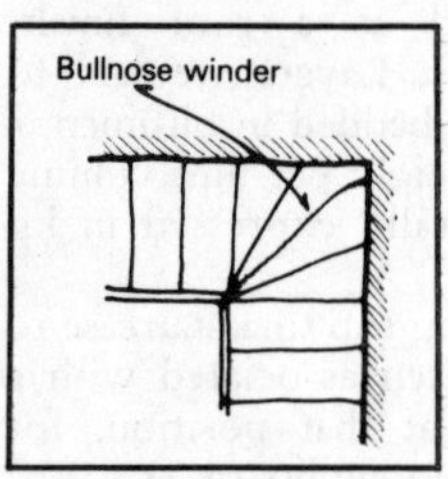

bull stretcher A stretcher laid as a **quoin**, with the exposed **arris** rounded. cf. **brick**.

bund or bund wall A low wall built around the seating of an oil storage tank or similar vessel, enclosing an area sufficiently large to contain the contents of the tank should leakage occur.

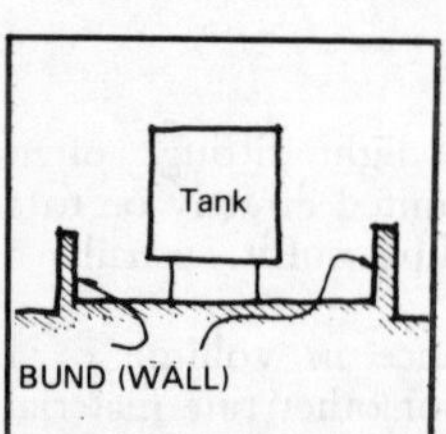

bungalow siding (USA) **Weather-boarding**.

buoyancy The natural tendency of air to rise when there is a temperature differential. The force that causes **stack effect**.

burl A **burr**.

burning in The fixing of a lead **flashing** into a dove-tail groove in a wall by **caulking** with molten lead.

burning off The softening of an old paint film with a **blow lamp**, thus making it easy to scrape off.

burning rate See **combustion** rate.

burnt clay Clay burnt in a kiln to make bricks, tiles and earthenware goods, as opposed to baked clay as in **adobe**.

burnt lime Quick lime (CaO)

burr 1. The curly grain **figure** obtained by cutting through the enlarged trunks of certain trees, such as walnut, the excrescence in the tree growth giving strong colour contrasts in the markings. 2. The rough and often sharp edge left on metal by a cutting tool.

burring reamer A tool used in a **brace** to remove the fine burrs still adhering to the inside of a pipe after cutting.

bush A metal lining to a cylindrical hole.

bush hammering The **tooling** of a concrete or stone surface using a light percussive tool, driven usually by compressed air, to provide a texture to the surface which improves its appearance and weathering properties.

bushing A pipe fitting for jointing two pipes of different diameters, threaded on the inside and outside, used in place of a **taper pipe** in restricted spaces.

butane A hydrocarbon of the paraffin series (C_4H_{10}) used in a liquefied form as a fuel.

butt 1. The thicker end of a **shingle** or any other component of variable thickness. 2. To abut, or meet without overlapping.

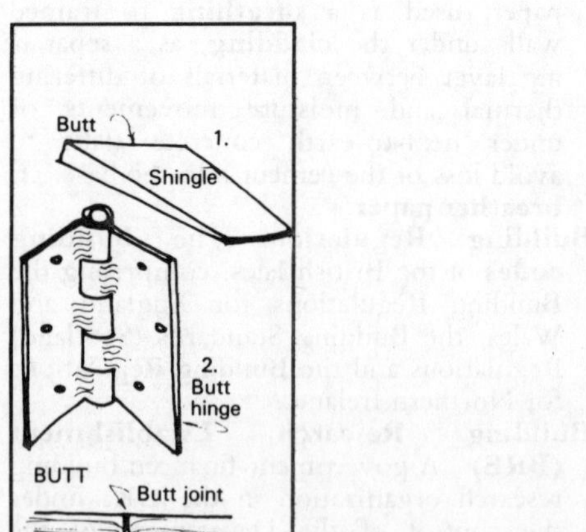

butterfly fastener A **cavity fixing** device used in thin-wall cellular construction (such as plasterboard-faced studwork), which consists of a long **machine screw** with two spring-loaded arms, connected to a nut, which open once inside the cavity. By operating the screw these can be drawn against the back surface of the lining, spreading the load of the fastener over a large area of lining.

butterfly roof A roof in which there are two pitched surfaces inclined towards the centre of the building and not towards the outside.

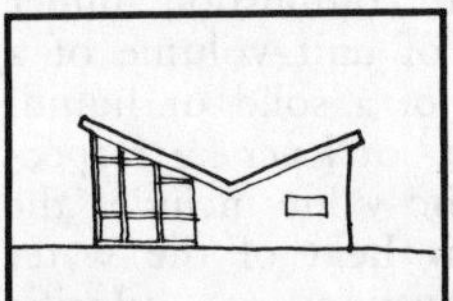
BUTTERFLY ROOF

butterfly wall tie A **wall tie** made of galvanized steel wire twisted into the form of two triangles with apexes touching.

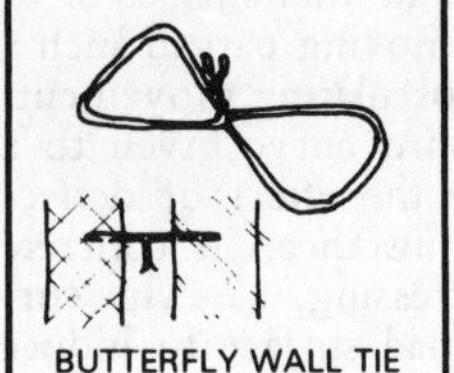
BUTTERFLY WALL TIE

C

cabinet file A single-cut, smooth, half-round file used to finish wood joints.

cabinet scraper or scraper plane A tool similar to a **spokeshave**, but with a thin, flat blade of steel set almost vertically. It is drawn over a wooden surface to remove plane marks prior to sandpapering.

cabin hook A simple piece of ironmongery used to secure a cupboard door or casement, consisting of a hooked bar which engages in a **screw eye**.

buttering Spreading mortar on the **perpend** face of a brick before laying it.

buttering trowel A bricklayer's trowel which is slightly smaller than a **brick trowel**.

butt gauge A **marking gauge**.

butt hinge A hinge intended to be sunk into the edge of a door and into the **hanging stile** so that the two surfaces fold together. The ordinary steel butt hinge is cheap and durable.

butt joint 1. A joint between two materials or components of the same material, in which their squared ends meet but do not overlap or penetrate each other. 2. In veneering, the joint perpendicular to the grain.

button or button catch A simple catch for a cupboard door in the form of a small length of wood or metal held loosely by a screw so that it can be positioned across the **meeting stiles** of two doors, or the junction between a door and its frame.

button-headed screw A **screw** with a hemispherical head.

buttress A **pier** or short thickening of a wall to provide stiffness or additional support under a point of vertical load or to withstand a sideways thrust.

butt stile The **hanging stile** of a door.

butt veneer The strong curly grain figure of a veneer cut from that portion of the trunk of the tree which is joined by the roots.

butt weld A **butt joint** between two pieces of metal, formed by a **weld**.

butyl rubber A synthetic rubber.

buzz saw A **circular saw**.

by-pass A layout of pipes which direct the flow around, rather than through, a particular piece of equipment or pipework.

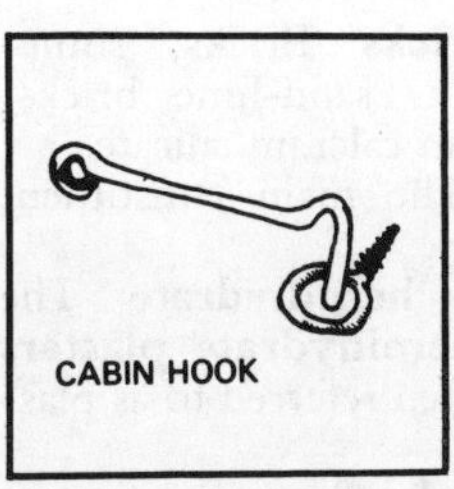
CABIN HOOK

cable The means of conveying electric current. Cables are conductors surrounded by insulation. The conductors are usually of copper (having a low electrical resistance) although aluminium and other metals are sometimes used. The insulation is either rubber, paper, or PVC, all of a high electrical resistance. Sizes of cable are quoted according to the cross-sectional area of the conductor (1, 1.5 and 2.5 mm^2). Above these sizes multi-strand conductors are used so as not to lose flexibility, *eg* 4 mm^2 cable contains 7 strands, each 0.85 mm diameter.

cable trunking A fabricated system of linear enclosures of rectangular cross-section, assembled together by connectors and having one removable side; used for the protection of electrical cables.

cadmium plating A protective finish given to minor items of steel ironmongery such as **nails** and **screws.** If chromated it takes paint more easily. cf **chromating**.

caisson A boxlike structure sunk below water or ground level surrounding an area of work in which further excavation work or constructional work is to take place. The caisson is pumped dry of water or cleared of soil in each case.

caking A defect of paint in which the dense pigments settle into a mass which is not easily dispersed by stirring.

calcination The process of heating a solid to produce a material capable of being used as a plaster or forming the base for a plaster. Limestone and chalk are calcined to form quicklime; gypsum to form hemihydrate and anhydrous calcium sulphate.

calcite A crystalline form of calcium carbonate ($CaCO_3$).

calcium carbonate The main constituent of limestone and chalk ($CaCO_3$).

calcium chloride ($CaCl_2$) An **accelerator** no longer used in structural concrete in the UK.

calcium hydroxide **Slaked lime** ($Ca(OH)_2$).

calcium oxide The main constituent of **quick lime** (CaO).

calcium silicate bricks Bricks, sometimes referred to as sand-lime bricks, which are made from calcium silicate.

calcium sulphate The main constituent of **gypsum** ($CaSO_4$).

calcium sulphate hemihydrate The basis of retarded **hemihydrate plasters** ($CaSO_4.\frac{1}{2}H_2O$), often referred to as plaster of Paris.

calculated brickwork Structures comprising walls of loadbearing brickwork whose structural performance, and therefore thickness, is calculated rather than arrived at by rule of thumb. This form of construction is more economic than framed structures for low or medium rise buildings of limited span, having repetitive patterns of internal walls on each floor.

callus The abnormal formation of tissue around the area of an injury to a tree.

calorie A unit of heat, being the amount of heat required to raise the temperature of 1 kg of water at 15 °C by 1 °C. It is now superseded by the **SI unit** of energy, the **joule**.

calorific value The amount of heat liberated by the complete combustion, under specific conditions, of unit volume of a gas or unit weight of a solid or liquid, expressed in J per m^3 or J per kg respectively. Gross calorific value includes the release of the **latent heat** of the water produced by combustion; net calorific value does not.

calorifier A vessel through which circulates, in a sealed enclosure of pipes, steam or hot water which transfers its heat to the water in the surrounding vessel. cf. **indirect cylinder.**

cam A non-circular plate on a spindle, the turning of which has the effect of increasing the distance between the spindle and the edge of the plate at a given position, causing it to bear on another surface or to operate some other moving part in such a way as to create an oscillating movement.

camber 1. The upward curve given to a beam to counteract the effect of deflection, achieved, for instance, in concrete by means of pre-stressing. 2. The curvature given to a road surface to induce drainage of the surface water or to assist vehicles in cornering.

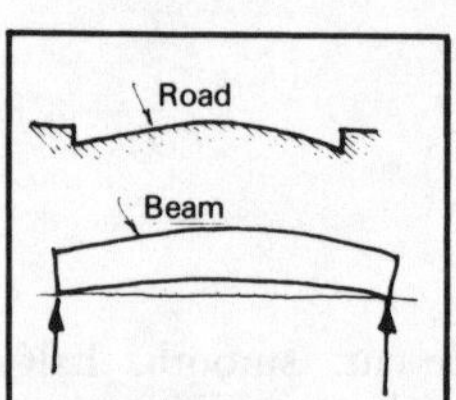

camber arch See **arch**.

camber board A **template** used in the construction of a chamber.

camber slip A piece of wood with a **camber** in its upper surface used in the **centering** of flat brick arches to ensure that the bricks in mid span are set above the **springing line**.

cambium Layers of actively dividing cells between the bark and the wood of a tree.

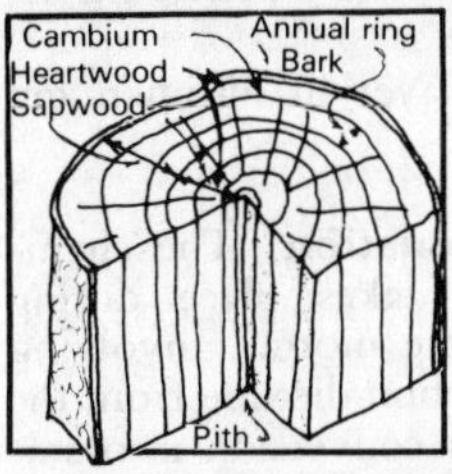

came The **glazing bar** in **leaded lights**, made of lead or copper and of an H-shaped cross section, into which adjoining pieces of glass fit.

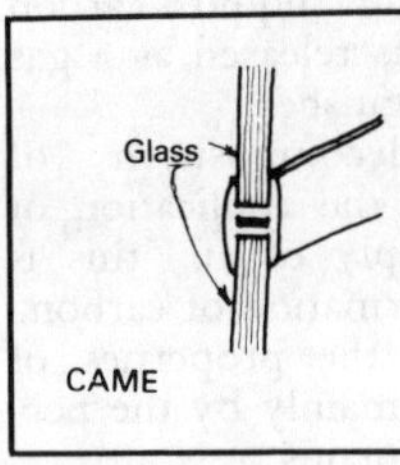

camel-hair mop A dome shaped brush with soft hair.

camp ceiling (Scotland) The ceiling of a room within the roof, having four sloping surfaces.

candela (cd) An SI unit of luminous intensity. Candelas per m^2 is the SI unit of **luminance**.

candle lamp A decorative lamp having its bulb in the shape of a candle flame.

cant 1. To tilt. 2. To cut the **wane** from a log.

cant brick A splayed **brick**.

cant course A course of stones laid with the natural bedding of the stone vertical.

cantilever A beam or slab built into the structure, or otherwise fixed, at one end and totally unsupported at the other end.

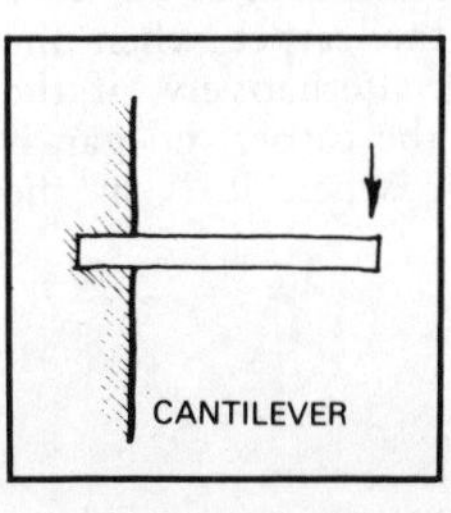

cantilever bracket A bracket in the form of a **cantilever**, often built into the wall or hooked into a metal upright attached to the wall, to withstand the load placed upon it.

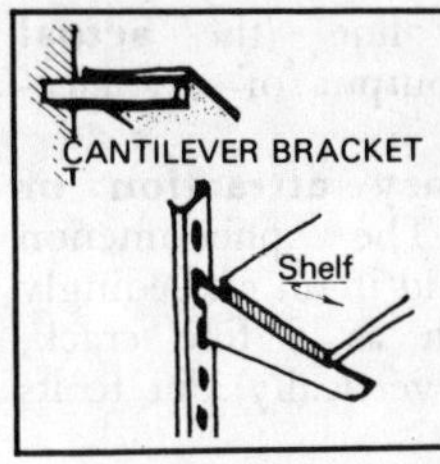

cantilever step A step in a flight of steps or a staircase (once of stone, now usually of concrete) which is built into the side wall of the stair and is unsupported at its other end. Sometimes the **riser** of the step will bear for its whole length on the **tread** of the step below it.

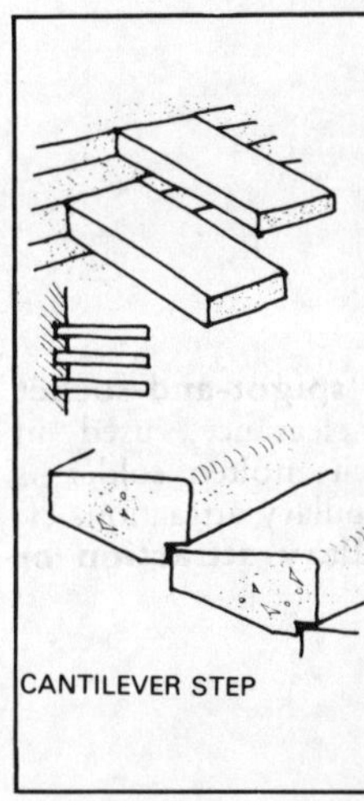

canting strip A **water table**.

cant strip (USA) A **tilting fillet**.

cap 1. A plate, often moulded, on top of a post, such as a **newel** to provide a decorative finish and cover the **end grain**. 2. That part of a lamp which fits into the lampholder. 3. A cover with internal threads which closes the end of a pipe.

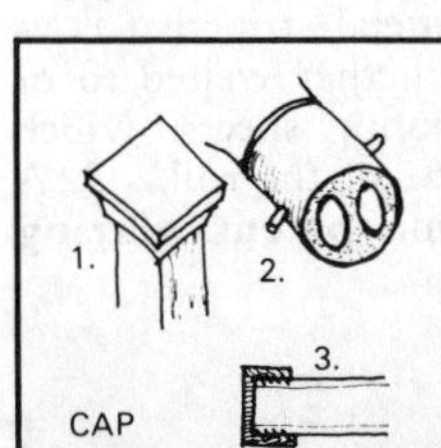

capacity 1. The volume contained in a vessel. 2. The amount of liquid contained in a vessel when filled to 75 mm below the overflow. 3. The amount of liquid contained in a cistern when filled to the marked water line (the **actual capacity**). 4. The output of any electrical apparatus.

capillarity or capillary attraction or capillary action The phenomenon associated with a liquid in an exceedingly confined space, such as a fine crack, where it flows (even vertically) due to its own surface tension.

capillary groove 1. A horizontal groove in a vertical face into which a lead **undercloak** is dressed. 2. A groove cut in the face of one or both of two adjoining components to form a space and thus break the effects of capillary attraction in the crack between the two components.

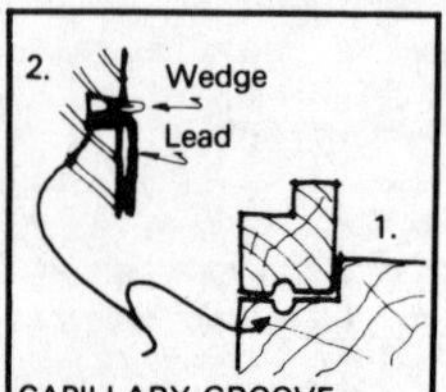

CAPILLARY GROOVE

capillary joint A **spigot-and-socket joint** with a fine clearance, used in plumbing, into which molten solder is caused to flow by capillary attraction. cf. **Capillarity or capillary attraction or capillary action**.

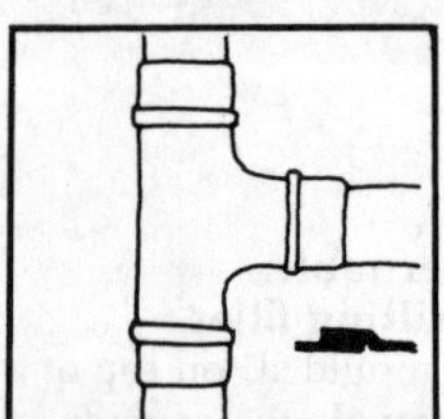
CAPILLARY JOINT

cap iron A **back iron** of a **plane**.

capping 1. The top of a low internal wall or feature which does not reach the ceiling, *eg* **dado** capping 2. In **flexible-metal roofing**, the metal strip that covers the wood **roll**, whether welted to or separate from the roofing sheets, which are dressed up the side of the roll. 3. A metal section in some **patent glazing** systems that fixes the glass and covers the upstand of the **glazing bar**. 4. The sealing of the end of a pipe in a plumbing installation with a **cap**.

cap sheet The top layer in bitumen felt **built-up roofing**.

capstone A **coping**.

carbonating or carbonation The chemical process which takes place during the hardening of lime mortar, involving the absorption of carbon dioxide from the air and the mortar's conversion into stable **calcium carbonate**. This can be expressed as: $Ca(OH)_2 + CO_2 = CaCO_3 + H_2O$; or hydrated lime + carbon dioxide = calcium carbonate + water.

carbon dioxide fire extinguisher A fire extinguisher containing liquid carbon dioxide (CO_2) which is released as a gas on activating the extinguisher.

carbonization The decomposition of organic substances by the application of heat in a limited supply of air, this is accompanied by the formation of carbon.

carbon steel A steel, the properties of which are determined mainly by the percentage of carbon it contains.

carborundum A carbide of silicon (SiC) obtained by heating coke with sand in an electric furnace. It is extremely hard and is used in **non-slip nosings** to stairs and as an **abrasive**.

carcassing 1. The formation of the structure before lining out. 2. The installation of plumbing or gas pipework and electrical conduits.

carpenter's hammer A **claw hammer**.

carpentry The timber work consisting of structural carcassing (floors, roofs, studwork, etc.) as opposed to finished timber work (architraves, skirtings, etc.) which is **joinery**.

carpet strip A timber or metal strip fixed to the floor beneath a door, which is the thickness of the carpet against which it stops. Its use prevents the foot of the door from dragging on the carpet when the door is opened, or, alternatively, if the door is cut to clear the carpet, no gap is left below the door when it is in the closed position.

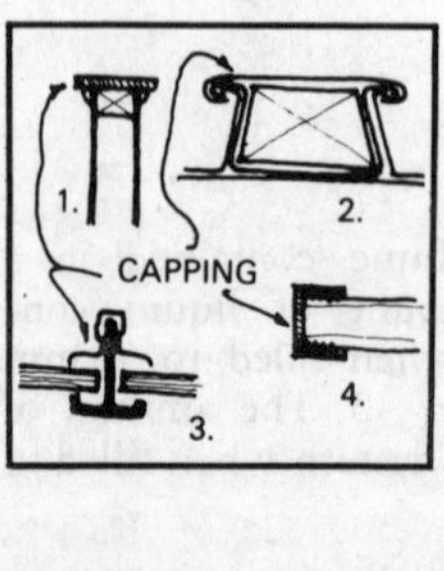

CAPPING

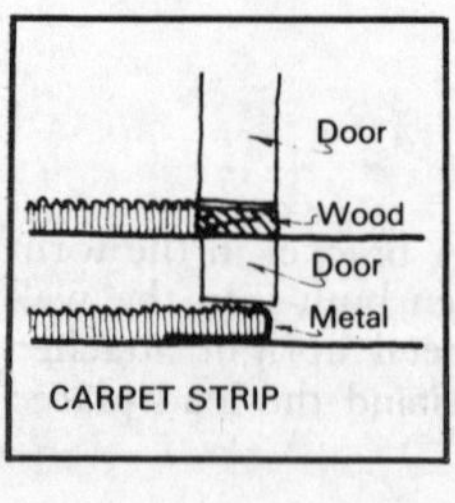

CARPET STRIP

carriage An inclined timber placed midway between the two strings of a **stair**.
carriage bolt A **coach bolt**.
carrying capacity The size of current which a **cable** or **fuse** can convey without causing the overheating which would result in excessive voltage drop or the fuse blowing.
cartridge fuse A **fuse** in an incombustible tube which protects the installation from fire when the fuse melts or blows.
carved brickwork Brickwork laid with very fine joints, which is subsequently carved in low relief.
case 1. That part of a latch (usually in box form) into which the bolt mechanism is assembled. 2. (Scotland) A **cased frame**. 3. A surface layer which has been hardened by a change in the composition of the material, by heat treatment, or by a combination of both. cf. **case hardening**.
cased beam A structural steel beam which has been surrounded with fire resistant material (concrete, asbestos insulation board etc.) to protect the steel from the effects of fire for a stated period of time.

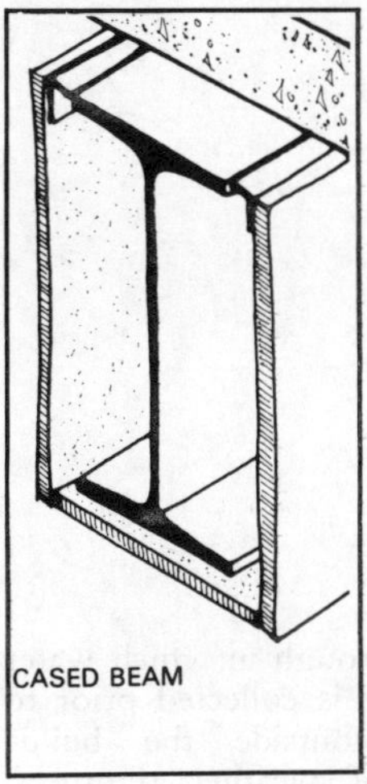

CASED BEAM

cased column A structural steel column which has been surrounded with fire resistant material (concrete, asbestos insulation board etc.) to protect the steel from the effects of fire for a stated period of time.
cased frame The hollow frame of a counterweight-operated **sash window**, containing the sash weights and pulleys.
case hardening 1. Hardening the surface of a material by changing its composition followed by suitable heat treatment. This is effected by carbonizing (the introduction of carbon into the surface by heating to, and holding at, a temperature above the transformation range whilst in contact with a source of carbon) or cyanide hardening (the introduction of carbon and nitrogen into the surface by heating to, and holding at, a suitable temperature whilst in contact with molten cyanide). 2. In timber, the condition in which the outer layers have undergone drying and become set without corresponding shrinkage, causing stress between the inner and outer layers.
casein glue A wood adhesive made from a protein precipitated from skimmed milk and other reactants. It is more water-resistant than animal or fish glues and has reasonable gap-filling properties. It is water-soluble before it hardens. Lime is sometimes added to improve its resistance to bacterial attack. cf. **gap-filling glue**.
casement door A fully glazed door or one of a pair of doors, sometimes referred to as a French window. The door is always hinged.

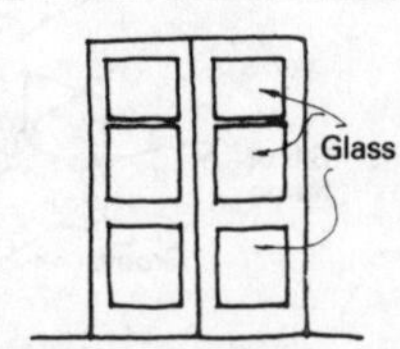

CASEMENT DOOR

casement stay A piece of ironmongery used to retain a **casement window** in an open position.
casement window A window in timber, metal or plastic, a part of which is hinged to open. Usually the main **lights** are side-hung and the smaller lights (night ventilators) are top-hung.
casing 1. The internal lining to a window or door opening, usually in wood. 2. A boxing on the internal surface of a wall or ceiling containing pipe runs.
casting resin A synthetic resin in liquid form that can be poured into moulds and thus shaped without pressure into solid articles; often a **phenol formaldehyde resin** or **epoxy (or epoxide) resin**.
cast-in socket A female threaded cylinder cast into concrete to receive a bolt fixing.
cast iron An alloy of iron and carbon containing more than 1.7% carbon (generally 2.4 – 4.0%). Silica, manganese, sulphur and phosphorus are also present.
cast steel The term applied to carbon tool steel made by the high frequency crucible or other melting process.

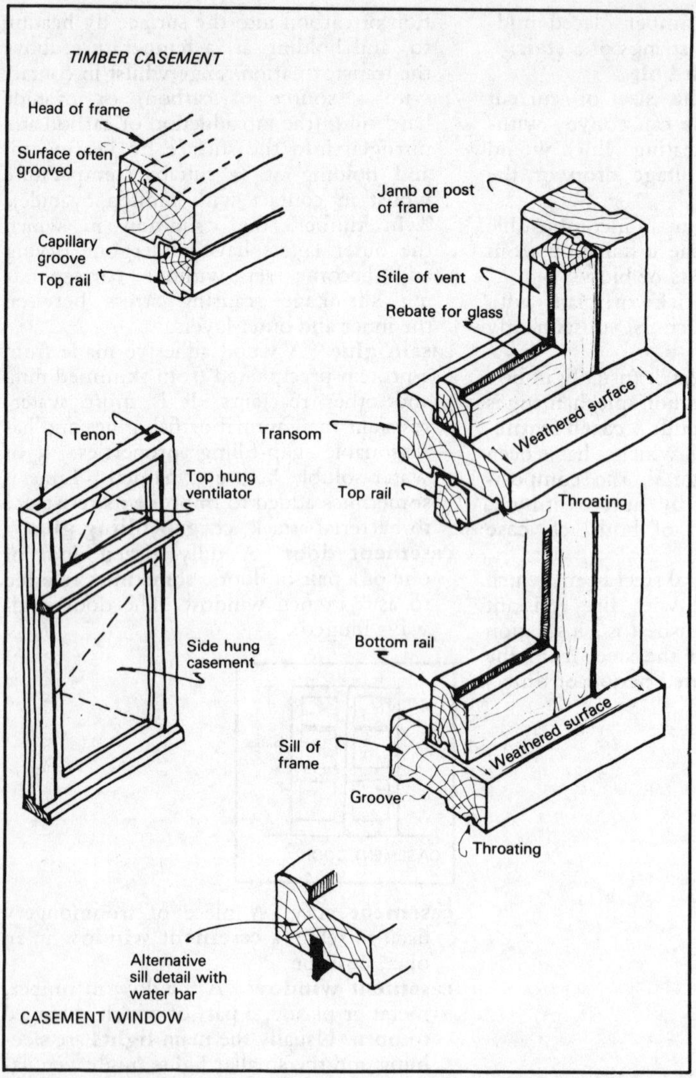

CASEMENT WINDOW

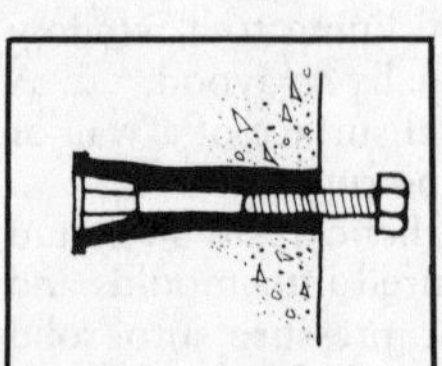
CAST-IN SOCKET

cast stone See **reconstructed stone**.

catalyst A substance added in small quantities to start or accelerate a chemical reaction, but which remains itself unchanged.

catch That part of a fastening that secures the latch.

catchment tray 1. In **open joint** cladding, a horizontal trough in which water behind the cladding is collected prior to being discharged outside the building. 2. In tests of weather tightness, collection vessels at various points of the test specimen to measure water penetration at those points.

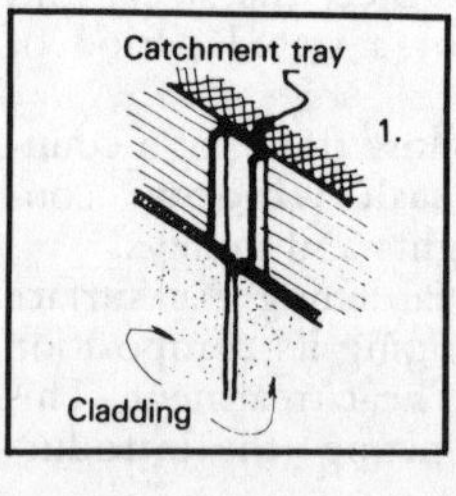

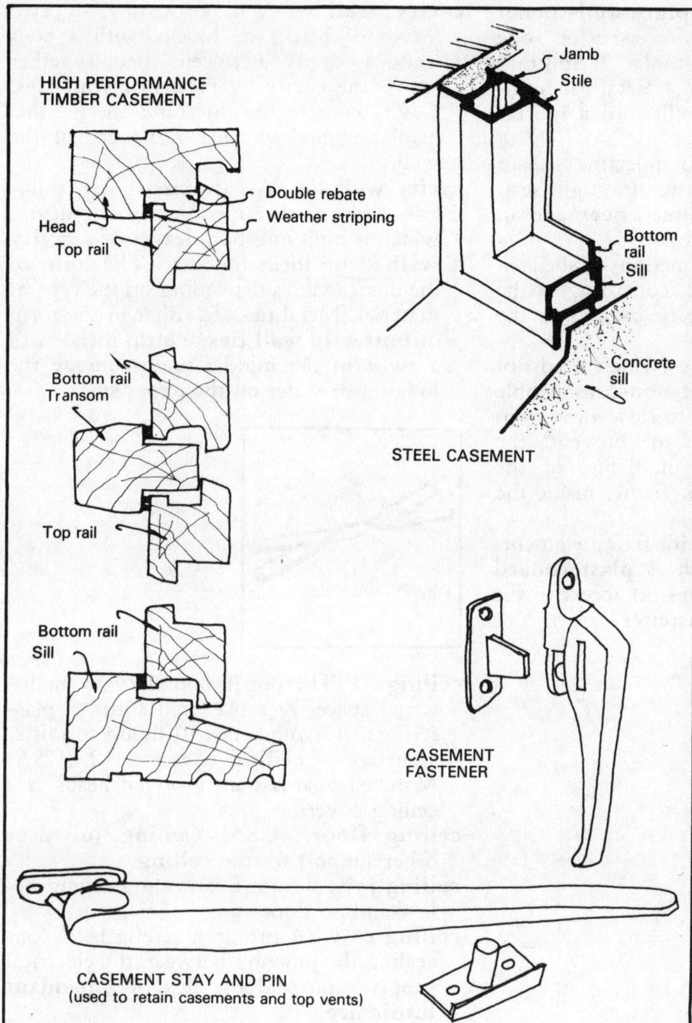

CASEMENT WINDOW (CONT)

catch pit 1. A chamber at the entrance to a drainage system into which solid matter sinks, thereby being prevented from blocking the drain. 2. A reservoir to receive surface water drainage.

cat eye (USA) A **pin knot**.

cathedral glass A rolled translucent glass one surface of which has a specific type of texture giving it a degree of obscuration. The degree of obscuration varies according to the texture.

cathode The electrode through which a direct current leaves an **electrolyte** (in electrolysis) and at which the positive ions are discharged and the negative ions are formed, or other reducing reactions occur.

cat ladder 1. An arrangement on a sloping roof to give a foothold and protect the roof covering; sometimes referred to as a duck board. 2. A vertical ladder giving access to a loft or an access platform.

caulked joint A **spigot-and-socket joint** in which the jointing material, such as lead wool or asbestos rope, is compacted by means of caulking tool and hammer.

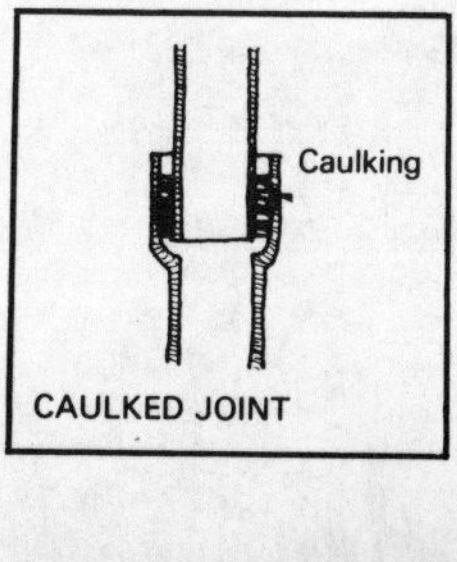

CAULKED JOINT

caulking 1. Filling a **spigot-and-socket joint** with lead wool or asbestos rope driven in by a caulking tool. 2. Splitting and twisting the ends of a metal bar to increase its grip when built into a mortar joint.

caulking gun A tool for injecting sealant into joints to produce a weathertight seal.

cavil An axe with a pointed **peen** and an axe blade for cutting stone.

cavitation The phenomenon associated with the flow of liquid, consisting of the formation and collapse of cavities in the liquid.

cavity barrier A device (which need not necessarily be made of non-combustible material) which is used to close a cavity in a structural element to prevent the penetration of smoke or flame, or the movement of smoke or flame, inside the cavity. cf. **fire stop**.

cavity fixing A device for fixing elements to a cellular base, such as **plasterboard partitioning**. It requires no access to the rear cavity. A **blind fastener**.

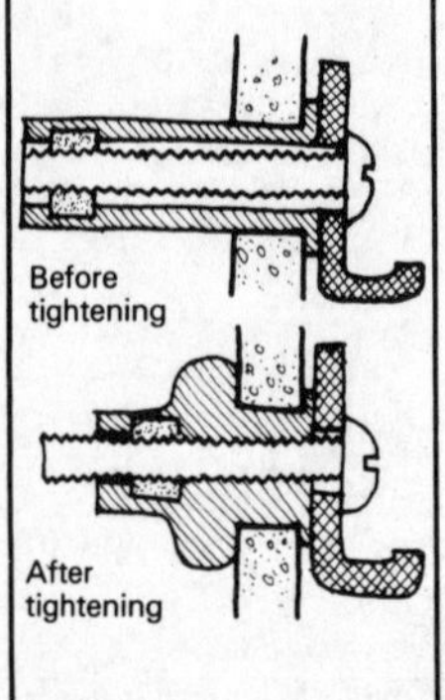

CAVITY FIXING

cavity flashing See **cavity tray**.

cavity tray A **dpc** which crosses the cavity of a **cavity wall** above a bridging of the cavity, and which slopes towards the outside in order to direct any water in the cavity away from the inner leaf.

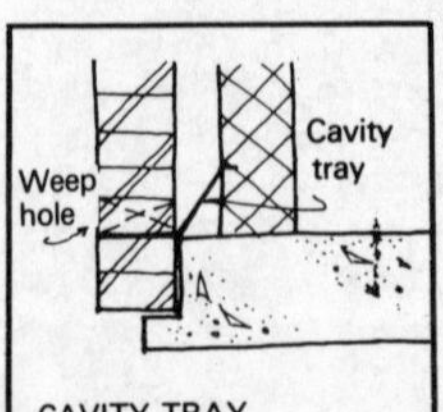

CAVITY TRAY

cavity wall A wall consisting of two leaves of bricks or blocks with a continuous cavity between, tied together across the cavity by means of **wall ties**. Cavity construction increases the thermal insulation and weather resistance of the wall.

cavity wall tie A galvanized steel, stainless steel or other metal or plastic device which is built into both leaves of a **cavity wall** to tie them together. The form of the device varies depending on the type of material. Metal ties are either in the form of **butterfly wall ties** or strip metal with a twist in the middle to discourage the lodging of water on the upper surface.

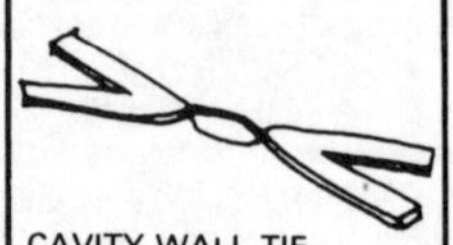
CAVITY WALL TIE

ceiling 1. The upper boundary to an internal space, *eg* a plastered soffit, a plasterboard (or other board) lining to joists, a surface of **ceiling tiles** etc. 2. (USA) Matched boards with grooved beads as a ceiling covering.

ceiling floor (USA) **Ceiling joists** or other support for the **ceiling**.

ceiling joist A joist carrying a ceiling below and no floor above.

ceiling rose A fitting at ceiling level concealing the junction between the electrical supply cable and the flex of a **pendant luminaire**.

ceiling tile A decorative or plain tile, with or without fire resistant properties, used to form a ceiling surface, often suspended below the structural floor or roof and resting in, or supported by, a light metal framework. Ceiling tiles can also be stuck to an existing ceiling surface for decorative, acoustic or thermal effect.

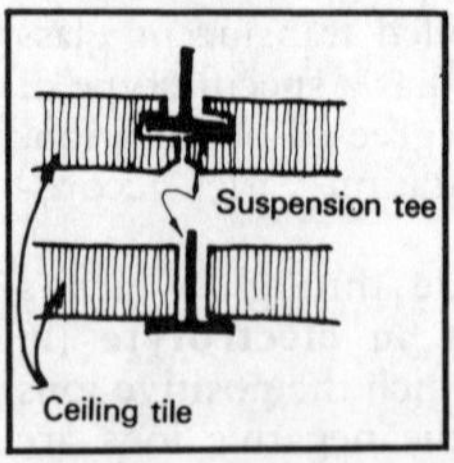

ceiling trimming The framing of the **ceiling joists** around a chimney breast.

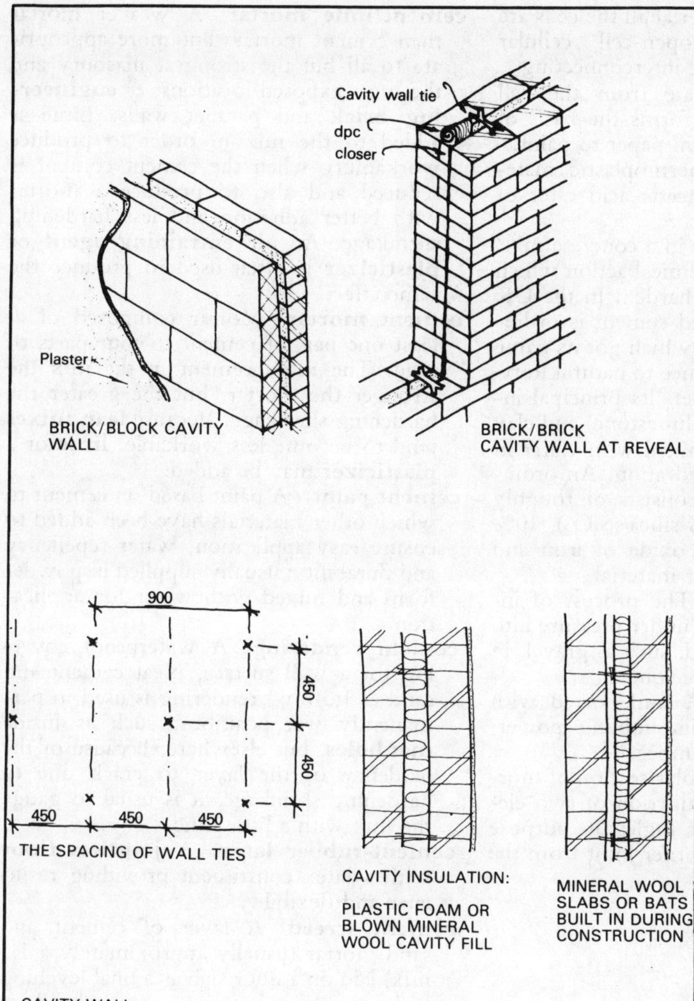

CAVITY WALL

ceiling void The space above a **suspended ceiling**, often used for the containment of services.

CEILING VOID

cell 1. A small cavity surrounded partially or completely by an enclosing wall. 2. A complete electrolytic system comprising a cathode, an anode and an intervening electrolyte.

cellar rot See **wet rot** (***Coniophera cerebella***).

cellular block or cellular brick A **block** or **brick** with one or more moulded holes or cavities which do not entirely pass through the block, and with the solid material amounting to 50–75% of the total volume. cf. **hollow block**.

cellular board Plywood, the core of which consists of a cellular construction, with at least two cross-band plies on either side of the core.

cellular concrete See **aerated concrete (autoclaved aerated concrete)**.

cellular material Material having many cells dispersed throughout its mass. In closed-cell cellular material all the cells are non-connecting; in open-cell cellular material all the cells are interconnecting.

cellulose A carbohydrate from the cell walls of plants which forms the basis of numerous products from paper to paint.

cellulose acetate A thermoplastic material derived from an acetic acid ester of cellulose and plasticizer.

cement A **binder** used in a concrete mix. It is involved in the chemical action which causes the concrete to harden. In the UK the most generally used cement is ordinary **Portland cement** which got its name because of its resemblance to natural Portland limestone when set. Its principal ingredients are chalk (or limestone) and clay and it hardens when mixed with water in a process known as hydration. An ordinary Portland cement consists of roughly 60% lime (CaO), 20% silica (SiO_2), 10% alumina (Al_2O_3), 3% oxide of iron and small amounts of other material.

cementation process The process of injecting **cement grout** under pressure into certain types of ground, such as gravel, in order to render it more solid.

cement-coated nail A **nail** coated with cement to improve its holding power, particularly in green timber.

cement fillet A triangular section of mortar placed across the junction of two elements meeting at right angles, its purpose being to protect the corner joint from the ingress of water.

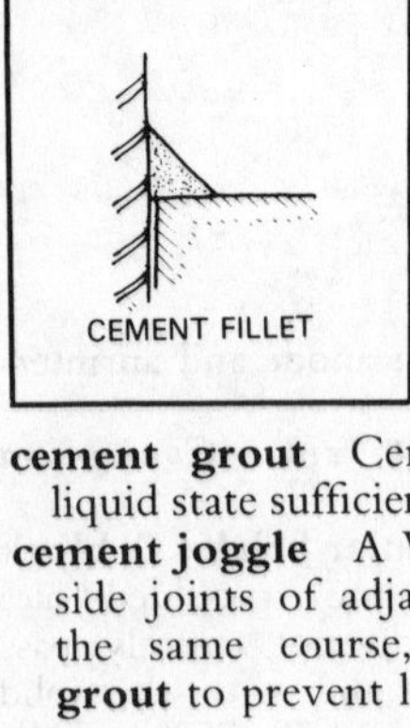

CEMENT FILLET

cement grout Cement and water in a liquid state sufficiently thin to be poured.

cement joggle A V-shaped sinking in the side joints of adjacent walling stones in the same course, filled with **cement grout** to prevent lateral movement.

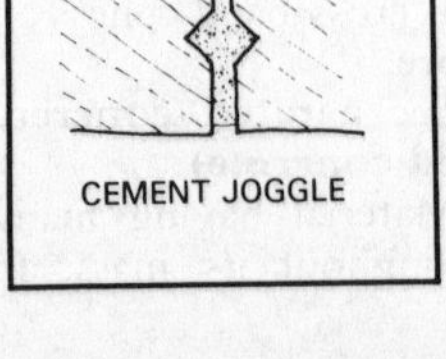

CEMENT JOGGLE

cement/lime mortar A weaker mortar than cement mortar, but more appropriate to all but the strongest masonry and the most exposed locations, *eg* **engineering brick** and parapet walls. Lime is added to the mix in order to produce workability when the cement content is reduced and also to produce a mortar with better adhesion and less hardening shrinkage. An **air entraining agent** or **plasticizer** is often used to produce the same effect.

cement mortar Mortar composed of at least one part of cement to four parts of sand. The more cement in the mix the stronger the mortar, but the greater the hardening shrinkage. Because **lean mixes** tend to become less workable, **lime** or a **plasticizer** may be added.

cement paint A paint based on cement to which other materials have been added to ensure easy application, water repellency and durability; usually supplied in powder form and mixed with water for application.

cement rendering A waterproof covering for a wall surface. Neat cement and sand (a 1:3 mix) rendering is used in permanently wet positions, such as inside **manholes**, but elsewhere, because of the tendency of the layer to crack due to hardening shrinkage, it is usual to gauge the mix with a little lime.

cement-rubber latex A **jointless floor** with a latex constituent providing resilience and flexibility.

cement screed A layer of cement and sand mortar (usually approximately a 1:3 mix) laid on a floor slab as a final levelling and smoothing layer to receive the floor finish; often 38–50 mm thick.

cement slurry A liquid cement-water mix used to wash wall and floor surfaces prior to their receiving a further treatment. The slurry provides a **key**.

cement-wood floor A **jointless floor**, now rarely used in the UK, consisting of cement, sawdust and pigment. It was not suitable for wet areas.

centering A temporary supporting framework, usually of timber members,

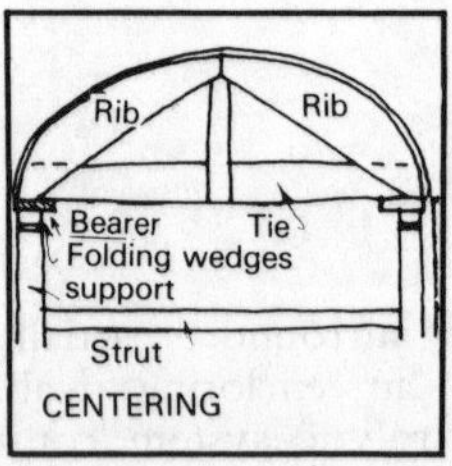

CENTERING

made to support an arch or dome structure until the materials of construction have hardened sufficiently to be self-supporting.

central heating A form of heating, either dry (**warm air heating**, electric **underfloor heating** or off-peak storage blocks) or wet (hot water or steam heated radiators or convectors) which heats the whole (or substantially the whole) of a building, as opposed to a system using individual sources of heat in different rooms.

centre bit A wood **bit** for use with a **brace**, having a central point and two side cutters for drilling deep holes. The first side cutter describes a circular groove around the central drilling; the second side cutter clears the wood between the groove and the centre drilling.

centre-hung A description of a window that is operated by a **pivot hinge** on each **jamb** of the frame.

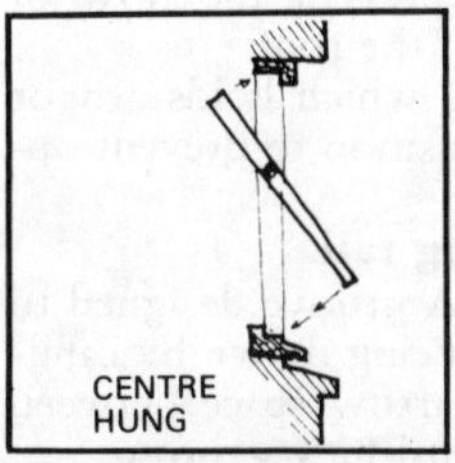

centre nailing The fixing of slates by nailing along a line slightly above the head of the slate in the course below and just above the middle of the slate being fixed. In areas of high wind speeds, slates fixed in this way are less likely to be stripped than those with end nailing. There is, however, only one layer of slate over each nail hole.

centre of gravity A point in or near a body about which all its parts balance. The weight of a body can be considered as acting through its centre of gravity.

centre-to-centre A method of dimensioning on drawings, which is based on establishing the measurements between

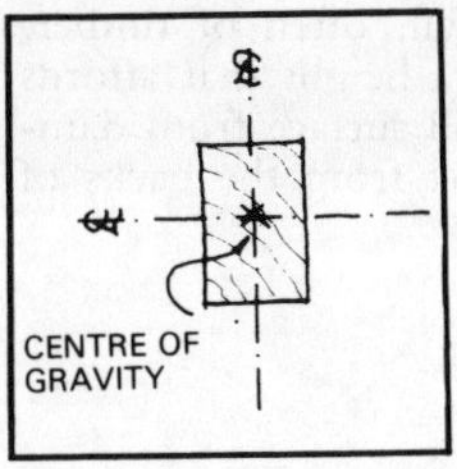

the centre lines of elements – particularly repetitive elements such as columns – thereby reducing the number of dimensions required to set out a structure.

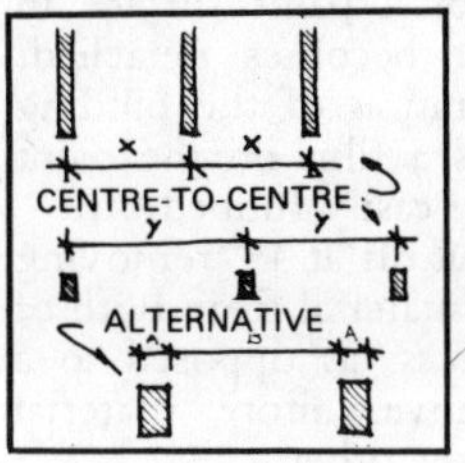

cesspit or cesspool A large underground chamber built in brick or concrete with a waterproof rendering, or sometimes preformed in **glass reinforced plastic**; provided where there are no main drainage services, for the collection of the foul drainage. Cesspits are periodically pumped out. cf. **septic tank.**

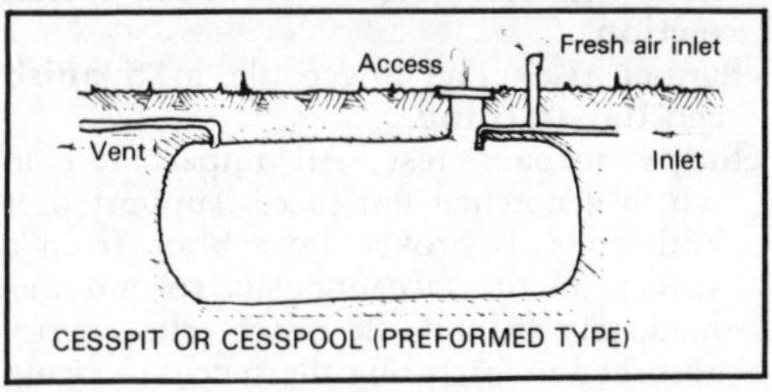

chain A measuring device used in land surveys where long distances are to be measured, consisting of a series of heavy wire sections (usually each 300 mm long) linked together and fitted with brass swivel handles at the ends.

chain link fencing A diamond-shaped mesh of galvanized steel or plastic-coated steel wire, which is supported from steel or concrete posts to form fencing.

chain saw A power driven saw consisting of a chain with projecting cutting picks, travelling round a frame.

chain tongs A plumber's tool for gripping heavy pipes, consisting of a chain connected to a toothed bar.

chair rail A **dado** rail, often of timber, placed on a wall at a height that affords protection to the wall surface from damage caused by impact from the backs of chairs.

chalking A defect of a paint surface in which the pigment becomes detached, due to the disintegration of the binding medium, and forms a film on the paint surface which can be easily rubbed off.

chamfer A corner cut off at 45° removing an equal amount of material from both of the two adjacent faces, as opposed to a **bevel**, which removes more material from one face than the other.

chamfer stop 1. A brick which stops a chamfer; often referred to as a plinth stop or a cant stop. cf. **brick**. 2. A chamfer that dies away into a sharp **arris**.

channel 1. In drainage, a semicircular open pipe. cf. **block channel** and **anti-splash device**. 2. A metal section with a cross-section in the shape of a square U. cf. **rolled steel joist (RSJ) or rolled steel channel** (**RSC**) and **cold-rolled section**.

channel tile The lower tile in **Spanish** and **Italian tiling**.

charpy impact test An impact test in which a notched test piece, supported at both ends, is broken by a blow from a striker on the face opposite to and immediately behind the notch, the energy absorbed in fracturing the specimen being recorded.

charring rate The rate at which light, friable, mainly carbonaceous residue forms on wood or other organic matter as a result of incomplete combustion. Timber is, in fact, protected to some degree by the formation of this charcoal on its surface since it provides an insulating layer and slows down combustion. All timbers char at a predictable rate which is in the region of 20 mm per half hour.

chase A groove cut or formed in a wall, roof, ceiling or floor in order to conceal electric conduits or service pipes, or into which flashings may be wedged. cf. **duct.**

chase mortise A type of **mortise** used to frame a timber in between two others which are already fixed, a sloping or tapering chase being cut to the bottom of the mortise to allow the cross-piece of the frame to be slid into position.

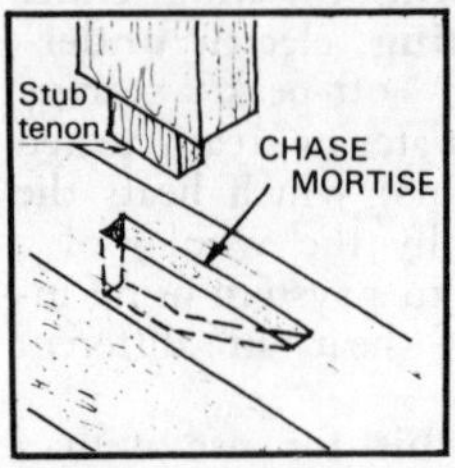

check 1. A crack caused by seasoning stress. It occurs along the grain of timber and is restricted to the surface layer. The defect is called checking. 2. A defect of a paint film in which the paint film cracks completely, causing a breakdown of the coating. 3. (Scotland) A **rebate**.

checked back Rebated. cf. **rebate**.

check-fillet In asphalt flat roofing, an asphalt upstand to prevent the flow of water off the edge of the roof.

check lock A device which holds a door lock in the locked position to prevent operation with a key.

check rail A **meeting rail**.

check throat (ing) A groove designed to prevent water from being drawn by capillary action into a narrow space between two members. cf. **capillary groove**.

cheek The side of a **dormer** (**window**).

cheek nailing (Scotland) A method of double nailing slates in which a hole is pierced near one side of the slate and a notch is cut in the other side.

cheese head A shape of head sometimes used for **machine screws** in which the head is cylindrical rather than domed, *ie* like a cheese.

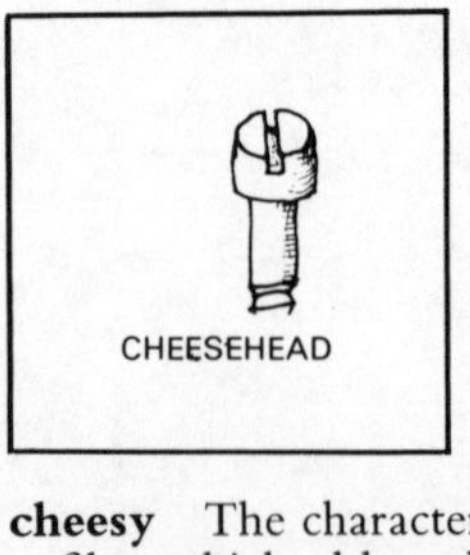

cheesy The character of a paint or varnish film which although dry is mechanically weak and rather soft.

chemical anchor An **anchorage fixing**, usually into a concrete element, based on a strong two-part adhesive being released into a pre-drilled hole and setting into it a metal stud. The two chemicals of the adhesive are contained in separate sachets in the fixing device and it is the act of inserting the device in the hole, or the stud into the device, that mixes the two together and commences the chemical setting of the adhesive.

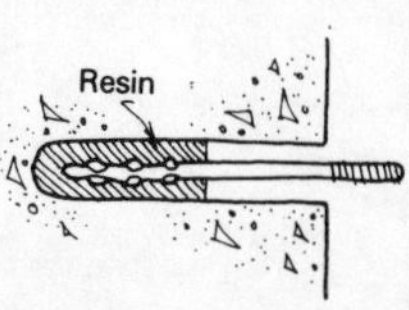

CHEMICAL ANCHOR

chemical closet A closet, not connected to a drain, that uses a liquid reagent as a deodorant.

chemical foam extinguisher A fire extinguisher from which chemical foam is expelled when the chemical solutions, stored separately within the body of the extinguisher, are caused to mix and react.

chequer work Masonry walls built of two different materials in alternating squares.

chestnut paling or cleft chestnut paling Fencing composed of light chestnut poles, cleft and bound together by two or three lines of galvanized wire. Connected to timber posts, these form a cheap and easy-to-erect fence, usually from 900 to 1,800 mm high with **pales** at 50 to 100 mm centres. The paling is made up in rolls for easy handling. A heavier form of chestnut paling fencing is less frequently seen. In this case the heavier cleft pales are driven into the ground and then bound round with wire.

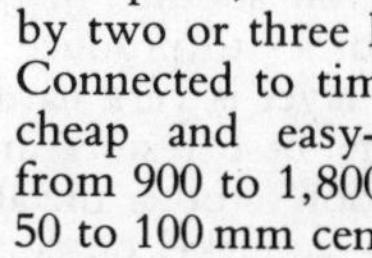

CHESTNUT PALING

chilling A defect of paint which has been stored at low temperatures.

chimney A hollow structure, constructed of either brickwork or masonry, in which the internal cavity is continuous from a fireplace to the open air, or a metal or asbestos-cement **flue** pipe fulfilling the same function of conveying to the atmosphere the smoke and combustion fumes from a fire or boiler.

chimney back The wall behind a **fireplace**. In the case of back-to-back fires this can be one wall which forms a back to both.

chimney block (USA) A precast concrete sectional tube used as a **flue lining**.

chimney breast The housing of a **fireplace** and **flue** in the form of a projection into the room; constructed of the same materials in which the wall is constructed. cf. **breast**.

chimney can (Scotland) A **chimney pot**.

chimney gutter A **back gutter**.

chimney lining A **flue lining**.

chimney pot The topmost feature of a **flue**, usually in the form of an earthenware pipe, projecting above the brickwork of the chimney to discharge the smoke and combustion fumes above the level of the brickwork.

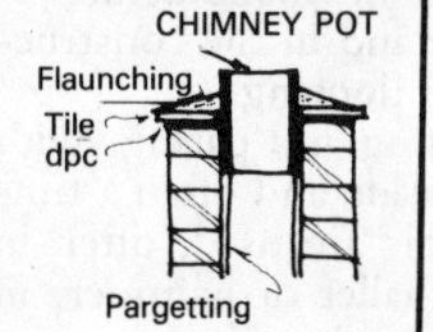

chimney shaft A term usually applied to a large chimney from a boiler installation, which encloses the **flue** or flues from that installation; nowadays often constructed of precast concrete sections.

chimney throating That part of a **flue** above the flue gathering, where the flue opening takes on the size and shape it will maintain for its remaining height – usually as close as possible to the fireplace.

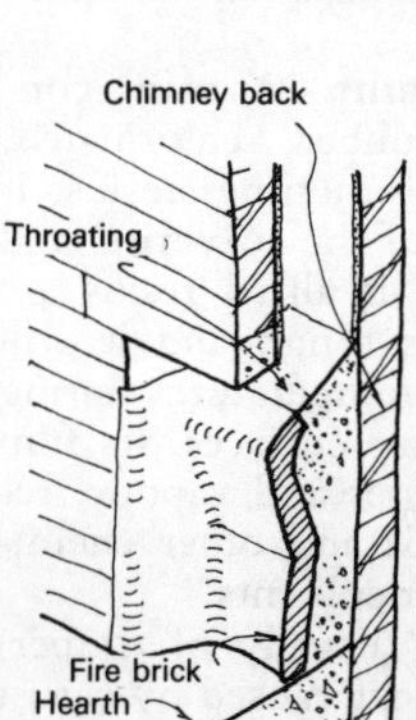

CHIMNEY THROATING

china clay A primary or secondary clay consisting of comparatively coarsely crystalline kaolinite; it is not very plastic and becomes white on firing. China-clay rock is the parent material of china clay, but contains debris which is eliminated in the refining of china clay.

chipboard A **building board** (sometimes called a **particle board**) made from timber waste which is finely chipped and compressed with thermo-setting resin binders. Sheet sizes are usually 1,200 mm wide by up to 3,000 mm long. Chipboard has a moisture movement equivalent to timber along the grain, and some grades can be very sensitive to moisture. This has led to the introduction of moisture resistant grades with a sealed surface for use in places where it might become damp during construction or condensation might be experienced. Chipboard is only about one-third the strength of timber and is used primarily in the manufacture of fittings and furniture and in the construction of sheathing and flooring.

chisel A tool for cutting and paring, with a long steel cutting blade and often a timber handle. Such tools are used, often in conjunction with a mallet or hammer, in woodwork, masonry and steelwork.

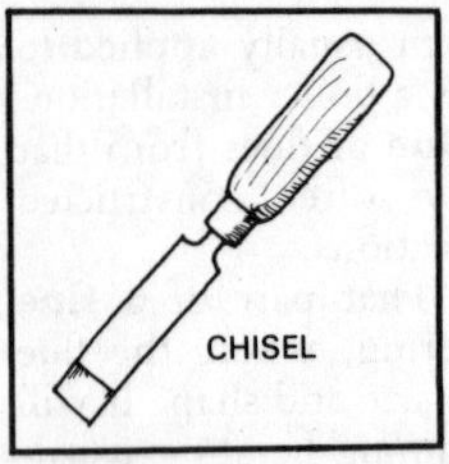

chisel knife A tool which is similar to a **stripping knife** but with a narrow blade up to 38 mm wide.

chlorinated rubber paint A paint consisting of natural rubber, chlorinated, with plasticizers and sometimes resins. It dries by evaporation of the **solvents**, and by partial **oxidation** if alkyd resins are present. Its surface is tough and it will tolerate not only low temperatures during drying but also alkaline surfaces. Its film is impermeable to water and vapour, resistant to acids, alkalis and other chemicals, but not to oils or solvents.

chock A small block (usually of timber) used to resist movement caused by thrust or pressure.

choke A device included on an electrical circuit to control the flow of current. It provides a voltage pulse whenever the circuit is made; used to start a **fluorescent lamp**.

chord The long top or bottom member of a built-up beam, both of which are equivalent to the flanges in a **rolled steel joist/channel**, being the primary tension and compression members of the assembly.

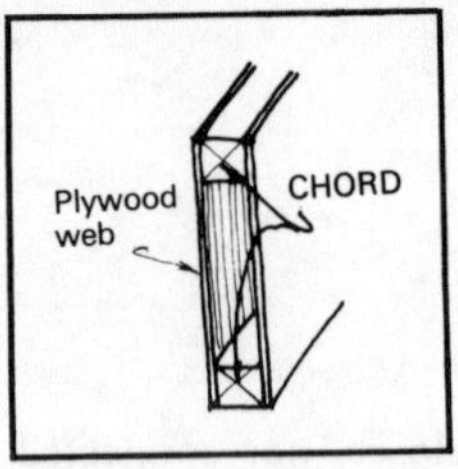

chute An enclosed shaft used to transfer material from one level to another by gravity, *eg* a refuse chute in high-rise flats.

chromating 1. A method of coating magnesium alloys by dipping them in hot solutions of alkaline dichromate or chromic and nitric acids. This is not an electrolytic process. 2. The treatment of ferrous metals with chromate primers (lead or zinc) to discourage rusting.

chromium plating The electrolytic deposition of chromium on another metal for protection and in order to produce a shiny appearance. The layer is very hard. On iron and steel the best results are obtained by the deposition of other metals before the chromium – *eg* nickel on copper.

cill See **sill**.

cinder block (USA) A **clinker block**.

circuit 1. In a hot water system, an assembly of pipes and fittings through which water circulates. 2. In electrical installations, a cable which starts from and returns to a **distribution board (panel)** having serviced a number of lighting points, **socket outlets** or pieces of electrical equipment, the whole being protected by a **fuse** at the distribution board.

circular saw A mechanical saw consisting of a toothed steel disc which is usually fixed in a work bench.

circulator A water heating appliance, often gas-fired, connected to a storage **cylinder** or tank from which the hot water can be drawn. The connections are made by **flow and return pipes** in which natural circulation takes place.

cistern 1. An open-topped tank, rectangular or circular, for the storage of cold water obtained from the mains supply. From the cistern the water is fed into a domestic hot water system, to individual cold water draw-off points or into a wet central heating system. It is usually made of galvanized steel, asbestos-cement or plastic. 2. See **flushing cistern**.

cladding A generally lightweight material used to cover the exterior of a building structure, often a framed structure but sometimes a structure lacking the necessary water-resisting characteristics (such as solid **insulating brick** walls, which may be clad with **tile hanging**). Examples include asbestos-cement and metal sheeting, **weather-boarding**, tiles and slates (natural or asbestos-cement). Generally cladding is substantially watertight, the exception being **open-joint** cladding. Heavyweight precast concrete wall panels are sometimes referred to as cladding panels.

clamp 1. A short piece of metal or slate bedded into sinkings in adjacent stones or pre-cast concrete components to tie one component to the other. 2. In joinery, a tool for squeezing together pieces of wood which are being glued. It is removed once the glue has hardened. 3. A metal strap fixed to the back of a door frame and built into the wall. 4. A stack of bricks piled together in a kiln for burning.

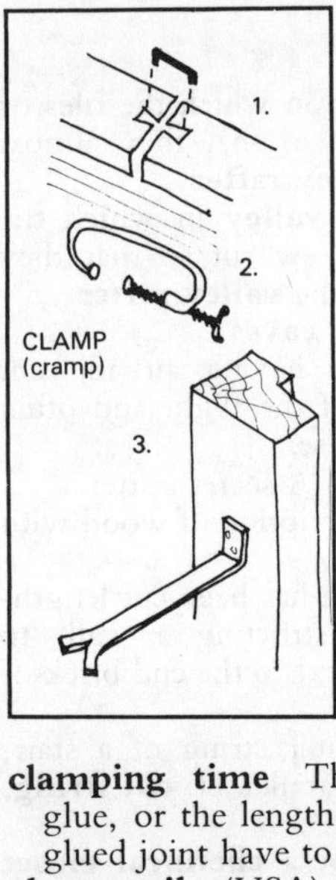

clamping time The setting time of a glue, or the length of time the parts of a glued joint have to be clamped together.

clamp nail (USA) A nail used to secure a mitre joint.

clapboard A term used predominantly in the USA for **weather-boarding** in which the boards are feather-edged and overlap each other, and are not rebated or tongued and grooved. cf. **feather edge**, **rebate**, **tongued and grooved joint.**

clasp nail A cut nail used in heavy carpentry fixings and for fixing such elements as door linings and skirtings to masonry. It is difficult to extract and varies from 25 to 200 mm in length. Sometimes it is used in place of **flooring brads**.

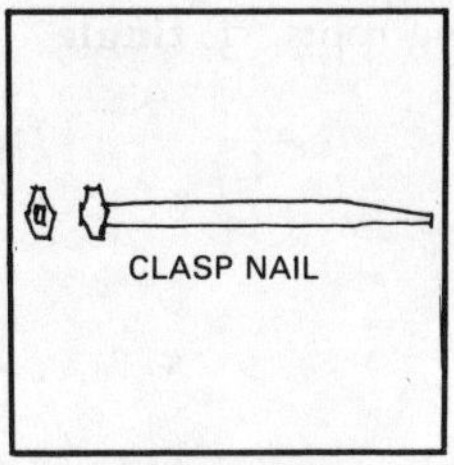

claw A tool for drawing nails out of wood or other material. It has a split end which fits under the nail head. cf. **claw hammer**.

claw hammer A hammer used in woodwork, whose **peen** is in the form of a **claw** for drawing nails.

claw hatchet A **shingle** hatchet.

clay tile 1. A **roofing tile** made of burnt clay in either flat, pan, single-lap or other form. cf. **single-lap tile**, **pantile**. 2. A **quarry tile**.

cleaner's sink A sink set at normal height, but with taps set at a high level, and having protection to the front edge of the sink. cf. **bucket sink**.

cleaning eye A removable cover in a pipe which allows access for cleaning. cf. **access eye**.

cleaning hinge A long-legged window hinge which holds the open casement clear of the stile, thus allowing the outside of the glass to be cleaned from inside. Also known as an **offset hinge**.

cleanout (USA) An **access eye**.

clear A description applied to timber that is free from visible defects and imperfections.

clear anodized aluminium Aluminium with a substantially colourless, translucent anodic oxide coating (often referred to as natural or silvered anodized aluminium).

clear span The distance between the two facing surfaces of a supporting structure carrying a beam, slab or truss.

cleat 1. A small piece of timber or steel fixed to one member and used to support or locate another. 2. In roofing, a piece of metal used at intervals to hold down **flashings** and **cappings** or to fix replacement slates in existing roofs. cf. **tingle**.

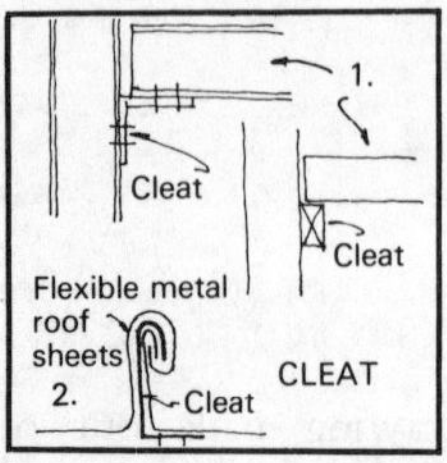

CLEAT

cleavage plane A plane which bears a geometric relationship to one or more of the axes of a crystalline system and along which slip and fracture most readily occur.

cleft chestnut paling See **chestnut paling**.

cleft timber Timber which has been split along the grain.

clenching or clinching Bending over the protruding point of a nail which has been driven right through a piece of wood.

clink (Scotland) A **welt**.

clinker Sintered or fused ash from furnaces which, if it contains little unburnt coal, is a good aggregate for concrete.

clinker block A concrete **building block** made using **clinker** aggregate.

clip A small, shaped piece of metal used for fixing one component to another, *eg* a pipe clip, metal roofing clip, etc.

clipped eaves In pitched roofs, **eaves** which do not overhang the wall face by more than the width of the gutter.

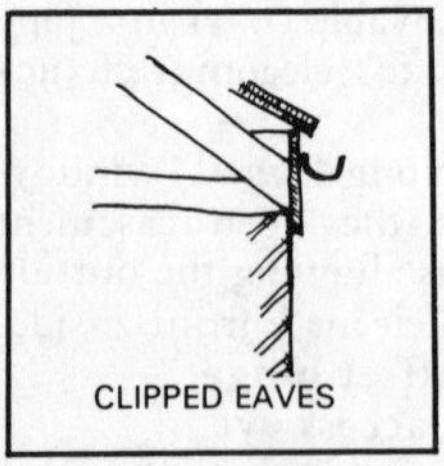
CLIPPED EAVES

clipped gable (USA) A hipped gable **roof**.

Clo A unit of measurement of the insulation value of clothing. 1 Clo is roughly equivalent to the insulation of a normal suit (approximately 0.155 m^2 C/W).

close-boarded A structure, such as a roof, which is covered with boarding nailed so that each board is touching its neighbour in a butt joint.

close-boarded fencing Fencing consisting of vertical boards nailed to rails between posts. The boards can be either butted, rebated or feather-edged. cf. **butt**, **rebate**, **feather edge**.

close-contact adhesive A synthetic resin adhesive suitable for use only in those joints where the surfaces to be joined can be brought into close contact and where the glue line need not exceed 0.13 mm in thickness. It is an adhesive which does not have gap-filling characteristics. cf. **gap-filling glue**.

close-coupled roof A roof in which the **common rafters** are joined at **wall plate** level by **ties** (in effect the **ceiling joists**). This type of roof is suitable for building widths of up to 3,800 mm.

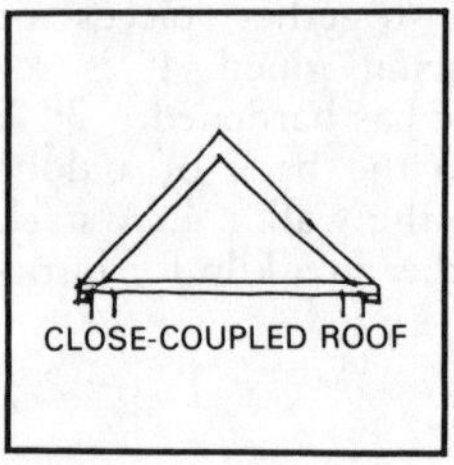
CLOSE-COUPLED ROOF

close-cut hip A **hip** in which the tiles or slates are skew cut so that they almost meet above the **valley rafter**.

close-cut valley A **valley** in which the tiles or slates are skew cut so that they almost meet above the **valley rafter**.

closed eaves **Boxed eaves**.

closed stair A stair having an adjacent wall on each side of the flight and often with a door at its base.

closed valley (USA) A secret gutter.

close grained A description of wood with a fine grain.

closer A brick which has been cut lengthwise; used, in constructing a wall, to close up the bond next to the end brick of a course. cf. **bond**.

close string The outer string of a stair, having both edges parallel. cf. **cut string**, **stair**.

closet 1. A privy, or a **chemical closet** or **water closet**. 2. (USA) A small room or cupboard.

closing stile The **stile** farthest from the hinges.

closure A **closer**.

clout nail A round headed wire nail used for the rougher applications in timber-to-timber fixings, as well as for fixing roofing felt, slates and plasterboard; lengths vary from 10 to 100 mm and diameters from 2 to 4.5 mm; made from steel, copper and aluminium alloy.

CLS timber sizes The standard method of sizing timber in North America (Canadian lumber sizes).

club hammer A small but relatively heavy hammer with a double face, used by bricklayers and masons.

clutch head The driving profile of a screw which is not intended to be removed. It is based on a **slot head** from which the anti-clockwise face has been chamfered off to remove any purchase for the **screw driver**.

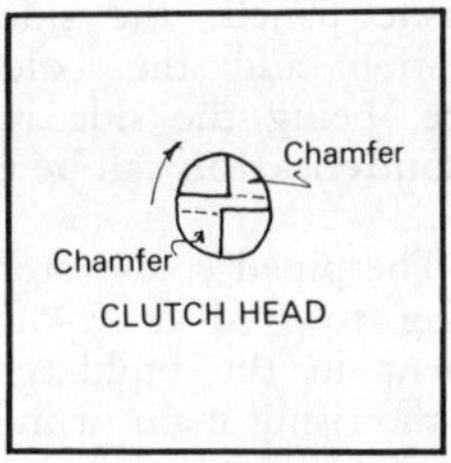

coach bolt In wood construction a round-headed bolt with a square thickening of the shank under the bolt head to avoid rotation of the bolt when the nut is tightened. In USA, a carriage bolt.

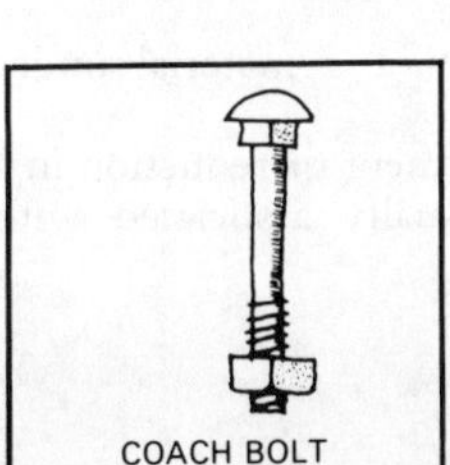

coach screw A large (6 mm diameter or above) gimlet-pointed square-headed screw for making wood fixings. It is driven by turning the head with a spanner after pre-drilling a starter hole.

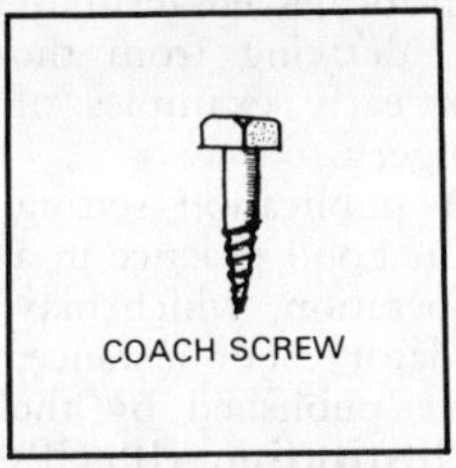

coal tar epoxide paint A two-part preparation, one part consisting of coal tar/epoxide resins, the other being an amine or polyamide curing agent. The two parts are mixed together before use.

coal tar pitch A black or dark brown, solid or semi-solid, fusible and agglomerative residue from partial evaporation or fractional distillation of coal tar and coal tar products.

coarse aggregate An inert material, such as gravel or broken stone, which is mixed with **fine aggregate** and **cement** to make **concrete**. It is of such a particle size as to be largely retained on a 4.76 mm square sieve.

coarse stuff Lime-based material used for the first and second coats of three-coat plasterwork. It was mainly used with **lime plaster** and is little used with **gypsum plaster**. cf. **fine stuff**.

coat 1. A layer of a surfacing material such as plaster or asphalt which is placed in a single application. 2. A film of paint or varnish laid on in a single application and allowed to dry before a further coat is applied. (See also **undercoat** and **gloss** coat).

coated macadam or tarmacadam A road-making material consisting of graded and interlocking aggregate coated with tar or bitumen, or a mixture of the two, and compacted.

co-axial feeder A type of cable used in the transmission of radio frequency power and consisting of concentric inner and outer **conductors** insulated from one another.

cobble 1. A rounded stone used in combination with others to give a rough-surfaced paving. 2. To pave with cobbles.

cobbled Paved with cobbles.

cobwebbing During spraying, the creation of fine filaments, rather than the normal atomized particles, of the material being sprayed.

cock A valve in a pipeline for controlling the flow of liquid or gas through the pipe. (**stop** cf. **cock**).

cocking piece See **sprocket**.

cockspur fastener An absolescent term for a casement fastener, deriving from the ornamental shape of early examples of this piece of ironmongery.

Code of Practice A publication setting down the standards of good practice in a particular trade or operation, which may or may not be mandatory. For instance, the codes of practice published by the **British Standards Institution** (BS:CP) are not mandatory, though the US **building codes** are.

coefficient of elasticity See **modulus of elasticity**.

coefficient of expansion The expansion per unit length, area or volume of a material per degree rise in temperature, known respectively as the coefficient of linear, superficial or cubical expansion.

coefficient of thermal expansion See **coefficient of expansion**.

coefficient of utilization A numerical factor used in calculating the number of light fittings needed for an installation. It is based on room dimensions and the fact that all **lumens** emitted by a lamp do not reach the **working plane**, some being trapped in the **luminaire**, some absorbed and some illuminating nearby surfaces.

coffer dam See **caisson**.

cohesion The attraction between the molecules making up the mass of a liquid or a solid, which, for instance enables drops and thin films to be formed.

cohesive soil A soil which contains clay and which will form a coherent mass.

cold asphalt A close-textured **coated macadam wearing course** in which the aggregate will completely pass through a 6 mm sieve for the fine grade and substantially pass through a 10 mm sieve for the coarse grade. The aggregate is coated with a binder (usually bitumen) and the mixture is adjusted to allow spreading and compaction of the material without heating.

cold bridge A ready path of heat transmittance through a structure. A part of relatively high **U value** when compared with the rest of the structure.

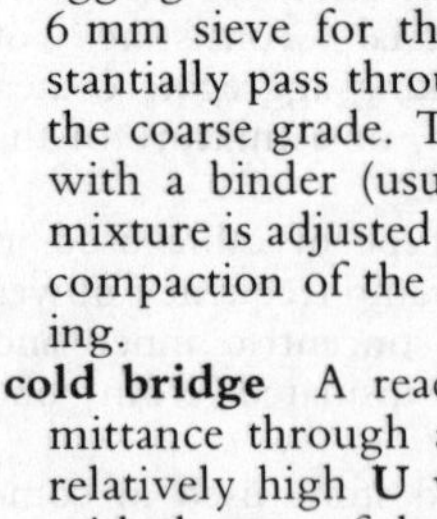

COLD BRIDGE

cold-rolled section A light gauge steel section, usually in the form of a lipped angle or channel or a Z section, used to construct structural steel framework. cf. **zed purlin**.

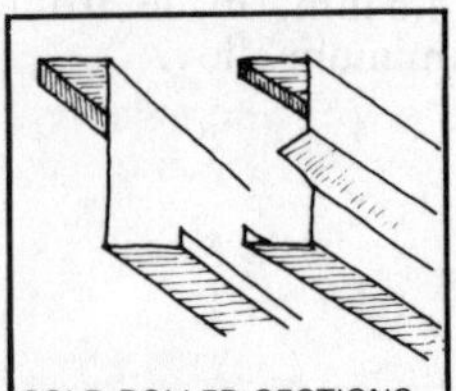
COLD ROLLED SECTIONS

cold rolling The passing of a sheet or strip of metal, at or near atmospheric temperature, between a pair of rotating rollers. The reduction in thickness may be slight, but the shape of the sheet or strip may be substantially altered. The process results in a smooth surface finish.

cold roof A roof structure with the insulating layer below the roof void. cf. **warm roof**.

cold-setting adhesive A synthetic resin adhesive, such as **urea formaldehyde** (**UF**), which will harden when mixed with an acid accelerator. The process can often be speeded up by the application of heat. cf. **thermo-setting** adhesive (resin).

cold-side In composite panels, the side between the insulation and the cold ambient temperature, being the side in which **interstitial condensation** can be a danger.

cold water service The piped cold-water supply to a building to feed draw-off points and equipment in the building, either directly from the rising main or indirectly through a cold water storage tank.

cold working The operation of permanently altering the shape or dimensions of metals at or near atmospheric temperature, as in **cold rolling**, pressing or bending.

collapse The failure of a material under load.

collar 1. An enlargement or reduction in a pipe's diameter, usually associated with

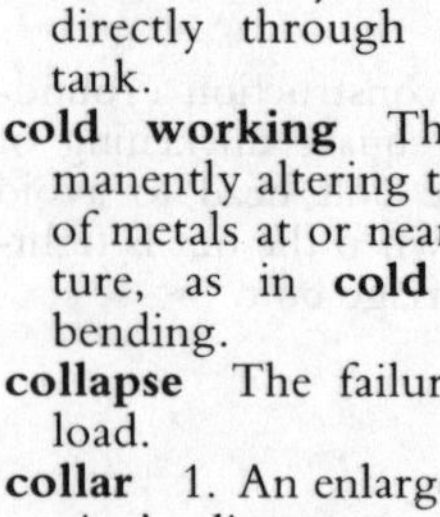

COLLAR

the making of a connection between pipes. cf. **spigot-and-socket joint**. 2. An upstand of roof finish around a vertical pipe passing through the roof, so designed as to produce a weathertight joint. 3. A **collar beam**.

collar beam A horizontal beam above the level of the wall plate which ties together an opposing pair of **common rafters** and is often positioned roughly halfway up their length.

collar beam roof A roof construction consisting of pairs of **common rafters**, each pair tied together by a **collar beam** approximately halfway up the rafters, thus providing additional headroom in the roof above **wall plate** level. cf. **close-coupled roof**.

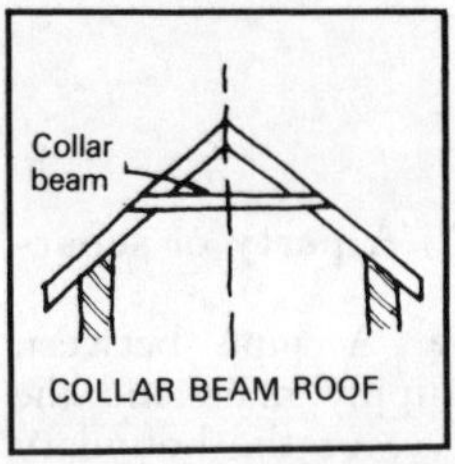

collimation line See **line of collimation.**

colonial siding Plain, square-edged **weather-boarding** most commonly used in the USA and consisting of boards 225 to 300 mm wide.

colonnade A row of **columns**; often outside the line of the external wall of a building and supporting a series of lintels which in turn support a roof over a pedestrian way which runs between the columns and the main part of the building.

colour anodizing Anodizing followed by dyeing the **anodic coating** in a solution of organic dyestuffs or inorganic compounds.

coloured cement Cement with which mineral pigments have been mixed to add colour; used particularly in mortar, so that the joints harmonize with the colouring of the brickwork.

colour fastness The ability of a colour not to fade or change as a result of the action of light, air or water.

colour rendering The effect an artificial light source has on the appearance of a colour compared with its appearance under natural daylight.

column A vertical compression member designed to carry an **axial load**. It may be made of steel or other metal, brick, concrete or stone. When made of steel or cast iron it is also known as a **stanchion**.

column casing The lining or encasement of a steel column with fire-resistant materials (brick, concrete, asbestos-cement insulation board, sprayed asbestos etc.) to provide that member with protection from the effects of fire for a stated period also the materials so used.

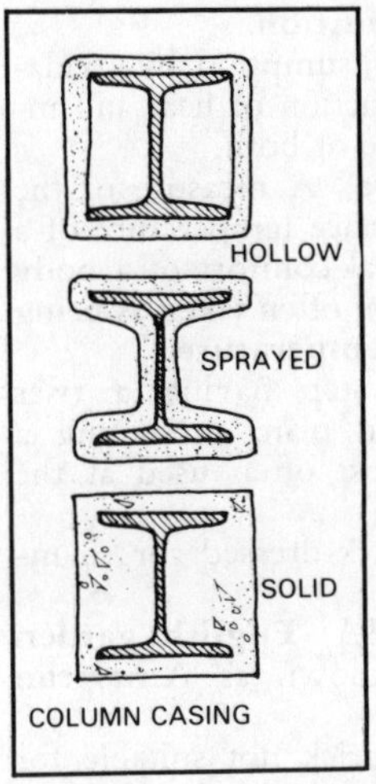

comb 1. A toothed metal plate for scoring the surface of a plaster coat to provide a key for the next coat. 2. A toothed metal plate for spreading adhesive on a flat surface. 3. A thin spring-steel tool used for **graining**.

combed joint An angled joint formed by the engagement of a series of complementary parallel tenons. cf. **dovetail joint**). Sometimes this joint is referred to as a **finger joint**. Depending largely on the glue for its strength, the joint is completed by a dowel driven through the 'stack' of tenons.

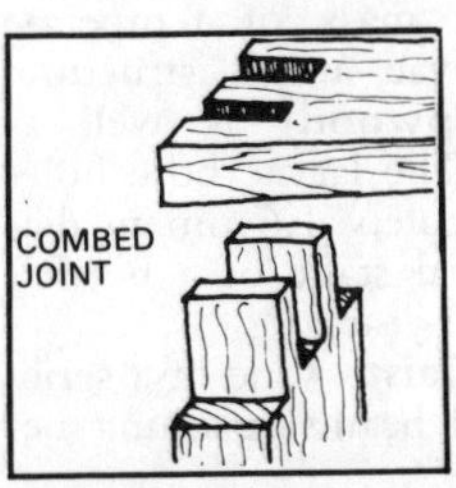

combination cylinder or combination tank A hot water **cylinder** (either **direct** or **indirect**) combined with a cold water feed tank in one package unit.

combination grate A back-to-back arrangement of cooking range in the kitchen heated by a solid-fuel-burning fireplace in the sitting room; rarely seen today.

combined system A drainage system in which foul drainage and surface water drainage is discharged into the one sewer. cf. **foul drain**, **surface water drain**, **separate system**.

combustible Capable of undergoing **combustion**.

combustible material Material capable of supporting **combustion**.

combustion The consumption by oxidation, with the production of heat and incandescence or flame or both.

comfort temperature A measure of the effect of air and surface temperature of a room on the thermal comfort of a body occupying that room; often taken as being the **dry resultant temperature**.

commode step A step having a riser which is curved on plan, presenting a convex surface. Most often used at the foot of a staircase.

common ashlar Pick-dressed or hammer-dressed **ashlar**.

common bond (USA) **English garden wall bond**; also known as **American bond**.

common brick A brick not suitable for facing purposes or for heavy loadbearing applications, but useful as a backing to exterior skins of **facing brick** or other facing material. Bricks in this class tend to be highly absorbent, and also inconsistent in colour. Often referred to in the plural as commons.

common dovetail A dovetail joint in which both members joined show end grain.

common flue A flue taking the products of combustion from two or more appliances.

Common Furniture Beetle (*Anobium punctatum*) A wood boring beetle indigenous to the great mass of temperate Europe, whose larvae attack structural timber (usually **sapwood**) as well as wooden furniture. The larvae bore holes which are approximately 1.6 mm in diameter, and the larval stage of a beetle's life cycle is at least 2 years.

common (or floor) joist One of a series of timbers or small beams spanning between walls or beams, or between beam and wall, to which are nailed the floor boards or floor decking which they support.

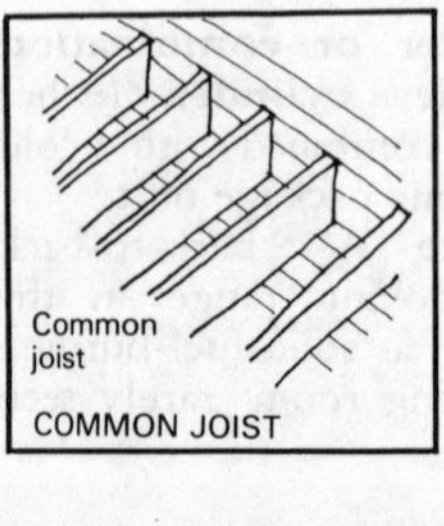

COMMON JOIST

common rafter A sloping timber component of pitched roof, usually about 100 ×50 mm, fixed to a **wall plate** at its foot and a **ridge** at its head and spanning between these, or between each of these and an intermediate **purlin** where the roof span or length of slope makes this necessary.

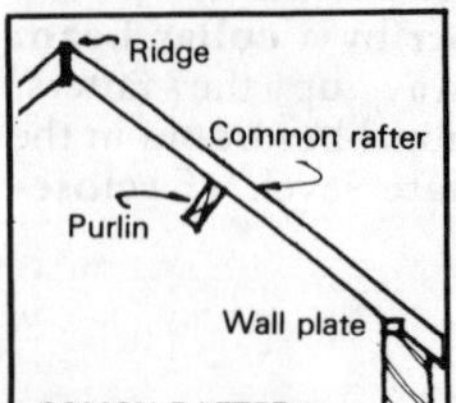

COMON RAFTER

common wall (USA) A **party** or **separating wall**.

communicating pipe A pipe between the Water Board's supply main and the consumer's stop valve, or the boundary of the consumer's site.

compaction The process of consolidating the particles of a material by rolling or other mechanical means.

compartment floor/wall A fire-resisting floor/wall used to divide a building into separate compartments. cf. **compartmentation**.

compartmentation The division of a building into compartments by means of fire-resisting elements of structure (**compartment floor wall**) in order to contain within its compartment of origin, for a stated period of time, any firing occurring in the building.

compass saw A wood saw with a blade tapering to a point. It is used for cutting around sharp corners.

compatibility The ability of a material to exist in close contact with another similar or dissimilar material without breakdown (or other degrading effects) occurring in either material. For instance there should be compatibility between the undercoat and the top coat in a paint system.

completion date The date, entered into a building contract, by which time the works are programmed to be completed and handed over to the client, and from which point the **defects liability period** commences.

compo 1. A mortar made up of cement and lime. 2. A lead alloy of which pipes are made for use in gas installations to make somewhat flexible connections to items of equipment.

component A unit contributing to the construction of a whole building, such as a wall panel; or a part which, in conjunction with other parts, makes up an **assembly**.

composite board A board made up of more than one type of material and deriving its performance from a combination of the properties of the individual materials, *eg*. metal-faced plywood, or insulation-backed plasterboard.

composite brick A brick consisting of two or more layers of material of differing composition or texture.

composite construction Different materials used in conjunction in order to take advantage of their various properties.

composite truss A **truss** containing members, both of steel and timber; steel is usually used for the tensile members.

composite window A window consisting of two or more separate window units joined together by one or more coupling members.

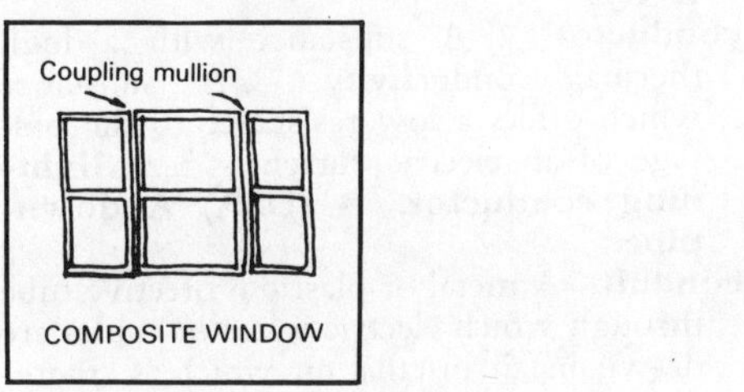

COMPOSITE WINDOW

composition cork Agglomerated cork made with the addition of a binder derived from a material other than cork.

composition roofing (USA) Bitumen felt roofing.

composition shingles (USA) Imitation **shingles** made of bitumen felt.

compound shake Several types of **shake** appearing close together in one piece of timber.

compressed rock asphalt surfacing A **wearing course** consisting of powdered **rock asphalt** compressed whilst hot.

compressed straw slab or strawboard A building board made from compressed straw faced on each side by a strong paper. It has good thermal insulation, but is vulnerable to moisture.

compression Deformation by pressure cf. **compressive stress**.

compression failure A permanent deformation or a fracture caused by excessive **compressive stress**.

compression joint A joint used in light-gauge copper plumbing in which pipes are connected by screw fittings which, as they are tightened, compress wedge rings into the walls of the pipes and secure a seal. This method does not require any form of heat. In one type of compression joint (manipulative) the pipe ends have to be opened out with a special tool. In the other type (non-manipulative) the pipe ends require no special preparation.

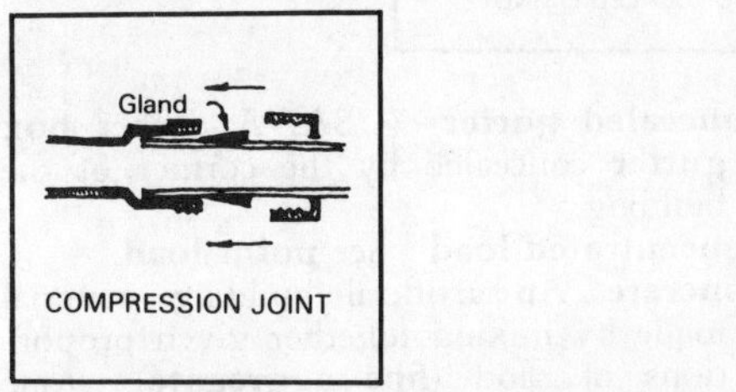

COMPRESSION JOINT

compression seal A seal that functions solely by virtue of being compressed between adjacent **components** in a **dry joint** and does not depend on adhesion to the components; sometimes referred to as a **gasket**.

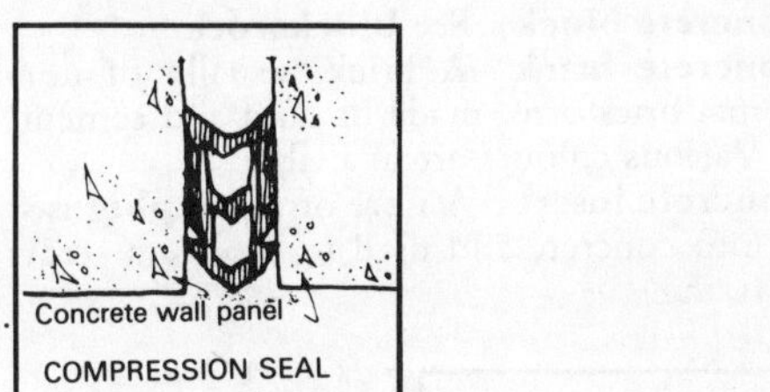

COMPRESSION SEAL

compression test A test in which a specimen is subjected to increasing **compressive stress** or to a given compressive stress to determine its strength and/or elasticity under these conditions.

compressive deformation See **compressive strain**.

compressive strain The change in length per unit of original length as a result of **compressive stress**. It is expressed not in dimensions but as a ratio.

compressive strength 1. The ability of a material to withstand **compressive stress** 2. The compressive stress at which a material fails.

compressive stress The compressive force per unit area of the initial cross section of a material applied to that material in such a way as to compress it, expressed in MN/m^2.

compressor A machine which draws in a gas at one pressure and delivers it at a higher pressure.

concealed fixing A fixing which is made without the fixing device being apparent. cf. **secret nailing**.

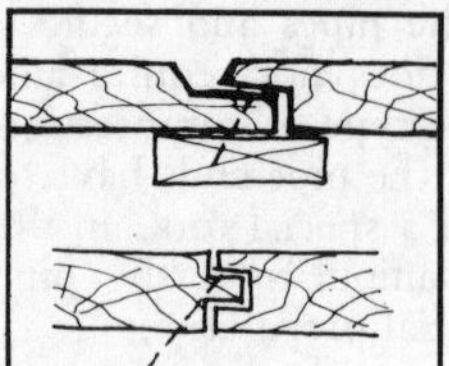

CONCEALED FIXING

concealed gutter (USA) A timber **box gutter** concealed by the cornice of the building.

concentrated load See **point load**.

concrete An artificial building material made by mixing together given proportions of sand (**fine aggregate**), stone (**coarse aggregate**), cement and water. The concrete hardens, by the hydration of the cement, into a stone-like mass similar in appearance and properties to some natural limestones. Concrete differs from mortar in that it contains coarse aggregate; mortar does not.

concrete block See **blockwork**.

concrete brick A brick, usually of normal brick size, made of sand and cement. Various colours are available.

concrete insert A fibre or metal **plug** cast into concrete and used to receive a screw fixing.

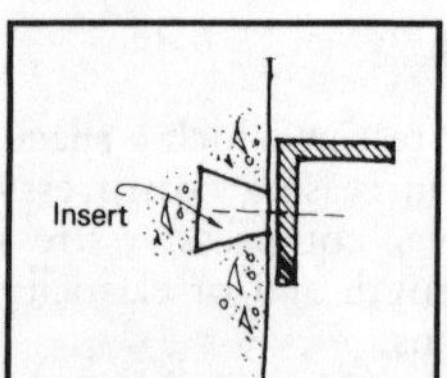

CONCRETE INSERT

concrete nail (USA) A **masonry nail**.

condensation 1. The formation of water on cold surfaces when the adjacent air is cooled below its **dew point**. cf. **interstitial** and **surface condensation**. 2. A chemical process used in the manufacture of some **synthetic resins** involving the combination of molecules with the elimination of water.

condensation groove or condensation channel A profile designed to collect **condensation**, usually from the inside of window glazing or **patent glazing**, and discharge it through a tube to the outside of the building.

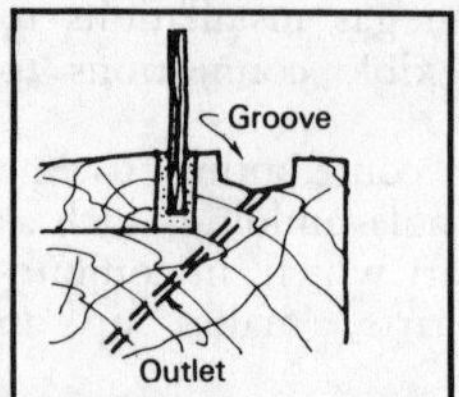

CONDENSATION GROOVE

condenser A **heat exchanger** in which the vaporized refrigerant, after compression to a suitable pressure, is liquefied by the transfer of heat to an appropriate external cooling medium.

condominium A collection of properties rented or brought by a number of different individuals, but linked by common agreements.

conductance See **thermal conductance**.

conduction The transfer of heat through a solid material from a region of higher temperature to a region of lower temperature, the heat energy passing from molecule to molecule without visible movement of the material.

conductivity (k) See **thermal conductivity**.

conductor 1. A substance with a high thermal conductivity. 2. A substance which offers a low resistance to the passage of an electric current. 3. A **lightning conductor**. 4. (USA) A **downpipe**.

conduit A metal or plastic protective tube through which electric wires or cables are drawn in an installation which is, therefore, easily re-wired when necessary. It can be embedded in plaster, screed or concrete, or placed within the thickness of framed floors, ceilings and walls.

conduit box A **junction box**.

conduit bushing An internally smooth, threaded sleeve at an outlet from a conduit which prevents injury to the enclosed cable.

conical (or batten) roll A roll joint in **flexible metal roofing** formed over a wooden roll which is nailed or screwed to the roof boarding and has a triangular cross sectional profile with a bluntly rounded apex.

Coniophora cerebella See **wet rot**.

connection The fixing detail between two building components, such as that between two elements of a steel frame.

connector A mechanical fixing device for connecting together relatively small sections of timber to create a framework, as in **roof trusses** or **trussed rafters**. Devices included in this category are steel

split-ring connectors, **shear plates**, **toothed connectors** and **nail plates**.

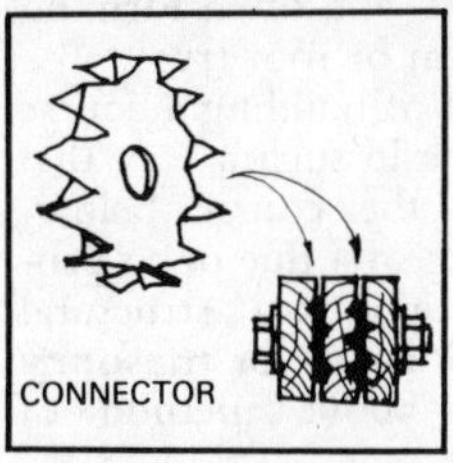

consistency 1. The viscosity of a paint or varnish, which is judged from the material's behaviour when stirred or applied by brush. 2. The capacity of fresh concrete or mortar to resist flow. 3. The general ability to remain true to the same properties, shape or movement patterns.

construction joint A joint, often in a concrete slab, between concrete which has been placed earlier and is already set and newly placed concrete. The position is often chosen for a **movement joint**, as cracking can often take place along this line.

consumer's terminal The demarcation between the electricity board's cable and the consumer's wiring; usually adjacent to the main switch.

contingency allowance A small allowance of time in a building programme to compensate for infrequent, unforeseen happenings which could extend the programme if no such allowance were made.

contingency sum A sum of money included in a building contract to cover the cost of unforeseen work during the course of the contract.

continuous beam/slab A beam or slab which is continuous over one or more intermediate supports, as distinct from a series of independent beams or slabs, each spanning between two supports.

contract An agreement between an employer and a building or civil engineering contractor in which the contractor undertakes to complete certain construction work for a specific sum of money. cf. **form of contract**.

contract document A document which is used as a means of defining the scope of a contract and is therefore considered as being part of the contract agreement. Usually these documents are named in the **form of contract** and can be drawings, specifications, bills of quantities or schedules. Each document is signed by both parties to the contract.

controlling dimension A dimension between key reference planes, such as that between floor level and floor level, or centre line and centre line, and within which a number of components and assemblies are to be installed. cf. **dimensional co-ordination**.

controlling line A line representing a key reference plane, such as the plane forming the boundary of a zone (floor, roof or wall). cf. **dimensional co-ordination**.

controlling zone A zone between key reference planes provided for a floor, roof, loadbearing wall or column. Such a zone is large enough to contain both the structure and the finish. cf. **dimensional co-ordination**.

convection The transfer of heat in a liquid or gas by the upward movement of the hotter part of the medium, its place being taken by the colder part which moves downward, thus setting up **convection currents**.

convection current That circulation movement within a liquid or gas which is caused by convection.

convector A space heater comprising an enclosure containing a heating element and having air grilles at the top and the bottom. Air drawn in through the bottom grille is heated by the element, rises and flows out of the upper grille to heat the room by **convection**.

conversion 1. The process of sawing timber from logs. 2. A slow and not immediately reversible change in the crystalline structure of a material resulting from **heat treatment**. 3. The alteration of an existing building so that it is suitable for a different use.

conversion coating A coating on the surface of a metal consisting of a compound of the metal produced by chemical or electrochemical treatment; such as chromate films on zinc or cadmium and oxide films on steel. **Anodizing** fulfils the definition, but is not usually referred to by this description.

converted timber Square sawn timber.

cooler A **heat exchanger**, usually consisting of tubes or plates containing refrigerants at a low temperature, which absorbs heat from the substance with which it is in contact.

cooling tower A structure used for cooling condenser water by evaporation, the water trickling down inside the open-topped tower over a system of slats. Considerable heat is lost to the air in this process, a fact which has led to alternative means of disposing of the waste heat, sometimes, in **district heating** schemes.

co-ordinating dimension 1. The dimension of a **co-ordinating space**. 2. A dimension common to two or more building **components** to permit their assembly together.

co-ordinating plane A plane of reference on which a building **component** or **assembly** is co-ordinated with another.

co-ordinating size The size of a **co-ordinating space** allocated to a component, which includes allowances for the joints and tolerances.

co-ordinating space A space bounded by **co-ordinating planes**, allocated to a **building component** or **assembly** and including allowances for joints and tolerances. cf. **dimensional co-ordination**.

cope 1. A **coping**. 2. To cover the top of a wall with a coping. 3. To fit one **moulding** to another without mitring. cf. **mitre**.

coping 1. A protection to the head of a wall formed usually by a projecting course of stone or precast concrete slabs, **weathered** and throated, or sometimes by **engineering bricks** or metal. cf. **throating**. 2. Splitting stones by drilling a series of holes on the intended line of fracture and driving in steel wedges.

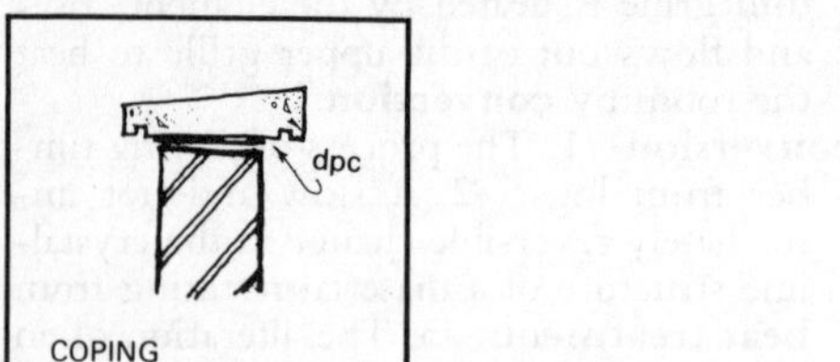

COPING

coping saw A **bow saw** with a narrow blade about 150 mm long and 3 mm wide, used to cut sharp curves.

coping stone A stone forming part of a coping.

copolymer A **polymer** consisting of molecules of more than one kind of structural unit.

copper glazing Glazing using copper **cames**. cf. **electro-copper glazing.**

copper plating Electro-plating with copper to form a protective layer. It is also used under **chromium plating**.

copper roofing **Flexible-metal roofing** made up of copper sheets joined as appropriate, by seams, **conical rolls** or **drips** and forming a weatherproof layer. The sheets are from 0.45–0.70 mm thick and are fully supported on decking.

copper slate See **lead slate**.

coppersmith's hammer A hammer with a long, bent ball **peen** used for beating copper.

corbel A brick, stone or concrete element, built into and projecting from a wall to support a load, and often forming the support for a beam or roof truss.

corbelling 1. The act of building a course of brickwork or stone in such a way that it oversails slightly the course below, either in the gathering of a flue or to provide a ledge to support a structural element. 2. The brickwork or **masonry** resulting from the above method of building.

corbel plate Flat, cranked, cranked and fish-tailed or flat and fish-tailed steel plates bedded into **mortises** in a structural backing to provide a **cantilever** support for a facing layer.

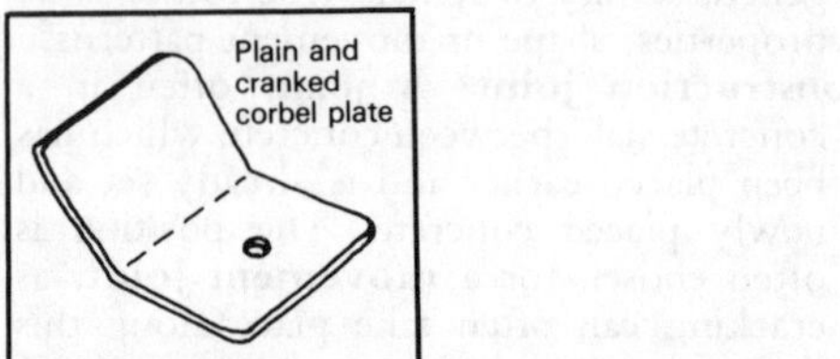

CORBEL PLATE

corbie step gable See **crow step gable**.

core 1. The softer central areas of case-hardened steel. 2. A cylindrical sample of hardened concrete obtained by a core cutter. 3. A cylindrical sample of material obtained by driving a hollow-core drill into the ground to ascertain the depth and composition of the various strata. 4. A filling of undressed stone behind a facing layer. 5. The inner layer of a sheet of **blockboard** or **composite board**, etc., or of a **flush door.**

coreboard A stiff wood-based board made up of strips of wood glued together to form a core and faced on each side by a veneer whose grain runs at right angles to the grain of the core strips. Different types of core are indicated by the use of different names for the coreboard, such as **laminboard**, **blockboard** and **battenboard**.

core rail The steel bar beneath (sometimes let into) a timber handrail, to which metal **balusters** are connected. Also used

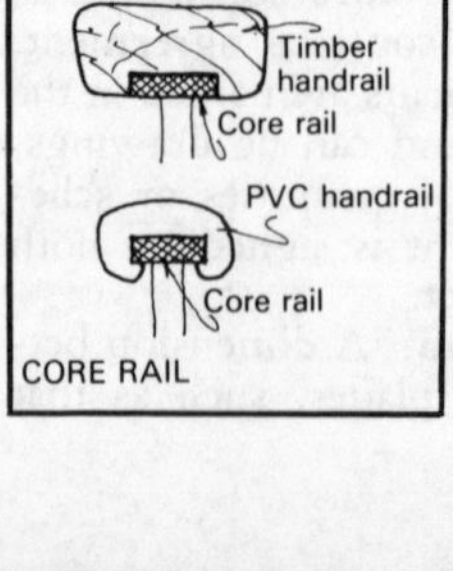

CORE RAIL

to describe the steel rail that receives a plastic handrail.

cork The bark of the cork oak, indigenous to the Mediterranean areas and North America.

corkboard Granulated cork compressed and baked to form slabs for flooring, wall covering or special insulation applications.

corner bead An **angle bead**.

corner chisel A **chisel** with an L-shaped, double ended blade used to cut out **mortises.**

cornerlocked joint A **combed joint**.

corner post A post at an angle of a building in **timber framed construction**.

cornice A moulding at the top of a wall. It can be on either an external wall, in which case it is used to throw rainwater clear of the wall below, or an internal wall, where it forms a decorative junction between wall and ceiling.

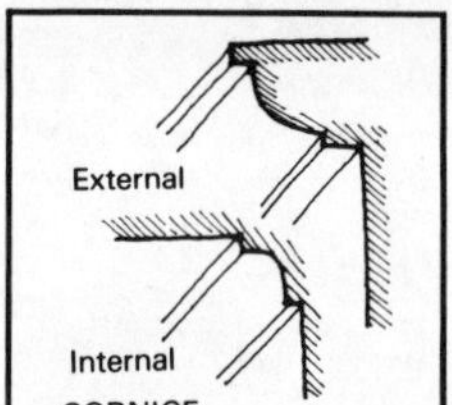

CORNICE

corrosion The chemical or electrochemical reaction of a metal with its environment resulting in degradation of the metal. cf. **rusting**.

corrosion fatigue Weakening experienced in stressed metal, accelerated by **corrosion**.

corrosion inhibitor A chemical such as sodium nitrite or chromate which when used in paints helps them to protect metals from **corrosion**.

corrugated fastener A fixing device in the form of a corrugated piece of metal which has one edge sharpened. It is driven across the joint between two timber members to hold them together, where good appearance is unimportant.

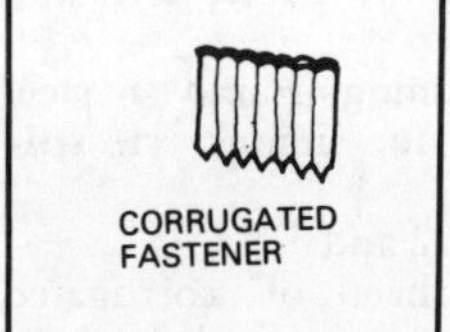
CORRUGATED FASTENER

corrugated sheet Metal, plastic or asbestos cement wall or roof cladding which gains increased resistance to bending from its corrugated profile and has the advantage of lightness combined with good spanning ability.

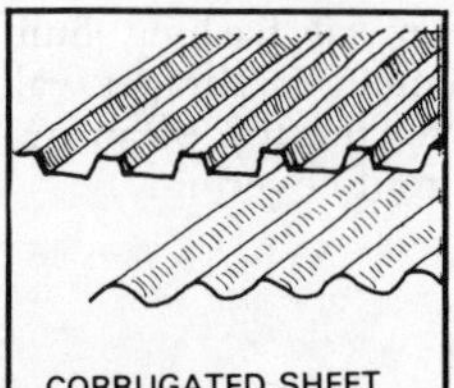
CORRUGATED SHEET MATERIAL

corrugated sheet nail A nail with a round, nipple or spring head in galvanized steel or aluminium; used to fix corrugated sheeting.

cost plan An elemental breakdown of the estimated cost of a building, in which the cost of each element of structure and finish is estimated and each of these estimates is then used as a target cost which is not to be exceeded. The design of the building may well have to be tailored to these targets. The process is a control mechanism to ensure that the total building cost is contained within the estimate.

cost plus contract A contract undertaken on the basis of the actual cost to the builder of the labour and materials used to undertake a job plus a percentage to cover his overheads and profit. It is a form of contract used normally only for small, emergency works, due to there being no assurance to the client of the end cost of the work.

counter batten 1. One of a series of battens fixed after the boarding and felt have been fixed on a roof, being parallel to the **rafters** and nailed over them. The slating or tiling battens are then nailed to the counter battens. This type of construction provides a drainage path below the roofing battens for any driven rain or snow which has gained access. 2. A batten fixed across several boards to stiffen them.

counter flap hinge A hinge usually fixed to a counter flap, which not only allows the opened flap to fold back on to the

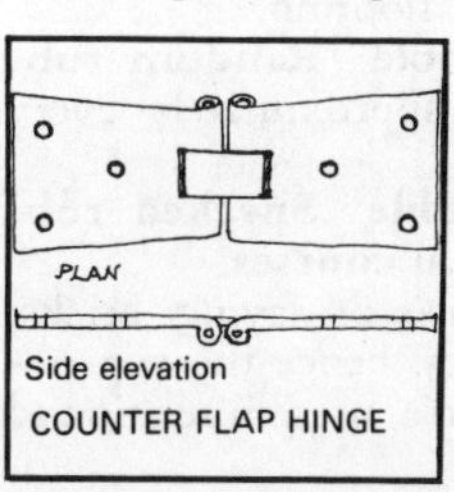

COUNTER FLAP HINGE

counter but also presents a flat surface on top when the flap is closed. This is achieved by means of an intermediate jointed piece let into the two main hinge flaps.

counter flashing A metal flashing built into the joint of a chimney or parapet wall and turned down over the top of an upstanding flashing or roof covering.

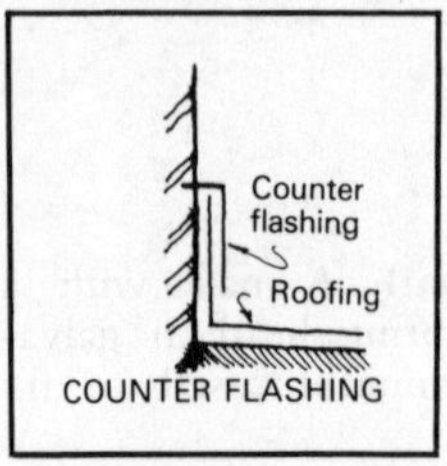

COUNTER FLASHING

counter floor The lower of two sets of floor boards, the joints running counter or diagonal to those of the upper set of boards. The boarding under a **parquet** floor. In the US it is referred to as a blind floor.

countersinking A conical sinking made in timber or other material by a countersink **bit** to enable the head of a countersunk screw to be driven flush with the surface of the material.

countersunk head A screw or rivet head having a conical shape, so that it may enter the countersunk workpiece sufficiently for the top of the head to be virtually flush with the surface of the workpiece.

countess slate A size of slate which in imperial terms was 20″ long ×10″ wide. This has been roughly converted into metric measurement as 500 mm long × 250 mm wide.

couple roof A **close-coupled roof**.

coupling 1. A collar fitting to join two screwed pipes, consisting of a short, internally threaded tube. 2. In tubular scaffolding, a fitting which clamps two or more tubes together.

course A horizontal layer of bricks, stones, blocks, slates etc. including the thickness of any mortar that may be necessary to bed the components of the layer. The term is sometimes applied to rows of wood block flooring.

coursed random rubble **Random rubble** laid to course approximately every 300 mm.

coursed snecked rubble **Snecked rubble** built to occasional **courses**.

coursing The practice of laying bricks, stones etc. in courses; hence the expression 'bringing to course' used in relation to **rubble walling**.

coursing joint A **bed joint**.

cove or coving A concave moulding at the junction between a ceiling and a wall.

coved ceiling A ceiling that is linked to the wall beneath by a concave **moulding**.

cove lighting Artificial, **indirect lighting** from a source above a **cove** or **cornice** or similar projection on a wall. The light is directed upwards on to the ceiling, from where it is reflected downwards in a pleasantly subdued fashion.

cover 1. The covered width of a slate, tile or similar coursed roofing unit. 2. The distance (*ie*, the thickness of concrete) between the outer surface of any reinforcement and the nearest surface of the concrete in which it is placed.

cover fillet or cover strip A narrow strip of material covering a joint between materials in the same plane or at right angles to each other. cf. **cover mould**.

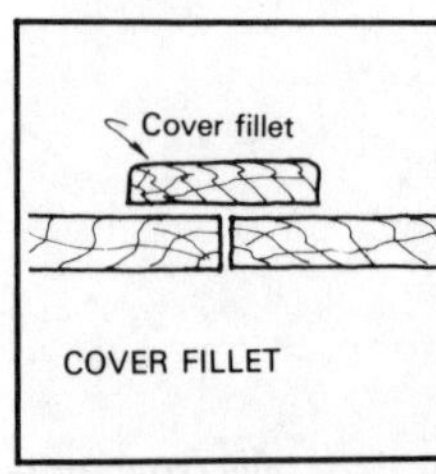

COVER FILLET

cover flap A panelled flap which covers **boxing shutters** when folded back.

cover flashing Similar to a **counter flashing**. cf. **raking flashing** and **stepped flashing**.

covering capacity The area which can be covered satisfactorily by a given quantity of paint, varnish, etc.

cover mould A moulding planted to cover a joint between two flush surfaces. cf. **cover fillet or cover strip**.

cowl A cover, which may be fixed or rotating, plain or louvred, attached to the top of a **chimney** to reduce or prevent down-draught.

cradle A suspended platform with guard rails, used to gain access to the external face of a tall building for maintenance and repair work.

cradling Rough framing round a steel beam as a support for linings. cf. **soldiers**.

cramp See **clamp** 1, 2 and 3.

cranked sheet A sheet of corrugated asbestos or metal bent at an angle to form either a ridge piece to a **double-pitched roof** or to link wall cladding and roof cladding.

crawling Defect appearing in a gloss paint or varnish finish before drying, revealing the undercoat or primer.

crawlway A working duct (usually underground) at least 1 m high, but not high enough to walk in.

crazing 1. Hair cracking of the surface of concrete or cement rendering, generally caused by excessive water content of the mix or over-trowelling. 2. In plasterwork, the cracking of the finishing coat and its lack of adhesion to the undercoat, caused by a weak undercoat.

creasing Two or three courses of plain roofing tiles at a **sill** or under a brick-on-edge **coping**, projecting beyond the wall surface by about 38 mm and in the latter case often protected on the upper surface by a **cement fillet** to throw off the rainwater.

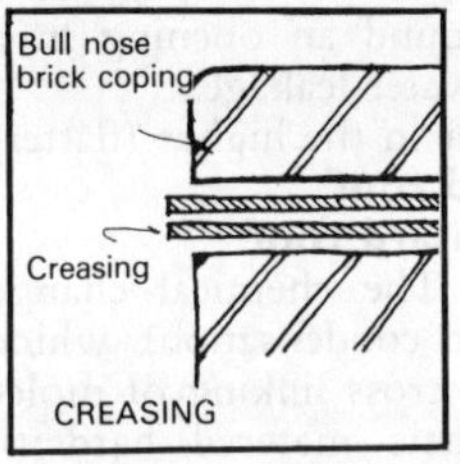

CREASING

creep The slow plastic deformation or movement of a material owing to inherent properties of the materials.

creosote A material used for the preservation of rough timberwork; it is manufactured from coal and wood-tar by distillation.

cricket (USA) In a **back gutter** to a chimney, a **saddle** to despatch water to either side.

cripple Any framed member which has to be shorter than its fellows, either at an opening and reducing the span of the opening (as in the case of a cripple stud) or in a position such as that of a jack-rafter in a hipped roof.

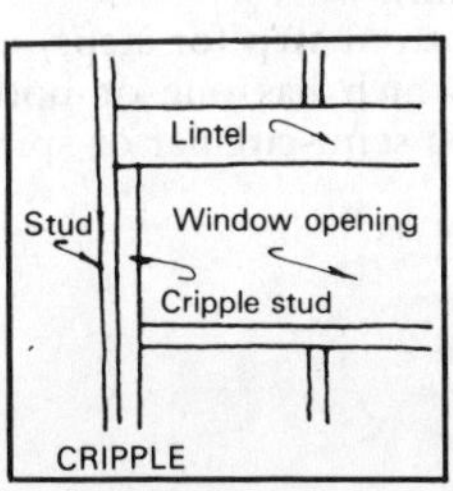

CRIPPLE

critical path diagram A multi-activity network programme which highlights those activities of which the duration is critical in the attainment of the overall programme. It also shows which activities have some **float** time, or capacity to be extended in duration without affecting the overall programme.

crocodiling A defect on a painted or varnished surface, characterized by a pattern of **crazing** that resembles a crocodile's skin.

cross band In **plywood** and **coreboard** the veneer on either side of the core, with its grain at right angles to the grain of the core. In three-ply material, the cross bands are the outer veneers.

cross bridging (USA) **Herring-bone strutting**.

cross-cut 1. To cut a piece of timber at right angles to the grain. 2. A saw-cut made at right angles to the grain of a piece of timber.

cross-cut saw A **saw** with its teeth set and sharpened to cut across the grain of wood. The larger the saw, the coarser its teeth; a 350 mm cross-cut saw has 32 to 40 points per 100 mm, whilst a 650 mm cross-cut saw has 24 to 32 points per 100 mm.

cross fall A gradient across the narrower of the two horizontal dimensions of an object or structural element.

cross furring (USA) **Brandering**.

cross garnet A **strap hinge** in which a long strap is screwed or bolted to the door face, the strap being hinged to an upright plate, screwed to the door frame. For most types of joinery this hinge is no longer used, though it is still used for **ledged and braced doors**.

cross grain 1. Grain which does not run parallel to the length of a piece of timber; it may be **end**, **diagonal**, **spiral** or **interlocking grain**. 2. Grain of face veneers in **plywood** which runs at right angles to the longer axis of the board.

cross hair A fine line on the diaphragm of a **theodolite** or **level** used to mark the position through which precise readings can be taken from a **levelling staff.**

cross joint See **perpend**.

cross-lap joint (USA) A halved joint between two pieces of timber meeting or crossing at right angles. cf. **halving joint (halved joint)**.

cross nogging **Herring-bone strutting**.

cross peen That part of a hand **hammer**, which is wedge shaped and on the opposite side of the head to the hammer face. The wedge is at right angles to the handle of the hammer. cf. **straight-peen hammer**.

cross-section A section at right angles to the length of a building, assembly or component; a drawing showing such a section. cf. **longitudinal section**.

cross tongue A piece of plywood or slip of timber glued into opposing saw cuts to stiffen the joint between two components.

cross wall construction A form of construction used in buildings of considerably greater length than width and consisting of repetitive subdivisions (as in a terrace of houses). The periodic cross walls are constructed as the main loadbearing elements of the building, all floor and roof loads being conveyed to them rather than to the front and back walls.

cross welt A seam between adjacent sheets of **flexible-metal roofing** and at right angles to the length of the sheet, *ie* across the slope of the roof.

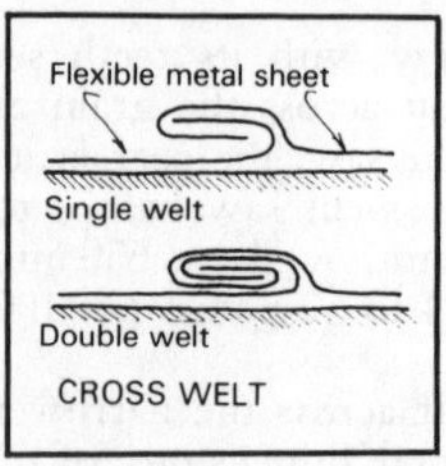

cross wires See **cross hair**.

crow bar An iron bar, tapered at one end and flattened to a wedge shape at the other, used as a lever for moving heavy objects. cf. **pinch bar**.

crown 1. The highest part of the cross-section of a cambered road. 2. The highest part of an arch.

crowsfoot or crowsfooting Minor wrinkling of paintwork resembling the imprint of a bird's foot.

crow step gable A gable whose profile is made up of a series of horizontal steps.

crushing strength The maximum load per unit area that a material will withstand before failure.

cube test A standard test to determine the strength of concrete, involving the application of a compressive force on a standard test cube of stated size and shape.

cubical aggregate Aggregate made up of angular particles having length, breadth and thickness substantially equal.

cubic content The space contained within the external surfaces of the walls and roof and the upper surface of the lowest floor of a building: the volume of the building.

cubing The process of working out the volumes of a building or of certain **items** in a **Bill of Quantities**.

culvert A structure in the form of a large pipe for the total enclosure of a watercourse beneath a road, building, etc.

culvert brick A tapered brick such as could be used to construct a culvert. cf. **brick**.

cup 1. A warping of flat sawn timber such as floor boards, in which the long edges bend upwards; hence 'cupping'. 2. A hollow metal truncated core with a rounded lip, fitted into a **countersinking** and used in conjunction with a screw fixing. It is used mainly to enable removal and replacement of the screw to be made without detriment to the surrounding timber, though it is used occasionally simply for decorative effect.

cupboard latch A simple catch, such as a ball catch, used to secure a lightweight door. It engages by spring action when the door is closed.

cup joint A **blown joint**.

cup shake A **ring shake**.

curb An upstand either to the edge of a carriageway or around an opening in a flat roof to avoid water leakage.

curb rafter A rafter in the higher (flatter) slope of a **mansard roof**.

curb roof See **mansard roof**.

cure or curing 1. The chemical change (polymerization or condensation) which occurs resulting in cross linking of molecules when a plastic material hardens; caused either by heat in the case of **thermo-setting** resins, or by the addition of an accelerator in the case of cold-setting resins. 2. The process of ensuring the hardening of concrete after placing by preventing it from being affected by excessive evaporation or extremes of temperature.

curing agent An **admixture** introduced into a material or mixture to start the chemical process of setting or hardening, or to assist such a process.

curl The fine figure obtained on a veneer or a worked surface of wood following skilful conversion of the timber from the crotch of a tree (*ie* the junction between a branch and the trunk).

curtail step The bottom step (or steps) of a flight of **stairs** which has one or both ends extended into a semi-circular or spiral return.

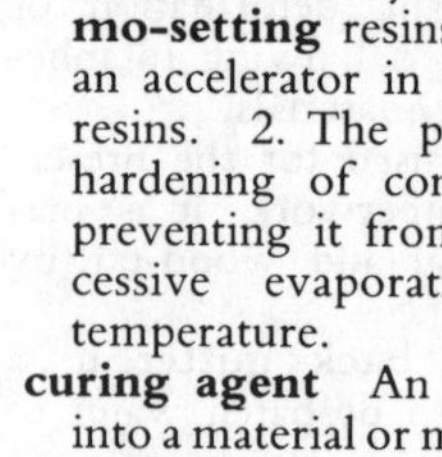

curtaining The sagging of a paint film on a vertical surface causing festoon markings; usually the result of a too-thick coat of paint being applied, or uneven brushing out.

curtain wall An infilling wall to a frame structure, which carries no load from the rest of the structure and is designed simply to withstand wind pressure and support its own self-weight. It may be composed of a light metal framework with opaque infill panels and glazing within

curtilage The total land area attached to a dwelling house.

cushion 1. Padstone. cf. **Pad or padstone**. 2. The seating (usually of asbestos, plastic or lead) of a sheet of glass in **patent glazing**.

cut and fill The execution of earthworks involving the excavation of cuttings and the construction of embankments, as in terracing. In the design of such works one endeavours to balance, as nearly as possible, the cubic content of the excavated earth against the cubic content of earth required to form the built-up contours.

cut-and-mitred hip or cut-and-mitred valley A **close-cut hip** or **valley**.

cut-and-mitred string A **string** which is cut on the upper edge to the profile of the stairs but which conceals the end grain of the **risers** by being mitred to them.

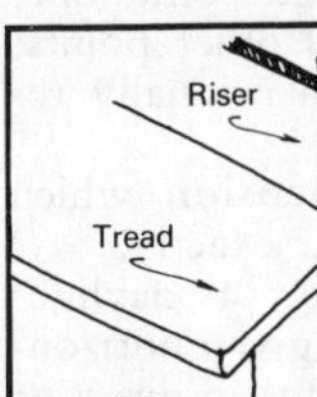

CUT-AND-MITRED STRING

cut brick A brick that has been cut to shape using a bricklayer's **axe** or **bolster**. It is more roughly finished than a **gauged brick**.

cut nail A heavy carpentry **nail** of rectangular cross-section, made by cutting a sheet of steel plate, as opposed to forging wire to make **wire nails**. Cut nails cannot be bent over and clenched like wire nails. cf. **clenching**.

cut-out A circuit breaker in an electrical circuit, designed to break if the designed capacity of the circuit is exceeded.

cut string An open **string** of a stair in which the upper edge is profiled to receive the **risers** and **treads** of the stair, often with the treads overhanging the string.

cutting edge The transverse edge of each tooth on a saw, formed by the intersection of the flank and the face.

cutting in The practice of forming a clean line between one type of paint or colour and another on the same, or an adjacent, surface.

cutting iron The blade of a **plane**. cf. **back iron**.

cutting list A list of sized material required for a particular application, with the quantities and/or lengths of each size required.

cycle 1. A series of changes of physical state in which conditions at the end of the series have returned to what they were at the beginning, as in diurnal cycles of hot and cold ambient temperature. 2. An arbitrary unit of time equal to one cycle of **alternating current**, which in the UK equals 1/50 second. 3. The recurrent period of a sound wave or vibration, the frequency of which gives the sound its pitch.

cyclic conditions Environmental conditions which fluctuate in accordance with a regular pattern.

cylinder 1. A closed tank, usually circular on plan and domed on top, for storing hot water prior to its being drawn off for use. Often it is provided with an insulating jacket. 2. A unit separate from the lock which it operates, but fixed to it on installation. It contains one of a variety of key-operated mechanisms, often considered as being always **pin tumbler mechanisms**, but not invariably so.

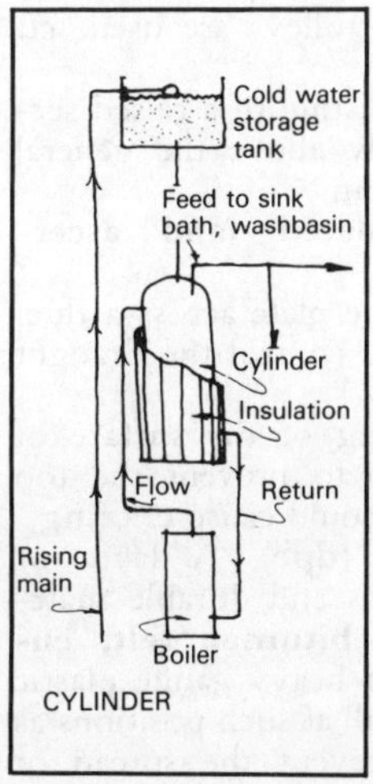

CYLINDER

cylinder latch A **night latch**.

cylinder lock A lock whose mechanism, which is generally provided by pin tumblers, is contained in a cylinder. cf. **pin tumbler mechanism, cylinder latch**.

cylinder rim night latch A **night latch** designed as a **rim latch**.

D

dado The lining or special finishing treatment given to the lower part of an internal wall which differs from the treatment given to the upper part in order to provide greater resistance to abrasion and impact or better protection against soiling. Treatments used include panelling, lining with a hard-wearing material or merely applying a type and/or colour of paint different from that applied to the upper part of the wall.

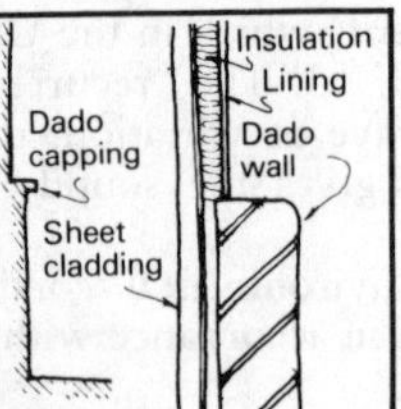

DADO

dado capping The head of a **dado**, which may be a timber capping to panelling or a moulded shape in the plasterwork or the capping to a brick wall forming a dado to a sheeted wall in an industrial building.

dado joint (USA) A **housed joint**.

dado rail Either the head of a **dado** (see **dado capping**) or an independent rail set on a wall at dado height to act as a protection to the wall surface, particularly in buildings in which trolleys are used. cf. **chair rail**.

dais A platform consisting of a raised section of floor slightly above the general floor level of the room.

damages See **liquidated (and ascertained) damages**.

damper An adjustable plate across a flue, duct or ventilator to control the draught or air flow.

damping The wetting of the surface of newly laid concrete to prevent the too rapid drying which could cause **crazing**.

damp-proof course (dpc) A layer or barrier of impervious and durable material, such as slate, **bitumen felt, engineering brick**, or heavy gauge plastic sheet, built into a wall at such positions as are necessary to prevent the spread of moisture in the wall by capillary action. Damp proof courses are located, for example, approximately 150 mm (not less) above the external ground level, below **copings**, in chimney stack walling just above the roof level and at window and door openings. cf. **tanking**.

damp-proofing The process of making a building proof against the penetration of dampness from adjacent ground or from driving rain by means of damp-proof courses, waterproof rendering, **tanking**, etc.

damp-proof membrane A continuous layer of impervious material incorporated in a solid floor or roof.

dancing step A tapered step in a **flight** of **stairs**, with the **tread** at its narrow end very little narrower than the parallel treads of the steps in the straight part of the flight. A dancing step, therefore, does not present the same hazard as a **winder** but is less economical in the use of space.

datum A known or assumed point, line, level or plane to which all other points, lines or planes can be dimensionally related.

datum dimension A **dimension** which locates a point, line or plane exactly.

daylight factor The ratio of daylight illuminance at a point on a given horizontal plane inside a building due to direct or indirect lighting from the sky, to the illuminance at a point on a horizontal plane exposed to an unobstructed hemisphere of sky. Direct sunlight is excluded from both values of illuminance.

daylight width The horizontal **dimension** between the **sight lines** of the frame

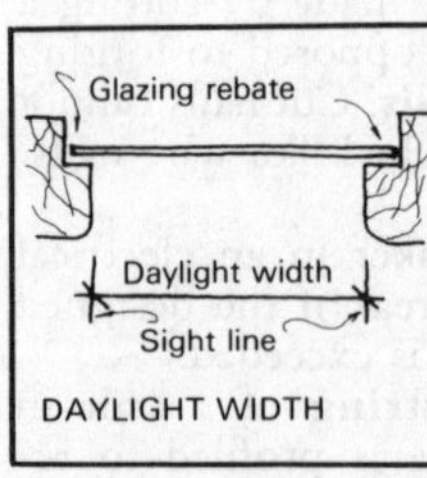

DAYLIGHT WIDTH

of a window, *ie* the total glass width less the widths of those parts of the glass obscured by the **glazing rebate**.

daywork A method of payment for building work (usually work of a small scale) involving the agreement of the hours of work and the quantities of materials used to undertake the work, and establishing the total payment to be made for that work by taking the actual cost of labour and materials to the general contractor and adding an agreed percentage for profit and overheads.

dead bolt A bolt, usually rectangular in cross-section and square-ended, which is shot by turning a key in a **lock**. cf. **right latch** and **barrel bolt**.

dead end A pipe with one end blanked off in a wet central heating system. The length of the dead end is measured from the last branch to the capped end.

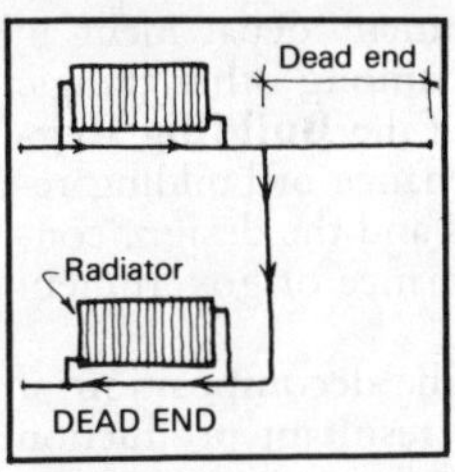

deadening See **pugging**.

dead knot A **knot** whose fibres are not intergrown to any great extent with those of the surrounding wood and which in consequence can be more easily knocked out than a **live knot**.

dead leaf See **standing leaf**.

dead leg A length of pipe in a hot water system leading merely to a draw-off point and not forming part of the circuit.

dead light 1. A window or part of a window which does not open. 2. A **light** in which the glass is fixed directly to the frame.

dead load The self weight of the structure, its finishes and any non-loadbearing elements of the building (such as partitions) and permanent racking for the storage of goods (but not the weight of the goods themselves). cf. **imposed load**.

dead lock A **lock** having only a **dead bolt**.

dead shore A vertical strut which supports a horizontal member (**needle**) which in turn provides a temporary support for a wall. cf. **shore**.

deal A piece of square-sawn softwood, 50 to 100 mm thick and 225 to no more than 279 mm wide. cf. **plank**.

deal frame A **frame-saw** used for cutting **deals** into timbers with smaller cross-sections.

Death-watch Beetle (*Xestobium rufovillosum*) A wood-boring insect 6–8 mm long, whose larvae inhabit mainly hardwoods subject to dampness or fungal decay. Although softwood attack is known, infestation is always confined to damp or decayed areas. Bore holes are 3 mm in diameter, loosely packed with bore-dust containing flattened spherical pellets.

debarking The removal of bark from a log or tree.

decay 1. Decomposition brought about by a fungus or other micro-organism, manifested in softening, progressive loss of strength and mass and often change in colour and texture. In timber it involves the decomposition of the cell walls. 2. Dilapidation. 3. A gradual wearing away of, say, stonework by the combined action of wind, rain, etc.

decibel A unit of sound, one-tenth of a bel, being a dimensionless unit used to compare sound intensities.

deck A platform. cf. **decking**.

decking 1. Prefabricated units of construction used to form floors or flat roofs. 2. In lightweight construction, the sheet material used to provide support to the weathering layer of a flat roof, or the sheet material used to support the finish of a suspended floor.

decorative laminate See **plastic laminate**.

decrement factor (f) The ratio of the cyclic **thermal transmittance** to the steady state **U value**.

deep bead A 50 mm or so tall board fixed to the sill of a sash window, allowing the lower sash to be raised to permit ventilation at the **meeting rails** only, without causing a draught, whilst the bottom of the window remains to all intents and purposes shut.

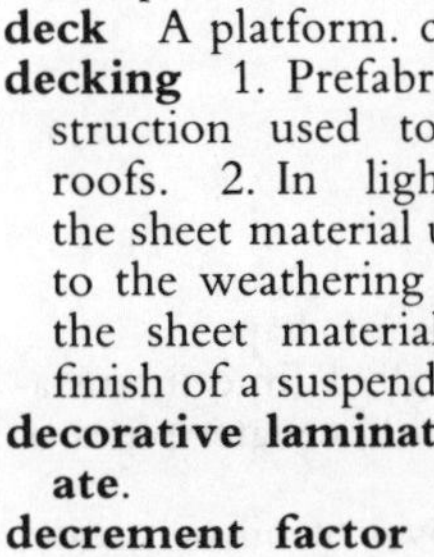

deep-seal trap An **anti-siphon trap**.

deep shakes Those **shakes** which are deeper than 5 mm in pieces of wood not more than 50 mm thick or 1/10th of the thickness of thicker pieces.

defect An inherent irregularity or weakness in a material, such as a **wane**, **shake** or **knot** in timber, or an irregularity introduced during manufacture or construction which detracts from the usefulness or suitability of a product for its required purpose, or an area showing signs of decay.

defects liability period Sometimes referred to as the maintenance period; a time after the practical completion of a building contract during which the contractor, as part of the contract obligations, is responsible for remedying any defect in the materials of workmanship that has become obvious and is not the result of either carelessness in the use of the building or normal wear-and-tear. The period is usually 6 or 12 months.

deflection The amount of bending of a structure when under load.

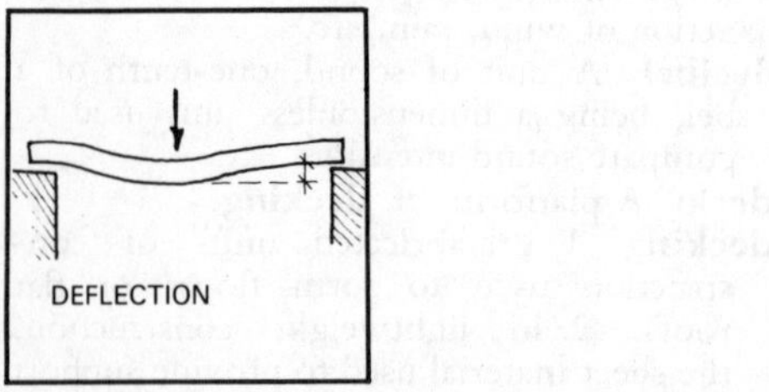

deformation A change of shape.

defurring The removal of lime incrustation from the inside of hot water pipes or cylinders.

degreasing The removal of oil or grease, usually by a suitable organic solvent or an aqueous detergent.

degree day value A figure which describes the coldness of a site and is based on the number of days per annum on which the temperature falls below that level at which heating is judged to be needed in a building. It is used to estimate the annual fuel consumption necessary to heat a building.

dehumidifier A device, often associated with air conditioning systems, which reduces the humidity of the air by cooling it, thus avoiding conditions which could lead to the formation of **condensation** on cold surfaces in a building.

delaminated joint A joint made by splitting the thickness of a piece of semi-rigid asbestos bitumen sheet, interleaving it with another similar piece and sealing the two together to form an impervious joint.

delamination The breakdown of the structure of a laminated material by the separation of its layers.

deliquescence The change undergone by certain substances which liquefy due to their absorption of water, usually from the air. Patches of chlorides occurring in plaster and brickwork may suffer from this defect, producing damp areas. The process involved is in direct contrast to that of **efflorescence**.

demountable Capable of being taken down and re-erected in some other location with little or no damage. Such items as partitions or even complete buildings may be demountable.

dense Having its constituent particles closely compacted together; close grained.

dense concrete Concrete in which the constituents are closely packed, resulting in a minimal number of voids.

density The mass per unit volume of a substance at a specific temperature measured in such units as kg/m^3.

Department of the Environment (**DoE**) The government department in the UK responsible, among other things, for the formulation of the **Building Regulations**, the maintenance of building research establishments and the design, construction and maintenance of government buildings.

depolymerization The decomposition of a polymer, with the resultant production of a monomer.

depth A measure taken downwards or inwards; *eg* of a **joist**, of a **manhole**, the vertical distance from the top of the manhole cover to the outgoing **invert**; of glazing, the distance between the top and bottom extremities of the glazed area measured in the plane of the glass; of a cupboard, the distance from the front of the cupboard to the back of it.

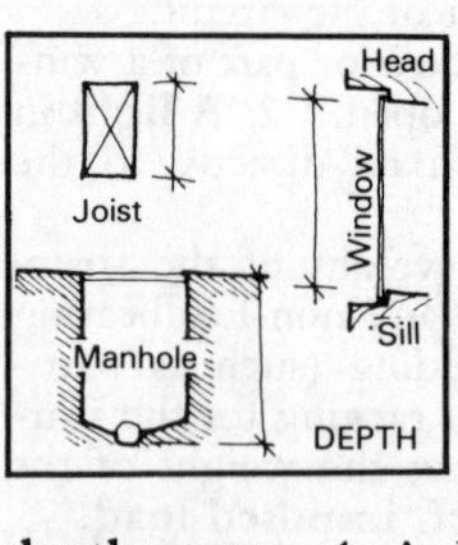

depth gauge 1. A device used to measure the depth of a hole or depression. There is considerable variation in the size and type of depth gauges, but the principle on which they are based is constant, a cross piece penetrated by a graduated rod, along which it slides. A clamp may be incorporated to fix the cross piece at a chosen point. With the rod standing in the sinking and the cross piece resting on the top of the sinking the depth is obtained. 2. A device which, when clamped to a drill, regulates the depth of hole bored.

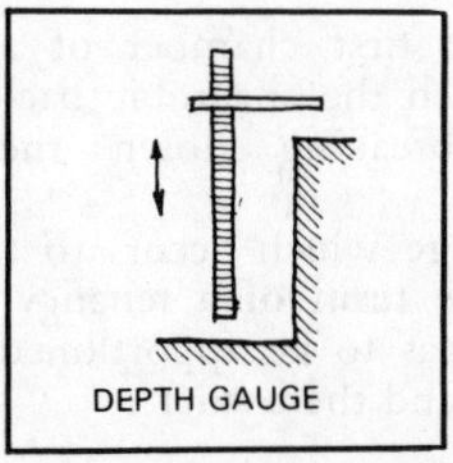
DEPTH GAUGE

descaling The removal, chemically or by abrasion, of scale (caused by corrosion or chemical deposit) from a metal element or pipe.

designed life Of a building or component, the period for which it is intended to last.

detail drawing A drawing of a part of a building which enables that part to be made and positioned within the building. It is usually drawn to a larger **scale** than **working drawings**, but there is no clear demarcation between the two types of drawing. Both are necessary for the construction of any but the simplest building.

detector A sensing device connected to a security alarm system, which is sensitive to temperature rise or smoke (in the case of fire protection systems) or the movement of an intruder (in the case of burglar alarm systems).

devil float A **hand float** with projecting spikes, used to score the surface of a coat of fresh plaster to form a **key** for a subsequent coat.

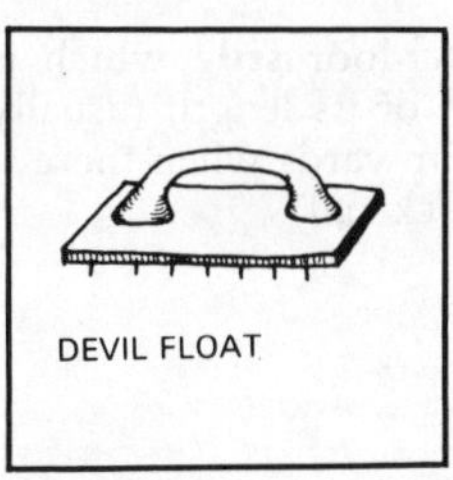
DEVIL FLOAT

devilling The scoring of the surface of a coat of fresh plaster to form a **key** for a subsequent coat.

dewatering The process of removing excessive water, as from a **caisson**, an excavation or a site.

dew point The temperature at which a given sample of moist air becomes saturated and **condensation** begins. The lower the temperature, the less moisture air is able to retain.

diagonal bond A form of bond used only in very thick walls, the brick courses being built diagonally across the wall and successive courses being laid in opposed directions. Bats are used to obtain a flush wall face. Also known as raking bond. **Herring-bone bond** is a form of diagonal bond.

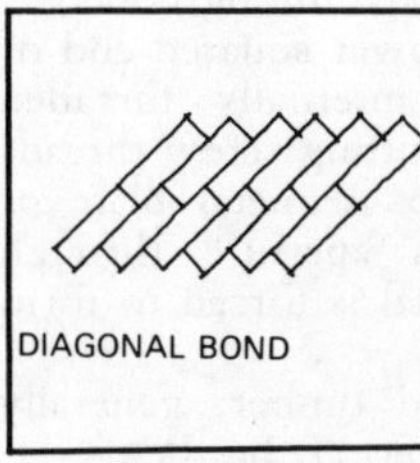
DIAGONAL BOND

diagonal brace A **brace** running from corner to corner of a rectangular frame. cf. **angle brace**.

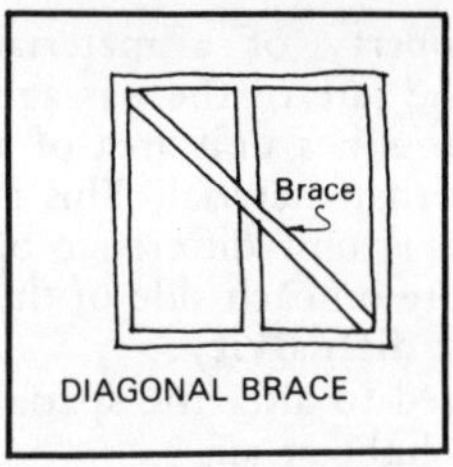

DIAGONAL BRACE

diagonal grain A defect in which the fibres run at an angle to, instead of parallel to, the length of a piece of wood. It is caused by faulty **conversion.**

diagonal slating Slates (usually of asbestos-cement) laid diagonally on a roof so that one diagonal of each slate is horizontal. The corners of this diagonal are cut off.

diamond matching See **four-piece butt matching**.

diamond saw A large **circular saw** used for cutting stone.

diamond washer A curved washer used with **corrugated sheeting material** to seal the hole through which the hook bolt (or similar fixing) passes to secure the sheeting. The curve of the washer matches the curve of the corrugations.

diaper work Decorative pattern in brickwork, achieved by so laying the **facing bricks**, as to give a diamond pattern of lighter or darker coloured **headers**.

diaphragm ball valve A float-operated valve in which the flow of water is controlled by a diaphragm.

diaphragm plate A stiffener placed between the webs of a box girder.

diatomaceous earth or diatomite A deposit, occurring as a whitish powder, which is composed of hollow siliceous skeletons of tiny marine or fresh-water organisms. It is resistant to heat and chemicals, and is used as an **extender** in paint, an **aggregate** in lightweight **building blocks** or flue bricks, and a constituent in fireproof cements and insulating materials. It is also used in certain water filtration systems for swimming pools.

die 1. The upper of lower squared end of a **baluster**. 2. An internally threaded steel block used for cutting screw threads on bars or pipes. 3. A metal plate or block containing an aperture through which a softer material is forced to form **extrusions**.

die square A squared timber, generally 100 × 100 mm or larger. cf. **baulk**.

differential pressure The air pressure variation that can be expected between different faces of a building or element of construction.

diffusance That property of a material which determines the rate of the passage of water vapour through a unit area of a specific thickness of that material. This is assessed when there is unit difference of water vapour pressure on each side of the material. cf. **vapour diffusivity**.

diffuser A device used to alter the spatial distribution of heat, light or air.

diffuse radiation In terms of solar radiation that radiation which does not result from the direct incidence of solar rays on an object – the type of radiation experienced on overcast days.

diffuse reflection The scattered reflection of light or sound from a surface, such as that of light from a matt, white sheet of paper, which is equal in all directions.

diffuse-reflection factor The ratio of the amount of light which is diffusely reflected from a surface to the total amount of light falling upon that surface.

diffusion A spreading or scattering or distribution; that change in the distribution of molecules or ions which is brought about by normal thermal agitation. The mixture of one with another of gases or liquids which are in contact.

diffusion treatment A treatment of timber in which preservative, usually waterborne, is applied to the surface of green timber in a paste or concentrated solution and gradually moves into the wet wood under the force of the concentration gradient. Double diffusion treatment is the steeping of timber in two successive and different salt solutions.

diffusivity The property of a material which is independent of thickness and is a measure of the rate at which vapour will pass through the material when a difference of pressure exists between the air on opposite sides. It is the reciprocal of **vapour resistivity** and is measured in gm/MN.

digestion tank The first chamber of a **septic tank** in which the anaerobic bacteria commence breaking down the sewage.

dilapidations Damage which occurs to a property during the term of a tenancy, the cost of which has to be apportioned between the tenant and the owner.

diluent A **thinner**.

diluent air Air admitted or induced into a flue to dilute the products of combustion.

dimension 1. A measurement in length, breadth or thickness. 2. (In the plural). The specific size of an object.

dimensional co-ordination The application of a range of related dimensions to the sizing of building components and assemblies and to the building incorporating them.

dimensional stability That property of a material or component which enables it to maintain its original shape and dimensions at all times and under all conditions.

dimension shingles **Shingles**, usually of western red cedar, cut to uniform rather than random widths.

dimension stone A term sometimes used for an **ashlar**.

diminishing courses Courses of slates in which the **gauge** diminishes from the **eaves** to the **ridge**. The slate widths may also diminish, provided a satisfactory bond is maintained.

diminishing piece or diminishing pipe A **taper pipe**.

diminishing stile A door **stile** which is narrowed for a part of its length (usually from the **lock rail** upwards when there is glazing above the lock rail).

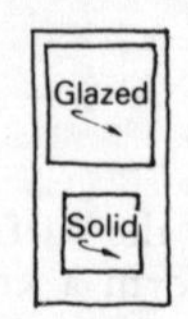

DIMINISHING STILE

DIN Deutsche Industrie Norm – German industrial standard, which is similar in concept to other national standards, such as, the British Standards; one of a wide-ranging system of standards which includes the construction industry.

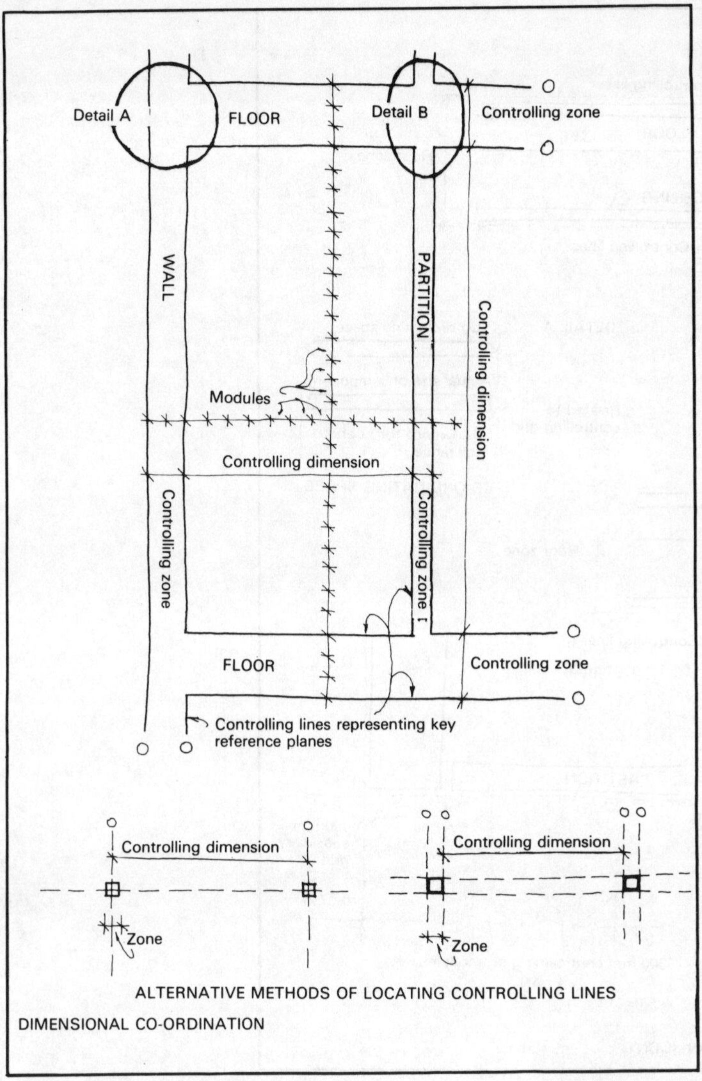

dinging A rough, single-coat, sand/cement **stucco** on walls, sometimes marked to imitate masonry.

direct current (dc) Electrical current which flows perpetually in one direction; that is, the **terminals** of the system remain permanently either positive or negative. cf. **alternating current**.

direct cylinder A hot water **cylinder** into which hot water passes directly from a **boiler**, being stored in the cylinder until it is drawn off. cf. **indirect cylinder**.

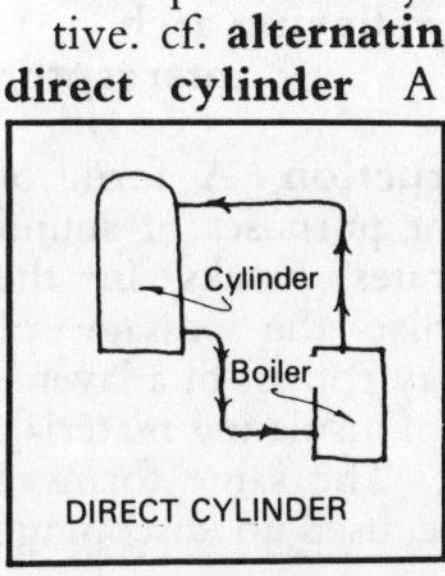

direct glazing Glazing directly into the structural surround of an opening and not into a frame which sits within the opening.

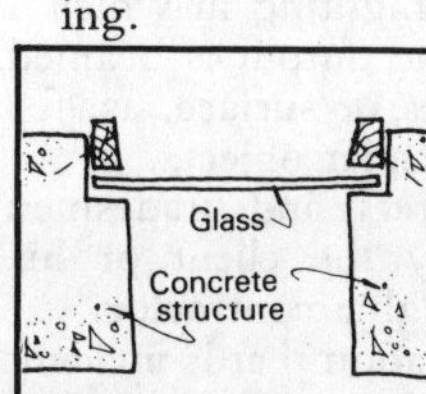

direct heating The heating of a room by radiation, the source of which is in the

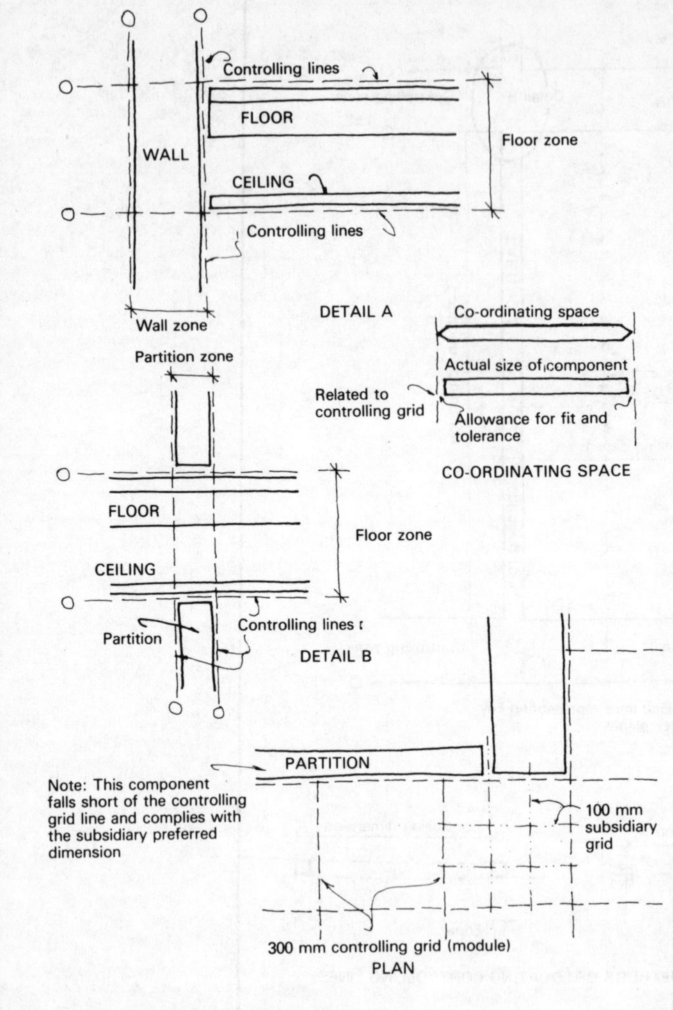

DIMENSIONAL CO-ORDINATION (CONT)

room itself and may be, for instance, a solid fuel fire, or a gas or electric fire.

direct hot water system A system in which water passes through and is directly heated by a boiler to provide domestic hot water.

directional lighting Lighting in which a high proportion of the output is beamed towards a specific area or surface, as, for instance, on to a particular object.

direct labour Labourers and tradesmen employed directly by the client or his agent instead of through a contractor.

direct radiation Radiation that is incident upon the receiving object or absorber.

dirty money Additional payment to operatives for working in difficult or unpleasant conditions.

discharge lamp A lamp in which the light is produced, either directly or by means of phosphors, by an electric discharge through a gas, a metal vapour or a mixture of several gases or vapours.

discharge pipe A pipe which conveys the discharge from sanitary appliances.

discharging arch A **relieving arch**.

disconnecting trap See **interceptor trap**.

discontinuous construction A form of construction that, for purposes of sound insulation, incorporates breaks in the structure to minimize the passage of sound. The break may consist of a layer – or a series of pads – of insulating material, or an air space, etc. The same form of construction may be used to discourage

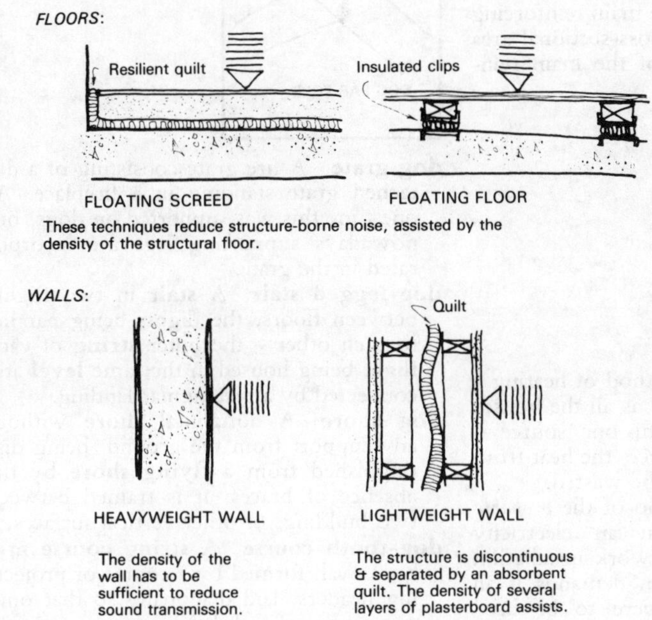

DISCONTINUOUS CONSTRUCTION

the passage of vibration from plant or equipment into the structure of a building.

disc sander A small **sanding machine**; one form consists of an attachment to an electric hand drill in the form of a rubber disc forming a backing to a replaceable **glasspaper** disc.

dishing A sinking in the surface of a material, often for drainage purposes.

dispersion A distribution or scattering. A term used, for instance, in relation to the small, suspended drops of liquid in an emulsion.

distance piece A short piece or block of wood or other material used to hold two components apart by a desired distance.

distemper A heavily pigmented paint in which the **binder** is size. It is used only for internal painting. Washable distempers include some drying oils.

distemper brush A flat **brush**, 125 – 250 mm wide, with long, closely packed bristles.

distributed load A load that is evenly spread. cf. **point load**.

distribution board or distribution panel An insulating panel containing terminals and fuses or circuit breakers, etc., for the distribution of power supplies from the incoming line to one or more branch circuits, each branch having its own fuse or circuit breaker.

distribution box See **junction box**.

distribution line The main electrical feed

which is separated into branch circuits at a **distribution board or distribution panel**.

distribution pipe Any pipe conveying water from a storage cistern.

distribution steel (reinforcement) Steel bars in a reinforced concrete slab which run at right angles to the main reinforcing steel and have a total cross-sectional area of about 10% of that of the main reinforcement.

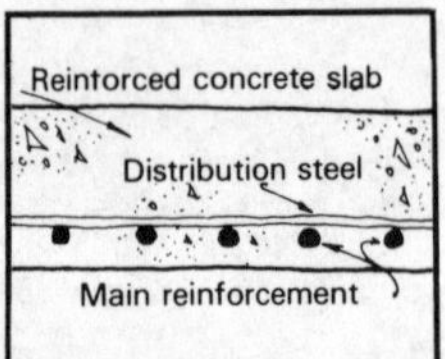

DISTRIBUTION STEEL

district heating The method of heating a group of buildings (such as all the houses on a housing site) from one source – usually an industrial source, the heat from which would otherwise be wasted.

diversity factor The ratio of the *probable* maximum demands on an electricity supply system or a pipework installation to the *possible* maximum demands if all outlets or appliances were to be used simultaneously. It is a factor used in the design of the systems.

division wall A wall that subdivides a structure in order to restrict the spread of fire. cf. **compartment floor/wall** and **separating wall/floor.**

dog 1. A **corrugated fastener**. 2. A U-shaped spike for fixing together heavy timbers, such as a dead shore and a needle. 3. A name for various mechanical devices used for gripping, such as a grappling iron of the type used in pairs with chains for gripping and hoisting an object. 4. One of a pair of irons used for supporting burning wood in a fireplace, or, at one time, for supporting a loose fire grate. cf. **dog grate.**

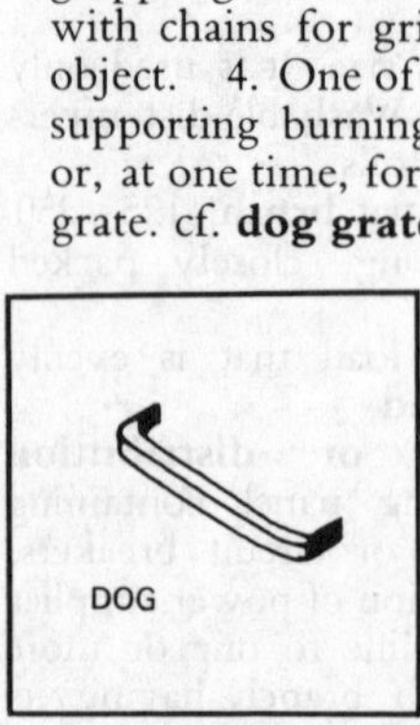
DOG

dog ear (fold) A box-like corner formed in a flexible metal sheet by folding, not cutting, the metal. It may be used to provide an upstand or downstand of the sheet.

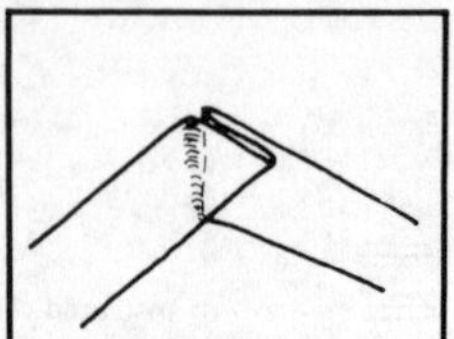
DOG EAR FOLD

dog grate A fire grate consisting of a detached grate standing in a fireplace. At one time this was supported on dogs, but nowadays supporting legs are incorporated in the grate.

dog-legged stair A **stair** in two flights between floors, the flights being parallel to each other – the outer **string** of each flight being housed in the same **level** and connected by a rectangular landing.

dog shore A horizontal **shore** without any support from the ground, being distinguished from a **flying shore** by the absence of braces. It is framed between two buildings or other vertical surfaces.

dog-tooth course A **string course** in a brick wall formed by a course of projecting headers, laid diagonally so that only one corner of each brick projects.

dome A hemispherical **vault**, circular on plan.

domelight A **rooflight** made up of a single sheet of glass or plastic, curved in a dome-like form.

door buck (USA) A door **sub-frame** of wood or pressed metal to which the **door case** is fixed.

door case See **door lining**.

door casing (USA) The **architrave** or other **trim** to a door opening.

door chain A device to prevent a door from being opened more than a short distance. It consists of a chain attached to the door frame, the knobbed end of which engages in a slotted fixture on the door. This allows the door to be opened a few centimetres but restricts further opening until the chain is disengaged from the inside.

door cheeks The **jambs** of a door frame. Also called door posts.

door closer A device for closing a door automatically, a common type being a sprung device fixed to both the door and the frame or to the door and the floor. A check action is often incorporated to ensure that the final closing is slow and quiet.

door frame The frame to a door, consisting of a head and two jambs, to one of which the door is hinged. The frame usually is rebated and is of a stouter cross section than a **door lining**. cf. **rebate**.

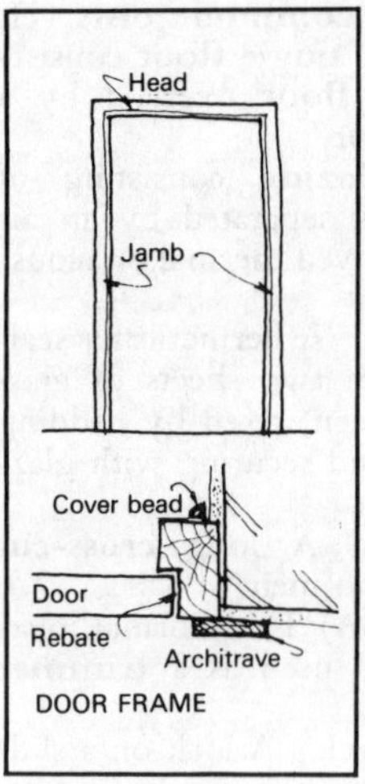

DOOR FRAME

door furniture The various items of ironmongery attached to a door which relate to its operation and locking (*ie* handle, knob, **lock, bolt, finger plate, escutcheon**, etc.

door head The top member of a **door frame**.

door jamb One of the vertical members of the door frame.

door lining A lightweight alternative to a **door frame** (usually only for interior doors). The lining extends to the full width of the **reveal** and covers both sides and head. It is occasionally rebated for the door, but more often has a **planted-stop**. cf. **rebate**.

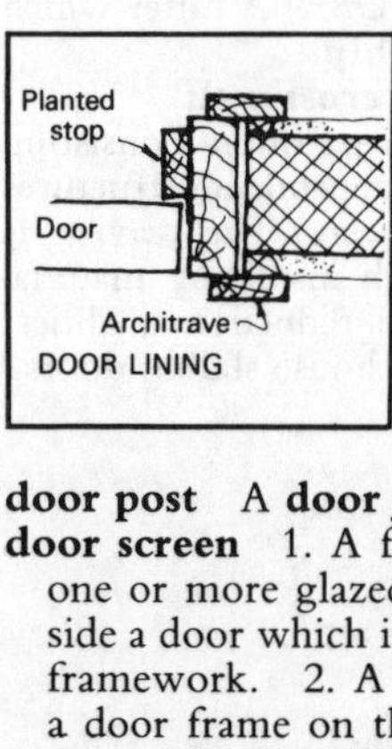

DOOR LINING

door post A **door jamb**.

door screen 1. A framework made up of one or more glazed **lights** around or beside a door which is hung within the same framework. 2. A wire screen hinged in a door frame on the outside of the main door to exclude flies when the main door is open.

DOOR SCREEN

doorset An assembly including a **door frame** or **lining**, a door in one or more leaves hinged to the frame, and the hardware or **door furniture**. It may also include a sill, an over-panel and a side panel.

door sill An external door **threshold**.

door stop 1. A rebate cut from the solid frame, or a **planted** batten on a **door lining**, against which the door closes. 2. A catch set in the floor to hold a door open, or a device fixed to the floor or to a wall to prevent the door from opening too far.

dormer (window) A vertical window set into and projecting from the slope of a pitched roof, and having its own pitched, swept or flat roof.

DORMER WINDOW

dormer cheek The vertical side of a **dormer (window)**.

dot 1. A wiped, soldered or leadburned covering to a screw which is securing a sheet of lead cladding to timber boarding on a steeply sloping or vertical surface (*eg* on a **dormer cheek**). The fixing area is dished and the dot fills this sinking. 2. A dab of plaster used with others to secure **dry lining**.

dote or doat Early **decay** of timber, indicated by discoloration in the form of dots or speckles; hence the adjective **doty**.

doty Term applied to timber which is beginning to **decay**.

double-action hinge A door hinge which enables the door to be swung in either direction by pushing or pulling from either side and which usually is sprung to close the door after it has been opened.

double ball catch A friction catch used mainly for cupboard doors, in which a staple on the door passes between the jaws of the catch which house two spring-loaded balls. These fall back into place behind the thick part of the staple, thereby retaining the door.

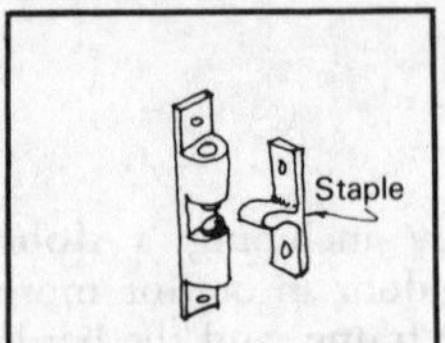

DOUBLE BALL CATCH

double bead Two parallel **beads** separated by a **quirk**.

double boxed mullion A mullion separating adjacent sash windows and containing two sets of counterweights or counter balance springs for the **sliding sashes** on either side.

double-bridging Two rows of herringbone strutting which divide the span of a floor into three equal parts.

double connector A short piece of pipe with a thread at each end used to make a connection into a gas supply pipe.

double door A pair of doors, often with rebated **meeting stiles** (unless they are **swing doors**). cf. **folding door**.

double-door bolt An **espagnolette bolt**.

double-dovetail key A hardwood **cramp**, shaped like two **dovetail** pins joined at their narrow ends, set into a butt joint between two timber members to hold them together. Also known as a dovetail feather.

DOUBLE DOVETAIL KEY

double eaves course A double thickness of **plain tiles**, **slates** or **shingles** at the foot of a roof slope or area of **tile hanging**.

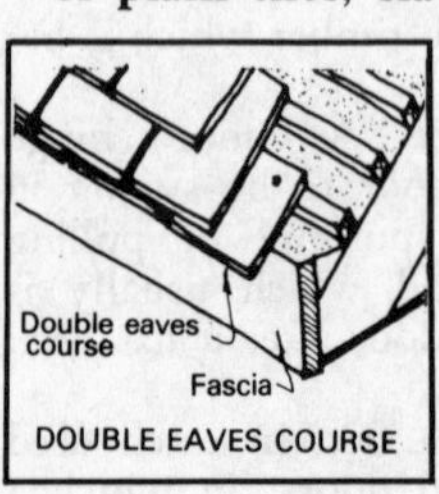

DOUBLE EAVES COURSE

double Flemish bond Brickwork which shows **Flemish bond** on both faces of the wall. cf. **bond**.

double floor 1. A floor made up of more than one span of **common joists.** cf. **single floor**. 2. A **single floor** consisting of a **counter floor** overlaid by a second, finished floor.

double glazing **Glazing** consisting of two layers of glass separated by an air space, to give improved thermal or acoustic insulation.

double glazing unit A hermetically sealed unit made up of two sheets of glass with a cavity between, fixed by bedding in glazing rebates and securing with glazing beads.

double-handed saw A long **cross-cut saw** operated by two men.

double header (USA) Two normal joists nailed together and used as a **trimmer joist** at an opening.

double hook bolt lock A lock on a sliding door containing two hooked bolts, usually projecting in opposite directions, and a fixed pin which lines up the lock and the **striking plate** when the door shuts.

DOUBLE HOOK BOLT LOCK

double-hung window A vertical sliding **sash window**.

double jack-rafter (USA) A rafter which joins a **valley** and a **hip**.

double lock welt A **cross welt**.

double partition A partition consisting of two parallel independent structures with a cavity between. This cavity is sometimes filled with insulating material to give better sound reduction qualities, or it may be used to house sliding doors.

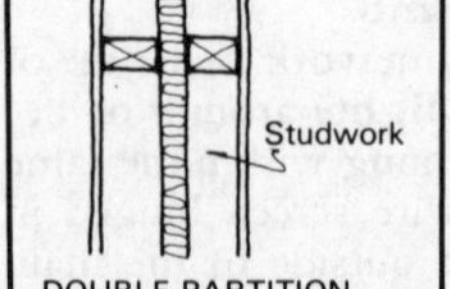

DOUBLE PARTITION

double-pitch roof or double-pitched roof 1. A **roof** with two sloping surfaces, which slope in different directions from a **ridge**. cf. **mono-pitched roof**. 2. A **mansard roof**.

double quirk bead A **bead** set into a surface, and having a **quirk** on each side.

double rebated A frame with two **rebates** either both on the one side to provide two **weather checks** or on opposite sides of a wide frame to allow a door or window to be hung on either side.

double-return stair A **stair** with one wide flight up from the lower floor to a landing, and two flights (one on each side) from the landing to the upper floor.

double-roll verge tile A **single-lap tile** with a roll on each edge so that both **verges** are similarly edged with a roll.

double Roman tile A **single-lap tile** with a roll up the centre which matches the edge roll. cf. **Roman tile**.

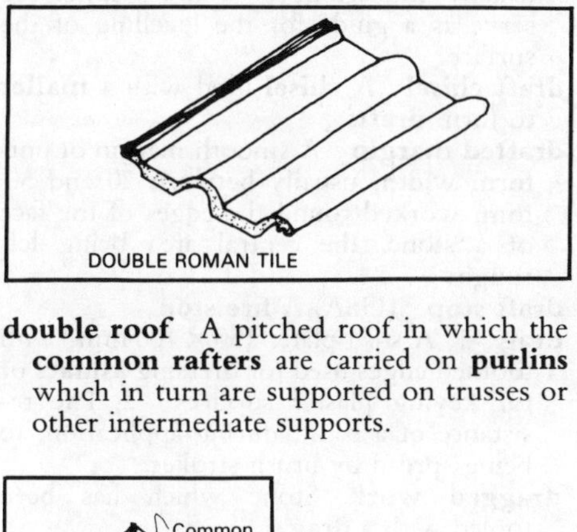

DOUBLE ROMAN TILE

double roof A pitched roof in which the **common rafters** are carried on **purlins** which in turn are supported on trusses or other intermediate supports.

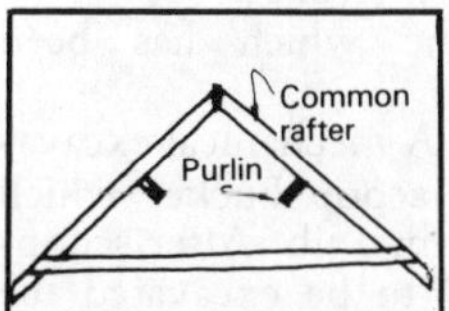

DOUBLE ROOF

double shear A member suffers double shear when it is resisting **shear** stress along two section planes, as in the case of a **rivet** joining three plates.

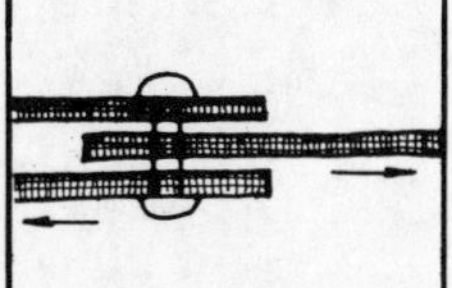

DOUBLE SHEAR

double skirting A higher than normal **skirting (board)** made up of two pieces of wood rebated together.

double socket A stoneware pipe fitting comprising a short pipe with a socket at each end for joining the **spigot** ends of two pipes in the same alignment.

double tenon or double tenon joint Two tenons formed within the thickness of a member making up a multiple tenon joint. Also known as a **twin tenon**.

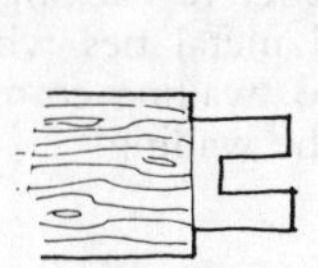

DOUBLE TENON

double-throw lock Any lock whose dead bolt, after the first turn of the key, can be thrown a second time to project further into the **keeper** by a second turn of the key.

double time The payment of double the normal hourly rate for work outside the normal working hours; *ie* week-end working or night work.

doubling course A **double eaves course**.

doubling piece A **tilting fillet**.

dovetail (joint) A joint similar to a **combed joint**, but having the interlocking tenons (or pins) fan-shaped (thicker at the end than at the root). It is used in making drawers or boxes in fine joinery.

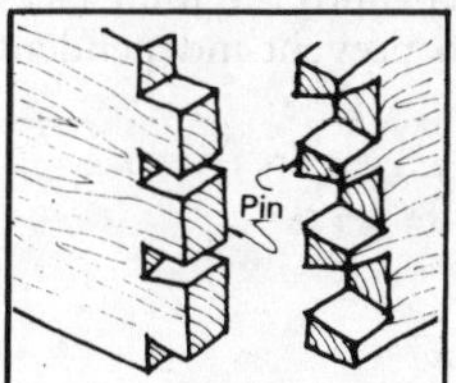

DOVETAIL (JOINT)

dovetail cramp A slate or metal **cramp** in a double-dovetail shape used in stonework.

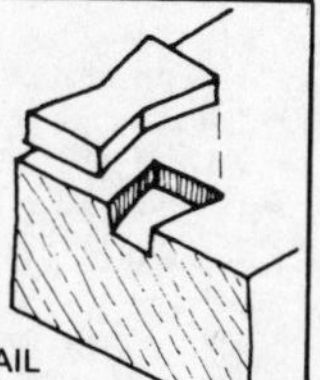

DOVETAIL CRAMP

dovetail feather A **double-dovetail key**.

dovetail halving (dovetail halved joint) A halved joint in which the halved pieces are dovetailed. cf. halving joint (halved joint).

dovetail saw A *back saw* about 200 mm long and with approximately 7 points to 10 mm.

dovetail slot and anchor A fixing device consisting of a metal channel insert, narrower at its open end than at its base, which is cast into a concrete backing to receive dovetail shaped metal ties which are fixed to, or cast into, walling components, thus anchoring the walling.

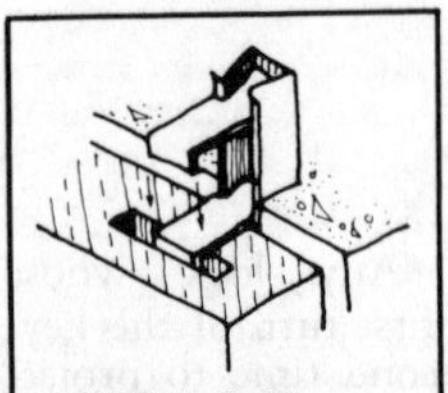

DOVETAIL SLOT

dowel 1. A short, round hardwood rod used instead of, or in conjunction with, a **tenon** for connecting two pieces of wood together. Used with a tenon it penetrates the complete joint, including the tenon. Used without a tenon it fits into opposed holes in the pieces of wood to be joined. It should be grooved to allow air and excess glue escape. 2. A short steel rod cast into concrete to locate an adjacent component which has a matching hole or socket. 3. A short piece of metal or slate bedded in sinkings cut into the joint faces of adjacent stones to prevent independent movement.

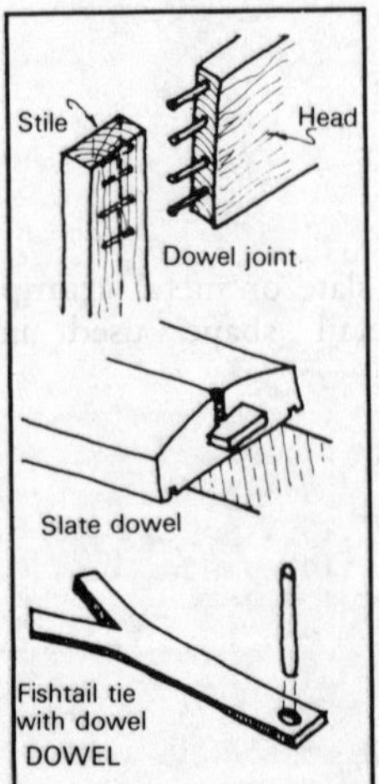

DOWEL

dowel pin 1. A short **wire nail** pointed at both ends. 2. (USA) A headless nail with a barbed shank which is driven through a **mortise-and-tenon joint** to fix it permanently.

dowel plate A perforated steel plate, its perforations being the size of **dowels**. It is used to verify the sizes of dowels or to trim dowels to size by driving oversized pegs through the required size of hole.

dowel screw A **woodscrew** threaded at each end.

downdraught A current of air down a chimney due to a cold flue or a faulty flue.

downpipe 1. A **rainwater pipe**. 2. That portion of a urinal **flush pipe** assembly which connects the **flushing cistern** to the **sparge** pipes.

downspout A **rainwater pipe**.

draft A smooth margin or strip worked on the face of a rough squared stone, usually the width of a draft chisel, to serve as a guide for the levelling of the surface.

draft chisel A **chisel** used with a **mallet** to form **drafts**.

drafted margin A smooth margin of uniform width, usually between 20 and 50 mm, worked round the edges of the face of a stone, the central area being left rough.

draft stop (USA) A **fire stop**.

drag 1. A steel plate, 150 × 100 mm, with toothed edges used for dressing **ashlars** or for keying plaster surfaces. 2. The resistance of a paint, during application, to being spread by brush strokes.

dragged work Stone which has been tooled with a **drag**.

dragline excavator A mechanical excavator consisting of a scoop bucket which swings on chains from a jib. After scooping up the material to be excavated the bucket is dragged back towards the machine by means of a wire rope.

dragon beam or dragon piece A horizontal timber member into which the foot of a **hip rafter** is framed. It bisects the angle of the **wall plates** at the corner of a building and its inner end is carried by an **angle tie**, sometimes called a **dragon tie**.

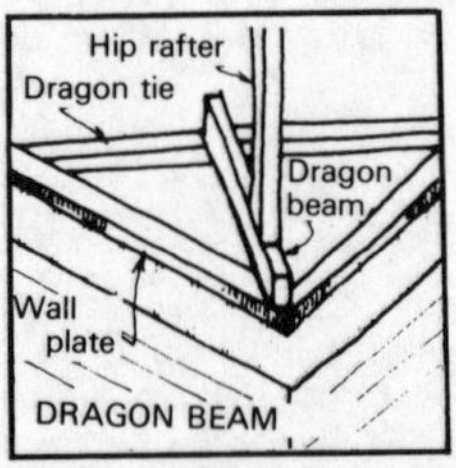

DRAGON BEAM

dragon tie An **angle tie** supporting a **dragon beam**.

drain A pipe, an open channel or underground conduit, etc. for the conveyance of surface, sub-soil or waste water or sewage.

drainage area In open **drained joints**, that part of the joint on the weather side of the components within which rainwater drains away without reaching the air-tight seal at the rear.

drainage channel A way created within a component to drain away water, whether this has penetrated from outside or is due to condensation, without harm to the structure.

drain cock A **cock** placed at the lowest point of a water system or wet central heating installation for draining the system.

drained glazing A glazing system that provides **drainage channels** within rebates to drain away harmlessly any water that penetrates the **glazing compound** – particularly used where glazing is by **double glazing units**.

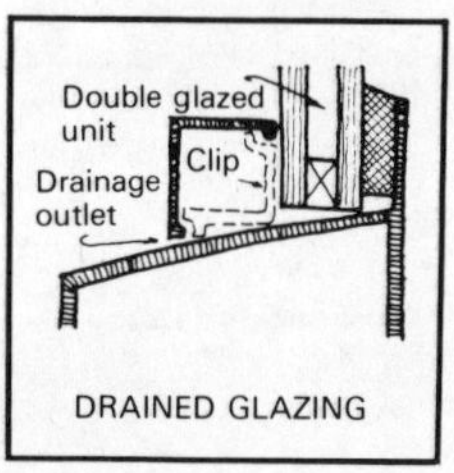

drained joint An open joint so designed that any water entering the joint drains harmlessly away without reaching the air-tight seal at the rear of the joint.

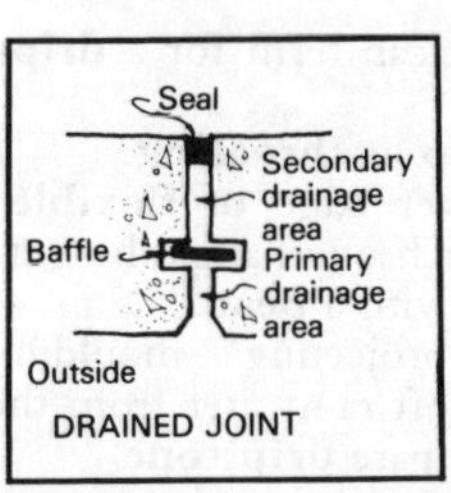

drain pipe A cylindrical (or occasionally oval) pipe of salt-glazed earthenware or stoneware, metal, glass, pitch fibre, plastic or concrete used to convey waste effluent or sewage from an appliance or a building.

drain plug or drain stopper A device for temporarily sealing off a portion of a drain sometimes for testing purposes.

drain rod One of a set of flexible rods which connect one to the other by screw fittings. They are used to clear blockages in a drain by pushing the soft plug head on the leading rod through the drain run from access point to access point.

drain shoe A drain fitting consisting of a short length of horizontal pipe with either a vertical or a horizontal socketed inlet and having an access opening into which may be fitted a grating or an access cover.

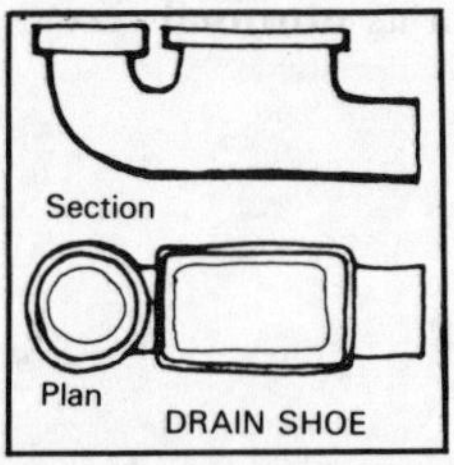

drain test The testing of a drain for leakage. This is always done, for instance, prior to the back filling of the trench. Tests may make use of water, air or one of various chemicals.

draught 1. A current of air, especially through gaps in the structure of a building (which provides fortuitous ventilation) or in a chimney. 2. In **drawboring**, the amount by which two or more holes are out of alignment to ensure a tight joint when a pin or dowel is driven through.

draught bead A **deep bead**.

draught fillet In **patent glazing**, a strip to seal the glass to the glazing **purlin**.

draw bolt Any small hand-operated (as opposed to key-operated) bolt, such as a **barrel bolt**.

drawbore pin A tapered steel pin used in **drawboring** to bring holes into alignment, following which it is withdrawn and the **trenail** is inserted.

drawboring The practice of drilling holes through mortise and tenon pieces slightly out of alignment (usually about 3 mm) so that when a **drawbore pin** is inserted it cramps the pieces tightly together.

draw-in system An electrical installation in which the cables run in conduits or ducts, thus allowing their easy removal and renewal when necessary.

drawn glass Glass usually, for construction work, in sheet form, made by a continuous mechanical drawing operation.

draw-off pipe A single pipe for drawing off water from a hot water circuit, a storage cylinder or tank.

dress 1. To plane and sandpaper timber 2. To cut and shape stone. 3. To apply a dressing to.

dressed 1. Having any kind of worked finish. 2. Of slate, having a bevelled edge as left by a dressing knife or guillotine as opposed to a sawn edge which is square. 3. (Scottish) **Wrot**.

dressed and matched boards Planed **matchboards**.

dressed size The finished size of timber, which is usually approximately 9 mm less in each direction than its **nominal size**.

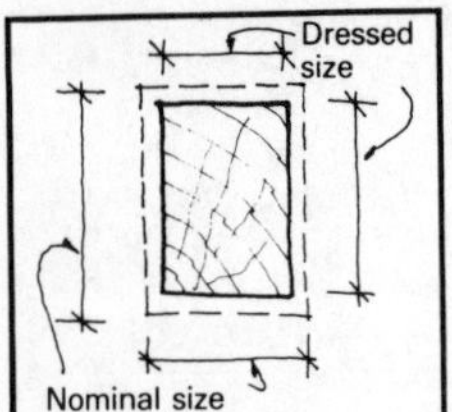

DRESSED SIZE

dressed stone Stone that has been squared all round and smoothed on the face.

dressed timber Timber which has been planed on one or more surfaces.

dresser A mallet used for flattening or shaping sheet metal, especially lead.

dressing 1. The action of beating a sheet of metal to the required shape. 2. The process of treating a surface by applying a preservative, or the coating of preservative thus applied. 3. The application of a layer of material on to land, etc. or the material thus applied, *eg* a dressing of top soil. 4. An ornamental moulding.

dressing compound Any bituminous or other material used hot or cold for top **dressing** the exposed surface of **roofing felt**.

dressing iron A 450 mm long steel **straight edge** with spikes at each end for fixing to a work bench. It is used in dressing **slate**, to obtain a clean, straight edge, the slate being laid over the iron to the appropriate amount and struck with the **zax**.

drier A compound which encourages the **oxidation** of **drying oil** in paints or varnishes.

drift bolt A fixing for heavy timbers consisting of a steel pin (usually not less than 21 mm diameter) driven into holes of a slightly smaller diameter bored in the timbers.

drift plate A steel plate for dressing one lead sheet over another.

drift plug A wooden plug driven through a lead pipe to straighten out a kink in it.

drill A tool for forming a hole in a material.

drilling 1. The act of drilling a hole. 2. A hole formed by a **drill**.

drip 1. A **throating**; 2. The undercut edge of an asphalt apron. 3. A strip of roofing felt or metal projecting beyond and fixed under or between the layers of the roof covering at the **eaves** or **verges** and subsequently turned down at the edge; sometimes referred to as a **drop apron**. 4. A step formed in a flat roof or gutter covered by **flexible-metal roofing**, being at right angles to the direction of fall and at the junction of two sheets. 5. The groove or recess formed on the underside of a projection from a wall, so designed as to encourage rainwater to fall off rather than flow back towards the wall.

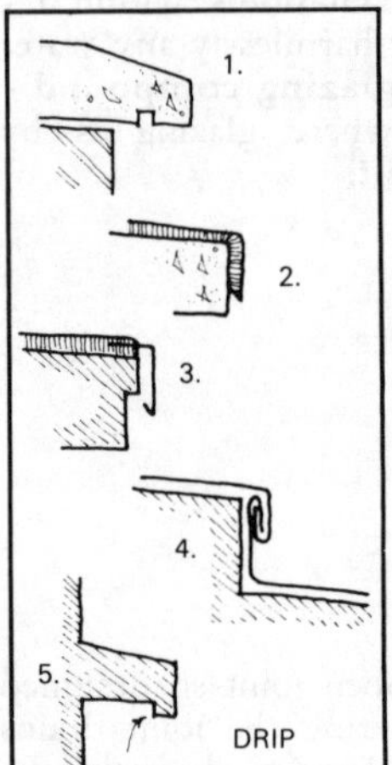

DRIP

drip cap The American term for a **dripstone**.

drip channel A **drip** or **throating**.

drip edge The lower edge of **flexible-metal roofing** which overhangs the gutter, often stiffened with a **bead**.

drip mould A projecting moulding arranged to throw off rainwater from the face of a wall. Compare **dripstone**.

dripstone A weathered projection over a door or window opening with a **drip** on its underside to throw off rainwater flowing down the face of the building. Known as a **drip cap** in the USA. cf. **drip mould**.

drive screw A steel nail, usually galvanized, with a steep **screw thread**, intended to be driven into timber with a hammer and withdrawn by a spanner.

DRIVE SCREW

driving profile The shape formed in the head of a screw which allows it to be driven by means of a screwdriver of a particular type. cf. **slot head**, **Philips head** and **Pozidriv head**.

driving-rain index A figure based on a combination of annual rainfall and average wind speed to give a measurement of exposure, such that

$$\frac{\text{annual rainfall (mm)} \times \text{average wind speed (m/s)}}{1{,}000} = \text{driving-rain index } (\text{m}^2/\text{s})$$

driving-rain rose A diagrammatic method of relating both the amount of driving rain and its direction for any specific area or point.

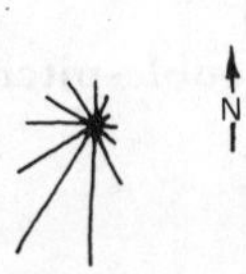

DRIVING-RAIN ROSE

drop A service feed (either pipe or cable) from a high level distribution run to a fitting.

drop apron That strip of metal, at the edges of **flexible-metal roofing**, which is fixed vertically downwards at **eaves, verges** and **gutters**, being held by a **lining plate**.

drop ceiling A **suspended ceiling** or false ceiling, being below the structural ceiling.

drop connection A **back drop**.

drop escutcheon A small metal plate pivoted above a keyhole to cover the hole when the key is not in the lock, usually matching the **escutcheon** in size.

drop-point slating **Diagonal slating.**

drop siding Rebated and overlapping or tongued and grooved **weatherboarding**.

drop system A heating system in which the **flow pipe** rises directly from the boiler to the highest point in the system and feeds downwards from there.

drop window A **sash** window in which the sashes slide completely inside the hollow sill wall to give an unobstructed ventilation area.

drowning pipe An inlet pipe to a **cistern**, which enters the cistern below the water level to reduce noise.

drunken saw A **circular saw** which is deliberately set slightly off the perpendicular to its own shaft so that it makes a wide cut.

dry area A narrow roofed **area** between the external basement wall of a building and the **retaining wall** for the surrounding ground.

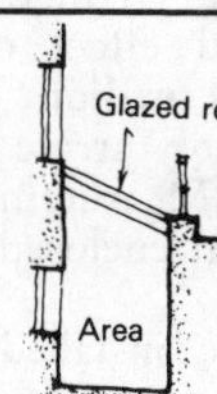

DRY AREA

dry construction Building as far as possible without wet trades, such as ***in situ*** concreting and plastering, and making use, instead, of prefabricated components and assemblies in order to eliminate, or reduce to the minimum, the drying out period.

dry hydrate **Hydrated lime** powder.

drying The hardening of a coat of paint or varnish by evaporation of the **vehicle** or by chemical change (usually **oxidation**) or by a combination of both these methods.

drying oil An oil of animal or vegetable origin which has the property of hardening by **oxidation** to a tough film when exposed to the air in a thin layer. **Linseed oil** is the commonest drying oil.

drying shrinkage Shrinkage of concrete, timber, etc. caused by evaporation of the water content.

dry joint A joint using a **gasket** and not relying on either a setting compound (**mortar**) or a non-setting **sealant** (**mastic**).

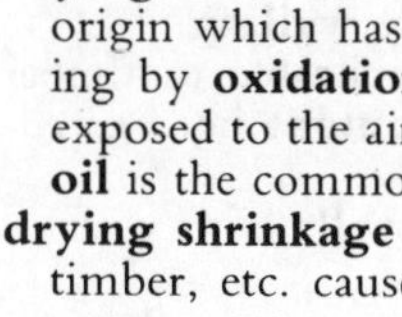

DRY JOINT

dry lining The technique of surfacing walls with **plasterboard** instead of applying wet plastering.

dry masonry Walling laid without **mortar**.

dry mix 1. The gauged ingredients of **mortar** or **concrete** mixed together without adding water. 2. A concrete mix with the correct water-cement ratio (as opposed to one with too much water, which is a wet mix).

dry press A method of making **reconstructed stone** with a very dry mix to facilitate early removal from the mould.

dry-press brick (USA) A **brick** of good quality made from nearly-dry clay pressed into moulds.

dry resultant temperature A method of measuring the combined effect of **air temperature** and **mean radiant temperature** of a room to arrive at a **comfort temperature**. Measurement is made by a thermometer enclosed in a blackened globe.

dry riser A vertical pipe installed in a building for fire-fighting purposes, being fitted with inlet connections at fire brigade access level and outlet valves at specific points in the building. The pipe is normally dry, but is capable of being charged with water, usually by pumping from the fire service appliance.

dry rot (Merulius lacrymans) A wood-destroying fungus which attacks wood (particularly **softwood**) in damp unventilated conditions, and consists of cotton-wool like growths and a network of thin threads (hyphae). The fungus breaks down the cellulose in the wood and the timber becomes brittle and suffers from cuboidal cracking.

dry stone walling **Dry walling**.

dry stress A **stress** applicable to timber having a **moisture content** not exceeding 18%.

dry walling **Rubble walls** built without **mortar**.

dry wood Timber after seasoning having, in the UK, a **moisture content** from 15% to 23%.

dual system A **two-pipe system**.

dubbing out The process of filling in hollow places in a solid background with coarse stuff before **rendering** or the application of plaster.

dub off To remove **arrises**; as might be done in the case of a **tenon** to enable it to enter a **mortise**.

duckbill nail A chisel-pointed nail which is easy to clench. cf. **clenching**.

duckboard 1. A narrow slatted board which may be used to form a path over, wet ground or a wet floor, etc. 2. A **cat ladder**; a board with cleats nailed on it to provide a protection for a roof slope and a foothold for workmen operating on the roof.

duck-foot bend A **rest bend**.

duct 1. A subway, **crawlway**, **chase** or **casing** which accommodates services pipes or cables in a building. 2. A tube of metal, wood, plastic, etc., round or rectangular in section, through which air is passed for forced-draught ventilating or air-conditioning purposes.

ductility The ability of a material to undergo cold plastic **deformation**, usually by being subjected to tension or beating, whilst retaining strength and freedom from cracks.

dumb waiter A lightweight **lift**, electrically or manually operated, for conveying food or crockery etc., between a kitchen and a dining area on different floors.

dummy 1. A tool for straightening large lead pipes, consisting of a lump of lead or iron on the end of a long cane. 2. A round-headed hammer of zinc or lead with a short wooden shaft, used in conjunction with wooden-handled **chisels** or **gouges** to work soft stone.

dumpy level See **level**.

duo-pitched roof A **double-pitch roof**.

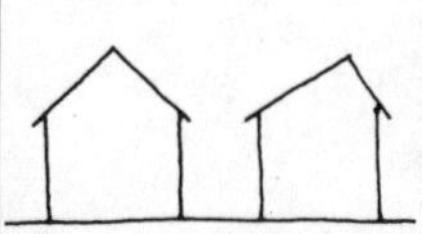

DUO-PITCHED ROOF

duplex apartment (USA) A **maisonette**.

duplex dwelling (USA) A two-family dwelling in which the living units are arranged one above the other.

durability The quality of being able to withstand decay or wear or chemical attack.

dust dry A stage in the **drying** of a finish, after which dust will not adhere to the surface.

dusting 1. The conversion to a powder of the surface of a material, either as a result of wear or due to a faulty mix. 2. The application of a material in powder form.

dusting brush A round or flat soft bristle brush for removing dust from a surface prior to painting.

Dutch barn A lightweight steel-framed structure without wall cladding, with an arched roof consisting of braced trusses and, usually, corrugated sheeting.

Dutch bond A modification of **English bond**, having alternate courses of headers and stretchers. Each stretching course begins at the quoin with a three-quarter bat, and every alternate stretching course has a header placed next to the quoin three-quarter bat.

Dutchman A piece of wood driven into a joint which has been badly cut; hence, also, a piece of material used to cover up a mistake, in carpentry or other trades.

dwang 1. (Scottish) **Strutting** between floor joists. 2. A **crow bar**.

dwarf wall A low wall such as that supporting the joists of a suspended timber ground floor.

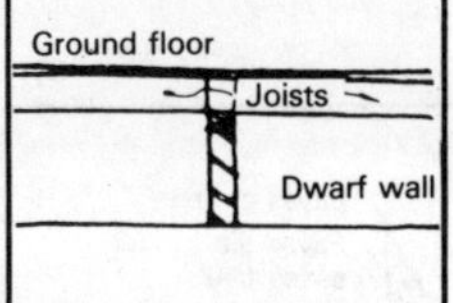

DWARF WALL

dye A colouring material which, unlike a **pigment**, colours by penetration.

dyke (Scottish) A **dry wall** in stone.

dynamic pressure The total pressure on an object minus the static pressure.

dynamic strength The resistance to suddenly applied or changing loads.

E

ear A projecting lug from a pipe used to fix it to a wall.

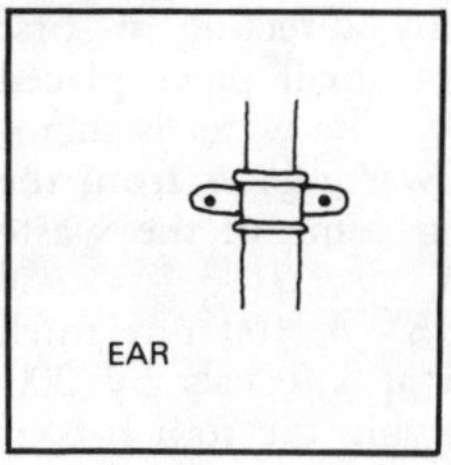
EAR

earth 1. Soil, the term is loosely used for any excavated material. 2. An electrical connection to earth through an **earth electrode**.

earthed circuit An electrical **circuit**, one or more points of which are intentionally connected to earth.

earthed concentric wiring A cable consisting of two conductors, one of which is a metal tube which is earthed. The other conductor, which is surrounded by insulation, is contained within this tube.

earth electrode A metal plate, water pipe or other conductor electrically connected to earth.

earthenware Pottery made from brick earth; it is softer than **stoneware**. Exposed surfaces are often coated with an impervious glaze fixed to the body by firing. This may be transparent or opaque, white or coloured.

earthing The action of effecting an electrical connection between an electrical apparatus or an electrical **circuit** and earth.

earthing lead The conductor which makes the final connection to an **earth electrode**.

earth plate An **earth electrode** consisting of a large copper plate sunk in damp ground.

earth pressure The pressure exerted by the ground behind a **retaining wall**, and usually considered as acting at the natural slope of the particular soil, its **angle of repose**.

eased arris An **arris** that has been slightly rounded.

easement A liability attached to land, whereby some person other than the owner has certain clearly defined rights over that land in perpetuity; alternatively, a right over land granted in perpetuity by the owner to some other person for a specific purpose, such as passage, the laying of drains etc.

easing 1. The act of planing the frames of opening lights of windows or the edges of a door to avoid sticking due to too tight a fit within the **rebate**. 2. The shaping of a curve so as to avoid an abrupt change of curvature.

eastern closet See **squatting closet**.

easy-clean hinge See **offset hinge**.

eaves The bottom of a pitched roof slope,

or the edge of a flat roof, usually overhanging the wall.

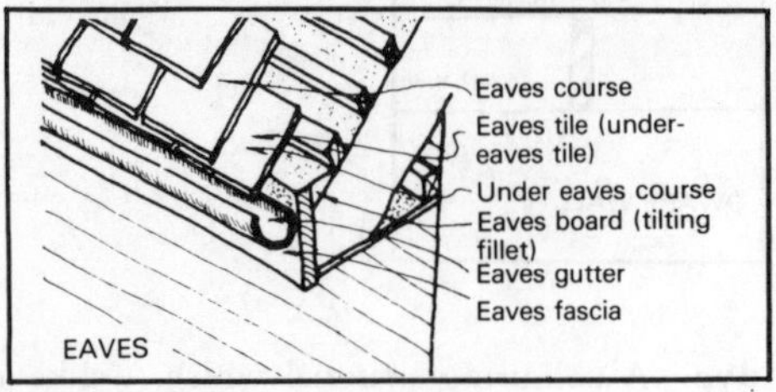

EAVES

eaves board A **tilting fillet**.

eaves course The first course of **plain tiles**, **slates** or **shingles** together with the course of plain tiles on which the first course of **single-lap tiles** is bedded. cf. **double eaves course**.

eaves fascia A vertical board nailed to the feet of the rafters and providing a fixing for the **eaves gutter**. Sometimes the fascia projects above the rafters and serves as a **tilting fillet**.

eaves flashing 1. A **drop apron** from an asphalt flat roof dressed into the **eaves gutter**. 2. In corrugated sheeting, the flashing unit which closes the corrugations at the eaves and forms a **drip** into the **eaves gutter**.

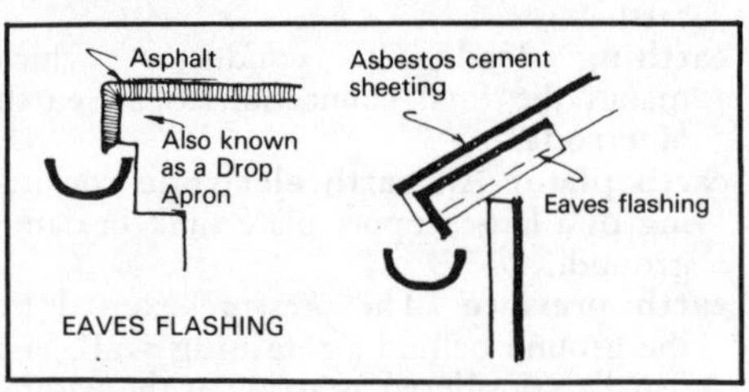

EAVES FLASHING

eaves gutter The rainwater **gutter** into which water from the roof discharges.

eaves plate A **wall plate** which spans between interrupted sections of wall and, between the walls, supports the rafters.

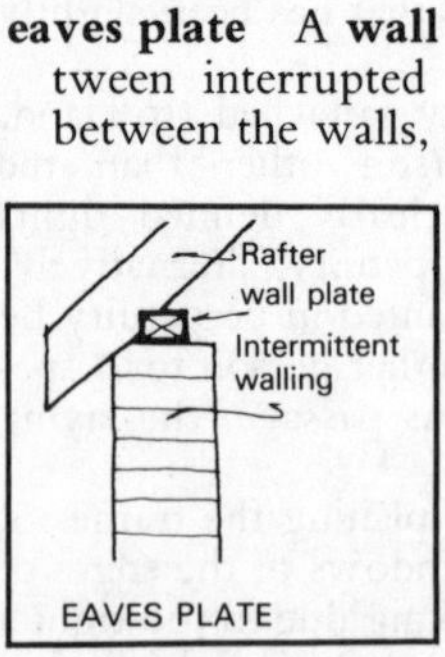

EAVES PLATE

eaves tile A short tile used in the **under-eaves course** in plain tiling cf. **double eaves course**, **plain tile**.

ebonite A hard, black, material made by treating rubber with sulphur, zinc oxide and carbon black. It is used for electrical insulation.

eccentric load A load which does not act through the **centre of gravity** of a structural member, or along its axis, and as a result produces a non-uniform stress distribution.

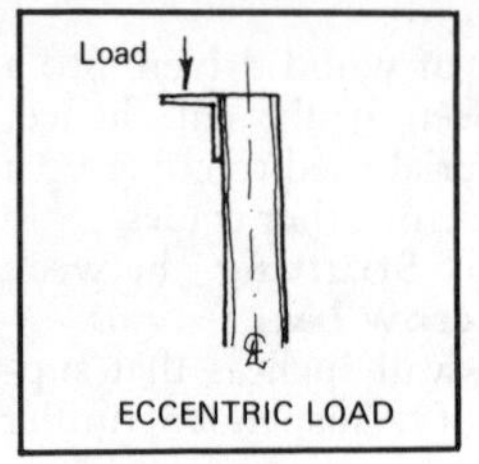

ECCENTRIC LOAD

echo A sound received by means of the reflection of sound waves from a hard surface. It is discernible by the human ear only if the path of the reflected sound, from its source to the ear, is significantly longer than the path of the direct sound. The effects of echo can be reduced by the application of sound absorbent materials to the reflecting surfaces.

economizer A device which pre-heats water before it passes into a **boiler**, or similar apparatus, by directing it first through a battery of small pipes placed across the boiler flue. The water is therefore, heated by the waste gases from the boiler, thus allowing some of the waste heat to be recovered.

economy wall (USA) A 100 mm thick brick wall stiffened at intervals by 200 mm thick **piers** carrying the roof trusses and projecting outwards on both sides of door and window openings.

edge bedding See **face-bedded**.

edge grain The grain seen in **quarter-sawn timber**; *ie* wood that is **converted** so that its **growth rings** are at 45° to the face of the piece.

edge isolation See **expansion strip**.

edge joint A joint made between two veneers in the direction of the grain. cf. **butt joint**.

edge nailing **Secret nailing** of floor boards etc.

edge-shot board A **board** with a planed edge.

edge tool A tool such as a **hatchet**, **chisel**, **plane**, **gouge** or knife, which has a cutting edge.

edge trimmer A plane for making a square edge on small wood pieces. It has a perpendicularly recessed sole.

edging See **lipping**.

edging strip The **lipping** to the edge of a flush door, etc.

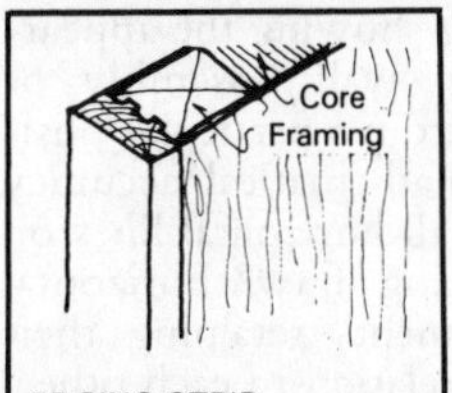

EDGING STRIP

edging trowel A rectangular trowel with one edge bent down for use in trimming the edges of kerbs etc.

EFAB seal An **evacuated tube gasket** of Swedish design.

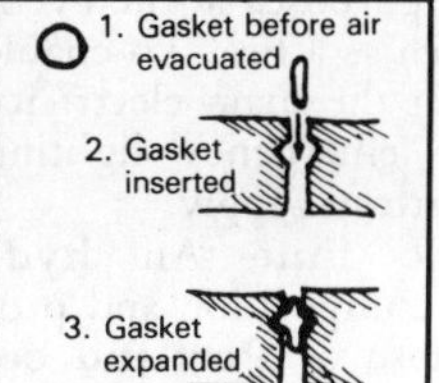

EFAB SEAL

effective ambient temperature A suitably weighted mean between the **air temperature** and the **mean radiant temperature** of the surroundings.

effective depth The depth of a reinforced concrete beam or slab as measured from the surface of the concrete on the compression side to the centre of the tensile reinforcement.

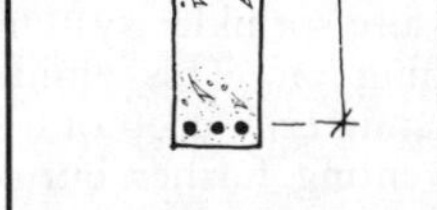
EFFECTIVE DEPTH

effective span The horizontal distance between the centres of the two bearings of a beam or slab, or (in the case of a continuous beam) the distance **centre-to-centre** of the supports, as opposed to the **clear span**.

effective temperature An arbitrary index of the degree of warmth or coldness felt by a human body in response to the combined effects of temperature, humidity and air movement.

efflorescence The development of a crystalline deposit on a brick or cement surface due to the evaporation from the wall of water containing soluble salts, the salts therefore being left behind on the wall surface. The effect is harmless and will eventually cease when all the salts have been brought to the surface. In the meantime, the salts may be washed or brushed off the wall if this is desirable.

effluent The outflow from a **sewage treatment plant** or from an industrial process.

eggshell finish A paintwork finish which has more gloss than a matt finish, but does not reach the degree of reflectivity of a gloss paint.

ejector grille An output grille on a ventilation system which, due to the positioning of the outlet louvres causes the ejected air to be directed in divergent streams.

elastic deformation A change of dimension produced by a **stress**, the deformation disappearing when the stress is removed.

elasticity The ability of a material to return to its original size or shape after being subjected to tension, compression or deformation.

elastic limit The limiting value of the deforming force beyond which the original shape or dimension of a body or material is not completely recoverable after the force is removed.

elastic method of design A method of designing structural steel or reinforced concrete based on the assumption that the materials are elastic within the range of permissible stresses and that the modular ratio is constant.

elastic modulus See **modulus of elasticity.**

elastomer A macromolecular material such as, for instance, neoprene or natural rubber, which after substantial deformation returns rapidly to approximately its initial dimension and shape once the stress in released.

elastomeric sealant A sealant based on polysulphide rubbers, silicone rubbers or polyurethane and some butyl mastics which is plastic when applied and cures to form a compound with rubber-like properties. Such sealants have varying degrees of plastic flow properties.

elbow A sharp corner in a pipe, usually of 90°, as opposed to a **bend** which is curved, not angular.

elbow board A **window board**.

electrical resistance The resistance to the flow of an electric current in a conductor. It depends on the material and temperature and is proportional to the length of

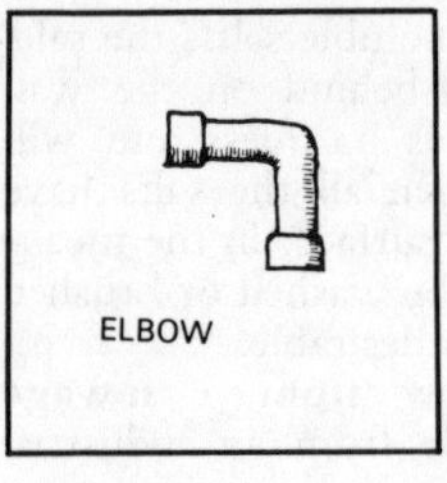

the conductor and inversely proportional to its cross-sectional area.

electric drill An electrically operated hand tool with interchangeable **bits** for drilling holes in wood, stone, concrete, brick or metal.

electric panel heater A **panel heater** which achieves its heat by the electrical resistance of its heating **element**.

electric screwdriver An electrically operated hand tool, similar to an electric drill, which is used to drive screws both speedily and with an even force which ensures consistent tightening. A clutch slips when the required torque is reached.

electric storage heater An electric heater which depends on the heating up of a block of material with a high **thermal capacity**, the heat being radiated and convected during the subsequent period, giving a more or less even heat output. Some storage heaters are fan-assisted.

electro-copper glazing A method of securing accurately cut pieces of glass which are positioned between copper **cames**, the whole assembly then being pressed closely together. Additional copper is next added to the cames by electrodeposition brought about by placing the assembly in an **electrolyte** and wiring the cames as the **cathode**.

electrode boiler An electric **boiler**, usually larger than domestic size, which, unlike the **immersion heater**, does not depend on the heating up of an **element**, but passes an alternating current through the water.

electrolyte A solution capable of conducting electricity.

electrolytic corrosion Corrosion resulting from the contact of two different metals when an electrolyte is present and current flows. Sometimes referred to as galvanic corrosion.

electro-plating The electrodeposition of one metal on another to provide a coating with properties different from those of the base metal.

element 1. Part of a building or structure having its own functional identity, such as a **foundation, roof, wall**, etc. 2. A heat source, such as a wire with a high **electrical resistance**, or a hot water tube with integral fins to increase surface area.

elevation A drawing showing the appearance of a building, wall, assembly or component viewed from a particular position; drawn with mathematical accuracy and no perspective, all horizontal lines on the building, etc. being drawn horizontal and all vertical elements retaining their true proportions in relation to each other.

elevator (USA) A **lift** for passengers or goods.

elliptical stair A **stair** which on plan has a well in the shape of an ellipse.

emergency lighting In buildings to which the public have access, a secondary means of providing minimum lighting, sufficient for escape purposes in the event of an emergency such as a fire. To enable it to function during the main electricity supply failure, the emergency lighting usually runs off a battery supply.

eminently hydraulic lime An **hydraulic lime** whose composition and properties approach those of **Portland cement**, such as lime made from limestone of the Blue Lias formation. It is sometimes called natural or Roman cement and is not produced to a large extend in the UK, where raw materials to produce Portland cement are readily available.

emission The release of radiant energy.

emissivity The ratio of the thermal radiation from unit area of a surface to the radiation from unit area of a full emitter (a black body) at the same temperature and in the same surroundings.

emulsifier system An automatic fire fighting method of dealing with old fires based on a high pressure sprinkler system directed at the burning oil. This emulsifies the oil, thus coating each drop of oil with water and preventing further burning.

emulsion paint A **dispersion** of one liquid in another (usually water) to form an **oil-bound paint**, latex emulsion or coloured bituminous emulsion paint. Emulsion paints harden by **evaporation** of the water and not by **oxidation** as is the case with oil paints.

enamel 1. A **hard gloss paint** with a high **gloss** due to its considerable **varnish** and reduced **pigment** content. Enamels flow well, but require good undercoats due to their poor **opacity**. 2. Vitreous enamel is a gloss surface coating fired on to cast iron or steel articles. It is more hard-wearing than enamel, but is subject to chipping.

enamelled brick A **glazed brick**.
encase To cover with another material (as in encasing steelwork in concrete for **fire protection**), or to surround by a framework and **lining**.
encased knot A **dead knot** more or less surrounded by bark or resin.
encaustic decoration Decoration burnt on to tiles, bricks, porcelain or glass.
enclosed fuse (USA) A **cartridge fuse**.
enclosed knot A **knot** which does not appear on the surface of a piece of timber.
enclosed stair A **closed stair**.
enclosure wall (USA) An external non-loadbearing wall of a framed building.
end grain The surface of timber exposed when it is **cross-cut**.
end joint A **butt joint**.
end-lap joint An **angle joint** formed by halving together two timber components which meet at right angles. cf. **halving joint** (**halved joint**).

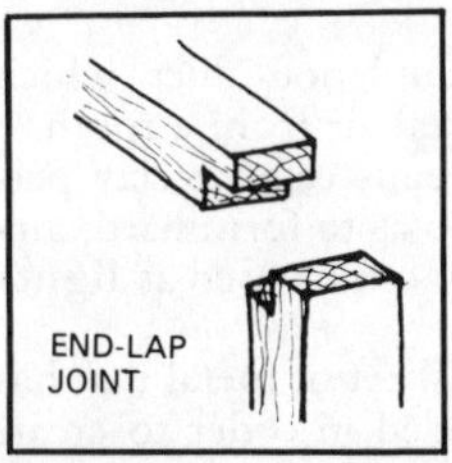

END-LAP JOINT

endless saw A **band saw**.
engineering brick A dense brick with a high crushing strength. In the UK, Class A engineering bricks have a compressive strength of not less than 69.0N/mm^2 and an average water absorption of not more than 4.5%. Class B engineering bricks have a compressive strength of not less than 48.5N/mm^2 and an average water absorption of not more than 7.0%.
engineer's hammer A hammer weighing from 31 g to 1.3 kg with a flat striking face and either a ball, cross or straight **peen**.
English bond A brick bond with alternating courses of **headers** and **stretchers**. See **bond**.
English cross bond **English bond** but with a **header** placed next to the **quoin** stretcher in alternate stretcher courses, thus displacing these stretcher **perpends** from vertical alignment.
English garden well bond **English bond** in which only the fifth, sixth or seventh course is a course of headers. Also referred to as American bond and in the USA as common bond.
English roof tile (USA) A single lap tile overlapping at the sides within its own thickness so that both the upper and lower surfaces are smooth.

ENGLISH ROOFING TILE

environmental temperature A simplified equivalent to the **comfort temperature**, combining **air temperature** with **mean radiant temperature**.
epoxide resin paint A pigmented solution of an epoxide resin, which (just before use) is mixed with a **curing agent**.
epoxy paint A paint based on an epoxy resin.
epoxy or epoxide resin A class of synthetic resin made by the interaction of epichlorhydrin and a phenol such as disphenol, widely used for making high strength **adhesives**, etc.
equilibrium A state of balance; either in mechanical terms, in which moments of action and reaction are balanced, or in physical terms, such as **moisture content** or temperature, in which a body neither loses nor gains moisture or heat.
equilibrium moisture content The **moisture content** of seasoned timber, etc., which has reached an **equilibrium** with the humidity of the surrounding air and which will remain constant if the temperature and humidity of the environment remain constant.
equivalent temperature A method of measuring the combined effect of **air temperature**, **mean radiant temperature** and air movement in a room on bodily comfort. It takes no account of humidity and is measured by a **eupatheoscope**.
erection The positioning and fixing of the parts of a building, particularly the structural frame.
ergonomics The study of the efficiency of persons in their working environment. It is thus important in the design of work stations, chairs, tables etc. to suit the body's requirements and avoid fatigue.
erosion The wearing away of a surface layer by environmental or mechanical abrasion.
escalator A moving stair on an endless belt.

escape stair A stair required by law to facilitate the escape of a building's occupants in case of fire. It may be on the inside or outside of the building shell and need not necessarily be used as part of any normal circulation route.

escutcheon A metal plate round a key hole.

escutcheon pin A small brass nail up to 12 mm long used to fix **escutcheons** and similar small items of architectural ironmongery.

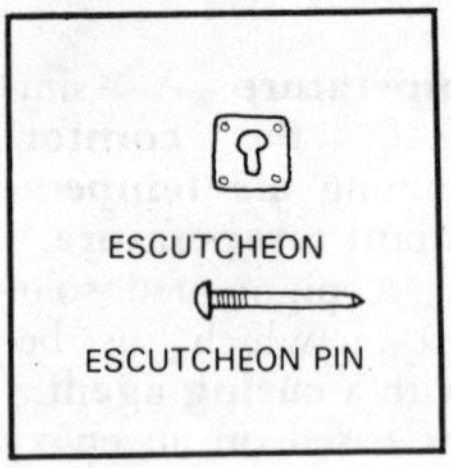

espagnolette bolt A fixing for tall windows and **casement doors** in which bolts are driven home simultaneously at the top and bottom of the window or door by turning a centrally positioned handle.

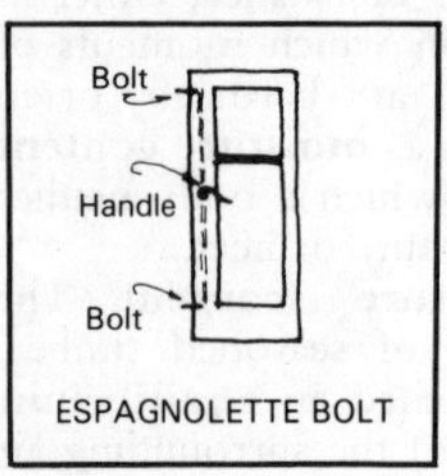

establishment charges **Overheads**.

estimating Assessing the cost of building work by establishing a **rate** for each activity (including labour and material costs) and multiplying these rates by the **quantities** involved. Less accurate methods of estimating can involve the establishment of the cost per m^2 of floor area, or per m^3, of similar buildings recently constructed and applying such cost to the building in question.

etching 1. The marking of the surface of glass or metal (often in a decorative pattern) using an acid. 2. The removal of the surface of concrete or reconstructed stone with acid to expose the **coarse aggregate**.

etch primer A primer based on zinc chromate butyral resin to which a phosphoric acid **hardener** is added, used to achieve maximum adhesion of a paint film to aluminium, zinc or zinc coated surfaces.

eupatheoscope A black electrically heated cylinder developed by the BRE (Building Research Establishment) for use in estimating **equivalent temperature**.

evacuated tube gasket A tube gasket from which the air is evacuated prior to placing, after which the vacuum is released to provide pressure to seal the joint.

evaporation 1. The loss of moisture from a liquid due to vaporization. 2. The drying of **varnishes**, **emulsion paints** and **lacquers** by the loss of vapour, as opposed to drying by **oxidation** causing the hardening of **drying oils**.

even-textured In timber, a grain showing little difference between spring and summer growth.

exfoliated vermiculite Vermiculite which has been heated to cause its expansion to 10 to 15 times its original volume, thereby forming a lightweight material.

exfoliation The flaking of stone due to weathering.

exhaust shaft A ventilation duct which removes contaminated air from a room.

expanded clay Vitreous cellular clay pellets burnt in a kiln so as to form hard, air-filled particles which can be used as **lightweight aggregate**.

expanded metal A sheet of metal that has been cut and expanded in order to create a mesh, which can be used as a support for plastering or as reinforcement for light concrete work. It is a term often incorrectly applied to any mesh of steel wires.

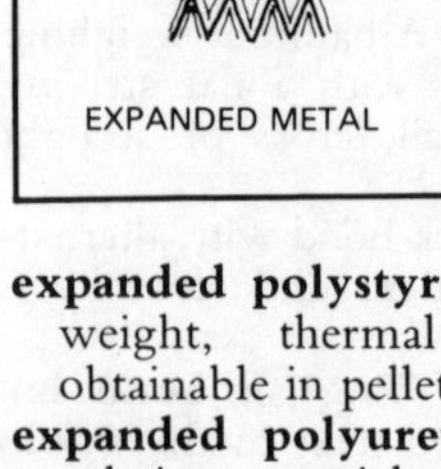

expanded polystyrene A cellular, lightweight, thermal insulating material obtainable in pellet, block or sheet form.

expanded polyurethane A foamed insulating material which can be foamed *in situ*, if required, and has good adhesion to most surfaces; often used in **sandwich panels**.

expanding anchor A fixing device used to make a fixing to concrete, brick or stone elements. Part of the device expands, on installation, against the sides of the pre-drilled hole in which it is placed, thus prohibiting its withdrawal. A heavyweight **plug**.

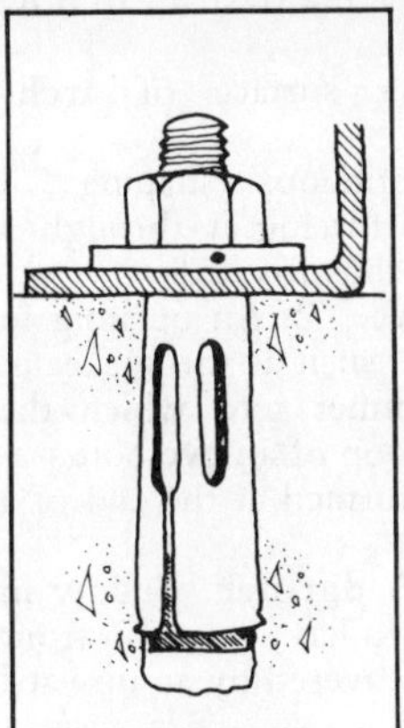

EXPANDING ANCHOR

expanding bit A drill bit with a cutter that can be adjusted to different radii.
expanding plug A **drain plug**.
expansion Increase in volume. cf. **coefficient of** linear or thermal **expansion**.
expansion joint See **movement joint**.
expansion pipe In a hot water system, a pipe leading from the **cylinder** to discharge over the cold water storage **cistern**, thus providing a safe escape route for steam or water should the water in the system boil.
expansion sleeve A sleeve or short section of tube made of metal, asbestos or plastic, built into a wall or floor and through which a slightly smaller diameter pipe passes. This allows the smaller pipe to expand or contract without damage to itself or to the structure.

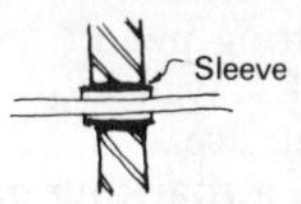

EXPANSION SLEEVE

expansion strip A strip of compressible material which allows two parts of the structure (made of similar or dissimilar material) to move independently or react to thermal and moisture movement; also used to give that discontinuity of structure which discourages sound transmission through the structure. cf. **discontinuous construction**.

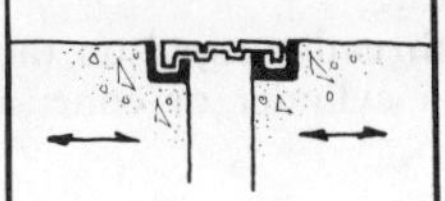

EXPANSION STRIP

expansion tank In a hot water system, a tank above an **indirect cylinder** which allows the water in the primary circuit to expand on heating up.
exposed aggregate finish A finish to concrete in which the **coarse aggregate** is exposed either by laying a bed of aggregate in the **formwork** before pouring the concrete, or by **aggregate transfer**, or by the removal of the sand and cement surface of the hardened concrete by **acid treatment**, **bush hammering** or **grit blasting**.
exposure The extent to which a site suffers from the effects of the weather; usually measured by its **driving-rain index**, and often associated with the number of days each year during which the site experiences frost.
extended price The **rate** in a **Bill of Quantities** multiplied by the appropriate **quantity** to give a cost for the item.
extender 1. A white, inorganic, finely crushed powder with low opacity added to paint to adjust its film-forming and working properties; common examples are **asbestine**, **diatomaceous earth**, **mica** and silica. 2. A substance. such as wood flour, added to synthetic resin **glue** to cut the cost or to increase its spreading capacity.
extending ladder A telescopic **ladder**.
extension bolt Usually a **barrel bolt** with a long handle to facilitate the operation of the bolt.

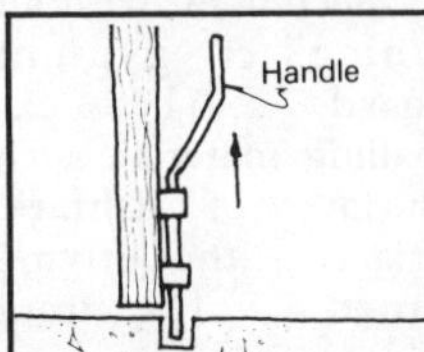

EXTENSION BOLT

extension rule A wooden **rule** in two parts which slide relative to each other, making it possible, for instance, to take interior measurements such as those between door linings.
exterior plywood **Plywood** in which the glue is moisture resistant, thus allow-

ing the plywood to be used externally, given a suitable coating.

external thread A **thread** formed on the external surface of a cylinder or cone; a male thread.

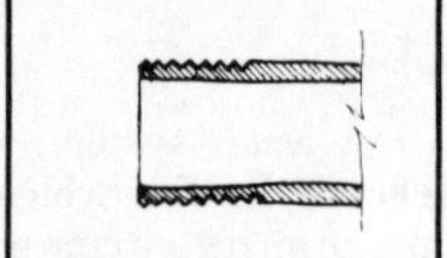
EXTERNAL THREAD

external vibrator A vibrator clamped to the **formwork** and used to ensure the correct consolidation of a concrete pour. cf. **surface vibrator** and **poker vibrator**.

external wall A wall of which at least one face is exposed to the weather or to the earth – an enclosing element of structure.

extra Work not included in the original **contract**, which has to be ordered by the architect by issuing a **variation order**.

extract system A ventilation system which extracts contaminated air from the inside of the building by electrically-driven fans, thereby reducing the internal pressure and encouraging fresh air to flow into the building.

extrados The upper surface of **arch-stones**. cf. **arch**.

extrusion The continuous shaping of plastic material by forcing it through a die, or the product thus formed.

eye 1. An **access eye**. 2. An opening in a metal component, such as the socket in the head of a hammer into which the handle fits, or the loop of an eye bolt.

eye bolt The loop formed at the end of a steel wire or bolt.

eyebrow dormer A **dormer** window in a roof surface: it often has no roof in front of it, but is always covered by an upward sweep of the roof.

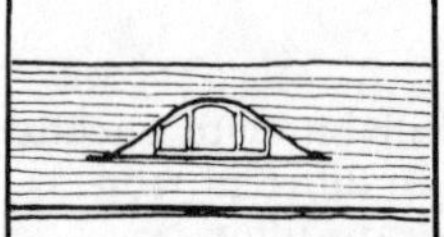
EYEBROW DORMER

F

fabric 1. The shell of a building. 2. Wire mesh reinforcement such as that used in suspended or next-to-earth concrete slabs.

façade The face of a building.

face 1. The broad surface of **square-sawn timber**. 2. The side with the best appearance (as of **plywood** or **core-board**). 3. The cutting edge of a **saw-tooth**. 4. The surface of gypsum wall-board which can be decorated without the need for **skimming**. cf. **gypsum plasterboard/wallboard**. 5. The exposed surface of a walling material, such as the exposed surface of **ashlars**. 6. The working surface – the driving face – of a **hammer**. 7. The front of a wall or building.

face-bedded Of stonework, not laid on its **natural bed**. Only **arch-stones** should be laid in this manner, since vertical positioning of the natural bed in these circumstances can lead to flaking.

face brick (USA) **Facing brick**.

faced plywood **Plywood** faced with a material other than a wood **veneer** (*eg* metal or plastic).

faced wall A wall of **facing bricks** and **common bricks** bonded together, as opposed to a **cavity wall**. Other facing materials, such as **reconstructed stone** or natural stone, can be used.

face edge The first edge of a piece of wood to be prepared, being that from which the other edges are measured.

face hammer A mason's hammer with a striking **face** and a cutting **peen**.

face joint The part of a wall cross joint which shows on the surface.

face plate That part of a **marking gauge** which in use is pressed against the face of the wood.

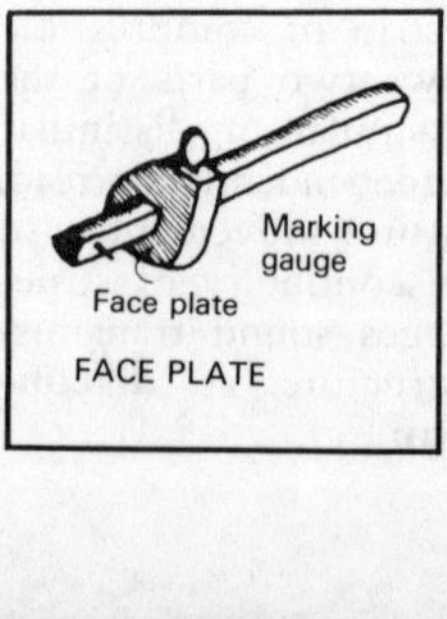

FACE PLATE

face putty In putty glazing (as opposed to **bead** glazing), the triangular fillet of **glazier's putty** on the outside of the glass.

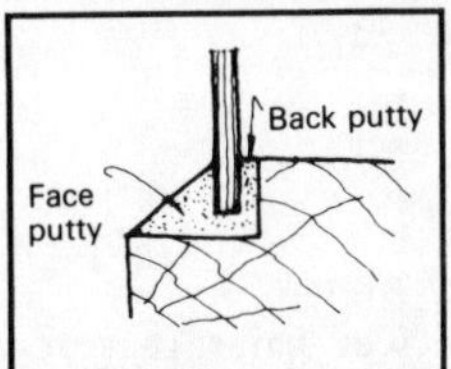

FACE PUTTY

face side The exposed face of a material. It is prepared first and used as a datum for further finishing operations on that material.

face string (USA) The **outer string** of a **stair**.

face veneer A **veneer** chosen for its decorative effect rather than its strength.

facing 1. A piece of non-structural joinery (*eg* **skirting**, **architrave**, etc.). 2. The act of preparing the surface of a material. 3. A material used by virtue of its appearance to face a less attractive material.

facing brick A brick used for its appearance rather than its strength. Facing bricks vary considerably in colour and texture. cf. **common brick** (**commons**).

facing hammer (USA) A **hammer** used for dressing stone and concrete, with a notched rectangular head.

factor of safety The ultimate stress of a material divided by the **permissible working stress**. A number by which the **breaking weight** (**load**) is divided to give the safe or **permissible working load.**

fadding Applying shellac lacquer with a pad called a fad.

fading The bleaching of a paint surface (or other decorative finish) due to ageing or weathering, which can be corrected by a coat of varnish. Not to be confused with the **chalking** of a paint surface.

faience Glazed **terra cotta**, used at one time as a facing for walls, though now rarely used.

fair cutting The cutting of facing brick with a **trowel**, **bolster** or **scutch**. Always assuming a 112 mm half brick thickness, it is measured in a **Bill of Quantities** in linear metres.

fair-faced Applied to brick or block walling, neatly built with smoothly pointed joints. Often used in referring to internal walls which are not to be plastered and may be left either untreated or with a paint finish.

fall An inclination, such as the slope given to a flat roof in order to convey rainwater to the outlets or gutters, or the inclination of a drain.

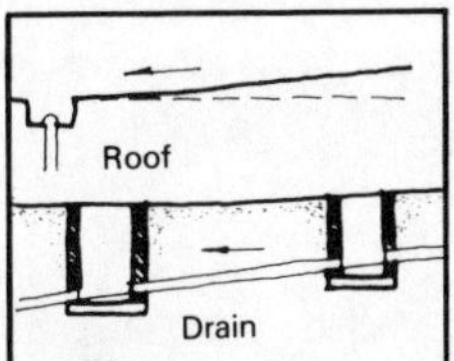

FALL

fall bar 1. A primitive door latch consisting of a pivoted wooden bar falling into a **keeper** and opened from one side through a hole in the door. 2. A **thumb latch**.

fall pipe A rainwater pipe.

false ceiling See **suspended ceiling**.

false header A half brick, used in bonding, which appears on the surface of the wall as a **header** but is only half the usual length of a brick.

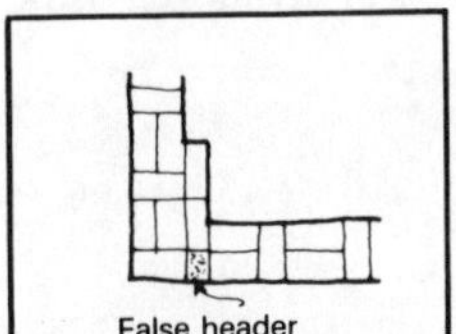

FALSE HEADER

false heartwood Wood which, though *not* heartwood, has the appearance of **heartwood** due to unusual growth, **fungus** or as a result of frost action.

false tenon A loose **hardwood** tenon used instead of a tenon cut from one of the timbers to be joined. This action is taken when a tenon so cut would prove too weak.

falsework **Formwork**, **shuttering** or **centering** for concrete.

fan A floor of scaffold planks cantilevered out over a footpath, street, etc. and sloping slightly upwards towards the outer edge. It is constructed to catch debris during demolition work or alterations.

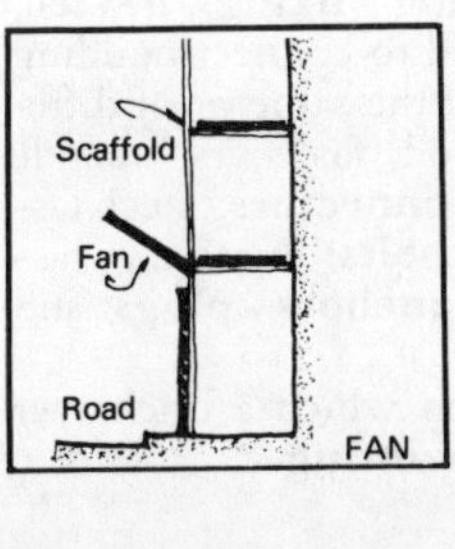

FAN

fang 1. The **tang** of a steel tool. 2. The fish-tailed end of a rail built into a wall.

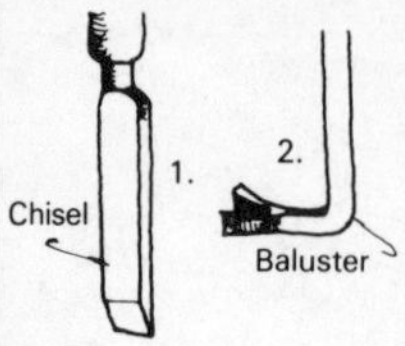

FANG

fanlight A glazed **light** over a door, usually contained within the door frame.

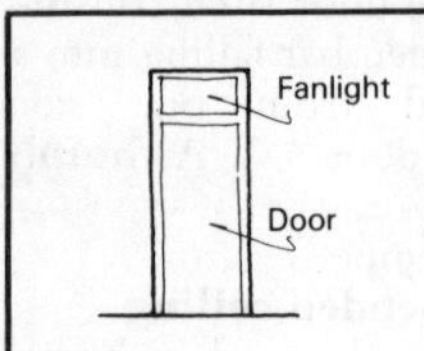

FANLIGHT

fan truss A **roof truss** in which there are both inclined and vertical struts. cf. **fink truss**.

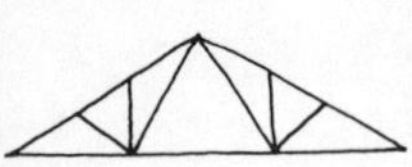
FAN TRUSS

fascia (board) 1. An **eaves fascia**. 2. Any deep board set vertically on edge on a wall face, such as the name board over a shop front.

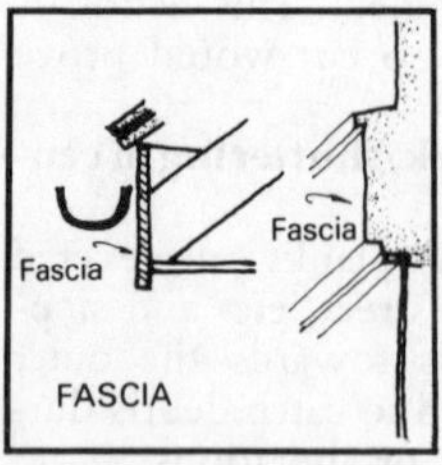

FASCIA

fastener A mechanical **fixing device**, usually of metal, used to connect building components either of the same or of different materials. Wood fasteners include **nails**, **screws** and **connectors**; steel fasteners, **rivets** and **bolts**; masonry fasteners, **expanding anchors**, **plugs** and **chemical anchors**.

fat board A board on which a bricklayer carries **mortar** for **pointing**.

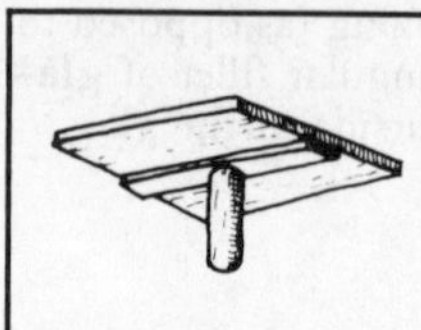
FAT BOARD

fat edge A ridge of wet paint that accumulates at the bottom of a vertical painted surface when the paint has been applied too thickly, or has been insufficiently brushed out, or is such that it flows too easily.

fatigue The deterioration in strength or resistance of a material due to repeated application of stress.

fat lime **High calcium lime**.

fat mix A rich **mortar** mix containing more cement (and lime) than normal. A **rich mix**.

fat mortar A **mortar** that sticks to the trowel; the opposite of **lean mortar**.

fattening The increased **viscosity** in a paint that has been stored for a long time; but is not sufficiently thickened to make it unusable.

faucet 1. (USA) A tap. 2. The socket end of the pipe in a **spigot-and-socket joint**.

feather A **cross tongue** jointing **matchboards**. It may be worked on the long edge of one of the boards, fitting into a corresponding groove in the adjacent board, or may be a loose slip.

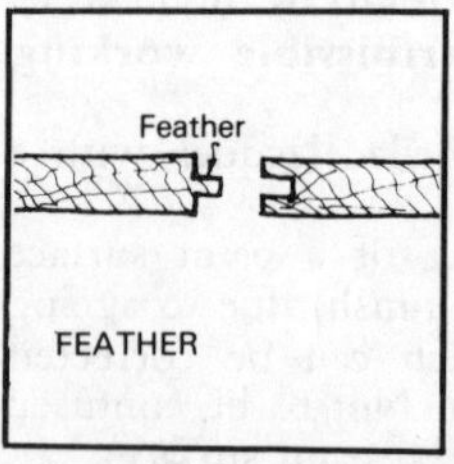

FEATHER

feather edge 1. A tapered edge. 2. A **feather-edge rule**.

feather-edged board A tapered board (tapering from 9 mm to 6 mm edge to

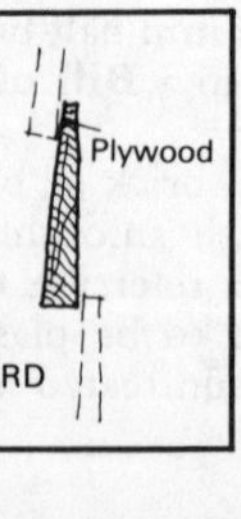

FEATHER-EDGED BOARD

edge) used for **weather-boarding** or close-boarded fencing.

feather-edged coping A **coping** with a wedge-shaped or splayed cross-section.

FEATHER-EDGED COPING

feather-edge rule A plasterer's **rule** (450 – 1800 mm long) with one edge tapered in thickness. It is used to work angles.

feather joint A joint between ploughed edges of adjacent timber members, using a **cross tongue**.

FEATHER JOINT

feather tongue A **cross tongue**.

feebly hydraulic lime Lime burnt from limestone containing 6–12% clay.

feed cistern A cold water storage **cistern**, which is supplied from the service mains through a **rising main** and **ball cock**, and is used to provide cold water to the hot water system and, usually, to all other cold water points in the building, except those specifically for drinking purposes.

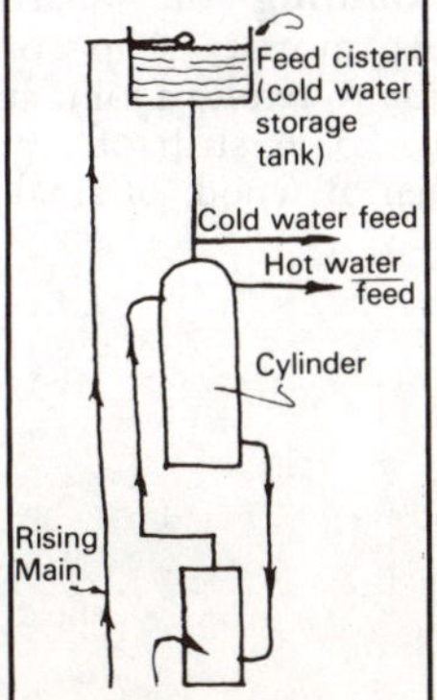

FEED CISTERN

felt See **bitumen felt**.

felt-and-gravel roof (USA) A roof covered with **bitumen felt** protected from solar radiation by gravel.

felting down Removing the gloss from a paint or varnish **film** with a felt pad and **abrasive** powder with a lubricant (often water).

felt nail A **clout nail**.

female thread A **thread** formed on the inside of a pipe or tube.

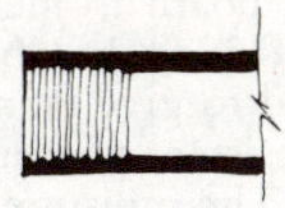

FEMALE THREAD

fence 1. A means of enclosure of open ground, to define site boundaries or provide security. 2. Part of a joiner's **plough**, parallel to the line of a cut and holding the blade at a constant distance from the edge of the wood. 3. A guide for timber on a saw bench.

fender A **baulk** of timber laid on the ground to protect the uprights of scaffolding from being hit by vehicles.

fender wall A **dwarf wall** supporting three edges of the hearth slab in a suspended ground floor.

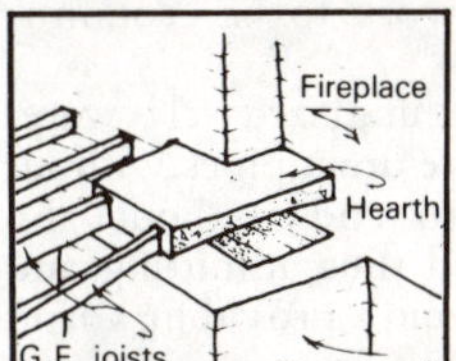

FENDER WALL

fenestration The arrangement of window and door openings in a building's **façade.**

ferritic steel Stainless steel containing not less than 11% chromium and more chromium and less carbon than **martensitic stainless steel**.

ferro-concrete An obsolete name for **reinforced concrete**.

ferrous metal A metal containing iron.

ferrule 1. In plumbing, a short length of tube, such as a **sleeve piece**. 2. The metal band round the handle of a chisel to prevent it from being split by the **tang** of the blade.

festoon staining A **pattern staining** visible on external walls. It is caused by differential rainwater flow down their surfaces and an insufficiently protective **coping**.

fettling Removing roughness from a casting and generally finishing it off.

fibre board A wide variety of boards made mainly from wood fibre and falling broadly into categories of **insulating boards** and **hardboards**. The insulating boards (**softboards**) result from a board's not being compressed during manufacture; hardboards are more dense and result from compression (during manufacture) to either medium board (sometimes referred to as panelboard) or hardboard. Some boards are treated to give flame retardant and moisture resistant properties.

fibre saturation point The moisture content of wood (usually about 30%) at which the cells contain no water, but the cell walls are saturated. Further seasoning causes shrinkage, but increases strength; above fibre saturation point no further dimensional change takes place and strength remains approximately constant.

fibrous concrete Concrete, such as **glass reinforced concrete** (GRC), containing fibrous **aggregate** (glass fibre, asbestos etc.) to produce a lightweight concrete of varying characteristics depending on the aggregate used. Such concrete can have very high strength.

fibrous plaster Plaster castings made up of plaster reinforced with canvas and wood laths and cast in moulds, therefore allowing repetitive work to be economically undertaken.

field drain Round, unglazed clayware, concrete or pitch fibre drain pipes without sockets, laid end to end without any jointing medium and thus admitting and conveying water and providing land drainage.

fielded panel A raised panel, as, for instance, on a panelled door. cf. **raised and fielded panel**.

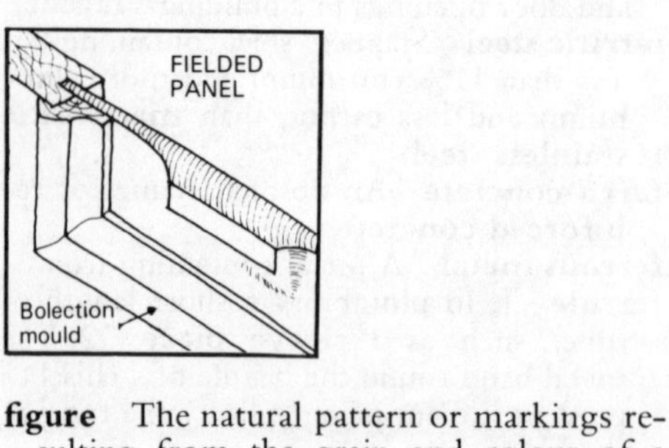

figure The natural pattern or markings resulting from the grain and colour of a wood, and varying according to the method of cutting from the log.

figuring (USA) Taking off **quantities** from drawings for the preparation of an estimate.

filament lamp An **incandescent lamp**.

file A tool, usually of steel and available in many sizes and shapes, for abrading, smoothing or reducing materials.

filled joint A **one-stage joint** made by either **mortar**, **sealant** or compressive **gasket**, as opposed to a **drained joint**, which is a **two-stage joint**.

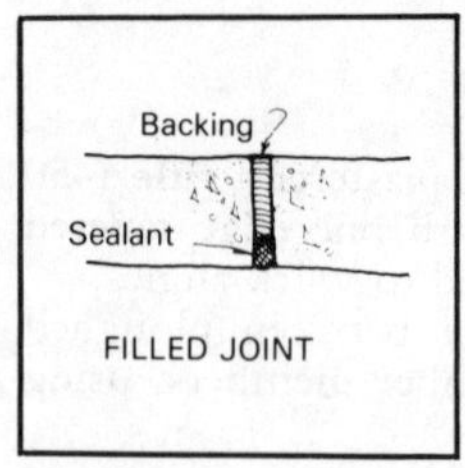

filler 1. A material added to plastics, having a function equivalent to that of an **extender** in **glue** (*ie.* varying the mechanical properties or reducing the cost). 2. A setting paste used to fill indentations in surfaces which are to be painted.

filler joist floor A suspended floor consisting of a series of small beams or joists at relatively close spacing and with clay or concrete hollow blocks spanning between them.

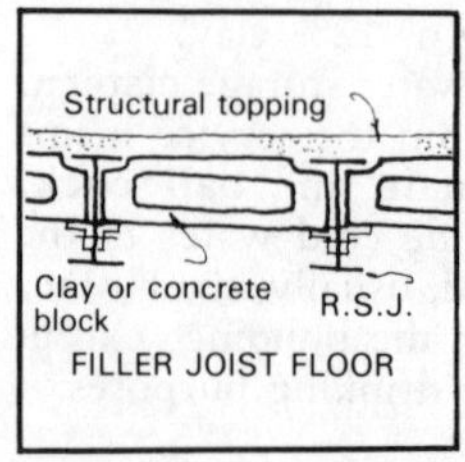

fillet 1. A small **moulding** of square cross-section. 2. A mortar strip of triangular cross-section to render a joint at an angle waterproof. 3. A strip of any material, though often of wood, of small cross-section.

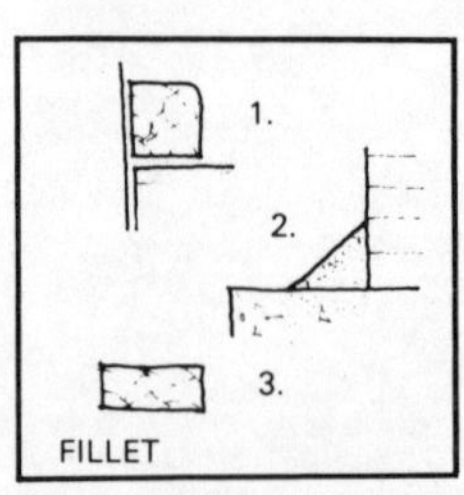

fillet chisel A mason's tool used for fine working.

filling-in piece A timber component, such as a **jack rafter**, shorter than similar neighbouring components.

filling knife A knife used for placing **filler**, similar to a **stopping knife** but more flexible.

filling piece A small piece of timber planted in a large piece to give a plane surface.

fillister 1. A **rebate** in a **glazing bar** to receive glass and putty. 2. A **plane** used to make fillisters.

film A thin layer of material deposited or formed on another, as a layer of dried paint or varnish (possibly consisting of several coats).

film building or film forming The property of a paint to form a strong, continuous and flexible **film** with good adhesive qualities.

film glue or film adhesive A thin solid sheet of **thermo-setting** adhesive (often **phenol formaldehyde resin** adhesive) used, for instance, in fine veneering where continuous adhesion is required and it is imperative not to wet the veneer and cause it to expand. The method is used also in making resin-bonded plywood.

filter bed The second stage of a sewage handling plant, in which the sewage is sprinkled on to, and passes through, a bed of **filter medium**, thus allowing the **aerobic bacteria** to complete the sterilization of the sewage, already commenced by the **anaerobic bacteria** in the **settling tank**.

filter medium The material in the **filter bed** of a sewage handling plant, usually **clinker** or broken stone, on which the aerobic micro-organisms, which assimilate and oxidize the organic matters in the sewage, can flourish.

final certificate The document produced by the architect or his quantity surveyor authorizing the final payment to the contractor for the construction of a building. It is produced after the settlement of the final account and the release of the **retention fund money** at the end of the **defects liability period**.

fine aggregate The sand in a concrete or asphalt mix, included to fill the interstices between the particles of **coarse aggregate** and thus eliminate unwanted air spaces and produce a dense mix. Fine aggregate should be well graded and mainly pass a 5 mm sieve.

fineness modulus A single-figure expression of the grading of an **aggregate**, obtained by adding together the percentage by weight of material retained on each of nine test sieves (38.1, 19.05, 9.53, 4.76, 2.40 1.20 mm and 600, 300 and 150 μm), then dividing by 100. This figure allows a comparison of aggregates for their relative overall fineness.

fine solder A more expensive solder than plumber's solder, made from tin and lead and having a very low melting point. It is used for making **blown joints**.

fine stuff The plaster used for the **finishing coat**.

fine textured A term used to describe a material which is not coarse in texture, as, for instance, a wood with very small pores which do not require filling before varnishing, as opposed to a coarse grained wood which requires filling.

finger joint A term usually applied nowadays to an **end joint** and not an **angle joint**. The joint consists of a series of interlocking fingers to join two pieces of timber in the same line, as opposed to a **combed joint** which is similar but joins pieces of timber at right angles.

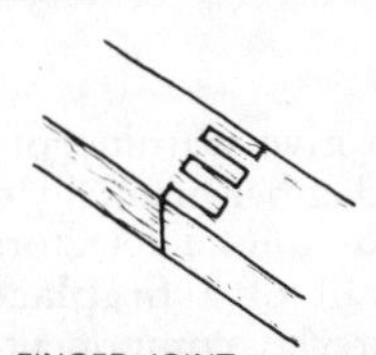

FINGER JOINT

finger plate A plate, usually of metal or plastic, fixed to the surface of a door near the **latch** and intended to protect the finish of the door from damage or staining.

fining off Applying the **finishing coat** of plaster or rendering.

finish 1. The standard of appearance and workmanship of a building, component or decorative treatment. 2. (USA) Fixed **joinery**.

finished floor level The level, related to some **datum**, of the completed floor of a building, *ie* the level of the top surface of the applied finish.

finishing carpentry (USA) **Joinery**.

finishing coat The top coat of a multi-coat system of **plastering** or **rendering**.

finishing off Preparing the finished surface of joinery.

finishing trade One of the trades involved in the final activities of a building contract, such as the fixing of joinery **trims**, plastering, painting, and installing the wall, floor and ceiling finishes.

fink truss A roof truss in which the struts are all inclined. cf. **fan truss**.

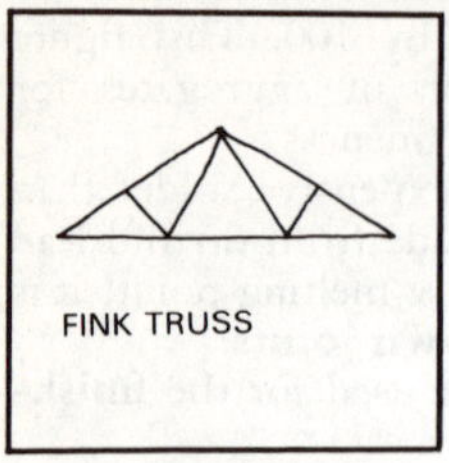

fir cone gasket A ridged **gasket** made of synthetic rubber or similar material and having a roughly triangular cross-section. It is used to form a seal between wall panels.

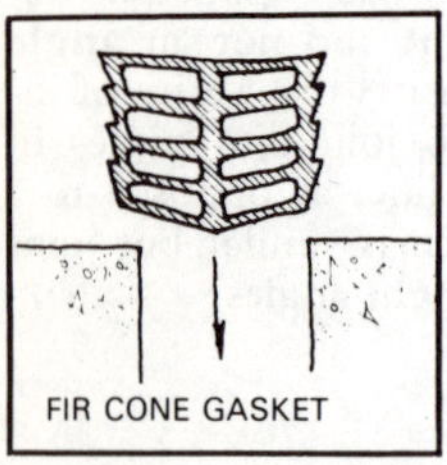

fire alarm A device to give warning of a fire. It may be activated either manually or automatically by heat or smoke detectors.

fire back The back wall of a **fireplace**, often consisting of a fireclay component.

fire break An obsolete expression for a fire-resisting subdivider of a building, such as a fire resisting wall or floor; now more usually referred to as a **compartment floor** or **wall**. Known as a **fire wall** in the USA.

fire brick A brick capable of withstanding temperatures up to 1,600 °C, made from clay with a huge quartz content.

fire check door A door which will provide a stated period of resistance of fire, while not achieving the full fire resisting rating of a **fire-resisting door**.

fireclay Refractory clay used for making **fire bricks**, having sizeable quantities of silica and alumina in its composition.

fired pin A hardened steel nail fired into masonry or concrete by an explosive charge in a gun.

fire escape stair See **escape stair**.

fire-extinguishing equipment Fixed or portable equipment for fighting fires in buildings, including **sprinkler systems**, **emulsifier systems**, **fire hydrants**, extinguishers etc.

fire hydrant A form of connection incorporated in a water main, to enable hoses to be attached by the Fire Service, either inside or outside a building. It varies from 19 to 63 mm in diameter.

fire load An assessment of the amount of heat (measured in Kw/m^2) that would be generated if a particular building and its contents were to be completely destroyed by fire. This figure is clearly affected by the quantity of combustible materials used in the construction and furnishing of the building.

fireplace A recess formed in a wall to receive a grating or other metal framework to support a fire. The recess is usually lined in **fire brick**.

fire point The lowest temperature at which a substance will ignite.

fireproof An obsolete term having no precise meaning. It is superseded by the term **fire resistance**, used in conjunction with a specified period of time.

fire protection The protection given by the encasing of structural members, such as steelwork or timber frames, to give these **elements** of structure the period of **fire resistance** required by the **Building Regulations**.

fire protective lining The construction used in encasing structural members to provide them with fire protection.

fire resistance The grading of a structure or element in respect of the period of time it will resist the passage of fire. The periods to be met are stipulated, in the UK, in the Building Regulations.

fire-resisting door A door that has been certified by test to resist fire for a set period, in respect of the door's integrity (it will not distort and release smoke and flame), stability (it will not burn through and disintegrate) and insulation (the temperature rise on the side of the door furthest from the fire is to be within stated limits).

fire-resisting glazing Glazed panels within restricted sizes, glazed in **wired glass** or **electro-copper glazing**.

fire-retardant coating See **flame retardant**.

fire stop A non-combustible material used to close the gap created by an imperfection of fit between elements or components in a structure, or to seal a cavity, against the penetration of smoke or flame. Compare **cavity barrier**.

fire vent An openable area in the enclosing wall or roof of a building, intended for releasing heat and smoke in the event of fire. It may be opened automatically or manually.

fire wall (USA) A **compartment wall**.

firing The burning of bricks and earthenware goods in a kiln.

firmer chisel A carpenter's or joiner's ordinary **chisel**. Stouter than a paring chisel but less robust than a mortise chisel.

firmer gouge A tool similar to a **chisel**, but having a curved blade with a cutting edge to cut grooves or recesses.

firring 1. Longitudinally splayed timber battens nailed to the top of flat roof joists, before the **decking** is fixed, to give the roof a **fall**. Also the process of nailing on such battens or strips. 2. The packing used to compensate for unevenness in joists and so produce a true and level upper surface. Also the process of applying such packing. 3. (USA) A cavity within an external wall, to provide thermal insulation and weather protection.

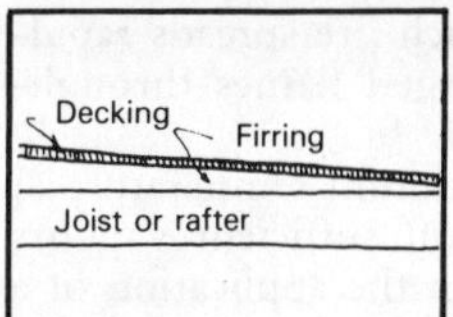

FIRRING

first fixings 1. The early work of the carpenter or joiner on site, *ie* the cutting and fitting of joists, roof trusses, floorboards, stairs and window frames. cf. **second fixings**. 2. **Grounds** to receive the later fixing of joinery items.

first floor In the UK, etc. the first full floor above **ground floor** level. (In the USA this is known as the second floor).

fish glue A **glue** similar to **animal glue**, but made from fish refuse.

fish plate The reinforcing plate (of metal or wood) placed across a lengthening joint and bolted or nailed to each of the joined components.

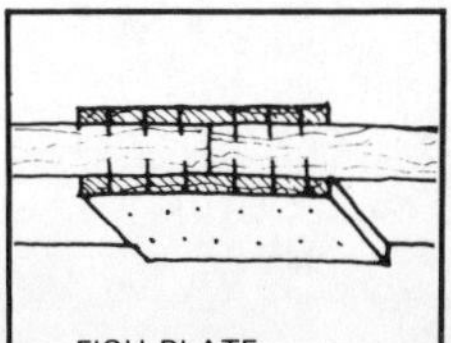
FISH PLATE

fish tail 1. The shape created at the ends of such components as **balusters** in order to give the component greater stability when it is set into a concrete element. It is formed by splitting the end of the component for a short distance and bending the halves in opposite directions. 2. A **hammerhead**.

fit The dimensional relationship between meeting components. It must reconcile the requirements of tolerances and clearances etc. between neighbouring components with performance requirements.

fitch A small, long-handled brush for painting areas having restricted access.

fitment Fixed furniture.

fitter's hammer An **engineer's hammer**.

fitting 1. In pipework, etc. a **bend, coupling, elbow, union** or similar accessory. A small auxiliary part. 2. A **fitment**. 3. The action of cutting and trimming a component to suit a particular location.

fixed joint A joint in a structural frame with restrains the member from turning, thus inducing a **bending moment** at the joint. cf. **pin joint**.

fixed light A **dead light**.

fixed-price contract A building contract entered into for a contract sum which is not subject to adjustment to compensate for **fluctuations** in the price of labour or materials. The contractor sets his **rates** so as to take account of the anticipated increases in price during the agreed contract period.

fixing See **fastener**.

fixing bracket 1. Any fixing accessory based on the design of an **angle bracket**. 2. In **patent glazing**, a device for securing the **glazing bars** to the structural frame.

fixing brick or fixing block A nailable brick or block made from sawdust and clay, **diatomaceous earth** or **lightweight concrete**. It is built into a wall to provide a fixing point for joinery items such as window frames, etc.

fixing device See **fastener**.

fixing fillet A thin slip of wood, the thickness of a mortar joint, inserted into a joint to provide a fixing for an item of joinery.

FIXING FILLET

fixing slip A **fixing fillet**.

fixture Anything that is fixed to the building and therefore becomes the landlord's property, *eg* sanitary fittings, plumbing, ceiling light fittings etc.

flagstone (flag) A slab of stone, **cast stone** or **concrete** used as a paving material, or used to provide a cover to a pit, etc.

flaking The detachment of thin particles from a surface, as from a paint film or a stone or other facing material.

flame cleaning The removal of mill scale and other contamination from weathered structural steelwork immediately prior to painting, using a hot flame.

flameproof luminaire An enclosed **luminaire** which satisfies the appropriate regulation for use in a situation where there is risk of explosion.

flame retardant A substance or treatment applied to a **combustible material** to decrease its tendency to propagate flame across its surface.

flame spread See **surface spread of flame**.

flammability The capacity to burn with a flame.

flammable A description applicable to any material that will burn with a flame.

flange A projecting part of a component, often (as in the case of a flange on a pipe) used in its fixing. In **RSJs** and **Universal columns or universal beams** the flanges are the top and bottom members of the section, as opposed to the **web** which joins them together.

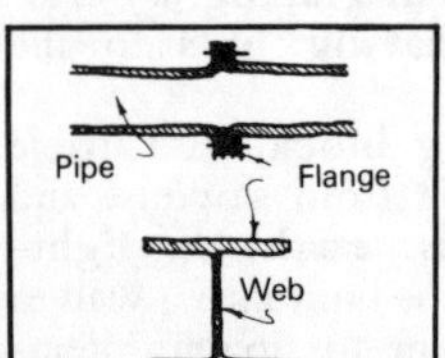

FLANGE

flank The **intrados** of an arch near its **springing**. cf. **arch**.

flank wall A side wall of a building.

flap The two flat plates of a hinge which are connected by a **pin** at the **knuckle**, one being screwed to the frame and the other to the **hanging stile**.

flash To make a junction of external building materials weathertight by the use of a **flashing**.

flash drying The forced drying of paint or varnish by exposing it to radiant heat for a suitable period.

flashing A strip of thin impervious material, often **flexible metal** (lead, copper or zinc) but sometimes bitumen felt, thick plastic sheet or asbestos-based material, used to weatherproof a joint between two materials in the external shell of a building (*eg* the joint between a roof covering and a vertical surface).

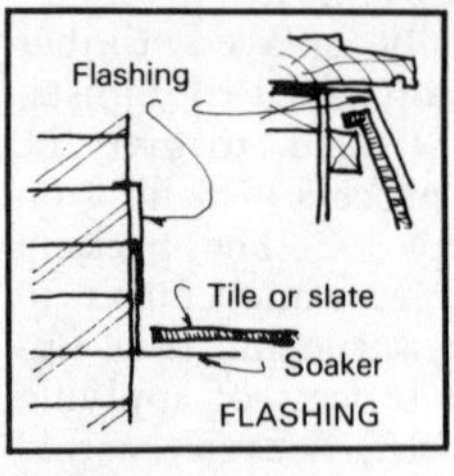

FLASHING

flashing board A board to which **flashings** are fixed.

flashover A stage in the development of a contained fire at which fire spreads rapidly to give large merged flames throughout the space.

flash point The minimum temperature at which liquid gives off sufficient vapours to produce a flash on the application of a small flame.

flat arch An arch with a level **soffit** and **extrados**. cf. **arch**.

flat coat 1. A coat of paint with a non-glossy finish; either a top coat or an undercoat. 2. A coat of **filler** applied prior to painting.

flat cutting The **re-sawing** of timber parallel to one edge of the original piece.

flat-drawn sheet glass See **sheet glass**.

flat grain The grain of **flat-sawn timber**, having annual rings at less than 45° to the face of the piece.

flat oil paint An oil paint which dries to a film with little or no gloss, usually having high pigment/binder ratios and relatively poor flow.

flat paint brush A metal-bound **brush** with bristles stiff enough to carry heavy varnish or paint, being between 12 and 150 mm wide.

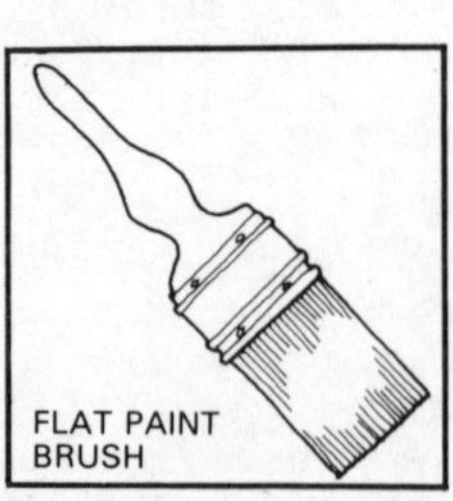
FLAT PAINT BRUSH

flat roof A roof with a slope of less than 10° to the horizontal.

flat sawing The practice of sawing logs with parallel cuts. Flat sawing is a method of **conversion** which wastes less timber than any other. cf. **quarter sawing**.

flat-sawn timber Timber produced by sawing logs with parallel cuts.

flatting down **Sanding** a painted surface with sandpaper or other **abrasive** to form a key for succeeding coats of paint.

flatting varnish An oil **varnish** containing substantial quantities of hard resin, making it suitable for use as an undercoating. It is easily flatted down.

flat varnish A **varnish** whose **gloss** has been reduced by additives.

flat wall brush A brush resembling a small **distemper brush**, but narrower, being approximately 125–150 mm wide.

flaunching 1. The cement mortar **fillet** surrounding a **chimney pot** and extending across the whole of the **chimney stack** to protect the top of the stack from rain penetration. 2. The act of placing this fillet.

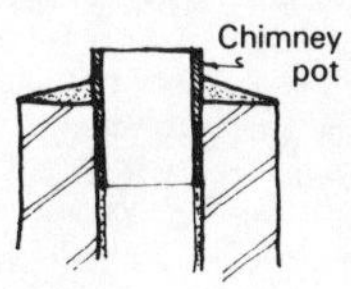

FLAUNCHING

flaxboard A **particle board** made from flax shives – the residue from the flax plant after the removal of the flax fibres.

Flemish bond A form of bonding of brickwork in which alternate **headers** and **stretchers** appear on every **course**. cf. **bond**.

Flemish diagonal bond A bond of brickwork in which a course of **stretchers** alternates with a course of alternating headers and stretchers, as in **Flemish bond**. A diagonal pattern appears on the face.

FLEMISH GARDEN WALL BOND

Flemish garden wall bond A **bond** of brickwork in which each **course** comprises a sequence of three **stretchers** and one **header**, each header being placed in the middle of the stretchers in the courses above and below.

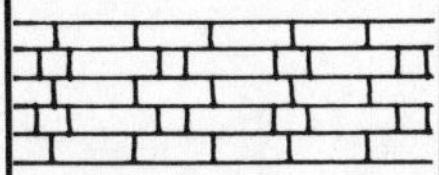
FLEMISH DIAGONAL BOND

fletton A cheap brick mottled pink and yellow, with properties similar to a **common brick** but with an improved appearance; made chiefly around Peterborough, from the local shale.

flex or flexible cord A flexible cable of small cross-section consisting usually of a large number of copper strands enclosed in rubber and a braided textile or **polyvinyl chloride** (PVC) plastic sheathing. It is used for supplying power to portable domestic apparatus, pendant lamps, etc.

flexible cable A power cable with one or more cores of such cross-section and fine stranding as to make the whole quite flexible.

flexible metal Sheet metal (copper, lead, zinc or aluminium) which is malleable and which, unlike corrugated metal, needs to be fully supported on a board decking when it is used for roofing.

flexible-metal roofing A roof covering made of **flexible metal** in which the individual sheets making up the roof are joined together by **seams**, **rolls** or **drips**.

flexibility In paintwork, the degree to which a paint film, after drying, is able to conform to the movement or deformation of its supporting surface without cracking or flaking.

flier 1. A step in a straight flight, with a rectangular **tread**, as opposed to a **winder**. 2. A **flying shore**.

flight A series of steps which joins one floor either to another floor or to a landing between floors. cf. **stair**.

flight hole The hole formed where the tunnel of a wood destroying insect (furniture, death-watch, or longhorn beetle etc.) reaches the surface of the wood and from which the adult beetle emerges.

flitch 1. A section of timber larger than 100 × 300 mm which is intended for reconversion. 2. A timber from which **veneers** are cut. 3. A stack of **veneers**

after cutting, piled in the order in which they were before cutting.

flitch beam A built-up beam made up of two timber beams with a steel plate sandwiched between them, the whole being bolted together at intervals, thus encouraging the composite construction to act as one member.

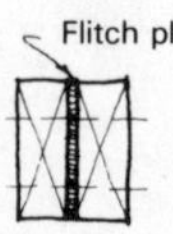

FLITCH BEAM

flitch plate The steel plate that is used to reinforce a **flitch beam**.

float A wooden or steel tool used by plasterers and screeders to produce the surface finish on each coat.

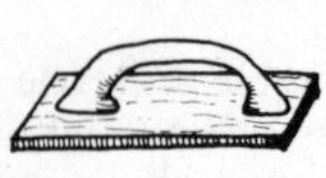

FLOAT

floated coat A plaster coat smoothed by a **float**.

floater (USA) A tool used for finishing mortar **screeds**.

float glass A transparent **glass**, the surfaces of which are flat, parallel and fire-polished so that they give clear, undistorted vision and reflection. It is manufactured by floating hot glass in ribbon form on a heated liquid of greater density than the glass.

floating 1. The act of levelling the **floating coat** of plaster with a **floating rule**. 2. The re-arrangement of pigment grains in a paint film when the paint is applied. Although this may result in a defect with some paints, with metallic paints this can be the intention.

floating coat The plaster undercoat immediately preceding the final coat.

floating floor The upper portion of a floor (including the flooring) when this is supported on a resilient layer or mounting to provide insulation against sound and vibration. It is a form of **discontinuous construction**.

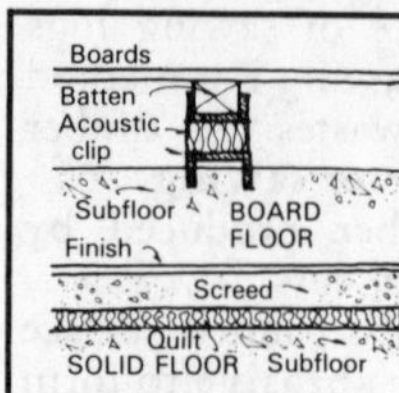

FLOATING FLOOR

floating rule A long wooden rule used for levelling a **floating coat** between **screeds**. cf. **feather-edge rule**.

float valve A **ball cock**.

floor chisel A **bolster** about 50 mm wide used to raise floor boards.

floor clip Sometimes called a bulldog clip; a sherardized steel clip which is pushed into a floor **screed** before it hardens. The clip is used to hold a **batten** to which the floor is fixed. If an insulating pad is included to reduce sound transmission it is called an **acoustic elip**.

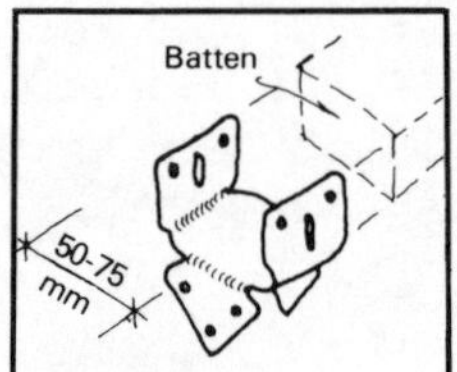

FLOOR CLIP

floor cramp A **cramp** used to force floorboards together before nailing them down.

floor framing **Common joists, strutting** and any supporting main beams.

floor guide A groove in a floor, usually in the form of a metal channel let into the floor, which acts as a guide for a sliding door.

flooring brad See **brad**.

floor joist A **common joist**.

floor line A mark on a wall or stanchion to show the level of the finished floor.

floor plan A horizontal section through a building, usually taken above the window sill level, showing the position and thicknesses of walls, the position of door and window openings etc.

floor socket outlet An electrical **socket outlet** set in the floor.

floor spring A sprung pivot set into the floor, flush with the finished surface, and used to control the opening and closing of a **swing door**.

floor stop A **door stop** set in the floor.

floor strutting **Strutting** between **common joists** at mid span, either in the form of **herring-bone strutting** or **solid strutting**.

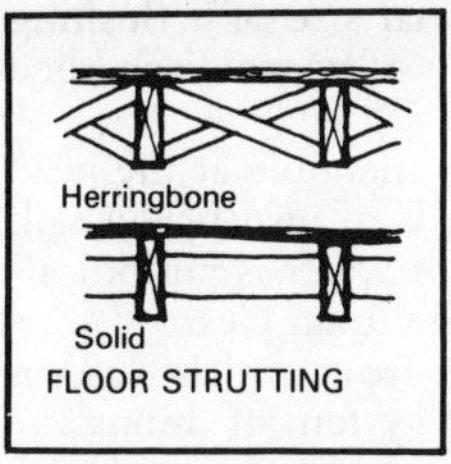

floor tile A thin flat tile, usually rectangular, made of clay, concrete, **linoleum**, cork, rubber, asphalt, vinyl asbestos, PVC or other plastic material set on a floor in either cement mortar, bitumen or other **adhesive** in order to provide a wearing surface. In addition such tiles may enhance the softness, thermal insulation and sound absorbence of the surface.

floor-to-ceiling height The height between the upper **key reference plane** of one floor and the lower key reference plane of the floor or roof above.

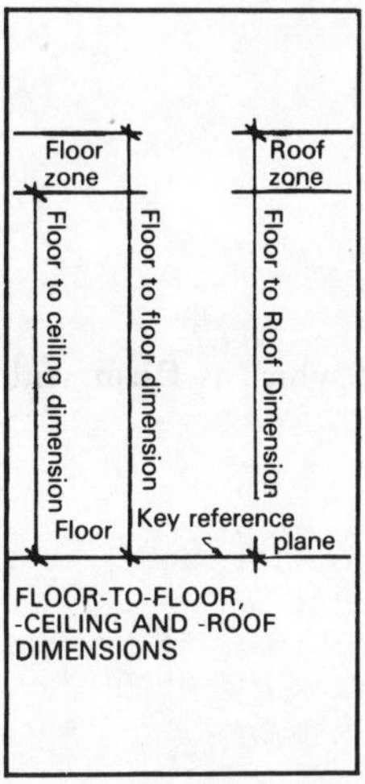

floor-to-floor height The height between the upper **reference plane** of one floor and the upper key reference plane of the floor above.

floor-to-roof height The height between the upper **reference plane** of one floor and the upper key reference plane of the roof.

floor varnish A quick drying, tough, abrasion-resistant varnish which is applied to floor boards, and is capable of taking a wax polish.

flow and return pipes Pipes connecting a hot water **boiler** to the **cylinder** to form the convection circulation route.

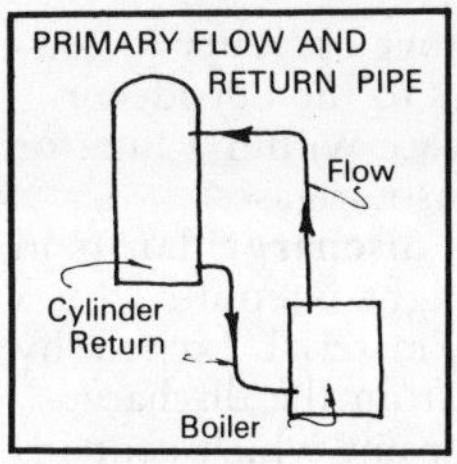

flow chart A graphical representation of the methods and sequences of solving a problem or undertaking an activity.

flow pipe The pipe conveying hot water from a **boiler** to a **cylinder**. cf. **return pipe**.

fluctuating stresses The pulsating or alternating **stresses** which result from the combined effect of **dead** and **live loads**.

fluctuation The amount by which the cost of labour and materials rises or falls during the course of building works. In some **forms of contract** these fluctuations can be adjusted in the cost of the work to the client; in **fixed-price contracts** no adjustment is permitted in the final contract figure to cover fluctuations.

flue A square or circular duct to convey smoke and combustion gases from a fireplace, boiler or heater to the outside air.

flue block A precast hollow block which, with others, forms a **flue**.

flue gathering The part of a chimney above the fireplace which is contracted by corbelling to the size of the flue and, possibly, changes direction.

flueless appliance Any combustion appliance for heating a room or for cooking which is not provided with a flue, the products of combustion being allowed to mix with the air of the room in which the appliance is situated.

flue lining The lining to a flue, constructed of fireclay, concrete, metal or asbestos pipe units from 75 mm diameter upwards. The metal or asbestos lining is used with efficient gas-fired or oil-fired boilers which have cool flue gases that could lead to condensation in the flue.

flue pipe A metal or **asbestos cement**

pipe from a boiler, stove or heater to convey combustion gases to the outside air.

flueway The clear space within a flue for the passage of combustion gases.

fluorescent lamp A **discharge lamp** in which most of the light is emitted by a layer of fluorescent material excited by ultraviolet radiation from the discharge.

fluorescent paint A paint which contains pigments which are capable of absorbing energy from the blue or ultra-violet end of the spectrum and re-emitting it in the form of light in the visible wavelengths, therefore appearing brighter than its surroundings. Such paint ceases to glow if the activating source is removed. cf. **luminous paint** and **phosphorescent paint**.

flush 1. A term applied to the surface of an element which is in one plane (*eg* a **flush door**) or is even or level with an adjacent surface. 2. To clean a pipe or channel or fitting by causing a rush of water to pass down it.

flush bead A **bead** set level with the surrounding material, but defined from it by a **quirk** an each side.

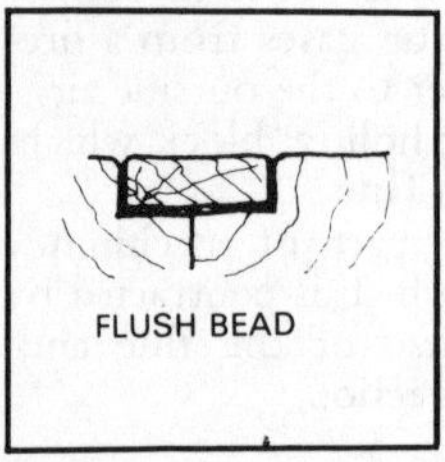

FLUSH BEAD

flush bolt A bolt for securing a door. It is let into the material of the door so that its front surface is flush with the door surface.

flush door A smooth-surfaced door, faced with **plywood**, **hardboard** or similar material and with a core that is of cellular, semi-solid, or solid construction.

flush eaves The **eaves** of a building when the **eaves fascia** is fixed directly against the wall face and there is no projection of the roof requiring a **soffit board.**

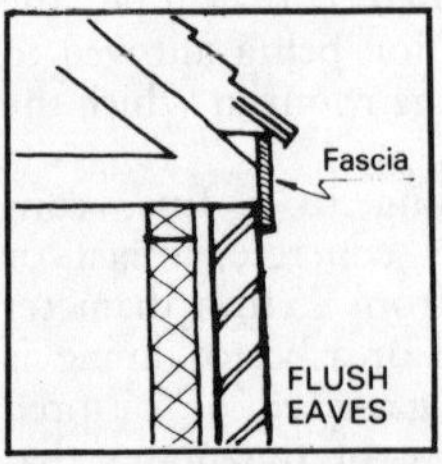

FLUSH EAVES

flushing cistern A cistern provided with a device for rapidly discharging its contents. It is used to clean sanitary appliances and carry away their contents to the drain. The nominal size of a flushing cistern is the quantity of water discharged at each flush.

flushing manhole A manhole at the head of a drain run which is of insufficient fall, into which a charge of water is periodically released to keep the drain clear.

flushing tank A tank from which water is discharged to flush a system of drains.

flushing trough A long water tank extending over a range of wcs and common to all. It is used particularly in institutional buildings, since it allows the flushing of several w.c.s. at short intervals without waiting for an individual **cistern** to fill.

flushing valve A valve which replaces a flushing cistern in some w.c.s. When operated it supplies a specific quantity of water to the **w.c. pan** and can be used repeatedly without having to wait for the cistern to refill.

flush joint A flat joint, smooth with the surfaces of the surrounding material.

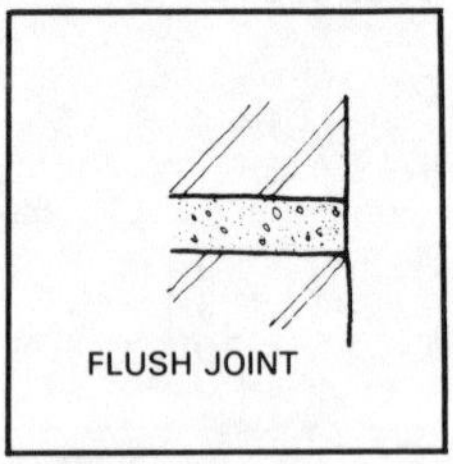

FLUSH JOINT

flush panel A panel which is **flush** with its frame.

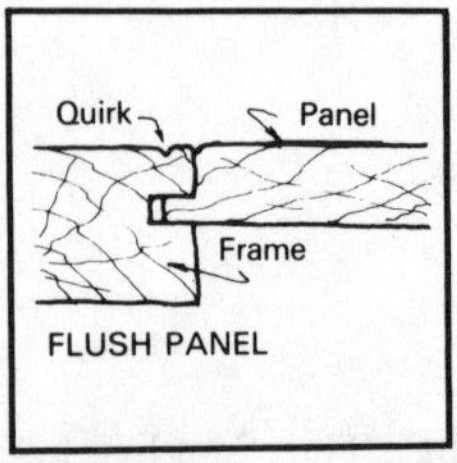

FLUSH PANEL

flush pipe The pipe which leads from a **flushing cistern** to a w.c., or the **sparge** pipe of a urinal.

flush soffit A smooth under-surface.

flush valve A **flushing valve**.

flute A vertical groove, usually semi-circular or semi-elliptical in plan, separated from the adjacent flute by a **fillet**, or meeting it in an **arris**.

flux A substance which is used in soldering, **brazing** or welding to increase the fusibility of the molten metal by dissolving the infusible oxide films which prevent adhesion. cf. **solder, weld**.

fly ash A fine dust, which may have pozzolanic properties, from the flue of power stations using pulverised coal. It is used as a partial substitute for cement in certain types of concrete, and is also used in brickmaking.

flyer See **flier**.

flying bond 1. **Monk bond**. 2. **American bond.**

flying scaffold A **scaffold** hung by ropes or cables from **outriggers**.

flying shore A horizontal strut, or a series of struts framed together, fixed above ground level between two walls. cf. **shoring**.

fly rafter A decorated **barge board**.

foamed blast-furnace slag A lightweight **aggregate** produced by water-cooling molten **blast-furnace slag**; the resulting steam produces expansion of the slag.

foamed concrete See **aerated concrete**.

foamed plastic Cellular plastic (polystyrene or polyurethane etc.) made directly from a liquid solution or dispersion; the term is sometimes applied to cellular plastics generally.

foamed slag A lightweight cellular material normally understood to be a material manufactured by treating molten blast furnace slag with sufficient water or other suitable medium to produce a dry, cellular product which is crushed and graded as required for use as a concrete aggregate. It consists chiefly of alumino-silicates of lime and magnesia in a glassy, partly crystalline or crystalline condition.

foam fire extinguisher A fire extinguisher from which chemical foam is expelled when the chemical solutions, stored separately inside the body of the extinguisher, are allowed to mix and interact.

foam hydrant A fire hydrant for obtaining either foam compound or solution from a piped supply.

foil A material of any width, in flat or coiled form, and in thicknesses up to and including 0.15 mm.

foil-backed plasterboard Gypsum plaster board with an aluminium foil bonded to its rear surface. This provides the board with increased thermal insulation properties (if associated with an air space) and increased resistance to water-vapour permeation.

folded flooring Floor boards which are sprung into place as opposed to being positioned using a **floor cramp**.

folded plate construction A method of spanning large openings with relatively thin, reinforced concrete slabs, or stressed skin timber frames, set at an angle to each other, thereby gaining additional stiffness.

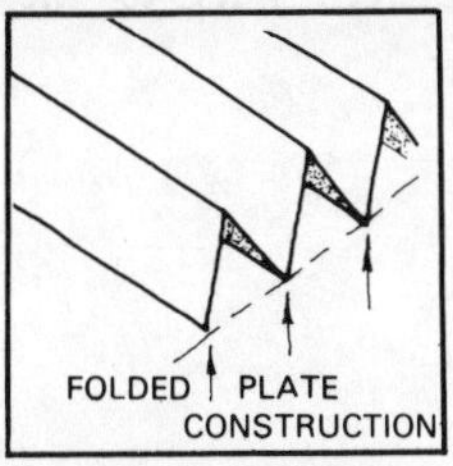

folding casement A pair of **casement windows** usually with rebated **meeting stiles** hung in a frame with no mullion between them.

folding door 1. A pair of doors, usually with rebated **meeting stiles**, hung in a frame with no mullion. 2. A door with two or more leaves hinged together so that they fold back to one side into a small space, only the end leaf being hinged to the door frame.

folding rule A **fourfold rule**, or a **zigzag rule**.

folding shutter A **boxing shutter**.

folding stair A **loft ladder**.

folding wedges Wedges, usually of timber, used in pairs (with their slopes opposed) for levelling and adjusting such items as **formwork** or temporary strutting.

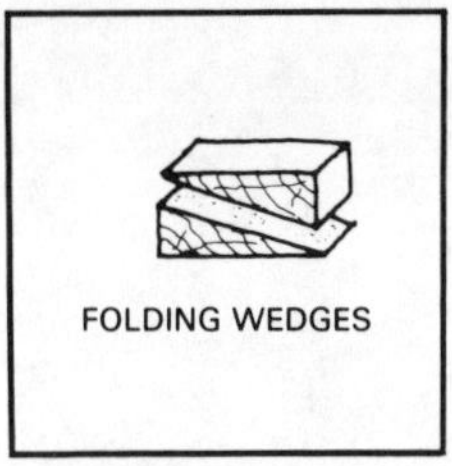

foot block An **architrave block**.

foot bolt A large **tower bolt** fixed vertically at the foot of a door.

foot cut The horizontal cut in a **birdsmouth joint** at the foot of a **common rafter**.

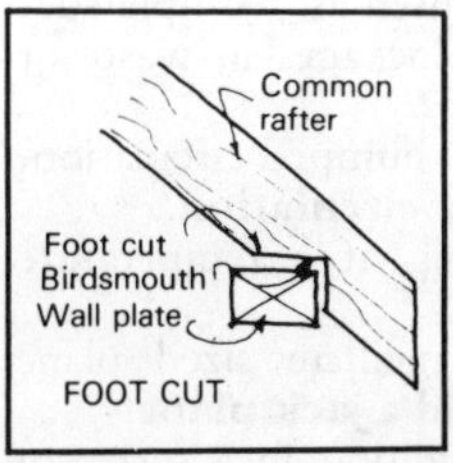

footing The widening of the base of a wall to spread its load over a greater area of subsoil; the term usually refers to the brick reverse corbelling above the concrete foundation, but can refer to the whole foundation.

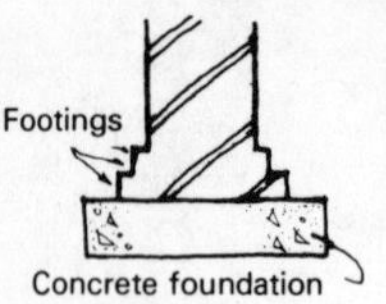

FOOTING

foot plate 1. A horizontal timber laid over the **wall plate** joining the foot of the **common rafter** to the **ashlering**. 2. A **sole plate**.

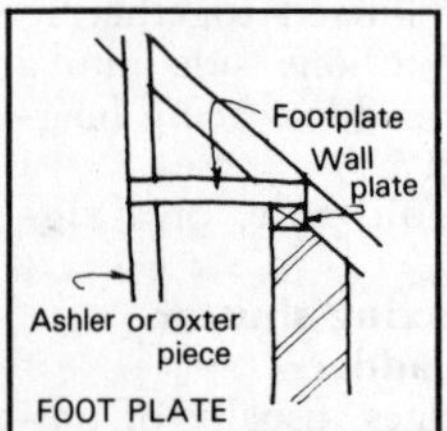

FOOT PLATE

footprints A pipe fitter's adjustable wrench with serrated jaws.

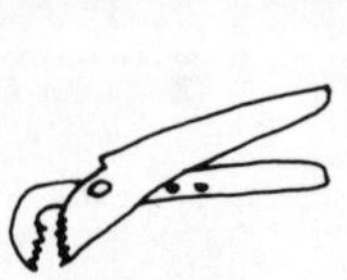
FOOTPRINTS

footstone A **gable springer**.
force That which tends to produce motion or change of motion in a body on which it acts. It is measured in newtons (*ie* kg m/s^2) representing mass × acceleration.
force cup A rubber cup fixed to a small wooden handle and used as a simple suction device to free blockages in waste or soil pipes.
forced circulation A pumped circulation, rather than a **gravity circulation**.
forced drying Drying at a temperature up to 66 °C.
fore plane An intermediate sized plane between a **jointer** and a **jack plane**.
foresight The last sighting in a series of readings taken in surveying before changing the position of the instrument. The point at which the foresight is taken becomes the first reading (or the **backsight**) from the new position of the instrument. Thus the two sets of readings can be inter-related.
forge welding Any welding process in which the weld is made by hammering, or some other impulsive force, while the surfaces to be mated are plastic.
forging 1. A shape produced by hammering or pressing, usually when the metal being forged is hot. 2. The act of forming a shape by hammering or pressing a piece of metal, usually when it is hot.
forked tenon A joint in which a **tenon** is cut in the middle of a long rail (across its length) and is straddled by an open or slot **mortise.**
formaldehyde See **synthetic resin**.
form of contract The particular type of building contract that is entered into by the employer, for whom the building is being constructed, and the contractor. There are various types of contract available for use on different types of project.
form of tender A form submitted to the prospective employer by a contractor, usually as a result of a competitive tender involving several competing contractors, on which the contractor has indicated his price for carrying out the required building work. He arrives at this figure either by pricing the **Bill of Quantities** for the work (prepared by the prospective employer's quantity surveyor) or as a result of taking off the quantities of labour and materials required for the job from drawings and a specification submitted by the architect.
forms See **formwork**.
formwork Temporary timber or metal work used to form a base and/or sides within which to pour *in situ* concrete.
Forstner bit A patent bit with a small centre point and a sharp ring at its outer edge for sinking **blind holes**.
fossil resin **Resin** which has become hardened through ageing in the ground; such as copal, amber and kauri which are used in varnish and paint making.
foul-air flue A duct used to draw the vitiated air from a room.
foul drain or foul sewer A **drain** or **sewer** intended to convey all manner of domestic and industrial effluent with the exception of surface water which is conveyed in a **surface water drain**.
foundation That part of a building which rests on or within the ground and which spreads the load of the building so as not to exceed the **bearing capacity** of the

subsoil. It can take the form of a strip of concrete (reinforced or unreinforced) below and wider than the loadbearing walls or columns, a set of **piles**, or a **raft foundation**.

foundation stone A large, commemorative stone set in a wall close to ground level, suitably inscribed on the outer face. There is a ceremony of 'laying the foundation stone'.

fourfold rule A pocket rule hinged to fold into four parts.

four-piece butt matching The practice of joining four sheets of **sliced veneer** with the best **figuring** of each sheet at the centre of the combined panel.

foxiness A term applied to a form of decay which affects hardwoods, causing reddish-brown staining.

foxtail wedging **Secret wedging**.

foxy A term applied to wood which is beginning to decay and has become dull red in colour.

frame 1. An assembly of timber components to form a **joinery** element, as in door frame, window frame etc. 2. A structural skeleton or framework of timber, steel or reinforced concrete components. 3. To connect components in order to create a structural framework.

frame construction 1. Timber construction, such as **balloon frame**, **braced frame** or **platform frame**. 2. Any steel or reinforced concrete framed building which relies for its stability on the framing elements and not on loadbearing walls.

frame corbel A **corbel plate** consisting of square bar bent to form a hoop shape.

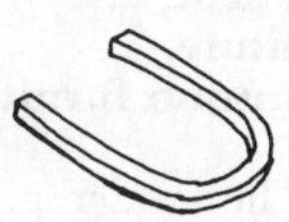

FRAME CORBEL

framed and ledged door A door similar to a **framed, ledged and braced door** but without diagonal braces.

framed door A door with a rigid frame consisting of top, bottom and **lock rails**, **hanging stile** and **shutting stile**.

framed floor A floor of **common joists** carried by **binders** which in turn are carried by beams; now entirely replaced by the reinforced concrete floor.

framed grounds **Grounds** framed like a door frame, with the head tenoned to the posts, and situated around openings to receive **joinery** fixings.

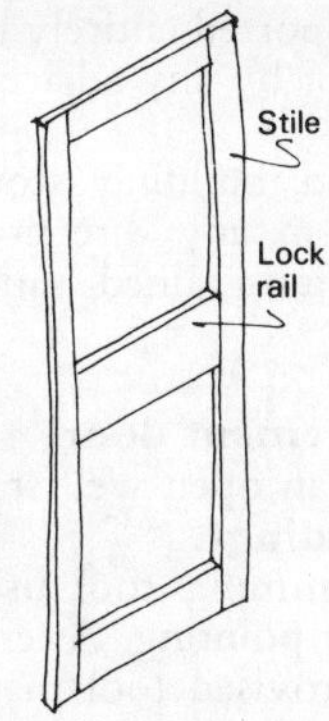

FRAMED DOOR

framed, ledged and braced door A wooden door which shows vertical boarding, two **stiles** and a top rail on its outside face. The top rail is rebated to receive the board ends. On the back of the door, horizontal **ledges** at the bottom and middle of the door, which are thinner than the complete door by the thickness of the boarding, are also visible, together with two diagonal braces.

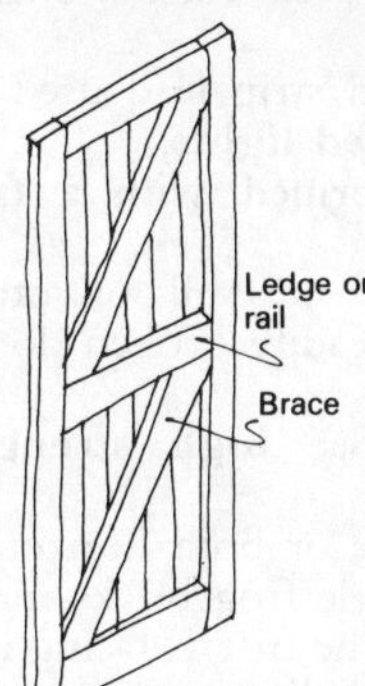

FRAMED LEDGED AND BRACED DOOR

framed partition A partition, usually a **stud** partition, in which the elements are framed together to provide additional strength (loadbearing or bracing).

frame saw 1. A power saw for wood or stone with one or several vertical or horizontal blades set in a frame. 2. A large **bow saw**.

framing square A steel **square**.

free-standing A vertical element, such as a chimney, which is supported entirely by its own strength and not by any adjacent structure.

freestone A fine-grained building stone which can be worked in any direction; usually limestone or fine-grained sandstone.

free stuff **Clear** timber.

French casement A **casement door**.

French flier A **flier** in an open well stair with **quarter-space landings.**

Frenchman A joint trimming tool used with a **jointing rule** for pointing. A term also applied to an improvised tool made from a bent over kitchen knife and similarly used with a jointing rule to trim mortar joints.

French polish Shellac dissolved in methylated spirits. Applied in numerous coats to wood surfaces to provide a high gloss.

French roof A **mansard roof**.

French window A **casement door.**

frequency The reciprocal of periodic time. When the independent variable is time, the unit of frequency is the Hertz (formerly cycles per second).

fresh-air inlet See **air inlet**.

fret saw A thin, narrow-bladed saw used to cut round sharp corners. The blade is kept in tension by a metal bow, usually 300–500 mm in length. A **jig saw** is a power-operated large scale version of this type of saw.

fretted lead H-shaped strip lead used to make **cames** for **leaded lights**.

fretwork Work performed with a **fret saw**.

friable The condition of soil or other material when it is readily broken down to a fine state.

friction grip bolt See **high strength friction grip bolt**.

frog A sinking in one or both horizontal faces of a **brick**. Single frog bricks make stronger walls when the frog is facing upwards, since it is then filled with mortar.

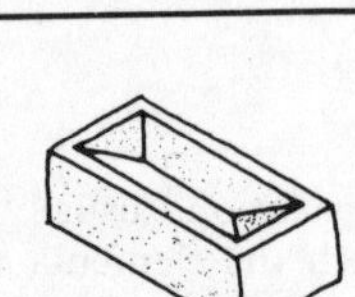

FROG

frontage The edge of a site which is parallel to the line of the roadway.

frontage line **Building line**.

front lintel The **lintel** supporting the outer skin of a **cavity wall**.

front putty **Face putty**.

frost cracks In timber, cracks caused by frost splitting the growing wood.

frost heart A deepening of colour of the **heartwood** of a tree due to frost action during growth.

frost heave The expansion of ground, particularly of clay subsoils, due to the freezing of the water it contains.

frowy A description of wood that is brittle or soft.

fugitive The description of colouring matter which readily suffers partial or total loss of its original colour on exposure to light or weather.

full A **joinery** term which is the opposite of **bare**: slightly oversize.

full coat The thickest coat of paint that can be applied without defect.

full gloss The highest grade of gloss paint.

full-size detail A drawing of a particular part of a building (usually joinery or metal work) to a scale of 1:1.

full-way valve A cock which, when fully opened, does not impede the flow of water; used where water pressure is very low.

functional capability The ability of a building component to fulfil its specified function.

fungicidal paint A paint which discourages the growth of fungi on its dry film; a property conferred by an additive although pigments such as zinc oxide may contribute.

fungus An organism that lives off the material on which it is situated. In the case of timber, such organisms can cause decay, as in **dry rot, wet rot**, etc.

furniture See **door furniture**.

furniture beetle See **common furniture beetle**.

furred A description of hot-water pipes, in **hard water** areas, which have become coated internally with lime and other salts deposited by the water.

furring 1. See **firring**. 2. The action of becoming **furred**.

furring strip A **rough ground**.

furrowed surface Vertical or horizontal **flutes** cut into **ashlar** at approximately 10 mm centres.

fuse A device for protecting a circuit against damage from excessive current flow by opening the circuit on the melting of the fuse element.

fuse box or fuse board A housing for **fuses**.

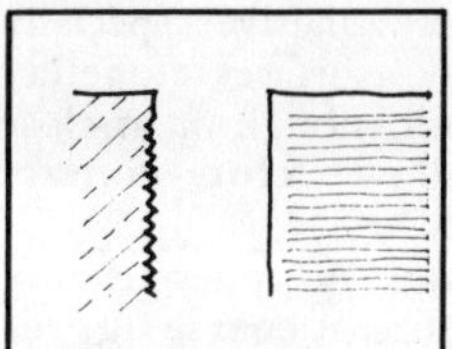

FURROWED SURFACE

fused plug An electrical plug containing a **fuse**, which protects the appliance to which it is fitted from excessive current flow.

fuse element The fusible wire in a fuse.

fuse link The device that holds a **fuse element**.

fuse-switch or switch-fuse A switch containing a **fuse**.

fusible link A piece of material with a relatively low melting point which, in case of a fire, melts and releases an automatically closing fire door, etc.

fusible plug A metal plug with a low melt point which will release steam in a boiler when the water level falls below the minimum safety level.

fusion welding Welding in which the weld is made between materials in a molten state without the application of pressure.

G

gabbart scaffold (Scotland) A form of timber scaffolding now obsolete in those parts of the world with plentiful tubular scaffolding. The **standards** comprise three **deals** bolted together, the centre deal being cut short at intervals to form a gap through which the **ledger** passes.

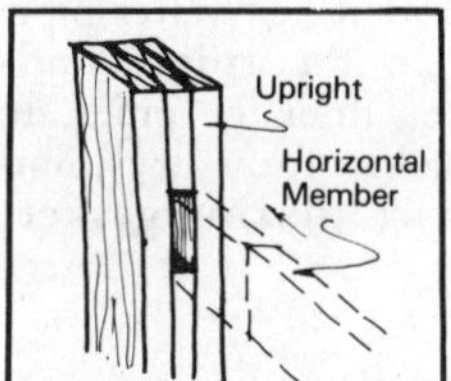

GABBART SCAFFOLD

gable Properly the triangular part of the end wall of a building with a **duo-pitched roof**. Often used loosely to mean the **gable wall**, or even the end wall of a narrow flat roofed building.

gable board A **barge board**.

gable coping The coping set on a gable wall when it projects above the line of the roof finish.

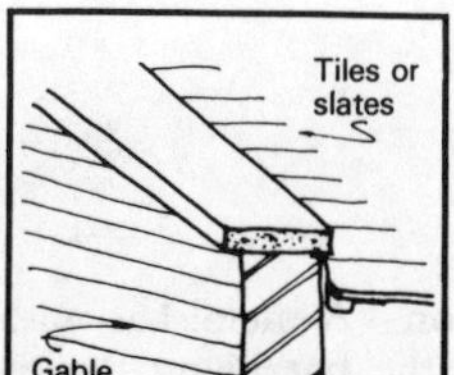

GABLE COPING

gable end A **gable**. Often used loosely to mean the **gable wall**; that end of the building which includes the gable.

gable post A short post at the apex of a **gable** used to secure the heads of the **barge boards**.

gable roof A **roof** with **gables** at each end.

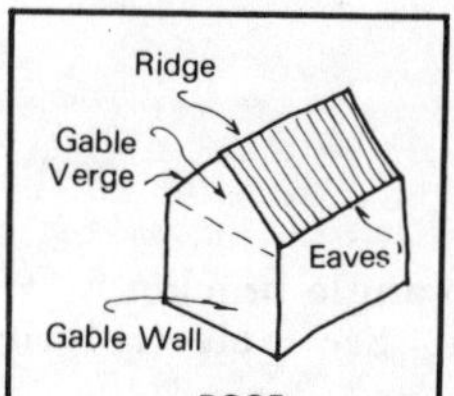

ROOF

gable shoulder The projection at the foot of a **gable coping** formed by the **gable springer**.

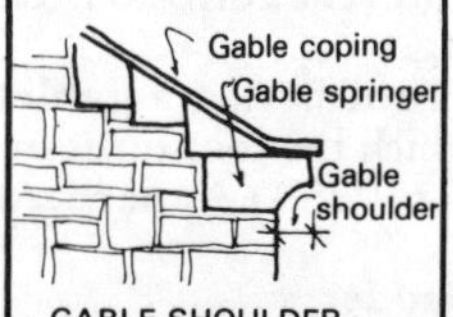

GABLE SHOULDER

gable springer An overhanging stone at the foot of a **gable coping** below the lowest **kneeler**.

gablet 1. A small gable over a dormer or in a **gambrel roof**. 2. A small gable-like decoration as, for example, over a niche or other opening.

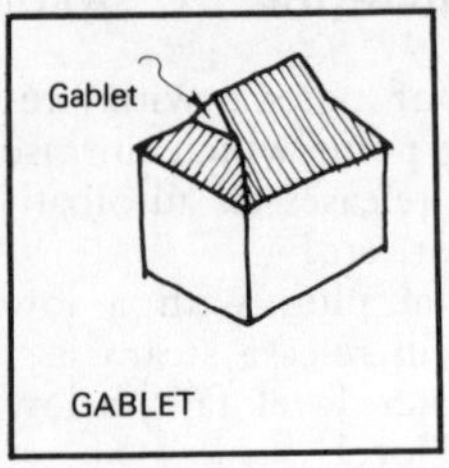

gable wall A wall surmounted by a **gable**.
gain A **mortise** or notch prepared to receive another timber or timber **connector**.
gallet A chip or splinter of stone.
galleting 1. The setting of small pieces of plain tile in mortar to form a seating for the ridge tile (and, sometimes, the hip) in **pantile** or **single lap tile** roofs; the small pieces of tile set thus. 2. The setting of **gallets** in the joints between rough masonry as decoration; the gallets set thus.

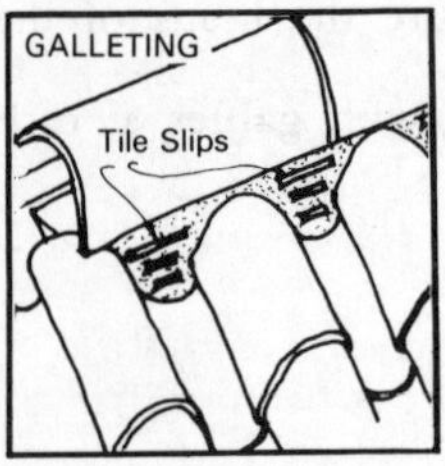

gallows bracket An **angle bracket**.
galvanic corrosion See **electrolytic corrosion**.
galvanized wire Wire which has been coated with zinc, the quality of the galvanizing being defined by a reference letter denoting the weight of the coating, its evenness and adherence.
galvanizing The coating of a ferrous metal with zinc to prevent corrosion. cf. **hot dip galvanizing**.
gambrel roof 1. A **roof** having a **gablet** at its apex, below which the roof turns into a **hipped roof**. 2. (USA) A **mansard roof**.
gang-board A **cat ladder**.
gangnail A punched plate fastener for timber joints with teeth punched out of the galvanized steel plate.
gang saw A **frame saw**.
gangway A temporary pathway made of **scaffold boards** to make access easier for men and wheelbarrows on rough sites.
gap-filling glue An adhesive specially formulated to stick surfaces together which are not smooth enough or in close enough contact to allow a **close-contact adhesive** to be used.
gap-graded aggregate A concrete mix made using a single size of **coarse aggregate**; used particularly for exposed aggregate finishes.
Garchey system A system for the conveyance by water, and the disposal at a central plant, of the bulk of domestic refuse from multi-storey dwellings. (Bottles, cans, etc. cannot be disposed of by this system).
garden wall bond See **English** and **Flemish garden wall bond**. A cheaper version of the particular type of bond, used only when the load to be carried is low.
garnet A **gallet**.
gas circulator A gas-fired appliance, connected to a **cylinder** and designed to supply hot water to it continuously. It is smaller and more efficient than **instantaneous water heaters**.
gas concrete See **aerated concrete**.
gasket A device used to make watertight a joint in a building shell, or between building elements. Such devices vary from simple hemp fibres bound round the threads of a screwed joint in a water pipe, or used as a seal in the **spigot-and-socket joint** between drainage pipes, to neoprene gaskets used to form dry joints between wall panels. cf. **glazing gasket**.

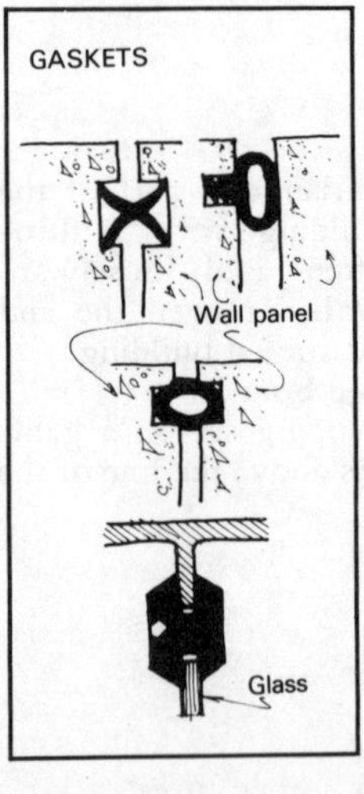

gate hook or gudgeon A metal bar with an upstanding pin, the bar being driven into a gate post or built into masonry, the pin receiving the gate hinge. cf. **band-and-hook hinge**.

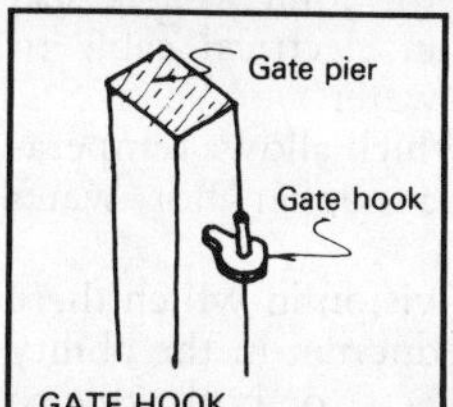

GATE HOOK

gate pier A gate post usually of brick, concrete or stone.

gate post Generally a timber post on which a gate is hung or against which a gate shuts.

gather To collect the **flues** from several fireplaces or other combustion appliances together into a **stack**.

gathering The contracting portion of the chimney passage, situated a short distance above the fireplace opening and reducing the passage to the size of the flue.

gauge 1. The proportions of different materials in a mortar or plaster mix. 2. To mix two or more materials in predetermined proportion. 3. The top to bottom measurement of the exposed part of a **slate** or **tile** (*ie* the distance between the bottom of the course above, to the bottom of the slate or tile in question). This is equivalent to the centres at which the battens are fixed. For **centre-nailed slates** the gauge equals

$$\frac{\text{length} \times \text{lap}}{2}$$

4. A wooden or metal boundary strip, similar to a plastering **screed**, used in asphalting. 5. To accelerate the hardening of plaster by the addition of **additives**. 6. The thickness of a metal sheet or strip or an instrument for determining such thickness. 7. Of bolts, the perpendicular distance between two adjacent lines of bolts when the lines of bolts are parallel to the direction of stress in the joint. cf. **pitch** (7).

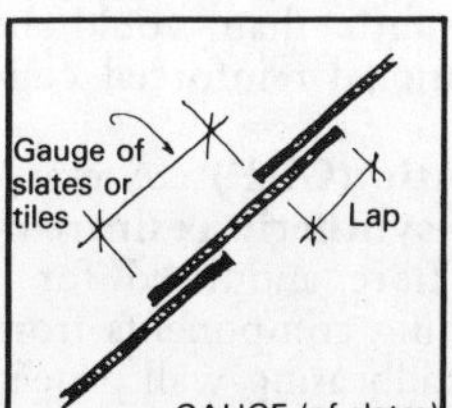

GAUGE (of slates)

gauge board A board about 900 mm square, usually on a stand, for carrying **plaster** and plastering tools during the application of plaster. cf. **gauging board**.

gauge (or gauging) box A **batch box**.

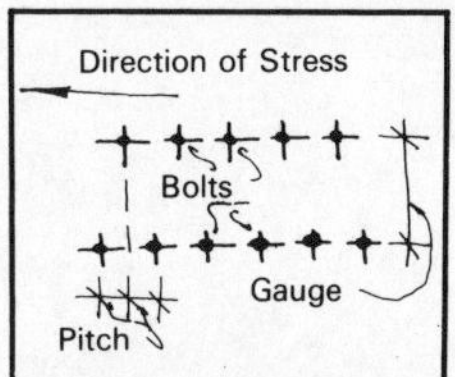

GAUGE (of Bolts)

gauged arch An **arch** built using **gauged bricks** with very fine joints.

gauged brick A soft brick, sometimes referred to as a **rubber**, used for forming **gauged arches** etc., because it can be rubbed on a stone or another brick to the exact shape required; now rarely used in this country.

gauged mortar **Mortar** which contains lime as well as cement and sand in proportions suitable for the bricks or blocks used. This produces a more workable mix then ordinary mortar and although less strong, it is more resilient and less inclined to shrink and cause cracking.

gauge rod A **storey rod**.

gauging 1. Making additions to a plaster mix to accelerate hardening. 2. Sawing or rubbing **gauged bricks** to size.

gauging board A **banker** for mixing mortar or plaster. cf. **gauge board**.

gaul A hollow in the **finishing-coat** of plaster.

G-cramp A steel screw cramp in the shape of the letter G, used to hold together components being glued.

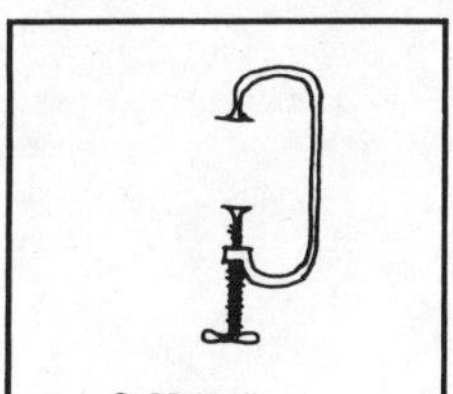
G-CRAMP

general arrangement drawing Drawing showing layout of a building or the components of its shell.

geometrical stair A **stair** with a continuous **string** round a semi-circular or elliptical well, having no **newel posts** and often no **landings**.

Georgian glass **Plate glass** with a reinforcement of square mesh steel wire embedded in it.

German siding **Weather-boaring** in which the boards are concavely rounded on their top edge and rebated on the inside of the bottom edge.

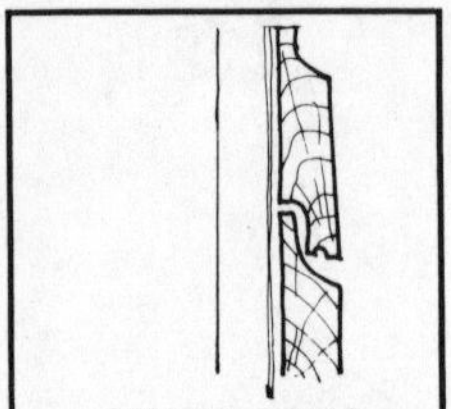
GERMAN SIDING

geyser An **instantaneous water heater** which delivers water to one fitting (or two adjacent fittings, if provided with a swivel nozzle) discharging directly over the fitting and not through a pipe, controlled by a tap.

gimlet A small tool for boring holes up to 6 mm in diameter in wood, having its handle at right angles to its axis. cf. **awl** and **bradawl**.

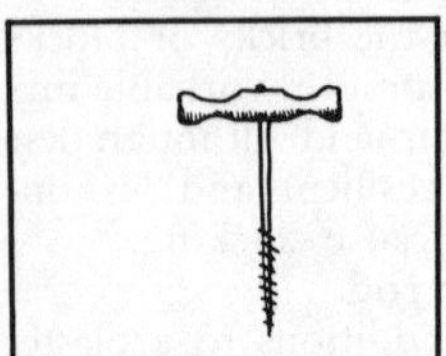
GIMLET

gimlet point The type of point on a **wood screw** which is intended to form at least part of its own hole and grip the wood at its point.

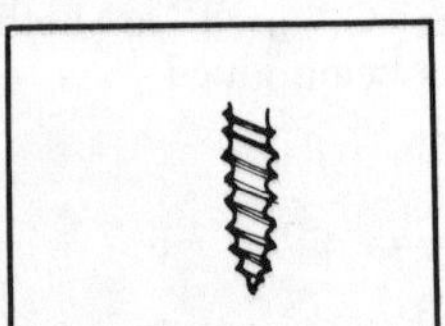
GIMLET POINT

gimp pin A small steel pin with a large flat round head and used particularly to fix upholstery materials to timber framework. Lengths are from 12.7 to 25.4 mm; diameters from 1.2 to 1.6 mm.

girder Originally, a main beam in floor construction; now generally applied to any built-up beam designed to support a heavy load.

girth The circumference of a round timber; circumferential measure of thickness.

girth strip A **ribbon board**.

gland 1. A compressible copper or brass ring used in a **non-manipulative joint** which is slipped over the tube and compressed and deformed on tightening the fitting, thus sealing the joint. 2. A seal used at the end of an electrical cable to prevent the entry of water.

gland joint A joint which allows temperature movement in a copper hot water pipe.

glare A condition of vision in which there is discomfort or a reduction in the ability to see significant objects, or both, due to an unsuitable distribution or range of luminance, or to extreme contrasts, or to a visible light source.

glass A transparent or translucent material used to allow the penetration of natural light into a building. Glass is in several forms; **float glass**, **heat-absorbing glass**, **obscured glass**, **plate glass**, **sheet glass** and **glass blocks**.

glass block or glass brick A hollow, translucent, non-loadbearing block made of glass and with a pattern moulded on to one or both faces to give a diffused light. It is used particularly in walls. (Glass blocks or lenses used in **pavement lights** are solid and are divided by reinforced concrete ribs; hence the obsolete expression 'glass-concrete construction').

glass cutter A tool which cuts glass by means of a diamond or a sharp, hard-metal wheel.

glass fibre Flexible fibres made from molten glass and used as reinforcement in **glass reinforced concrete** and **glass reinforced plastic**; it is also used in thermal insulation materials.

glasspaper An **abrasive** paper, not necessarily always composed of glass (flint, garnet, corundum and similar powders are used), in which the fine grit is bonded to cloth or paper and is used for smoothing many types of surfaces, particularly wood. There are several grades of fineness of grit.

glass reinforced concrete (GRC) A form of precast concrete which, because of the addition of glass fibre, is capable of producing thin panels with greater impact resistance and strength than could be obtained in conventional reinforced concrete.

glass reinforced plastic (GRP) A material produced by a **synthetic resin** reinforced with glass fibre and used for a wide range of building components from rooflights to non-loadbearing wall panels.

glass size The **glazing size**.

glass slate or glass tile A piece of glass made to the size of a slate or tile and laid along with the roofing in order to admit light into simple, un-insulated roof spaces which are not **under-drawn**; now largely obsolete.

glass stop 1. A **glazing bead**. 2. A device at the lower end of a **patent glazing** bar which prevents the glass panes from sliding down the bar.

glass wool **Glass fibre**.

glaze 1. To install glass in any sort of **light**. 2. A glass-like finish fired on to the surface of ceramic sanitary fittings, bricks and tiles, which provides waterproof protection and can be transparent, coloured or white. 3. To produce a glass-like finish on a material. 4. A **glaze coat**.

glaze coat A practically transparent coat of coloured paint put on in a thin coat to enhance the colour below.

glazed brick A brick with a surface that has been **glazed**.

glazed tile A ceramic **wall tile** (or, occasionally, floor tile) which has been **glazed** on its exposed surface to provide a decorative and long-lasting finish.

glazed ware or glazed stoneware Ceramic pipes and fittings used in drainage and **glazed** by the vapour of common salt thrown into the kiln during firing.

glazier's chisel A **putty knife** shaped like a chisel.

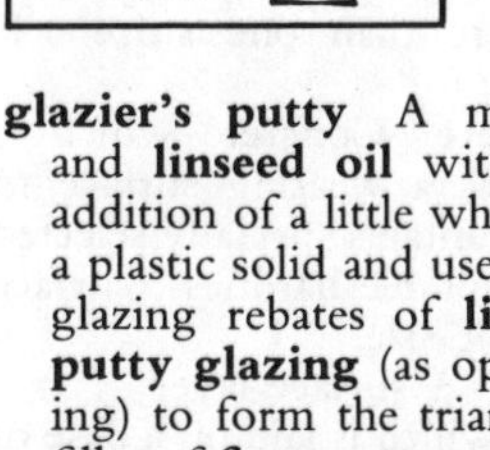

GLAZIER'S CHISEL

glazier's putty A mixture of **whiting** and **linseed oil** with, occasionally, the addition of a little white lead, produced as a plastic solid and used to bed glass in the glazing rebates of **lights**. Also used in **putty glazing** (as opposed to bead glazing) to form the triangular weatherproof fillet of **face putty** outside the glass.

glazing 1. The glass set in a **light**. 2. The act of setting glass in a light by means of putty, etc. or of furnishing a building with windows.

glazing bar A rebated wood or metal member which holds the glass in a window, rooflight or area of **patent glazing**.

glazing bead A small wooden or metal member, mitred at its corners, which holds the glass in place in the rebate of a window or door frame in **bead glazing**.

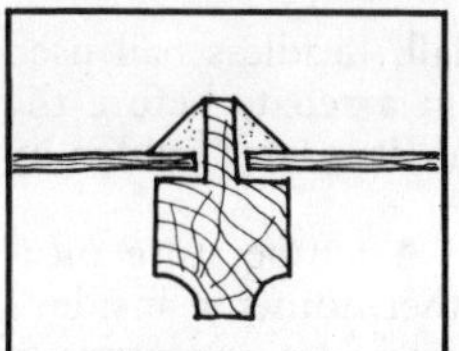

GLAZING BAR

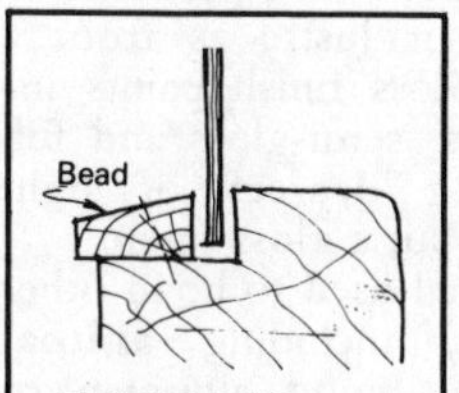

GLAZING BEAD

glazing compound A **sealant** used as an alternative to **glazier's putty** in glazing. It has a longer life, but is used only in **bead glazing**.

glazing gasket A **neoprene** (or similar) extrusion designed to retain glass within a frame and give a watertight joint without the use of a glazing **sealant**.

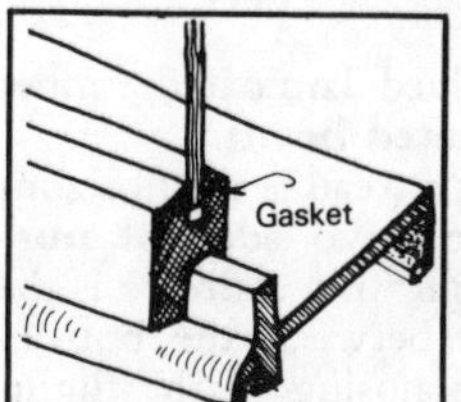

GLAZING GASKET

glazing rebate A **rebate** cut in glazing bars or window frames to receive the glass.

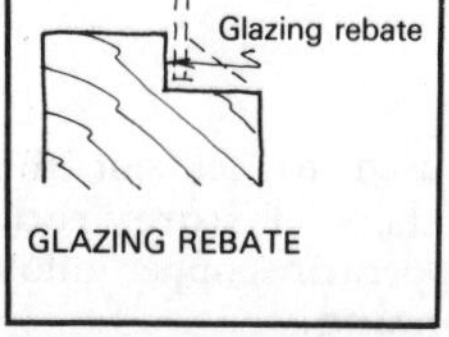

GLAZING REBATE

glazing size The true size of a piece of glass cut for glazing a particular aperture; usually about 3 mm less than the clear opening into which the glass fits to allow for thermal movement, though this dimension may be modified in the case of special types of glass, such as **heat-absorbing glass**.

glazing sprig A small, headless nail used to secure the glass in a rebate before the **face putty** is applied. It is later hidden by the face putty.

global temperature A temperature measured by using a thermometer inside a blackened globe. It provides a measure of the combined effect of **air temperature** and **mean radiant temperature** of a room, giving a **comfort temperature**.

gloss 1. Brightness or lustre as from a polished surface. Gloss finish paints include eggshell gloss, semi-gloss and full gloss in increasing degrees of light reflectance. 2. To put a gloss upon.

glue A liquid material used to bond other materials together, including **animal glue**, **casein glue**, blood albumen or soluble dried blood glues, vegetable glues, protein glues and **synthetic resin adhesives**. All have different performance characteristies in respect of water resistance, method and speed of set and gap-filling. cf. **gap filling glue**.

glue block An **angle block**.

glue kettle A pot, with a water jacket outside in the form of a larger pot, used for heating up animal glue.

glue line The thin surface of glue between two components.

glulam beam A glued laminated timber member. cf. **laminated beam**.

going The going of a tread is the horizontal distance between two adjacent **nosings**; that of the flight of a staircase is the horizontal distance between the bottom nosing and the top nosing of the flight. cf. **stair**.

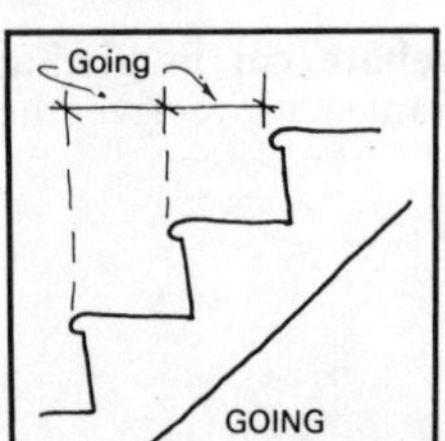

GOING

going rod A rod used to set out the **going** of a **flight** of stairs. cf. **storey rod.**

gold bronze A copper or copper alloy powder used in **bronzing**.

gold size 1. An **oleo-resinous paint** used to fix gold leaf. It quickly becomes tacky but hardens slowly. 2. An oleo-resinous varnish, with a high proportion of **driers**, used to make **filler**.

gold stoving varnish A transparent **varnish** which gives a yellow film on bright silvery surfaces, such as tin plate, by discoloration during **stoving.**

goods lift A **lift** used primarily to transport goods rather than people. cf. **passenger lift**.

gouge 1. A joiner's tool for hollowing out wood; used by carvers. 2. A mason's tool for carving stone.

gouge bit A **bit** with a rounded end.

gouge slip An **oilstone slip**.

graded aggregate **Aggregate** containing proportions, within specified limits, of different sized particles to ensure a dense concrete mix.

gradient Slope or inclination expressed as one unit vertically to the relevant number of units horizontally of the slope to the horizontal. The same ratio may be expressed as a percentage.

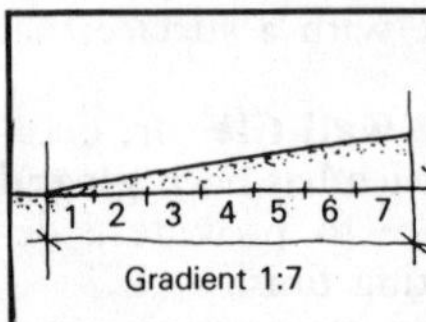

GRADIENT

graduated courses **Diminishing courses**.

graffito See **sgraffito**.

grain The pattern created by the annual rings and other growth patterns and fibre arrangements of wood.

graining The painting of a surface to resemble the grain of wood or the veining of marble, using a semi-transparent coating manipulated with combs, brushes or rags.

grand master key A key which operates the locks of more than one **suite**. cf. **master key**.

granolithic concrete Concrete which is suitable for use as a wearing surface to floors because it contains specially selected **aggregate** of a suitable hardness, surface texture and particle size.

granolithic finish A surface layer of granolithic concrete which is laid on a base of fresh, green or hardened concrete. It provides a hard wearing surface because it contains specially selected **aggregate**. cf. **green concrete**.

grappler A wedge-shaped, eyed spike driven into a brick joint at the head of a **bracket scaffold**.

gravel board A horizontal board at the base of a **closed-boarded fence** to protect the end grain of the vertical boards which are vulnerable to rot: should it rot it can be easily replaced.

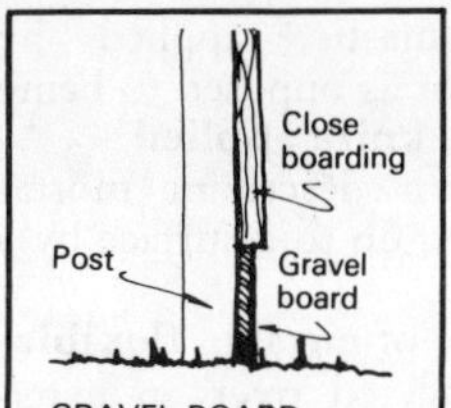

GRAVEL BOARD

gravel roof (USA) A flat roof of **bitumen felt** covered with a layer of gravel to protect it from solar radiation.

gravity circulation The movement of water in a hot water system which is not pumped, but whose flow is induced by the different densities of hot and cold water.

grease trap A large trapped **gully** fitted with a tray or basket within which grease congeals, thus preventing it from entering the drain and possibly causing a blockage.

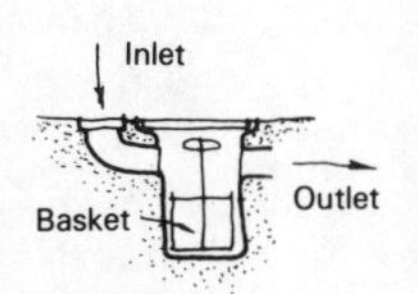

GREASE TRAP

greasiness A greasy surface on a paint film caused by a lack of **compatibility**.

green Term applied to bricks, concrete, timber, etc. in an unfinished or unseasoned state. cf. **green brick**, **green concrete**, **green timber**, etc.

green brick A clay brick before burning.

green concrete or green mortar Concrete or mortar which has taken its initial set but has not properly hardened. With normal **Portland cement** this state can exist for up to seven days and is associated with the concrete (or mortar) having a dark, greenish colour.

green stress The **stress** in timber with a moisture content in excess of 18% cf. **dry stress**.

green timber Unseasoned timber with a moisture content of around 50%.

grid line One of the basic lines forming the grid on a **grid plan**.

grid plan A plan in which a regular grid of lines in one direction or both directions coincides with a major structural components' centre lines or edges. **Dimensional co-ordination** systems are based on the application of a discipline of grid lines.

grille 1. An open screen of metal or wood used for security purposes or simply for decoration. 2. A grating through which air passes. It has no control arrangement (unlike a **register**).

grinder An **abrasive** wheel, usually power operated, for sharpening tools etc.

grinding slip An **oilstone slip**.

grindstone An abrasive wheel of natural sandstone turned at a relatively slow rate so as not to spoil the **temper** of the steel tools it is used to sharpen.

grinning through The showing of one coat of paint through another, due to inadequate thickness of the final coat, or to the incompatibility of the two paints, etc.

grit blasting The cleaning of a surface of metal, stone, concrete or brickwork by abrasion with a spray of fine grit. cf. **sand blasting** and **shot blasting**).

grommet or grummet 1. A device, similar to a washer, used to render a pipe **connector** waterlight. 2. Any small rubber plug used to seal a hole, particularly in thin metal.

ground 1. A **rough ground**. 2. Any surface that is, or will be, painted. 3. The first coat of paint, as in **ground coat**. 4. (USA) **Earth**.

ground beam A beam supporting the base of a wall, and spanning between either independent **pad foundations** or **pile caps**.

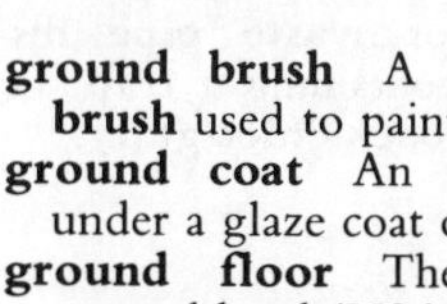

GROUND BEAM

ground brush A large round or oval **brush** used to paint large areas.

ground coat An opaque coat put on under a glaze coat or **scumble**.

ground floor The floor nearest the ground level (USA; the first floor).

ground floor plan The drawing comprising a horizontal section through the ground floor of a building, the section being usually located just above window sill level.

ground plate The **sole plate** of a timber framed building.

ground sill A **sole plate**.

ground water Water occurring naturally in the subsoil at or below the water table.

groundwork 1. Battens over boarding or **sarking felt** to received roof **tiles** or **slates**. 2. Literally, site work which takes place in the ground; *ie* excavation, drainlaying etc.

grout The material worked into the normal joints between tiles or slabs, also the material used to fill in voids in a wearing surface after grinding and before final polishing.

growth ring **Annual ring**.

grub saw A saw for hand cutting stone.

grub screw A headless, parallel-sided screw with a driving slot cut in one end, used to completely pass inside a threaded hole, as in the fixing of some door knobs.

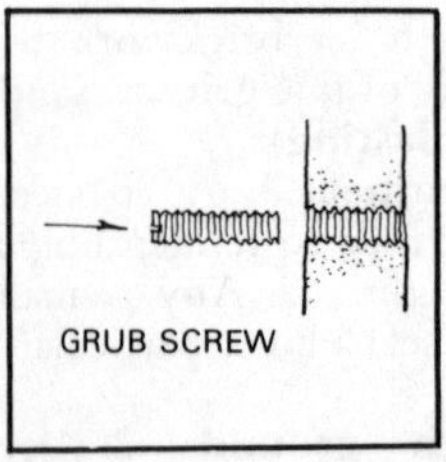

guard bead A bead mitred round the inside of a **sash window** to contain the lower sash.

guard board An on-edge **scaffold board** used to prevent objects from falling off the edge or a platform.

guard rail A handrail to a high level walkway or platform; particularly applied to scaffolding, or working or access walkways in industrial plant areas.

gudgeon 1. A metal dowel for locking together neighbouring stones. 2. A **gate hook**.

guillotine A trimming machine.

gullet The space between the teeth of a file or saw, also the length of a saw tooth from point to root.

gully or gulley A drain fitting over which **fall pipe** or **waste pipe** discharges; a usually containing a **trap**. cf. **trapped gully** and **back-inlet gully**.

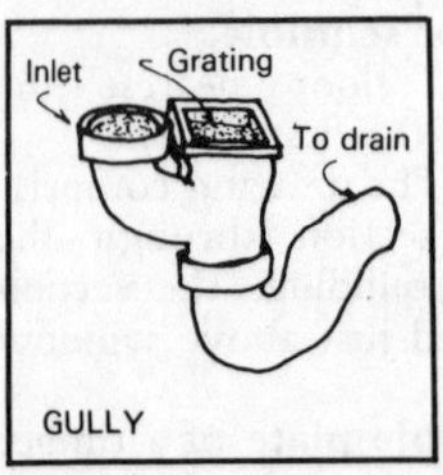

gummy Term applied to a sticky paint which has a heavy **drag** during brushing out.

gun applied Of mastic, applied by mechanical applicator as opposed to being applied by hand. cf. **knife applied**.

gunite A general term describing mortar or concrete projected on to a surface by a high pressure air jet.

gusset piece A piece of metal in **flexible-metal roofing** soldered over an external corner between the roof sheet and two adjacent vertical surfaces. cf. **dog ear**.

gutter A channel for the removal of rainwater, either on the edge of a road or roof or at the intersection of two roof planes. cf. **eaves gutter**, **box gutter**, **secret gutter** and **valley gutter**.

gutter bearer A short 50 × 50 mm timber which, with others, supports the boarding on which is laid the covering of a gutter, when the covering is metal, felt or asbestos based material.

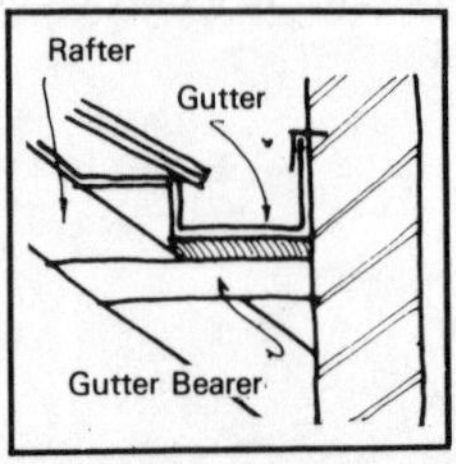

gutter board **Gutter bearer**.

gutter plate A **wall plate** below a metal-lined gutter.

gypsum ($CaSO_4$ $2H_2O$) The raw material of **gypsum plaster**, occurring naturally as alabaster, satin spar and selenite. Also used as an **extender** in some paints.

gypsum lath or gypsum plank Sheets of **gypsum plasterboard** in relatively narrow widths (600 mm), used for lining walls and ceilings, and usually scrimmed and skimmed. cf. **scrimming**, **skimming**.

gypsum plaster Plaster made by heating **gypsum** to drive off the water. There are various grades of gypsum plaster *eg* **anhydrous gypsum plaster**, **Keene's cement** (plaster) **plaster of Paris** and retarded **hemihydrate plaster**.

gypsum plasterboard or gypsum wallboard **Building board** with a core of **gypsum plaster** and a paper facing on both sides, in thicknesses from 9.5 to 19 mm. The board is either plastered or scrimmed and skimmed – or sometimes decorated directly with the joints covered with a **fillet** or (if the boards are feather-edged) filled. The feather-edged board is often referred to as gypsum wallboard. cf. **scrimming**, **skimming**.

H

hacking 1. A course of **rubble walling** in which single stones alternate with two stones, one above the other, to make up the depth of the course. 2. (USA) Laying bricks so that each course is inset from the course beneath; the opposite of **corbelling** 3. The process of making a surface rough in order to provide a key for rendering, etc.

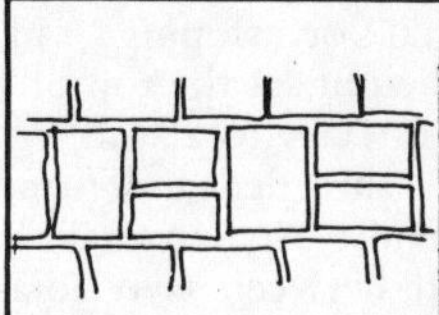

HACKING

hacking knife A knife used to remove old **putty** from a window frame before reglazing.

hacksaw A hand or mechanical saw for cutting metal, consisting of a thin, replaceable steel blade stretched tightly across a steel frame.

haft The handle of a tool such as a knife or an awl. cf. **helve**.

hair Animal hair used as reinforcement to lime plaster undercoats; now rarely used.

hair cracking Fine, random, cracking of a finishing coat (plaster, paint etc.) or concrete.

half bat A half brick cut across the length. cf. **brick**.

half-brick wall A brick wall that is the thickness of the width of a brick, thus being entirely constructed of **stretchers** (*ie* 113 mm thick).

half hatchet (USA) A carpenter's **hatchet** with a notch for drawing nails.

half-lap joint A joint formed by halving. cf. **halving (or halved) joint**.

half principal A **rafter** which does not reach the **ridge** of a roof.

half rip-saw A **hand-saw** with smaller teeth set closer together than is usual in an ordinary **rip-saw**. It is designed for cutting timber along the grain.

half-round Semi-circular.

half-sawn stone A quantity surveying term referring to a stone that has been sawn, half the cost of the cut being charged to the stone on each side of the cut.

half-space landing A **landing** joining two flights of opposed **stairs** between two storeys and extending across the width of both flights.

half span roof A lean-to roof. cf. **roof**.

halving or halved joint A method of forming an **angle joint** or a **lengthening joint** between two pieces of timber of equal thickness, in which half the thickness of each timber is cut away and the cut surfaces are placed together.

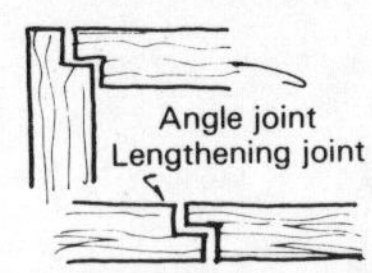

HALVING (OR HALVED) JOINTS

hammer A steel headed tool with a wood or metal handle which is set at right angles to the head. One end of the head (the **face**) is used for driving nails etc. the other end (the **peen**) may be hemispherical (**ball peen hammer**), or wedge-shaped (**cross peen** or **straight-peen hammer**).

hammer beam The short, horizontal, cantilevered **beam** in a **hammer beam truss** at the springing level of the arch brace of the truss.

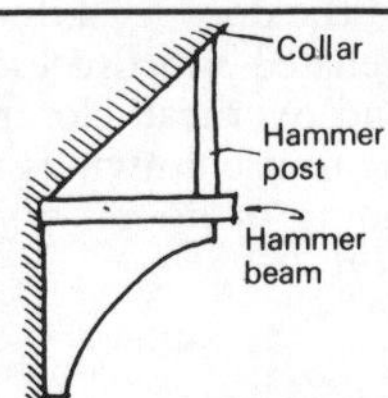

HAMMER BEAM

hammer beam truss A large timber roof truss developed in mediaeval times based on two horizontal and bracketed **hammer beams** at wall plate level, supporting vertical struts rising to the ends of a **collar beam** where it meets the **principal rafters**. The collar beam is set approximately halfway up the roof slope.

hammer-dressed stone Stone which has been roughly dressed at the quarry by means of a **hammer**.

hammer finish 1. A paint finish like hammered metal produced by spraying coloured enamel containing metal powder from a spray gun. 2. A finish obtained by **hammering**.

hammerhead The widening of a road at a dead-end, usually on one side of the road line only (single hammer head) to provide for vehicles turning. When the widening occurs on both sides of the road it is called a double hammerhead.

hammer-headed chisel Any mason's chisel with a flat conical steel head struck by a **hammer**, not a **mallet**.

hammer-headed key 1. A **double-dovetail key**. 2. A stone **cramp** like a **slate cramp**.

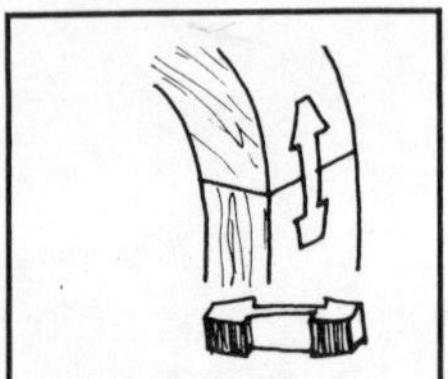
HAMMER-HEADED KEY

hammering Deforming sheet metal by hammering for decorative effect.

hammer post The post in a **hammer beam truss** with its base set on the **hammer beam**.

hand Term applied to a door or casement window which, in the UK, is said to be right-handed if the hinges are on the right hand side of the leaf when viewed from the side into which the leaf opens. In the USA, however, the terminology differs, and even in the UK various items of ironmongery are also handed and may not correspond to the hand of the door (*eg* a door needing a left hand rebated mortise lock could need a right hand overhead closer). It is therefore advisable to use drawings to communicate the handing of doors, windows and ironmongery.

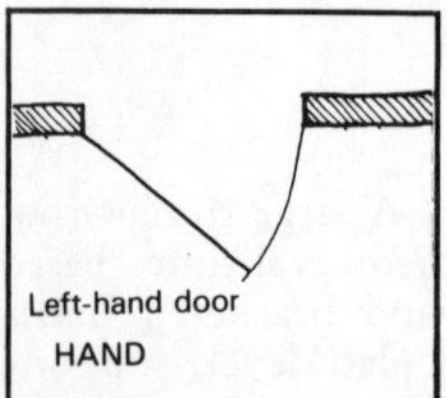

HAND

hand brace A carpenter's **brace**.

hand drill A boring tool, operated by hand to form holes of limited diameter in wood or metal. cf. **breast drill**.

handed A description of a building element which (as in doors and casement windows) can be either left or right-handed. A handed pair refers to two objects; one right-handed, the other left-handed. cf. **hand**.

hand float A wooden tool approximately 100 × 300 mm used for applying the **finishing-coat** of plaster.

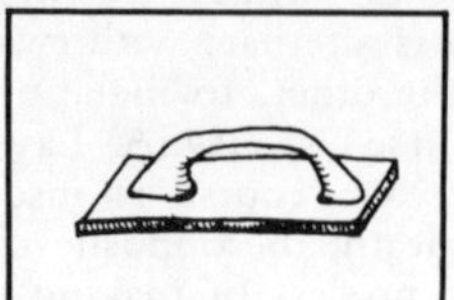
HAND FLOAT

handrail A horizontal or sloping rail, usually about waist height, at the top of a **balustrade** or fixed directly to a wall.

handrail bolt A bolt threaded and fitted with a nut at both ends; used to make a concealed connection between two adjacent lengths of **handrail**.

handrail punch A tool used to tighten the notched circular nut at one end of a **handrail bolt**.

handrail screw 1. A **dowel screw**. 2. A **handrail bolt**.

handrail scroll A spiral end to a **handrail**.

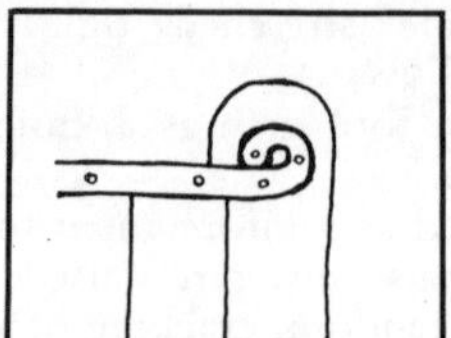
HANDRAIL SCROLL

handsaw Any saw held in the hand; *eg* **cross-cut saw**, **rip-saw**, **tenor saw** etc.

handscrew A **cramp**, usually with wooden jaws and screws.

hang 1. To fit a door or window by hinges into its frame. 2. To apply wallpaper to a wall by means of paste. 3. To suspend curtains from a rail or track by means of rings or hooks.

hanger 1. A vertical member, usually of steel strip, used to carry the weight of a suspended element (*eg* a suspended ceiling). 2. A **stirrup strap**.

hanging gutter (USA) A metal or plastic **eaves gutter** fastened to **rafter** ends or a **fascia**.

hanging stile The stile of a door or casement window to which the hinges are screwed.

hardboard A compressed **fibre board**. There are various densities depending on the pressure employed in manufacture, and most hardboards have one smooth

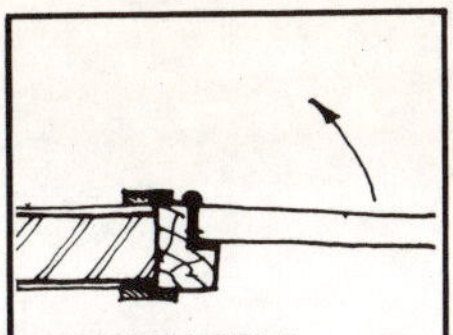
HANGING STILE

and one textured face. Thicknesses vary from 4 to 12 mm and sheet sizes from 1,200 or 1,500 mm wide × 2,400 or 2,700 mm long, although longer sheets are available. Varied face treatments can be obtained such as plastic faced, metal faced, veneer faced and other decorative or embossed surface treatments.

hard burnt 1. Describes a clay brick or tile burnt at high temperature, to give great compressive strength and low absorption. 2. A term applied to hard plasters like **Keene's cement**.

hardcore Consolidated broken brick or gravel used to form a level bed under next-to-earth concrete slabs and pavings of other materials.

hard dry A stage in the drying of paint when it is dried throughout its depth and nearly free from tackiness at which stage it can be flatted or another coat may be applied.

hardener A component of some **adhesives** which promotes setting. It can be in liquid or powder form.

hard finish A smooth plaster **finishing-coat** containing **gypsum plaster.**

hardness A term signifying, in general, resistance to cutting, indentation and/or abrasion. It is measured by various hardness tests depending on the material in question. cf. **international rubber hardness degree**.

hard plaster Plasters intended to resist impact; the hardest being cement/sand rendering, followed by **Keene's cement**. Gypsum plasters are harder than lime plasters.

hard putty **Hard stopping**.

hard solder Any solder which does not melt below red heat.

hard stopping A **filler** containing **plaster of Paris** which is mixed from powder into a stiff paste with water and used to fill deep holes in a **ground**.

hardware A loose term for **architectural ironmongery**.

hard water Water containing calcium and magnesium salts in solution. This causes difficulty in making a soap lather, and there is also danger of the salts being deposited in hot water pipes and boilers. cf. **furring**.

hardwood Wood from broad-leaved deciduous trees; all hardwoods are not necessarily hard.

hardwood floor block An element in a floor finish made up of many similar blocks. Each block is of hardwood, not less than 19 mm thick × not more than 88 mm wide and between 150 and 375 mm long.

harl 1. (Scotland) **Rough cast**. 2. To apply rough cast.

harling See **harl.**

hasp A hinged slotted arm or plate. cf. **hasp and staple**.

hasp and staple A simple fastening device consisting of a **hasp** which passes over a **staple**, through which is placed a padlock or peg.

HASP AND STAPLE

hatchet A small axe held with one hand; used for splitting or rough-dressing timber.

hatchet iron A **soldering iron** shaped like a hatchet.

haunch The abbreviated stump portion of a tenon, taking up the full width of the timber out of which it is formed, at the root of a **haunched tenon**.

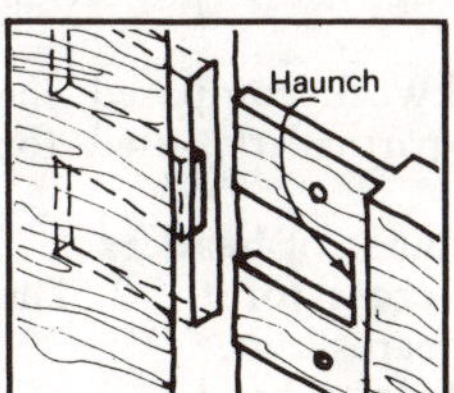

HAUNCH

haunched tenon A tenon from the width of which a part has been cut away, though not from the whole length of the tenon, leaving a haunch or stub tenon at its root.

haunching 1. Concrete round the sides of a buried stoneware drain pipe to support it above the bedding concrete. 2. A stub mortise for a **haunch**.

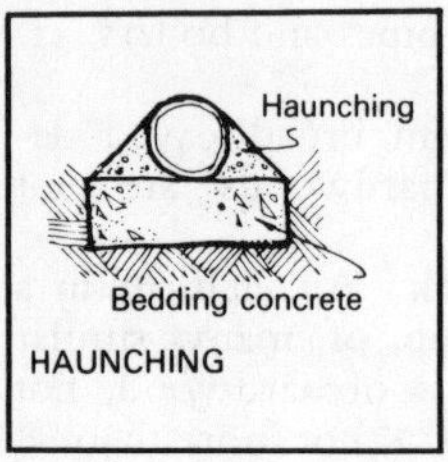

hawk A small board (300 × 300 mm) with a handle beneath, for carrying **mortar** or **plaster**.

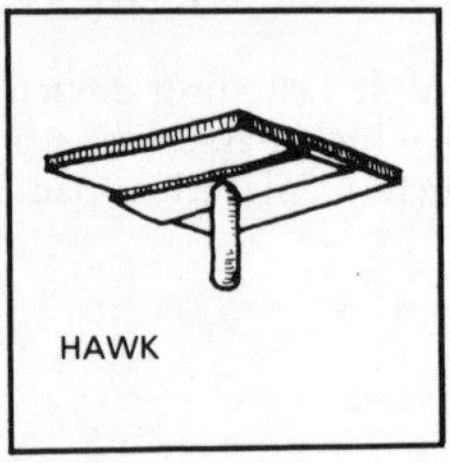

head 1. The upper member of a frame (door, window, **stud partition** etc.). 2. The upper part or capital of a column. 3. The larger end of a bolt or screw or nail. 4. The working end of a hammer. 5. The upper end of a slate.

head casing (USA) That part of an external architrave over the **head** of a door, usually capped with a **weathering** (drip cap).

header 1. A **brick** laid so that its length is at right angles to the face of the wall, so as to expose its short end. cf. **stretcher**. 2. (USA) **A trimmer joist** (sometimes referred to as a header joist).

head flashing A **flashing** like a small gutter round the edge of a projection through a roof.

heading bond Brickwork composed entirely of **headers**, particularly used for curved walling.

heading course A course of **headers**.

heading joint 1. A **cross joint**. 2. The line on which two boards butt.

head jamb (USA) A **door head**.

head joint (USA) A **cross joint**.

head moulding A moulding over an opening.

head nailing The nailing of **slates** at about 25 mm from their **head**, giving two-slates cover over all nail holes, but less stability in exposed locations, than **centre nailing**.

headroom The clear height from floor to ceiling. In **stairs** it is measured vertically from the **nosing**.

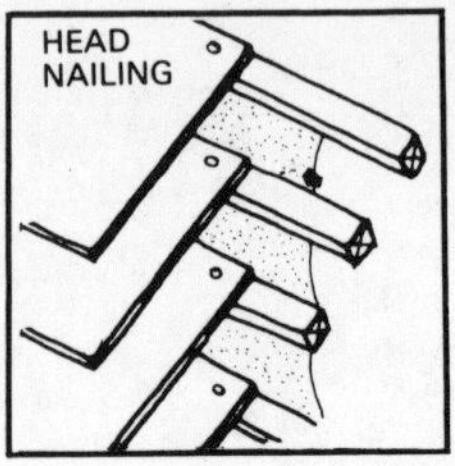

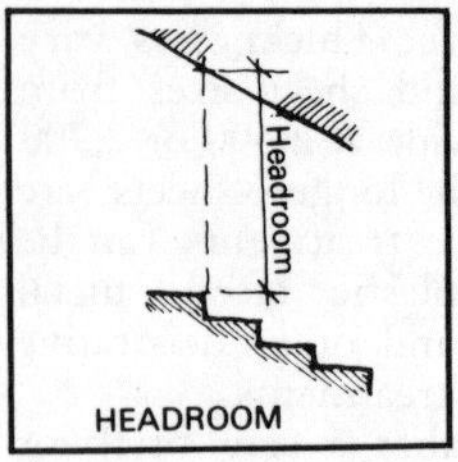

head weather moulding A small member framed into the **head** of a window frame to throw rainwater clear of the window.

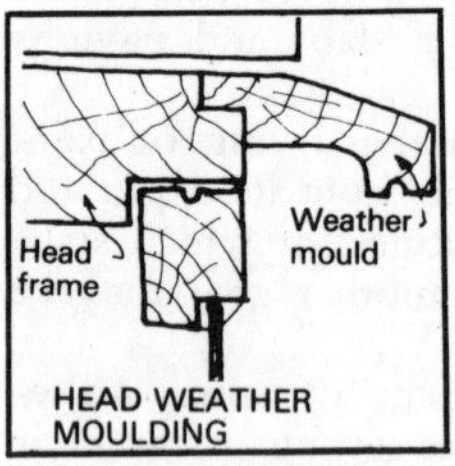

heart The centre of a log.

heart bond A bond in thick walls in which there are no **through stones**. Two **headers** meet in the centre of the wall with their joint covered by another header in the next course.

heartshake A radial **shake** originating in the heart of a log, in its **pith**.

hearth That non-combustible slab (stone or concrete) constructed below the position intended to be occupied by a fire. The hearth projects into the room to protect its floor or flooring from the danger of fire.

heartwood The dense and often dark-coloured wood which lies in the inner part of a trunk or branch; the superior timber in a log, as compared with the **sapwood**, which was the living tissue of the tree when felled and is softer and paler. cf. **pith**.

heat-absorbing glass A type of glass which does not allow the passage of some of the infra-red radiation of the sun. It also reduces some of the sun's visible spectrum.

heating See **central heating**, **storage heater**, **unit heater**, **radiant heater**, **convector** and **district heating**.

heat exchanger A device that passes heat from one liquid or gas to another, usually in the form of a network of tubes through which hot liquid flows, and which is set in a vessel in which the liquid to be heated is located. cf. **calorifier**.

heating element 1. The part of an electric heater which consists of a wire which is heated by the passage of an electric current. 2. Occasionally used to describe a finned pipe through which hot water passes and which is the means of warming air which is then distributed by convection currents.

heat insulation The **thermal resistance** of a material.

heat pump A heating device which transfers heat energy collected from a low temperature or low grade heat source (air, water or the ground) to a receiver (internal space, domestic hot water etc.) at a higher temperature.

heat-resistant paint (or enamel) **Paint** or **enamel** which may be used on hot surfaces and can be stoved at high temperatures.

heat treatment A process in which metal in the solid state is subjected to one or more temperature cycles to confer certain desired properties. Heating for the sole purpose of hot working is not included.

heavy-bodied paint 1. A viscous **paint**. 2. Paint that forms a strong film.

heel 1. The trailing end of a **plane**. 2. The lower end of the **hanging** stile of a door. 3. That part of a beam or **rafter** which rests on a support.

heel bead A strip of **glazing compound** or sealant between the edge of the glass and the frame in which it is set.

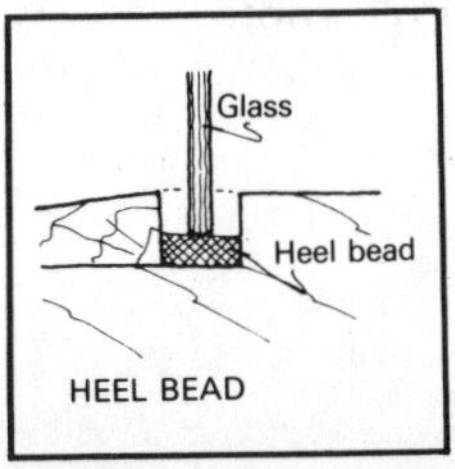

HEEL BEAD

height board A **storey rod**.

helical hinge A spring hinge for a swing door which is hung from its frame. cf. **floor spring**.

helve The handle of an axe, sledge hammer or similar heavy tool.

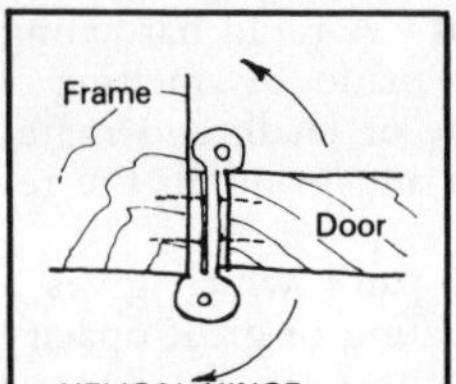

HELICAL HINGE

hemihydrate plaster A **gypsum plaster** in which **gypsum** ($CaSO_4$ $2H_2O$) is heated to drive off part of its water, becoming $CaSO_4.\frac{1}{2}H_2O$. This is the very quick-setting plaster called **plaster of Paris** and it has to be treated with a retarder additive to make it useful for normal plastering; hence retarded hemihydrate plaster.

herring-bone bond A form of **diagonal bond** or raking bond in which the bricks are laid to rake in opposite directions from the centre of the wall, to form a herring-bone on plan. It is a bond used also for brick pavings or rectangular tile pavings.

herring-bone matching **Book matching**.

herring-bone pattern The pattern formed by the laying of elements, such as brick pavers, to slope in different directions in alternate rows.

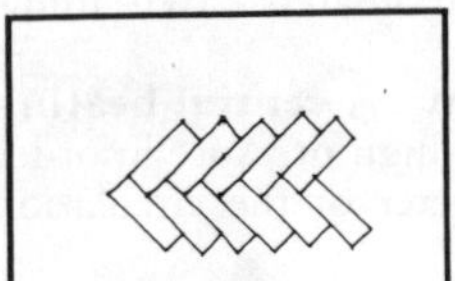

HERRING-BONE PATTERN

herring-bone strutting The light diagonal timber strutting fixed crosswise between **common joists** at their midspan to stiffen them.

hertz (Hz) A measure of **frequency**, *eg* the number of **cycles** per second produced in an alternating current supply (in the UK, 50 Hz).

hessian Coarse woven material of jute or hemp used to reinforce **fibrous plaster** and other materials (*eg* bitumen felt); also used as a decorative wall covering.

hew To shape timber with an axe or hatchet.

hewn stone **Hammer-dressed stone.**

H-hinge See **parliament hinge**.

hiding power The **opacity** of a paint. The power of a paint to obscure a black-and-white contrast.

high alumina cement A rapid hardening **hydraulic cement** made by melting a mixture of limestone or chalk and materials rich in alumina and grinding the resultant clinker.

high-build paint A paint which gives a particularly dense coating of great opacity or thickness; often the term refers to a textured paint.

high calcium lime A relatively pure lime (mainly CaO) giving a plastic putty. It can be mixed with **Portland cement**.

high density plywood **Plywood** manufactured at high pressures to form a much denser plywood than normal it has great strength but, generally, cannot be bent or nailed and has to be worked with metal-working tools.

highlighting Emphasizing the relief of a surface either by painting the raised portions a lighter colour or by means of artificial lighting.

high pressure mercury vapour lamp A lamp in which the light emission is produced by an electric discharge in mercury vapour at high pressure with or without the assistance of a fluorescent or translucent coating to the interior of the glass envelope.

high pressure sodium vapour lamp A **sodium vapour lamp** in which the partial pressure of the vapour during operation is approximately 100 millibars.

high-pressure system A **central heating** system operating at high pressure in order to reduce the diameter of the circulation pipes required

high strength friction grip bolt A bolt made of high-tensile steel, used in conjunction with high-tensile-steel nuts and hardened-steel washers, which is tightened to a predetermined **shank** tension. This tension produces a clamping force which transfers the loads between the connected members by friction and not by shear in, or bearing on, the bolt or plies of the connected members.

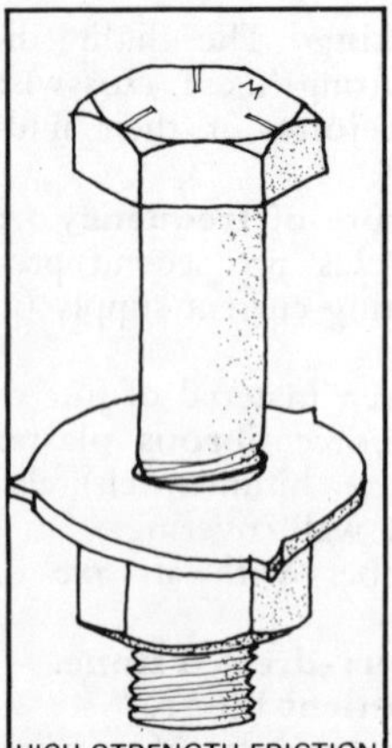

HIGH STRENGTH FRICTION GRIP BOLT

hinge A metal, pinned connection between, for example, a door, a gate or a casement window and its frame. There are many types of hinge including **butt, back-flap**, **band and look**, **counter flap**, **helical lift-off butt**, **parliament** and **rising butt**. Some types of hinge are symmetrical and are therefore not **handed;** others come in left-handed and right-handed versions.

hinge-bound door A door whose hinges have been too deeply set into the frame and which is therefore difficult to shut.

hip The external edge of the meeting of two roof slopes which occurs when the building is not provided with a **gable**. cf. **hipped roof**.

hip bath A bath in which one bathes in a sitting position.

hip capping 1. The top strip of roofing felt or other protection over a **hip**. 2. **Weaving**.

hip hook A curved metal bar fixed to a **hip rafter** and projecting upwards to hold the lowest **hip tile** in place.

hip knob A finial to a ridge where it meets a **hip**.

hipped end The sloping triangular end to a **hipped roof**.

hipped gable roof A roof which is hipped from the ridge to part of the way to the **eaves** and gabled from there downwards; the reverse of a **gambrel roof**. cf. **roof**.

hipped roof A roof having four slopes as opposed to two in a gable roof. The smaller slopes are triangular and are referred to as **hipped ends** and are bounded on their upper edges by **hips**. cf. **roof**.

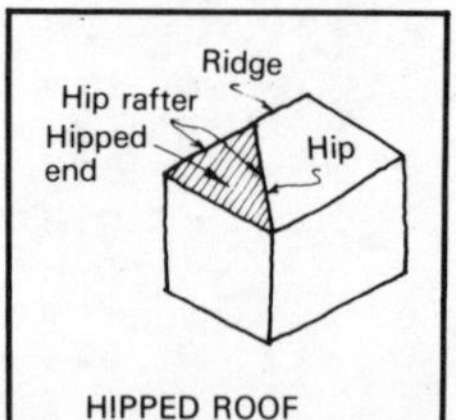

HIPPED ROOF

hip rafter A rafter forming a hip and on to which the **jack rafters** are spiked.

hip roll A round timber member with a V-cut in its underside to cover a **hip**, or its flexible-metal covering.

hip tile Clay, concrete or asbestos-cement tile which covers the ends of the roof tiles which abut in a **hip,** thereby rendering the angle waterproof. They can be angular, round or bonnet shaped. cf. **angular hip tile**, **bonnet tile**.

hoarding A high fence erected by a contractor round his site.

hod A timber or light metal tray, shaped like a box cut diagonally in two and fixed to a long handle; used for carrying bricks or mortar.

hoggin Coarse sand or fine **ballast**.

hogging The cambering of an otherwise horizontal surface or structural member.

hogsback tile A curved **ridge tile** which is parabolic rather than semi-circular in cross-section.

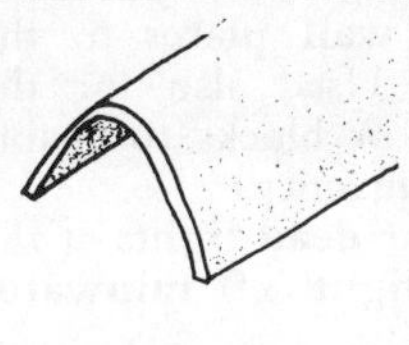

HOGSBACK TILE

holderbat A metal-collar fixing for a pipe, formed in two half-round parts capable of being clamped together and having a projecting leg on one part for fixing to a wall or, occasionally, a soffit.

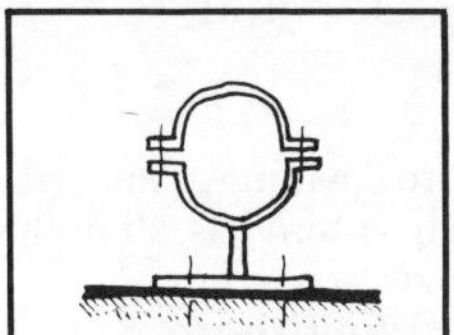

HOLDERBAT

holdfast A steel spike driven into a brickwork joint, with a flattened, eyed, piece on its outer end through which a fixing screw can be driven to fix joinery, etc.

holding-down bolt A bolt – often a **rag bolt** – which is cast into a concrete **foundation** or **foundation raft** and used to hold down steel or timber elements to the base.

holding-down clip In **flexible-metal roofing**, a folded clip shaped like a **capping**, but fixed to the roof **decking** to secure and join adjacent lengths of capping.

hole saw A drilling tool which greatly increases the diameter of hole that can be made with a normal drill. It consists of a tube with a serrated end which when revolved in the wood or metal cuts out a circular chase. It can be used for through drilling or merely cutting circular grooves for fixing shear plates or **split-ring connectors**.

holidays Areas of a surface which have been accidentally missed during painting.

holing Punching holes in slates by hand or machine.

hollow 1. A concave surface. 2. A **plane** for forming convex surfaces.

hollow-backed flooring Floorboards hollowed out on their undersides to improve both the ventilation and the bedding of the boards on the **joists**.

hollow bed A bed joint which is not filled in the middle. cf. **shell bedding**.

hollow block Concrete or burnt clay **building blocks** constructed with one or more cavities to increase lightness or thermal insulation. They are used to build external walls, partitions and **hollow tile floors**.

hollow chamfer A concave **chamfer**.

hollow clay tile See **hollow block**.

hollow-core flush door A **flush door** in which the facing plywood or hardboard is glued to a skeleton framework or core; a cheaper door than a solid-core door.

hollow glass block See **glass block**.

hollow partition 1. A **partition** built of hollow blocks. 2. A partition built in two leaves with a gap between for sound insulation or other purposes.

hollow plane See **hollow**.

hollow roll A **roll** used in the direction of fall to join flexible-metal sheet roofing and in which the adjacent sheets are bent together to form a cylindrical roll without the use of a **wood roll**.

hollow tile floor A concrete floor, originally of **in situ** construction in which lines of hollow clay blocks were included in the bottom of the slab, and concrete spines containing reinforcement ran between these lines. The hollow blocks reduced not only the amount of concrete required in the slab but also the overall weight of the slab. Today the most common floor using hollow blocks (clay or concrete) comprises precast concrete beams with blocks spanning between them and a topping of **in situ** concrete.

hollow wall 1. A **cavity wall**. 2. (USA) A wall built in two leaves, bonded together with bricks and not wall ties, as in a **rat-trap bond** wall.

hone or honestone A very smooth quartz stone used to finally sharpen a cutting tool after it has been rubbed on a coarse stone (**grindstone**). The surface is oiled before use. Hones can also be used for rubbing terrazzo or interior stonework. Honestone has been largely replaced now by emery and silicon carbide products.

honeycombing The separation of wood fibres due to drying stresses.

honeycomb slating **Diagonal slating** in which the slates have their tails cut off as well as their side points.

honeycomb wall A **half-brick wall** built in **stretcher bond** with a gap between the ends of stretchers thus providing the means of a ready passage of air; used particularly in **sleeper walls** under suspended timber ground floors.

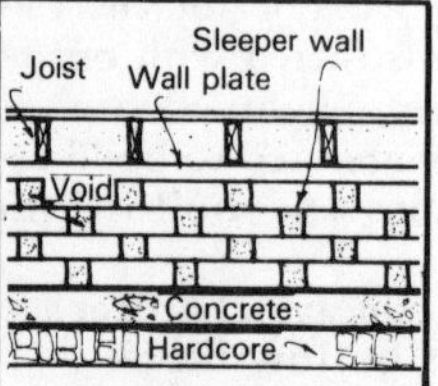

HONEYCOMB WALL

honing gauge A clamp to hold a **chisel** at a fixed angle whilst it is rubbed on a **hone.**

hood A canopy over a window, door, or other opening to throw off the rainwater.

hook The extension of the **cutting iron** past the **sole** of a plane.

hook-and-band hinge See **band-and-hook hinge**.

hook and eye A **cabin hook** and a **screw eye** in which it engages; used as a simple fastening for a door or casement window.

hook bolt A galvanized bolt formed out of a rod bent into a U bend at its unthreaded end and used to fix corrugated sheet cladding and roofing.

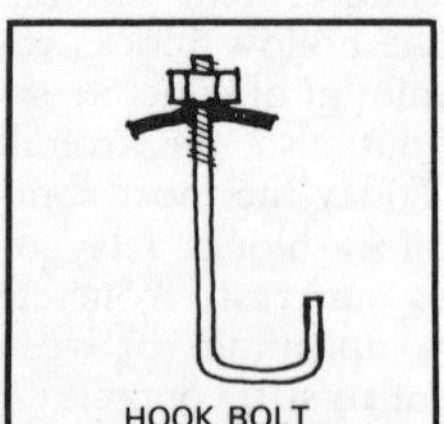

HOOK BOLT

hook bolt lock A lock having a hooked, rather than a straight, bolt.

Hooke's law The law stating that within the elastic range, the **strain** produced in a member is proportional to the **stress**.

hook joint A joint between the **meeting stiles** of doors, casements, etc. where an airtight seal is required, and in which the rebate in one stile is in an S-shape which fits into a similar groove in the other stile.

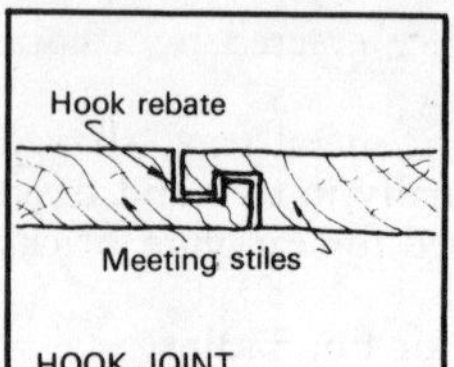

HOOK JOINT

hook rebate The S-shaped rebate in a **hook joint**.

hoop iron Thin strips of iron or steel used occasionally to reinforce bed joints of brickwork or hold **wall plates** to the brickwork beneath. Used also for the packaging of bricks or blocks to enable them to be lifted in quantity.

hopper The triangular **dead lights** at the sides of a **hopper light**. cf. **rainwater hopper**

hopper head A **rainwater hopper**.

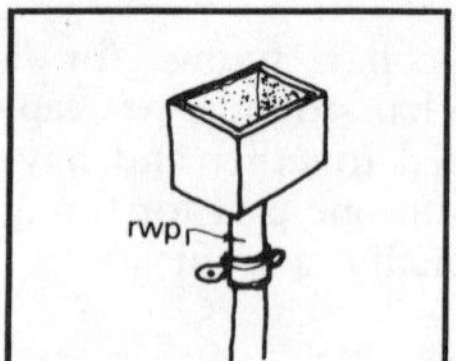

HOPPER HEAD

hopper light A bottom-hung, inward-opening **light** which often has draught preventing **hoppers** at each side.

horizontal shore A **flying shore**.

horn 1. An extension of the mortised member of a frame beyond the mortise to provide additional strength during wedging up or transportation; also used on frames with dowelled joints and usually trimmed off on site. 2. An extension of the stile beyond the meeting rail of a sash window to strengthen the frame and provide easier sliding; finished with a decorative moulding.

hose cock A tap with a nozzle that will connect to a hose pipe.

hose reel Fire fighting equipment, consisting of a length of tubing fitted with a shut-off nozzle and attached to a circular frame, with a permanent connection to a pressurized water supply.

hot-air seasoning The drying of timber in a **kiln**.

hot applied bitumen Bitumen applied in a molten state. cf. **cold asphalt**.
hot dip galvanizing The **galvanizing** of a component by dipping it in molten zinc, by which process alloy layers may be formed between the basic metal and the outer zinc layer. Under some circumstances the whole coating may consist of alloy layers, in which case the appearance may be grey or dull.
hotel lock A master-keyed lock having one or more of the following characteristics: a spring bolt which is operated by a handle on one side and a key on the other; a sliding bolt on the inside which prevents any key but the **grand master key** from entering the lock; a facility to lock the door with the grand master which allows no other key to unlock the door.
hot pressing Gluing in a press between heated **plates** or platens. It is used particularly with **thermo-setting** glues.
hot spraying Spraying paint which has been heated to make it less viscous, thus avoiding the need to add **thinners** which would reduce the paint film thickness.
hot surface The description of a surface which, when painted, absorbs an abnormal amount of paint.
hot-water cylinder A **cylinder** for storing hot water
housed joint A joint which is formed by means of a shallow sinking in one timber member to receive the end of another member, as in the joint between **tread** and **string** in a close string **stair**.

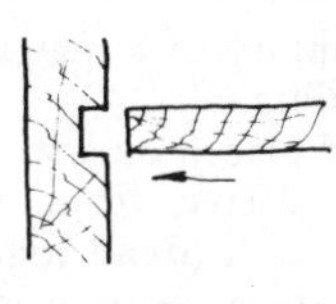

HOUSED JOINT

housed string A **close string**.
housemaid's sink A **bucket sink**.
housing 1. The shallow sinking in one of the timber members in **a housed joint**. 2. The action of joining one timber to another by placing it in a shallow sinking in the other timber. 3. A quantity of houses or flats.
hovelling Extending the chimney stack upwards with openings on all sides to improve the draught.
H-type gasket A form of structural glazing **gasket** with an H-shaped cross-section.
humidifier Plant that regulates the humidity of in-coming air in an air conditioning system.
humidity The amount of moisture present in the atmosphere. cf. **relative humidity**.
hungry A description of an over-absorbent surface which does not permit a good paint finish to be obtained with the normal number and quality of coats.
hurlinge A modified form of **butt hinge** designed for speedier fixing, due to the **hanging stile** and **frame** not needing to be worked to receive the hinge flap. The **flaps** close into the same plane, one flap being smaller than the other and the larger being cut out to receive the smaller.

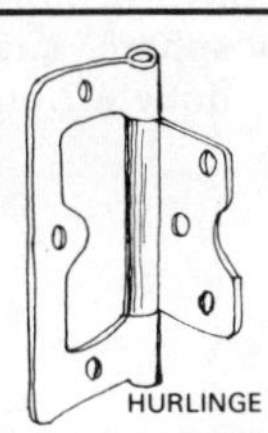

HURLINGE

hydrant A form of connection incorporated in a water main to enable a hose to be attached and a continuous supply of water obtained. cf. **fire hydrant**.
hydrated lime 1. **Slaked lime** ($Ca(OH)_2$) formed by adding water to quicklime (CaO). It is known as **lime putty**, after several weeks of treatment in water, and is used in lime plaster. 2. Commercially prepared $Ca(OH)_2$ supplied in bags as a dry powder which is ready for immediate use and does not require treatment in a **maturing bin**; now almost invariably used if lime plaster is required.
hydration The process by which **Portland cement** mixed with water develops a crystalline structure resulting in the setting and hardening of the cement. During hydration heat is given off together with small amounts of uncombined calcium hydroxide ($Ca(OH)_2$) and, provided the necessary water is available, this continues at a reducing rate even after setting.
hydraulic cement A cement like **Portland cement** that can harden under water.
hydraulic glue An old fashioned term for glue which is able partially to resist the action of moisture.
hydraulicity The property of a lime, cement or **mortar**, etc. which enables it to set in the absence of air and under water.

hydraulic lift A passenger or goods lift operated by a ram from beneath, the ram working in a cylinder to which liquid is admitted under pressure. The hydraulic lift has some advantages over the electric winding lift, especially that it does not require a lift motor room above the highest floor it serves.

hydraulic lime A description of lime which, like **Portland cement** mortar, can set under water because of the aluminium silicate content. Non-hydraulic limes (CaO) make workable 'fatty' plasters. **Eminently hydraulic limes** are 'lean' and least workable, but set under water in three days. **Feebly hydraulic** limes require 21 days to set under water.

hydraulic test A **water test** for drains.

hygroscopic Tending to absorb moisture readily, as from the atmosphere, and, in the case of solids, without liquefaction.

hyperbolic paraboloid roof A roof formed in **shell construction** (either of timber or concrete) over a square plan shape, in which one roof diagonal is a concave parabola and the other is a convex parabola. Two opposite corners of the roof are high and two are low, the lower corners needing to be tied together or buttressed to prevent the roof from spreading.

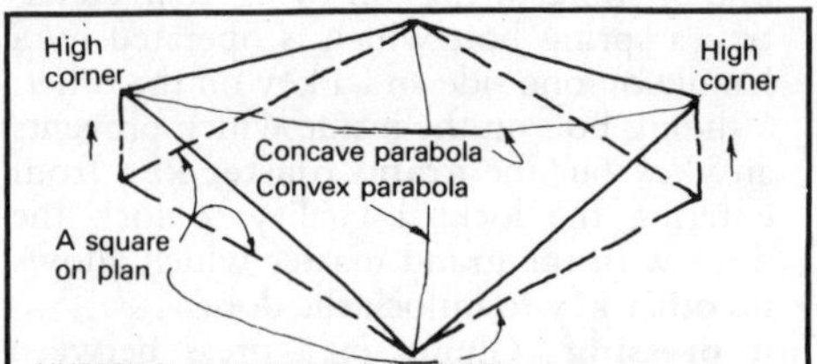

HYPERBOLIC PARABOLOID ROOF

I

idle time That part of **attendance** time when the worker has work to do but cannot undertake it because of bad weather, material shortage or the need for another trade's prior activity. Also the necessary period of waiting whilst another trade carries out certain operations.

ignitability The ability of a material to be ignited by a small flame.

illuminance The luminous flux density at a surface; *ie* the luminous flux incident per unit area, measured in lux.

illuminant 1. Radiant energy with a relative spectral power distribution defined over the wavelength range that influences colour perception. 2. Any kind of light falling on a body or scene. It may refer to the light source itself.

imbex The over-tile in a roof of **Spanish tiles** or **Roman tiles**. The imbex fits over the joint between a pair of **tegula** tiles.

imbricated 1. Said of slates or tiles which are laid so as to overlap 2. A term applied to any surface resembling overlapping tiles in appearance.

immersion heater An electric heating element designed to be installed in a water **cylinder** or **tank** which has been suitably insulated.

impact load An imposed load whose effect is increased due to its sudden application, as in the dropping of one object on another.

impact resistance The ability to resist a sudden blow.

impact sound transmission The degree to which noise produced by impacts on the structure in one room are transmitted to another room. cf. **structure-borne noise**.

impact strength The ability of a material to withstand shock loading.

imposed load Any load placed on a structure which does not derive from the weight of the structure itself (**dead load**). Imposed loads include those loads placed on the structure in the course of its normal use, such as the weight of people, furniture, movable equipment, cranes, vehicles, snow and wind loads; also referred to as live load and superimposed load.

impost A projecting capping stone on, or the top member of, a pier or pilaster from which an **arch** springs.

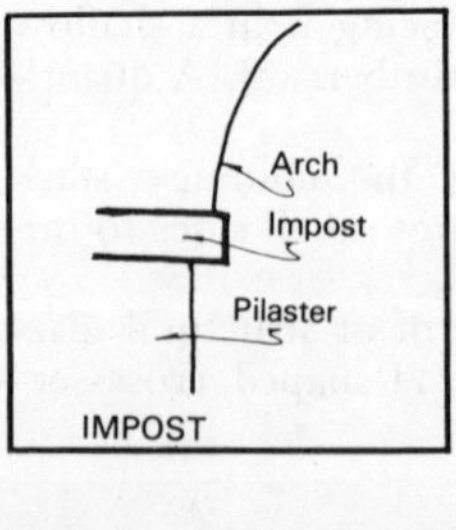

IMPOST

impregnated flax felt **Roofing felt** made of felted jute, flax or hair, water-proofed with coal tar pitch or similar.

impregnation The partial or complete filling of the pores of a material to impart to it special properties, as in the treatment of timber with **preservative**, either by pressure or double vacuum, which is more effective than brush application due to the greater penetration of the preservative.

improved wood Wood which has been processed, generally under pressure and at high temperature, with or without the addition of synthetic resin, so as to improve particular properties of the wood, such as mechanical strength or moisture resistance. The material may or may not be laminated.

improvement line The line of a proposed improvement in the width or re-alignment of a road.

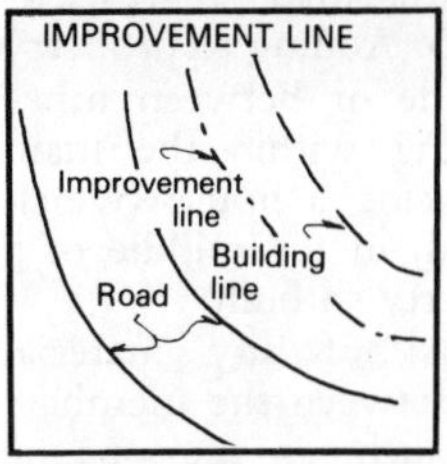

inbark Bark embedded in wood by a process of ingrowing.

incandescence The visible radiation from a heated substance.

incandescent lamp A light source whose visible radiation is produced by the heating of some material, such as the tungsten filament in a **tungsten lamp**. cf. **fluorescent lamp**.

incipient decay See **dote**.

incise To cut or carve.

inclined shore A raking **shore**.

incombustible The term (more correctly 'non-combustible') applied to a material which is incapable of supporting combustion, such as a metal, plaster, concrete, etc.

incompatibility The opposite of **compatibility**.

increaser A pipe which increases in diameter in the direction of flow; used as a coupling piece to join a small pipe to a larger one.

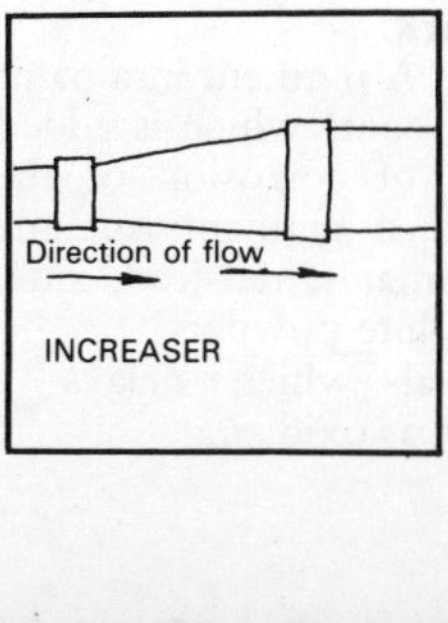

increment 1. The dimension, usually the smallest in a preferred range of dimensions, by which a component or assembly can be increased in size while remaining within the dimensional discipline of the building. 2. A small portion of material taken from a mass of material to provide a bulk sample.

incrustation 1. The furring up of hot water pipes and boilers in hard water areas. 2. A layer of corrosive material that builds up on walls in industrial areas and which, if not periodically cleaned off, can result in the deterioration of the walling.

indent The gap left in a course of brickwork or stone work for the future bonding in of new walling.

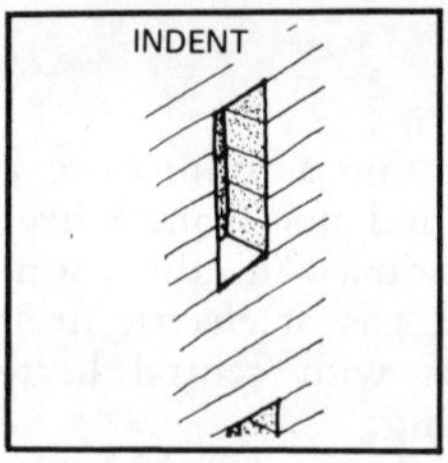

indentation hardness The total **force** in newtons required to produce a specified indentation under specific conditions, using a standard test piece with a standard apparatus and test procedure.

indented joint A **lengthening joint** in which the timbers being joined have notches cut in them to correspond with notches in a timber **fish plate** which is bolted to the main timbers, the notches being wedged.

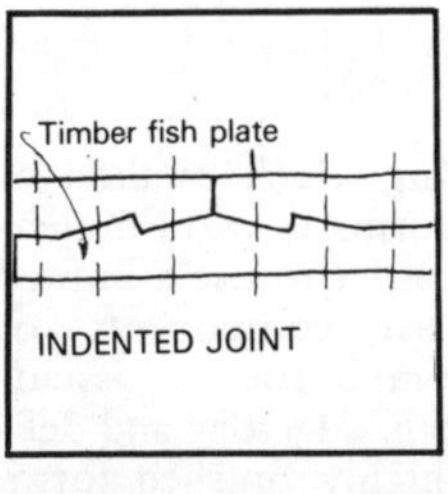

indenting **Toothing**.

independent boiler A separate boiler not fitted as part of an open fireplace, room heater or cooking range.

indeterminate frame A structural frame containing **redundant members**. Such a frame lacks triangulation, thus making the stresses difficult to determine.

indicator bolt A door bolt, usually used on a w.c. door, which indicates whether the cubicle is vacant or engaged.

indirect cylinder A type of hot water cylinder often used because of the danger of **furring** up of pipes and cylinders in hard water areas. It contains a heating coil (or **heat exchanger**) which is connected to the **primary flow-and-return** from the boiler. This heats the water in the cylinder, in contrast with the water in a **direct cylinder**, which is heated directly by the boiler.

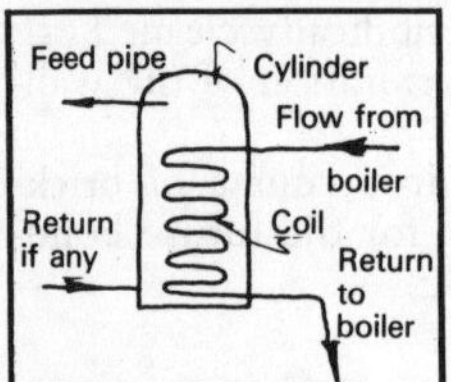

INDIRECT CYLINDER

indirect heating Heating a room from a distant heat source and not from a heat source actually positioned in the room (such as a solid fuel, gas or electric fire); usually synonymous with central heating. cf. **direct heating**.

indirect lighting Lighting in which the light source is concealed, and which results from light being reflected from the surfaces of the room rather than being transmitted directly from the light source.

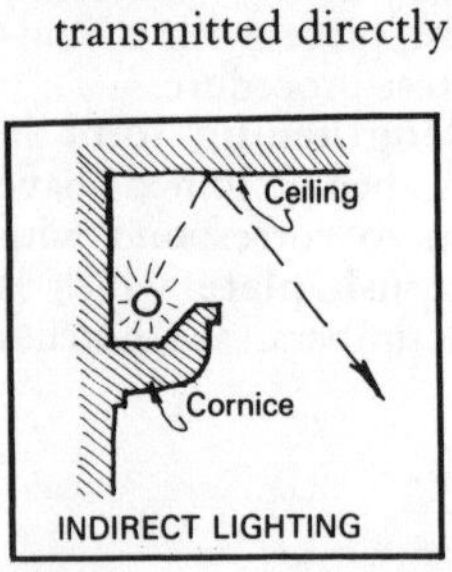

INDIRECT LIGHTING

industrialized building 1. A method of building which conforms to rigid dimensional disciplines in order to use a limited number of standard components or assemblies, these components or assemblies being produced in a factory and delivered to site in a highly finished form. The object of industrialized building is to achieve reduced cost by applying mass production techniques to a limited number of components and also to simplify and speed site construction by swift and easy assembly methods of large finished components or assemblies. cf. **system building**, and **prefabricated building**. The techniques of industrialized building are now being used substantially in many traditional buildings. 2. A building constructed according to the principles of building described in (1) above.

inert filler A filler not readily changed by chemical means.

inertia That property of a body which, independent of gravity, opposes any change in the state of motion or rest of the body.

inertia forces The **forces** produced by a change of velocity.

inert pigment A **pigment** which does not react chemically in a paint; often it is an **extender**.

infilling 1. Rigid material which occupies a space in a framework to provide weather protection, insulation, fire resistance or stiffness. 2. The correction of irregularities in a surface by filling the depressions with a material, or the material so used. cf. **dubbing out**. 3. Adding to property by building alongside or between other houses whilst staying within the main boundaries, *eg* replacing a house (which has been demolished) in the middle of a terrace, or the property so built.

infill panel A panel of any material occupying a space between the members of a framework, such as the opaque panels in a **curtain wall**.

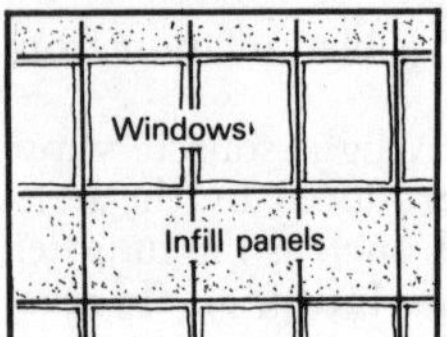

INFILL PANEL

inflammable Use **flammable**.

inflammability Use **flammability**.

infra-red drying Radiant-heat **stoving**.

infra-red radiation (IR) Radiation which is invisible to the human eye because it lies just beyond the red edge of the visible spectrum.

ingo or ingoing (Scotland) The **reveal** of a door, window or fireplace.

ingo plate (Scotland) A **reveal lining**.

ingrown bark **Inbark**.

inhibiting pigment A pigment in a paint (usually a **priming coat**) which is added to reduce the risk of corrosion of the material painted. Such pigments include zinc and other chromates, red lead, zinc, aluminium and graphite powders.

inhibitor A material which delays a chemical action such as oxidizing.

initial setting time The time required by a freshly mixed paste of water and cement (**mortar** or **concrete**) to acquire an arbitrary degree of stiffness.

inlaid parquet **Parquet** flooring assembled into (often) 600 mm square units on a backing.

inlay A decoration in which material of different colours from the background material is let into its surface as a series of **veneers**; usually applied to wood, **linoleum** or metal.

inner bead A **guard bead**.

insert 1. An inlay **veneer** filling a knot hole or other defect in plywood. 2. A plug, of wood, asbestos cement, etc. built into concrete to act as a fixing point.

inserted tenon A loose hardwood **tenon** inserted in the rails of oblique and circular work because the cross grain of a solid tenon would be too weak.

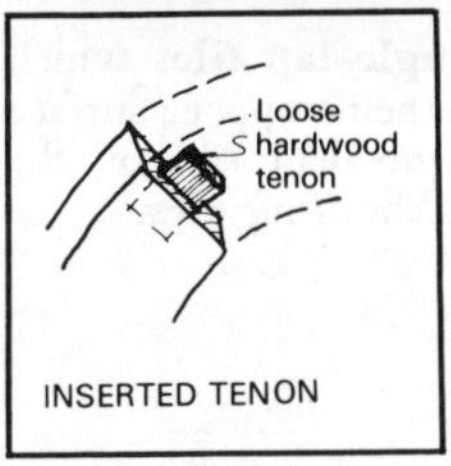

INSERTED TENON

inside-angle tool (USA) A plasterer's **angle float**.

inside glazing Glazing in an external wall with frames rebated on the inside, and therefore with the glass inserted into the frames from the inside of the building.

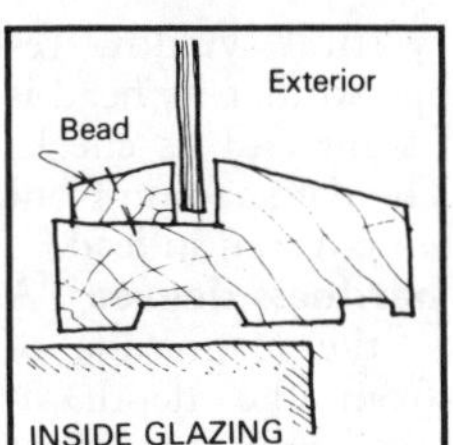

INSIDE GLAZING

inside trim (USA) The internal architrave to an external door or window.

in situ In position; a term used to refer to materials or components that are cast or assembled in their permanent position in a building or structure rather than being cast or assembled before installation (*ie* ***in situ*** concrete as opposed to **precast concrete**).

insoluble anode An anode which does not contribute metal ions to the **electrolyte** during electrolysis.

inspection chamber A shallow **manhole** of brick, concrete or plastic, positioned on a drain at a change of direction or where branches join the main drain. cf. **intercepting chamber**.

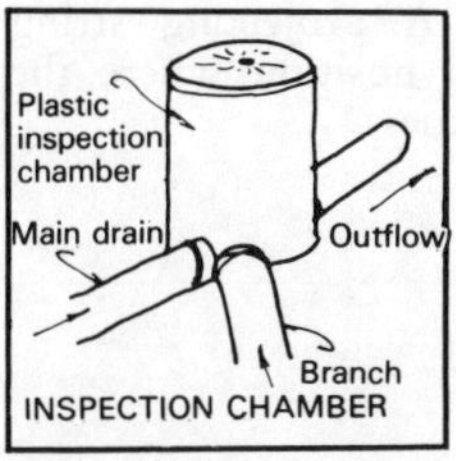

INSPECTION CHAMBER

inspection eye An **access eye**.

inspection junction A short branch drain leading up to ground level from a drain, and used to inspect the flow in the drain.

instantaneous water heater A water heater in which the action of turning on the hot water tap causes cold water to flow through a heat exchanger – this generates instant hot water. It has no hot water storage vessel.

insulated flange A flanged pipe-joint in which the nuts and bolts are electrically insulated from one, or both, flanges and the jointing gasket is non-conducting.

insulated flue pipe A metal or heavy-asbestos-cement **flue pipe** surrounded by a sealed air space or insulating material and protected from the weather by an outer casing.

insulating board Any sheet material, usually of low density (not greater than 350 kg/m^3), used primarily to give **thermal insulation**. Its **thermal conductivity** is not greater than 0.058 W/m °C.

insulating brick A brick which contains a high ratio of air cells to solid matrix.

insulation 1. Any means for confining heat, sound, electricity or vibration to a particular location. 2. A material which, because of its physical properties, impedes the transmission of heat, sound, electricity or vibration. Thermal insulation is a material with low heat conductivity (**k value**); sound insulation, a material with a high sound reduction factor, measured in dB; and electrical insulation, a material with high electrical resistance. Thermal insulation's effectiveness improves as density declines; sound insulation's as density increases.

insulation resistance The electrical resistance between two **conductors** or systems of conductors separated only by insulating material.

INT adhesive An interior adhesive or

glue that is resistant to cold water, but not resistant to micro-organisms.

intagliated Engraved or stamped in, as in **intaglio tiles**.

intaglio tile A tile with a pattern pressed into its surface.

intake belt course A projecting string course situated at a position where the wall reduces in thickness.

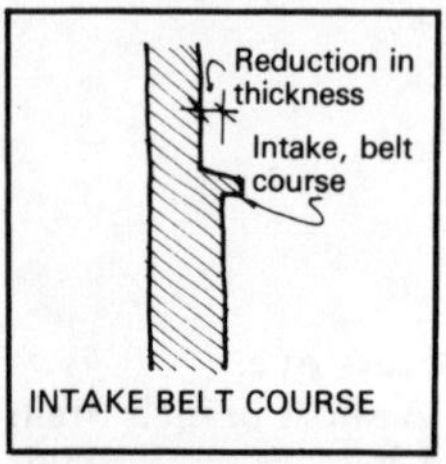

INTAKE BELT COURSE

intarsia **Inlay** work.

integral waterproofing Rendering waterproof without applying an independent **damp-proof membrane**. In concrete this is achieved by accurate proportioning of aggregates, cement and water and, possibly, by the addition of a waterproofing **admixture**.

intercepting chamber A **manhole**, often positioned at the end of a drain before it joins the sewer, which contains an **interceptor trap**. cf. **inspection chamber**.

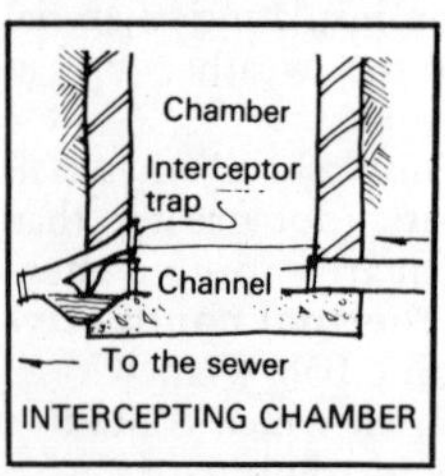

INTERCEPTING CHAMBER

interceptor trap A trap placed between a sewer and a drain to prohibit the passage of sewer gas or vermin into the building drain. Interceptor traps are now rarely required by local authorities.

interface The meeting plane of two materials.

intergrown knot A **live knot**.

interim certificate One of a series of certificates prepared by the quantity surveyor or architect authorizing partial payment for building works during the course of the work. cf. **final certificate**.

interior plywood A **plywood** manufactured using a **glue** which does not resist moisture, such as **animal glue**.

interlaced fencing Fencing made up of panels of interwoven very thin but wide **laths**.

interlocking grain Wood grain in which the fibres in one growth ring slope in one direction and gradually reverse their direction in the adjacent rings.

interlocking joint A joint in **ashlar** in which a projection on one stone is matched by a groove in the adjacent stone.

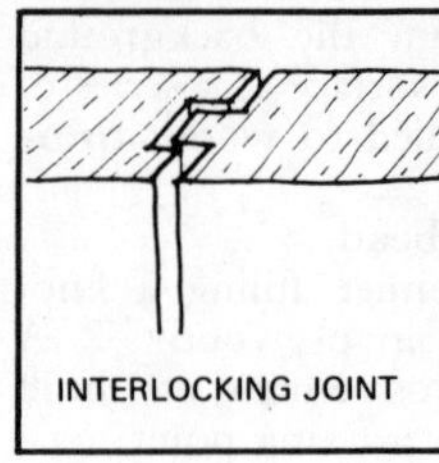
INTERLOCKING JOINT

interlocking paving Paving composed of small elements, usually made of concrete or burnt clay, which is laid on a bed of sand and is used for pedestrian and light vehicular surfaces.

interlocking tile **Single-lap tiles** which have grooves on their upper surface which mate with equivalent ribs on the underside of the neighbouring tiles.

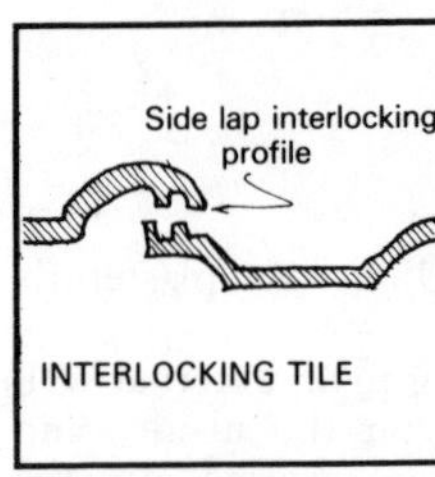

INTERLOCKING TILE

intermediate rafter A **common rafter**. cf. **jack rafter**.

internal dormer A vertical window recessed into a roof slope so that its head is under the main roof slope and its cheeks are within the roof. The flat space in front of the window is often covered in lead.

international rubber hardness degree A measure of hardness, the magnitude of which is derived from the depth of penetration of a specified indicator into a test piece under specific conditions. 0 degrees represents a material showing no measurable resistance to indentation and 100 degrees represents a material showing no measurable indentation.

International Standards Organization (ISO) A body which promotes 'the development of standards in the world, with a view to facilitating the international exchange of goods and services, and to developing mutual co-operation in the spheres of intellectual, scientific, technological and economic activity'.

international system of units A coherent system of units of measure founded on the metre, kilogram, second, ampere, kelvin (the unit of thermodynamic temperature), candela (the unit of luminous intensity) and mole (the unit of the amount of substance). cf. **SI unit**.

interstitial condensation **Condensation** which occurs not on the outside of a structural element but within it.

intertie A **nogging**.

intrados The undersurface of an **arch**.

intumescence A property possessed by certain materials (*eg* perlites) to expand permanently during heat treatment, forming vesicular texture. Intumescent material is used, for instance, around the edges of fire check doors) where it will expand when exposed to the heat from a fire, thus sealing the gap.

invert The lowest point of the internal surface of a drain, sewer or channel at any cross-section.

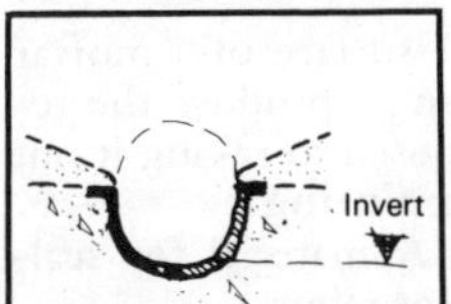

INVERT

inverted roof A flat roof (sometimes referred to as an upside-down roof) in which the weatherproof membrane is under the thermal insulation and acts as a combined weathering and **vapour barrier** layer.

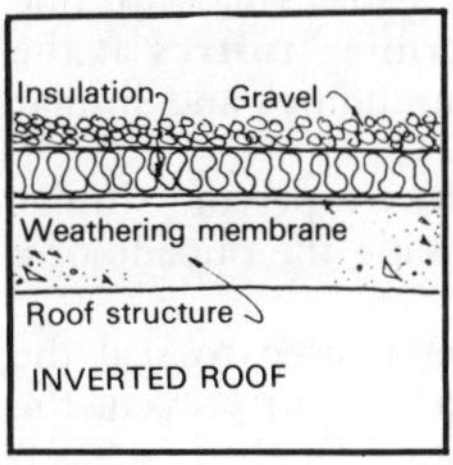

INVERTED ROOF

iron core A **core rail**.

ironmongery A loose description for all small metal components such as **door** and **window furniture**; sometimes referred to as architectural ironmongery.

irregular coursed rubble **Rubble** built in **courses** of varying depths.

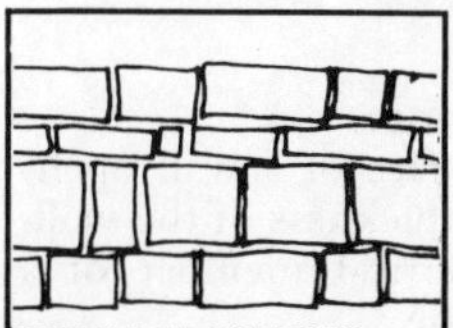
IRREGULAR COURSED RUBBLE

irreversible movement The movement of a structure or a building component caused by a permanent change in its physical condition, often as a result of ageing, *eg* the shrinkage of concrete or the expansion of newly manufactured burnt-clay products.

isolating membrane An **underlay**.

isolation strip An **expansion strip**.

Italian tiles Two differently shaped tiles which, used together, form a weatherproof roof covering. The imbex or over-tile is curved while the **tegula** or under-tile is a flat tray shape. cf. **roof cladding or roof covering**.

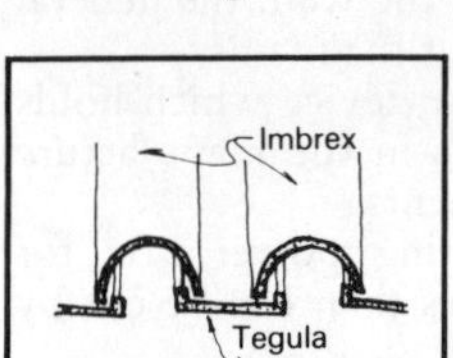

ITALIAN TILE

item A description of work and material or of one **labour** in a **Bill of Quantities,** together with a quantity, followed by a space in which the tenderer inserts his rate for undertaking the work.

J

jack A mechanical device for raising heavy loads through a short distance.

jack plane A **bench plane**, either wooden or of steel, used for the preliminary working of wood.

jack rafter A short **rafter** between a **hip rafter** and the **eaves**, or between a **valley** rafter and the **ridge**.

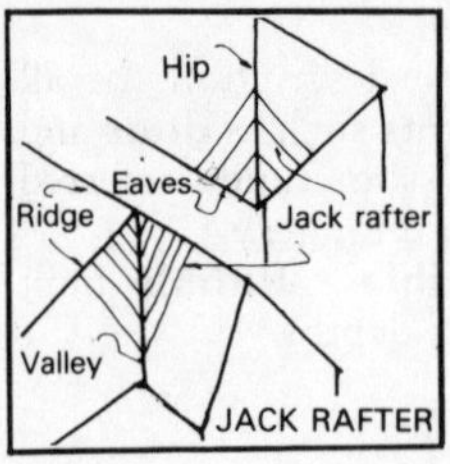

jack shore A **back shore**.
jamb 1. The vertical face of a wall opening which is the full thickness of the wall. cf. **reveal**. 2. A vertical member of a window or door frame.

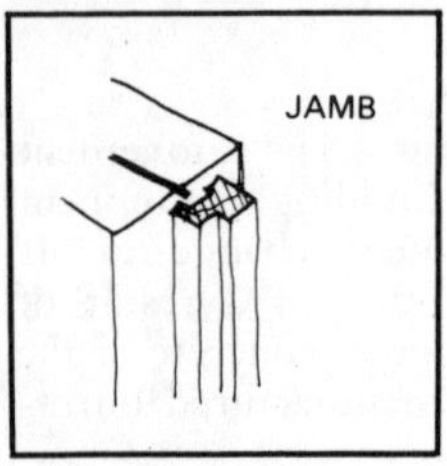

jamb lining A facing covering a **jamb**.
japanning An old term for a process of finishing metal by stoving, especially with high temperature black bituminous stoving enamel.
jemmy A small crowbar.
jib door A door designed to be inconspicuous and flush with the wall, the general decoration of which it maintains.
jig A clamp or similar device which holds work or guides tools in the manufacture of repetitive components.
jig saw A reciprocating power saw for cutting sharper curves than can be cut by a band saw.
job made (USA) An article made on a building site.
jog (USA) An offset or change in direction of a surface.
joggle 1. In blockwork or masonry, a recess in one block with a matching projection in the adjacent block to stiffen the **bond**. 2. The **mortar** filling matching recesses on adjacent blocks to provide a kind of dowel. 3. A **stub tenon**. 4. A metal **cramp**.

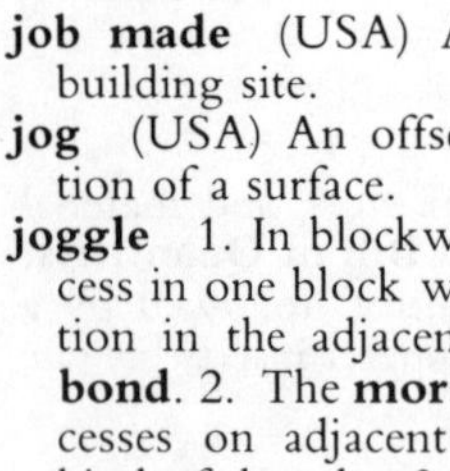

joggle post (USA) A **king post**.
joiner's gauge A **marking gauge**.
joiner's hammer A **hammer** with a cross **peen**.
joinery 1. Finished woodwork, such as **skirting boards**, **architraves**, doors, windows, etc., as opposed to carcassing timber. cf. **carpentry**. 2. (USA) The jointing of wood whether in carcassing timber or finished woodwork.
joint 1. A prepared connection between two components, usually involving a **bonding agent** or a **fixing device**. 2. A space between two adjacent components irrespective of whether it is filled or not.
joint bolt A **handrail bolt**.
jointer 1. A bricklayer's tool for finishing mortar joints. 2. A **plane** longer than a **try plane**.
jointer saw A machine for sawing stone.
joint fastener A **corrugated fastener** for joining together two pieces of timber.
joint filler See **filler**.
jointing Working the surface of a mortar joint while it is **green** to produce the required profile, as opposed to raking it out and refilling it, as in **pointing.**
jointing compound A material for sealing **spigot-and-socket** joints.
jointing plane A **jointer**.
jointing rule A bricklayer's straight edge used with a **jointer**.
jointless flooring Many types of flooring laid without joints other than **construction joints**, and including **asphalt**, **granolithic concrete** and **magnesite** (**composite**) **flooring**, **pitch mastic** and **terrazzo**.
joint rule A plasterer's steel rule with one end cut at 45° for forming **mitres** at the junction of cornice mouldings and similar locations.
joint runner Asbestos rope or similar material used for packing the outside of a pipe joint.
joint sealant A material used to seal the exposed surfaces of a joint to prevent the entry of water or grit.
joint tape Paper or paper-faced tape stuck over joints between wallboards cf. **scrim** or **scrimp**.
joist 1. One of a series of parallel timber or steel beams usually supporting a floor, ceiling or flat roof. Timber joists are often referred to as **common joists**. 2. (USA) Rectangular **lumber** from 50 up to (but not including) 125 mm thick by 100 mm or more wide, graded for strength when loaded on edge.
joist anchor A **wall anchor**.

joist hanger A steel strap or stirrup used to support the end of a **joist** by being either built into a wall or fixed to a **trimmer joist**.

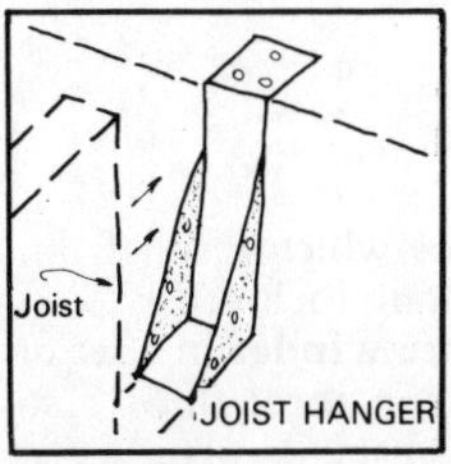

joule (J) An SI metric unit of work or energy equivalent to and superseding the calorie, kilowatt/hour, therm and British thermal unit. It equals force multiplied by distance (Nm). 1 J = 1 Nm.

jumbo brick (USA) A brick larger than usual in size.

jumper 1. In **snecked** or **squared rubble**, a taller than average stone. 2. A temporary electrical connection.

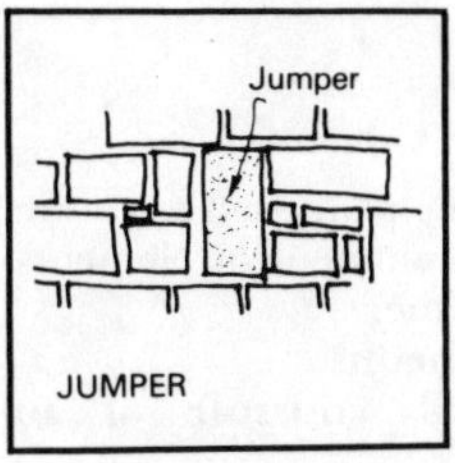

junction box A box in an electrical installation, used where connections are made between two sets of cables or at changes of direction to facilitate wiring.

K

Keene's cement An anhydrous gypsum plaster ($Ca\ SO_4$) made from selected high purity gypsum calcified at a higher temperature than other anhydrous gypsum plasters. It has a slow rate of set and is easily brought to a smooth, intensely hard finish.

keeper 1. The metal socket fitted on a door jamb to house the bolt of the lock in the locked position. 2. The metal loop over the fall bar of a **thumb latch** which limits its movement.

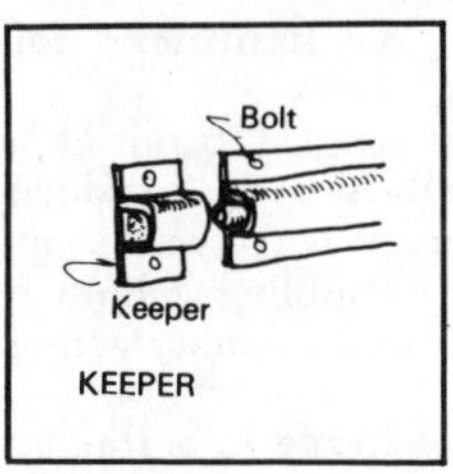

Kentish rag A form of **polygonal rubble** indigenous to Kent, using a local sandy limestone.

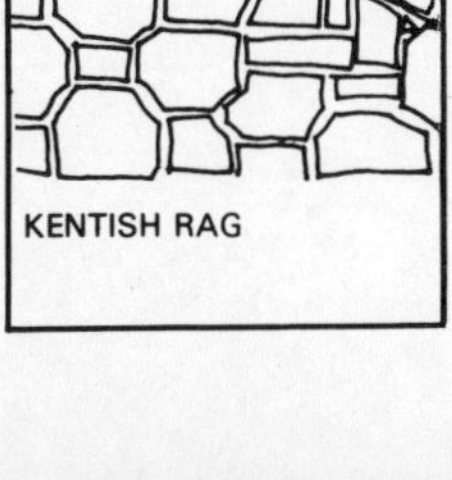

kerb See **curb**.

kerf The cut made by a saw.

kerfed beam A beam cut with several partial saw-cuts to allow it to be bent.

kerfing The technique of making saw cuts in one side of a piece of wood which do not pass through the wood. This allows the wood to be bent to produce curved features such as **curtail steps**.

kettle An open topped container with a semi-circular handle passing over the top; used as a container for glue or paint.

key 1. The roughness (possibly purposely produced) of a surface which enables a coat of **plaster**, **mortar**, or **concrete** to make a mechanical bond with it. 2. A small hardwood insert let into a joint to strengthen it. cf. **double-dovetail key** and **feather**. 3. A **counter batten** dovetailed across the back of boards to hold them flat. 4. A tool used by a bricklayer to make a **keyed joint**.

key block A **keystone**

key drop A **drop escutcheon**.

keyed dowel A description of a dowel which is grooved to allow air and excess **glue** to escape as the dowel is driven into position.

keyed joint **Bucket handle pointing**.

keyed mortise and tenon A **tusk tenon.**

keyhole saw A **compass saw** with a blade that tapers to a point.

keying-in The bonding of a new brick wall to an existing brick wall.

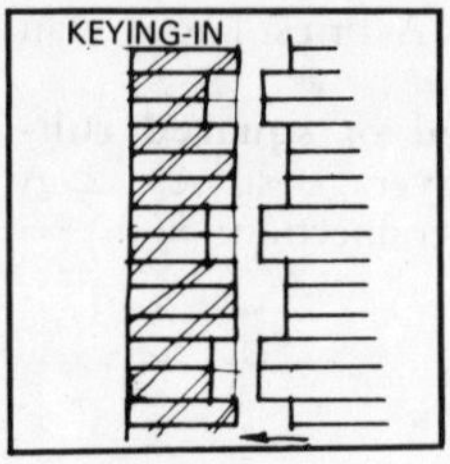

KEYING-IN

key plan A small scale plan used to locate particular items of equipment or elements of structure in a scheme.

key plate An **escutcheon**.

keystone The central **voussoir** of an **arch**.

kicking plate A metal plate fixed to the bottom rail of a door to protect it from accidental kicking during use.

kiln 1. A furnace in which cement, brick or lime is burnt. 2. A chamber over a furnace in which timber is seasoned. cf. **seasoning**.

kiln dry Kiln-seasoned timber with a moisture content of less than 12%.

kilogram (kg) A unit of mass in the *SI* system of units.

kilowatt (kW) A unit of power equal to a thousand **watts**.

king bolt A vertical steel rod between the **ridge** and the **tie beam** in a timber roof truss, used in place of a timber **king post**.

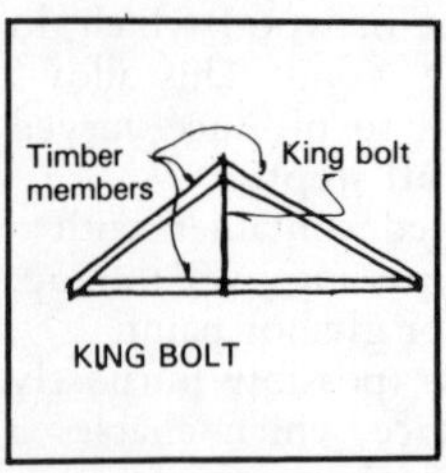

KING BOLT

king closer See **bond**. A brick which has had a corner cut off from the centre of one end to the centre of one side. It is used as a **closer** and is often referred to as a three-quarter brick, though this is an inaccurate description.

king post A vertical timber member in a king post truss extending from the ridge to the centre of the **tie beam**, which it supports. It is usually shaped with two **joggles** to receive the struts.

king post truss A wooden roof **truss**, consisting of two principal rafters with a horizontal **tie beam** joining their feet and a vertical **king post** between the tie beam and the ridge. Two struts prop the principal rafters, one from each side of the base of the king post. This type of truss is no longer used in the UK.

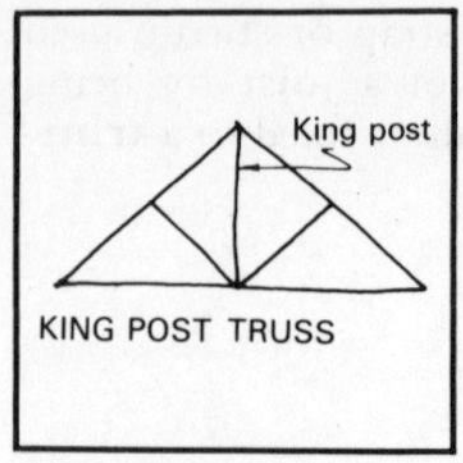

KING POST TRUSS

kiss marks The marks which result from bricks in a **kiln** touching each other.

kite winder The centre **winder** in a set of three on a stair turning through 90°; so named because of its shape on plan.

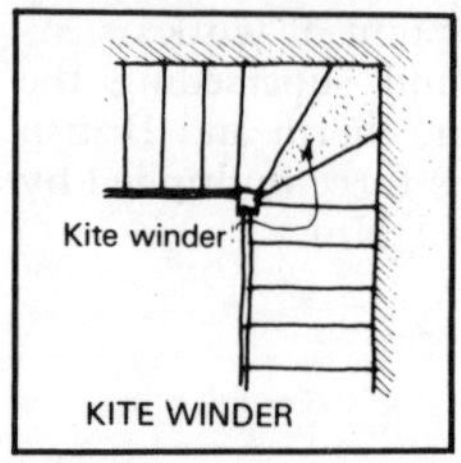

KITE WINDER

Knag gasket A drained glazing gasket developed in Norway.

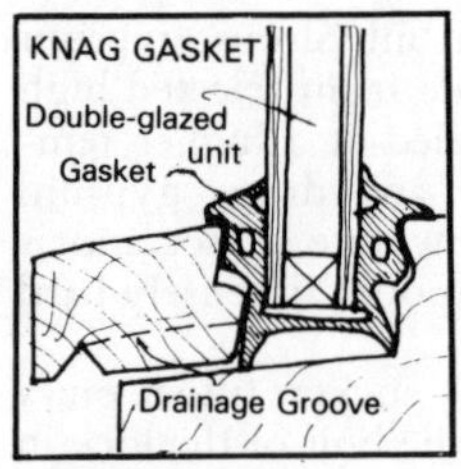

knapped flint A flint broken across the middle to show a dark face, and sometimes roughly squared.

knapping hammer A **hammer** for breaking and shaping stones.

knee 1. A sharp right-angled bend in a pipe; also called an **elbow**. 2. A sudden rise in a handrail when it is convex on its upper surface, thus resembling a human knee. 3. A curved metal member acting as a **corbel**.

knee brace An **angle brace** in a framed structure between a column and a truss or between the vertical member and the inclined member of a **portal frame**.

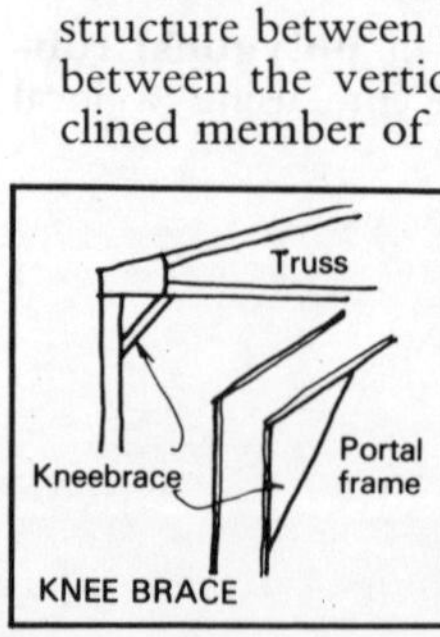

KNEE BRACE

kneeler A sloping-topped, but level-bedded, stone on a gable wall immediately below the **gable coping**.

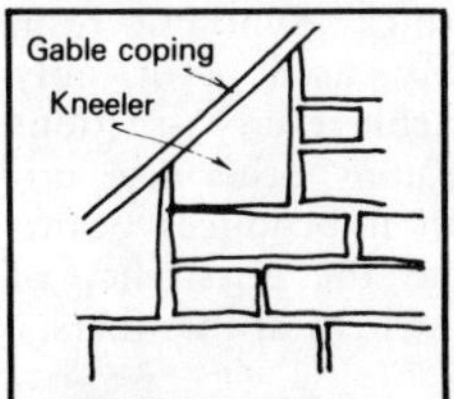

KNEELER

knife applied Of mastic when it is applied by hand as opposed to being applied by gun.
knobbing The act of dressing stone roughly at the quarry by breaking off projecting pieces.
knocked down Term applied to building components delivered to a site fully prepared and shaped and merely awaiting assembly; sometimes referred to as CKD or completely knocked down.
knockings Stone chips, smaller than **spalls**, knocked off in the process of chiselling or hammering.
knocking up 1. Mixing a batch of plaster, mortar or concrete. 2. The practice of trying to revitalize and make workable already set, or partially set, **plaster**, **mortar** or **concrete** (usually forbidden in specifications).
knot 1. The growth pattern on a piece of wood at the base of a branch growing from the main stem; in effect the hard portion of a branch enclosed in the natural growth of the tree. Knots which are dead, loose or unsound will reduce the strength of the wood, whilst those which are live will not reduce the strength. cf. **dead knot line knot**. 2. A bunch of bristles in a **knot brush**.
knot area ratio In a piece of wood, the ratio of the sum of the cross-sectional areas of all knots at a particular cross-section to the total cross-sectional area of the wood at that point.
knot brush A thick paint brush whose bristles are bunched in a series of round or oval groupings or knots.

KNOT BRUSH

knot cluster A number of small **knots** around which the fibres of the wood are completely deflected.
knotting A local sealing applied over **knots** in new wood to prevent the exuding of sap from the knot and the consequent disfiguring of subsequent paintwork.
knuckle The parts of a **hinge** which receive, and are pivoted about, the pin.

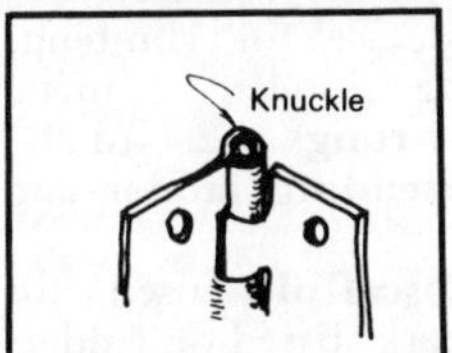

KNUCKLE

knuckle joint The joint between the two slopes of a **mansard roof**.

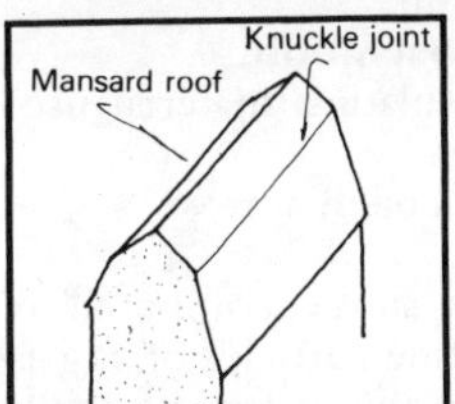

KNUCKLE JOINT

kraft paper A strong brown paper used as a facing to some insulating materials, or as a **building paper**.
K-value The **thermal conductivity** of a material.

L

labour An **item** in a **Bill of Quantities** consisting entirely of the work performed on a material, the material itself being measured in a separate item in the **Bill of Quantities.**
laced valley A **valley** in a tile or slate roof which has no **valley gutter** but has a **valley board** on which the tiles or slates on adjacent slopes intersect sharply. cf. **swept valley**.

lacing 1. In timbering for an excavation, the vertical member spiked to the sides of the strut or **walings** tying them together as a safety measure while excavation advances. 2. In **shoring**, a board connecting adjacent shores to ensure rigidity.

lacing course A **course** of brick, tile or dressed stone built into walls of **random rubble** or flint to give added stability and strength.

LACING COURSE

lacquer A glossy finish which dries solely by the **evaporation** of the **vehicle**.

ladder A portable device for climbing, formed of two long wooden or metal **stiles** spaced apart by **rungs** at 200 to 300 mm centres. cf. **extending ladder** and **step ladder**.

ladder scaffold A **scaffold** used for painting and light work, based on ladders braced together.

lag To wrap thermal insulating material around pipes, tanks or cylinders, for example, in order to prevent heat loss and discourage freezing up.

lag bolt (USA) A **coach bolt**.

lagging Thermal insulating material used to **lag** water pipes etc.

lag screw (USA) A **coach screw**.

laid on **Planted**.

laitance A scum or slurry composed of water, cement and fine particles of aggregate which forms on the surface of newly laid concrete or rendering, particularly when it is worked with a **float**.

lake asphalt Asphalt which is found in nature in a highly viscous condition.

lamina A thin layer or plate.

laminate 1. To impregnate layers of paper or textile with a **synthetic resin** and compress at high temperature to form a **plastic laminate**. 2. To build up a timber member or sheet of smaller pieces of timber glued together, as in the manufacture of a **laminated beam** or a sheet of **plywood**. 3. A laminated plastic, or other material similarly made.

laminated arch A wooden arch manufactured by the process of laminating small pieces of timber together. cf. **laminated beam**.

laminated beam A timber beam usually of substantial cross-section, formed by gluing together (parallel to the neutral axis of the beam) layers of timber approximately 25–30 mm thick. Synthetic resin adhesive is invariably used. Not only does this technique achieve cross-sections of timber of dimensions otherwise unobtainable today, but it produces beams of great strength and the possibility of constructing curved structural members.

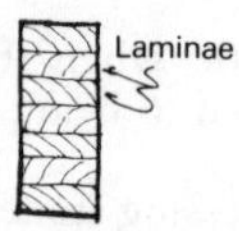

LAMINATED BEAM

laminated glass A sheet of glass, usually transparent, formed from interleaved, firmly adherent layers of glass and plastics material with glass layers outermost. Upon fracture, the glass is held together by the plastic.

laminated joint A **combed joint**.

laminated plastic sheet See **decorative laminate**.

laminboard **Coreboard** with the core made up of 3–7 mm wide strips of wood bonded together.

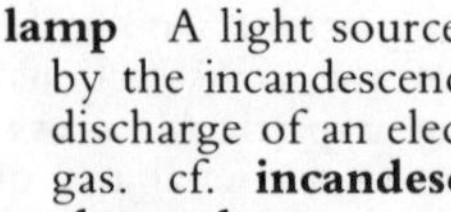

LAMINBOARD

lamp A light source which produces light by the incandescence of a filament or the discharge of an electric current through a gas. cf. **incandescent lamp** and **discharge lamp**.

lamp cord (USA) A **flex**.

lampholder or lamp socket An electrical fitting which is designed to hold an electric **lamp**, having contacts connected to the source of supply.

lamson tube A pneumatic tube for conveying documents in containers.

land drain A drain formed of unsocketed and sometimes perforated pipes laid in a trench and surrounded by freely draining material; used to drain away ground water.

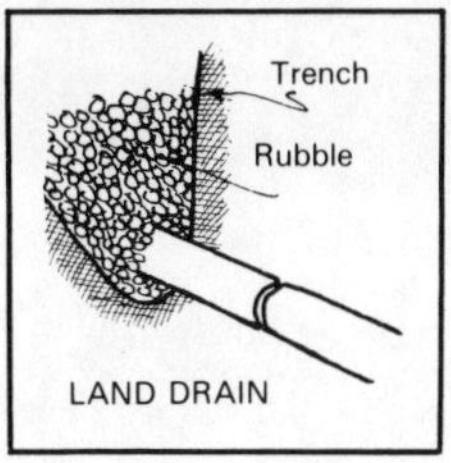

LAND DRAIN

landing A wide platform at the head of a flight of stairs. cf. **half-space landing** and **quarter-space landing**.

lantern light An upstanding glazed framework, usually with a duo-pitched roof, used to cover an aperture in a flat roof and admit light and air to the room below. Often the upstanding sides of a lantern light are openable for ventilation. cf. **rooflight**.

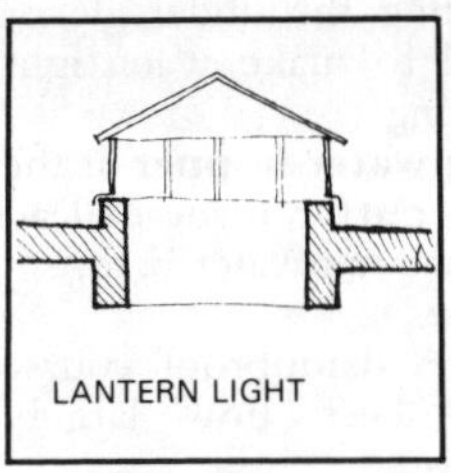
LANTERN LIGHT

lap The amount by which one material or component overlaps another at their junction; as in the amount courses of **slates** or **tiles** overlap each other. cf. **centre nailing** and **head nailing**, which give different amounts of lap.

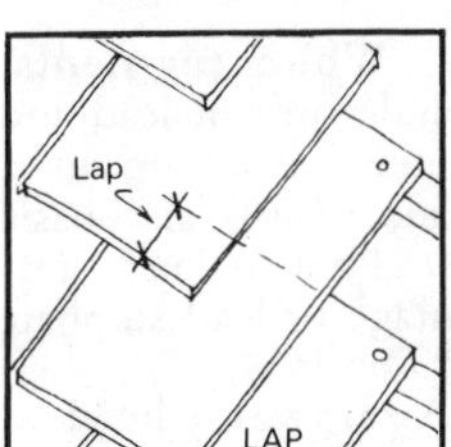

LAP

lap joint A joint between components in which the components overlap and are connected by bolting, nailing or screwing through (or gluing) the two thicknesses. A halved joint is a development of this. cf. **halving (or halved) joint**.

lapped tenons Two **tenons** which enter a mortise from opposite sides and overlap each other within the joint.

lap siding **Clapboard**.

large-panel construction A term derived from the early years of **industrialized building** and applied exclusively to sys-

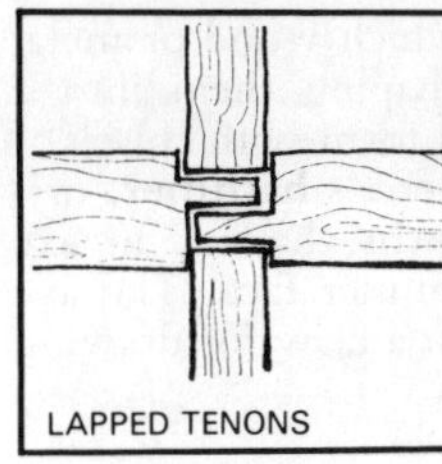
LAPPED TENONS

tem building based on the use of large precast concrete panels (floors, walls and roofs); now often used to indicate a building clad in large precast concrete panels supported by a steel or concrete frame.

latch 1. A simple door fastener, like a **thumb latch**, based on a bar pivoted on the door and engaging in a hook on the frame. 2. The bevelled metal tongue in a **mortise latch** or rim latch operated by the door handle and controlled by a spring. cf. **lock**.

latch bolt (USA) A **latch**.

latent heat The heat required to change the state of a substance without causing a change in temperature (*eg* the heat required to turn water at 100 °C into steam).

lateral support Support which restricts sideways movement.

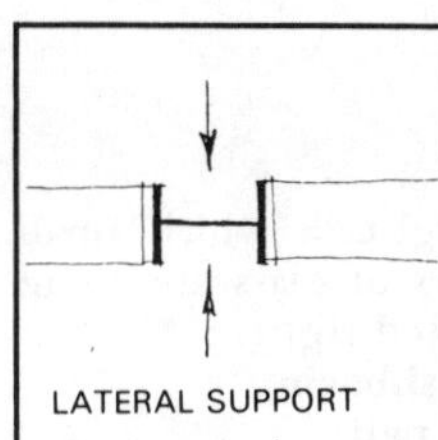
LATERAL SUPPORT

latex A colloidal aqueous dispersion of a **polymer**.

latex emulsion A **dispersion** in water of rubber or synthetic resins such as polyvinyl acetate (PVA).

latex foam rubber Cellular rubber made directly from liquid **latex**; the cells are either wholly or partly intercommunicating.

latex screed A flexible levelling **screed**, based on rubbery **binders**, used to smooth irregularities in the sand/cement screed, or power-floated concrete, prior to the laying of thin, floor finishes. The latex screed has sufficient adhesion to the substrate to allow thin, tapering layers to be used.

lath A strip of softwood of small cross-section (usually about 25 mm × 5 mm).

lathe A machine in which wood or metal pieces are turned, shaping them into a circular or cylindrical form with chisels.

lath hammer A plasterer's **hammer**, originally for nailing **laths**, having an axe edge as well as a hammer face. The axe side is nicked to form a claw for drawing nails.

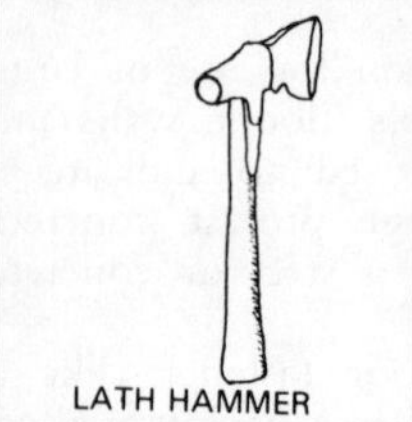

LATH HAMMER

lathing Any base for plastering, originally composed of a series of timber laths, but now often a metal framework. cf. **metal lathing**.

lattic beam or lattice girder A beam made up of diagonal **braces** between top and bottom chords.

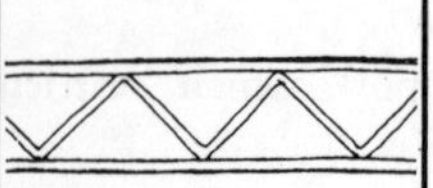

LATTICE BEAM

lattice window A **light** in which small diamond-shaped panes of glass are set in metal **cames**. cf. **leaded light**.

lavatory basin A **washbasin**.

lavatory pan A **w.c. pan**.

lay bar A horizontal **glazing bar**.

lay board A board fixed to the **rafters** of a pitched roof to receive the feet of rafters forming a subsidiary roof transverse to the main roof.

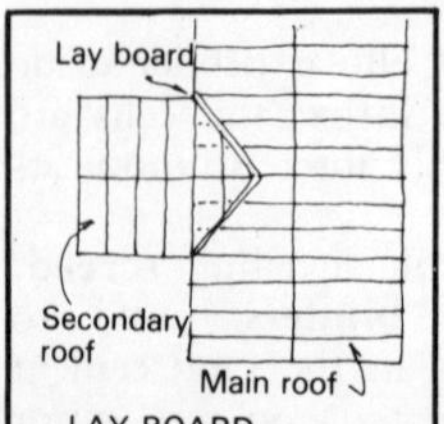

LAY BOARD

layer board The board forming the base of a **box gutter** and on which the lining of the gutter is laid.

laying trowel 1. A **brick trowel**. 2. A metal plastering trowel used to apply plaster to a surface; sometimes referred to as a laying-on trowel.

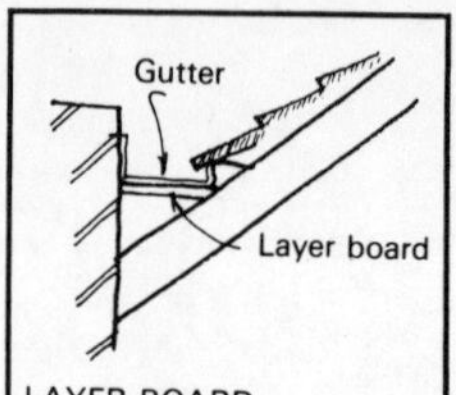

LAYER BOARD

lay light A **light** set horizontally in a ceiling.

lay panel A door or other **panel** with its length horizontal.

lead 1. A **conductor**. 2. (USA) A **racking back** corner in brickwork.

lead burning Welding lead without using solder.

lead-capped nail An American nail, with a lead washer forming the underside of the head; it is used to make watertight fixings of roof sheeting.

lead cesspool A **rainwater hopper** at the lower end of a **box gutter** made of lead and used to collect the rainwater before it enters the **downpipe**.

lead damp course A dampproof course consisting of lead sheet; now largely obsolete due to its cost.

lead dot See **dot**.

lead drier A lead compound which accelerates the hardening of **drying oils**; *eg* litharge, lead linoleate, lead resinate and other organic salts of lead.

leaded light A **light** made up of small panes of glass set in lead **cames**. cf. **lattice window**.

leaded zinc oxides **White pigments,** made from the sulphide ores of lead and zinc, burnt in together, resulting in a mixture of zinc oxide (ZnO) and basic lead sulphate ($PbO.2PbSO_4$) and described by the percentage of lead sulphate present (*eg* 15%, 25% or 35%).

leader head (USA) A **rainwater head**.

lead flashing A piece of sheet lead cut, shaped and dressed to cover a joint between two building materials, or two components of the same material, to avoid water penetration at that point.

LEAD FLASHING

lead flat A flat roof covered by lead **sheets** with **rolls** and **drips** at the junctions of sheets; rarely used today, because of its cost and weight, except for small or intricately-shaped areas.

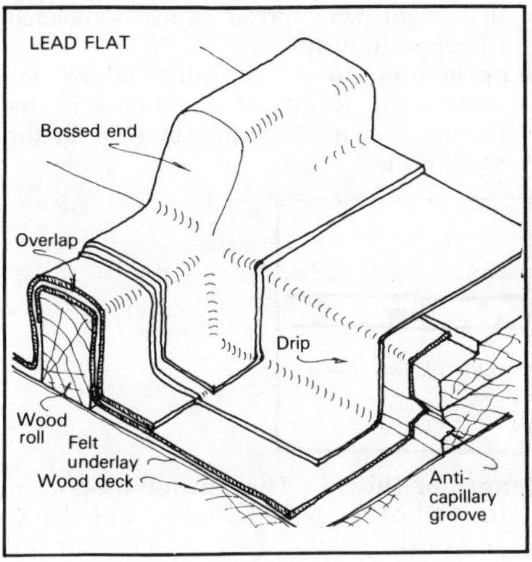

lead-free paint Paint without lead compounds and therefore particularly suited to locations where lead could contaminate food, etc.

lead glass Glass containing a high content of lead compounds, used as a transparent protective material against harmful radiation from X-ray and similar equipment.

lead glazing Glazing in which panes of glass are held in lead **cames**. cf. **leaded light** and **lattice window**.

lead joint A **spigot-and-socket joint** in cast iron pipes made by **caulking** with **lead wool** or by filling with molten lead.

lead nail A small copper alloy **nail** used to fix lead sheet roofing.

lead paint A paint containing lead **pigment**, particularly **white lead**, the manufacture of which is losing popularity due to the danger of poisonous white lead dust being inhaled or otherwise absorbed into the body.

lead plug 1. A small cylinder of lead driven into a hole in a wall to receive a screw fixing; now largely replaced by a variety of proprietary **plugs**. 2. A lead **cramp** between adjacent stones in a course.

lead-restricted paint A paint containing less than 5% lead oxide (PbO) and considered to be lead-free.

lead sheath An enclosure of lead around a steel **glazing bar** in **patent glazing**, usually embodying **lead wings** and **condensation grooves**.

lead slate A purpose-made **lead flashing** to waterproof the joint where a pipe passes through a roof.

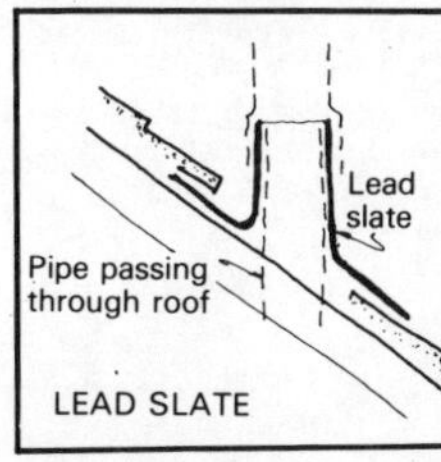

lead soaker A **soaker** made of lead.

lead spitter A short outlet from a lead **rainwater hopper** or **gutter** to a **down-pipe**.

lead tack A lead strip about 60 mm wide which fixes any free edge of a lead flashing, or holds a sheet at a roll or seam.

lead wedge A tapered piece of lead, made by beating folded scrap lead, used to fix a **flashing** into a **raglet**.

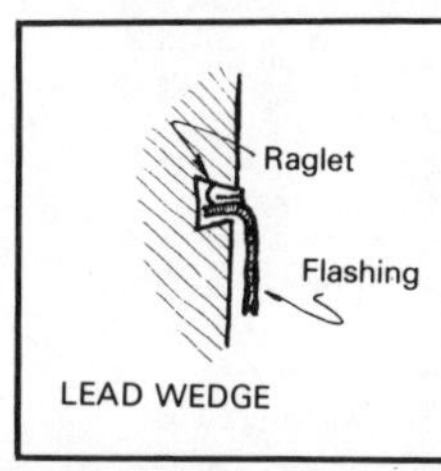

lead wing A projecting lead fin, part of a **lead sheath**, dressed down over the sheets of glass in **patent glazing** to retain the glass and to make the joint weathertight.

lead wool Fine strands of lead used for caulking spigot-and-socket joints in cast iron pipes.

leaf 1. One of a pair (or more) of doors or windows which make up a set. 2. In a cavity wall construction, one of the two skins of masonry material.

leafing The **floating** of metallic paints containing aluminium or bronze powder, so that the metallic elements lie flat to give good overall colour.

lean lime A lime that is less workable than a pure lime due to impurities. It is often **hydraulic lime**.

lean mix A **mortar** or **concrete** mix with little cement, which is harsh and difficult to spread, or a plaster that is unworkable. A **fat mix** is the opposite of a lean mix.

lean mortar Mortar having a lean mix, *ie* one with a low proportion of cement. The opposite of a **fat mortar**.

lean-to roof A **mono-pitched roof**, often abutting a higher building.

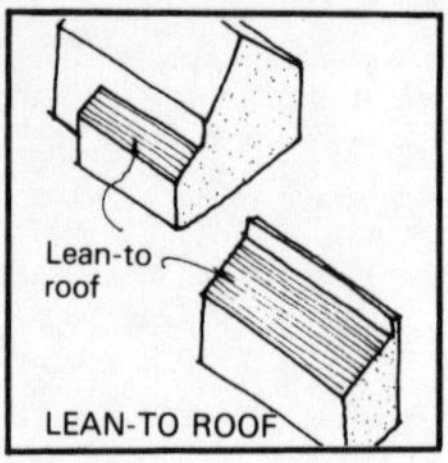

LEAN-TO ROOF

ledge One of the horizontal timbers on the back of a **batten door** or a **framed, ledged and braced door**.

ledged and braced door A **batten door** without a frame which is diagonally braced between ledges.

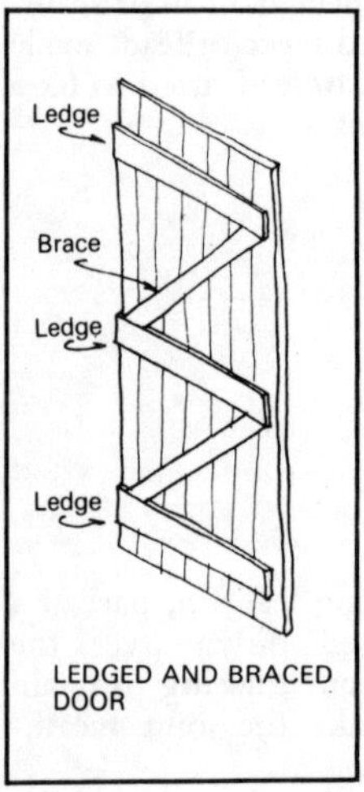

LEDGED AND BRACED DOOR

ledged door A **batten door**.

ledgement A **string course**, or a horizontal line of mouldings.

ledger In scaffolding a horizontal pole, parallel to the wall and fixed across a row of **standards**.

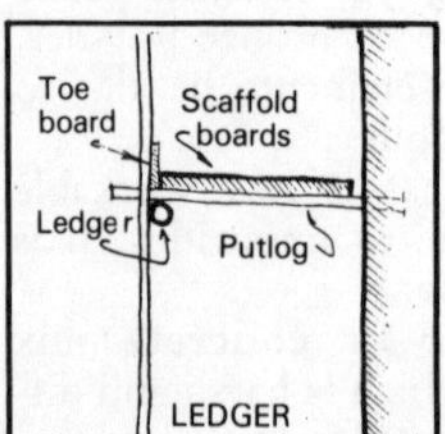

LEDGER

ledger board A **ribbon board** or ribbon strip.

left-handed door or left-handed window See **hand**.

left-hand thread A **screw-thread** that causes the screw to retreat from the operator when the screwdriver is rotating in an anti-clockwise direction. Viewed in elevation, the external thread inclines upwards from right to left, unlike the normal, right-hand thread which is inclined the opposite way.

lengthening joint A **joint** which increases the length of a component by joining a similar component to it in the same plane.

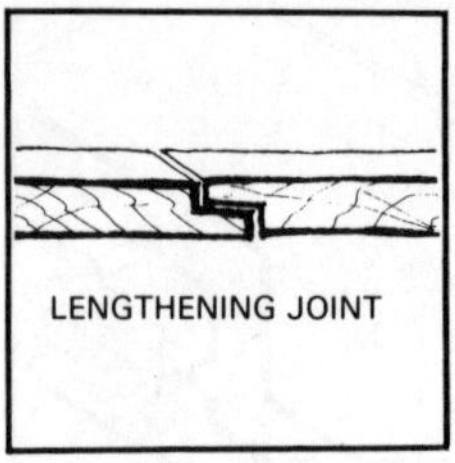
LENGTHENING JOINT

length of thread The dimension between the end of the bolt (including end champer) or the point of a screw to the last full **thread**.

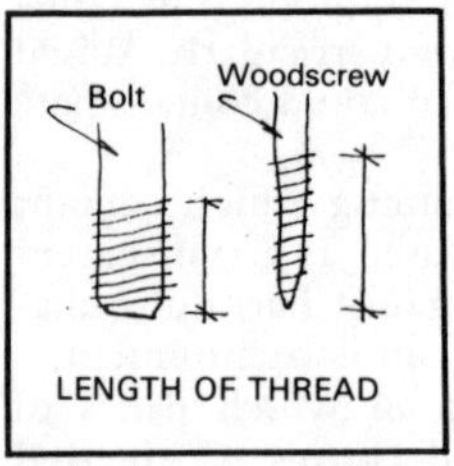

LENGTH OF THREAD

let in See **housing**.

letter plate A slotted plate with a sprung cover-plate over the aperture, designed to receive letters and usually set in a main entrance door or in the adjacent wall.

level 1. An optical surveying instrument based on a telescope; used to obtain the levels of various points in relation to a horizontal line (the **line of collimation**) with the aid of a **levelling staff**. There are various types of level, including the **dumpy level** and the quick-set levels. 2. A **spirit level**.

leveller A thin, horizontal stone in **snecked rubble** used to level up a section of walling to bring it on to course.

levelling 1. The operation of establishing the relative levels of various points on a site or in a building using a **level**. 2. The act of changing the contours of a site, reducing high spots and filling low spots, in order to produce a level plane. 3. The adjustment of a building element so that its upper surface is horizontal.

levelling rule A straight edge about 3 m long with an inset **spirit level** used to bring plastering screeds or dots to a uniform level.

levelling staff A staff, usually telescopic, with boldly printed dimensions which can be read through the telescope of a **level** or **theodolite** during surveying.

level survey A **survey** of land, with or without building *in situ*, involving the taking of a series of level readings all related to an **Ordnance Bench Mark** or **temporary bench mark**. This allows an accurate assessment to be made of the contours of the site with all its irregularities, the floor levels of buildings, inverts of drains etc.

lever action bolt A bolt, usually a flush bolt, operated by a spring lever and generally fixed in the face of a door.

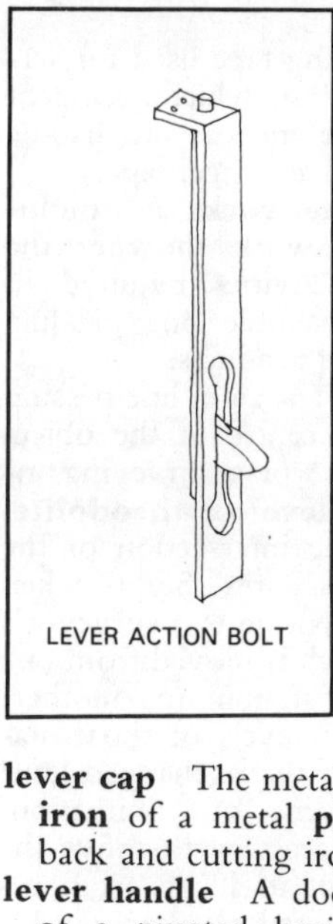
LEVER ACTION BOLT

lever cap The metal piece above the **back iron** of a metal **plane** which holds the back and cutting irons in place.

lever handle A door handle in the form of a pivoted horizontal bar, which is pushed downwards to withdraw the latch.

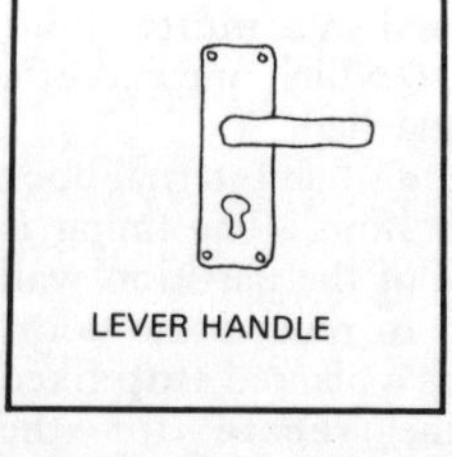
LEVER HANDLE

lever lock A door **lock** in which the turning of the key moves several levers to shoot the bolt (*eg* three-lever lock, four-lever lock etc.).

lewis A device, consisting either of two wedges of steel separated by a small steel plate or of two curved pieces of steel. It grips in a dovetailed **mortise** and thus acts as an anchor for a lifting ring or shackle in large blocks of stone or concrete.

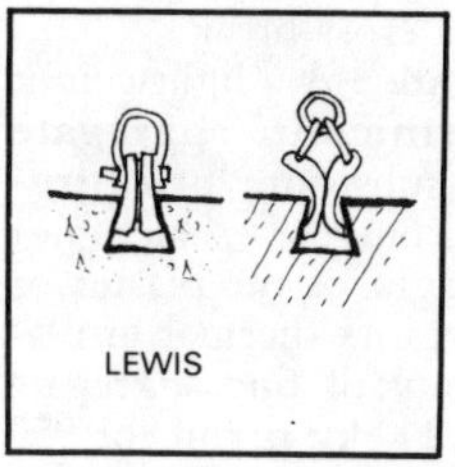
LEWIS

lewis hole A **mortise** cut in a stone or piece of concrete to receive a **lewis**.

lift A mechanical device in the form of a platform and enclosure (or car) which travels in a vertical shaft and is used for conveying people and goods from one level to another. There are two main types of large-scale lift, the electrically wound lift, in which the lift cage is suspended on cables and is wound up and down by means of a motor at its head, aided by counterweights, and the **hydraulic lift** operated by a ram from below.

lifting pins A **lewis**.

lift latch (USA) A **thumb latch**.

lift-off butt A **butt hinge** in which the part of the hinge fastened to the door can be lifted off the pin connected to the other half of the hinge which is fastened to the lining, merely by raising the door.

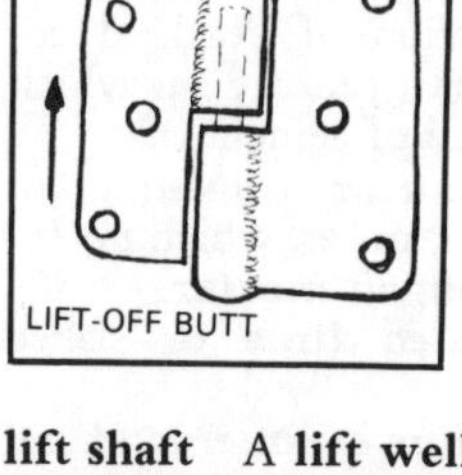
LIFT-OFF BUTT

lift shaft A **lift well**.

lift well The vertical compartment within which the **lift** car or compartment and, in the case of an electric lift, its counterweights travel.

light 1. A part of a window, fixed or opening, between two mullions or transoms or, in simple, single-light windows, between frames. 2. Visible radiation.

light gauge copper tube Copper pipe with **capillary joints** or **compression**

joints used for domestic plumbing applications when the wall thickness is too thin for screwed joints.

lightning conductor A thick copper **lead** connected to **earth** and projecting above the building in a pointed terminal; it reduces the risk of the building being struck by lightning.

lightning shake A compression failure of timber appearing as a cross break.

lightweight aggregate A lightweight material, such as **vermiculite aggregate** or **perlite**, used as a substitute for **aggregate** in plaster or concrete, which not only reduces the weight of the plaster or concrete but improves its thermal insulation. The bulk density of fine aggregate should not exceed 1,200 kg per m^3 or 950 kg per m^3 for coarse aggregate when oven dried at 105 °C (± 5 °C).

lightweight concrete Concrete which is lighter than normal concrete, due to its being aerated (see **aerated concrete**) or containing **lightweight aggregate**. Lightweight concrete is used where strength is not a major requirement but where the dead weight of the structure needs to be kept to a minimum or its thermal insulation needs to be high.

light well See **air shaft**.

lignin A constituent of wood consisting of resins that impregnate and bind the wood fibres together.

lime A substance produced by heating chalk or other naturally occurring forms of calcium carbonate to 825 °C or more in a kiln. This produces **quicklime** (CaO). When this is soaked in water (**slaking**) **hydrated lime** is formed – the form of lime most commonly used in building.

lime ash **Small lime**.

lime concrete A form of concrete used before the introduction of Portland cement in the nineteenth century, in which lime was used instead of cement.

lime mortar A **mortar** consisting of lime, sand and water and in which no cement is used. cf. **gauged mortar**.

lime paste **Hydrated lime** or slaked lime.

lime plaster A mixture of **lime**, sand and hair.

lime powder The power resulting from **quicklime** being air slaked, and consequently useless for building. cf. **air slaking**.

lime putty The material obtained from a **maturing bin** in which **quicklime** soaked in water (slaked) and passed through a 3 mm mesh has been allowed to settle for about a month.

lime tallow wash A **limewash** mixed with tallow, which can be used on bituminous surfaces (*ie* to produce a reflecting finish on bitumen felt).

limewash A milk-like mixture of **quicklime** and water, possibly with other additives.

limit state The state reached by a structure, or part of a structure, when it is rendered unfit for use or when it ceases to fulfil the function or satisfy the conditions for which it was designed.

line A cord used for setting out building work, particularly brickwork, by establishing the proposed line or level of a component or group of components.

linear expansion See **coefficient of linear expansion**.

line level A small **spirit level** which can be set on a bricklayer's **line** and is used to level the line to an accuracy of about 3 mm in 3 m.

linen tape A measuring tape used for setting out and measuring, which, being of glazed linen, is light and easy to handle but is not as accurate as a steel tape.

line of balance network A multi-start, single-end network showing the sequences of the activities required to manufacture and assemble one product or a batch of identical products.

line of collimation The sight line passing through the optical centre of the object glass of the telescope of a surveying instrument such as a **level** or **theodolite**, and also through the intersection of the **cross hairs** or cross-wires. Sights taken through the instrument on to a surveyor's **levelling staff**, which is moved from one strategic point or station to another, establish the relative levels of those stations by reference to the unchanged level of the horizontal line of collimation. When it becomes necessary to move the surveying instrument itself, the staff remains in its last-sighted position until a **backsight** has been taken on to it to establish the relative level of the new line of collimation of the re-positioned instrument.

line pin A nail inserted in a mortar joint at the end of a wall, to which one end of a bricklayer's **line** is attached.

lining 1. The surround of an internal door to which the door is hung. The lining is usually the thickness of the partition wall and is either rebated to receive the door, or more normally has a planted **stop** fixed to it to form the **rebate** for the door. 2. The sheet material (**insulating board**, **plasterboard** etc.) fixed to framework as in a partition or a ceiling. 3. Troughs and ridges in a paint film in the direction of brushing, usually indicating a lack of compatibility between the paint and the surface to which it is applied.

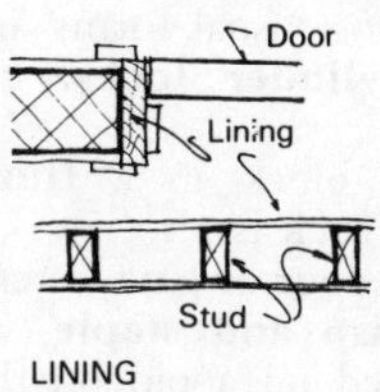

LINING

lining paper A fairly thin white paper pasted on to a wall surface to cover defects in the surface prior to painting or wallpapering.

lining plate A metal strip in **flexible-metal roofing** which is nailed to the **eaves** or **verge** and holds the main roof sheet by being hooked to it.

lining tool or liner A small flat **fitch** with an inclined edge used for painting lines.

link dormer A large **dormer** which links two parts of the roof together or incorporates a feature such as a chimney. It may have **lights** at its sides.

linoleum A floor covering manufactured by pressing or calendering on to jute canvas, a mass consisting of oxidized and/or polymerized **linseed oil**, rosin and/or resin, cork or wood flour, colouring materials, inorganic fillers and other additives. The finished thickness varies from 2–6.7 mm and the standard width of sheet is 1,800 mm.

linseed oil An oil used in **paint**, **varnish** and linoleum manufacture. It is obtained by crushing the seed of flax, and darkens and thickens to a tough film following **oxidation**.

lintel or lintol A **beam** placed over a door, window or other opening and usually carrying the weight of a wall over the opening; on occasions it may carry floor or roof members instead of, or as well as, a wall above.

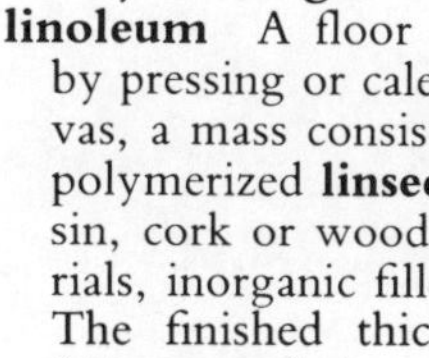

LINTEL

lip The projecting section of a **striking plate** which is bent to protect the frame and to depress the head of the latch bolt and guide it towards the **keeper**.

lipping A strip of wood on the edge of a built-up and veneered board or door, etc. to cover the edge of the **veneers** and the **core** (*eg* the **shutting stile** of a flush door is always lipped, and all edges are so treated in high quality flush doors).

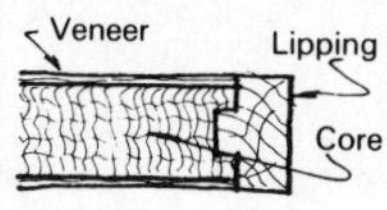

LIPPING

liquidated (and ascertained) damages A charge made against the builder for not having reasonable justification for failing to complete the building work by the **completion date**. The sum is usually stated in the **form of contract** as £X per week of delay, and these monies are deducted from any sum still owing to the builder.

liquid drier **Soluble drier**.

listing 1. The operation of removing **wane** or waney edge. 2. A narrow edge of a board.

litharge (lead monoxide PbO) A **drier** and **pigment**, coloured pale yellow to brown, used in paint-mixing.

lithopone A white opaque **pigment**; a co-precipitate of barium sulphate ($BaSO_4$) and zinc sulphide (ZnS); used in interior paints.

live edge A wet edge of paint which can still be blended with newly applied paint without the overlap showing.

live knot A **knot** that is sound and firm due to its fibres being intergrown with the wood.

live load The superimposed load on a structure (*ie* all loads other than the **dead load**). **Imposed load** is often considered a preferable term.

live wire A **conductor** with an open connection to an electrical source.

load A **force** acting on a structure or a structural member.

load a pipe To insert a **bending spring** into a pipe before bending the pipe. The bending spring prevents the pipe from distorting during bending. Other fillings can be used, such as sand.

loadbearing A description of a structural member whose function is to carry loads imposed upon it, as well as its own weight and any wind pressure on its surface.

loadbearing fixing Any fixing designed to support the dead weight of one or more cladding units and to transfer this load directly to the structure, as well as holding the cladding unit in place as would a **restraint fixing**.

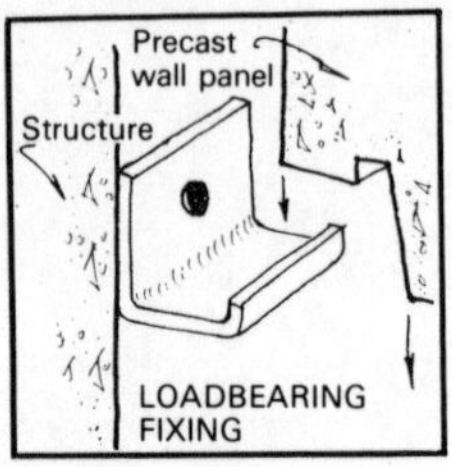

LOADBEARING FIXING

loadbearing tape **Pre-shimmed tape**.

load factor The numerical value by which a load, which would cause failure of a structure, is divided to give the **permissible working load** on the the structure.

load factor method of design A method of structural design based on a suitable **load factor** or ratio of the ultimate strength of the member or structure to its **permissible working load**.

load indicating bolt (LIB) A high strength **friction grip bolt** which indicates, by the compression of pads under its square head, when the bolt has been tightened to the correct degree.

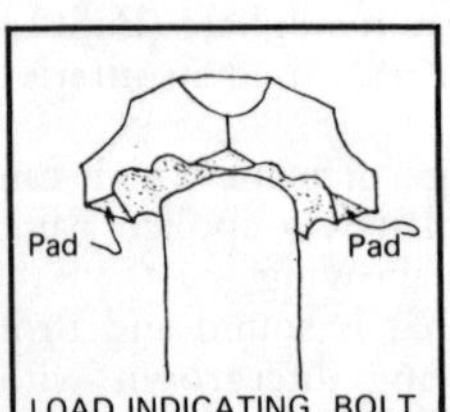

LOAD INDICATING BOLT

loading coat or loading slab A concrete slab laid over asphalt **tanking** to prevent the tanking from being displaced by water pressure beneath it.

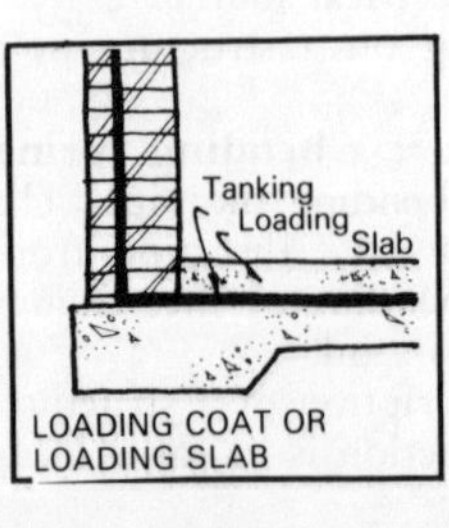

LOADING COAT OR LOADING SLAB

location plan A plan showing the size of a building site and its relationship to adjacent existing roads, footpaths and buildings. It may also include the outline of a proposed new building.

lock A device used to fasten a door, etc., and operated by a key which shoots a bolt into a keeper. The most usual forms are **mortise, rim** or **cylinder locks.** cf. **latch**.

lock block A wood block in a **flush door**, into which the **lock** is set.

locking bar A simple door or gate fastening, similar to a **hasp and staple**, in which a bar is pivoted on a pin on the door, hooks over a staple and is secured with a padlock.

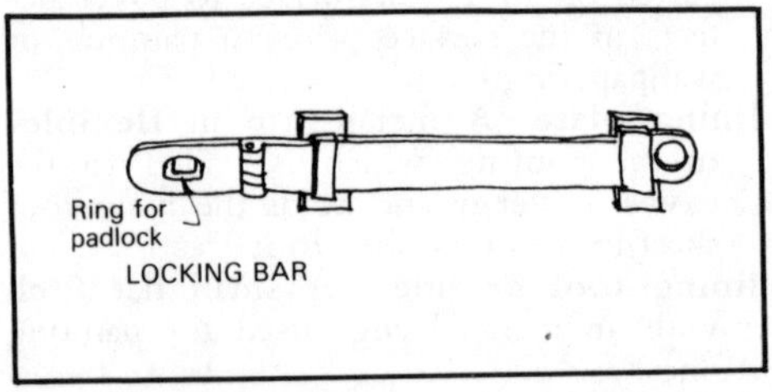

LOCKING BAR

locking stile The door **stile** on the edge which carries the lock. cf. **hanging stile**.

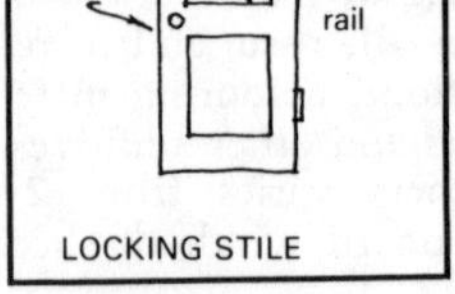

LOCKING STILE

lock joint A **seam** in **flexible-metal roofing**.

lock rail The central **rail** in a door which usually carries the **lock**.

lock stile A **locking stile**.

loft A storage space within a pitched roof.

loft ladder A folding ladder fixed to the trap door into a **loft** or roof space, which unfolds to give occasional access to the loft.

log A length of tree trunk after felling, barking and trimming.

London stock See **stock brick**.

long dummy A plumber's tool for straightening kinks in lead pipes.

long float A **float** which needs two men to operate it because it is so long.

longhorn beetle (*Hylotrupes bajulus*) A wood destroying insect that spends its larval stage boring in sapwood, leaving recognizable oval flight holes (usually more than 3 mm in diameter) and fibrous bore-dust (sometimes in the form of cylindrical pellets). The beetle is indigenous to many parts of Europe and a restricted area of the UK.

longitudinal section A **section** parallel to the long dimension of a building, assembly or component; a drawing showing such a section. cf. **cross-section.**

lookout (USA) A short wooden bracket which supports the overhang of a roof.

looping in A method of wiring, in which one cable is permanently connected to the lampholder, the other passing through the switch.

loop vent (USA) A **ventilation pipe** which is a continuation of the **soil pipe** above the highest branch.

loose butt hinge See **lift-off butt**.

loose-fill insulation Insulation material in a granular or loose fibre form. It may be used between rafters or studs or in cavity walls to increase the insulation value.

loose knot A **knot** which is not held fast and is therefore a defect in structural timber.

loose-pin hinge A **butt hinge** in which the **pin** can be withdrawn to allow the door to be unhung without unscrewing the **plates** or flaps.

loose tongue A **cross tongue**.

lost-head nail A round wire nail with a head of very little greater diameter than the nail, intended to be punched below the surface of the wood.

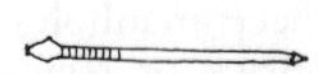

LOST-HEAD NAIL

loudness level The intensity of sound above the threshold of audibility measured in phons and estimated by comparison with a reference sound having a loudness level of 40 phons.

louvre 1. A ventilator consisting of horizontal sloping slats which allow the passage of air but exclude rain. 2. A **grille** on the outlet of a ventilating duct.

low pressure mercury vapour lamp A **discharge lamp**, with or without a coating of phosphor to the envelope, in which during operation the partial pressure of the vapour does not exceed 1 millibar.

low pressure sodium vapour lamp A **discharge lamp** in which the partial pressure of the vapour during operation does not exceed 9.05 millibars and which produces its light mainly by sodium radiation.

low-pressure system A hot water system that relies on **convection** currents caused by the difference in temperature between the water in the **flow** and **return pipes** (*ie* a system that does not rely on a pump for its operation).

lug 1. A small projection from a pipe or frame, often used to fix the component. 2. A terminal on the end of a wire to facilitate the making of a good electrical connection.

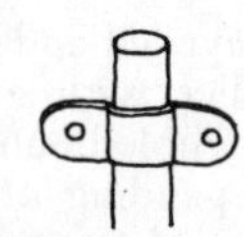

LUG

lug sill A **stooled sill**; one which is of greater length than the distance between the jambs of the opening, and has its projecting ends built into the wall.

lumber (USA) Converted logs which have been sawn and sometimes re-sawn. In the UK this term is properly restricted to square-edged sawn hardwood of random widths, but is now often used for all sawn timber, as in the USA.

lumber core (USA) **Coreboard.**

lumen (L) A measure of the amount of light emitted by a point source or received by a surface. One lumen is equal to the amount of luminous flux emitted by a point source with a luminous intensity of 1 **candela** falling on a rectangular surface, all points of which are equidistant from the source and with its sides the same length as its distance from the source.

luminaire A light fitting.

luminance The brightness of a light source or lighted surface measured photometrically (not subjectively) and expressed in **candelas** per m^2.

luminescence The phenomenon in which a substance absorbs primary radiation which gives rise to a later emission of light by the substance.

luminosity The sensation that a source is emitting more or less light than other sources. The common term for this is brightness, which today is more properly restricted to a description of colour.

luminous efficacy The method of expressing the efficiency of a lamp. It is derived by dividing the **lumens** output by the **watts** consumed and is expressed in lumens per watt (L/W).

luminous paint A paint which exhibits fluorescence or phosphorescence.

lump hammer A **club hammer**.

lump lime Sometimes called best hand-picked lime; large lumps of the best quality quicklime and without an ash content.

lump-sum contract A **fixed price contract** usually undertaken on the basis of drawings and a specification and without a **Bill of Quantities**. A form of contract suitable only for small scale work.

lux The unit of illuminance; a measure of light falling on a surface equal to 1 lumen per m^2.

lying panel A **lay panel**.

M

macadam Broken stone levelled and consolidated by a heavy roller with gravel filling the interstices, the whole bound by water, bitumen or tar depending on the quality of the surface required. cf. **coated macadam**.

machine screw A metalwork fixing similar to a lightweight, fully-threaded bolt, intended to be used with a nut or threaded socket; there are various styles of **head**.

made ground, or made-up ground Ground whose level has been raised by means of earth, hardcore, etc. brought from elsewhere.

magazine boiler A solid fuel boiler having an integral bunker with capacity to hold a 24 hours' supply of fuel.

magnesite (composition) flooring A jointless flooring composed of burned magnesite mixed with **fillers** such as wood flour or sawdust, and ground silica, powdered limestone, powdered asbestos or sand, gauged with a solution of magnesium chloride. It is laid in one or two layers up to 19 mm thick and has good resistance to cracking and abrasion.

magnesium-oxychloride cement Magnesite flooring.

main beam A beam that transfers its load on to columns or loadbearing walls at both ends. cf. **secondary beam**.

maintenance The treatment and repair of a building structure so that it remains capable of fulfilling its function in spite of the wear and tear resulting from its use.

maintenance factor A numerical factor included in certain lighting calculations to allow for loss of light output due to the collection of dust and dirt on the light fitting; often taken as 0.8.

maintenance period The **defects liability period**.

maisonette A self-contained flat on two levels; in the USA it is called a duplex apartment.

make good To bring back to an 'as-new' condition after work has been completed.

male thread A **thread** formed on the outside of a pipe, tube or solid cylinder.

mall A heavy **mallet** or **beetle**.

malleability The property of a metal which allows it to be hammered easily into a thin sheet.

mallet A tool like a **hammer**, but having a wooden head or one made of rubber or raw-hide.

mallet-headed chisel A mason's chisel with a rounded steel head meant to be struck with a **mallet**.

mandrel A cylindrical piece of hardwood pushed through a lead pipe to straighten, enlarge or regularize it.

manhole A chamber constructed to give access to a drain or sewer or to other underground services; deep manholes are usually constructed of brick or concrete, shallow manholes are often prefabricated in earthenware or plastic.

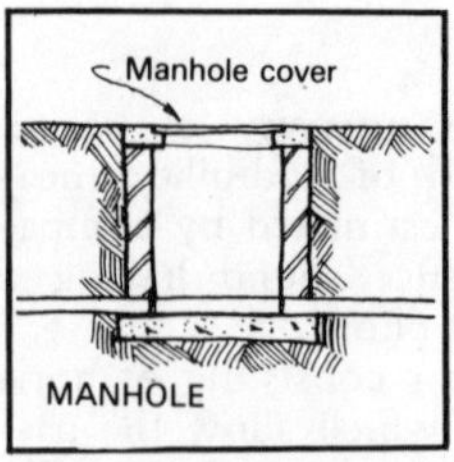

manhole cover A removable access plate over a **manhole** which allows work to be carried out on the services; usually designed to be airtight.

manipulative joint A type of **compression joint** in which the ends of the tubes being joined are slightly opened, so that a **gland** is usually unnecessary.

mansard roof A pitched **roof** with two slopes on each side of the ridge, the upper slope being shallow, the lower slope being steep.

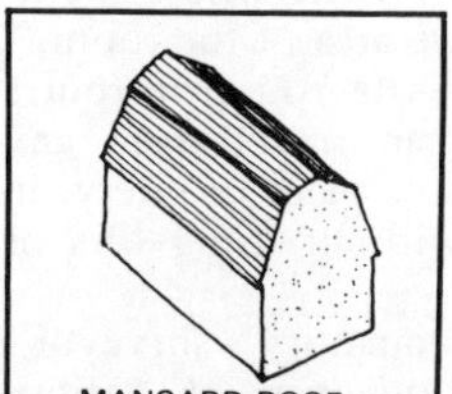

MANSARD ROOF

manual fire alarm system A fire alarm system initiated by hand.
manufacturing size A size which is within a specified permissible deviation from a **work size**.
marbling The reproduction of the pattern of marble, or other stone, in paint.
margin 1. The **gauge** of a slate or tile. 2. The projecting of the **closed string** of a stair above the line of the **nosings**. 3. The exposed face of a **stile** or **rail**. 4. A border round a hearth. cf. **drafted margin**.
margin light A narrow **pane** at the edge of a **sash**.

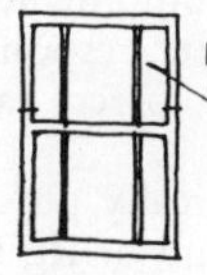

MARGIN LIGHT

margin trowel A plasterer's trowel for laying margins and working internal angles. It has a square U-shaped cross-section with two parallel, square-ended sides.
marked face The **face side** of timber.
marking gauge A joiner's tool used to mark lines parallel to the face of a piece of wood by sliding a hardwood block along the face and marking the line by a steel point at the further end of a bar that passes through the block. The distance between the block and the point can be adjusted by sliding the bar through the block and holding it in the required position by a wooden screw.

MARKING GAUGE

marquetry The decorating of a timber surface by inlaying into it pieces of contrasting wood, or occasionally metal, mother of pearl, ivory etc.
martempering Quenching steel from a temperature above the transformation range to some temperature slightly above the upper limit of **martensite** formation, holding at that temperature long enough to permit equalization of temperature without transformation of the **austenite,** followed by cooling in air. This results in the formation of martensite which can be tempered as required.
martensite A hard constituent produced when steel is cooled from the hardening temperature at a speed greater than its critical cooling rate.
martensitic stainless steel A chromium steel containing not less than 11% chromium; it may be strengthened and hardened by quenching and tempering. It is a magnetic steel.
masking Protecting a surface from adjacent painting by sticking or fixing tape or paper on to the surface.
masonry 1. The craft of stone preparation and walling. 2. Stonework and, often, other forms of mass walling (*ie* brickwork and blockwork).
masonry cement A hydraulic cement consisting of a mixture of Portland cement with a very fine mineral filler and an **air entraining agent.** It has good working properties deriving from the plasticizing effect of the additives.
masonry fixing A **fixing device** used to fix stonework and concrete cladding panels, including **cramps**, **corbel plates**, **anchor bolts** etc.
masonry nail A zinc-plated hardened steel nail, which may be either hand driven or fired into concrete, stone or brickwork.
mason's mitre A joint in stone that gives the appearance of a mitred joint. The intersection, however, is carved out of the solid stone and the actual joint is a butt joint away from the corner.
mason's putty A mortar used for pointing **ashlar**; it is made from **lime putty**, stone dust and Portland cement in a mix of 5:7:2.
mason's scaffold A **scaffold** which, unlike a bricklayer's scaffold, is entirely self-supporting and is not supported in the

wall by **putlogs** because the holes to receive them would deface the wall.

mason's stop A **mason's mitre**.

mass concrete Concrete without reinforcement, usually forming large foundations or retaining structures.

master key A key which opens a **suite** of locks, each of which is operated by a different key.

mastic A non-hardening adhesive composition; the term is loosely used to describe a plastic filler, stopper, putty or adhesive, but is not to be confused with the term gum mastic which relates to a natural resin. cf. **sealant**.

mastic asphalt A type of asphalt composed of suitably graded mineral matter and asphaltic cement in such proportions as to form a coherent, voidless, impermeable mass, solid or semi-solid under normal temperatures, but sufficiently fluid when brought to a suitable temperature to be spread by a hand float.

mastic asphalt surfacing A wearing course formed by spreading hot **mastic asphalt**, with the addition of chippings, by hand floats or machine.

mastic seal See **adhesive seal**.

matchboarding or matched boards Boards specially cut at the edges to enable close joints to be made, either by means of tongues and grooves or rebating. When matchboarding is used for lining, the joints may also be beaded or vee-jointed to hide any shrinkage.

matched floor A floor made of **matchboarding**.

matching 1. **Matchboarding** 2. Arrangement of **veneers** to achieve a decorative effect by exploring their colour and figure; cf. **book matching** and **four-piece butt matching**.

matt (finish) A uniform finish of a fine texture virtually lacking reflectivity, *ie* non-glossy.

mattock A tool similar to a **pick axe** used for grubbing up tree roots and loosening hard ground; one end is broadened like an adze, the other is pointed like a pick.

maturing bin A tank or lined pit into which **milk of lime** is run and allowed to settle and mature for several weeks, after which it is dug out as **lime putty**. A now largely obsolete site practice.

mat well A depression in the floor immediately inside an external door to contain a doormat.

maul A heavy wooden **mallet**.

maximum demand The greatest possible instantaneous electric power demand, used as a method of charging in some electricity tariffs.

mean radiant temperature The sum of the product of surface temperatures and surface areas taken over the whole room, divided by the surface area of the room.

means of escape A safe route or routes by which persons can travel from any point in a building to a place of safety, in the event of fire, without using lifts or escalators.

measurement The quantity surveyor's assessment of the quantity of various materials needed to construct a building, based on the working drawings.

measuring frame A **batch box**.

mechanical engineering In building terms, the heating, cooling or ventilating of a building including the design of all related plant and equipment. Some specialist installations, such as lift installations, also fall into this category, but are usually designed and carried out by specialist engineers and subcontractors. It also covers some aspects of plumbing, (the domestic hot water installation is usually undertaken by the mechanical engineer). Mechanical engineering sometimes merges with electrical engineering, for example, whilst a mechanical engineer would be responsible for the installation of electrically controlled equipment, the electrical engineer would be responsible for running a supply of the correct capacity to that equipment.

mechanical saw A mechanically powered saw, such as a **circular**, band or **jig saw**.

mechanical ventilation The ventilation of an internal space by means of an electrical fan, with or without associated duct work. The fan normally extracts from the space air which is then replaced by air from adjacent spaces. cf. **natural ventilation**.

medium The liquid constituent of a paint which, on hardening, becomes the **binder** of the film.

medullary ray A **wood ray**.

meeting rail One of the two rails of double opening **lights** of a window which come together when the lights are closed.

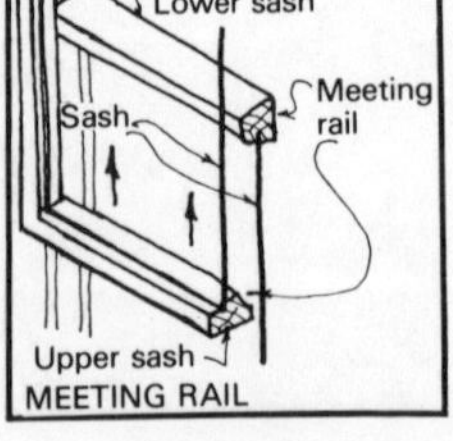

MEETING RAIL

meeting stile One of the two middle **stiles** which come together when two **folding doors** are closed.

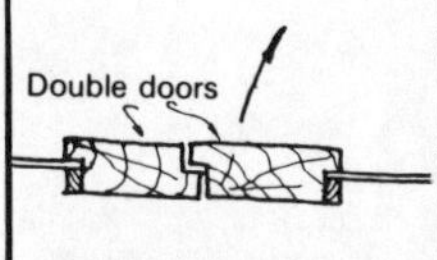

MEETING STILE

melamine formaldehyde A **synthetic resin** used for gluing or surfacing laminates.

melamine laminate See **decorative laminate**.

melamine-surfaced chipboard Resin-bonded **chipboard** with a decorative, smooth **melamine formaldehyde** surface. A cheaper, less durable version of laminate-faced chipboard.

member A **component** in an assembly of parts, *ie* a component in a frame or truss.

membrane Usually a thin sheet or layer of impervious material used to withstand water penetration, as in a next-to-earth ground floor slab.

mending plate A flat steel plate drilled to receive countersunk screws, used to repair a break in a timber component by screwing to sound wood on either side of the break.

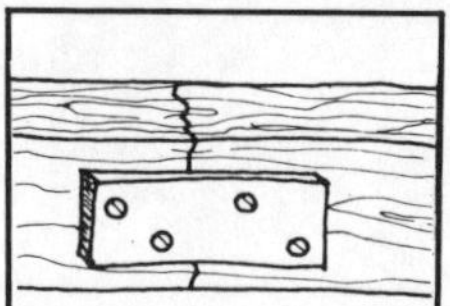

MENDING PLATE

mensuration The measurement of lengths and the calculation of lengths, areas and volumes.

Merulius lacrymans See **dry rot**.

mesh 1. In concrete slab reinforcement, an arrangement of bars or wire normally in two directions at right angles, tied or welded at the intersections or interwoven. 2. Expanded metal diamond mesh; metal punched with slots and then expanded to create a diamond-shaped network.

metal coating The application of a thin metal coating (nickel, zinc, copper, cadmium, chromium, aluminium etc.) to a corrodible metal to protect it from corrosion. cf. **galvanizing, sherardizing** and **chromium plating**

metal cramp A bent metal bar used to secure adjacent stones. cf. **cramp**.

metal lathing **Expanded metal** used as a base for plastering either over irregular backings or a backing which provides little or no key.

metal-sheathed mineral-insulated cable An electrical cable consisting of a copper wire, or wires, inside a copper tube which is filled with mineral insulation, usually magnesia. It can withstand a degree of overloading and is fire-resistant.

metal trim **Angle beads**, **architraves** and **skirtings** made of sheet metal, fixed before plastering and incorporated in the plaster surface.

metal valley A **valley gutter** lined with flexible metal.

mezzanine An intermediate level between two main floor levels.

mica A group of minerals with excellent cleavage characteristics allowing very thin sections to be obtained (as in a **mica-flap valve**). Mica is also used in a finely crushed form as an **extender** in some paints.

mica-flap valve A one-way valve providing fresh air into a drain above the **interceptor trap** and comprising a free-hanging flap made of thin mica: now rarely used.

micro-bore (heating) system A very small-bore, wet central heating system in which there is a manifold closely situated to a group of radiators, to which the flow and return pipes from the boiler are installed and which serves the radiators by very small (6 mm diameter) flow and return pipes. cf. **small-bore (heating) system**.

mid-feather 1. The leaf of brickwork separating two flues. A **withe**. 2. A **parting slip**.

MID-FEATHER

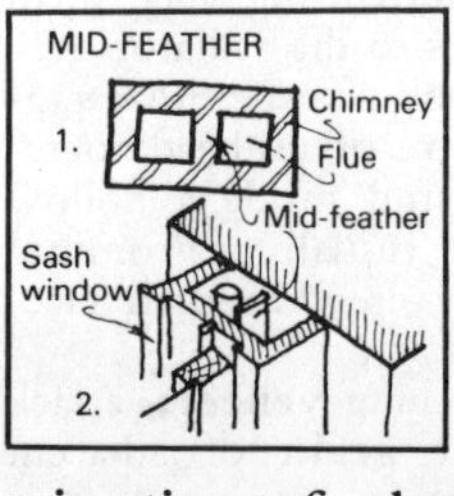

migration of plasticizer The loss of mass of a plastic component due to some of its plasticizer being absorbed by an adjacent material (*eg* plasticizer of PVC tile flooring absorbed by decking).

mild steel Carbon steel containing approximately 0.12 to 0.25% of carbon.
mild steel reinforcement Bars made of steel containing 0.12 to 0.25% carbon, used to reinforce concrete (*ie* to withstand tension forces) and having a tensile strength of 250 N/mm^2.
milkiness A defect of varnish which gives the film a whitish, translucent appearance.
milk of lime **Slaked lime** in water.
milled lead Lead rolled into sheets from cast slabs.
mill finish A finish of aluminium in which the surface is left without treatment and allowed to weather naturally. cf. **anodizing**.
mill scale A layer of black oxide of iron produced during the hot rolling of steel.
millwork (USA) Prefabricated joinery. cf. **prefabrication**.
mineral fibre A generic term for all non-metallic inorganic fibres.
mineral-insulated cable See **metal-sheathed mineral-insulated cable**.
mineral streak A green or brown discoloration of hardwoods which is an aesthetic defect only.
mineral-surfaced bitumen felt A **bitumen felt** used as a **cap sheet** on built-up roofing, its upper surface finished with a dressing of slate or other stone particles. It is used on felt roofing with a slope of over 10°, whilst lower pitches are usually finished with a plain cap sheet and chippings because the chippings afford greater ultra-violet and thermal protection.
mineral wool A generic title for mineral fibres of a woolly consistency, normally made from molten glass, rock or slag.
miniature circuit breaker A compact mechanical device for making and breaking an electrical circuit both in normal conditions and, automatically, in abnormal conditions such as overcurrent and short circuit.
mini-bore (heating) system A **small-bore (heating) system** using very small flow and return pipes to the radiators.
mirror screw A wood screw with a tapped hole in the centre of its head to receive the threaded stud inside a hollow dome. This dome (usually chromium plated) conceals the screw head in face-fixed items such as mirrors.
mismatch 1. In matching **veneers**, a lack of fit in **figure** or **grain** of adjacent veneers. 2. A bad fit at a joint.
mission tile (USA) A **Spanish tile**.
mist coat A very thin, sprayed coat.
mitre An **angle joint** between two members of similar cross-section, each cut at the same angle (45° for a right-angled joint) and butted so that the line of the joint bisects the angle made by the two members. (USA, miter).

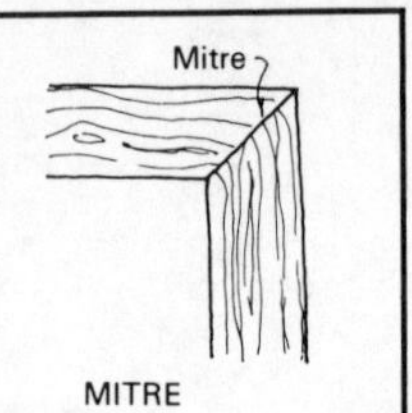

MITRE

mitre bevel In glass cutting, the 45° **bevel** (unless another angle is specified) of the edge of glass with the extreme point of the corner slightly arrised.

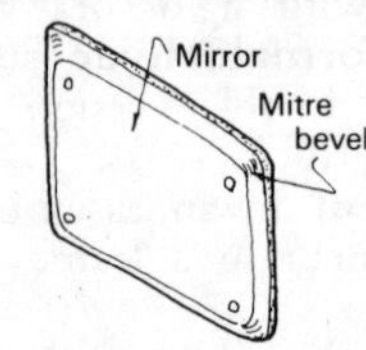

MITRE BEVEL

mitre block A device used in the cutting of **mitres** consisting of a rebated block of wood in which 45° saw cuts have been made.

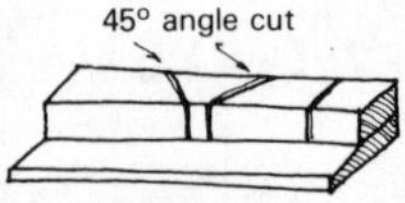

MITRE BLOCK

mitre brad A **corrugated fastener**.
mitred-and-cut string A **cut-and-mitred string**.
mitred border The margin of a hearth.
mitred cap A **newel** cap into which the **handrail** is mitred.
mitred closer A **brick closer** cut at an angle.
mitred hip A **close-cut hip**.
mitred knee The mitred meeting of the horizontal part of a **stair handrail** and a steeply falling part.
mitre dovetail A dovetail joint in which the pins are cut so as not to be visible and only the **mitre** shows.
mitred valley A **close-cut valley**.
mitre joint A **mitre**.

mitre (mitring) machine A **trimming machine**.
mitre saw A **tenon saw**.
mitre square A **bevel** in which the blade is set at 45° to the stock.
mitring Making a **mitre**.
mix 1. The proportions of the ingredients in **concrete**, **mortar** or **plaster**. 2. A batch of **concrete**, **mortar** or **plaster** after mixing.
mixing valve A valve in which separate supplies of hot and cold water are mixed, the outlet temperature being either manually or thermostatically controlled.
MOATS Methods of assessment and test, published by the Agrément Board in the UK.
modular brick A **brick** of a size that is consistent with the principles of metric modular design. Actual sizes of bricks available in the UK are 288 × 90 × 90 or 65 mm and 190 × 90 × 90 or 65 mm.
modular component A building component whose **co-ordinating sizes** comply with a **modular system**.
modular co-ordinating Dimensional co-ordination.
modular grid A reference grid in which the distance between consecutive parallel grid lines is a **module** or multiple of a module.
modular masonry unit (USA) A brick or building block which (including joint) courses in multiples of 100 mm vertically. In plan the unit is also a multiple of 100 mm in both directions allowing for one joint in each direction.
modular plane One of the planes bordering and defining a **modular zone** within which is housed a component or group of components.
modular system The use of a **planning grid** based on a module or multiples of that module, on the lines of which all major elements of structure and divisions of space fall (see **dimensional co-ordination**).
modular zone A zone between **modular planes**, provided either to house a component or group of components (which need not necessarily fill the space), or to be left empty.

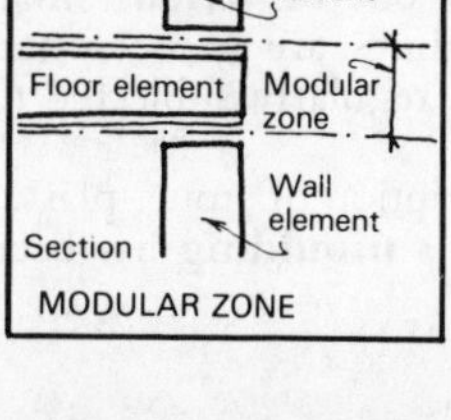

module 1. A convenient unit of size used in single or multiple units to create a **planning grid**. 2. One completed unit or section of a prefabricated building where several such sections are used side by side to create the whole building.
modulus of elasticity The ratio of **stress** to **strain** in a material over the range for which this remains constant (the elastic range). Sometimes known as Young's modulus when referring to **tension** and **compression**; or modulus of rigidity when referring to **shear**.
moisture barrier An imprecise term which can mean either a **vapour barrier** or a **damp-proof course**.
moisture content The quantity of water in a material, usually expressed as a percentage of its dry weight. Moisture content is particularly important in wood for carpentry and joinery. At a moisture content of 20% it is practically immune from fungal attack.
moisture equilibrium A condition reached by a material, such as wood, at a given temperature and **relative humidity** at which it no longer absorbs or desorbs more water than is necessary to maintain a stable moisture content.
moisture expansion Increase in the volume of a material brought about by absorption of moisture.
moisture gradient The variation in **moisture content** between different surfaces of a building component (*eg* a piece of wood, or a wall) due to evaporation or absorption of moisture from one side only.
moisture movement Reversible dimensional change produced by a component absorbing or losing water.
moler brick or moler block An insulating brick or block made from **diatomaceous earth**.
moment of force The product of a force and the distance between the point at which the force operates and the position where the moment of force is to be determined.
moment of inertia (I) That property of a structural member which is made up of the sum of its particles multiplied by the squares of their distances from the **neutral axis**. It is the resistance of the section to rotation.
moment of resistance (R) The resistance of a beam to forces inducing bending, made up of the permissible stress of the material of construction and the **moment of inertia** of the beam.
monitor roof A flat or pitched roof hav-

ing a continuous **rooflight**, usually across the full width of the span.

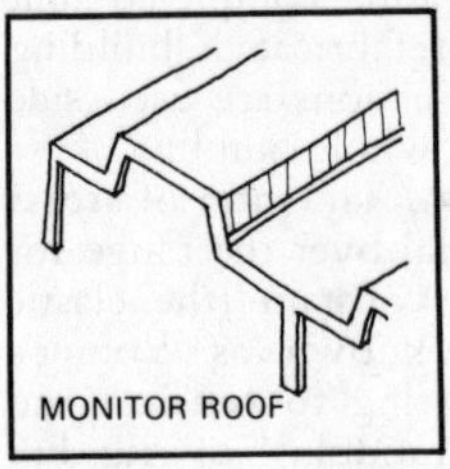
MONITOR ROOF

monk bond **Flemish bond** brickwork in which the sequence of two **stretchers** and one **header** is repeated in each course.

MONK BOND

monkey tail A scroll pointing downwards at the end of a **handrail**.

monkey-tail bolt An **extension bolt.**

monolithic screed A floor screed laid immediately following, or within a short time of, the laying of the concrete slab.

monomer The unit molecule from which a polymer is built up.

mono-pitch roof A single slope pitched roof.

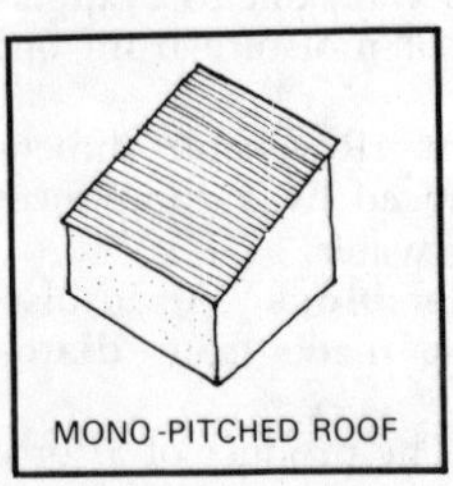
MONO-PITCHED ROOF

mopstick handrail A handrail of a generally circular cross-section except for a small flat surface underneath.

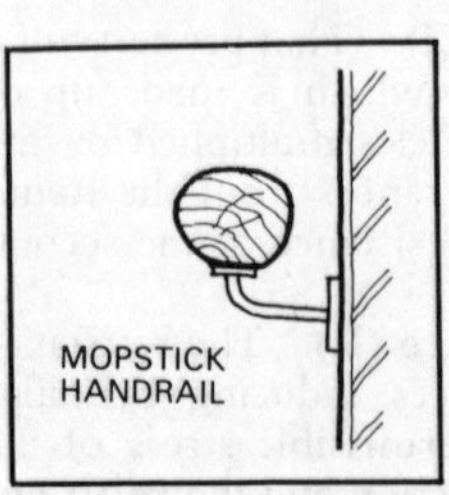
MOPSTICK HANDRAIL

mortar A mixture used to bed bricks, blocks or stones, containing either sand and cement, sand and lime, or sand, lime and cement. Other additives such as **plasticizers** may be included. cf. **masonry cement**.

mortar board A **hawk**.

mortar-cube test A test of the strength of a **mortar** mix, involving the crushing of a standard cube made from the mix, in a standard way having allowed it to harden for a specified time.

mortise 1. A rectangular slot cut in one member to receive a tenon cut in another; usually in joinery, when the mortise width should not exceed one-third of the width of the timber into which it is cut. 2. A rectangular sinking in a stone to receive a **cramp**.

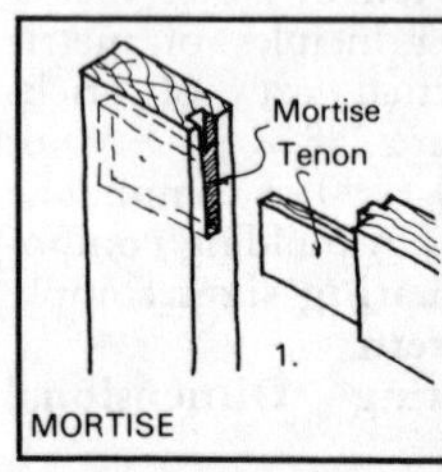

MORTISE

mortise-and-tenon joint A joint, usually between members at right angles to each other, in which a **tenon** is cut in the end of one member, with fits into a **mortise** cut in the other (*eg* between a door **rail** and **stile**).

mortise chisel A strong, stiff chisel meant to be struck with a hammer and used to cut out mortises.

mortise joint A **mortise-and-tenon joint**.

mortise latch A door **latch** set into a **mortise** cut in the **stile**. cf. **rim latch**.

mortise lock A door **lock** set into a **mortise** cut in the **stile**. cf. **rim lock**.

mortising machine A power-operated machine for cutting mortises in timber.

mosaic Small pieces of ceramic or glass cemented together, usually on to a flat backing surface, to create a pattern or design.

motorized valve A valve operated by an electric motor.

mottler A flat thick paint brush for **graining** or **marbling**.

mould A **form** for casting precast concrete units. 2. Any one of various small fungi which sometimes are to be found on walls which are regularly subjected to condensation.

moulded The description of stone, plaster or wood on which a **moulding** has been cut.

moulded plywood **Plywood** bent during gluing to form a permanently curved form.

moulding 1. The act of shaping a piece of material. 2. A shaped piece of material (often wood) such as a **quadrant** or **bolection mould**. 3. A projection or groove on a surface used as decoration or to shed water.

moulding machine A machine for cutting mouldings in wood or stone.

moulding plane A hand **plane** used to cut **mouldings** in wooden members.

mould oil Oil or emulsion applied to the face of **forms** to act as a release agent.

mouth The slot in the sole of a plane through which the **cutting iron** projects.

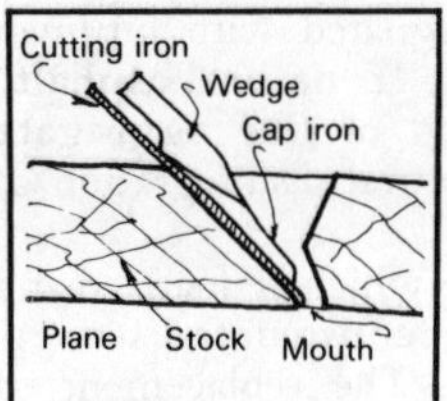

MOUTH

movement joint A straight, wide joint formed in a vertical or horizontal plane (wall or slab) and rendered weatherproof by pointing with a flexible non-setting **sealant**, or filled with a flexible **gasket**, or covered by a metal cover fixed to one side of the joint only. The joint is intended to allow all normal thermal, moisture or other movements expected of the material making up the plane to take place, and the jointing must be sufficiently flexible and the joint sufficiently wide to allow this to happen. Movement joints are, in effect, planes of weakness which prevent any build-up of stress which might result from the natural movement characteristics of the component.

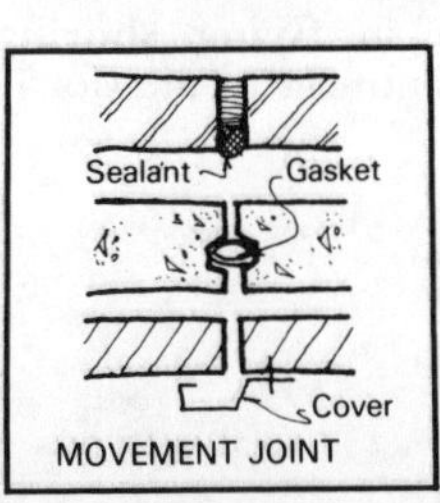

MOVEMENT JOINT

MR adhesive An adhesive or glue that is 'moisture resistant' that is it will be moderately resistant to the weather, will withstand cold water for long periods and hot water for short periods, and is resistant to micro-organisms. A typical member of this category is **urea formaldehyde** adhesive.

mullion A member that divides a door or window vertically into **lights**; not to be confused with **glazing bars** which divide a light into panes and can be vertical or horizontal. cf. **transom**.

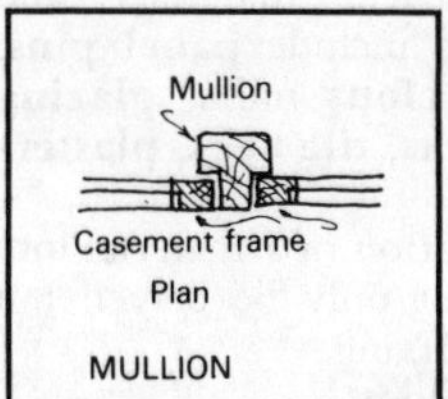

MULLION

multiple glazing Glazing composed of more than one sheet of glass, for reasons of thermal or sound insulation. The sheets may be bonded together in **sealed units** or used in separate **lights**.

multi-point water heater A gas, or electric, instantaneous water-heater which supplies more than one tap.

multi-unit wall (USA) A wall built of two or more half-brick thicknesses.

Munsell system A reference system for colour based on the three attributes of hue, value (lightness) and chroma (**saturation**).

Munsell value The estimated lightness of a colour on a scale of 10 equal sensation intervals extending from ideal black (0) to ideal white (10).

muntin 1. A vertical member in a framed door which separates the **panels**, *ie* a member framed between **head** and **rail**, or between **rail** and **rail**. 2. (USA) A **glazing bar** or a **mullion**.

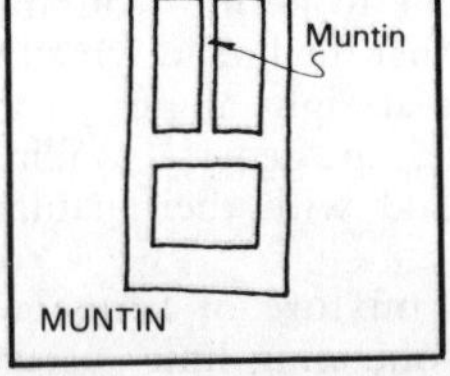

MUNTIN

mushroom head A head shape of a screw which is circular in plan and in the shape of a mushroom in elevation.

N

nail A simple form of mechanical fixing device used to fix two or more components together, made of metal and placed by driving with a **hammer**. Nails fall into two broad categories, **wire nails** and **cut nails**, and can have a variety of head styles (**countersunk**, **cheese**, **pan** and **lost-head**), shank cross-section (round, oval or rectangular), materials and finishes. Nail types include **panel pins**, **escutcheon pins**, **clout nails**, **glazing springs**, **brads**, **tacks**, **tile pegs**, **plasterboard nails** etc.

nailable The description of a material into which **nails** can not only be driven but also make a secure fixing.

nail float A **devil float**.

nailing block A **fixing brick**.

nailing ground A **rough ground**.

nail plate A metal mechanical fixing device used to connect pieces of wood which lie in the same plane as each other. It usually consists of a thin metal plate (frequently galvanized steel) either punctured with holes, through which nails are driven, or with integral nail-like teeth pressed out of the plate.

nail punch A short, blunt, steel tool used to drive a **nail** below the surface of a wood component. One end is intended to be hit by a **hammer**; the other tapers to the diameter of a small nail head.

narrow-ringed timber Wood with **annual rings** close together due to its slow growth; generally stronger than quickly grown timber.

natural ageing See **age hardening**.

natural asphalt A mixture of bitumen and considerable quantities of inert mineral matter, which occurs naturally in oil-bearing strata.

natural bed A plane parallel to the strata in which a sedimentary stone occurs in the quarry. For stone to be most durable it should be cut so that the line in which it is to be stressed is at right angles to its natural bed; hence, in general walling stones should be laid with their natural bed horizontal.

natural cement A mixture of limestone and clay, or clay containing lime, occurring naturally and producing a **hydraulic cement** when burnt.

natural circulation The movement of heated or cooled air, water or other fluid by **convection** rather than by any mechanical means.

natural draught A movement of air caused by a difference of pressure between internal and external areas, or one internal area and another. For example, the reduction of pressure in a room due to warmed air rising up a chimney can cause natural draughts.

naturally seasoned See **air seasoned**.

natural resin A member of a group of glassy, amorphous, organic solids secreted by certain plants (such as copal by trees) and insects (shellac). It is insoluble in water, but soluble in many organic solvents.

natural rock asphalt A consolidated calcareous rock impregnated with bitumen by a natural process. cf. **natural asphalt**.

natural sand A sand or **fine aggregate** produced by the natural disintegration of rock.

natural stone Stone which is quarried and cut, in contrast to **reconstructed stone**.

natural ventilation The replacement of air in rooms without resort to fans (*ie* by means of windows, louvres and ventilation grilles). cf. **mechanical ventilation**.

neat A description of **cement** or **plaster** mixed with water and used without the addition of sand or lime.

neat (or finished) size The term applied to the dimensions of a carpentry or joinery component after cutting and planing.

neat work Brickwork which is above the ground level and is therefore visible.

needle 1. A short, horizontal beam of wood or steel which is placed through a wall when its means of support is about to be removed, *eg*, during **underpinning**. It supports the wall (in conjunction with other **props** or **shores** during such building work and is itself supported on a pair of **dead shores**. 2. A horizontal steel or timber component in **flying shoring**, which acts as an abutment to the sloping shores. cf. **shore**.

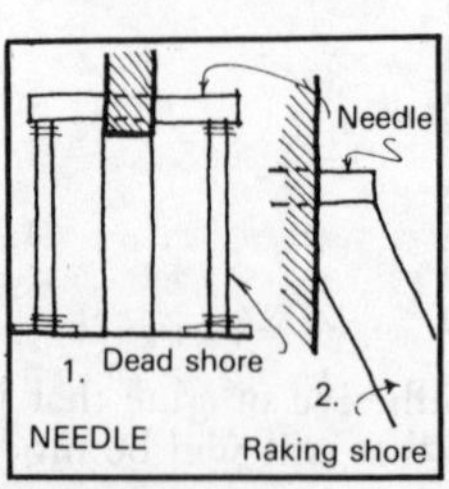

NEEDLE

needle bath A **shower** with multi-directional jets, mainly horizontal.

needle scaffold A **scaffold** hung from **needles** driven into the wall.

neoprene A synthetic rubber, consisting of the polymer polychloroprene.

neoprene paint A paint based on a type of synthetic rubber, usually of a two-part type with a vulcanizing agent used as a catalyst. This type of paint is both chemical resistant and weather resistant.

nest of saws A set of saw blades which can be used in the same handle, the blade chosen depending on the type of work being undertaken.

net floor area The usable floor area of a building, or part of a building, including all relevant floor levels, but excluding such things as staircases, landings, partitions, chimneys, built-in cupboards and service areas ancillary to the usable area.

network A graphical representation of activities and/or events in a project with their inter-relationships and dependencies. cf. **activity-on-arrow network** and **activity-on-node network**.

network analysis A technique for presenting information to assist in the planning and control of projects, in which the sequence and logical inter-relationships of all activities are represented by a diagrammatic **network**.

neutral axis That plane, in a structural member which is being subjected to bending, where the longitudinal stress is zero.

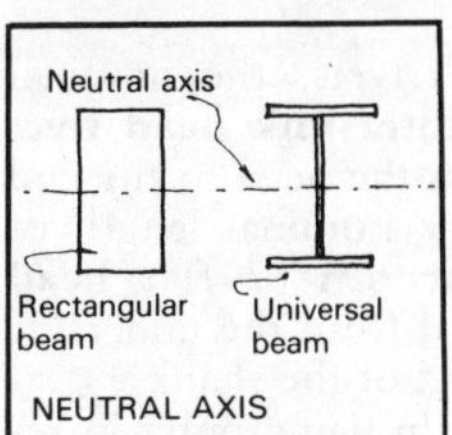

NEUTRAL AXIS

neutralizing The preparation of a **concrete**, **cement**, **mortar** or **plaster** surface to prevent the free **lime** in the base from attacking the paint with which the surface is to be treated.

newel or newel post 1. A post in a flight of **stairs** carrying the ends of the **outer string** and **handrail** and supporting them at a change in direction. 2. In a spiral stair, the central column or post carrying the inner ends of the **treads**.

newel cap A wooden piece fixed on top of the **newel** post.

newel drop The projection of a **newel** below the soffit of a **ceiling**, usually as a decorative feature.

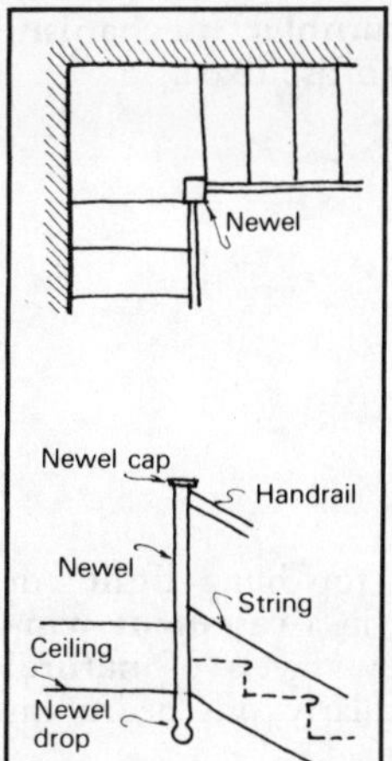

NEWEL

newel joint A joint between a **newel** and the **string** or **handrail**.

newton (N) A unit of **force**. 1 N is the force required to produce an acceleration of 1 m per s^2 in a body with a mass of 1 kg (1N = 0.102 kg force).

nib 1. On a tile, the downward projecting lug which hooks over a tiling **batten**. 2. The top edge of an asphalt upstand which fits into a chase in the wall. 3. A solid particle which projects above a film of **varnish** or **paint** and which, with others, produces a finish which is called 'bitty'.

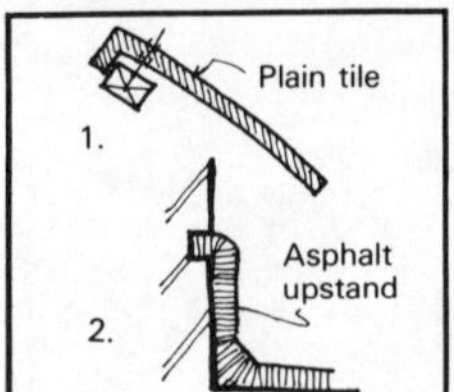

NIB

nib guide A **straight edge** nailed on the **floating coat** of a ceiling which is to receive an ***in situ*** cornice mould. It is used with a **running rule** to provide control in the forming of the mould.

nicker 1. A **centre bit**. 2. A mason's broad chisel for cutting a groove in a stone before splitting it.

night latch Any latch having a single spring bolt, withdrawn from the outside by key and from the inside by a knob or handle. It usually has a thumb slide or the equivalent to hold the bolt in either the withdrawn position or the locked position when desired. Night latches are generally made with a **pin tumbler mechanism** and can be rim or mortise fixed.

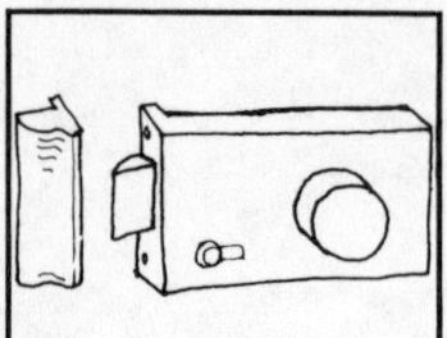

NIGHT LATCH

night vent A small top hung **light** or other small opening in a **casement window** to provide low levels of **natural ventilation**, particularly in bedrooms when they are occupied.

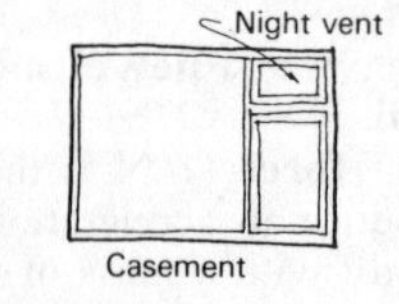

NIGHT VENT

nippers Two curved levers hinged together and used as a grab attached to the lifting hook of a crane. The action of lifting the nippers closes the levers. Used for moving large blocks of stone, etc.

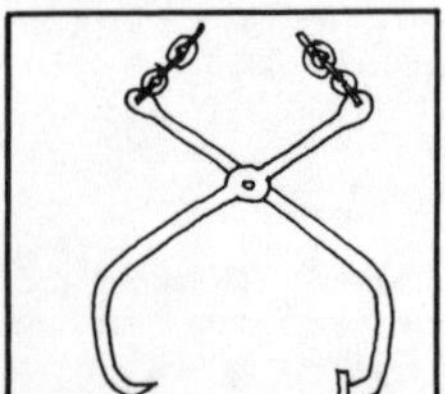

NIPPERS

nipple 1. A small valve for releasing air from hot-water systems; it is positioned on radiators or high points in the system. 2. A short pipe threaded on the outside at both ends with a **taper thread** for joining internally threaded pipes. 3. A point for the injection of grease into a machine part.

node 1. The point in a **network** at which arrows start and/or finish. cf. **activity-on-node network**. 2. The junction of a number of members of a **space frame**.

no-fines aggregate **Aggregate** in which there is a minimum of particles passing a 10 mm test sieve.

no-fines concrete Concrete made without any **fine aggregate**. cf. **no-fines aggregate**. As a result, it contains large pores which prohibit the capillary passage of water. Although it has low moisture movement and can be plastered or rendered readily because of its texture, it has relatively low strength. cf. **capillarity**.

nog 1. A **fixing brick** or block. 2. A **nogging**.

nogging 1. Horizontal timber members between **studs** in timber-framed walls or partitions. They are used to stiffen the studs. 2. **Brick nogging**.

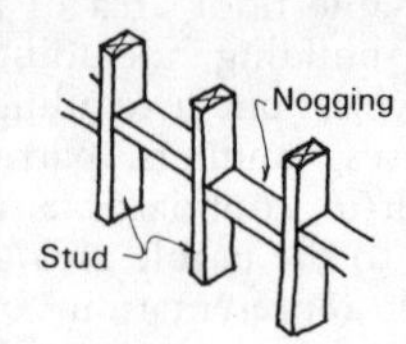

NOGGING

noise Sound which is undesired by the recipient.

noise absorption The attenuation of sounds brought about by this absorption by the surrounding structure and furnishings as a result of their density, structure or anechoic finishes.

noise insulation See **sound insulation**.

noise level See **loudness** (**level**).

nominal capacity The total volume of a **cistern**, **tank** or **cylinder** calculated from the external dimensions. cf. **actual capacity**.

nominal length Of rivets, the nominal length of a flat **countersunk head** rivet being measured from the head to the end of the shank and the nominal length of **round**, **pan**, **mushroom** or **flat head** rivets being measured from the underside of the head to the end of the shank.

nominal size A size in name only; in reference to timber this is the size of the unwrought timber (*ie* sawn but not yet worked or planed), usually about 6–8 mm larger than the finished or **dressed size**. In reference to manufactured products it is the intended size, which in practice may be subject to plus or minus tolerances.

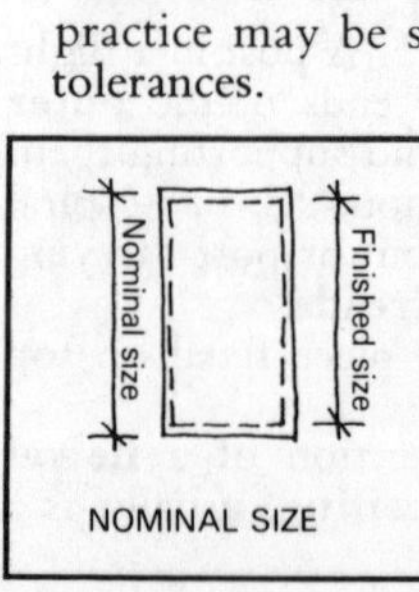

NOMINAL SIZE

nominated subcontractor The supplier of labour and materials who is named in the **Bill of Quantities** as the one to undertake a particular part of a project, and with whom the contractor must place the relevant subcontract.

nominated supplier The supplier of materials or goods who is named in the **Bill of Quantities** as the one from whom the contractor must obtain such materials or goods.

non-combustible The description of a material which is incapable of supporting **combustion**. (This term is preferred to 'incombustible').

non-ferrous The description of a metal which does not contain iron.

non-flammable The description of a material which is incapable of burning with a flame.

non-hydraulic lime **High calcium lime**.

non-manipulative joint A joint between pipes, such as a **compression joint**, which requires no work to the pipe ends other than cutting square.

non-return valve A device that prevents the reversion of flow of gas or liquid.

non-reversible movement That movement of a structure or component which is due to the physical characteristic of its composition and is a one-way dimensional change, *eg* the shrinkage of a concrete frame.

non-slip nosing A **nosing** of a **stair** which contains a material such as carborundum which discourages slipping.

Norfolk latch A **thumb latch**.

normal roll pantile A **pantile** in which the roll is parallel from head to tail.

north-light roof A **double-pitched roof** having its two planes at different angles, in the northern hemisphere the northerly plane is at a steeper slope, in the southern hemisphere the southerly plane is steeper.

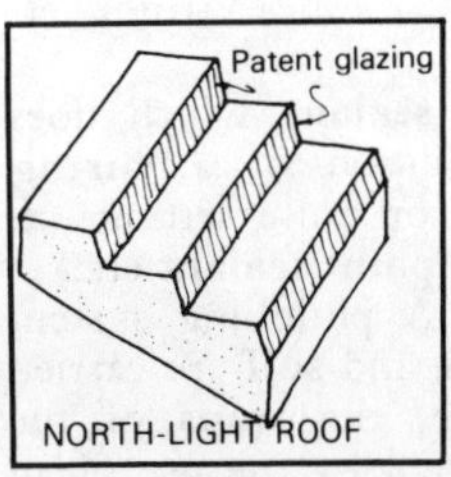

NORTH-LIGHT ROOF

nose 1. A blunt overhang or **nosing**. 2. The lower end of the **shutting stile** of a door or **casement window**.

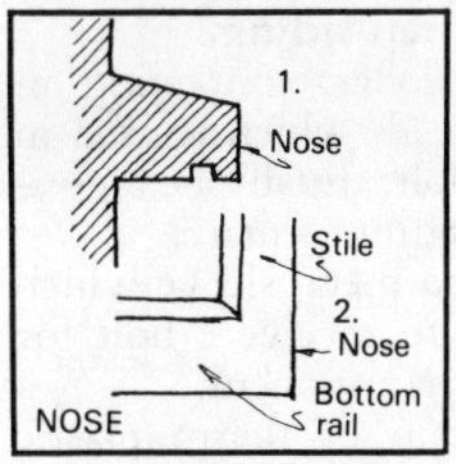

NOSE

nosing A usually rounded and slightly overhanging edge to a **stair tread**, flat roof, window sill etc.

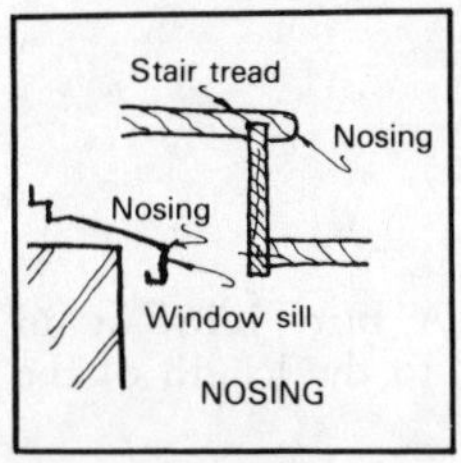

NOSING

nosing line The inclined line joining the upper edges of the nosings of a stair and from which the **margin** of a **close string** is measured.

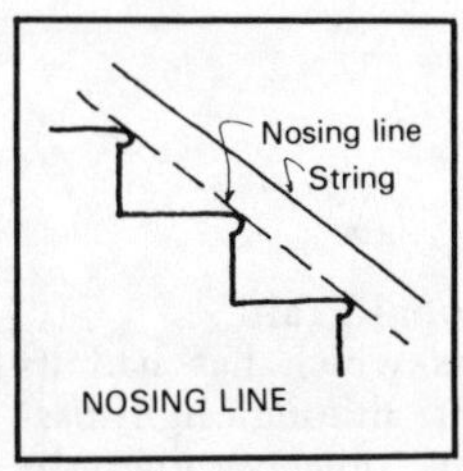

NOSING LINE

notch A groove in one component to receive another component.

notching The joining of two components by cutting a part out of one or both.

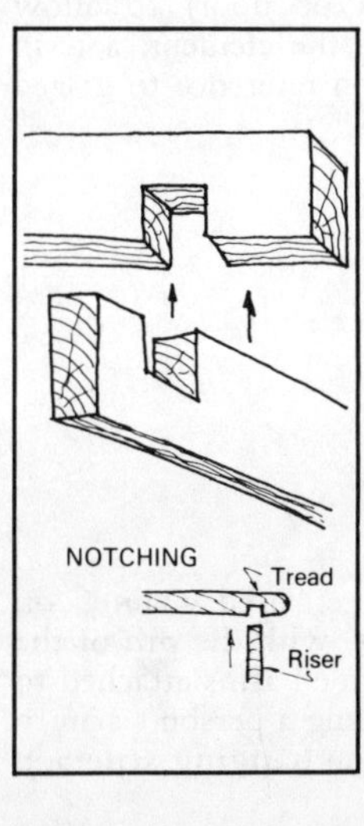

NOTCHING

novelty siding **German siding**.

nut The thick metal collar, containing an internal coupling thread, which is used in conjunction with a bolt; usually hexagonal in shape, but sometimes square.

nut socket A threaded metal sleeve which is cast into concrete to receive a bolt for the fixing of another component.

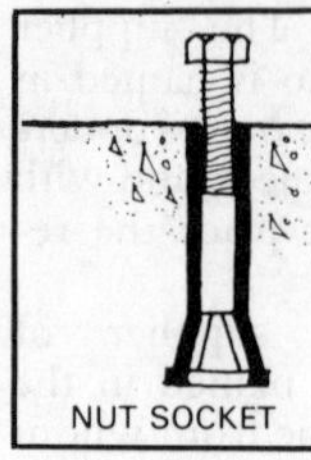
NUT SOCKET

nylon One of a group of thermoplastic polyamides with high softening temperatures, strength and toughness and self-lubricating properties.

O

oblique butt joint A **butt joint** at an angle other than 90° to the length of the components.

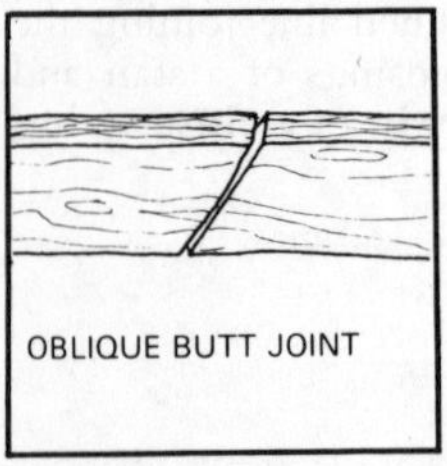
OBLIQUE BUTT JOINT

oblique grain **Diagonal grain**.

obscured glass **Glass** which has had its surface treated so that, although light passes through the pane, objects cannot be seen through it. Treatments include sand blasting and decorative patterns moulded into the surface of the glass.

observation panel A glazed panel in a solid element (wall or door) to allow observation through the element; a term used particularly with reference to glazed panels in flush doors.

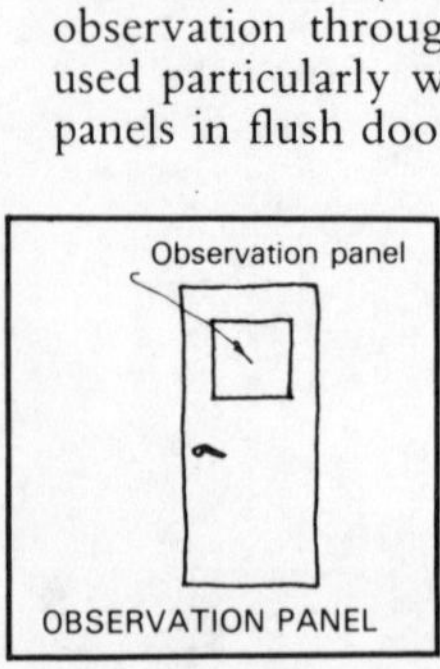

OBSERVATION PANEL

offset hinge A hinge, used mainly on **casement windows**, with the **pin** of the hinge offset on extended arms attached to the **flaps**, thus allowing a person's arm to be passed between the **hanging stile** and the frame to clean the outside of the window; sometimes called an easy clean hinge.

ohm The unit of electrical resistance.

oil-bound water paint A **distemper** containing **drying oil**.

oil paint A paint in which the non-volatile portion of the **medium** consists solely of **drying oils**.

oil slip An **oilstone slip**.

oil stain A thin oil paint with little pigment

oilstone A **hone**.

oilstone slip A small curved-edge **hone** for sharpening **gouges** and the concave **cutting irons** of **planes**.

oil varnish A clear or tinted finish which may be used on timber internally or externally, depending on the particular grade of **varnish** employed.

oleo-resinous paint A paint composed of drying oils in conjunction with hardening resins, the latter being either natural or synthetic.

olive See **gland**.

oncosts Contract **overheads**.

one-part adhesive An **adhesive** which does not require the addition of a **curing agent** to encourage or cause setting. cf. **two-part adhesive**.

one-part sealant A **sealant** which does not require the addition of a **curing agent** to encourage or cause setting. cf. **two-part adhesive** (**paint sealant** etc.)

one-pipe system 1. A plumbing system in which both **waste** and **soil** are carried by a common pipe, the **traps** of the fittings being protected by the use of an **anti-siphonage** pipe. cf. **single-stack plumbing system**. 2. A wet heating system in which both flow and return connections of radiators are connected to a single circulating pipe. cf. **two-pipe system**.

one-stage joint A joint, such as a **filled joint**, that relies on only one defence against the ingress of water.

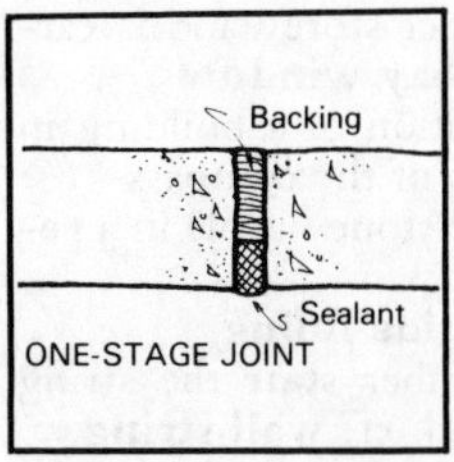

opacity The **hiding power** of a paint; the opposite of transparency.

opal glass Glass which is opalescent or white in appearance; made by adding fluorides such as fluorspar or cryolite, to the molten glass. It has good powers of diffusion.

opaque Having a resistance to the passage of light; totally absorbent of light rays of a specified wavelength.

open assembly time The time which elapses between the application of **glue** to components which are to be bonded and the bringing together of the components.

open circuit A circuit within an intruder alarm system which, when closed, creates an alarm.

open cornice (USA) **Open eaves**.

open defect Any defect in timber taking the form of a hole or split, *eg* a **knot** hole or **check**.

open eaves **Eaves** in which the underside of each rafter is exposed, *ie* eaves having no **soffit board**.

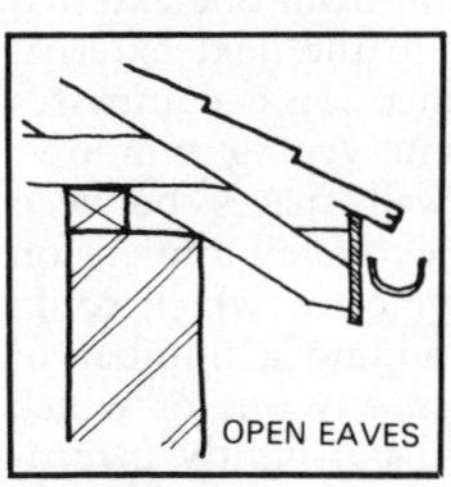

open fire A solid-fuel burning fire in a fireplace as opposed to an enclosed heater or stove.

open floor A suspended floor in which the joists are not underdrawn by a ceiling.

open grained A description of coarse-textured wood with annual rings set far apart.

opening leaf The hinged leaf of a **folding door** which normally is in continuous use, as opposed to a standing or dead leaf. cf. **standing leaf**.

opening light A window **light** which may be opened as opposed to a **dead light** which is designed not to be opened.

open joint A joint in **rain screen cladding**. No seal is used, but water passing through the joint is captured by trays or shields and drained harmlessly away.

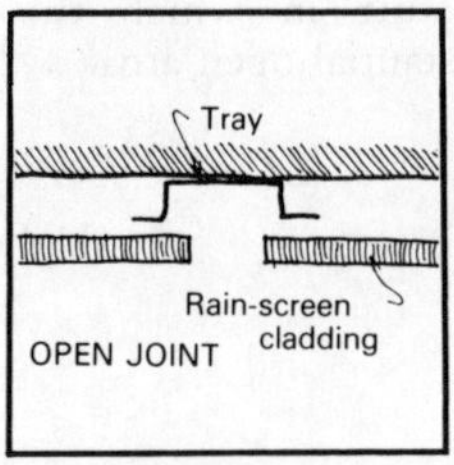

open mortise A **mortise** which is open on three edges, being made in the end of a member. Also known as a slot mortise.

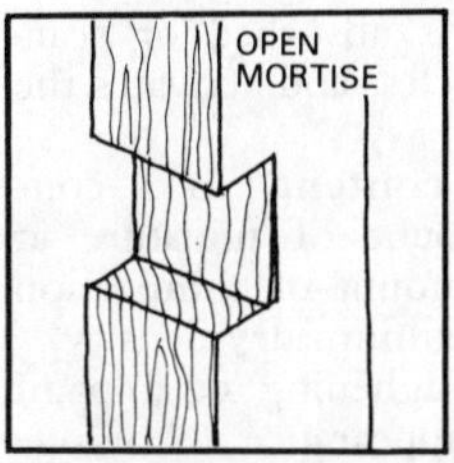

open-newel stair A stair without **newels**, as a **geometric stair**; a stair having successive flights rising in opposite directions about a rectangular well.

open planning The designing of a building without fixed partitions, except round stair wells, lifts and amenity rooms.

open roof A pitched roof which is not under-drawn by a ceiling and therefore leaves the **rafters** exposed.

open slating Slates laid with a gap between adjacent slates on the same **course**. The gap is usually restricted so that there is at least 100 mm side lap.

open stair (USA) A **stair** which has no wall on one or both sides. cf. **closed stair**.

open string A **cut string**.

open tender A **tender** which is advertised and in which tenderers are not selected by the client or his advisers. Contractors can apply for inclusion in the list of tenderers.

open valley A valley in which the roof covering elements are set so as to expose the valley gutter; as opposed to a **secret gutter**. cf. **swept valley**.

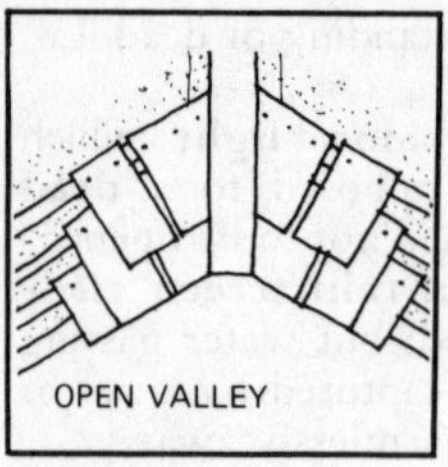

open-well stair A **stair** in which the **flights** enclose a substantial open area.

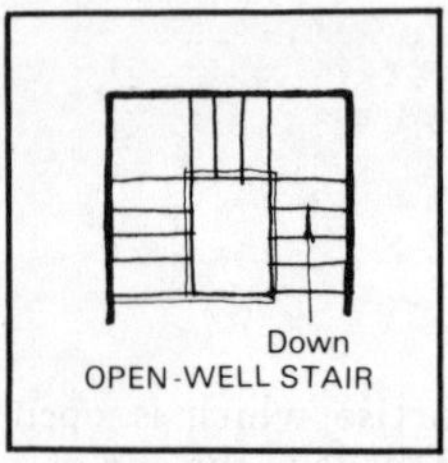

optical smoke detector A form of fire detector in which a photoelectric cell responds when light is absorbed or scattered by smoke particles, and activates the alarm.

optimum moisture content In a concrete mix, the amount of moisture at which a specified amount of compaction will produce the maximum dry density.

orange peel The roughening of a paint surface, similar in appearance to orange peel, caused by poor spraying techniques.

ordinary Portland cement See **Portland cement**.

ordinary quality brick A brick which can be used for external walling, but which, because it usually has a greater absorption and lower density than a **special quality brick**, is not recommended for positions of extreme exposure.

Ordnance Bench Mark A **bench mark**, distinguished by a broad arrow surmounted by a horizontal line, officially established by the Ordnance Survey and representing a level related to the Ordnance datum.

Ordnance datum A level established with reference to heights shown on an Ordnance Survey map.

Ordnance Survey (OS) A survey of Great Britain covering land, building, roads, etc. Based on the original triangulation made by the Board of Ordnance it is published as maps which give the whole country a unified reference system.

organic solvent preservative A solution of various chemicals in an oil solvent (usually volatile) or sometimes heavier oils, which is used to treat timber. After treatment, the volatile solvent evaporates leaving the preservative in the wood. Among the toxic substances used are pentachlorophenol, chlorinated naphthalenes and naphthenates of copper and zinc.

oriel window or oriel A window which projects from an upper storey and is carried on **corbels**. cf. **bay window**.

orientation The position of a building in relation to the points of the compass.

outband A **stretcher** stone visible in a **reveal**.

outer lining An **outside lining**.

outer string In a timber **stair** the string furthest from the wall. cf. **wall string**.

outfall The place of discharge of a sewer.

outlet 1. A discharge point from a container or gutter. 2. A **socket outlet**.

output The capacity of a heating appliance or boiler.

outrigger 1. A projecting beam or assembly of beams, joists or scaffold tubes or proprietary brackets to which the upper ends of suspension members of a **flying scaffold** or similar construction are secured. 2. Extendible structural members on a mobile crane which increase the effective base and stability of the crane in use.

outside casing An **outside lining**.

outside glazing Glazing in which the glass is placed into the frame from outside the building.

outside lining The members forming the outside of a **cased frame**.

oven-dry timber Wood dried in a ventilated oven at 103 °C (±2 °C) until there is no further fall in moisture content.

overall dimension A dimension which encompasses a series of other dimensions, *eg* the dimension from one external corner of a building to the next external corner when that dimension encompasses the dimensions of intervening windows or doors and the wall spaces between them. Measuring the overall dimension avoids any cumulative error which could result from merely adding a number of smaller measurements, any one of which or all of which could be slightly inaccurate.

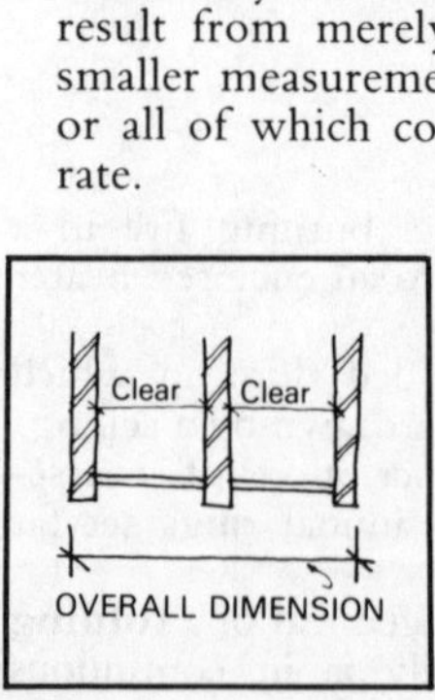

overcloak In **flexible-metal roofing**, that part of the upper sheet which overlaps the lower sheet at a **drip**, **roll** or **seam**.

overflow pipe A pipe positioned above the normal water level in a **tank** or **cistern**, thus allowing excess water to flow harmlessly to waste in the event of the **ball valve**, or similar device, failing to close.

overgrainer A brush like a long thin **mottler** used for **graining** and **marbling**.

overhand work External bricks laid from inside the building rather than from an external scaffolding.

overhang The part of a building or component which projects beyond the structure that supports it.

overhanging eaves **Eaves** in which the rafters and roof finish project beyond the outside surface of the external wall cf. **flush eaves**.

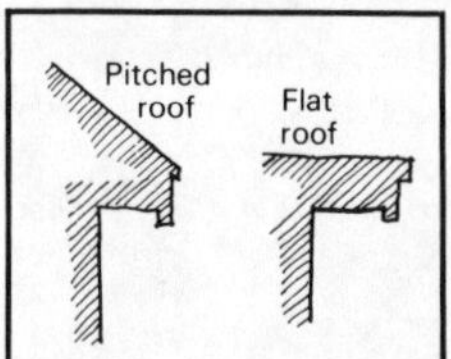

OVERHANGING EAVES

overhead door A door of one or more leaves that opens by being raised and slid into horizontal tracking at **door head** height.

overheads The costs of operating a site and running a contracting organization which have to be recovered not through an individual price in a **Bill of Quantities** but by being spread over all the **items** in the contract. Overheads include the costs of office staff, administration, accountancy, heating, lighting and telephones and, on the site, site administration, accommodation, temporary electricity supply and usage, temporary roads, scaffolding, hoardings etc.

overlay flooring **Parquet strip flooring**.

over-purlin lining The internal lining of a sheeted roof in which the lining sheets are carried over the top of the roof **purlins**. cf. **under-purlin lining**.

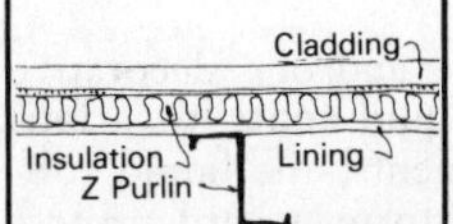

OVER-PURLIN LINING

oversailing course A brick or stone **string course** or **corbelling**.

oversite concrete A layer of concrete laid on the earth under a ground floor, usually 100 to 150 mm thick.

overtime Payment for work outside normal working hours, the remuneration being at a higher rate (time-and-a-half, double-time) than for normal working.

oxidation 1. The formation of oxides or other compounds on metals as a result of the combination of oxygen with the metal, as in the **rusting** of ferrous metals. 2. The hardening of **drying oils** by the air as a result of their absorption of oxygen to form a durable **film**.

oxter piece The vertical member in **ashlering**.

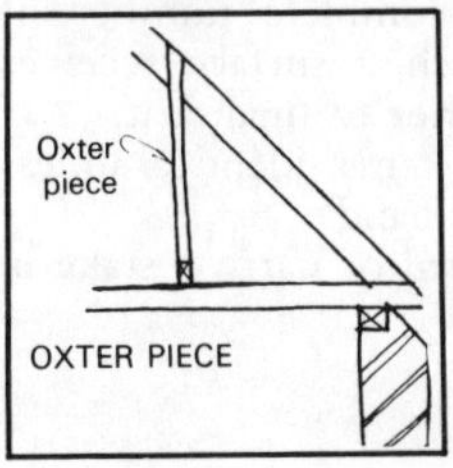

OXTER PIECE

oxychloride cement See **magnesite (composite)** flooring.

P

packing A small piece of material used to fill an oversized hole, *eg* small stones that fill gaps in **rubble walling**.

pad or padstone A stone, or now more often a precast concrete block, placed in a **loadbearing** wall below a point of load, *eg* at the seating of an **RSJ**, to spread the load in the wall.

pad foundation An isolated concrete foundation.

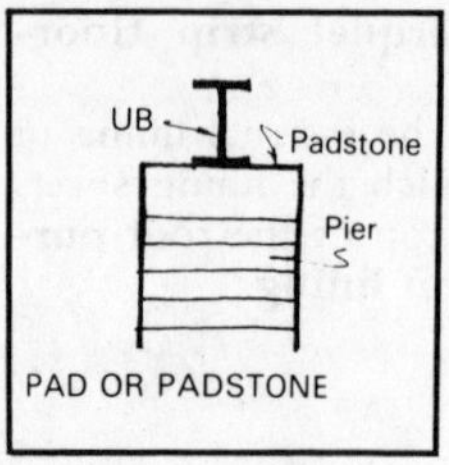

paint A protective and/or decorative material applied as liquid **coats** to various surfaces and components, the liquid subsequently drying to form a hard protective **film**.

painter's putty **Glazier's putty** used as a **filler**.

paint harling Paint-coated chippings thrown on to a sticky paint film to give a textured effect.

paint kettle A small steel pail used to hold paint during painting operations.

paint remover or paint stripper A liquid which when applied to a paint or varnish film softens it so that it can be easily scraped off.

paint system The complete number of coats of paint which a surface receives from **sealer** or **primer** to final coat.

pair Two matching items, identical unless they are of opposite hands.

pale An upright board or narrow stake in a **fence** or **palisade**.

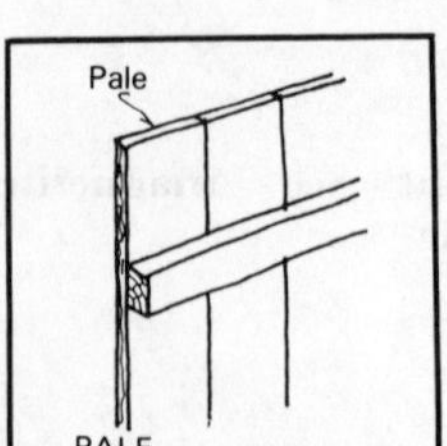

paling A run of fencing composed of pales.

palisade An enclosure or **fence** made up of vertical members or **pales**.

pallet A **fixing fillet**.

pan-and-roll roofing tiles (USA) **Italian tiles**.

pane 1. A sheet of glass cut to size to fit between the **glazing bars** or **frames** of a window or the **stiles** and **rails** of a door. 2. A **panel**. 3. The **peen** of a hammer.

panel 1. The timber, glass or other sheet material fitted into the rebates of a frame. 2. A brick, stone or precast concrete infill between steel or concrete structural frame members. 3. A single span or **bay** of a continuous concrete slab.

panel heater A radiant heater often set flush with the wall or ceiling surface and having a flat front plate heated either by a concealed coil of hot-water pipes or by an electric element.

panel heating Heating achieved by means of **panel heaters.**

panelled door A door made up of an outer framework of **stiles**, **head** and **bottom rail** with intermediate framing members (**rails** and **muntins**) forming a series of apertures which are filled with **panels** of wood or glass.

panel pin A small-headed, fine-gauge wire nail for fixing light timber components, mouldings or **plywood**. It can be easily punched home and the hole filled. Lengths from 15 to 75 mm and diameters from 1 to 2.6 mm.

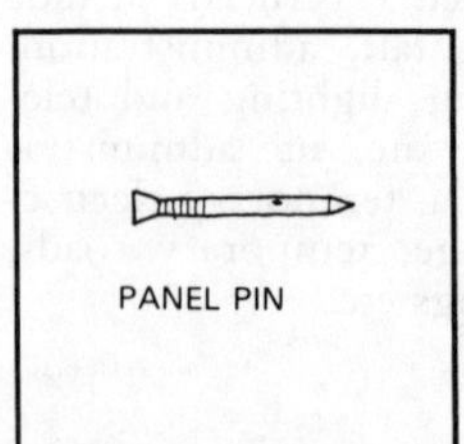

panel saw A **cross-cut saw**.

panel wall An external wall in framed construction, which receives support from the frame but carries only its own weight.

pan head screw A particular style of **machine screw** head, which is cylindrical with its upper edges rounded.

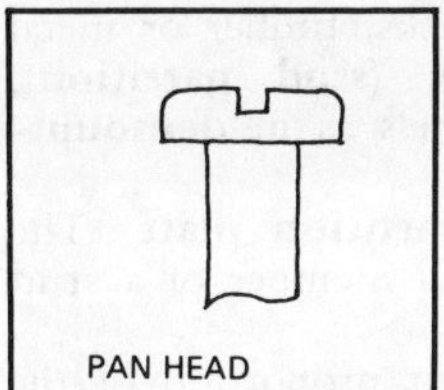

PAN HEAD

panic bolt A bolt for use on an emergency exit door. It provides connected top and bottom fastenings operated by a horizontal bar at waist height, so that in case of panic the pressure of people against the bar unfastens the bolts, allowing the door to swing open outwards. Because there is no operating mechanism on the outside of the door this type of bolt is also used where it is necessary to provide an exit from a building whilst barring entry.

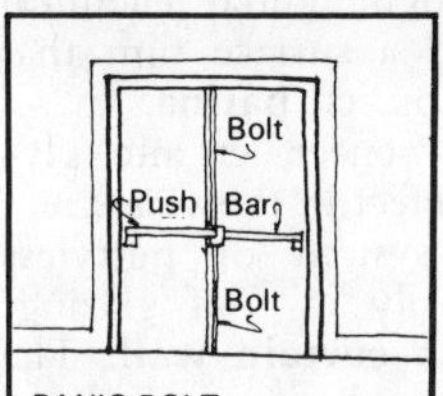

PANIC BOLT

pantile A traditional **single-lap** tile with a cross-section in the form of a flattened S shape, each tile on a roof overlapping the adjacent tile on the right (looking from the ground) and the tile in the course below. The traditional pantile has no grooves at either horizontal or vertical overlap, but modern versions (interlocking pantiles) do have such grooves, which coincide with reciprocal grooving in the lapped tiles. Pantiles are generally secured by nailing and have a ledging **nib**.

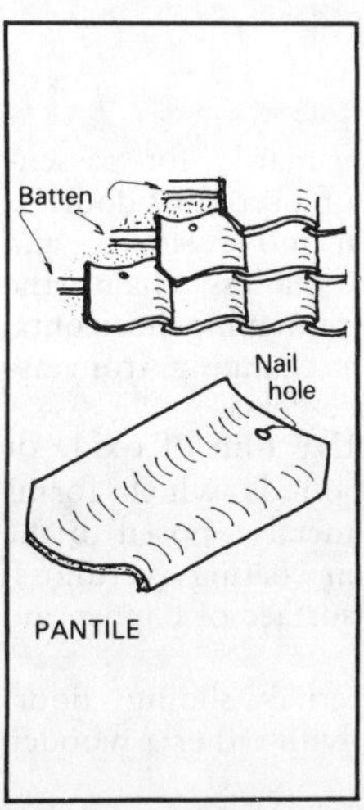

PANTILE

paper felt A thin felt composed of compressed cellulose fibre.

parabolic arch See **arch**.

parallel coping A coping, without **weathering**, usually used to cover a sloping wall top such as a **gable**.

parallel gutter A **box gutter**.

parallelogram of forces A graphical method of determining the resultant of two forces, in which the two sides of a parallelogram represent the two forces drawn to scale and the diagonal of the parallelogram represents the direction and size (to scale) of the resultant force.

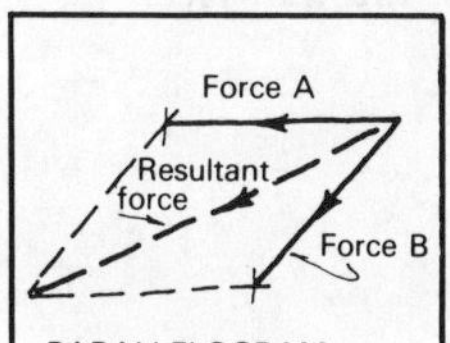

PARALLELOGRAM OF FORCES

parallel thread A screw thread of uniform diameter as used for a **bolt** or **machine screw** cf. **taper thread**.

parapet or parapet wall A low wall protecting the edge of a balcony or bridge, or that part of the external wall of a building that continues above the roof and is thus exposed on both front and back faces.

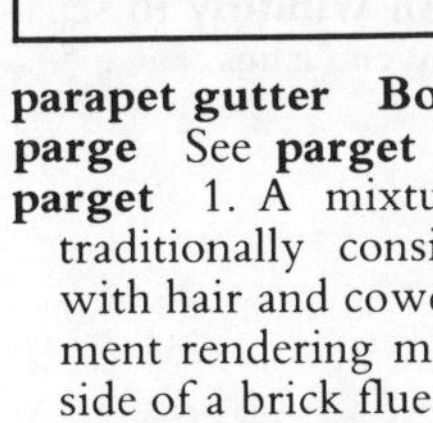

PARAPET (WALL)

parapet gutter **Box gutter**.

parge See **parget** 1.

parget 1. A mixture used in rendering, traditionally consisting of **coarse stuff** with hair and cowdung, now usually a cement rendering mix. It is used on the inside of a brick flue. 2. Ornamental work in plaster; a facing of plaster with designs either in relief or indented, used as a wall decoration, particularly to outside walls in Suffolk and Essex.

pargeting 1. The operation of rendering the inside of a brick **flue** to assist airtightness. 2. (USA) The operation of rendering the inner face of an outer leaf of **cavity** wall. 3. Historically, the operation of plastering with repetitive patterns to outside walls particularly in Suffolk and Essex.

parget-work See **parget** 2.

Parian cement A **gypsum plaster** similar to **Keene's cement**.

paring chisel A long, thin-bladed, level-edged chisel which is used by hand and not intended to be struck with a **mallet**.

paring gouge A thin, long **gouge** sharpened on the inside face.

parliament hinge A **hinge** with plates projecting and the **knuckle** offset from the leaves to form an H shape. When fixed the knuckle projects in front of the wall face, allowing the door or shutter to fold through 180° and be restrained in the open position against the wall face.

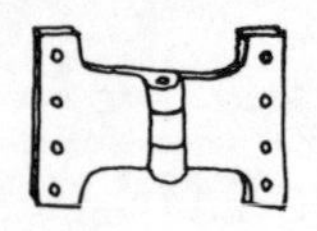

PARLIAMENT HINGE

parquet A flooring made up of thin pieces of hardwood (6.4 to 9.5 mm thick) of a predetermined size and shape glued direct to a subfloor in patterns, or pre-glued to a backing and laid in panels on to the subfloor. cf. **wood block flooring**.

parquet strip flooring A flooring made up of hardwood strips in random lengths, **tongued and grooved** and end-matched. Strips are 9.5 mm finished thickness and are glued and **secret nailed** to the subfloor.

particle board **Chipboard**.

parting bead A narrow, vertical strip of wood fixed to the **pulley stile** of the **cased frame** of a **sash window** to separate the upper and lower sashes.

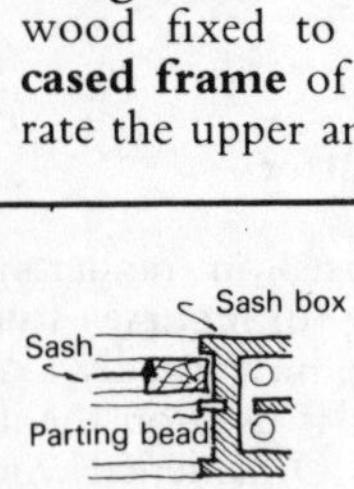

PARTING BEAD

parting slip A narrow, vertical strip of wood suspended from the soffit lining of a **sash window** to separate the two weights. Also known as a mid-feather.

partition A wall, usually non-loadbearing, separating adjacent rooms and made of bricks, blocks, timber or metal framing and lining (**stud partition**), or prefabricated panels as in **demountable** partitions.

partition head or partition plate The uppermost horizontal member of a **stud partition**.

partition factor That proportion of the radiant heat which is absorbed by the glass of a window and later released to the internal environment.

party fence A fence separating two properties, the upkeep of which is the joint responsibility of both owners.

party wall A **separating wall** between adjoining buildings.

passenger lift A **lift** primarily used to transport people. cf. **goods lift**.

passings The amount by which one flashing sheet overlaps the next.

passivity The condition of a metal or mineral when a slight initial chemical attack has produced a surface film that prevents further action. cf. **patina**.

patch An **insert** of veneer let into plywood to replace a defect in the veneer.

patent glazing A system of puttyless glazing used primarily in roof glazing, but occasionally as a **curtain wall**. The sheets of glass span between inclined **glazing bars** of steel, aluminium or other metal (timber is rarely used today) having rebates designed to drain to the outside of the building any water which penetrates the system.

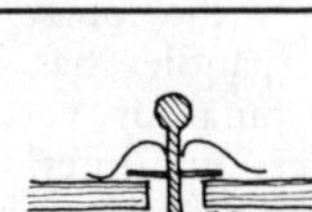

PATENT GLAZING BAR

paternoster A lift, primarily for passengers, which consists of a series of doorless compartments which move slowly and continuously on an endless chain, the compartment floors remaining horizontal at all times, whether changing from ascent to descent or vice versa.

patina A thin protective film of oxide or other metallic compounds which forms on the surface of a metal exposed to the air, such as the green coating (verdigris) which forms on the surface of copper and copper alloys.

patio door An external sliding door, usually fully glazed, with either a wooden or a metal frame.

patterned glass Glass having one flat face and one textured or patterned face, its degree of obscurity depending on the pattern. Patterns include reeded, ribbed and hammered.
pattern staining A discoloration of the internal surface of a wall or ceiling, usually reflecting the structure behind the surface, which takes place due to the differential thermal insulation of the structure between and at the framing positions.
pave To construct a **pavement**.
pavement 1. A footway for pedestrians, treated with asphalt, concrete, flags, pavings etc. to withstand expected wear and weathering. 2. Any surface that has been treated with asphalt, concrete or bitumen to withstand expected traffic loads and weathering.
pavement light A **light** made up of solid **glass blocks** set into a concrete or cast iron frame, positioned in a pavement and giving light to a basement.

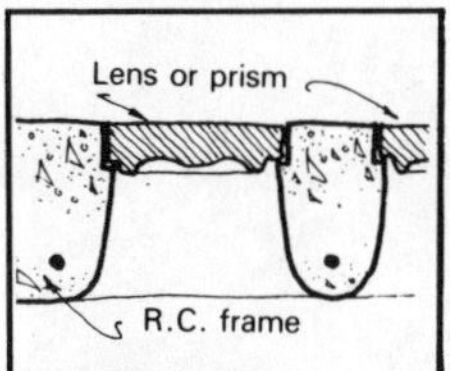

PAVEMENT LIGHT

pavement prism A **glass block** in a **pavement light**.
paver A very hard brick or concrete block of brick shape used for the surfacing of a **pavement**.
paving flag or paving stone A rectangular slab of stone or concrete used for the surfacing of a **pavement**.
peacock's-eye veneer A **veneer** figured like a bird's-eye.
pearl The surface texture of an acid-frosted electric lamp.
pebble dash 1. An external rendering finished by throwing small stones against its unset surface. 2. To render with pebble dash.
pebble walling A wall built of rounded pebbles and constructed in a similar manner to flint walling.
pedestal washbasin A **washbasin** which is supported from the floor by a column-shaped base.
peeler log A log used for the **rotary cutting** of **veneer**.
peeling 1. **Rotary cutting**. 2. The loosening of a paint film from its backing.
peen The blunt, wedge-shaped or ball-shaped end of a **hammer** head, opposite the striking **face**.
peen hammer A mason's hammer with no flat striking **face** but with two cutter **peens**.
peg 1. A hardwood or metal rod passing through a roofing tile to hold it in place. 2. A wooden **dowel**. 3. A metal pin which secures the glass in a metal window frame.
peggies Small random slates.
peg stay A casement stay which operates by the engagement of a peg through one of the holes in its length.

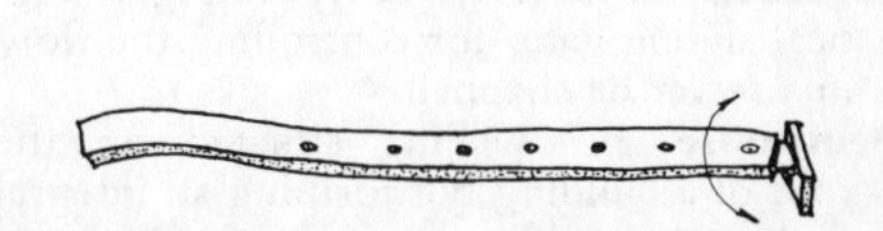
PEG STAY

pellet A small circular piece of timber covering the head of a countersunk screw.
pelmet A fitting at the head of a window which covers the curtain rail or blind.

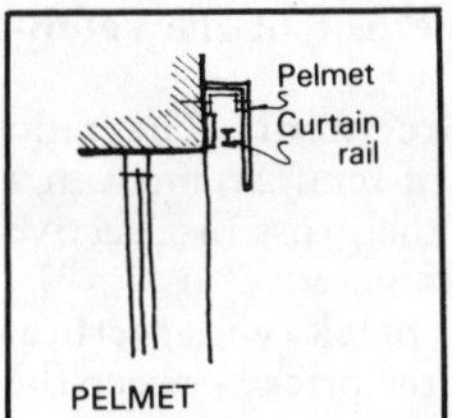

PELMET

pencilling Painting the mortar joints of brickwork to emphasize their pattern.
pencil round Description of a rounded angle with a radius similar to that of an ordinary lead pencil.

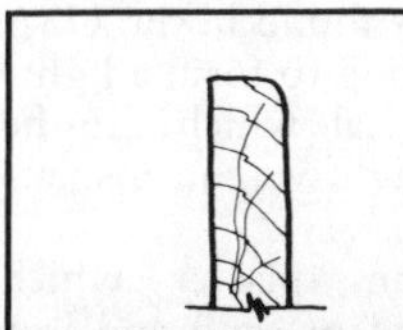
PENCIL ROUND

pendant luminaire A **luminaire** provided with a cord, chain or tube, etc. which enables it to be suspended from a ceiling or a wall support.

pendant post In a **hammer beam** roof truss, the vertical member which runs down the wall face from the **wall plate** to the corbel which carries the **hammer beam truss**. The hammer beam runs across its head.

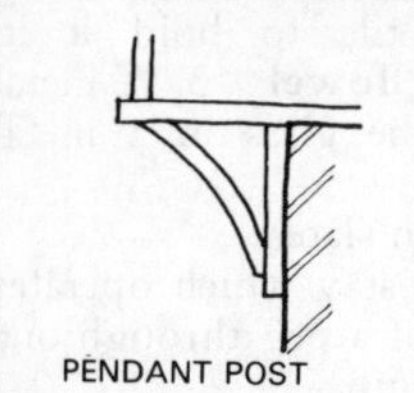

PENDANT POST

penstock A device, incorporating a vertical sliding gate, for controlling the flow in a sewer or channel.

penthouse A dwelling situated on the roof of a building but forming an integral part of the building.

penthouse roof A **mono-pitch roof**.

penultimate certificate The document produced by the architect or his quantity surveyor authorizing payment to the contractor at the practical completion of the works. This consists of the total value of the labour and materials of the construction, less a suitable amount for any aspect still to be resolved in the settlement of the final account and one half of the **retention fund**.

percentage of reinforcement The ratio of the sectional area of reinforcement in a concrete member to the gross or effective sectional area of the concrete.

perforated brick A **brick** with vertical perforations through the brick between the bedding plane and the top surface.

performance specification The detailed description that states the performance required of a component or assembly and which may refer to standard tests.

pergola An open-topped structure of intersecting beams carried on posts; designed to support climbing plants.

perlite A volcanic glass found in the USA which expands on heating to form a lightweight granular material which can be used as **aggregate** in lightweight, insulating concrete or plaster.

perlite plaster Gypsum plaster which contains **perlite** instead of sand and is a thermally insulating lightweight plaster.

permanent shuttering **Formwork** which is not struck after the concrete has set but remains in position as part of the structure.

permeability The rate of flow of a fluid or water vapour through a material per unit area and unit pressure gradient. It is the **vapour diffusance** of a material divided by its thickness.

permissible manufacturing deviation The maximum amount of dimensional tolerance (plus or minus) acceptable in a component without contravening the requirements of fit.

permissible working load The maximum load a structural member should be allowed to carry, being the maximum load which it can carry (its **ultimate load**) divided by a **safety factor**.

permissible working stress The ultimate **stress** of a material divided by the **safety factor**; the stress that can be safely sustained by a structural component under particular conditions of service and load.

perpend 1. A vertical joint in brickwork or masonry. cf. **bed joint**. 2. A corner of brickwork erected before the rest of the wall and carefully plumbed.

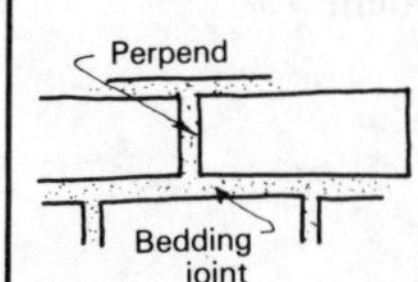

PERPEND

perpend stone A **bond stone**.

pervious Allowing penetration by liquid.

pet cock A small valve or **plug cock** which is used to release air from a hot water system or release water in a slow controlled flow into an **automatic flushing cistern**.

petrifying liquid A **thinner** for some types of **distemper** or a protective coating for masonry.

petrol-intercepting chamber or trap A **trap** which receives water from garage wash-down areas and filling station forecourts before it passes into the drains. It consists of three ventilated chambers separated by scumboards which trap the floating petrol and oil and retain them within the trap.

PFA See **pulverized fuel ash**.

phenol formaldehyde resin (PF) A **synthetic resin** which forms a **thermosetting** glue which is moisture-resistant, even boil-proof, and is immune to bacterial attack.

Phillips head A recessed driving profile of a **wood** or **machine screw** with a cruciform recess needing a special **screwdriver**. This profile aids non-slip driving. cf. **slot head** and **clutch head**.

Phillips screw A screw with a cruciform slot needing a special screwdriver.

Phillips screwdriver A screwdriver with a pointed head of cruciform section for use in driving Phillips screws.

phon The unit of the objective loudness of sound; the decibel unit of the 1 kHz intensity-level scale which is used in deciding the apparent loudness of a sound either by subjective comparison or by objective comparison.

phosphating The protection of metal by hot phosphoric acid as a pretreatment to a finish.

phosphorescent paint A **paint** which absorbs visible or ultra-violet radiation and emits it after the source of radiation has been removed. cf. fluorescent paint and **luminous paint**.

piano hinge A long hinge with continuous plates, knuckle and pin as used on a piano lid or for hingeing together two long, thin sections of timber, metal, etc.

pick A digging implement with two long sharp points at right angles to the **helve**; used to break up tarmacadam or loose rock. cf. **pick axe**.

pick axe A **pick** (often referred to as a navvy pick) with a sharp point on one side of the head and a **chisel** edge on the other.

picket A **pale** in a fence.

pick hammer A slater's tool which can be used to draw or drive slating nails and also to form nailing holes in slates. It has a head which is sharply pointed at one end – and has a striking face at the other end. Set at right angles to the head is a forked device for drawing nails.

picking Forming a surface on stone or concrete by striking with a sharp steel point to produce a series of closely spaced pits. cf. **bush hammering**.

picking up 1. **Pulling up**. 2. The joining up of a **live edge** of paint with a new coating.

pickling 1. A treatment for the removal of **rust** or **mill scale** from steel by immersion in an acid solution containing an inhibitor. Pickling should be followed by thorough washing and drying before painting. 2. The process of removing **paint** and **varnish** with an alkaline preparation or strong solvent.

pieced timber A piece of timber from which a defective piece as been cut, the resulting gap being made good by a sound piece of wood, cut and fitted into the gap; usually the gap is cut with a **dovetailed** cross-section.

piend (Scotland) A **hip**.

pier 1. A short buttress, or thickening of a wall on one or both sides, to stiffen the wall, provide a greater area of support under a vertical load or withstand diagonal stress. The pier is fully bonded to the main wall. 2. The brickwork between door or window openings. 3. The support or **pillar** for an **arch**, bridge or beam.

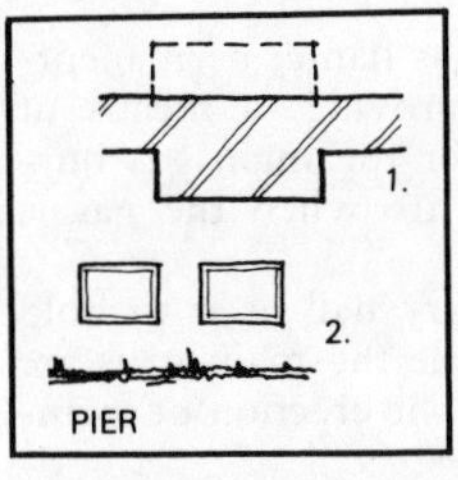

pigeon-holed wall A **honeycomb wall**.

pigment The insoluble dispersed particles in a paint which give the dried **film** its colour and opacity. Often used today to include **extenders** as well as the white and coloured pigments.

pilaster A **pier**; often treated decoratively.

pile A slender member driven or screwed into, or formed in the ground to provide support for the structure above. The pile is driven either to a stratum which provides a safe load-bearing base for the pile or to a depth which ensures sufficient friction between the sides of the pile and the surrounding subsoil to support the loading of the building. cf. **sheet pile**.

pile cap 1. An ***in situ*** concrete block enclosing the top of a **pile** or group of piles and forming the seating for the **ground beam**. 2. A metal cap or helmet temporarily fitted over the head of a precast **pile** to protect it during driving.

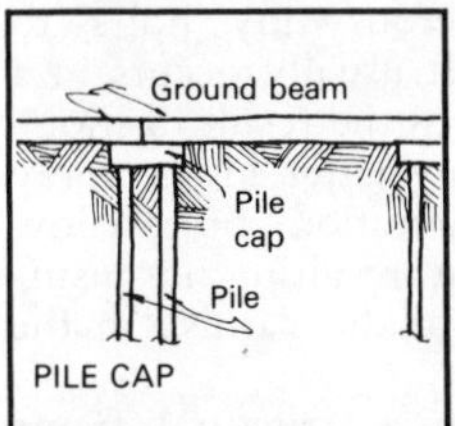

piling 1. The act of driving or forming **piles**. 2. The phenomenon of a paint **film** becoming thick and uneven during brush application due to its drying too fast.

pillar A freestanding vertical member, usually rectangular or polygonal on plan.

pillar tap A water tap with a vertical inlet, used on **washbasins** and baths and fixed through a hole in the horizontal surface of the basin or bath.

pilot hole A small diameter hole drilled as a guide before the drilling of the main hole.

piloti A **column** or **pier**, usually one of a series of similar columns or piers, which carries a building above an open ground floor space.

pilot light A small gas flame, permanently burning, which provides a means of automatic ignition for the main gas burners in a boiler or fire when the gas is turned on.

pilot nail A temporary nail used to hold timbers together while the main nails are driven; often used in the erection of formwork.

pin 1. A slender **wire nail** (*eg* **panel pin**) 2. A **trenail** or **dowel**. 3. A **dovetail** tenon inserted into a dovetail joint. 4. The metal dowel in the **knuckle** of a **hinge**. cf. **pintle**. 5. To wedge brickwork up to a wall or floor above with slates bedded in mortar.

pinch bar A bent steel bar, between 12 and 19 mm diameter with a claw at the bent end and a **chisel** point at the other. When it is over 900 mm long it is called a **crow bar**.

pinch rod A batten used in a similar way to a **storey rod** for checking the width of a building aperture.

pine shingles European **shingles** made from pine wood.

pin hinge A **loose-pin hinge**.

pinhole The flight hole of a pinhole borer, a wood destroying insect which attacks only green timber.

pinhole borer A wood-boring insect which attacks only green timber.

pinholing A defect in a **varnish** film which causes numerous tiny holes to appear in the film. It usually occurs in a spray coat and is often the result of moisture or other foreign matter in the spray tubes, too thick application, or too low pressure of spraying resulting in insufficient breaking up of the varnish in the gun.

pin joint A joint in a structural frame which restrains the member in position but allows it to turn. There is therefore no **bending moment** at the joint. cf. **fixed joint**.

pin knot A knot smaller than 6 mm diameter.

pink primer A **priming** coat for wood which originally contained white or red lead.

pinning (Scotland) A stone with a contrasting colour or texture set in a wall along with others to form a chequered effect.

pin rail A wooden board fixed to a wall surface, to which are fastened hat and coat hooks.

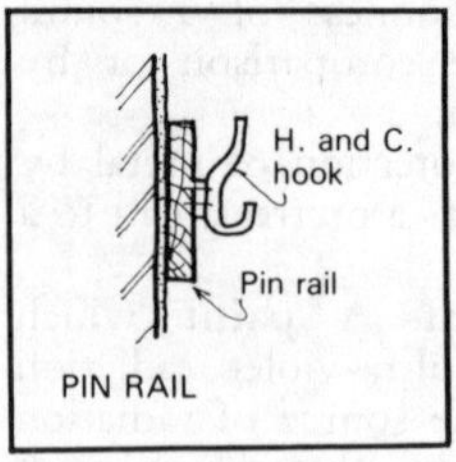

pintle A **pin** in a hinge.

pin tumbler mechanism A locking mechanism consisting of a cylindrical plug rotating in a body and movable detainers in the form of pairs of pins and drivers (pin tumblers) which fit, together with their springs, in holes in the plug and body. In the secure position the drivers bridge the interface between the plug and the body, thus preventing the plug from turning. The mechanism is operated by the turning of a key and by a connector bar, thrower, cam or other device attached to the end of the plug to turn with it to operate the bolt.

pipe A hollow cylindrical tube of plastic, metal, asbestos cement, burnt clay or concrete used to convey water, sewage, air or gas.

pipe cutter A tool for cutting steel **pipes** by means of metal cutting discs. Some of the metal is forced into the pipe during cutting and its original diameter has to be recovered by the use of a **burring reamer**.

pipe drill A tubular **plugging chisel** which cuts round holes in brickwork for wooden **plugs**.

pipe duct A **duct** designed to accommodate pipes.

pipe fitting See **fitting**.

pipe hook A **fastener** with a spiked end which is driven into a mortar joint in a wall or into a timber. The other end of the fastener is in the shape of a curved saddle to support a pipe.

pipe sleeve See **expansion sleeve**.

pipe stopper A **screw plug** for drain testing.

pipe tongs **Footprints**.

pipe wrench A heavy wrench with serrated jaws for gripping and screwing pipes.

pitch 1. A black or dark brown, solid or semi-solid, fusible and agglomerative residue remaining after partial evaporation of the fractional distillation of tar. The term pitch should always be qualified with the name of the material used to produce it, *eg* **coal tar pitch** 2. The ratio of the height to the span of a **stair** or pitched **roof**, or its angle of inclination to the horizontal. 3. The distance between parallel objects set at uniform spacing *eg* the distance between reinforcing bars in reinforced concrete. 4. The distance between adjacent nosings of a **stair**. 5. The slope of the **face** of a sawtooth measured from the perpendicular to the line of its points. 6. Of thread, the distance, measured parallel to the axis of the screw, between adjacent crests of **thread**. 7. Of bolts, screws, nails etc., the distance between adjacent fixings in the same line or, when two or more lines are set parallel to the direction of stress in a joint, the distance between adjacent staggered bolts in different lines.

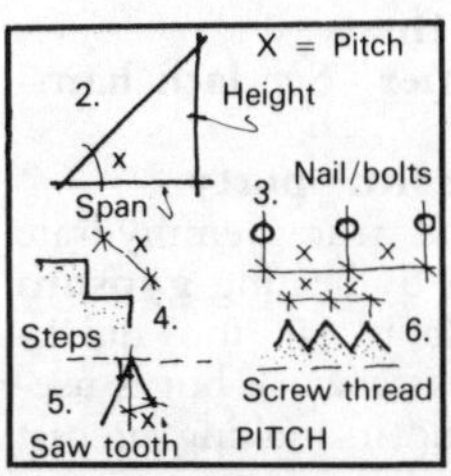

pitch board A triangular **template** used to set out lines to which the **strings** of a **stair** must be cut or **formed**, the sides corresponding to the **rise**, the **going** and the **pitch**.

pitched roof A roof having a plane or planes inclined at a greater angle than 10° to the horizontal. cf. **flat roof**.

pitch-faced stone A stone whose face has been worked at the quarry by means of a **pitching tool**.

pitch fibre A preformed, felted fibrous material impregnated with coal-tar pitch or bitumen compounds under vacuum and pressure.

pitch fibre pipe A pipe made of **pitch fibre**, suitable for soil and surface water drainage.

pitching piece In a stair, the horizontal timber carrying the joists of the **landing** and the **carriages** of the **stair**.

pitching tool A **hammer-headed chisel** with a thick broad edge about 125 mm long; used to produce **pitch-faced stone**.

pitch mastic A mixture of **aggregate** and **coal tar pitch** which is fluid when hot and can be used as a topping for **jointless flooring**.

pitch pocket A gap between **growth rings** in some **softwoods**, containing resin.

pith The cylindrical centre of a log.

pith ray A **wood ray**.

pitting 1. The **blowing** of plaster. 2. Small surface cavities in a metal caused by chemical or atmospheric attack.

pivot A stump, pin or centre on which a moving part may swing.

pivot hinge An alternative to the more usual butt hinge for use on doors and windows, using a pair of pivots on which the frame is swung. Windows may be pivoted horizontally or vertically, with the possibility in the latter case of the pivots being set off-centre. **Floor springs** (particularly double action floor springs) for doors are often referred to as **spring pivots**.

pivot-hung window An opening **light** which is hinged at positions along opposite edges (both sides or top and bottom) thus causing part of the window, on opening, to project inside the building and part to project outwards. cf. **projecting top-hung window**.

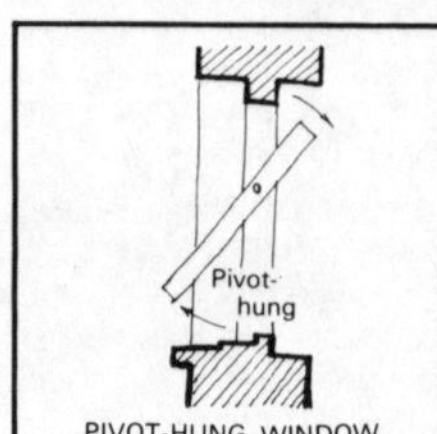

plain ashlar Surfaced stone smoothed with a **drag** or similar tool.

plain-sawn timber **Flat-sawn timber**.

plain tile A flat roofing-tile of concrete or burnt clay with a slight, convex camber, approximately 260 × 160 mm, with two nibs and two nail holes. Each tile on a roof overlaps two **courses** below it.

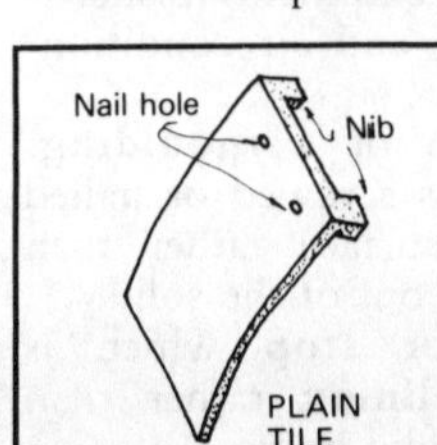

plan A horizontal sectional drawing at a particular scale, the scale chosen depending on the degree of detail to be shown. cf. **floor plan**, **roof plan**.

planceer piece See **soffit board**.

plane A tool for smoothing and reducing the thickness of wood. cf. **badger**, **beading tool or bead plane**, **smoothing plane**, **rabbet plane**, **universal plane**.

plane iron The cutting iron of a plane, as opposed to the **back iron**.

planer A **planing machine**.

plane stock The body of a **plane** that holds the **plane iron** and the **back iron**.

planing machine A machine which is used to smooth a wood surface or to reduce the thickness of a piece of wood. It can also be used to undertake other tasks, such as **moulding**, chamfering etc. cf. **chamfer**.

plank 1. A piece of **softwood**, 50 to 100 mm thick × 275 mm or more wide. cf. **deal.** The term should not be used of hardwood. 2. (USA) A piece of timber more than 25 mm thick laid with its face horizontal, like that of a floor board.

plank-on-edge floor (USA) A floor in which the joists are laid touching each other to give a certain degree of fire resistance. The finished floor is laid directly on to the joists (*ie* there is no **decking**).

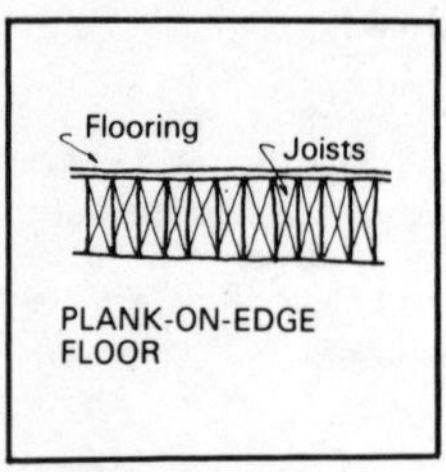

PLANK-ON-EDGE FLOOR

planning grid A network of horizontal and vertical parallel lines at equal spacing used, for instance, by an architect as an aid to designing the internal layout of a building. This grid may, but need not, coincide with a modular grid.

plant 1. Site equipment such as concrete mixers, hoists, cranes, diggers etc. 2. The mechanical equipment associated with lifts, heating and air conditioning systems, etc.

planted A description of a **moulding**, strip or cove which is screwed or nailed into position on a surface rather than being cut or moulded out of the solid.

planted stop A **door stop** which is **planted** on to the **lining** rather than being cut out of the solid lining.

plaster A substance based on **Portland cement**, **gypsum plaster** or **lime putty** mixed with sand and applied to wall and ceiling surfaces in a series of coats to provide a smooth, hard surface when set.

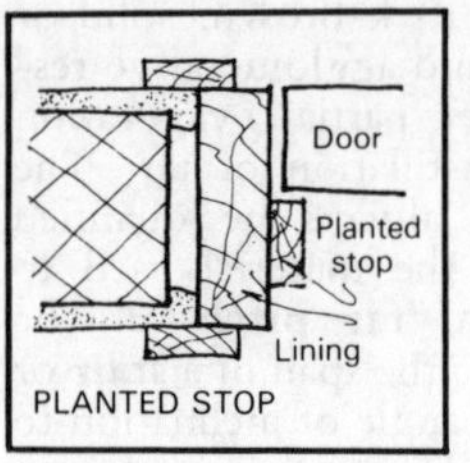

PLANTED STOP

plaster base The ground for a plaster finish, such as brickwork, masonry, **plasterboard**, **insulating board**, **metal lathing** etc.

plaster bead An **angle bead**.

plasterboard The usual name in the UK for **gypsum plasterboard**.

plasterboard nail A large round-headed nail, galvanized or sherardized, used to fix plasterboard to **studs** or **joists**. cf. **galvanizing**, **sherardizing**.

plaster dab A small mass of **gypsum plaster** which, along with others, is used to fix plasterboard sheets to a brick or block backing.

plasterer's float See **float**.

plasterer's lath hammer See **lath hammer**.

plasterer's putty See **lime putty**.

plaster of Paris The true hemihydrate plaster, obtained first by heating **gypsum** ($CaSO_4$. ½H_2O). It is far too quick-setting for general plasterwork but is useful for small areas and in making precast mouldings. To extend the setting time a **retarder** (keratin derivative or lime with an activator) is added to form a **retarded hemihydrate plaster**.

plaster slab Precast partition blocks made of **gypsum plaster** laid in cement mortar or with gypsum plaster as mortar or grout.

plastic 1. The description of an easily workable plaster or mortar. 2. See **plastics**.

plasticizer 1. An **admixture** in mortar or concrete, which increases workability, usually by air-entrainment. The finished mortar or concrete has greater frost-resistance, but slightly reduced strength, but this reduction in strength can be offset by the fact that the admixture allows a reduced water:cement ratio. 2. An additive used during the manufacture of a plastic material; usually a non-volatile solvent added to reduce the brittleness and increase the flexibility of the finished plastic material.

plasticity 1. The property of a plaster or mortar to work easily, sticking readily to the trowel, but smooth to spread. The use of an **air entraining agent** admixture helps to produce these characteristics in cement mortar. Gypsum plaster possesses these characteristics naturally. 2. Generally, the property of a material that allows it to be shaped without cracking and to retain its new form.

plastic laminate A decorative laminate, comprising layers of paper impregnated with melamine resin under pressure, at high temperatures, to form a hard, thin, scratch-resistant material which may be used to surface chipboard for worktops, etc. The top layer of paper is printed with a decorative pattern.

plastic paint A paint which can be manipulated after application to produce a **textured finish**.

plastics A generic name for a group of polymeric materials which under heat and pressure become plastic, when they can be shaped, moulded or extruded, and later harden upon cooling. They are typically of organic or synthetic composition, usually based on synthetic resin or on modified polymers of natural resins, and are formed by a process of molecular growth known as **polymerization**. Originally plastics were based on natural **monomers** but today the majority of plastics are made from derivatives of coal, tar, mineral oil (petroleum) and natural gases. Thermoplastic plastics can be resoftened by heat, thermosetting plastics cannot.

plastic wood A paste of nitrocellulose, wood flour, **plasticizers** and resins used to repair wood and fill holes in wooden members. Its surface can be painted soon after use.

plastisol A suspension of finely divided resin particles (often PVC or copolymer) in a **plasticizer**, used to coat metal cladding and other exterior components. After application the coating is heated and the plasticizer diffuses into, and softens, the resin particles which fuse to a continuous film without significant loss of volatile matter.

plate 1. A horizontal timber member, usually about 100 × 50 mm, often supported throughout its entire length, as in a **wall plate** or **sole plate**. 2. (Scotland) A broad thin board.

plate cut A **foot cut**.

plate girder A heavy-duty steel beam of webs and flanges made up of steel plates and angles.

plate glass See **polished plate glass**.

platform frame A form of timber framed construction in which the floor panels extend over the wall frames below, forming a platform for the erection of the wall panels for the next floor. cf. **balloon frame**.

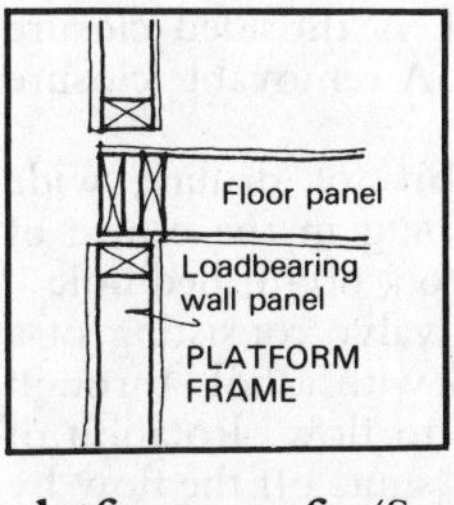

PLATFORM FRAME

platform roof (Scotland) **Flat roof**.

plenum system An **air-conditioning** system in which the conditioned rooms are maintained at a pressure above atmospheric pressure by forcing the conditioned air into the rooms, usually at high level, and withdrawing vitiated air at low level, or allowing it to dissipate through gaps in the enclosure if no recirculation is intended.

pliers A gripping tool, pivoted like a pair of scissors and with various styles of jaw depending on the size of the pliers and their intended use. Wire cutting blades may be built into the jaws.

plinth 1. A projecting course or courses at the base of a wall. 2. The cuboidal projecting base of a column or pedestal. 3. The slightly projecting or slightly recessed base of a piece of furniture.

PLINTH

plinth course(s) The course forming the plinth to a wall, or the courses forming the **plinth** to a brick wall.

plough 1. A **plane** designed for cutting grooves in wood, usually along the **grain**. It is provided with a movable **fence** which allows the position of the groove in relation to the edge of the piece of wood to be adjusted. 2. To cut a groove in.

ploughed-and-tongued joint A **feather joint**.

plough strip A strip of wood which has been ploughed; it is used to hold the edge of a drawer bottom.

plow (USA) A **plough**.

plug 1. A small peg or piece of timber, fibre, metal or plastic driven into a hole cut in a wall, to receive a screw or nail fixing. 2. A **bag plug** or **screw plug**. 3. An electrical connection that fits into a **socket outlet**. 4. A threaded closure piece for a pipe. 5. A removable closure for a waste outlet.

plug-centre bit A **bit** for drilling wide holes in which the plug in the centre of the bit is inserted into a pre-drilled hole.

plug cock A simple valve consisting of a tapered plug pierced with a hole through which liquid is able to flow. Rotation of the plug through 90° shuts off the flow by blocking it with the undrilled part of the plug.

plugging The act of drilling a hole in mass walling and driving in a **plug** to receive a screw or nail fixing.

plugging chisel or drill A short, steel, hand-held tool which is struck with a **hammer** to form holes in a wall to receive **plugs**. cf. **pipe drill**.

plug tenon A short **tenon** projecting from the foot or head of a post and used to locate and fix it.

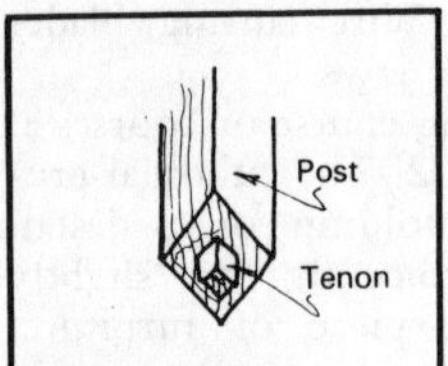

PLUG TENON

plumb 1. Vertical. 2. To make vertical.

plumb bob The small weight which hangs on the end of a **plumb line**.

plumb cut (USA) The vertical cut in a **birdsmouth joint** at the foot of a **rafter** where it fits on to a **wall plate**. cf. **foot cut**.

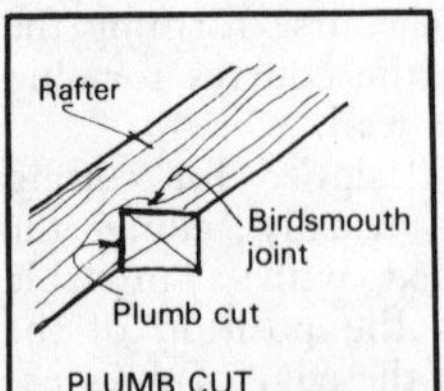

PLUMB CUT

plumber's solder An alloy of lead and tin, mix proportions varying from 1:1 to 3:1, used for jointing lead pipes.

plumbing 1. The craft or the operation of installing sanitary fittings, above ground drainage and hot and cold water services in a building; also the services themselves. The plumber may install the wet heating system, but this is more properly the work of the heating engineer and is not included in the plumbing section of a **Bill of Quantities.** The domestic hot water system may be installed by the heating engineer, but the last 450 mm of pipe work to each tap or other outlet is included in the plumbing. 2. Using, a **plumb line** to achieve verticality.

plumb level A **spirit level** with a small bubble at right angles to the main bubble of the instrument to establish whether a vertical surface is plumb.

plumb line A cord with a **plumb bob** on one end to ensure that the cord, if allowed to hang freely, hangs vertically. The cord is braided to avoid spinning.

plumb rule A narrow board used to achieve verticality, having a plumb bob suspended from the top and hanging freely in an egg-shaped hole at the bottom. When the bob hangs centrally in the hole the edge of the board is plumb.

plummet A **plumb bob**.

ply 1. A thin sheet or **veneer**, usually of wood (as in **plywood**, **coreboard** etc.) but sometimes of metal or plastic. 2. One sheet of **roofing felt** in a built-up roof finish.

plymetal **Plywood** faced with a metal on one or both sides.

plywood A timber sheet product consisting of a number of **veneers** of wood bonded together with adhesive. A **balanced construction** using odd numbers of veneers is usually used and the finished thickness is from 3 to 25 mm. The **grain** of adjacent veneers is aligned in opposite directions. Plywood has better strength characteristics and greater dimensional stability than natural wood. Its durability depends on the type of timber used for the veneers and the type of adhesive (**WBP**, **BR** and **MR**, etc.). The plywood grade is specified in accordance with the grade of adhesive and the quality of its surface veneers (Grade 1, 2 or 3 veneers).

plywood parquet Squares or tiles of **plywood** with a thick hardwood, top veneer, usually laid with alternating **grain**, the squares being pinned to the subfloor and the nails punched and filled before the hardwood is glasspapered and polished.

pocket 1. An opening in a wall in which a beam is to be inserted. 2. The aperture in the **pulley stile** through which the sash weight is passed when fixed to the **sash cord** of a sash window.

pocket piece The piece of the **pulley stile** of a **sash window** which is removed to form the **pocket** and can be replaced after the sash weights have been fixed.

pocket rot Small areas of decay in wood which eventually become round holes.

pock marked **Orange peel**.

point 1. The sharp end of a **saw-tooth**. 2. An electrical outlet, whether **socket outlet**, **lampholder** or other terminal, from which power can be drawn. 3. Any outlet on a gas system.

pointing 1. The act of raking out mortar joints to a depth of about 19 mm and pressing into them surface mortar, often of a different colour. **Jointing** is more durable because the bedding mortar is worked to give the required joint profile at the time of laying the bricks, so it is not necessary to disturb the bedding mortar. 2. The filling of the joints between **ridge** or **hip tiles** with mortar, or the filling of joints between wall or floor tiles with **grout**.

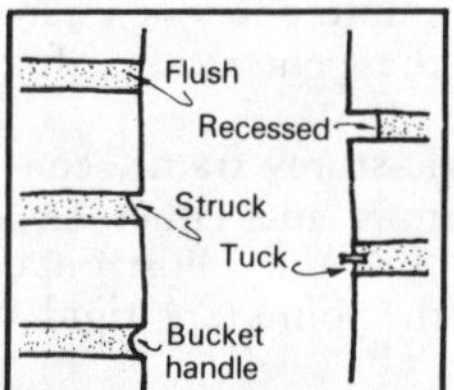

POINTING

point load A concentrated load which is applied over a relatively small area, such as below a beam seating or the foot of a column, as opposed to a **distributed load**.

point of contraflexure The position in a **fixed jointed** or **continuous beam** or column at which the tensile and compressive stresses reverse.

point of gross leakage In the testing of a component (*eg* a window) for rain penetration, the pressure difference across the component at which the amount of water penetrating increases to such a volume that there would clearly be a risk of damage to the component, or the building fabric, or inconvenience to the occupants of a building in which such a component was fitted.

point of initial leakage In the testing of a component (*eg* a window) for rain penetration, the pressure difference across the component at which water penetration is first visible, but in insufficient volume to cause damage to the component, or the building fabric, or to cause inconvenience to the occupants of a building in which such a component was fitted.

poker vibrator A device for vibrating concrete mechanically to ensure that the pour is correctly consolidated. The poker is inserted at intervals into the concrete and consolidation is complete after the air bubbles have stopped rising. cf. **external vibrator** and **surface vibrator**.

pole plate In large-scale timber pitched-roof construction, a horizontal member parallel with the wall resting on the **tie beams** or **principal rafters** of a truss and supporting the feet of the **common rafters** and the inner edge of the **box gutter**.

poling board One of a number of short vertical boards set against the face of an excavation in order to prevent the soil from collapsing into the trench or excavated area.

polished plate glass Good quality glass with perfectly flat, parallel surfaces resulting from grinding and polishing both surfaces. cf. **float glass**.

polished work Crystalline building stone (limestone, marble or granite) which has been treated with **abrasives** to produce a glass-like surface.

poll 1. The striking face of a hammer. 2. To split (knap) flints.

poll adze A **adze** which has a blunt head opposite the cutting edge.

polycarbonate A tough, scratch-resistant thermoplastic **polymer** containing carbonic acid ester linkages which can be produced in a transparent form, thus proving useful as a glazing material where shatter resistance is essential or in areas of anticipated vandalism.

polychromatic finish 1. A multi-coloured finish. 2. A metallic lustre and iridescent finish produced by lacquers or **enamels** containing metal flake powders and transparent colouring matter.

polyester resin A synthetic resin, either **thermoplastic** or **thermo-setting**, used in laminated construction with glass fibre to give high strength, as in reinforced translucent sheeting. It is made by reacting organic acids and alcohols. Those used in paint are called **alkyd resins**.

polyethylene A **thermoplastic** made by compressing the heated gas ethylene, and produced in medium or high densities. It is chemically inert, electrically insulating and used, for instance, in floor covering, pipe and bottle manufacture.

polygonal rubble **Rubble walling** made up of stones with many sides, such as **Kentish rag**.

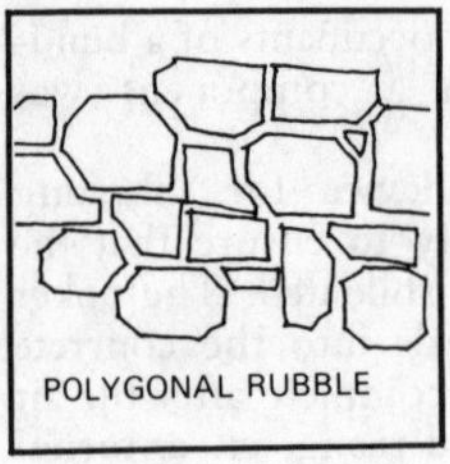

polyisobutylene A thermoplastic material produced by the **polymerization** of isobutylene.

polymer A compound whose molecule is formed of a chain or grid-like linking of molecular units (**monomers**) in a process known as polymerization. The polymer is likely to have different characteristics from the monomer.

polymer impregnated concrete A concrete mix into which a polymer has been introduced either during mixing or after placing. The effect of the polymer is to improve the strength of the concrete by filling all the voids which would otherwise occur in conventional concrete. In addition, water absorption is reduced and the concrete has greater dimensional stability.

polymerization The linking together of like molecular units (**monomers**) to form a chain or grid-like structure (a polymer). The process of polymerization is usually brought about by subjecting the raw material of the monomer to one or more influences such as light, heat, or pressure or to the action of a **catalyst**.

polypropylene A chemically close relative of **polythene**, based on the propylene **monomer**, but with a higher softening temperature and greater resilience.

polystyrene A **thermoplastic**, used in building mainly in its expanded form as a lightweight insulating material, being a polymerized form of styrene **monomer** (manufactured by reacting benzene with ethylene). cf. **polymerization**.

polytetrafluorethylene (PTFE) A plastics material used in the jointing of pipes.

polythene An abbreviation for **polyethylene.**

polyurethane A group of plastics of complex chemical structure derived from the reaction of a polyisocyanate with a polyhydroxy compound normally of polyester or polyether structure. It gives toughness, flexibility and adhesion to paints and coatings. In building this group of plastics is used especially in a foamed form as an insulant (thermal and acoustic) with resilient or rigid characteristics. It is also resistant to water vapour transmission.

polyvinyl acetate (PVA) A vinyl plastic made from vinyl acetate **monomer** which can be emulsified in water for use as a **paint** base or **adhesive**. It can also be used in a concrete mix to give resilience, and added to a **plaster** or **rendering** mix (or some flooring) to improve bonding.

polyvinyl chloride (PVC) A polymer made from vinyl chloride **monomer** in both rigid (unplasticized) and flexible (plasticized) forms. Plasticized, it is a tough rubber-like material with good chemical resistance and non-flammability, used for floor and wall coverings; unplasticized, it is used for roof sheeting, rainwater goods and plumbing fittings.

poor lime A **lime** containing impurities which are insoluble in acids.

popping **Blowing** in plasterwork.

pores In timber, small round holes which convey sap and are seen in the end grain of hardwood.

porous Containing minute pores or interstices which allow the penetration of a liquid.

portal frame A single-storey frame, consisting of two columns and either two inclined members or one horizontal member, in which the joints are rigid.

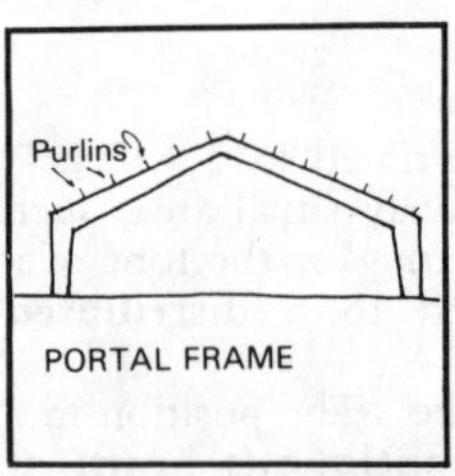

Portland blast-furnace cement A cement differing from ordinary **Portland cement** in that it is an interground mixture of up to 65% of blast-furnace slag and ordinary Portland cement. It is a low-heat cement, slow in its early hardening, but able, ultimately, to equal or exceed the strength of ordinary Portland cement. Because of its high resistance to sulphate attack it is often used for marine construction.

Portland cement **Cement** which is manufactured from the burning of chalk (or limestone) and clay, and is composed of approximately 60% lime (C_aO), 20% silica (SiO_2), 10% alumina (Al_2O_3), 3% oxides of iron and small amounts of other materials. It hardens by **hydration**. It originally acquired its name because of its resemblance, when set, to Portland limestone.

post A vertical support of a building frame or partition, particularly in timber. When in a partition it is also known as a stud.

post and wire fence A cheap form of barrier fence consisting of timber, concrete or metal posts supporting a series of wires; designated according to the number of strands (three-strand, four-strand, five-strand wire fence etc.).

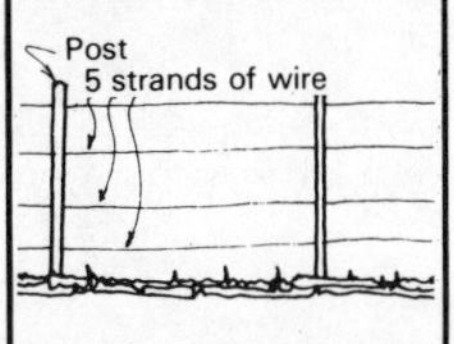

POST AND WIRE FENCE

post-tensioned concrete See **prestressed concrete**.

pot floor A **hollow tile floor**.

pot life The maximum length of time that a mixed glue remains usable. cf. **shelf life**.

pot type boiler A boiler in which the combustion chamber is surrounded by a water jacket, thus ensuring that most of the heat passes to the water.

pouring rope A **joint runner**.

powder post beetle (***Lyctus brunneus***) A wood destroying insect that attacks the sapwood of certain hardwoods. Flight holes are about 2 mm in diameter and bore dust is a very fine flour-like powder.

power float A mechanically-operated trowel having a rotary steel blade, principally used for finishing floors.

pozidriv head A recessed driving profile of a **wood** or **machine screw** similar to a **Phillips head** and requiring a special **screwdriver**. Ease of screw placement and non-slip driving are the benefits of this profile.

pozzolana Originally a natural volcanic material, but this term now includes other natural and artifical materials like diatomaceous earth, calcined clay and pulverized fuel, all having **pozzolanic properties**.

pozzolanic properties The ability to combine with lime at ambient temperature and in the presence of water in order to produce compounds having hydraulic properties.

preamble The introduction to each **trade** in a **Bill of Quantities**.

preboring for nails Drilling holes approximately 0.8 × the diameter of a nail to receive the nails when there is a danger that the driving of the nails without predrilling would split the timber.

precast concrete Concrete in units such as blocks, beams, etc. which are cast separately before they are fixed in position.

precast concrete floors A floor made up of precast concrete units such as beams, slabs or hollow tiles.

precast stone **Reconstructed stone**.

precision bolt A bolt with a smaller range of acceptable tolerances than a **black bolt**, made of carbon or alloy steel and supplied heat-treated after manufacture (dull black) or with a bright finish. Generally precision bolts cover higher performance grades than black bolts.

pre-cure The setting of **glue** in a joint before the surfaces have been clamped together.

prefabricated building A building the greater part of which is constructed in a factory; the term is usually reserved for a small building that can be transported in one finished section to site, or in a few easily connected sections. cf. **industrialized building**.

prefabricated tie (USA) A form of **wall tie**.

prefabrication The operation of constructing parts of a building (*eg* door sets and roof trusses) or whole buildings in a factory.

preformed tape A sealant in the form of a strip for simple economic application.

preliminaries The introductory clauses of a **Bill of Quantities** which set out the basic conditions which apply to the undertaking of the work.

pre-mixed plaster A bagged plaster, often containing lightweight aggregate such as **perlite** or **vermiculite**.

preservative 1. A chemical which can be applied to timber to protect it from fungal (and often insect) attack by rendering it poisonous to the spores of fungi (or insects). Application is by brush, spray, steeping or pressure impregnation. Materials include derivatives of coal tar or wood tar, organic solvents consisting of a toxic chemical in an oil solvent, and aqueous solutions of one or more toxic salts (copper sulphate, zinc chloride or aluminium sulphate).

pre-shimmed tape A loadbearing **glazing compound** in strip form, including a rod of synthetic rubber to act as a **distance piece**.

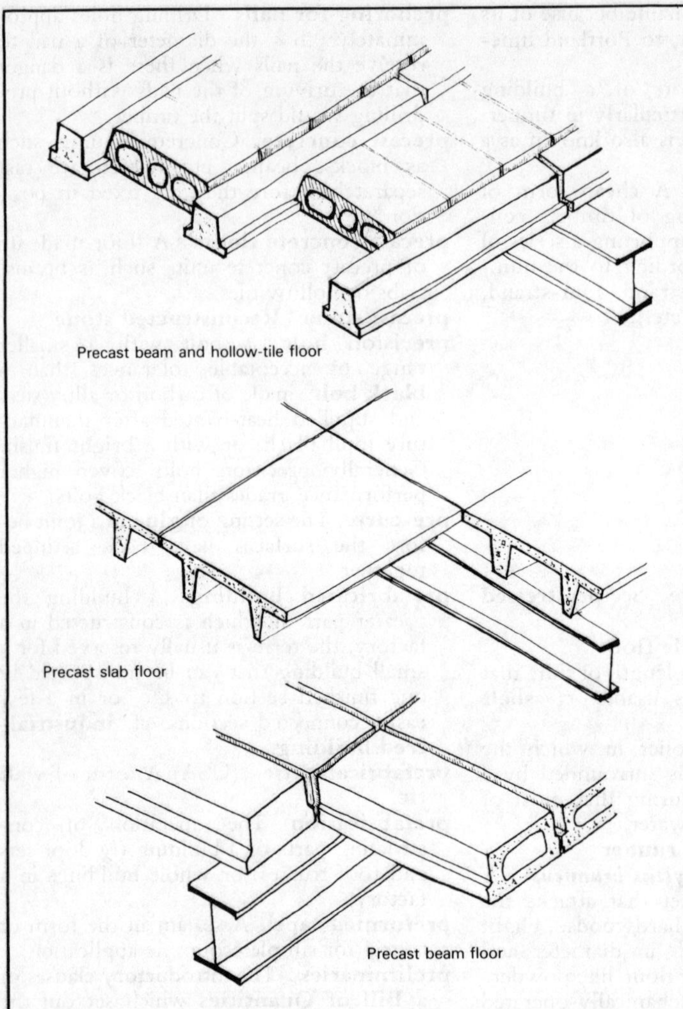

PRECAST CONCRETE FLOORS

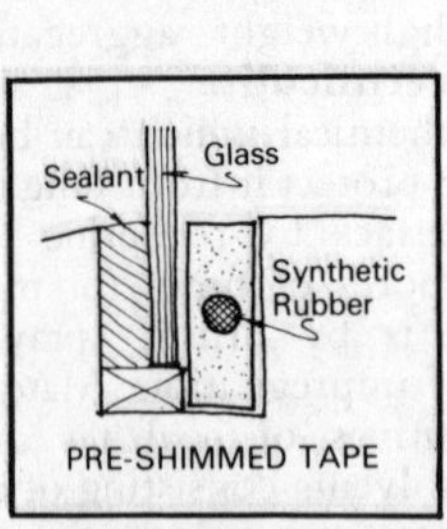

PRE-SHIMMED TAPE

pressed brick A **brick** manufactured by pressing (cf. **wirecut brick**) which is distinguished by sharp **arrises** and smooth surfaces; it is more dense than most bricks.

pressed steel Sheet steel which has been hot pressed into a particular profile, such as that for a window **sill**.

pressure gun A tool, like a grease gun, with which sealant is applied.

prestressed concrete Concrete that is given a compressive stress by its reinforcement in order to allow it to carry the tension stresses to which it may be subjected, thus allowing thinner concrete sections to be used. Pre-tensioning of concrete involves the stressing of the wires before the concrete is cast (as opposed to post-tensioning, in which the wires are stressed after the concrete has set).

pre-tensioned concrete See **prestressed concrete**.

priced bill A **Bill of Quantities** which has been priced by the contractor (*ie* he has added his rates for each operation and multiplied this by the **quantity** (extended) to arrive at his total **tender**) and is used as one of the **contract documents** to control the work.

pricking up Scoring the first coat of plaster to form a key for the succeeding coat.

prick punch A tool used to locate the centre of holes and make a start prior to nailing or drilling. It is similar to a **nail punch** but with a point.

primary energy The total energy calculated before losses brought about by conversion of that energy into usable energy of various forms (*ie* the amount of electricity, oil, gas, etc. used).

primary flow-and-return pipe See **flow and return pipes**.

prime cost item or sum A figure entered in the **Bill of Quantities** as being the sum to be paid to the contractor for a specific item and therefore included in the contractor's tender figure. This sum is adjusted during the contract to cover the actual cost of the item.

primer 1. A **priming coat**. 2. A bituminous coating on a roof decking on which the first layer of roofing felt is laid.

priming coat The first coat of paint applied to a previously unpainted surface or a surface from which all previous paint has been stripped. It may partially seal the surface of porous materials, or inhibit corrosion, and will form a good base to which the next paint film can adhere.

principal 1. A **principal rafter**. 2. A **roof truss**.

principal rafter The rafter in a roof truss which supports the **purlin**, which in turn supports the **common rafters**.

processed shake Common, sawn, western red cedar **shingle** which has been treated to look like a split shingle. cf. **shake**.

production drawing A **working drawing**.

profile 1. A horizontal board, set up just outside the proposed foundations of a building, supported on uprights and fixed so that its upper surface is on a datum level (*eg* ground floor level) and marked with nails or saw cuts to show the lines of dig, position of wall face etc. Usually there are two profiles at each corner of the building. 2. A **template** for shaping a mould.

programme The expected timing of the progress of a building operation as illustrated on the **progress chart**.

progress chart A wall chart often in the form of a **bar chart** showing all site op-

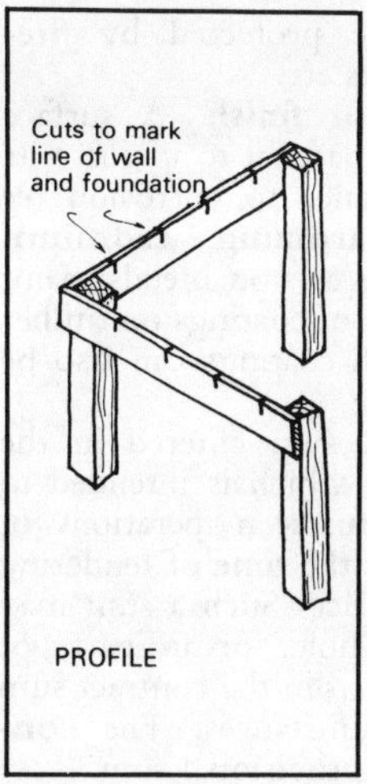

erations and their sequence against a time scale.

projecting scaffold A **bracket scaffold**.

projecting top-hung window An opening **light** hinged at the top of the jambs so that as the window is opened the top rail of the opening light drops slightly below the head frame. The whole of the opening light projects outwards. cf. **pivot-hung window**, **top-hung window**.

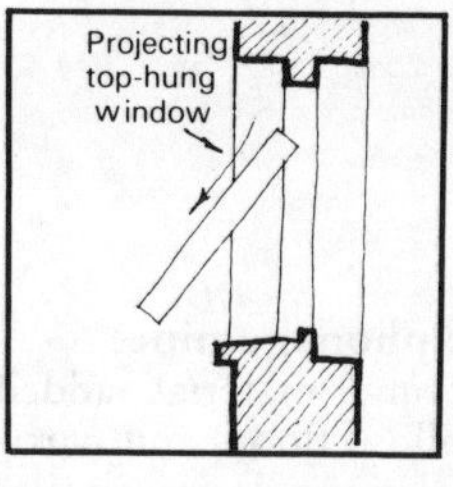

project network A **critical path diagram** illustrating the anticipated progress of a building operation and showing the sequence of operations and their logical inter-relationships and the dependencies of one operation on another.

prop An upright wood or steel member supporting temporary **formwork**.

protected escape route A means of escape providing a degree of safety in a fire due to the fire resistance of its enclosing structure. A route can consist of corridors and/or stairs in **protected shafts**.

protected shaft A stairway, lift, escalator, chute, duct or other shaft, which establishes a connection between different compartments which are enclosed by **compartment floors or walls**, and is itself required to be protected by fire-resisting walls, doors etc.

protective coating or finish A surface coating given to a material to increase its durability or resistance to corrosion (*eg* **galvanizing**, **sherardizing**, **cadmium plating**, **anodizing** etc. on metals; paint or textured waterproof coatings on timber and plywood). Such coatings can also be decorative.

provisional sum A sum entered in the **Bill of Quantities** which is intended to cover the cost of unforeseen operations, or operations which at the time of tendering are impossible to price. Such a sum may be expended in whole, or in part, or withdrawn entirely from the contract sum depending on circumstances. The **contingency sum** is a provisional sum.

pry bar A tool for drawing nails similar to the claw of a **claw hammer** but not so sturdy.

PTFE **Polytetrafluoroethylene**.

P-trap A trap, usually part of a w.c. pan, with a horizontal outlet and shaped like a letter P lying horizontally with its curved section downwards.

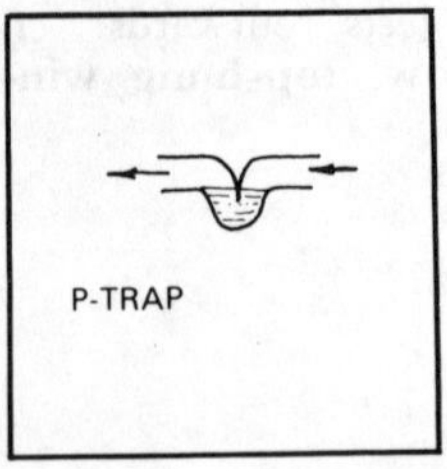
P-TRAP

puff pipe An **anti-siphonage pipe**.

pugging Soundproofing material added to the cavities of hollow floors and partitions, usually sand, slag wool, or a similar material.

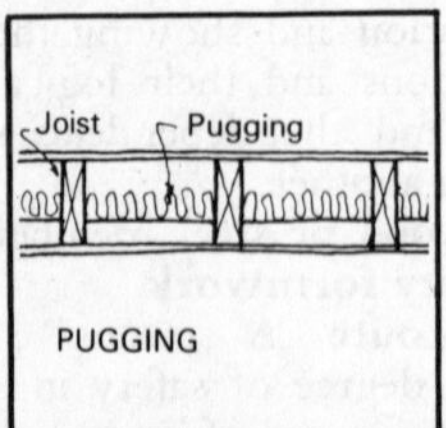

PUGGING

pull (handle) A handle for opening a drawer or cupboard door.

pull box A box in a conduit system at which point the electrical cables can be drawn through the conduit. cf. **draw-in system**.

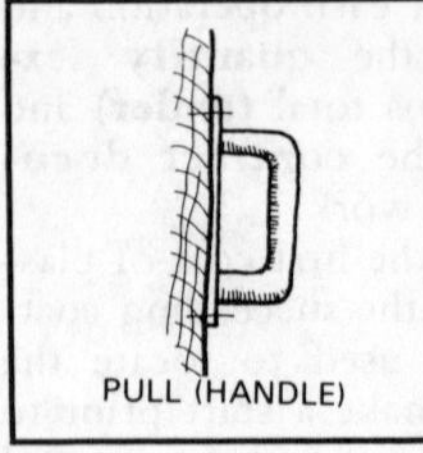
PULL (HANDLE)

pulley head The head of the cased frame of a **sash window**.

pulley stile The vertical board between the sash and the sash weight compartments in the **cased frame** of a **sash window**. The **sash pulleys** are secured to the pulley stile.

pulling A **drag**.

pulling up The softening of a dry **coat** of paint or varnish when another coat is put on, which makes brushing difficult.

pull-out strength The **withdrawal load** of a nail or a series of nails.

pulverized fuel ash (PFA) The ash of pulverized fuel, recovered from the flue gases of power stations and used as a lightweight **aggregate**.

pumice concrete A lightweight concrete which uses pumice as coarse **aggregate**.

pumice stone An **abrasive** for use before repainting, formed from the vesicular material obtained from the surface froth on a gaseous lava.

punch 1. A tool for making holes by shearing out a piece of material, or for driving home a plug, etc, when struck with a hammer. cf. **nail punch, handrail punch, prick punch** or **solid punch**. 2. A mason's chisel with a 100 mm cutting edge.

punched work **Ashlar** faced with diagonal strokes created by a punch.

purlin A horizontal beam at right angles to the **principal rafters** or trusses and carried by them or supported from or by the internal walls. It supports the **common rafters**.

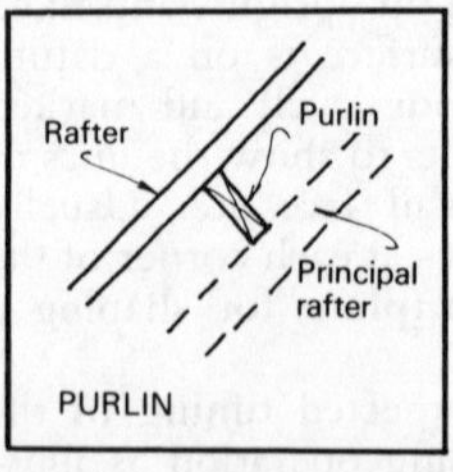

PURLIN

purlin roof A roof in which the purlins are carried on cross walls, or propped off the cross walls; usually a roof of domestic scale, now largely replaced by **trussed rafters**.

purpose-made brick A brick made to a special shape.

push plate A metal plate on the **locking stile** of a door at a suitable level to be pushed by the hand and used, particularly on **swing doors**, to open the door. The plate protects the door surface. cf. **finger plate**.

putlog A short horizontal length of scaffold tube which supports the **scaffold boards** in a bricklayer's scaffold. The putlog is supported in the wall at one end, the other end resting over a **ledger**.

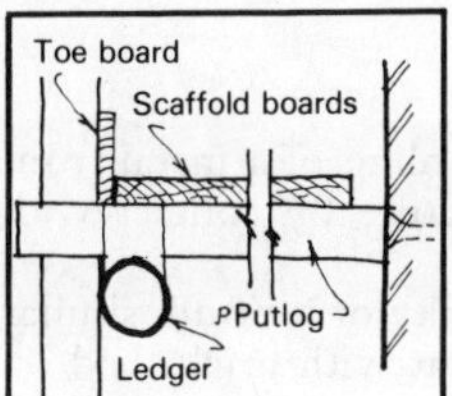

PUTLOG

putlog hole A hole left in a brick wall to receive a **putlog**.

putty See **glazier's putty**, **lime putty**, **mason's putty** and **white lead putty**.

putty glazing A glazing system in which the glass is held in position by **glazing sprigs** and **glazier's putty** and not by a bead. cf. **bead glazing**.

putty knife A glazier's knife for applying **face putty** to a **glazing bar**.

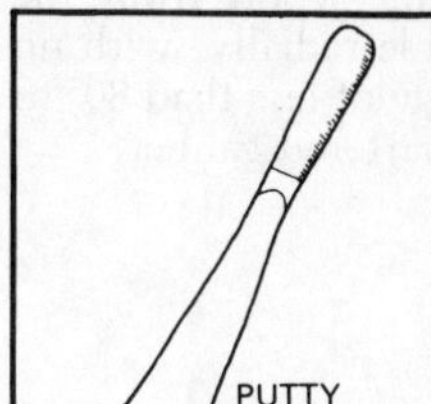

PUTTY KNIFE

PVA **Polyvinyl acetate**. cf. **latex emulsion**.

PVC **Polyvinyl chloride**.

pyramidal light A **roof light**, square or polygonal on plan, whose sides slope inwards to meet in a point.

Q

quadrant 1. A curved, metal **casement stay**. 2. A timber mould shaped in cross-section like a quarter circle.

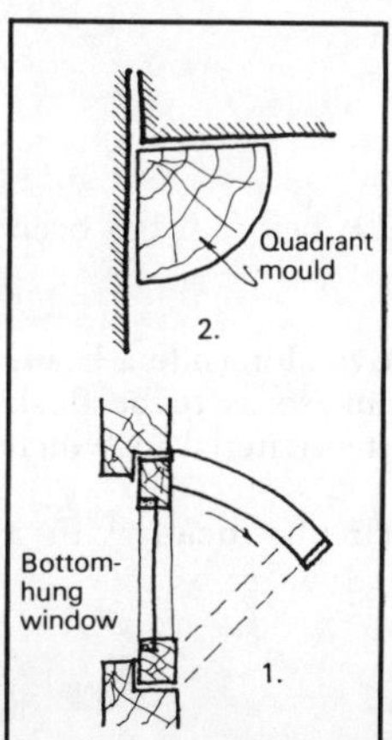

QUADRANT

quality control The inspection methods implemented in a factory or on site to ensure that a product maintains accepted minimum standards of quality, *eg*, the mix of concrete etc.).

quantities The amounts of building materials or building operations needed to construct a building which are written into a **Bill of Quantities**.

quarrel A **pane** of glass in a **leaded light**.

quarry A **quarry tile**.

quarry face The natural face of a stone as it has been quarried.

quarry sap The moisture in stone which has been freshly quarried.

quarry stone bond Any bond in **rubble walling**.

quarry tile A burnt clay tile, usually used for flooring (though occasionally for wall tiling) and obtainable in a limited range of colours (black, buff, heather and red), being unglazed but non-porous. Sizes are usually 225 × 225 mm or 100 × 100 mm.

quarter **Quarterings**.

quarter bend A 90° bend in a pipe; other angles are proportional to this (*eg* a 45° bend is a one-eighth bend).

quartered Quarter-sawn.

quartered log A log cut into four quarters for conversion by quarter-sawing.

quarter-girth rule A method of calculating the volume of timber in a log by taking the cross-sectional area of a square with a side equal to ¼ × the girth of the log at its middle point.

quartering 1. Wood sections of area 645 to 2580 mm^2. 2. Small sections of wood used as studs in partitioning. 3. **Quarter-sawing**.

quarter round A **quadrant** mould.

quarter sawing Sawing wood from the log as nearly as possible radially, with no growth ring at an angle of less than 80° to the surface in fully-quartered timber.

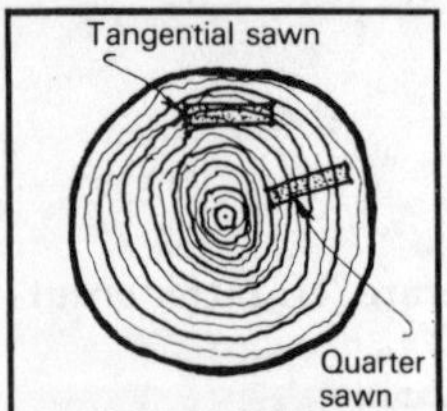

QUARTER SAWING

quarter-sawn timber Timber converted by **quarter-sawing**.

quarter-space landing A square landing at which a **stair** turns through 90°, having sides which are the same length as the treads of the rest of the stair.

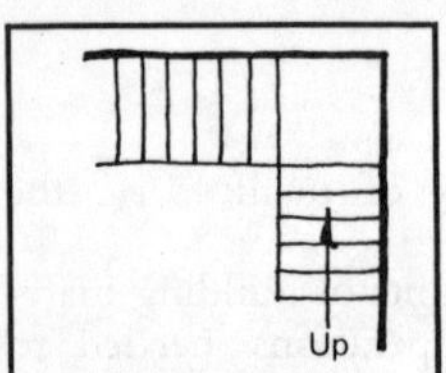

QUARTER-SPACE LANDING

quarter-turn stair A stair which turns through 90° by means of a quarter-space landing.

quartz-halogen lamp A tungsten filament lamp in which the filament is enclosed in a quartz bulb containing halogen gas.

quartzite tiles A non-slip, hardwearing floor finish composed of tiles quarried from natural crystalline rock of schistose formation; sizes vary with the quarry of origin.

queen bolt A steel bolt used instead of a **queen post** in a **queen post truss**.

queen closer A **brick** cut in half along its length to present a half **header** in the bond.

queen post One of two vertical members, set at about one-third span spacing in a **queen post truss**.

queen post truss A timber roof truss, now virtually obsolete, which has two **queen posts** at one-third span spacing with horizontal straining beams connecting the heads and the feet of the posts and two struts (from the feet of the posts to the mid-points of the principal rafters); in use prior to the development of **trussed rafters**.

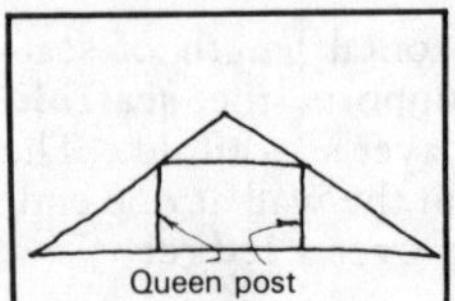

QUEEN POST TRUSS

quenching Rapid cooling of a metal from a treatment temperature by contact with water, air or oil.

quetta bond A brickwork **bond** similar to **rat-trap bond** but with bricks laid on bed and not on edge as is the case with rat-trap bond. The wall is usually one and a half bricks wide and the bond leaves gaps in the centre of the wall, which are filled with **grout** and reinforcement as the wall is built. Both faces of the wall are in **Flemish bond**.

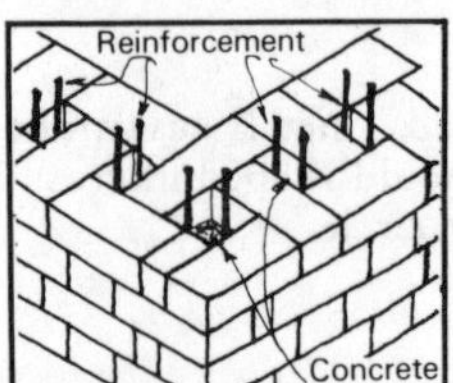

QUETTA BOND

quicklime Lime (CaO) before it has been slaked.

quilt See **blanket**.

quirk A narrow groove alongside a bead, when the bead is sunk so as to be flush with the surface of the material in which it is worked.

quirk bead A semicircular **bead** with a

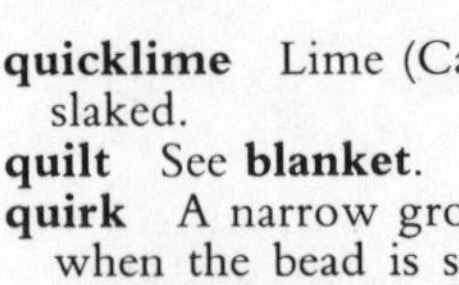

QUIRK BEAD

quirk at one side to mark the edge of a board. A double quirk bead has quirks on both sides.
quirk router A **plane** used to cut **quirks**.
quoin 1. The external corner of a building. 2. A brick, set of bricks or a large stone laid to form an external corner, often emphasized by line, decoration, moulding or colour for aesthetic effect. cf. **block quoin**.
quoin header A corner **header** in the face wall, that becomes a **stretcher** on the return wall.

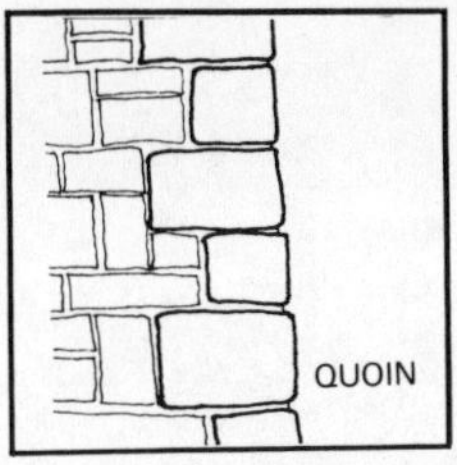

R

rabbet See **rebate**.
rabbet plane A plane with a cutting iron set at the edge of the sole to enable **rebates** to be cut.
raceway (USA) A rectangular duct in which cables pass through a building.
racking back The practice of building up the corners in brickwork before the rest of the wall, the unfinished end being stepped or racked back at an angle to avoid a vertical line of junction when the rest of the wall is built.
radial brick A **brick** tapering on plan, used to build circular brickwork.
radial shrinkage The drying shrinkage of wood at right angles to the **growth rings**.
radial step A **winder**.
radiant heater A heater which relies primarily on **radiation** as opposed to **convection** to distribute its heat. It can consist of either a glowing element backed by a reflecting surface, or a heated dull plate.
radiation 1. The dissemination of heat from a specific source by invisible rays, which do not heat the gas or vacuum through which they pass, but heat only solid objects on which they fall. 2. The dissemination of all forms of energy from a specific source.
radiation fire detector A detector which responds to **radiation** emitted by a fire.
radiator A piece of heating equipment used to convey heat to a room (not exclusively by means of **radiation** – often also by **convection** currents). It usually consists of a container of large surface area, through which hot water circulates. It can also be a movable piece of equipment in the form of an oil-filled electric radiator or an electric fire.
radiofrequency heating A method of rapid heating generated by a high frequency source and used in gluing thick **plywood** assemblies.
rafter A sloping timber in pitched roof construction stretching from **ridge** to **wall plate**. It may be a **common rafter** or a **principal rafter**.

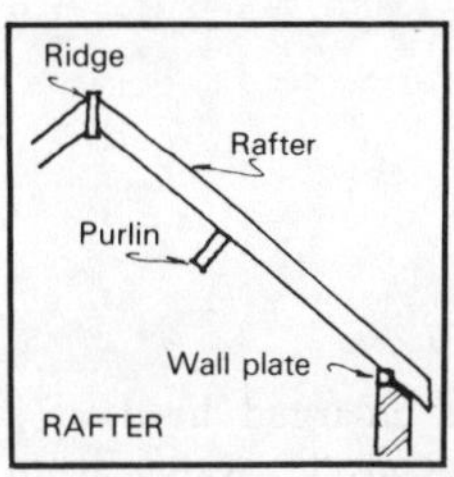

rafter filling Brick filling between the feet of rafters at wall plate level.
raft foundation A foundation in the form of a reinforced concrete slab of an area equal to, or greater than, the base area of the building.

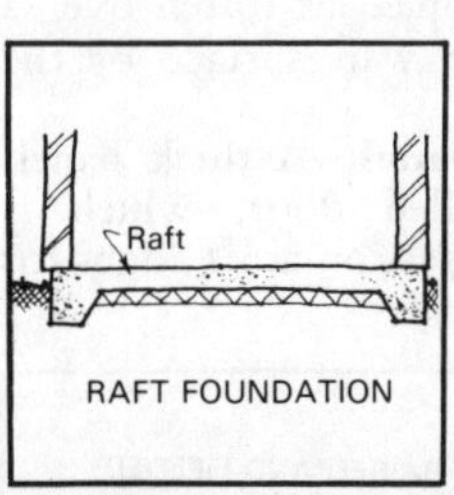

rag bolt A bolt with a deformed end to give greater hold when cast into concrete.
rag felt (USA) **Bitumen felt**.
raglet A groove, sometimes **dovetailed**, cut into either a masonry or brickwork surface or a mortar joint to receive the edge of a lead **flashing**.

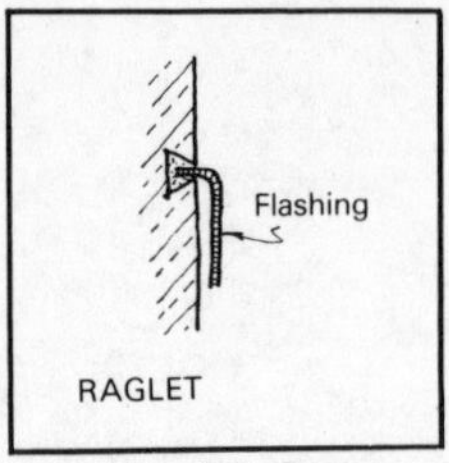

ragstone Coarse-grained sandstone, (*eg* **Kentish rag**.

rail 1. A horizontal member in a framework, as the rail of a door (**bottom rail**, **top rail lock rail**). 2. A **handrail**. 3. Any horizontal member in a fence.

rail bolt A **handrail bolt**.

railing An open fence with posts and rails.

rain leader (USA) A **downpipe**.

rain screen cladding Open-joint **cladding** designed to provide substantial protection to the wall structure behind by encouraging rainwater to drain away in the ventilated cavity behind the cladding.

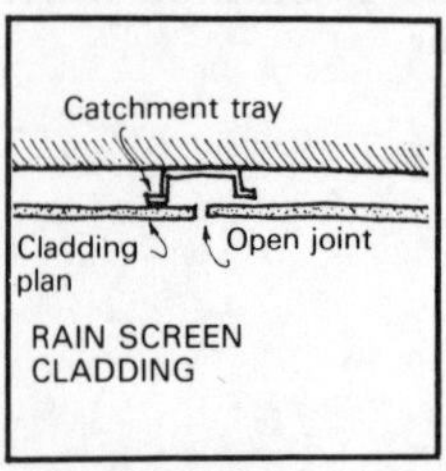

rainwater head The enlarged head of a **downpipe**, which collects water from gutters.

rainwater hopper A hopper-shaped **rainwater head**.

rainwater pipe (rwp) A **downpipe**.

rainwater shoe A short, bent fitting at the foot of a **fall pipe** which discharges rainwater into the open air (often over a **gully**) clear of the wall surface of the building.

raised and fielded panel A thick panel, usually in a panelled door, which is shaped to a thinner section at its edges for tonguing into the stile.

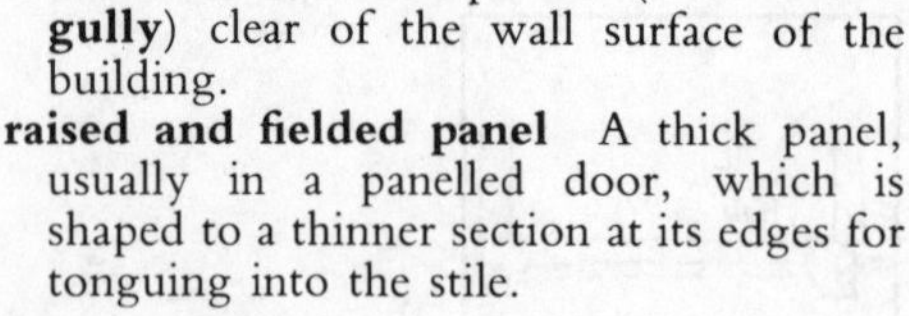

raising plate A **pole plate** or **wall plate**.

rake An angle of inclination.

raked joint A mortar joint which has been cleared of mortar to a depth of about 19 mm before **pointing** the joints or plastering the wall.

rake moulding (USA) A sloping **moulding** at the top of a **barge board** just below the tiles.

raking back **Racking back**.

raking bond **Diagonal bond**.

raking cornice or coping A **cornice** or **coping** surmounting a **gable**.

raking flashing A sloping cover-flashing used in stonework in which the top of the flashing is parallel to the roof and is let into a **raglet**. cf. **stepped flashing**.

raking out Cleaning mortar out of **joints** before **pointing**.

raking riser A **riser** which is not vertical but overhangs part of the **tread** below.

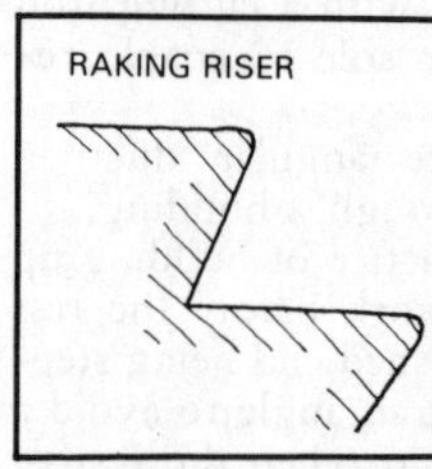

raking shore A long sloping member in **shoring** which is supported at ground level on a **sole plate** and abuts the wall of the building which it is temporarily supporting, being supported at the top by a **needle**, a **cleat** and a **wall piece**.

ramp 1. An inclined area of road, pathway or corridor to make a transition from one level to another without the use of steps. 2. A bend in a **handrail** or **coping**, concave on its upper surface.

random ashlar (USA) **Coursed random rubble** which contains squared stones.

random courses Courses of varying depths, either in walling or slating.

random rubble Walling using irregular shaped and sized stones without courses.

random shingles **Shingles** of a uniform length but varying width.

random slates **Slates** of varying widths. Slates of varying length can be laid in **diminishing courses**.

random-toothed ashlar Stone finished by **batting**.

random-tooled ashlar Stone finished with groovings cut irregularly.

range masonry (USA) **Regular-coursed rubble**.

ranging line A string stretched between **profiles** to establish the line of the face of a foundation or wall.

rank set The opposite of a fine set of a plane, in which the **back iron** is set leaving a big space between it and the edge of the **cutting iron**; used in rough work.
rapid hardening (Portland) cement A **Portland cement** that is finer than normal Portland cement and hardens more rapidly after setting.
rasp A plumber's file.
ratchet brace or drill A carpenter's brace or drill for use in confined spaces where a full turn of the tool is impossible. It is fitted with a ratchet and pawl which allows anticlockwise movement of the handle to be effected without any movement of the tool head.
rate The unit cost of a material or an activity, which is filled into an **item** in a **Bill of Quantities** and extended by multiplying with the quantity of that material or activity.
rate of growth A guide to the quality of timber, judged from the number of growth rings in the timber measured radially. If rings are widely spaced this indicates rapid growth and often, in softwood, less strength.
rat-trap bond A **bond** in brickwork in which bricks are laid on edge to build a one-brick wide wall. Bricks on each face are alternating **headers** and **stretchers**, which leaves a cavity between the stretchers. It is a cheap form of wall construction. cf. **Quetta bond**.

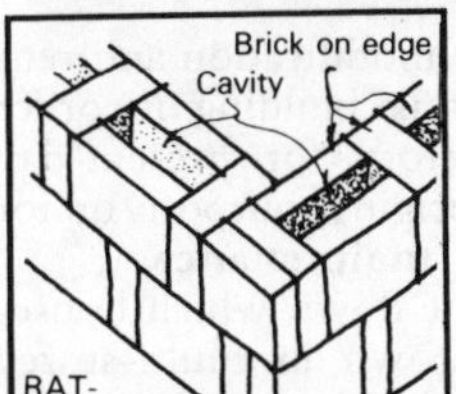

RAT-TRAP BOND

raw linseed oil Refined linseed oil which has not been boiled. cf. **boiled oil**.
ray A **wood ray**.
ready mixed concrete Concrete which is delivered to site in a plastic condition and requires no further treatment before being placed.

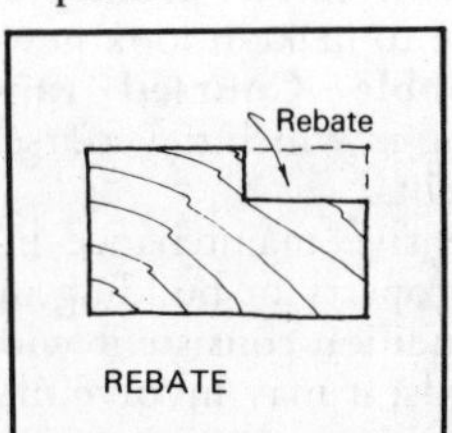

REBATE

rebate A long step-shaped recess cut into the edge of a timber component, as in a **glazing rebate**.
rebated weather-boarding **Weather-boarding** which is wedge-shaped and rebated on the inside edge of the lower face to fit over the thin edge of the board below.

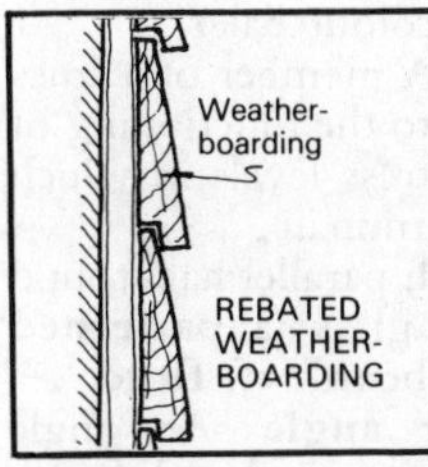

REBATED WEATHER-BOARDING

receptacle (USA) A **socket outlet**.
receptor (USA) A shower bath tray.
recessed head screw A **wood** or **machine screw** with a head profile other than a normal slot, *ie* with a **Phillips head** or **Pozidriv head**.
recessed pointing **Pointing** in which the **mortar** of a mortar **joint** is set back from the face of the brick or stone to give a strong shadow. It does, however, provide a ledge on which water can rest.
reciprocating drill A joinery drill for drilling small holes, consisting of a steeply-threaded shaft carrying the chuck and a sleeve which, when pushed down the shaft, rotates the drill. When the sleeve is returned up the shaft, however, it does not rotate the drill.
reconditioning A remedial treatment for collapsed hardwood (hardwood that has suffered irregular shrinkage) or warped hardwood, involving high temperature steam treatment.
reconstructed stone An imitation of natural stone, produced by mixing crushed stone with cement to give an even-textured 'stone' which is much cheaper than the natural stone from which it has been made.
rectangular hollow section (RHS) A structural steel section available in various sizes and consisting of a hollow tube of rectangular cross-section.
rectangular tie (USA) A wall tie made of bent wire in the form of a rectangle.
rectifier A device for converting alternating electrical current into direct current.
red lead A red **inhibiting pigment** made up of a mixture of oxides of lead (mostly Pb_3O_4) and used on timber and steel. It is poisonous.

red oxide A red **pigment** which does not inhibit corrosion.

reduced level The finished level of a site after excavation has taken place, expressed in relation to a prescribed datum.

reducer 1. A **thinner**. 2. In plumbing, a pipe of reducing diameter, reducing in the direction of flow.

reducing power The ability of white **pigment** to make a colour paler.

redundant member A member of a truss which is unnecessary to the functioning of the framework, the stress levels in which are statistically indeterminate.

reeded Decorated with parallel half-round **beads**, as in reeded glass (a **patterned glass**) or reeded hardboard. cf. **flute**.

re-entrant corner or angle An angle which points inwards in a closed figure (such as the outline of a building), being above 180° as viewed from the inside; an

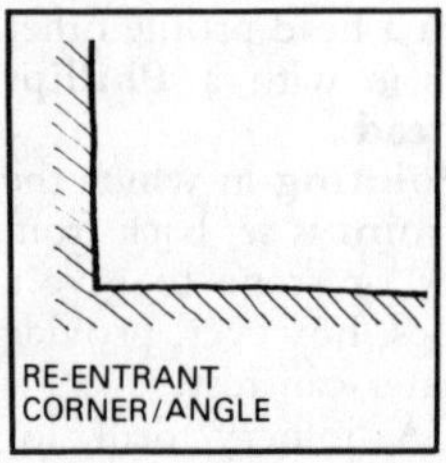

internal angle; the opposite of an external angle or **salient** corner.

reference plane A boundary of a building element, component or **zone** to which measurements are taken in **dimensional co-ordination**.

refined tar Coal tar which has been brought to a high temperature, from which water and some volatile oils have been removed by distillation.

reflectance A measure of the ability of a surface to reflect visible light, expressed as the ratio of the intensity of the reflected light to that of the incident light, striking at an angle normal to the surface.

reflection The return of incident visible radiation from a surface without change of frequency.

reflection coefficient The ratio of sound energy reflected from a surface to the incident sound energy.

reflection factor A numerical factor which expresses the extent to which a surface will reflect light. It is expressed as a percentage, *eg* a reflection factor of 45% indicates that of the light which falls on the surface 45% is reflected.

reflectivity The ratio of the amount of thermal radiation reflected from a surface to the incident thermal radiation.

reflector A device, dependent on the phenomenon of **reflection**, which is used to alter the spacial distribution of luminous flux from a source.

refraction A change in the direction of radiation as it passes through an optically non-homogeneous medium or from one medium to another.

refractory A substance that is able to resist high temperatures; used in lining furnaces, flues, etc.

refractory cement A form of cement capable of withstanding very high temperatures.

refractory concrete A concrete which withstands very high temperatures, made of high-alumina cement and refractory aggregate such as broken firebrick.

refractory mortar A mortar specially formulated for use in setting boilers, etc.

refrigerant The fluid which is alternately vaporized and compressed to liquid in the operating of a **refrigerator**.

refrigerator A cold compartment which is reduced in temperature by the action of a **refrigerant** which expands into a gaseous form and so takes heat from the compartment; the refrigerant is then turned into a liquid (outside the compartment) by a compressor in a finned heat exchanger, thereby giving up its heat to the surrounding air.

refurbishment The modification and renovation of an existing building in order to make it satisfactory for present-day use, either for its original purpose or for some other use. cf. **maintenance**.

refuse chute A chute down which household rubbish is thrown in multi-storey buildings, such as blocks of flats. The rubbish is collected in containers at the base of the chute.

register 1. A grille with a **damper** to control the volume of air passing through it into a room. cf. **grille**. 2. A **damper** to control a chimney draught.

reglet A **raglet**.

regrate To remove the surface from previously **hewn stone** to make it look new.

regular-coursed rubble **Coursed random rubble** walling in which the courses are of uniform height.

rehabilitation Extensive maintenance intended to bring a property or building up to an acceptable condition consistent with present-day standards; it may involve improvements.

reinforced bitumen felt A saturated fibre bitumen felt with a reinforcement of hessian.
reinforced came A **came** in a leaded light which is not made entirely of lead, but is lead-covered steel.
reinforced concrete Concrete into which steel reinforcing bars or mesh have been set, particularly to counteract tensile stresses. Reinforced concrete can be either ordinary concrete, or **prestressed concrete.** cf. **mass concrete.**
reinforced masonry Walling of stone or **building blocks** reinforced with steel bars or **mesh** in the vertical or horizontal joints or cavities.
reinforced woodwool **Woodwool slabs** containing lengthwise reinforcement in the form of wood **battens** or pressed steel sections to enhance the slab's spanning capability.

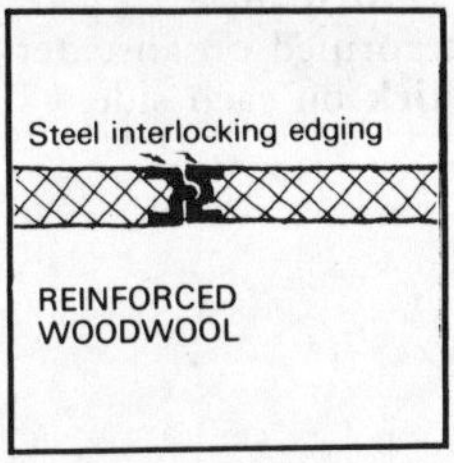

reinforcement Rods, bars or fabric, usually of steel, embedded in concrete to resist, particularly, tensile stresses.
rejointing **Pointing.**
relative humidity (RH) The ratio between the actual water vapour pressure of a sample of air at a particular temperature and the maximum vapour pressure the sample could contain at the same temperature, expressed as a percentage.
relay A control which uses electromagnetic or electrothermal means to operate electrical contacts.
release agent A substance, usually applied to the face of **formwork**, which discourages adhesion between the concrete and the formwork.
relieved shank The description of the **shank** of a bolt which is of a smaller diameter than the crest of the thread.

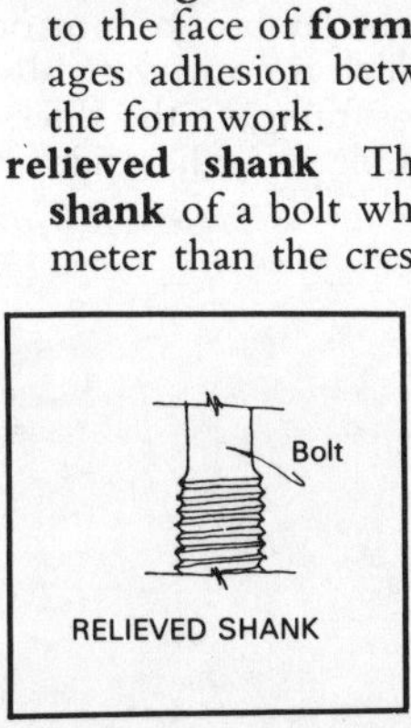

relieving arch An **arch** built over an opening in a brick or masonry wall which is spanned by a **lintel**, and which relieves the lintel of some of the load of the wall above.

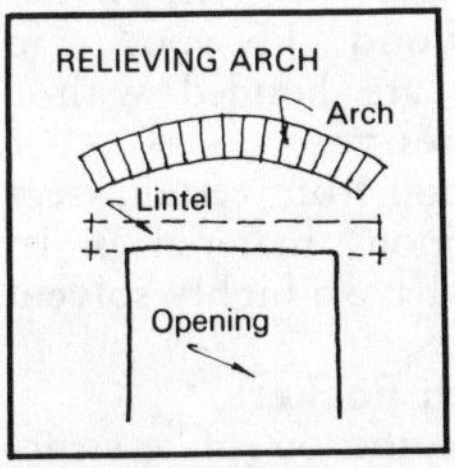

relish The depth of projection of a **haunch** from the point of a tenon.
render and set Two-coat plasterwork; *ie* a **render coat** covered by a **finishing-coat.**
render coat 1. The first coat of a multi-coat plastering system; *ie* the **coarse stuff** or the first coat of gypsum plaster applied to a wall or ceiling surface. 2. One or more coats of sand and cement applied to an external wall surface, the inside surface of a manhole, etc, to provide a waterproof layer.
render, float and set Three-coat plasterwork.
rendering A surface application of cement and sand or similar mix to an external face of a manhole, etc., to provide a surface, for reasons of appearance or to make the wall more weatherproof.
resaw A circular saw (or a band saw) used to saw boards, planks and other material.
re-saw To rip sawn timber into smaller sizes.
reseal trap A trap below a washbasin or sink, used where there is a danger of siphonage. The trap contains an enlarged chamber which retains a body of water until the siphon is broken, wherupon the body of water falls and stabilizes, thus resealing the trap. This device is not universally accepted.
residual tack A fault of paint finishes in which the film does not harden.
resilience The ability of a material to recover its original dimensions after deformation.
resin A product obtained from the sap of plants or pine trees. There are gum resins, hard resins and oleo-resins. Hard resins are insoluble in water but can be dissolved in organic **solvents** or vegetable oils. Gum resins are soluble in water and are used in glues. Oleo-resins are distilled from dead pine wood or bled from the

living tree and, in a distilled form, become **turpentine**. cf. **synthetic resin**.

resin-bonded Glued with **synthetic resin**. This usually gives the joint some moisture resistance.

resin-bonded chipboard See **chipboard**.

resin-bonded plywood Plywood in which the **veneers** are bonded with a **synthetic resin adhesive**.

resinous timber Wood from certain trees which contains resinous material in its cells. The resins can have a highly solvent effect on many paints.

resin pocket A **pitch pocket**.

resonance The phenomenon of a structure's response to sound stimuli, producing sympathetic vibrations at particular frequencies.

resorcinol formaldehyde resin A **synthetic resin** of the phenolic type which produces a thermosetting glue with a high resistance to moisture.

resorcinol resin A **synthetic resin** of the phenolic type made from resorcinol.

rest bend A right-angled bend at the foot of a vertical waste pipe where it connects to the main drain.

restraint fixing A mechanical **fixing device** which holds a component, such as a wall panel, in position, but does not carry its weight. cf. **loadbearing fixing**.

retaining wall A structure designed to support a higher level of earth on one side than on the other by withstanding the lateral pressure exerted by it on the rear of the wall.

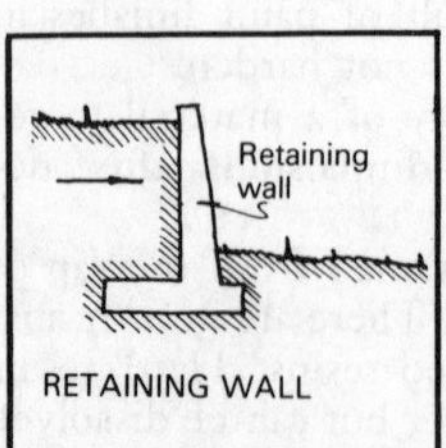

retarded hemihydrate plaster A gypsum plaster manufactured by the addition of a retarder to a hemihydrate plaster (plaster of Paris). cf. **hemihydrate plaster**.

retarder An **admixture** added to a hemihydrate plaster or a mix of concrete or mortar to reduce its rate of hardening or setting; it can also be coated on the inside of concrete shuttering.

re-tempering The undesirable practice of remixing mortar or plaster after it has begun to set.

retention fund or money A percentage of the money owed to a contractor for carrying out a building operation, which is held until the end of the **defects liability period** and until any defects discovered during that time are remedied. The retention money is then paid to the contractor.

return 1. The change in direction of a wall or component of a building, often at right angles. 2. A **return pipe**.

return bead A **bead** formed on an external angle, with a **quirk** on each side.

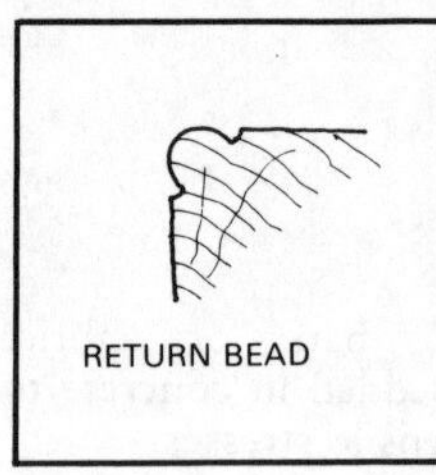

returned end The end of a **moulding** which is shaped to the same profile as the main part of the moulding.

return pipe A pipe in a circulating hot water system which conveys the cooling water, after it has flowed through the system, back to the boiler. cf. **flow pipe**.

return wall A short length of wall at an angle (usually a right angle) to the main length of wall.

reveal That part of the jamb of a door or window opening which is not covered by the door or window frame, *ie* the thickness of the wall visible on either side of the frame.

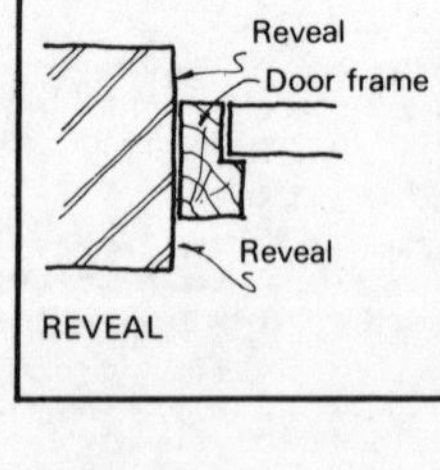

reveal lining The finish to a **reveal**.
reverberation The persistence of sound due to repeated reflections at the boundaries.
reverberation period The length of time, in seconds, taken for a sound of a particular frequency to decrease by 60 dB after the sound source has been silenced; it is dependent on the volume and **absorption** of the room.
reverse A **template** used to check the accuracy of a plaster **moulding** and cut to the reverse shape of the moulding.
reversible lock A lock which can be used on either **hand** of door.
reversible movement The temporary movement of either a structure or a building component due to its reaction to changes in temperature of humidity. cf. **irreversible movement**.
revetment A facing of stone or other material which is laid on a sloping earth surface to maintain the slope in position or to protect it from erosion.

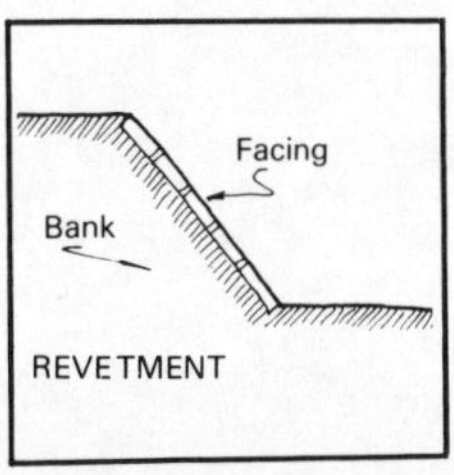

REVETMENT

revolving door A four-leaf door, the leaves being fixed at right-angles to each other and pivoted at their junction so that the door revolves within a matching circular enclosure. There are **wiping seals** on each leaf so that, in any position, the door acts as a barrier to draughts while allowing the entrance or exit of one person at a time in the space between adjacent leaves; used primarily in public buildings. Leaves can be locked in parallel pairs in the open or closed position.
rhone (Scotland) An **eaves gutter**.
riband 1. In **formwork** the board which runs across the head of the struts under a reinforced concrete beam. 2. A **rail** in a **palisade**.
ribbing The ridged surface of timber caused by differential shrinkage of summer and spring growth, and emphasizing the **annual rings**.
ribbing up The practice of gluing together **veneers** of wood to form circular joinery items.
ribbon 1. In walling, an occasional course of ornamental slates or tiles. 2. A **ribbon board**.
ribbon board In a **balloon frame**, a **joist** housed into the studs to support the floor joists.

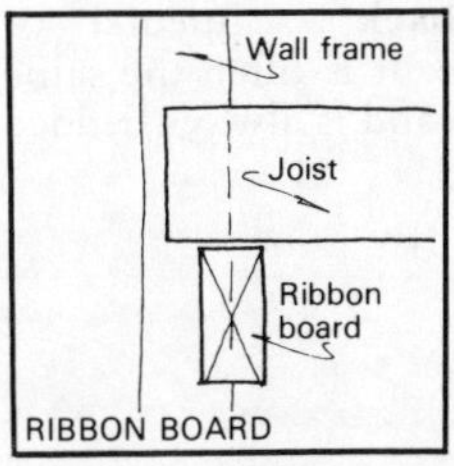

RIBBON BOARD

ribbon courses In roofing, slates or tiles laid to varying **gauges** to produce alternately long and short exposed courses.
ribbon rail A **core rail**.
ribbon saw A narrow **band saw** with a blade about 50 mm wide.
ribbon strip A **ribbon board**.
rich lime **High-calcium lime**.
rich mix A plaster, concrete or mortar mix which contains a greater proportion of gypsum plaster or cement to aggregate than is usual.
riddle A coarse sieve.
rider shore A short **raking shore** carried by a **back shore** rather than on a sole piece on the ground. cf. **shoring**.
ridge The summit-line of a pitched roof, usually horizontal.
ridge (board) In a **double-pitched roof**, a horizontal board to which the upper ends of the **rafters** of the opposing slopes are fixed.

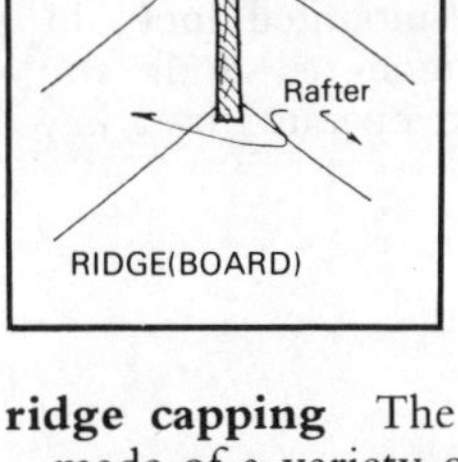

RIDGE(BOARD)

ridge capping The covering to a ridge, made of a variety of materials depending on the roof covering. The term refers particularly to pre-formed asbestos-cement or metal capping pieces to sheeted roofs.
ridge course The top course of tiles or slates on a pitched roof which is lapped by the **ridge tile** and is often shorter than other courses.
ridge pole A **ridge**.
ridge roll A **hip roll**.

ridge stop A **flexible metal** flashing at the abutment of a **ridge** and a wall rising above it, being dressed over the ridge and a short distance up the wall.

ridge tile The covering to a **ridge**, made of burnt clay or concrete and usually of half round, **hogsback**, segmental or angular cross-section. It is often the same shape as the **hip tile** and is always bedded in cement mortar.

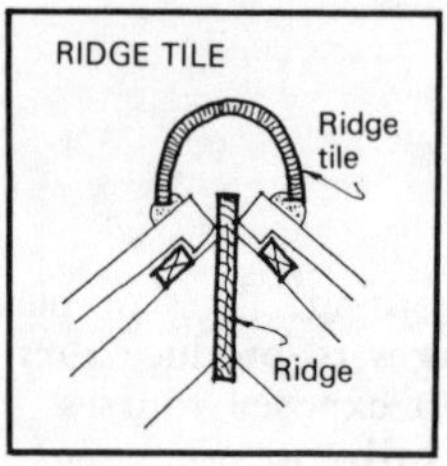

riding 1. The description of a door which touches the floor as it opens. 2. The description of a joint that does not meet evenly along its joining surfaces, *ie* it meets at the centre of the joint and is open at both ends.

riffler A rasp used by a mason for working concave surfaces.

rift sawn **Quarter sawn**.

right-hand thread A thread which causes the screw to retreat from the operator when the screwdriver is rotated in a clockwise direction.

right of way The right of a person or persons to pass over land on foot or otherwise. The right may be subject to conditions and restrictions of use.

rim latch A surface-mounted **latch**, in a metal box housing mounted on the **shutting stile** of a door; usually operated by a knob.

rim lock A surface-mounted **lock**, in a metal box housing mounted on the **shutting stile** of a door; operated by a key.

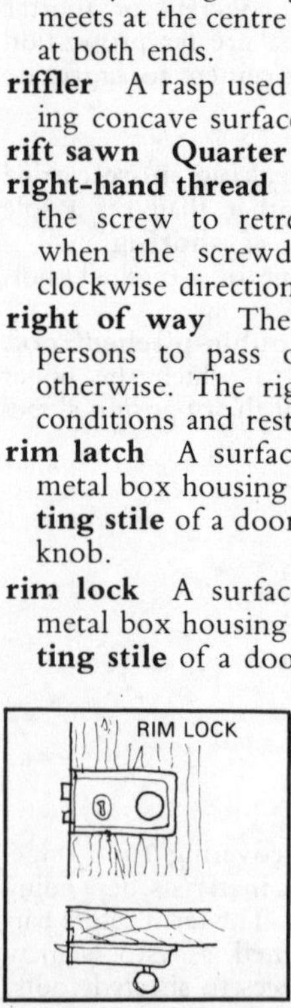

rindgall A **callus** in timber.

ring course The nearest course to the extrados of an arch.

ring main A method of electrical wiring to a number of **socket outlets** using two lengths of cable which together form a ring. Each **plug** contains its own fuse in this method. This is now the generally accepted method of wiring socket outlets in the UK.

ring shake A **shake** along a growth ring, usually in the heart of mature wood. cf. **shell shake**.

rip To saw timber parallel to the grain.

ripper 1. A long, thin, cranked-bladed tool used by slaters to cut the **slate nails** when a roof is being repaired. 2. A **rip saw**.

ripple finish A paint finish, usually achieved by **stoving**, which is uniformly wrinkled.

rip saw A **handsaw** used for cutting timber parallel to the grain, having widely spaced **points**.

rise 1. The distance between the **ridge** of a roof and the top of the supporting walls. 2. The distance between the **springing line** of an **arch** and the highest point of the **intrados**. 3. The vertical distance between one **tread** and the next in a stair.

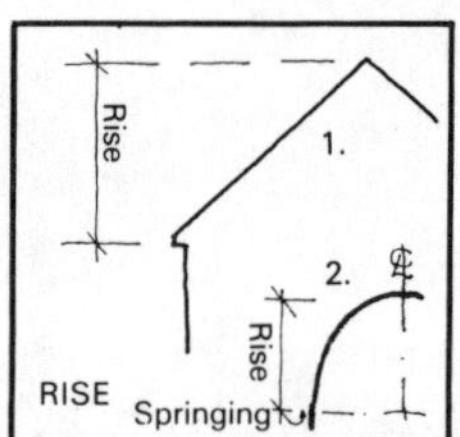

rise-and-fall table A bench for a circular saw, which can be raised or lowered relative to the saw blade.

rise and run An expression of the pitch of a member in the terms of a vertical height per metre of horizontal run.

riser 1. The vertical (or near vertical) face of a step. 2. In **snecked rubble**, a stone that is deeper than one **course**.

rising-butt hinge A **hinge** with a helical bearing surface between the two leaves, causing the door to rise about 12 mm as it

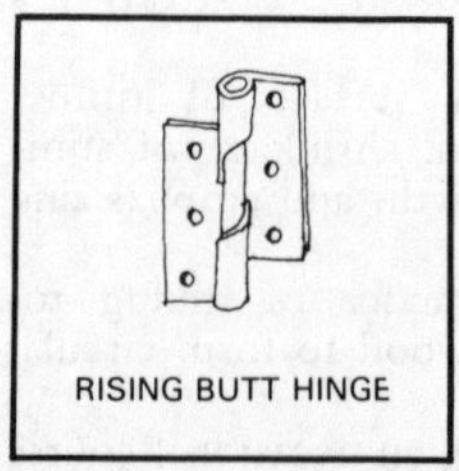

opens. This tends to close the door automatically. Doors hung on rising-butt hinges clear carpets as they open. They can also be unhinged by lifting them off the hinge **pin**.

rising main A main water, gas or electric service which, having entered the building below ground level, rises to a main metering or distribution point, or passes through one or more storeys of the building, or from one property to another positioned above.

rive To split **shingles** or **laths**.

riven lath A plaster **lath** that has been split rather than sawn and is thus less liable to damage from unintentional splitting.

rivet A metal fixing device with one head which is passed through a hole drilled through the components to be fixed, after which the shank of the device is deformed to form another head, thus clamping the components together.

rivet plug A fixing device for joining two thin materials (light gauge steel or plastic sheets) when there is access to one side only. The device consists of a tough and resilient nylon plug which is expanded on the farther side of the components being joined by inserting a wood screw or machine screw.

riving knife A steel blade behind a circular saw blade, which projects up from a bench and ensures that the wood being cut divides smoothly to avoid binding on the saw blade.

rock asphalt A naturally occurring form of **asphalt**.

rock faced Pitch-faced stone.

rocking frame A moving frame on which **moulds** are oscillated after they have been filled with concrete, to compact the concrete.

rod 1. A board, such as a **storey rod**, on which the dimensions of an assembly are set out in full size. 2. To clean drains.

rodding 1. The cleaning of drains or clearing of blockages, by means of **drain rods**. 2. (USA) Using a **floating rule** to level plaster.

rodding eye A drain **access eye**.

roll A wooden member of more or less curved cross-section, depending on the type of **flexible-metal roofing** involved, used as an aid to the joining of adjacent sheets of flexible-metal roofing on their longer edges.

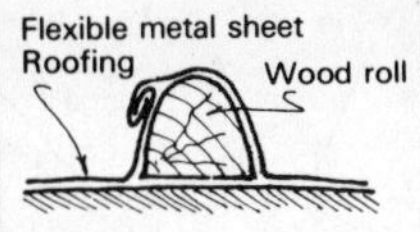

ROLL

roll-capped ridge tile A **ridge tile** surmounted by a cylindrical projection.

rolled steel joist (RSJ) or rolled steel channel (RSC) A structural mild steel section in an I or U shape, formed by hot rolling and used to construct steel building frames; now complemented by a range called **universal beams** or **universal columns**.

roller blind A window blind, usually internal and spring-loaded, which retracts above the window opening, sometimes into a pelmet-like box.

roller (rolling) shutter A shutter, usually of steel or aluminium, which is used to cover large entrance openings or windows. The shutter is wound on to a spindle which is suspended in a shutter box at the head of the opening, and is operated either manually by chains or by an electric motor.

roll roofing (USA) Any roofing material sold in rolls like **bitumen felt**.

Roman brick (USA) A narrow brick, approximately 50 mm deep including one mortar joint.

Roman cement Originally **pozzolana**, but in the UK in the nineteenth century the term was used to describe a cement, (the forerunner of **Portland cement**), which was made by calcining hard nodules of marl found in London clay.

Roman mosaic A **terrazzo** laid with 12 mm square pieces of marble placed by hand to form geometric patterns.

Roman tile A single-lap roofing tile with a single roll (single Roman tile) or a double roll (double Roman tile).

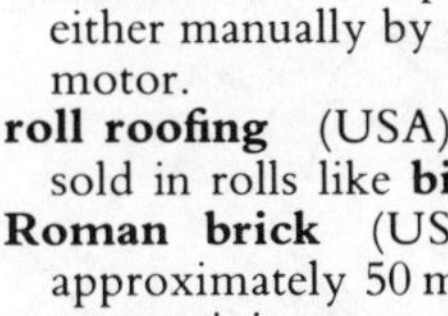

ROMAN TILE

rone See **rhone**.

roof The capping of a building, either flat or pitched, designed to protect the building from the elements. The shape of the

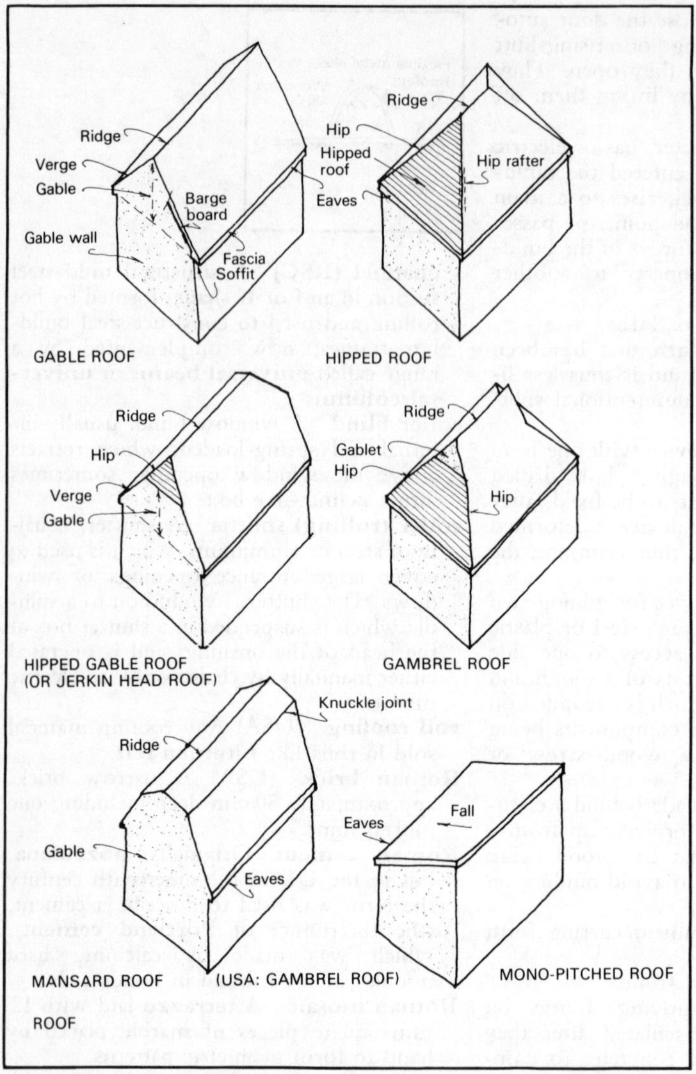

roof is dictated by its structure and its covering.

roof boarding or sheathing Boards nailed to **common rafters**; previously tongued and grooved boarding, now usually plywood or similar sheet boarding. It provides a base for asphalt, roofing felt or **flexible-metal roofing**; additionally, in high standard tile and slate roofing it is used with counter battens to provide extra bracing to the roof structure and additional insulation and protection to the **sarking felt**. This latter use of roof boarding is particularly common in Scotland, where it is called **sarking**.

roof cladding or covering The weatherproofing layer or elements of a roof, *eg* tiles, slates, asbestos-cement sheets, metal sheets, flexible metal roofing, bitumen felt roofing, asphalt etc.

roof decking A term applied to many different types of material which span between roof joists to provide a base for the roof covering. These can vary from simple sheet materials, such as plywood, chipboard or woodwool slabs to composite panels containing insulation, or even roof covering. Built-up decking units are also available, such as timber or asbestos-cement decking units or metal decking.

roof guard See **snowboard**.

roofing felt Sheets of fibres treated with

coal tar pitch or bitumen to produce a waterproof membrane and used as a **sarking felt** or in **built-up roofing**.

roofing paper See **building paper**.

roof(ing) tile A small element of roofing which, with others, forms a waterproof **roof cladding or covering**; made of concrete, burnt-clay or asbestos-cement. The main types of tile are **plain tiles**, **single-lap tiles** (pantiles, interlocking tiles etc.) and **Italian** or **Spanish tiles**.

roof ladder A **cat ladder**.

roof light A means of gaining light (and, maybe, ventilation) through a roof; the term includes **lantern lights**, **skylights**, **domelights** etc.

rooflight sheet 1. A corrugated sheet of transparent plastic material used to form rooflight areas in a sheeted roof. 2. An asbestos-cement roof sheet which has an opening for glazing in it and is set on an upstand above the general sheeting level.

roof plan A view of the roof from above, usually showing roof slopes, **gutters**, rainwater outlets, **rooflights** etc.

roof space The space between the ceiling of the topmost storey and the roof.

roof terminal (USA) The open end of a ventilation pipe above the roof.

roof truss A wooden or metal frame which spans a building or a section of a building and supports the roof covering. Traditional forms of truss include **king post** and **queen post trusses** both of which are now largely replaced by **trussed rafters** and forms of steel roof trusses. cf. **bowstring roof truss**, **northlight roof**.

room-sealed boiler A gas boiler which is a **balanced flue appliance**.

root 1. The part of a **tenon** which joins the **shoulders**. 2. The point of the internal angle between **saw** teeth, or screw threads.

ropiness A defect in a paint surface caused by the brush marks not having flowed out, due either to poor flow properties of the paint or to brushing after the paint film has begun to harden; hence the description, a ropey finish.

rose 1. A decorative plate through which a door handle passes. 2. A plate or boss on a ceiling through which an electric light flex hangs.

rose bit A countersink bit for wood.

rosin A natural **resin** obtained from pine oleo-resin (turpentine) after the removal of the volatile fraction.

rot The decay of timber due to infection by a wood-destroying fungus.

rotary cutting A method of cutting **veneer** from a log which, having been soaked, is revolved in a lathe against a long knife. Most veneers are cut in this way except for some decorative veneers which are cut by **slicing**.

rotary veneer A **veneer** cut by rotary cutting.

rough arch A **relieving arch**.

rough ashlar Stone as brought from the quarry.

rough back A rough end of a stone which is hidden in a wall.

rough bracket A bracket under a timber **stair**.

rough carriage A carriage under a timber **stair**.

rough cast An external rendering of **coarse stuff** which is roughened and then finished by having fine shingle thrown against it, it is often coloured.

rough coat A **render coat**.

rough cutting The cutting of common brickwork, measured in a **Bill of Quantities** as an area. cf. **faircutting**.

rough floor (USA) A floor of rough boards, usually square edged, on which the finished floor is laid; often the two floors are separated by building paper.

rough ground A piece of timber of small cross-section, nailed or plugged to a wall or other surface to receive the fixings for a joinery item or lining etc.; often the rough ground is the thickness of the plaster coating and is used to stop the plaster against.

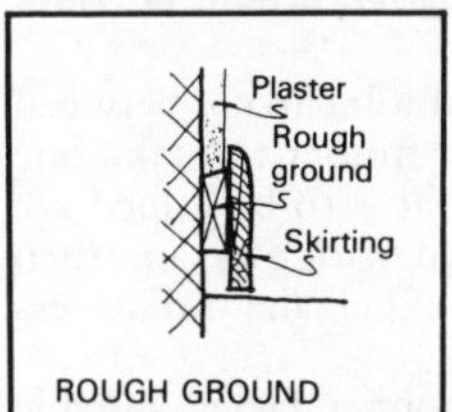

ROUGH GROUND

roughing-in Performing the first rough work of any trade.

roughing-out In carpentry, roughly shaping a piece of wood before carrying out the more accurate shaping work.

rough string A **carriage** under a timber stair.

rough work Brickwork which will be hidden eventually by **plaster**, **facing brick** etc.

rounded step A **bullnose step**.

round head A term applied to the head of a nail, screw or bolt which is segmental or flat in elevation and round in plan.

round-log construction The practice of constructing walls by laying logs, one on top of the other. At the corners of the building, opposing logs are halved together and pass each other.

rout To cut and smooth wood in the shape of a groove with a **router** plane.
router 1. A **plough**. 2. The side wing of a **centre bit** which ploughs out the wood in a circular form. 3. A hand-held machine used to rout out timber.
rowlock A brick-on-edge course of brickwork.
rowlock arch (USA) A brick **relieving arch** made up of concentric courses of headers set on edge.
rowlock-back wall A brick wall backed by bricks laid on edge.
rowlock cavity wall A wall built of **rat-trap bond**.
RSJ A **rolled steel joist**.
rubbed finish 1. A concrete finish produced by rubbing down with a carborundum stone or other abrasive. 2. A paint finish that has been flatted down. cf. **flatting down**.
rubbed joint A glued joint made between two narrow pieces of timber to make one wider piece. The surfaces to be joined are planed smooth, coated with glue and then rubbed together to expel air and excess glue.
rubber A brick without a **frog**, suitable for rubbing to shape for gauged brickwork. cf. **gauged brick.**
rubber hardness degree See **international rubber hardness degree**.
rubber latex A colloidal aqueous dispersion of rubber.
rubbing 1. **Flatting down** a paint film. 2. Rubbing with an abrasive.
rubbing stone A grit stone used for rubbing bricks.
rubble 1. Broken brick, concrete and similar material. 2. Stone which has not been worked, apart from being, sometimes, roughly squared. cf. **rubble walling**.
rubble ashlar A **rubble** wall faced with **ashlar**.
rubble drain A trench dug to falls and partially filled with broken stone or similar coarse materials, normally used for draining surface water from a building site.

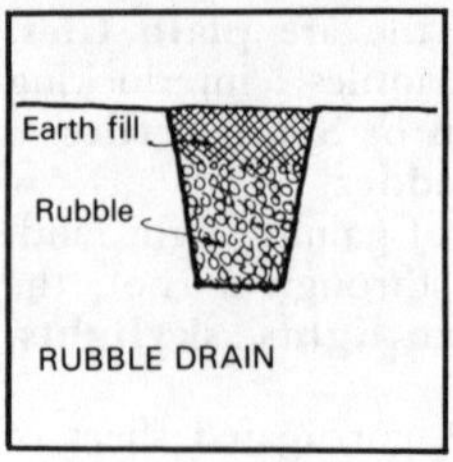

rubble walling Stone walls made of stones which are not finely worked and therefore have joints wider than in **ashlar** walls; the work can be **random rubble**, **snecked rubble**, **coursed rubble** or **polygonal rubble**.
rule 1. A straight edge of any length, divided for measuring. 2. A plasterer's straight edge for working plaster; of various types such as **floating rules**, **joint rules**, **levelling rules** and **running rules**.
run 1. A **barrow run**. 2. A length of pipework, cable or services. 3. The flow of an over-thick paint film before it has hardened, resulting in a defect in the smoothness of the paint film.
rung A horizontal bar in a ladder.
run line A straight line painted by using a **lining tool** and straight edge or by stencilling.
runner 1. A horizontal timber across the top of ceiling joists in a pitched roof, hung from the purlin and lessening the span of the ceiling joists. 2. A horizontal timber carrying joists under **formwork** under a concrete slab. 3. The guide in front of a **plough**.
running bond **Stretcher bond**.
running-off Applying a finishing coat of plaster to a moulding.
running plank A plank in a **barrow run**.
running rule A **straight edge** nailed to the floating coat below a cornice **moulding** which is to be run.
rust The coating of red or yellow oxide of iron produced on the surface of iron or steel when it is exposed to a humid atmosphere – not to be confused with white rust, which is a term loosely used to describe the corrosion products or certain non-ferrous metals.

rusticated ashlar **Ashlar** in which the stones are left with a rough face which stands proud of the joint.

rustic brick A **facing brick** which has had a textured surface applied by covering with sand (sand-faced brick) or by impressing it with a pattern.

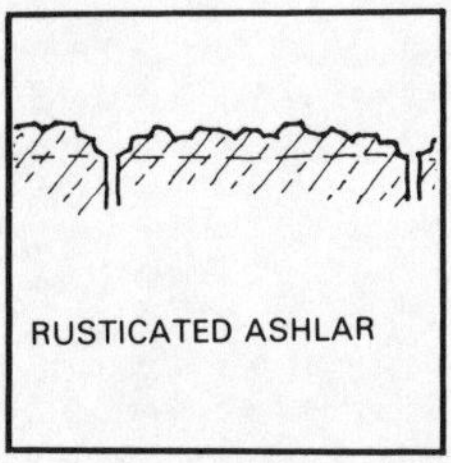

rustic joint Joints sunk back from the surface of stone in stone walling.

rustic siding **Drop siding**.

rustic slates **Random slates**.

rusting The formation of **rust** on ferrous metals due to the action of moisture.

rust pocket An **access eye** at the foot of a cast iron ventilation pipe for the removal of rust.

rybat(e) (Scotland) A **stretcher** stone in a jamb or opening.

S

saddle 1. A **flexible metal** flashing dressed to fix under slates or tiles at the intersection of a **dormer** ridge or subsidiary roof and the main roof. 2. A fitting for making a drain connection to a sewer, set over a hole cut into the sewer. 3. A **bolster**. 4. A fixing lug that passes over a pipe or conduit and is fastened down each side.

saddle-back board A **carpet strip**.

saddle-back coping A **coping** with a triangular shaped top, a sharp apex and flat flanks.

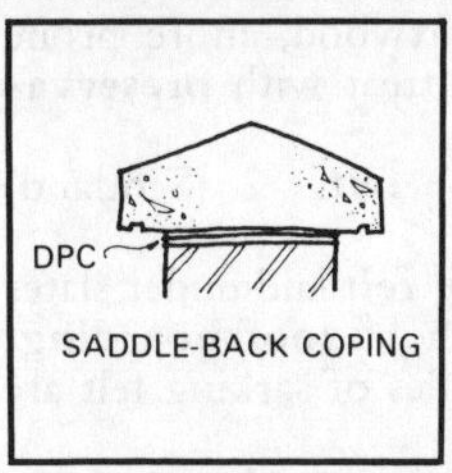

saddle bar A horizontal metal bar which supports and stiffens **leaded lights**.

saddle joint A **joint** between the stones of a cornice in which the stones are profiled into a saddle shape at the joint in order to throw water away from the joint.

saddle piece A **flexible metal** saddle that forms a watertight junction between the end of a **roll** and an **abutment**.

saddle roof A term applied to a **duo-pitched** roof with gables.

saddle scaffold A scaffold, used in the building and repair of chimneys, which is built over the ridge of the roof.

saddle stone The **apex stone** of a gable.

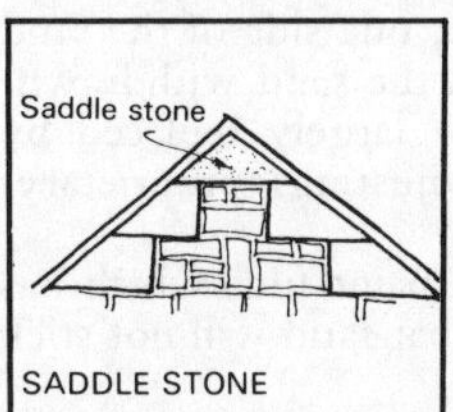

safety arch A **relieving arch**.

safety factor See **factor of safety**.

safety glass Glass which is treated to make shattering (particularly splintering), or breaking less likely. This category includes glass reinforced by wire mesh (as in **Georgian glass**), glass that has been toughened by heat treatment (**armour-plate glass** or **toughened glass**) or glass laminated with transparent plastic sheets.

safety lighting A system of lighting, supplied from a source separate from the general lighting, which is installed in buildings occupied by the public to assist them to leave the premises safely without the aid of the general lighting in the event of a mains power failure. If the building, or a part of it, has inadequate daylight, safety lighting is kept on at all times when the public are in the building.

safe working load See **permissible working load**.

sagging See **curtaining**.

sailing course A **string course**.

St. Andrew's cross bond See **English cross bond**.

salient A term applied to an external corner as opposed to a **re-entrant corner or angle**.

sally 1. A re-entrant angle cut in a timber component, such as a **birdsmouth joint**. 2. The projecting tongue of a **scarf joint**.

salt glaze A glaze obtained on stoneware by shovelling salt into the hot kiln.

sand Fine aggregate resulting from the natural disintegration of rock or from the crushing of quarried rock or gravel.

sand blasting An abrasive method of cleaning or wearing down a surface in which sand in a stream of air at high pressure is thrown at the object to be abraded. Used, for example, in the production of a textured finish in hardened concrete, or the matting of a gloss surface.

sand box A box full of dry sand used to support a timber post which in turn supports the **formwork** of a reinforced concrete horizontal member. When the formwork is to be struck, one side of the sand box is removed and the sand withdrawn. The method is now largely replaced by the use of screw-adjusting, proprietary, tubular steel props.

sand-dry surface A paint film which has dried to the extent that sand will not stick to it.

sanded bitumen felt A **bitumenous felt** which is surfaced on each side with a dressing of fine sand.

sander A **sanding machine**.

sand-faced brick A **facing brick** with a coating of sand on at least one stretcher and one header face to give a textured appearance.

sanding The smoothing of wood surfaces with **glasspaper** or **sandpaper** either by hand or by machine. The same process is called **flatting down** when a paint finish is being sandpapered.

sanding machine A power tool for smoothing surfaces with **glasspaper** or other **abrasives**.

sanding sealer A sealer for wood which allows the surface to be sanded after sealing.

sand-lime brick A **calcium silicate brick**.

sandpaper An **abrasive** paper made of sharp sand stuck to cloth or paper. cf. **glasspaper**.

sandwich beam A **flitch beam**.

sandwich panel A composite panel, usually comprising a relatively hard outer layer or layers (metal, plywood, plasterboard, plastic etc.) bonded to a core of foamed plastics or a cellular material, combining strength with lightness and a degree of thermal insulation.

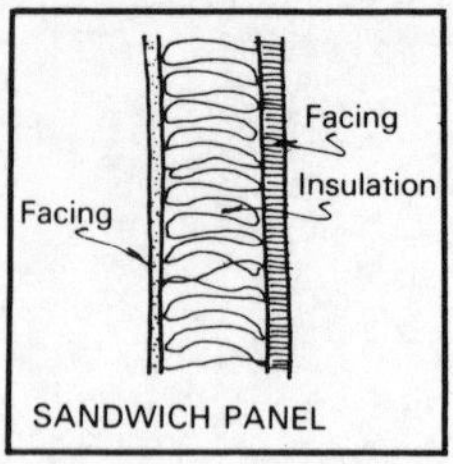

sanitary appliance A fixed appliance in which water is used either for cleansing, culinary or drinking purposes before passing to waste, or for the flushing away of soil or waste matter.

saponification In general, the formation of soap by the reaction a fatty acid ester and an alkali. In painting practice, the decomposition of the medium of a **paint** or **varnish** film by alkali and moisture in a substrate, such as new concrete or renderings based on cement, sand and lime.

sap rot **Sapwood** of abnormal colour with yellowish-brown or pinkish-brown tinges, with or without reduction of hardness. Occurs in cut wood as a result of the action of wood-destroying fungi.

sap stain **Blue stain**.

sapwood The outer, more recently grown wood of a tree. It occurs between the bark and the **heartwood** and is lighter in colour than the heartwood, more prone to **rot** but easier to treat with **preservative**.

sarking 1. **Sarking felt**. 2. (Scotland) **Roof boarding**.

sarking felt **Roofing felt** laid under slates or tiles with or without **roof boarding**. Some insulating grades of sarking felt are now available.

sash A sliding **light** in a **sash window**. The term is usually reserved for vertically sliding lights, as opposed to horizontally sliding lights.

sash and case window (Scotland) A **sash window**.

sash balance A spring which controls the moving lights of a **sash window** in place of sash weights, pulleys and cords.

sash chain In heavy **sash windows**, a chain which replaces the normal **sash cord**.

sash chisel A **small-bladed chisel**.

sash cord The cord attached to a sash, which passes over the pulley and is connected to the **sash weight**.

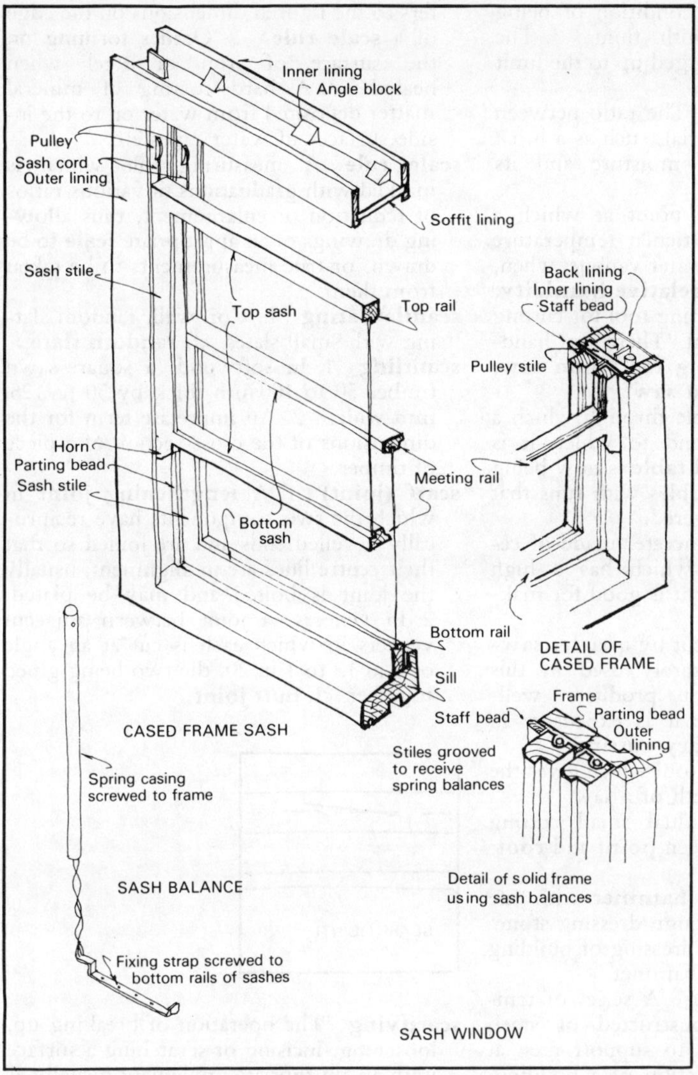

sash door A half-glazed door.

sash fastener A bolt, pivoted on the top of the **meeting rail** of one **sash** and engaging in a **sneck** or **keeper** on the top of the meeting rail of the other sash.

sash lift A **pull** or hook on a **sash** which is used to assist in its opening or closing.

sash lock A **sash fastener**.

sash pocket See **pocket**.

sash pulley One of the two pulleys per **sash** which are set in the **pulley stiles** and over which the sash cords run.

sash run (USA) A **pulley stile**.

sash weight The counterweight used in a **sash window**. There are two counterweights per sash, enabling the sash to be positioned at any chosen point from fully closed to fully open, the counterweights also easing the movement of the sash. The weights are housed, and move, within the **cased frame**, being attached to the sashes with **sash cords** or **sash chains** and suspended over **sash pulleys** attached to the **pulley stiles**.

sash window A window in which the two **opening lights** slide vertically in a **cased frame**, balanced by **sash weights** or **sash balances**.

satin finish A fine-textured matt finish.

saturated roofing felt A roofing felt which is saturated, usually, by bitumen, but has no surface dressing of bitumen.

saturation 1. The degree to which a colour departs from white and approaches pure colour. 2. The condition of being thoroughly soaked with fluid. 3. The condition of being charged up to the limit of capacity.

saturation coefficient The ratio between the capacity of a material, such as a brick or stone, to absorb moisture and its amount of pore space.

saturation point The point at which a sample of air at a particular temperature can contain no more water vapour; when, in fact, it is at 100% **relative humidity**.

saw A steel-bladed cutting tool for cutting wood, stone or metal. There are hand-held versions including the **tenon saw**, **rip saw** and **cross-cut saw**.

saw bench A steel table through which a circular saw passes and to which it is fixed. A **rise-and-fall table** is now being superseded by fixed tables with runs that can be raised and lowered.

sawdust concrete Concrete, made of cement and sawdust, which has a high moisture movement but is good for making fixing blocks.

sawn veneer Veneer cut by **quarter sawing** (slicing), now rarely used in this country, although it produces well-figured veneer, since it is expensive in waste timber. cf. **rotary cutting**.

saw set An adjustable tool which gives the correct **set** for the teeth of a saw.

saw-tooth The individual small cutting blades of a saw, between **point** and **root**.

sax A slater's **zax**.

scabbing hammer A **hammer** with one pick point used for rough dressing stone.

scabbling The rough dressing of building stone with a pick or hammer.

scaffold or scaffolding A series of temporary platforms constructed of steel, light alloy or timber to support men at work on the construction of a building.

scaffold board A softwood board, often bound at its ends with hoop iron, which with others forms a platform on a **scaffold** used by men working on the construction or repair of a building. Scaffold boards can also be used to construct other access paths on sites, such as **barrow runs**.

scaffold pole A component of a **scaffold** framework, once made of larch poles, now normally in the UK made of tubular steel or aluminium alloy.

scagliola Plasterwork coloured to look like marble and polished; common in the seventeenth and eighteenth centuries.

scale 1. The ratio of reduction or enlargement in the drawing of an object; also refers to the figured dimensions on the edge of a **scale rule**. 2. Oxides forming on the surface of iron or steel when heated. 3. A hard coating of mineral matter deposited from water on to the inside surfaces of water pipes etc.

scale rule A measuring rule which is marked with graduations in various ratios of reduction or enlargement, thus allowing drawings of an appropriate **scale** to be drawn, or true measurements to be taken from them.

scantle slating In Cornwall, random slating with small slates. cf. **random slate**.

scantling 1. In softwood, a square-sawn timber 50 to 100 mm thick by 50 to 125 mm wide. 2. An imprecise term for the dimensions of the cross-section of a piece of timber.

scarf (joint) 1. A **lengthening joint** in which the two components have reciprocally bevelled ends and are joined so that their centre lines are in alignment; usually the joint is bolted and may be plated. 2. In veneers, a joint between adjacent veneers in which each is cut at an angle of 1 in 12 to 1 in 20, the two being glued together. cf. **butt joint.**

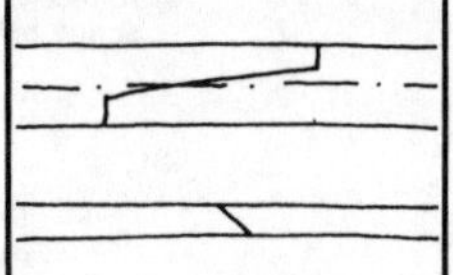

SCARF (JOINT)

scarifying The operation of breaking up, loosening, incising or scratching a surface with an appropriate implement, usually as a preparation to resurfacing.

schedule of dilapidations A list, prepared at the termination or expiry of a lease, of all repairs to be undertaken by the outgoing tenant.

schedule of prices An alternative to a **Bill of Quantities** in certain simple types of project. A list of **items** without quantities is compiled and the tenderer is invited to set a **rate** against each item. In large work this method can lead to inflated prices unless the tenderer is given an idea of the quantities involved.

scissor truss A roof truss in which the strut supporting the centre of one rafter is attached to the foot of the opposing rafter. From the crossing of the struts (or scissor members) there is a supporting post to the ridge.

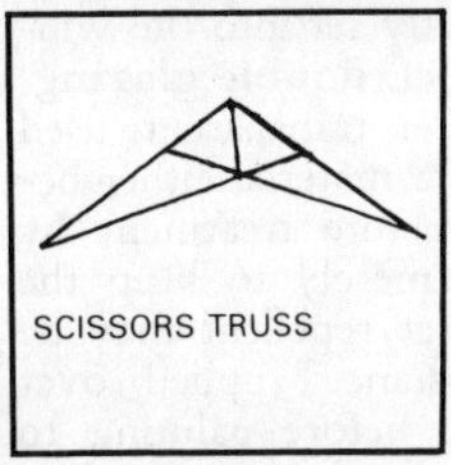

score To scratch a surface to obtain a better mechanical bond.
Scotch bond **English garden wall bond**.
scraper A **cabinet scraper**.
scraper plane See **cabinet scraper**.
scratch awl An **awl**.
scratch coat The first coat of plaster on lathing.
scratcher A **comb**.
scratching Laying the first coat of plaster and roughening its surface ready for the next coat.
scratch work See **graffito**.
screed 1. A line of plaster or of concrete carefully laid to the level of the finished surface and acting as a guide for the **rule**, when plastering, or the **screed rail**, when concreting. 2. A wood or steel straight edge used as a temporary alternative to (1). 3. A layer of mortar from 25 to 63 mm thick used to level off a concrete floor and produce a smooth surface for a later finish.

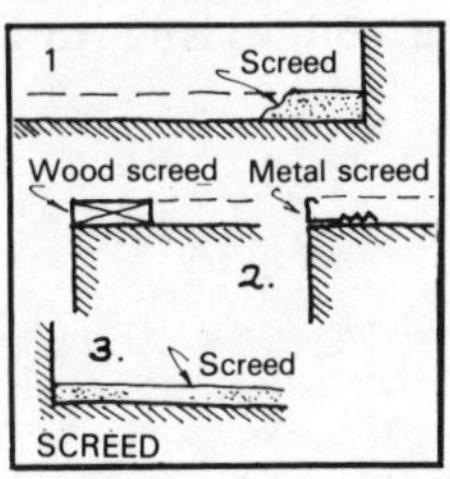

screed rail A heavy **rule** used to level the surface of concrete or screed.
screw A fixing device with a **thread** on its **shank**. **Woodscrews** have a spiral thread and a pointed end; **machine screws** have a helical thread and a blunt end for use with a nut or for screwing into metal. All screws except **grub screws** and **dowel screws** have heads of various styles with **slot**, **Phillips**, **Pozidriv** or **socket** driving profiles. cf. **coach screw**, **drive screw**, **recessed head screw**.
screw clamp A **handscrew**.
screw-down valve A cock, similar to a domestic water tap, that operates by the screwing down of a jumper.
screwdriver A tool for rotating a screw, with a blade to match the driving profile of the screw (**slot**, **Phillips** or **Pozidriv**).
screwed connection Any threaded connection to which pipes or apparatus can be fitted.
screwed pipe A gas or water pipe threaded externally at its end and joined to the next pipe by a fitting threaded internally. Greater diameters of similar pipe are sometimes used for rails, crush barriers and other structures.
screw eye A wood screw with a loop in place of a head; used with a **cabin hook** as a simple door or window fastener.

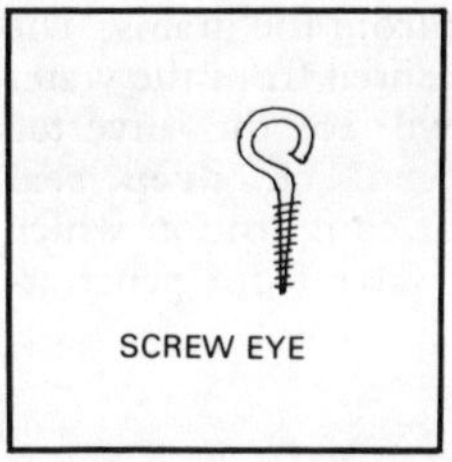

screw gauge The diameter of screws defined in a series of whole numbers (*eg*, No. 2 = 2.08 mm, No. 4 = 2.74 mm, No. 8 = 4.17 mm).
screw nail A **drive screw**.
screw pile A cylindrical **pile** fitted with a screw point which bores its way into the earth when it is turned.
screw plug A drain plug, used during a drain test, consisting of a rubber ring which expands to block the end of a length of drain when two steel plates (one on each side of the rubber) are screwed together.
screw thread See **thread**.
scribe 1. To cut one member to fit the often irregular surface of another. 2. To score or incise with a pointed tool: to fit by so marking.
scribed joint A joint between mouldings, in which one moulding is cut to receive the other, *ie* they are not mitred. cf. **mitre**.
scriber A pointed tool for scribing lines, sometimes in the form of a pair of dividers.
scrimming The setting of **scrim** over joints between sheets of gypsum plasterboard, or other backing material, before plastering.
scrim or scrimp Coarse canvas, or mesh of other material, set over joints in a

backing material before plastering to avoid the plaster coating cracking at that point. Also used to reinforce **fibrous plaster**.

scrub board (USA) A **skirting board**.

scrub plane A plane which removes deep shavings because of its rounded **cutting iron**.

scumble A low opacity, light-coloured paint used to achieve broken colour effects by softening or modifying the **ground coat**, which is deliberately allowed to grin through. cf. **grinning through**.

scutch A bricklayer's tool, similar to a small hammer, but with a **cross peen** on both ends of the head, used to cut bricks.

scutcheon An **escutcheon**.

seal 1. Water contained in the **trap** of a gully, w.c. or waste pipe which prevents the escape of foul air from the drains. The depth of a seal is measured from the water level vertically down to the inverted crown of the U-bend. cf. **deep seal trap**. 2. A device or composition which prevents air and/or water from penetrating a joint.

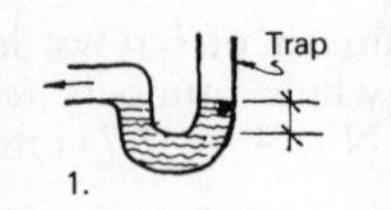

SEAL

sealant 1. An adhesive composition applied to a joint by hand, gun, knife or trowel, by pouring or in strip form, with the intention of creating a **seal** between adjacent components and maintaining this despite movement in the joint. Sealants are therefore expected to maintain their flexibility for a considerable time and to adhere well to the surrounding components. 2. A paint or other coating intended to seal and render impervious the surface of a material. cf. **sealer**.

sealed flue A **balanced flue appliance**.

sealed unit A multi-glazed unit consisting usually of two sheets of glass with a space between, the unit having been hermetically sealed after the air has been withdrawn. Sealed units are directly set into the window glazing rebates. cf. **double glazing**.

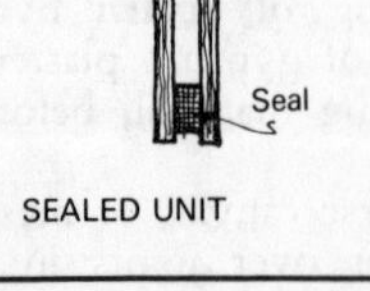

SEALED UNIT

sealer 1. A liquid, often transparent, used to close the pores of a material either before decoration or before treatment by another material or merely to keep the surface clean. A water repellent may be included. 2. A substance applied over bitumen or creosote before painting to prevent their bleeding through the paint film.

sealing compound 1. A **sealant**. 2. A cold-applied bitumen applied to **roofing felt** laps.

seam A joint between two sheets of **flexible-metal roofing**, formed by bending up both sheets and doubling them over together. A **standing seam** is applied to the longitudinal edges of the sheets; a **cross welt** or **double-lock welt** is usually applied to the ends of sheets (*ie* across the fall of the roof).

seamer A specially shaped pair of pliers used to form **seams** in **flexible-metal roofing**.

seam roll A **hollow roll**.

seasoning 1. The drying of timber (either by natural means or in a kiln) to the specific **moisture content** required for its ultimate use. 2. The drying, and consequent hardening, of stone. cf. **quarry sap**.

seasoning check A **check** which occurs during seasoning.

secondary beam A beam that transfers its load at one end or at both ends on to a **main beam**.

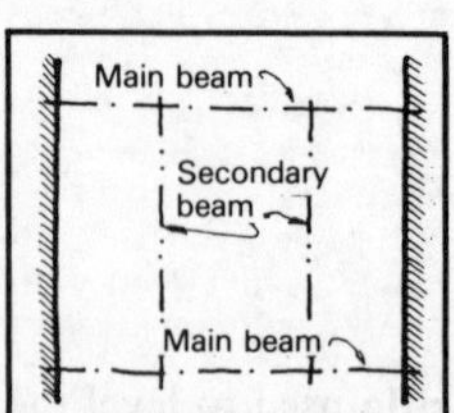

SECONDARY BEAM

secondary circuit The flow and return pipes through which water circulates between the **cylinder** and the draw-off points. cf. **primary flow-and-return**.

second fixings Items which are fixed after plastering; *ie* **architraves**, **skirting boards**, cupboards. Plumbing and services trades also need a second visit to site to carry out their second fixings. cf. **first fixings**.

second moment of area The sum of the products of the elements of area of a section and the squares of their distances from the axis.

seconds Second quality materials or goods.

secret dovetail A **mitre dovetail**.

secret fixing A method of fixing which cannot be seen once the fixing is complete.

secret gutter A valley gutter which is almost completely hidden by the oversailing of the slating. cf. **open gutter**.

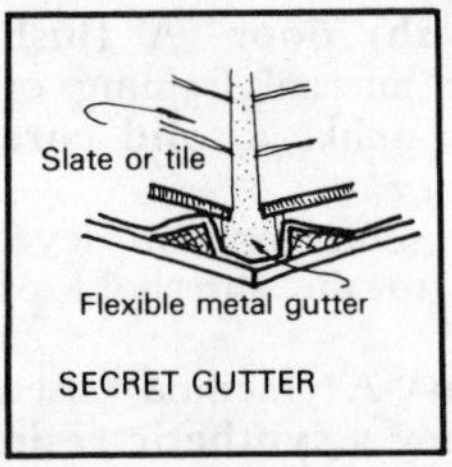

SECRET GUTTER

secret joggle A **joggle** in an arch in which the interlocking is not visible on the face of the arch.

secret nailing Nailing which cannot be seen on the exposed surface of the component being fixed, as in the nailing of tongued and grooved boards.

SECRET NAILING

secret tack A method of fixing large lead sheets on a steeply sloping surface, in which a lead strip is soldered to the back of the sheet, passed through a slot in the **roof boarding** and fixed by screws to the inside surface of the boarding.

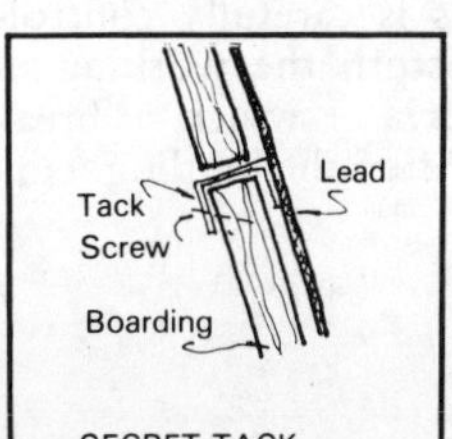

SECRET TACK

secret tenon A short **tenon** that fits into a **blind mortise**; *ie* it does not pass through the mortised wood to appear on the opposite surface.

secret wedging A method of fixing a secret tenon by inserting wedges into saw cuts in its end – the wedges driven up the tenon as the tenon is inserted into the **blind mortise.**

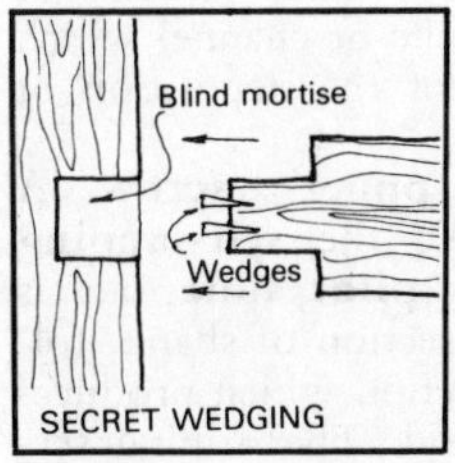

SECRET WEDGING

section 1. A building material formed to a definite **cross-section** but unspecified length; often manufactured by a continuous process such as rolling, drawing. extruding etc. 2. A drawing of a building, assembly or component showing all parts which can be 'seen' from an imaginary vertical section line through a particular position in the building, assembly or component. The section will show both the parts of the object that have been 'cut' by the section line, and the parts which appear in **elevation** (*ie* not intersected by the section line). cf. **cross-section**, **longitudinal section**.

sectional insulation Thermal insulating material shaped to fit round a pipe or fitting.

section modulus Of a section, the **second moment of area** divided by the distance from its axis to the most remote point of the area.

security glazing Glazing carried out in transparent material, such as rigid plastics, laminates of glass and plastic, wired glass etc. which provide some specified level of protection against attack. cf. **safety glass**.

sediment pan A removable bucket for the collection of oil, grease etc. in a gully. cf. **yard gully**, **grease trap**.

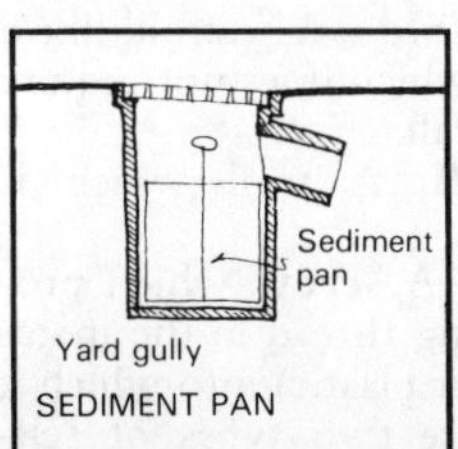

SEDIMENT PAN

se-duct A vertical flue for a number of gas appliances in a multi-storey building, supplying combustion air to the appliances as well as taking the products of combustion to the outside air.

segregation The differential concentration of the constituent materials in mixed concrete resulting in non-uniform proportions of **coarse** and **fine aggregate** throughout the mass.

self-cleansing velocity That velocity of liquid flowing in a pipe or channel which is required to prevent the deposition of solids, etc.

self-drilling, self-tapping screw A **screw** which, unlike the **self-tapping screw**, requires no **pilot hole** but is formed with a drill section of shank, followed by a screw section which produces its own mating thread. The drilling section passes through the base material before the thread-forming screw reaches the metal.

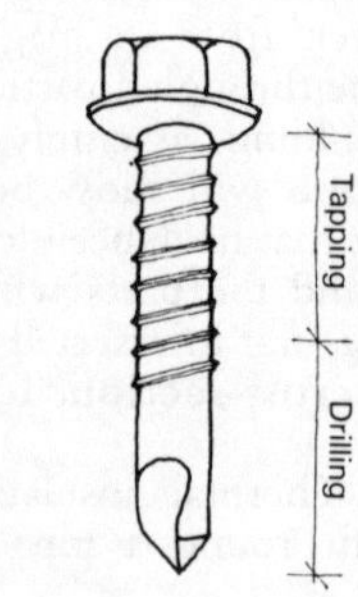

SELF-DRILLING SELF-TAPPING SCREW

self-faced stone Stone that splits cleanly to give a face that needs no further dressing.

self-finished roofing felt Roofing felt that has been saturated with bitumen and dressed with it and, often, treated with talc.

self-supporting scaffold A scaffold like a **mason's scaffold** which does not require support from the wall.

self-supporting wall A wall which is non-load-bearing.

self-tapping screw A **screw** which produces its own mating thread in the material (usually metal or plastic) into which it is driven. There are two types of self-tapping screw: a thread-forming screw which forms its mating thread by displacement rather than by the removal of any material (this can be used only with materials sufficiently soft to allow this) and a thread-cutting screw which cuts its mating thread. Both types are driven with the aid of a **pilot hole.** cf. **self-drilling, self-tapping screws.**

semi-engineering brick A **brick** of slightly less crushing strength than an engineering brick but with a higher crushing strength and less absorption than a **common brick**.

semi-hydraulic lime A lime which is halfway between **high calcium lime**, which is non-hydraulic, and **eminently hydraulic lime**. It is almost as workable as high calcium lime but has greater **hydraulic** properties.

semi-solid core (flush) door A **flush door** in which the internal framing or core contains voids, unlike a **solid core flush door**.

sensation level The sound pressure level which corresponds to the threshold of hearing.

separate application A method used sometimes in applying a **synthetic resin** adhesive, in which one of the surfaces to be bonded is treated with the resin and the other with the **accelerator**. Setting commences when the surfaces are brought together. The method avoids any waste.

separate system A drainage system in which surface water (storm water) and soil drainage are run in separate pipes.

separating layer A layer of material between screed and sub-floor which is laid to prevent adhesion between the two.

separating wall or floor A wall, or floor, which separates two properties, as a wall between two houses or a floor between two flats (where one flat is above the other) or a wall or floor between a dwelling and another class of building.

septic tank A large underground tank for the treatment and purification of **sewage** (for populations up to 100) when no sewer is available. Designs and sizes vary, but septic tanks consist of two or more chambers; the first being a digestion tank, the second a **settling tank**. Flow into these chambers is carefully controlled so as not to disturb the working of **anaerobic bacteria** which break down the solids. After the settling tank

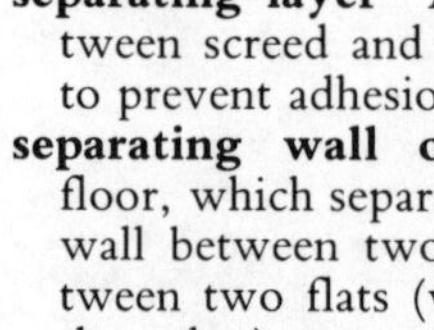

SEPTIC TANK

the effluent is passed through a filter medium in a filter chamber and thence is allowed to dissipate through **soakaways** or into a dyke or stream.

sequence of trades The order in which the various building and service trades carry out their work in a new building. This is the order in which the trade sections occur in a **Bill of Quantities** or **specification**.

service cable The supply authority's cable to the supplier's fuse box.

service core The collected services in a building, often collected into a prefabricated module. In a domestic building the service core is likely to contain **boiler**, hot water **cylinder**, cold water **storage tank**, and major plumbing runs, both for feed and waste, and may contain metering points for gas and electricity.

service lift A lift for carrying goods, usually restricted to a floor area of 1.20 m^2.

service main The pipe or cable used for conveying gas, water or electricity to buildings in a developed area, and from which service connections are made to the individual properties.

service pipe A gas or water pipe between the **service main** and the supplied premises.

service road A subsidiary road connecting a more important road to adjacent buildings and properties which may have no direct access to the more important road. The service road may be used as a secondary access to shops and stores so that parked delivery vehicles are on the service road instead of blocking the main road.

services The electrical, **plumbing** and mechanical services in a building, including specialist installations such as telephones, fire and intruder alarm and detection systems, lift installations etc.

set 1. The slight bend given to the point of a saw-tooth so that the **kerf** is slightly wider than the saw blade, thus preventing the saw from binding. Alternate points are bent in opposite directions. 2. The first hardening of concrete, mortar or plaster (the initial set). 3. Of a coat of plaster, the final coat of multi-coat plasterwork. 4. A **nail punch**.

setback The stepping back of a building to a deeper **building line** above a certain level, required on certain city sites in order to preserve the required amounts of light and air in the street.

set screw A **grub screw**.

sett A small rectangular block of stone, about 180 mm deep by 120 mm wide and from 100 to 180 mm long; formerly used for surfacing roads, now used simply for decorative paving.

setting 1. The action of giving a **set** to a saw. 2. The first hardening of concrete, mortar or plaster; sometimes used in relation to the hardening of glue. 3. The act of positioning a lintel, beam etc. on its bearing surfaces. 4. The brickwork which supports and encloses a boiler or furnace.

setting block A block of resilient, non-absorbent material placed in the **glazing rebate**, with others at the sill, to ensure that the sheet of glass is central in the frame and the edge clearances are maintained.

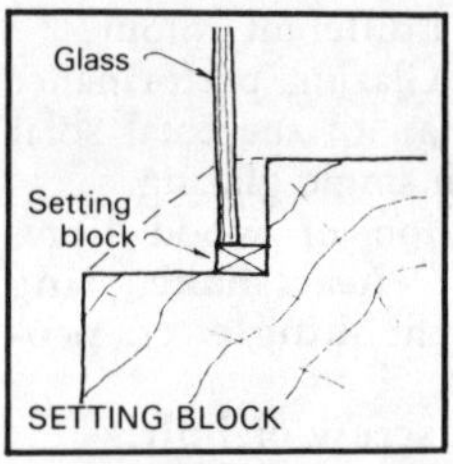

setting coat A finishing coat of plaster.

setting out The operation of marking out with pegs the position of a building or roadway on a site, or marking out the position of walls on a floor slab etc.

setting time The time taken for the chemical or physical action by which an **adhesive** changes to a hardened state. In respect of concrete, it is the time required for concrete to take its initial set. cf. **initial setting time**.

setting up The thickening up of paint during storage. If it cannot be thinned by stirring it is not suitable for use.

settlement Minor movement of the foundation of a building, after it has been loaded by the full weight of the building. It is generally of a limited nature, both in amount and extent, not causing major cracking or distress of the structure. cf. **subsidence**.

settling or settlement tank The chamber in a **septic tank** in which solids are allowed to settle (part of the early treatment of sewage).

sett paving A surface made up of rectangular blocks of stone (setts) laid in a regular arrangement upon a prepared road base.

sewage Water-borne domestic waste conveyed in sewers. It may also include trade effluent, surface water and ground water.

sewage treatment plant Any purification plant, from large sewage works to the domestic **septic tank**, which renders **sewage** innocuous.

sewer Pipes, channels or other underground structures for the conveyence of water and **sewage**; usually under the control of the local authority.

sewer brick (USA) An **engineering brick**.

sewer connection 1. The length of drain pipe between the last **manhole** on a drain or private sewer and a main **sewer**. 2. That part of a private sewer or drain which lies beneath a public highway.

sgraffito A plaster decorative surface achieved by scratching the top coat of plaster while it is soft to expose the coat beneath which is of a different colour.

shading coefficient Glazing performance expressed as a fraction of the total solar transmission through single glazing.

shake 1. The separation of wood fibres along the grain. cf. **heartshake**, **ring shake**. 2. A handsplit **shingle**. cf. **processed shake**.

shank The shaft of a **screw** or **bolt**.

shaping (of a saw) The second operation of putting a cutting edge on a saw; after **topping**, the teeth are filed to a uniform size and shape. After shaping, the saw is **set** and sharpened.

sharpening (of a saw) The final operation of putting a cutting edge on a saw after it has been **set**, performed with a taper saw file.

sharp paint A flat paint like a **primer** or **sealer**, which dries quickly by **evaporation** and has a strong pigment.

sharp sand Sand whose grains are angular, not rounded, and free from clay or other alien material; suitable for making mortar or concrete.

shear 1. The sideways sliding movement of a layer or component relative to parallel adjacent layers or components due to an imposed load. 2. An abbreviation for **shear strain**.

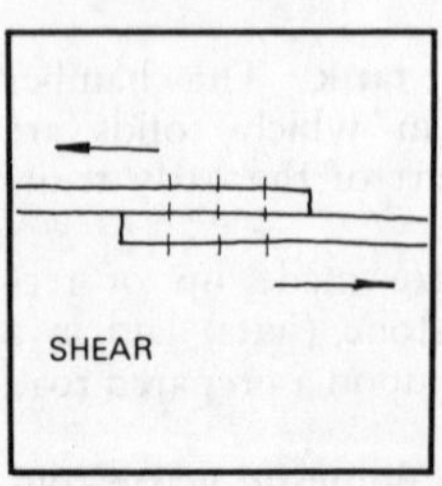

SHEAR

sheariness A defect in a paint **film** which should appear glossy, but because of a greasy surface, lack of **compatibility** or other cause appears oily.

shear plate A circular timber connector plate with a projecting perimeter flange on one face, used in conjunction with a bolt.

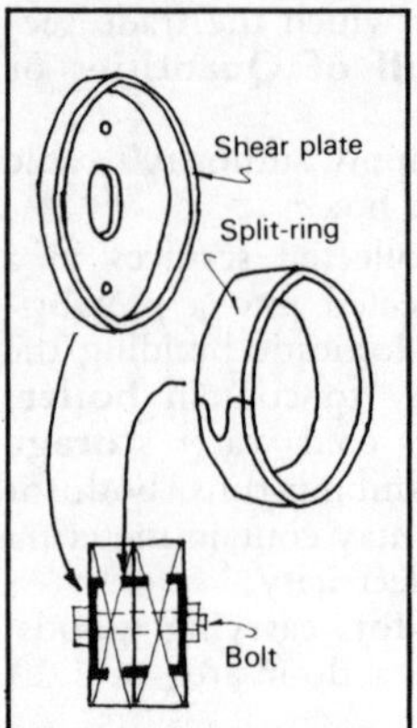

SHEAR PLATE AND SPLIT RING

shear resistance The resistance to the sliding of one component over another.

shear strain Relative deformation in shear.

shear stress **Stress** parallel to the area being considered.

sheathing Close-boarding or timber sheet material, such as **plywood** or **chipboard**, nailed to the outside of a timber frame or roof rafters (cf. **roof boarding**) to form a base for later cladding and to provide bracing for the frame.

sheathing felt An **underlay** felt under asphalt roofing to isolate the roofing from the roof structure.

sheathing paper **Building paper**, particularly when fixed to **sheathing**.

sheen A dull gloss effect, such as that sometimes seen when flat paint films are viewed obliquely in certain light conditions.

sheet 1. (Metals) The term applied to steel which is thinner than plate; copper, aluminium or zinc which is less than 9.5 mm thick and more than 0.15 mm thick (below this range it is called foil) and more than 450 mm wide (below this width it is called strip). 2. (Materials other than metal) The term applied to timber-based or **plaster**, **plastics** or **asbestos-cement** materials, etc. in standard sizes of up to 1,200 mm wide by lengths of 2,400 mm or more and of varying thicknesses depending on the material.

sheet glass Glass with fire-finished surfaces which are never perfectly flat and parallel, thus producing a certain degree of distortion of vision and reflection; available in the UK in 2, 3 and 4 mm thicknesses and in three building qualities and one horticultural quality. cf. **float glass**.

sheeting clip A cranked clip fixed to the lower end of an **asbestos-cement** sheet.

sheeting rail A rail or tube secured to a vertical member at the side or end of a structure for the attachment of side wall **cladding**.

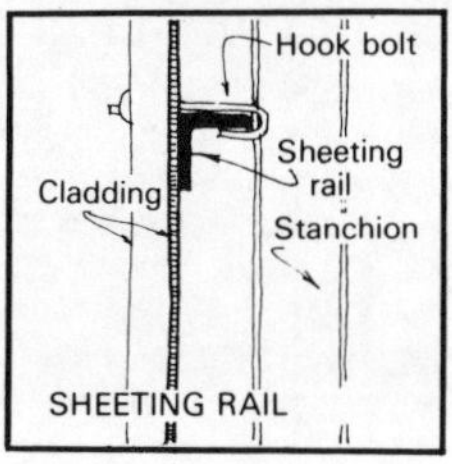

sheet pile One of a row of **piles** driven or constructed in the ground adjacent to one another to form a continuous wall which resists lateral forces or reduces seepage (*eg* in defence work or river banks etc.). Sheet piles usually interlock, one with another, and may be vertical or inclined.

shelf life The length of time a **glue** can be stored before it is mixed and still remain usable.

shellac A natural **resin** used in **varnishes**, **French polish**, **knotting**, **abrasives** etc.

shell bedding A method of laying concrete and clay blocks in which a strip of mortar along the front and back edges of the blocks is used instead of a solid bed of mortar. This method is usually applied to hollow blocks and is known to increase their resistance to rain penetration.

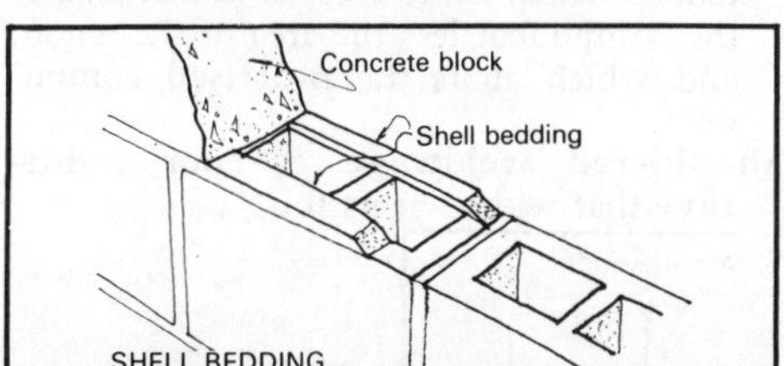

shell construction A method of spanning large open spaces using very thin (less than 75 mm thick) reinforced concrete curved slabs. The curved shape of the slabs permits their extreme thinness and resulting reduction in **dead load** and **reinforcement**. Early forms were the **barrel vault** and dome; today the conoid and **hyperbolic paraboloid roof** are frequently used.

shell shake A **ring shake**.

sherardizing The process of coating iron and steel components with a zinc-iron alloy by diffusion. The components are heated to 370 °C in a container together with zinc dust. cf. **galvanizing**.

shim 1. An **insert** in a **veneer**. 2. A metal packing piece used in levelling an assembly or component on its foundations or bearing surface.

shingle A sawn timber tile used as a roof covering. It is often made of Western red cedar and reduces in thickness from the **tail** to the **head**.

shiplap boarding Rectangular **weatherboarding** with a **rebate** cut on each long edge to fit with the rebate on the adjacent board.

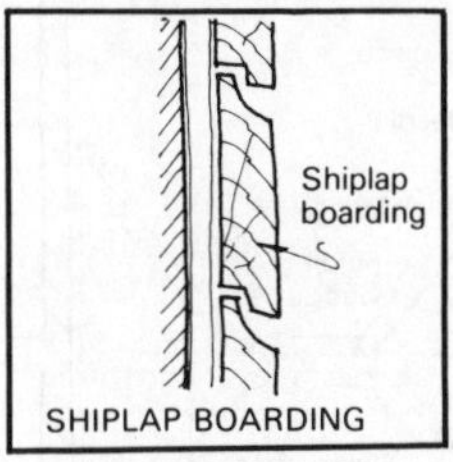

shoddy work 1. Granite stones less than 300 mm thick, each stone being squared. 2. Term applied to inferior, slipshod work.

shoe 1. The metal box-like socket giving support and protection to the end of a timber post. 2. A metal socket to form a joint where thrust from one component on to another is to be resisted. 3. The bent part on the bottom of a **fall pipe** or rainwater pipe to direct the flow away from the building. 4. In **patent glazing**, the fitting which secures the lower end of the glazing bar and acts as a stop to the glass. 5. The metal point fitted over the driving end of a pile.

shoot To plane the edge of a board to true it up.

shooting board A board which restrains another while its edge is being planed.

shooting plane A **jointing plane**.

shore A temporary support to a building structure; either sloping (**raking shore**), horizontal (**flying shore**), or vertical (**dead shore**).

shoring 1. The erection of heavy temporary timbering (**shores**) to support a building structure. 2. A collection of **shores**.

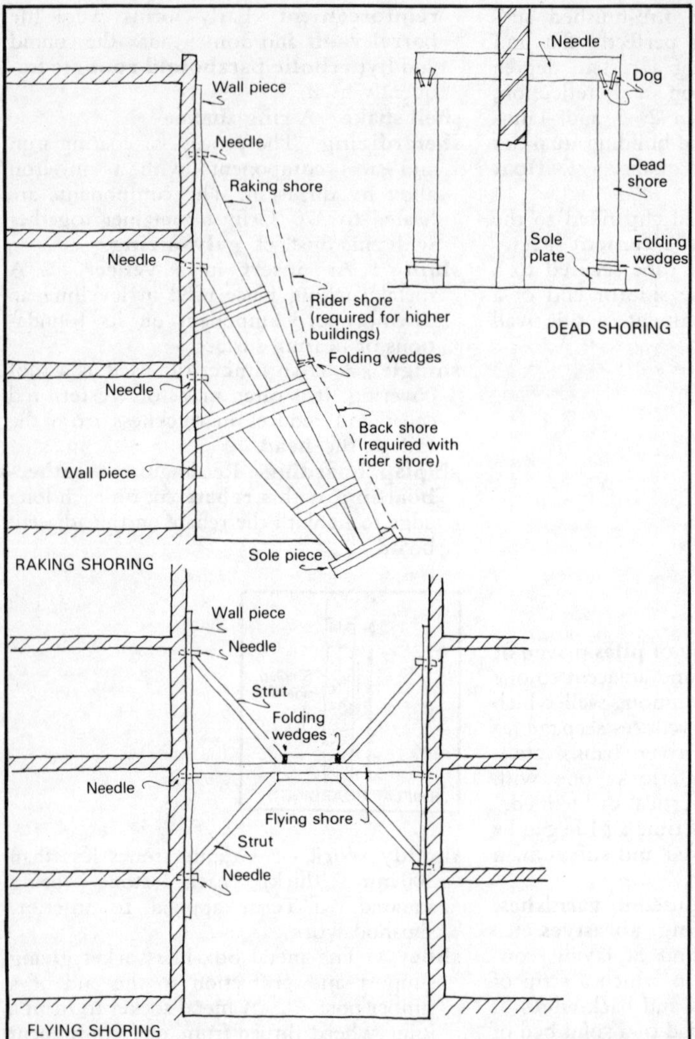

SHORING

short circuit An electrical defect caused, for example, by the positive and negative wires touching, resulting in a large passage of current which melts the **fuses** or other circuit-breakers.

shot blasting A process of surface treatment (cleaning or descaling) by flinging abrasive particles at the surface, generally carried in a high pressure jet of air.

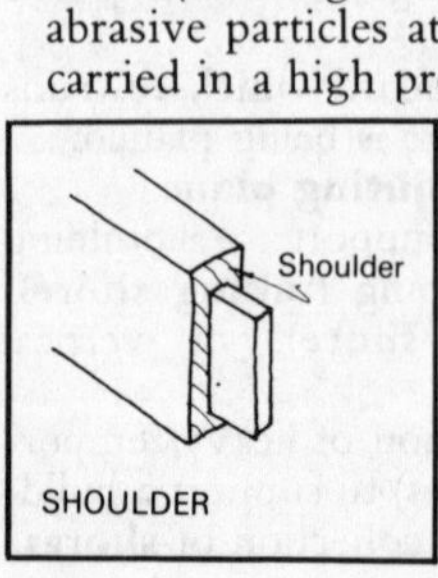

SHOULDER

shoulder The surface at the **root** of a tenon, which is the cross-sectional area of the component less the area of the tenon, and which abuts the **mortised** component.

shouldered architrave A door **architrave** that widens at its top.

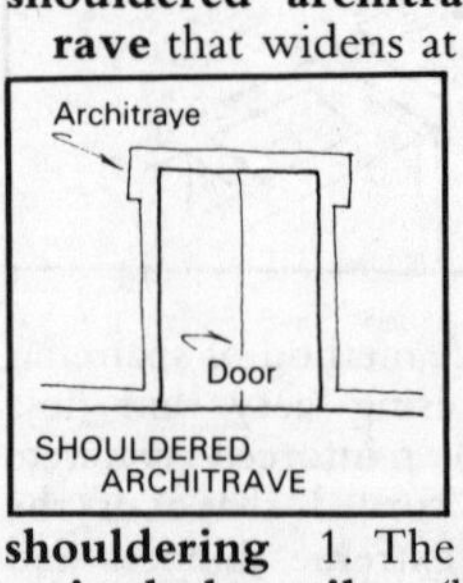

SHOULDERED ARCHITRAVE

shouldering 1. The splay cutting of some **single-lap tiles** (bottom left and top right hand corners) and some slates (top corners). 2. A thin bed of mortar to hold down slate **tails** in exposed areas; a form of half-**torching**.

shower A washing appliance which consists of a shower rose or spray head which discharges a fine spray of water on to the bather from above. The temperature of the water is usually controlled by a **mixing valve**. Shower fittings are either fixed over a bath, or installed in a special enclosure and the water is then contained by a curtain or the translucent walls and doors of the enclosure.

shower tray The base of a **shower** in the form of a shallow-sided sink with a **waste** outlet. The tray is the full size of the shower compartment base and is usually made of glazed fireclay or plastic.

shrinkage 1. The reduction in the dimensions of a material, usually resulting from a loss of moisture content, expressed as a percentage of its original size. This shrinkage is usually reversible on the material's taking up moisture again. 2. A non-reversible reduction in the size of a structure or component, such as that which occurs during the ageing of concrete.

shutter bar A pivoted bar for securing shutters in position over a window.

shuttered socket A **socket outlet** which, for safety, has its live and neutral sockets shuttered until the earth prong of the **plug** is inserted. This prong, being longer than the other two prongs, actuates the shutter springs thus allowing the entry of all three into their respective sockets.

shutter hinge A **parliament hinge**.

shuttering **Formwork**.

shutting post The post against which a gate shuts.

shutting stile The **lock stile** of a door; or the **meeting stile** of a folding door.

side cut Timber cut to avoid the **pith**.

side flight One of the return flights in a **double-return stair**; sometimes used as an alternative name for the stair type.

side flow The sideways flow of rainwater from the front face of components into the vertical joints between the components.

side gutter Any small gutter formed at the intersection of a roof slope and a vertical surface such as a **chimney** or **dormer cheeks**.

side lap 1. In roof tiling or slating, the amount by which a vertical joint between tiles or slates in one **course** is covered by the unit in the course above. 2. The side overlap of **single-lap tiles**.

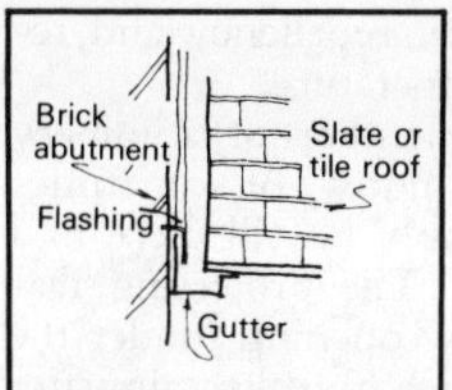

SIDE GUTTER

sidelight A margin light or a glazed panel beside a door in a **door screen**.

side rabbet plane A small **plane** used to smooth a **rebate** or a groove. It may be handed or universal.

siding 1. **Weather-boarding**. 2. (USA) Lightweight cladding of any material.

sieve A shallow box or tray with a base made of a mesh with perforations of a definite size or shape, used for separating and grading material.

sight line 1. A line on a drawing indicating the angle of visibility on bends or at road junctions. 2. A line of vision used in surveying or setting out a building or trench to establish the alignment of objects or levels.

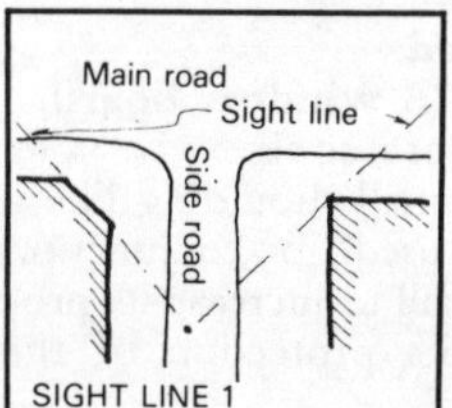

SIGHT LINE 1

sight rail A horizontal rail nailed to two posts and used to obtain levels and gradients by being viewed or sighted in relation to other similar posts.

sight size The actual size of a glazed opening between frame members.

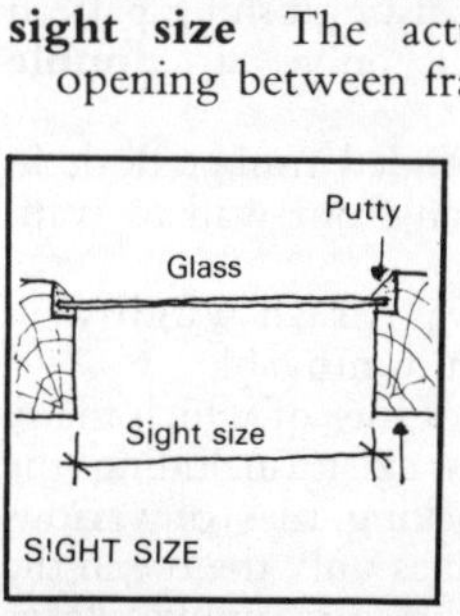

SIGHT SIZE

silica brick A firebrick to withstand high temperatures.

silicate paint A water paint containing sodium silicate; non-flammable and alkaline.

silicone One of a group of polymeric compounds based on silicon and oxygen, which has high water-repellency and resists extremes of temperature.

sill 1. The bottom member of a joinery assembly (door or window) or sometimes of a carpentry assembly (as sill piece in a **stud partition**). 2. The projecting feature below a window opening (under the window frame) which throws rainwater clear of the wall below; usually made of precast concrete, **reconstructed** (or natural) **stone**, or built up from flat tiles or bricks (often **bullnose** bricks).

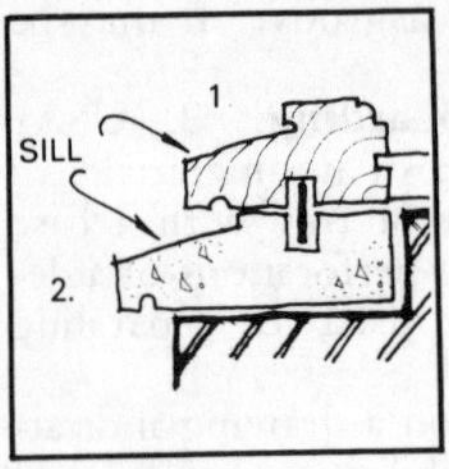

sill anchor A bolt which is set in the concrete or masonry base and is used to hold down the wall and partition frames of a **timber framed construction**. cf. **holding down bolt**.

sill bead A **deep bead**.

sill board (Scotland) A **window board**.

sill cock (USA) A **hose cock**.

sill-drip mould A small moulding like a **sub-sill** which is used in conjunction with a normal sized sill to increase its projection and hence its protection of the wall beneath.

silver brazing A method of forming a joint between light-gauge copper tubes.

single bridging **Herring-bone strutting**.

single Flemish bond **Flemish bond** brickwork with the distinguishing pattern visible on one face only. cf. **double Flemish bond**.

single floor A suspended timber floor in which the **joists** span from wall to wall. cf. **double floor**.

single-hung window A **sash window** in which only one sash in movable.

single-lap tile A roof tile, of which many shapes and patterns exist (including the **pantile** and interlocking tiles of various forms), which overlaps only the tile in the course immediately below, unlike **slates** and **plain tiles**.

single-lock welt A **cross welt**.

single-pitch roof A **mono-pitched** or **lean-to roof**.

single-point heater An **instantaneous water heater** supplying one tap only; as opposed to a **multi-point water heater**.

single roof A roof structure made up of **common rafters**, unsupported by **purlins**, **principals** or **trusses** but often stiffened and tied together by a tie at eaves level (a **close-couple roof**) or a **collar** at a higher level (a **collar beam roof**). cf. **double roof**.

single-sided gasket A form of glazing gasket that, unlike the **H** and **Y type gaskets**, retains the glass not between the arms of the gasket but between the gasket on one side and the rebate on the other.

single-stack (plumbing) system A **one-pipe system** from which all or most of the trap ventilating pipes (**anti-siphonage pipes**) have been omitted, in spite of the main vertical pipe receiving flow from a number of waste and/or soil fittings. This is made possible by the observation of certain stringent design rules.

sink A sanitary fitting used mainly for culinary and cleaning activities, usually with a hot and cold water supply and a trapped **waste**. It may be made of glazed earthenware, vitreous china, enamelled cast iron or stainless steel. Types vary widely and include the domestic sink, the commercial kitchen sink, **bucket** and **slop sinks**.

sinkage (USA) A recess in a floor, such as a **mat well**.

sink bib (USA) A tap for a kitchen sink.

sinking A recess cut in the general surface of a material, such as that for a butt hinge flap.

sintered steel A sintered material based on iron with intentionally added alloy elements.

sintering The fritting together of small particles to form larger particles or masses; a thermal treatment of a mixture of powders at a temperature approximating to the lowest melting point of any constituent.

siphonage The discharge of a liquid from a vessel through a pipe which first rises above the surface of the liquid before descending; the movement of the liquid is induced by suction aided by reduced pressure in the pipe.

siphonic closet A water closet which has a double trap, the fitting being flushed initially by the action of the discharge from the flushing cistern on the second trap, thus siphoning off the first trap and the contents of the pan. cf. **wash-down closet**.

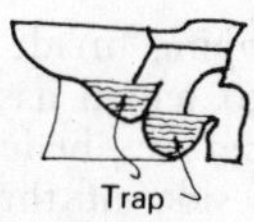

SIPHONIC CLOSET

site The land on which a building is being constructed.
site investigation The determination of the physical characteristics of a **site** in relation to how they will affect the design and construction of a building and the stability of adjacent structures; often including a subsoil investigation.
sitz bath A form of **hip bath**.
SI units A metric unit, such as a metre, kilogram candela, etc. which is an approved unit of measurement in the Système International d'Unités (SI) adopted in the UK at the time of metrication.
size A liquid sealer with which absorbent surfaces, such as new plaster, are often coated before receiving paint finishes other than emulsion paint; also used as a **binder** in **distemper**.
sized slates **Slates** of random length but uniform width.
sizing The operation of spreading **size**.
skeleton core The core of a flush door having a greater proportion of voids than a **semi-solid core** (flush) door.
skeleton core flush door A lightweight flush door with a **skeleton core**, thus making it a relatively inexpensive door.
skew 1. An oblique angle, hence 'on the skew' means 'out of square'. 2. A **kneeler**.
skewback A **springer**, or the upper surface of a springer.
skewback block A **gable springer**.
skew corbel A **gable springer**.
skew nailing Nails driven obliquely to the surfaces joined.
skew table A **kneeler** in a gable coping.
skid A length of steel or timber fixed under a large object, such as a prefabricated building unit, which allows it to be slid into place without the aid of a crane.
skiffling See **knobbing**.

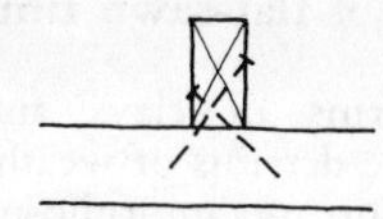
SKEW NAILING

skim (or skimming) coat A finishing coat of plaster applied either as a surface to a previous coat or coats of plaster, or as a finish over plasterboard.
skinning The forming of a skin on the surface of paint or varnish in the tin, caused by oxidation of the drying oil.
skip 1. A large receptacle for rubbish or demolition debris delivered to site empty and collected for disposal when full. 2. A break in the cover of a paint **film** or in the planing of a timber surface.
skirting An upstand of timber, ceramic tile, plastic, asphalt or other material covering the base of a wall to protect it from damage caused by knocking or kicking and to cover the junction between floor and wall finish; also used of the upstand of a roof finish against a parapet or abutment.

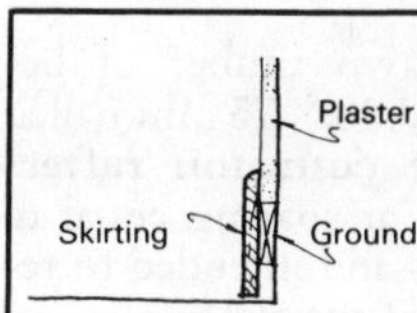

SKIRTING (BOARD)

skirting block An **architrave block**.
skylight A continuous **rooflight**, usually in a **pitched roof**.
slab 1. A thin flat piece of concrete or stone. 2. A concrete slab forming a floor.
slag 1. Non-metallic material formed during the treatment or purification of metal. 2. Non-metallic material resulting from chemical attack on a refractory product by material in contact with it.
slag wool **Mineral wool** produced from molten furnace slag, having high fire resistance and thermal insulation properties.
slaked lime **Hydrated lime** ($Ca(OH)_2$) -calcium hydroxide; produced by adding water to **quicklime** (CaO).
slaking The process of hydrating quicklime to produce hydrated lime (*ie* $CaO+H_2O=Ca(OH)_2$).

slap dash **Roughcast**.

slash grain The grain of **flat-sawn timber**.

slate Metamorphic forms of clays and shales formed from the detritus of weathered igneous rocks, or metamorphosed volcanic dust, with a dense laminated structure making it easy to split into thin slabs, used to form roofing elements of sizes from 750 × 400 mm to 250 × 150 mm. cf. **random slates**, **peggies**, **sized slates**). Slate is also used for cladding panels and (rarely, nowadays) **damp-proof courses**.

slate-and-a-half slate A slate of the same depth as the others on a roof, but wider by 50%; used at **valleys**, **hips** and **verges** to preserve the bonding pattern without resort to exceedingly small slates.

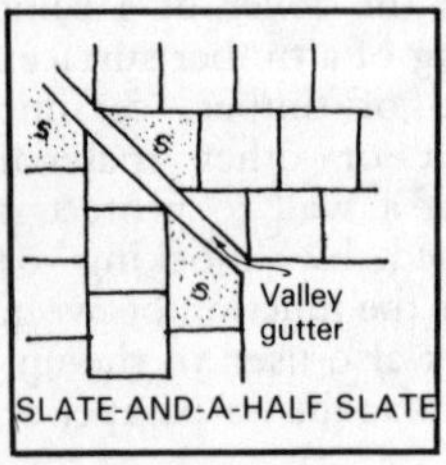

SLATE-AND-A-HALF SLATE

slate axe A **zax**.

slate batten Square-sawn timber of between 12 × 25 mm and 30 × 75 mm nailed horizontally over the **common rafters** (or **counter battens**) at spacing equal to the gauge of the slates and intended to receive the nail fixings of the slates.

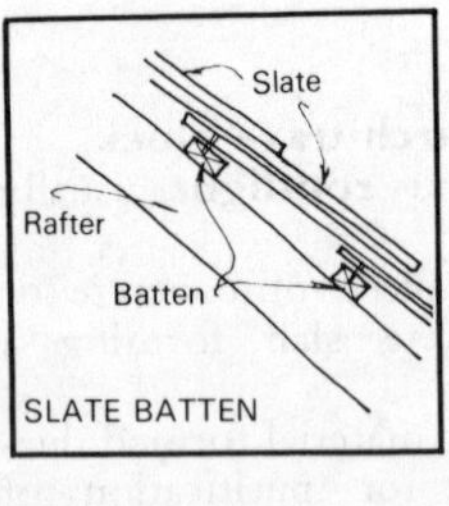

SLATE BATTEN

slate cramp A piece of slate shaped like a double dovetail, about 50 mm long × 25 mm across the widest part set in vertical **mortises** in adjacent stones to lock them together.

slate hanging **Slates** nailed to **battens** set on a vertical surface, to form a cladding.

slate nail A nail, usually non-ferrous, with a flat, thin head and a length of between 30 and 63 mm.

slate powder A very fine powder used as an **extender** in some paints.

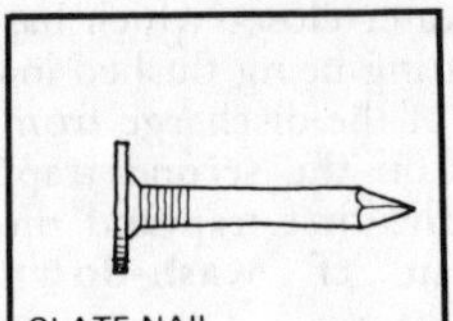
SLATE NAIL

slate ridge A ridge-capping made of a circular rod of slate, into which has been cut a V-shape on its underside, bedded on a heavy slate on each side of the roof apex.

SLATE RIDGE

sleeper clip (USA) A **floor clip**.

sleeper plate A **wall plate** on a **sleeper wall**.

sleeper wall A **dwarf wall**, usually of **honeycomb wall** construction to carry a **sleeper plate**, supporting floor joists.

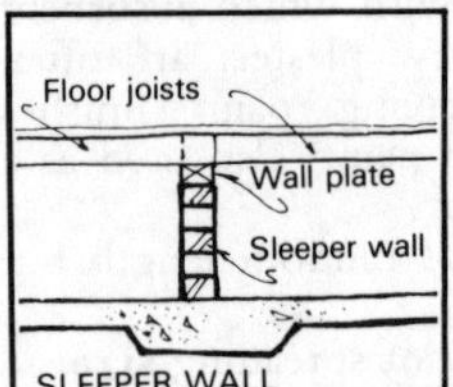

SLEEPER WALL

sleeve See **expansion sleeve**.

sleeve piece A short, thin-walled ferrule of brass or copper used when soldering a lead or copper pipe to one of a different material. cf. **solder**.

slenderness ratio The ratio of effective height (or, in the case of a wall, effective length, if this is less) to effective thickness.

sliced veneer **Veneer** cut by a long knife in a similar manner to the way in which a plane cuts wood; used mainly to cut figured veneer. cf. **rotary cutting**.

slicing The operation of cutting **sliced veneer**.

sliding door A door which is not hung on hinges but is suspended on a top track or set on rollers; it opens by sliding horizontally.

sliding folding-door or shutter A large scale door or shutter made up of a series of hinged leaves, which is suspended on a track at its head and opens by sliding sideways, while the leaves fold together in a concertina form.

sliding sash A **sash window** which slides vertically, or a horizontally sliding sash.

slip 1. A **fixing fillet.** 2. A **parting slip.**

slip feather A loose tongue used in a **feather joint** or similar.

slip form A system of **formwork** which can be moved slowly, and usually continuously, during the placing of concrete; movement can be either vertical or horizontal.

slip joint conduit Conduit (within which electrical cable passes) which is not screwed, one section to the next, but merely slipped one section into the socket of the next; it does not give an adequate electrical contact to use the conduit for **earthing.**

slip sill A non-stooled sill, or one that does not have squared ends for building into the wall at each side of the opening, but which sits between the reveals.

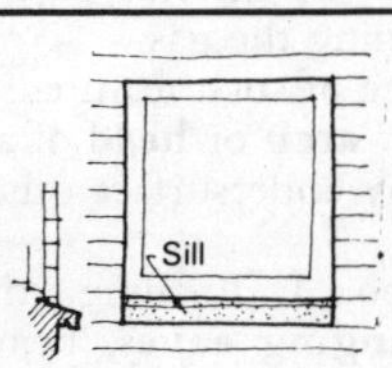

SLIP SILL

slip stone An **oilstone slip.**

slope of grain The angle formed by the axis of a piece of timber and the general direction of the **grain.** The steepness of this angle must be restricted in the case of structural timber to a maximum of 1:8 or 1:11, depending on the size of the member.

slop sink A rectangular sink set at low level and often provided with a metal, hinged grating on which to stand a bucket. The taps are set high enough on the wall to allow a bucket to be filled standing in the sink or on the grating.

slot head A driving profile of a **wood** or **machine screw** consisting of one straight slot cut across its head. cf. **clutch head, Philips head, Pozidriv head.**

slot mortise An **open mortise.**

slot screwing The screwing of boards on to a batten through slots, thus allowing some movement to occur. If shrinkage

SLOT HEAD

takes place the screws can be slackened off and the boards moved together; similar construction to that used on a wooden drawing board.

slotted angle A structural component made from cold-formed metal strips, generally in the shape of an angle, channel, tee or flat, into which has been stamped a repetitive pattern of perforations to allow different components to be fixed together by bolts.

slump test A method of assessing the consistency of freshly mixed concrete, plaster or mortar mixes by filling an open-ended cone with the material, removing the cone and measuring the amount the material settles or slumps.

slurry A mixture of certain materials, especially cement, and water (sometimes also containing sand), which has the flow characteristics of a liquid.

slurrying Protecting the surface of stonework by covering with a weak mix of lime, water and stone dust which can be washed off later.

small-bore (heating) system A pumped, wet, central heating system depending on a sealed pump capable of producing high pressure for its successful operation. As a result of the pressure produced by the pump the diameter of the flow and return pipes can be reduced in size (usually to about 12.5 mm in diameter). Small-bore systems are usually installed in small commercial and domestic buildings. cf. **micro-bore (heating) system.**

small lime The **quicklime** that remains, mixed with some ash and clinker, after the best hand-picked lime has been removed from a run of kiln lime; used to make black mortar.

smoke test An air test of a drain using smoke as a tracer medium.

smooth ashlar A block of squared stone with a smooth face.

smoothing plane A short bench plane about 200 mm long used for smoothing wood after rougher planes such as a **try plane** have been used.

smoulder To burn slowly without a flame, but usually with incandescence.

snake A tool used to unblock drains, comprising a long flexible spring.

snap (or snapped) header A half length brick, appearing on the face of brickwork as a header but, in fact, being a cut brick.

sneck 1. A term applied, regionally, to that part of a Norfolk latch which operates the **fall bar**. 2. A small squared stone in **snecked rubble** that levels up with the riser.

snecked rubble Masonry walling built of squared stones of varying size and built using a combination of **snecks**, **risers** and **levellers**.

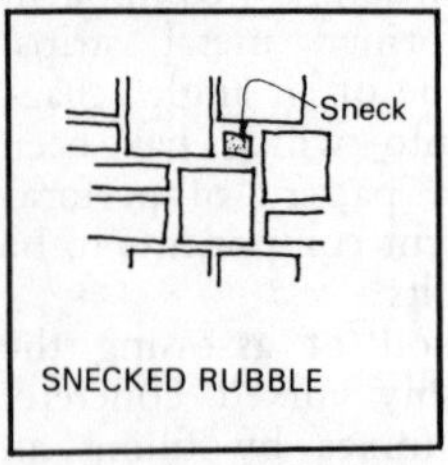

SNECKED RUBBLE

snips See **tin snips**.

snowboard A series of horizontal wooden battens nailed to vertical bearers with gaps between the battens, to restrain snow from slipping off a pitched roof on to a pathway or fragile roof below. The term also refers to a grid of timber slats placed over a **box gutter** to prevent it from filling with snow, but allowing water to drain into the gutter.

soakaway A pit dug into permeable ground, filled with hardcore and usually covered with earth. Surface water, or purified effluent from a **sewage treatment plant**, is drained into this and subsequently percolates into the surrounding ground.

soaker A piece of **flexible metal** which bonds in with tiles or slates at an **abutment** between a sloping roof and a vertical wall or at a **hip** or **valley**. It is bent upwards at an abutment or obliquely at a hip or valley to make a weathertight joint.

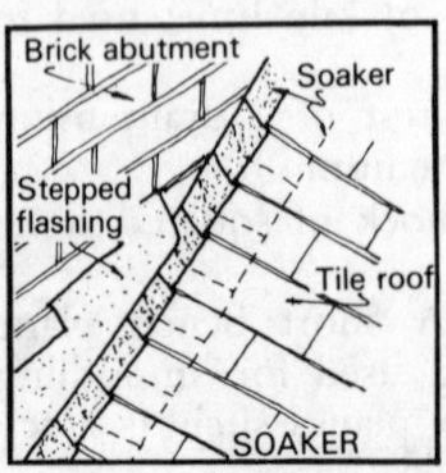

SOAKER

socket 1. The enlarged end of a pipe into which another pipe fits, as in a **spigot-and-socket** joint. 2. A coupling 3. The **mortise** of a **dove-tail joint.** 4. In a pivoted window, the aperture into which the pivot fits. 5. A **socket outlet**.

socket chisel A strong chisel, used with a mallet, with a socket at the base of its **tang** into which the wooden handle fits.

socket head A recessed **driving profile** of some **machine screws** or **set screws** which replaces the normal slot with a multi-sided recess. A tool with a special head is required to operate the screw, a fact which helps to prevent unauthorized removal of the screw.

socket outlet An electrical fitting, set in or on a wall or floor surface, into which a two or three-pin **plug** can be fitted to conduct electrical power to a piece of electrical equipment.

soda-lime process A method of water softening involving treatment with sodium carbonate (Na_2CO_2) to remove permanent hardness, and with lime (CaO) to remove temporary hardness.

sodium vapour lamp A lamp in which the light emission is produced by an electric discharge in sodium vapour with or without the assistance of a fluorescent or translucent coating to the interior of the glass envelope containing the gas.

soffit The undersurface of such features as a **fascia**, **stair**, **beam**, **arch** or **head** of an opening; generally any undersurface other than a ceiling.

soffit board The board forming the underside of **overhanging eaves**, being nailed to **rafters** or **bearers**.

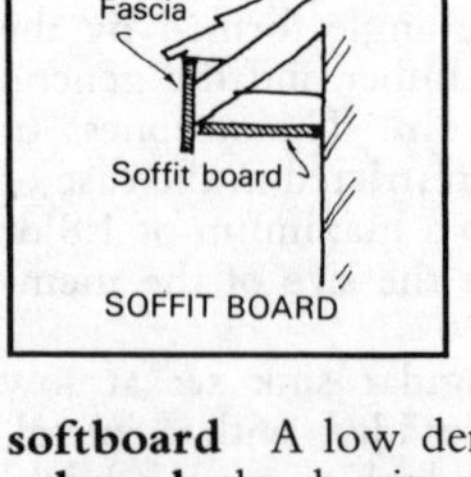

SOFFIT BOARD

softboard A low density fibre **insulating board**, the density not exceeding 350 kg/m^3

soft-burnt Of burnt clay products such as bricks or tiles, fired at a low temperature with the result that they have low compressive strength and high absorption.

soft sand **Sand** of which the particles are small and of rounded form.

soft solder A **solder** which melts below red heat. cf. **hard solder**.

softwood A description of wood which derives from trees from the botanical group gymnosperms; broadly these are conifers. Softwoods are often less hard than **hardwoods**, but not invariably.

soil 1. Earth; see **subsoil**, **vegetable soil**. 2. Foul **sewage**, as opposed to surface water, waste water, or subsoil drainage.

soil drain A drain for carrying foul sewage or industrial effluent.

soil pipe or stack A vertical, aboveground pipe which conveys **sewage** from fittings to the ground level where it enters the **soil drain**. Its head is taken through the roof and left open to ventilate the drain and prevent traps on the fittings from being siphoned off. cf. **siphonage**.

soil and vent pipe (S and VP) A **soil pipe**.

soil stabilization The treatment of soil to prevent erosion by wind, water or wear by over-growing or other methods; also the compaction of poor bearing soils by proprietary methods, such as soil compaction by vibration and pressure grouting etc.

sol-air temperature The equivalent of **environmental temperature**.

solar absorbtivity The ratio of the amount of solar radiation absorbed by a surface to that which is incident on the surface.

solar constant The amount of solar radiation reaching the earth's atmosphere (approximately 1,395 W/m^2).

solar construction Construction which attempts to make use of solar radiation when this is advantageous (*eg* for heating in cold weather) and exclude its effects when these are undesirable (*eg* glare, excessive heat gain).

solar control blind 1. A reflective window blind, manually or automatically controlled, which re-radiates some of the solar energy transmitted through the glazing, thus cutting down solar heat input. 2. An external window blind which is intended to shade the glazing from direct solar radiation.

solar reflecting surface A light-coloured finish applied to a flat roof covering (**bitumen felt** or **asphalt** etc.) which reflects some of the solar radiation falling upon it, thus reducing the temperature of the covering. White chippings or paint are commonly used for this application.

solder An alloy used to join two pieces of metal, having a lower melting point than the other metals. cf. **hard solder**, **soft solder**.

soldering iron A tool used to work solder, comprising a heavy working end, usually of copper, which can be heated up electrically or by other means, mounted on a thin metal shaft, which in turn is attached to an insulated handle.

soldier 1. A brick on end, one of several, forming a flat arch or decorative course. 2. An upright timber bearer wedged between the flanges of a steel joist and to which the beam casing is fixed. 3. A short upright **ground** used to fix a **skirting board**.

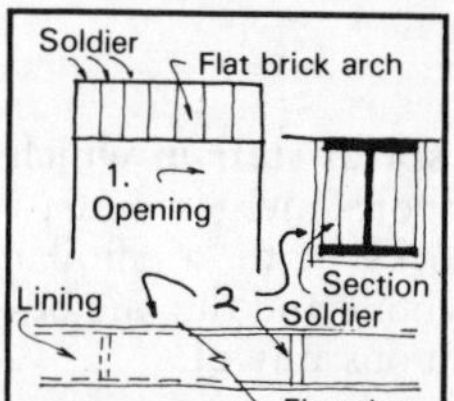

SOLDIER

soldier arch A **flat arch** in brickwork.

sole The under surface of a plane.

sole plate 1. The lowest horizontal member of a vertical frame, such as a wall panel or partition panel. 2. A **sill**. 3. A timber laid at an angle on the ground beneath the feet of **raking shores**, forming an abutment for them.

solid bossing The bossing of lead to shape, as opposed to soldering it.

solid bridging Horizontal **strutting** between floor joists using pieces of timber as deep, or almost as deep, as the joists. cf. **herring-bone strutting**.

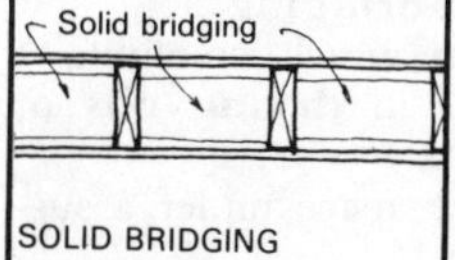

SOLID BRIDGING

solid core (flush) door A **flush door** which has a core made up in a similar manner to **coreboard**, without any voids, giving a door with good sound insulating properties. Some solid core doors have a solid **chipboard** core. cf. **semi-solid core flush door**, **hollow-core door**.

solid floor 1. In next-to-earth floors, a concrete slab on hardcore, as opposed to a suspended floor whether of timber joists or concrete. 2. Of a suspended concrete floor, a concrete slab without **hollow**

blocks or hollow precast beams. 3. **Plank-on-edge floor**.

solid frame A timber door frame in which the rebate is cut from the solid wood (*ie* the stop is not **planted**).

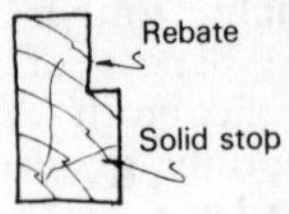

SOLID FRAME

solid-newel stair A **spiral stair** in which the step or its support merges into a cylinder that interlocks with a similar cylinder on the step above and the one below to form a continuous **newel**.

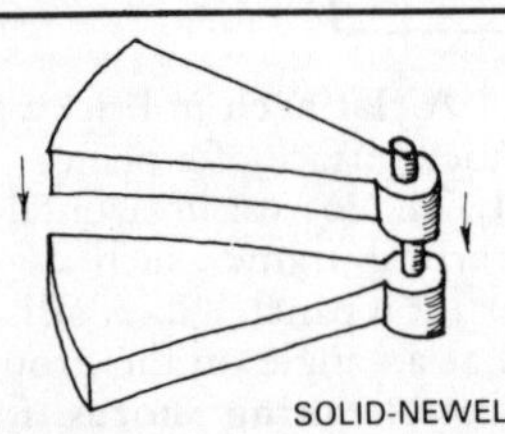
SOLID-NEWEL STAIR

solid punch A thick tool similar to a **nail punch**, for driving **bolts** out of holes.

solid roll The longitudinal joint between sheets of **flexible-metal roofing** in which the sheets are folded together over a **wood roll**. cf. **hollow roll**.

solid stop A door stop formed in a **solid frame** by cutting a **rebate**.

solid strutting **Solid bridging**.

soluble drier A **drier** which is soluble at normal temperatures in **drying oils** or hydrocarbon **solvents**.

solum (Scotland) The space under a suspended ground floor.

solvent 1. A liquid that dissolves solids (*eg* acetone). 2. In painting, a liquid used to dissolve or disperse binders. It evaporates during drying.

solvent weld A joint made between certain types of plastic in which the surfaces to be joined are smeared with **solvent** before joining, causing the surfaces to be welded together.

soot door A door at the bottom of a flue from which soot can be removed.

sound absorption coefficient A measure of the proportion of sound energy incident on a surface which is absorbed by that surface as opposed to being reflected.

sound boarding Horizontal boarding between floor joists to carry **pugging**.

sounder A device which converts electrical energy into a sound signal.

sound insulation 1. The means taken to reduce the transmission of sound. 2. The property of a construction (**eg partition** or **separating wall**) to resist the transmission of sound from one side to the other due to its mass or its **discontinuous construction**.

sound knot A knot that is firmly set in the wood and is free from decay.

sound propagation The wave process whereby sound energy is transferred from one part of a medium to another.

sound reduction factor or index A value, expressed in decibels (dB), which is a measure of the reduction of intensity of sound at a given frequency passing through a structure (*eg* wall, partition, floor etc.). It is 10 × the log to the base 10 of the reciprocal of the **sound transmission coefficient**.

sound transmission coefficient The ratio which the sound energy of a given frequency transmitted through a structure bears to that incident upon the structure.

sound transmission loss (USA) **Sound reduction factor**.

soya glue A vegetable **glue** made from soya bean meal.

space 1. Of a saw, the distance from one **saw-tooth** point to the next. 2. See **modular zone**.

spaced slating **Open slating**.

space frame or structure A method of spanning large areas without intermediate supports, based on a structural framework of tubes or small metal sections which function in three dimensions. The simplest version comprises an assembly of frames in the form of a series of repetitive equilateral prisms, point downwards, forming a flat, or nearly flat, deck framework. Other shapes include domes and barrel vaults.

space heating The heating of the interior of a building by **direct** or **indirect heating**.

spall 1. To break off edges of stone or concrete by slanting blows of a chisel. 2. A flake of stone or concrete broken off a large block, either accidentally or intentionally or by the action of the weather. 3. A **gallet.**

spalling The breaking away of thin flakes from the surface of case-hardened and other steel, or from surface coatings, or from stone or concrete.

span The distance between points of support.

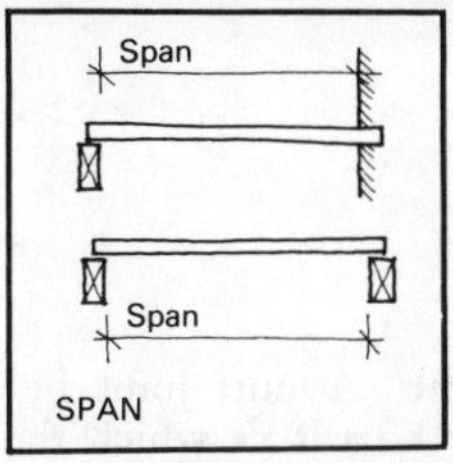

SPAN

spandrel 1. The roughly triangular wall above an arch **extrados**, and between it and an **abutment** and a horizontal **string course**, **coping** or similar feature above. 2. The infilling under the **string** of a stair. 3. (USA) The solid infilling wall between a sill and the window head below in a multi-storey building.

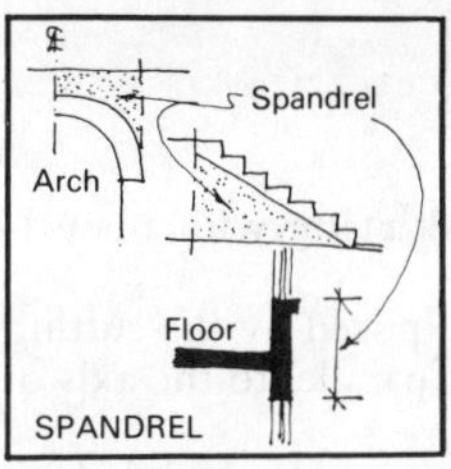

SPANDREL

spandrel step A solid stone or concrete step of triangular cross-section which, with others, produces a flush **soffit** to the **stair**.

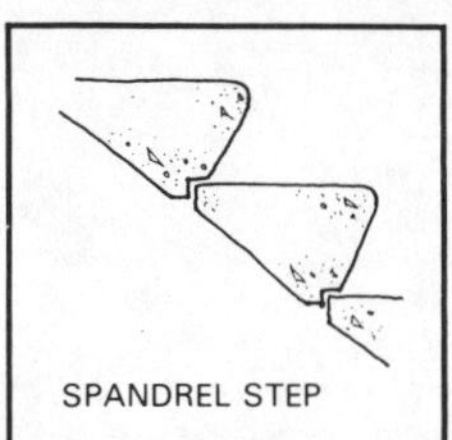
SPANDREL STEP

Spanish tile 1. A single-lap roofing tile, semi-cylindrical in cross-section, and wider at one end than the other. The tile system consists of an over-tile (imbrex) and an under-tile (tegula), both of approximately the same shape, the under-tile being slightly larger. 2. (USA) A **single-lap tile** similar to a **Roman tile**.

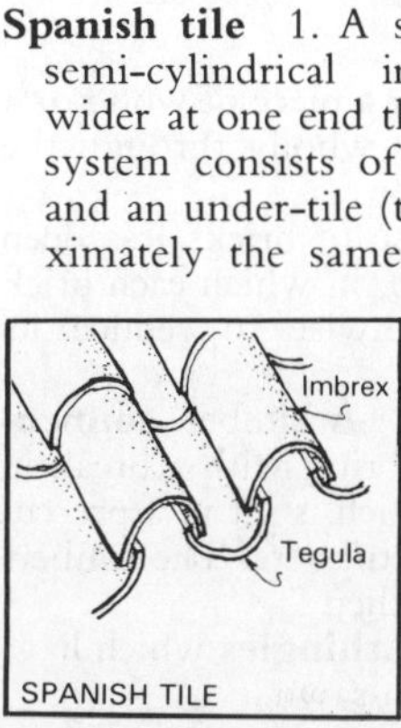

SPANISH TILE

span piece A **collar beam**.

span roof A **pitched roof**.

spar 1. In thatching, a thin split piece of hazel or willow, 600 mm long, pointed at both ends, bent double and driven like a **staple** into the thatch to hold the **withies** and other restraining elements at **ridge** and **eaves** in position. 2. A localized term for a **common rafter**.

spar dash See **pebble dash**.

sparge pipe A horizontal pipe which has perforations through which water is sprayed for cleaning purposes (*eg* on a **urinal** slab or in a tunnel shower).

sparrow peck A texture on plasterwork produced by a stiff broom; or on stone, produced by picking.

spatterdash A mix of cement and fairly coarse sand, prepared as a thick **slurry**, which is thrown on to dense brick or concrete backgrounds having poor suction. The spatterdash is then allowed to harden to provide a key for a later finish, such as a first coat of plaster.

special Any product which is not produced to the size, shape or quality of the standard range of products of that type.

special quality bricks or blocks Bricks or blocks which are durable when used in situations of extreme exposure where the walls may become saturated and frozen, *eg* **retaining walls**, sewage plants, parapets etc. **Engineering bricks** usually attain this standard of durability, **facing** and **common bricks** or blocks may do so, but cannot be assumed to.

specification A detailed description of a job, written in the **sequence of trades**, prepared to explain those things concerning a project which cannot be shown on a drawing, particularly the quality of materials and quality and type of workmanship. The specification should complement the drawings.

specific gravity The ratio of the mass of a given volume of a substance to the mass of an equal volume of water at a temperature of 4 °C. Masses are compared by weighing them.

specific heat 1. The amount of heat needed to raise the temperature of unit mass of a material 1 °C. This is a property of the particular material. 2. The ratio of the thermal capacity of any mass of a substance to that of an equal mass of water (usually at 15°C).

spigot The plain end of a pipe inserted into the **socket** in an adjoining pipe in a **spigot-and-socket joint**.

spigot-and-socket joint A joint made between pipes in which the plain end of one pipe (**spigot**) is inserted into the enlarged end of the next pipe (**socket**). The joint is then **caulked**; the material used for jointing depends on the material of the pipes.

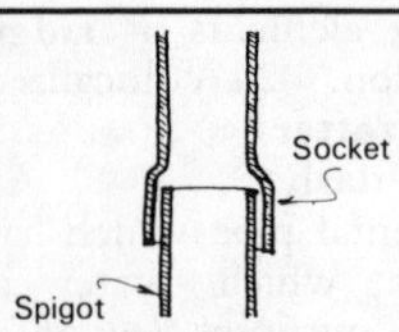

SPIGOT-AND-SOCKET JOINT

spindle 1. A piece of wood that has been turned, such as a **baluster**. 2. A small axle.
spine wall An internal loadbearing wall running in the direction of the main axis of the building.
spiral grain The pattern of grain which results from the distortion of the wood fibres due to the spiral growth of the tree.
spiral stair A **stair** which fills a circular space on plan and in which all the treads are winders; a solid newel is usual. Spiral stairs may be manufactured of stone, steel, cast iron, timber, concrete etc. or a combination of materials.
spirit level A tool used to establish the horizontality of a surface from the movement of a bubble in a glass tube which is nearly filled with spirit. The tube is set in a long **straight edge**.
spirit stain A dye dissolved in alcohol, used to darken a wood surface while emphasizing the grain.
spirit varnish **Varnish** made by dissolving a gum or resin in alcohol which dries by evaporation.
spit The depth of one spade blade, about 225 mm.
splashback An impervious surface protecting a wall surface behind a sanitary appliance, consisting of ceramic or other wall tiles, melamine-faced board or similar material.
splay A large **chamfer** across the full width of a surface.
splay brick A special **brick**, often called a cant brick, splayed on the header or **stretcher**.
splayed coping A **feather-edged coping**.
splayed ground A **ground** with a bevelled edge to act as a key for plaster. In this case the ground acts as a **screed**.

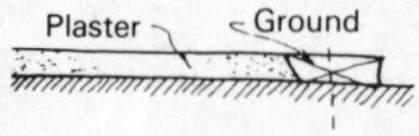

SPLAYED GROUND

splayed heading joint A butt joint between ends of floor boards in which the end cut is not vertical so that a slight overlap is formed between boards.

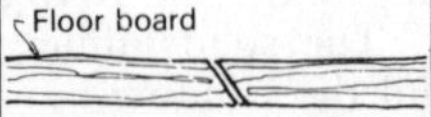

SPLAYED HEADING JOINT

splayed skirting A **skirting** with a bevelled top edge.
splay knot A knot exposed by the cutting of the timber almost parallel to the axis of the knot.
splice A lengthening joint in which halved timbers are glued together and the joint is then covered by steel or plywood plates on either side, bolted through the timbers or screwed to them.

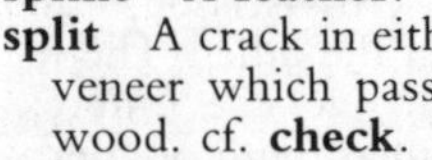

SPLICE

spline A **feather**.
split A crack in either a piece of wood or a veneer which passes wholly through the wood. cf. **check**.
split course A course of bricks less deep than a normal course, in which each brick has been cut lengthwise to reduce its depth.
split-ring connector A timber **connector** in the form of a ring with a break in its circumference which is set in a pre-cut ring groove in both timbers. The timbers are then bolted together.
split shakes Wooden **shingles** which have been split rather than sawn.

spokeshave A light **plane** used to shape convex surfaces, operated by holding the two handles (one on either side of the blade).

spot welding A process whereby a weld is produced at a spot in the workpiece between electrodes, the weld being approximately the same area as the electrode tips. Force is applied to the spot, usually through the electrodes.

spray coating A coating process in which powdered polymer is heated to fusing temperature in a cone of flame placed between the spray gun orifice and the substrate.

sprayed asbestos Asbestos fibres with additives, blown on to a surface by a **spray gun** to form a thermally insulating, non-combustible skin, from 3 to 150 mm thick.

spray gun A device which sprays paint in minute droplets or other coating material on to a surface by means of compressed air.

spray painting The application of paint by spraying, using compressed air through a **spray gun**. This is the best way of applying **lacquer**, but it is also a good method of applying water and oil paints.

spread Of adhesive, the area covered by a unit quantity of adhesive or the amount of adhesive required to cover a unit area.

spread of flame See **surface spread of flame**.

sprig A small wire nail with no head (*eg* a **glazing sprig**).

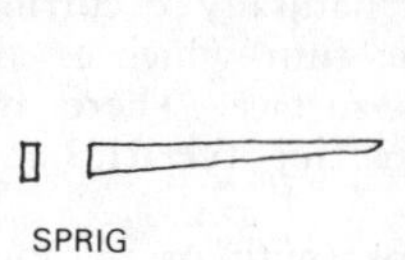

SPRIG

sprig bit A **bradawl**.

springer The first stone in an **arch**, which is bedded on the **springing line** and has an upper surface that is skewbacked.

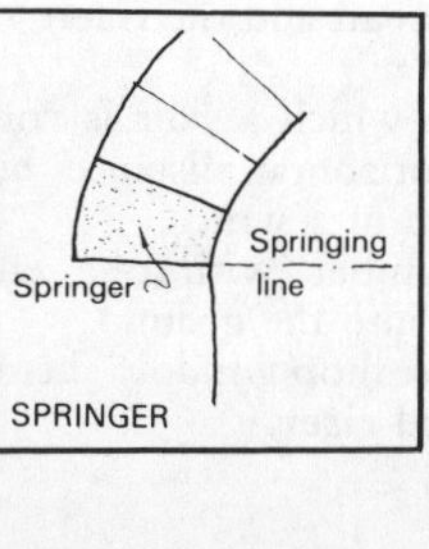

SPRINGER

spring-head roofing nail A galvanized **drive screw** for fixing sheet claddings.

springing line or springing The point at which the intrados of an **arch** moves away from the vertical line of the reveal below the arch, or the line which connects these points on either side of the arch.

spring pivot A **floor spring** (particularly a double action floor spring) for a swing door.

spring strip A form of metal weather stripping to doors or the opening lights of windows.

sprinkler system A system of water pipes fitted with sprinkler heads at appropriate intervals and heights, designed to control or extinguish a fire by discharging water through the heads, each of which (or each group of which) opens automatically at a specific temperature or by the operation of a fire detector.

sprocket A short tapered length of wood nailed to each **common rafter** close to the eaves to give there an angle less than that of the normal pitch of the roof (*ie* to give a slightly flatter slope at the eaves).

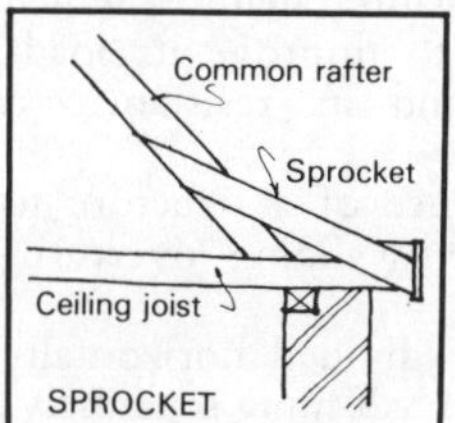

SPROCKET

sprung The description of timber that has **warped**.

sprung floor A form of timber floor (usually a strip floor) laid on battens supported on spring clips fixed to the substrate. This produces a resilient floor particularly suited to gymnasia and dance halls.

spud A dowel at the bottom of a door post to fix it to the floor.

spur A connection for a **socket outlet** from a **ring main**.

square 1. A tool of metal or metal and wood used by a carpenter for setting out right angles. 2. A pane of glass cut to a particular size, but of any shape. 3. A piece of square-section timber with a side of up to 150 mm.

square chisel A **mortising machine.**

squared rubble A stone wall made up of stones of varying sizes which are squared, but not **snecked**; usually coursed at every third or fourth stone and laid with fairly thin joints, though not as thin as in the case of **ashlar**.

square-edged timber Timber without **wane**.

square joint A **butt joint**.

square roof A symmetrical, **pitched roof** with opposing rafters meeting at right angles at the **ridge**, *ie* a roof with a pitch of 45°.

square-sawn timber A piece of wood sawn to a rectangular cross-section, with or without **wane**. cf. **squared-edged timber**).

square staff A rectangular bead, fixed at the salient corner of two plastered walls, as an **angle bead**.

squaring A process in the preparation of **Bills of Quantities** which follows the **taking off** and involves the calculation of the areas involved.

squatting closet A w.c. pan with an elongated bowl for installing with its top edge at or near floor level so that the user adopts a squatting position; often referred to as an Asiatic or eastern closet.

squint quoin A **quoin** enclosing an angle of a building which is not a right angle.

stabilized soil Any natural material which has been modified to improve its load-carrying capacity and its resistance to weather erosion.

stability The resistance of a structure to any form of collapse (*eg* sliding, overturning, etc.).

stable door A door divided horizontally in half and with each half hung separately.

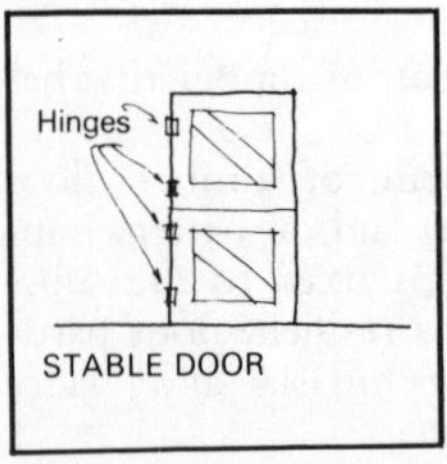

STABLE DOOR

stack 1. A **chimney stack** 2. A **soil pipe**.

stack effect The tendency of air to rise from lower to upper openings (*eg* in a chimney stack) in a building shell due to its **buoyancy**.

stadia The two short horizontal wires in the diaphragm of a **theodolite** or **level**, above and below the central **cross hair** respectively, used to measure distances when sighted against a **levelling staff**.

staff bead 1. An **angle bead**. 2. A **guard bead**.

Staffordshire blues A type of pressed or wirecut brick, which is extremely hard, dense and deep blue in colour; one of the best **engineering bricks** in the UK.

stagger 1. To dispose alternately on either side of a median line, as in lines of bolts, rivets, etc. where the fixings in one line are opposite the gaps between the fixings in the adjacent line. 2. The horizontal distance between the faces of adjoining properties in a terrace or pair when these are not built to the same building line (*ie* one is set back in relation to the other).

staggering Arranging in a staggered manner. This is a device used in the arrangement of rivets, etc. to avoid undue weakening of the section in which the rivets occur, since when staggered the rivet holes do not occur in as close an alignment as would otherwise be the case.

stain 1. A dye or other colouring matter held in solution or suspension in a vehicle and applied to an object or component to change its colour by penetration, rather than by obliteration as in a paint. 2. **Blue stain**.

stained-glass Glass making up a multi-coloured window in which the individual pieces of glass that make up the pattern have a colour fired into them.

stainers Coloured pigments which can be added in small quantities to give a paint a modified colour. Whilst stainers have the power to alter a paint's colour, they do not necessarily themselves have the opacity to give good obliteration.

stainless steel Steel containing chromium and nickel, having a resistance to corrosion conferred by a naturally occurring chromium rich oxide film which is always present on its surface. There are three types: **martensitic, ferritic** and **austenitic steel**.

stair A series of **steps** (with or without **landings**), together with any necessary protective devices such as **balustrades** and **handrails**.

staircase An expression now normally used for a stair; originally meaning the enclosure of a flight of stairs.

stair clip A clip which holds the stair carpet in place, being fixed at the re-entrant angle between the **tread** and the **riser**.

stairs A **stair**.

stairwell A **well** in which a stair is constructed, or the horizontal distance between parallel flights of a stair.

stake A timber member with one end pointed for driving into the ground.

stallboard A **sill** to a shop window, being above the **stallboard riser**.

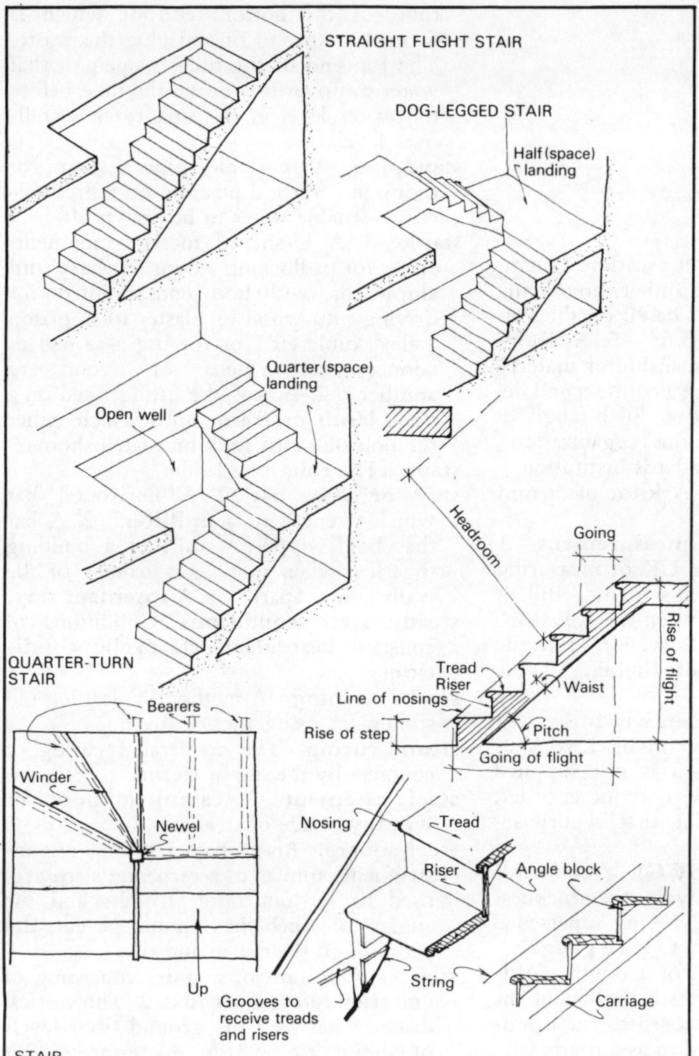

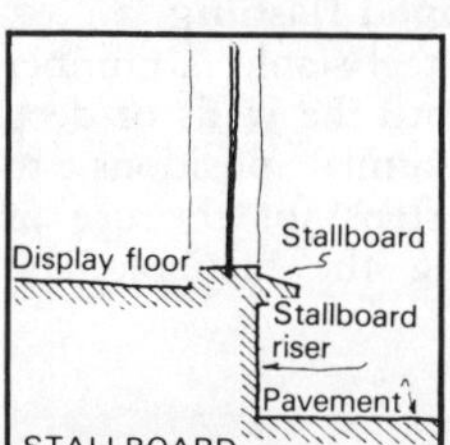

stallboard riser The vertical surface below a **stallboard**, from display floor level in the shop window to pavement level.

stanchion A vertical structural member, usually a steel universal column; less frequently, a reinforced concrete column.

stanchion base A concrete pad designed to distribute the load from a **stanchion** base plate.

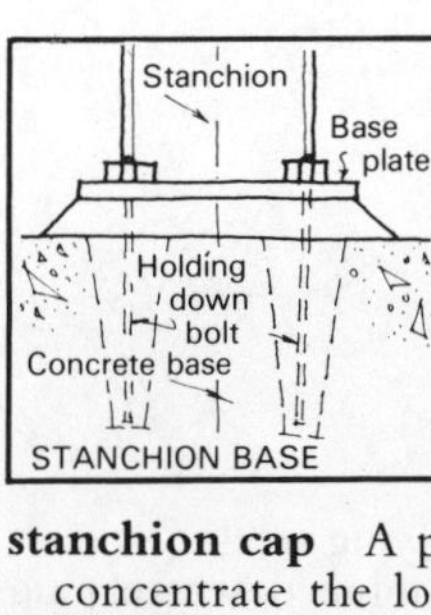

stanchion cap A pad or plate designed to concentrate the load imposed on a **stanchion**.

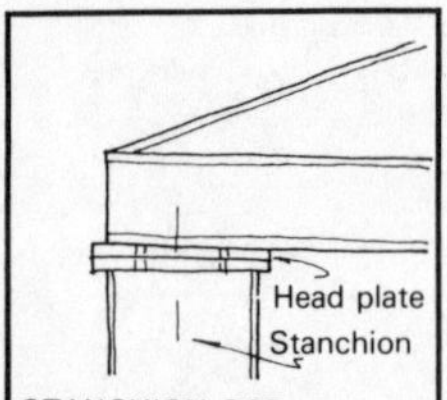

STANCHION CAP

standard 1. An upright scaffold member. 2. A measure of timber, now being superseded in the UK, based on the Petrograd standard of 165 ft^3. 3. A degree of excellence of workmanship or material expected in undertaking a contract and described in the specification. Such standards are published by various organizations, such as the British Standards Institution.

standard knot (USA) A **knot** of 36 mm diameter or less.

standard method of measurement A method adopted in the UK of measuring builder's work for inclusion in a Bill of Quantities, agreed between the Royal Institute of Chartered Surveyors and the National Federation of Building Trade Employers.

standard special An item which is a regularly required element in brickwork or drain laying but which is not supplied (although held in stock) without an order; as opposed to a **special**, that is purpose-made to order.

Standard wire gauge (SWG) A standardized method of specifying the thickness of metal now gradually being superseded by metric thicknesses. cf. **wire gauge**.

standing leaf The leaf of a double **folding door** which is mostly bolted in the closed position, as opposed to the **opening leaf**; often referred to as a dead leaf.

standing seam A **seam** in **flexible-metal roofing** used to joint the longitudinal edges of adjacent sheets (particularly on more highly inclined roofs) as an alternative to a **wood roll**. cf. **cross welt**.

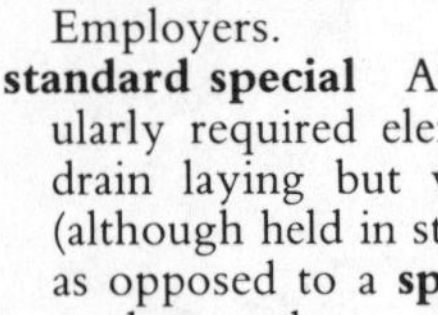

STANDING SEAM

standing timber Growing trees.

standing waste A combined **waste** plug and overflow for a sink, consisting of a tube, at the bottom end of which is formed a taper to fit and plug the waste. The top end of the tube is open so that water can overflow down the tube before the water level in the sink reaches spill-over level.

standpipe A portable pipe fitting for fixing in a vertical position on a fire hydrant to enable water to be drawn off.

staple 1. A U-shaped metal component, either for padlocking a door (cf. **hasp and staple**) or, with both ends pointed, for driving into wood or plaster to imprison a flex, cable etc., or for use as a nail to connect one piece of wood to another. 2. A box-like fitting fixed on a door **jamb** or **frame** into which either the bolt of a **rim lock** or a latch shoots.

stave The **rung** of a ladder.

stay or stay bar 1. A horizontal bar which strengthens a **mullion**. 2. A bar that holds opposite walls of a building together when there is a danger of the walls falling apart. 3. A **casement stay**.

steady state conditions Conditions of constant heat input. cf. **cyclic conditions**.

steam cleaning A method of cleaning old stonework using a jet of steam.

steam curing The accelerated curing of concrete by the use of steam.

steel casement A **casement door** or **window** made of steel.

steel square An L-shaped setting out instrument, similar to a carpenter's **square**, used to set out rafter lengths and the angles to which they should be cut, depending on their span and rise.

step 1. One unit of a **stair**, consisting of one **riser** and one **tread**. 2. The vertical distance between the ground floor levels of adjoining properties in a terrace or pair when these are not built with the same ground floor level.

step flashing A **stepped flashing**.

step iron A strong steel staple, a number of which are built into the walls of deep **manholes** and in similar positions, to provide projecting steps for the use of workmen descending the manhole and climbing up again.

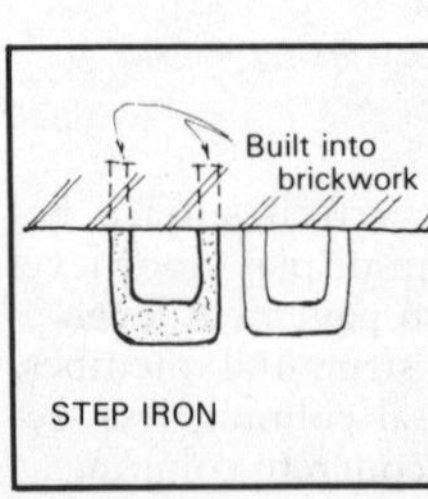

STEP IRON

step joint A notched joint between two timber members such as a **rafter** and a **tie beam**. It can be a single or double step joint, the latter being used to avoid weakening notched timber too greatly.

step ladder A ladder with rectangular **treads** (as opposed to **rungs**) which are horizontal when the ladder is in use and supported against its opposing prop.

stepped flashing A **cover flashing**, usually made of **flexible metal**, which helps to make the joint between a sloping roof and an abutting wall weathertight. The stepped flashing is dressed into the joints of the walling, stepping down from joint to joint, always keeping a minimum height of flashing of 75 mm. It overlaps the upstand of **soakers**.

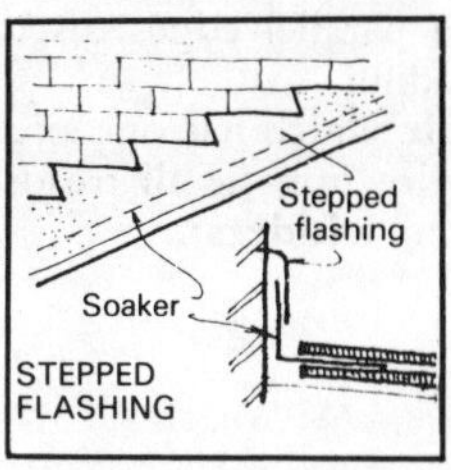

STEPPED FLASHING

stepped foundation A foundation in sloping ground, that follows the slope of the ground in a series of elongated steps, thus avoiding excessive excavation.

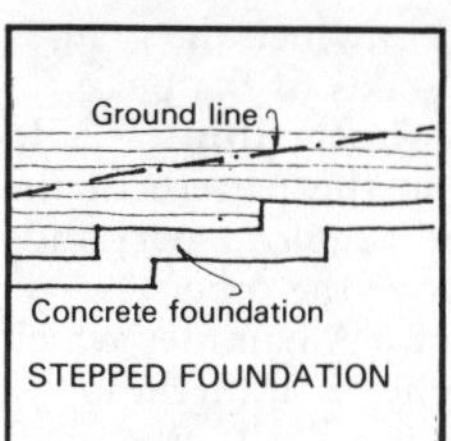

STEPPED FOUNDATION

step turner A hardwood tool for shaping **stepped flashings** so that they fit into brick joints.

sterilizing sink A metal sink incorporating a heater which is thermostatically controlled between 82° and 92 °C; used in commercial kitchens and similar locations.

stick-and-rag work **Fibrous plaster**.

S-tile (USA) A strongly curved **pantile**.

stile A vertical member of a frame (as in a **panel door**) to which the **rails** are dowelled or tenoned. cf. **closing stile** and **hanging stile**.

stillson A **pipe wrench**.

stipple 1. To dab a newly applied coat of paint with a **stippler**. 2. To break up the colour of a coat of paint with flecks of another colour, applied with a stippler.

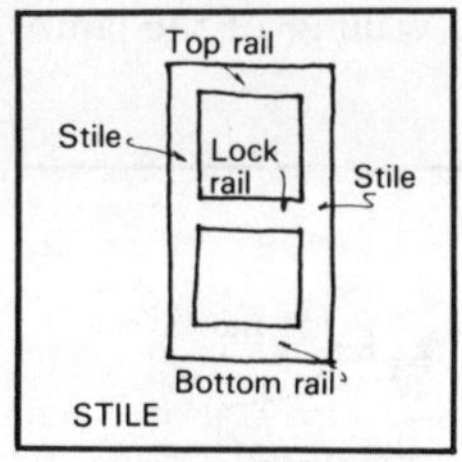

STILE

stippler A device, either in the form of a brush with many tufts of soft bristle, all ending in the same plane, or a rubber pad, used to remove brush marks and leave a wet paint coat with a slightly textured surface, or to break up the colour or texture of a paint surface.

stirrup strap A steel strap which supports the end of a horizontal beam and is itself built into the walling or supported from a post or beam.

stock 1. **Converted timber.** 2. The body of a plane, or the handle of another form of tool. 3. The tool that holds a **die** for cutting an external thread on a pipe. 4. A **stock brick**.

stock brick A brick commonly available in a district; hence the London stock, which is a yellow Kentish brick, still referred to in the south of England as a stock brick although it is no longer the most commonly stocked brick in London.

stock brush A brush used to wet a wall before the application of plaster.

stock lumber (USA) Pieces of wood sawn to sizes which are normally available on the market.

stone 1. A natural walling material (*eg* limestone, sandstone, granite etc.). 2. A **whetstone** or similar sharpening aid.

stone lime Any **lime** made from a material other than chalk.

stone saw A blade with no teeth, that is fed with water and an abrasive and is used to cut stone.

stone slate A thin stone used for roofing, varying from the relatively small Cotswold stone slate to the heavy Pennine stone slab.

stone tongs **Nippers**.

stoneware A hard ceramic material used for drainage pipes (usually **salt glazed**) and made from plastic clays of the Lias formation (approximately 75% silica and 25% alumina). cf. **earthenware**.

stooled sill A window sill in which the ends, which are built into the wall, are built up to coincide with the jointing of the walling and to provide a flat surface on which to bed the walling of the jamb. cf. **slip sill**.

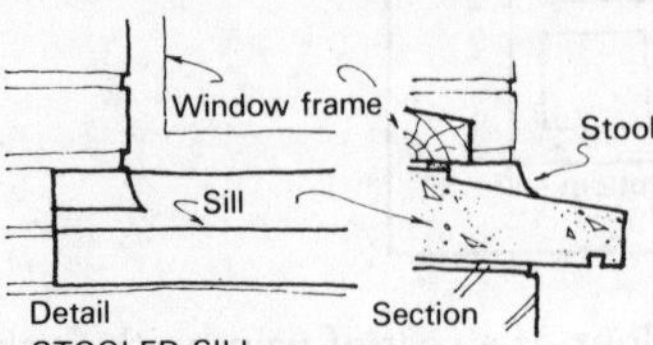

STOOLED SILL

stooling 1. The built up end of a **stooled cill** which is built into the walling. 2. (USA) A **window board**.

stoothing A wall constructed of **studs**.

stop 1. A moulding planted on, or cut out of, the door frame and against which the door closes. cf. **planted stop**. 2. The decorative end of a **stuck moulding**. 3. A **bench stop**.

stop bead (USA) **A guard bead**.

stopcock A **cock** on a gas or water pipe used to turn the supply on or off, but not to regulate the flow in the pipe.

stop moulding A **moulding** which ends at a stop and does not continue to the end of the member.

stopped chamfer A **chamfer** which merges into a sharp **arris**.

stopped mortise A **blind mortise**.

stopper or stopping 1. A **filler**. 2. **Hard stopping**.

stopping knife A glazier's knife used to smooth putty, with one rounded edge and one splayed edge.

storage heater A heater, usually powered by electricity, which consists of a substantial volume of material having a high thermal capacity, which is heated up at certain times of the day and stores the heat for radiation to the room at times when the power is not flowing.

storage tank A rectangular or circular tank used for the storage of cold water with which to feed either the hot and cold water domestic supplies of a building or the **wet heating system**; usually manufactured of asbestos cement, galvanized steel or plastic.

storage water heater A gas-fired water heater which is directly connected to its own insulated storage cylinder. cf. **gas circulator**.

storey The space between one floor and the floor above it, or a floor and the roof above it.

storey rod A measuring batten, cut to the exact height of a storey, on which are marked significant levels such as sill and window head heights, stair tread levels or brick courses.

storm clip A clip fixed on the outside of a **glazing bar** in **patent glazing** to hold down the glass.

stormproof window A now out-dated description of a high-performance window which has protection from air and rain penetration additional to that of an ordinary window.

stoving Drying a paint film by the application of either convected or radiated heat.

straddle pole The sloping **scaffold pole** laid on the roof surface in a **saddle scaffold**.

straddle scaffold A **saddle scaffold**.

straight arch A **flat arch**.

straight edge A long straight piece of wood or metal with parallel edges, used in **setting out** a building.

straight flight A **stair** which has one axis without change of direction (*ie* all treads are **fliers**; there are no **winders**).

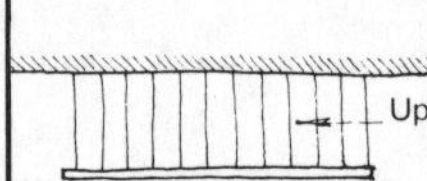

STRAIGHT FLIGHT

straight grain Wood in which the grain is parallel with the long axis of the piece.

straight joint 1. A **butt joint**. 2. In brickwork, a break in the pattern of the **bond** leading to one or more **perpends** being in line, one above the other.

straight-peen hammer A hammer which has, opposite to the hammerhead, a wedge-shaped **peen** parallel to the shaft of the hammer.

straight tongue A **tongue** formed in one edge of a board by two opposing rebates, intended to fit into a matching groove in another board.

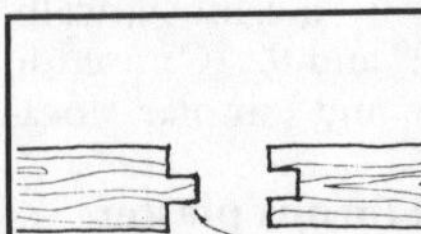

STRAIGHT TONGUE

strain The alteration of shape in a structural member when stressed. Strain equals deformation divided by original length.

straining piece In **flying shoring**, the horizontal element of the flying shore, forming an abutment for the inclined struts at each end.

S-trap A **trap**, usually part of a w.c. pan, resembling a letter S on its side and with an outlet that discharges vertically downwards.

strap anchor A steel plate which is fixed by **bolts** or **screws** to two floor joists as they abut over a support.

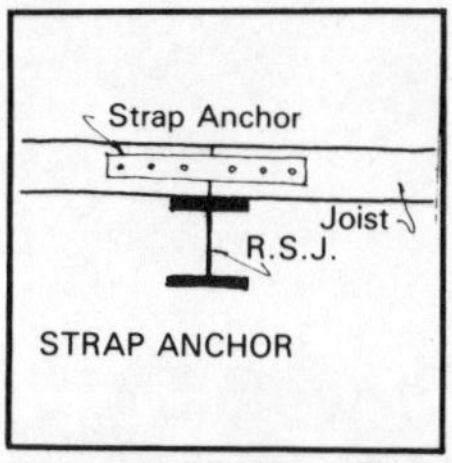

strap hinge A hinge with long plates or straps for bolting or screwing to a gate and gate post, as in a **band-and-hook hinge**.

strapping **Common grounds** on a wall forming the base for a lining.

strawboard A **compressed straw slab**.

stress (*f*) The internal force acting in a structural member resisting an externally applied force; expressed in load per unit area.

stressed skin panel A framework faced with a skin or skins of sheet material (*eg* plywood) on one or both sides, the fixing of the skins being so rigid that the whole assembly reacts to loading in an integral fashion, thus gaining a substantial part of its strength from the skin(s).

stress-graded timber **Converted timber** graded visually, or by means of a non-destructive testing machine, in relation to its likely strength. Visual grading takes into account the **rate of growth**, the number of **knots** and their type and size, the presence of **shakes**, the **slope of grain** etc.

stretcher A **brick** or stone laid with its long axis parallel to the length of the wall.

stretcher bond The bond obtained when a brick wall is built entirely of **stretchers**, being either a **half-brick wall** or a **cavity wall** with a half-brick outer leaf.

stretcher face The long face of a brick.

stretching course A course of **stretchers**.

striated finish A concrete finish in which the concrete is cast with a ribbed finish, the ribs (usually vertical) being partially broken or roughened to provide additional texture.

strike To remove the **shuttering** after the concrete has hardened sufficiently to allow this to be done without danger of collapse or damage.

striking plate A metal plate with one or more holes, screwed over a small **mortise** in a **door frame** or **lining**, into which the spring **bolt** of a **mortise lock** or a mortise **latch** engages when the door is shut. The lip of the striking plate is bent at an angle of about 30° to make the strike easier and smoother.

striking wedges **Folding wedges**.

string In a **stair** the inclined board on either side into which the **treads** and **risers** are housed, or which is cut to carry the treads and to mitre with the risers. cf. **outer string**, **wall string**, **close string**, **cut string**.

string course A decorative, often projecting, horizontal course in a wall, often lining up with window **sills** or **heads**. The projecting string course serves to throw rainwater clear of the wall.

stringer (USA) A **string**.

string piece A horizontal **tie** in a **Belfast truss**.

strip 1. A description of copper, zinc or aluminium sheet narrower than 450 mm and thinner than 9 mm but thicker than foil (0.15 mm). 2. **Square-sawn timber** less than 50 mm thick and 100 mm wide, as in hardwood flooring such as **parquet strip flooring**. 3. (USA) **Lumber** less than 50 mm thick and 200 mm wide.

strip flooring **Parquet strip flooring**.

stripping 1. Clearing a site of turf and vegetation before excavating. 2. Removing paint by burning with a **blow lamp** or applying a chemical paint stripper.

stripping knife A broad-bladed tool used to remove wallpaper or loose paint. The blade widens towards its square end and can be up to 100 mm wide.

strip slates Strips of mineral-surfaced **bitumen felt** cut to look like slates and laid in horizontal courses.

struck joint 1. A **weather-struck joint.** 2. A mortar joint similar to a **weather-struck joint**, but with the mortar sloping inwards from top to bottom and not the reverse direction. This joint is not recommended for external use as it provides a ledge on which water can rest.

structural Load-bearing; any part of a building that carries a load in addition to its own weight. This is a UK definition. In the USA 'structural' is given a less limited meaning.

structural clay tile (USA) A non-structural burnt-clay **hollow block**.
structural glazing gasket A glazing gasket of the H, Y-or single-sided type made of synthetic rubber or similar material, often incorporating a **zipper-strip**, which is fabricated to form a framework or 'ladder' containing several sheets of glass to make up a small **curtain wall**.

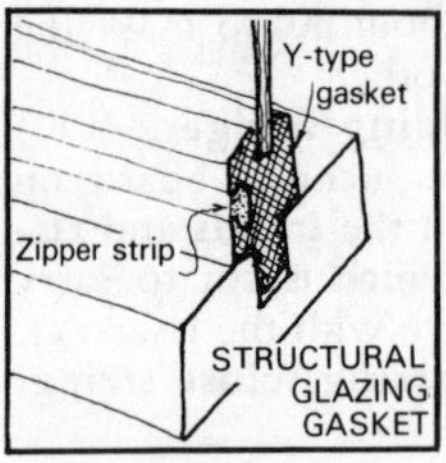

structural lumber (USA) **Square-sawn timber**, 50 × 100 mm or larger, usually **stress-graded timber**.
structural module A grid space on a **planning grid** which is used in planning structural elements.
structural steelwork A building frame made up of **rolled steel joists** or **universal beams and universal columns**, bolted, riveted or welded together. It may also contain built-up members, such as **lattice beams**, **rectangular hollow sections**, **cold-rolled sections** etc.
structure The loadbearing part of a building; the meaning is often extended to include the whole of the building shell.
structure-borne noise Noise conveyed by way of the structure of a building, often from one property to an adjoining one, usually having been caused by impact on the structure or connecting elements. cf. **airborne noise**.
strutting 1. Using temporary supports or struts, as in the supporting of formwork below a floor slab or beam. 2. **Solid bridging** or **herring-bone strutting**.
strutting piece 1. A **straining piece** 2. A piece of timber used in **solid bridging** or **herring-bone strutting**.
stub The **nib** of a **tile**.
stub tenon A tenon that fits into a **blind mortise**. cf. **secret wedging** and **wedged tenon**.
stuc Plasterwork intended to look like stone.
stucco 1. Smooth external plastering, usually of a lime: cement: sand mix with a greater volume of lime than cement. cf. **cement rendering**. 2. (Scotland) **Plaster of Paris**.
stuck moulding A moulding cut from the solid as opposed to a **planted** moulding.
stud 1. A vertical member in a timber or light steel framed partition, spanning between **sill** or **sole plate** and head piece, and often stiffened at mid-span by horizontal members or **noggings**. 2. A threaded rod set into a concrete or brick base material to facilitate the making of a fixing.

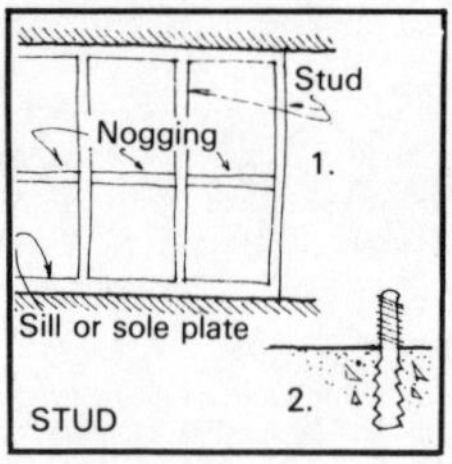

stud bolt An **anchorage fixing** device which, by the expansion of a part of the device in a hole in the base material (brick, concrete, or stone), fixes a threaded rod or **stud** in the base material to provide a means of attaching another building component to the base.

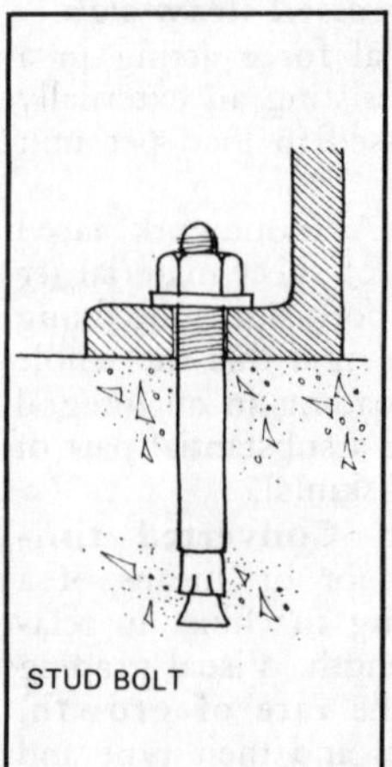

stud gun A cartridge-fired gun which shoots hardened steel pins or studs into concrete, brickwork or mild steel. The studs are of small diameter (6 to 9 mm) and have male or female threads. The gun has a safety device which prevents it from firing unless it is pressed against a solid surface.
stud partition A partition built of timber or light metal **studs**.
sub-base (USA) A **skirting board**.
sub-basement The second level of basement below ground floor level.

subcontract A part of a **contract** usually relating to specialist work, to be undertaken by a **subcontractor** but still under the overall responsibility of the **general contractor**.

subcontractor A specialist tradesman who undertakes part of a contract (a subcontract) under the control of the **general contractor**. cf. **nominated subcontractor**.

sub-floor The structural floor which carries the imposed load but which is covered by a floor finish.

sub-frame 1. A subsidiary frame set within the structural frame for the specific purpose of supporting a part of the building. 2. An outer frame for a window or a door, as in the case of a metal window set in a timber sub-frame.

subletting The practice of a **general contractor** of assigning sections of his contract, usually particular **trades**, to a **subcontractor** to carry out under the main contractor's overall control. This does not relieve the main contractor of the responsibility for assuring the satisfactory nature of the work. The architect's permission is required for such appointments.

submersible fitting A fitting, such as certain types of pump, designed to withstand indefinitely submersion in water to a specified depth.

subsidence The sinking or caving in of the ground, or the settling down of a structure to a lower level. The tendency of the subsoil under the **foundations** of a building, after being loaded by the full weight of the building, is to sink slightly. If this is limited and even in extent, the phenomenon is known as **settlement** and is considered quite normal. It should not lead to large cracking of the structure. If movement is extensive and uneven, leading to cracking of the structure, this is called subsidence and could be caused by insufficiently spread or inadequately constructed foundations, inconsistency in the subsoil which was unnoticed at the time of pouring the foundations, or some external cause such as dewatering of the subsoil by trees or mining activity.

sub-sill A subsidiary **sill** member fitted to the window frame after manufacture, with the intention of providing a greater projection of the sill and thus throwing off rainwater further in front of the wall face.

subsoil The ground which lies below the **vegetable soil**.

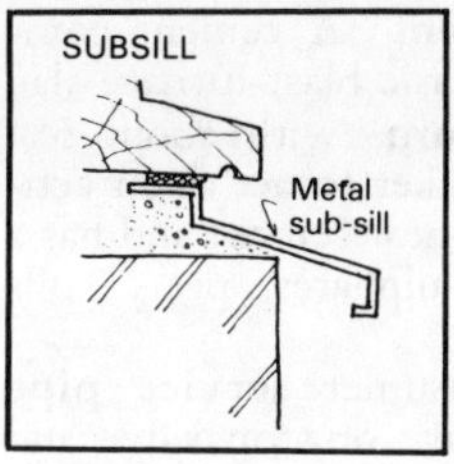

substation A room in a building, or a separate structure, in which are situated transformers to step down the high-voltage of incoming power to the correct voltage for use in the building. Main switch gear would also be included in this enclosure.

substrate A layer immediately under a layer of a different material to which it is stuck, *eg* a plywood floor deck may be a substrate for a PVC sheet floor covering.

substructure That part of a building or structure which is below ground level.

suction 1. The power which causes the adhesion of wet **mortar** to a brick, or wet plaster to a wall. 2. The power which causes the absorption of liquid from a paint by a porous surface, resulting in a poor finish. The surface should be treated with a sealer to prevent this absorption.

Suffolk latch A **thumb latch**.

suite A set of **locks**, all of which differ but can be operated by one **master key**.

sulphate resisting cement A modified **Portland cement** with improved resistance to chemical attack by the sulphate salts found in certain ground waters and in some building materials. These salts will cause softening and considerable expansion of normal Portland cement mortar or concrete.

sump 1. A pit below the floor of a building, or below an excavation level, into which unwanted water collects. 2. A chamber in a pumping installation.

sump pump A pump used to dispose of water that collects in a **sump**.

sun chart A chart forming a diagrammatic method of assessing solar radiation levels falling on a proposed building.

sunk draft A **margin** on a facing stone which is set below the rest of the face.

sunk face An **ashlar** face which is dressed below the level of the margins.

sunk gutter A **secret gutter**.

super An abbreviation for superficial, thus metres super means square metres.

superimposed load **Imposed load**.

superstructure All parts of a building or structure above ground level.

supersulphated cement A cement composed of 80–85% basic blast-furnace slag and 10–15% **gypsum**, with about 5% Portland cement clinker to act as an activator. This is a low-heat cement and has a high resistance to sulphates, peaty soils and oils.

supply pipe A consumer **service pipe** between the boundary or stop valve and the building.

surbase 1. A **dado capping**. 2. A **moulding** at the top of a **skirting board**.

surface condensation Condensation occurring on the surface of a building element. cf. **interstitial condensation**.

surface dry The stage in the drying of **paint** at which the surface has formed a dry skin, covering wet paint beneath.

surfaced timber Pieces of timber with at least one planed surface.

surface factor (*F*) That proportion of heat gain, at the surface of a building element subjected to cyclic input, which is re-admitted to the adjacent space. cf. **cyclic conditions.**

surface planer A steel-bed mechanical plane with a rotating adzing cutter between the two halves of the bed, the two halves being set at different levels but in parallel planes. The difference between the two bed levels represents the depth of material to be planed off.

surface A **surface planer**.

surface resistance The resistance of the inside or the outside surface of an enclosing element to the passage of heat, two components in the establishment of the total **thermal resistance** of the element (*R*). This value is influenced not by the material of the element but by the type of element (wall or roof) its surface **emissivity**, and, in the case of external resistance, the exposure of the element.

surface retardant A treatment which, when brushed on **formwork**, discourages the surface layer of the concrete from hardening, thus making the formwork easy to **strike** and giving a surface that can be readily roughened to form a good key for plaster.

surface spread of flame A characteristic of the surface of a combustible material, being its tendency to spread or discourage the spread of fire. The term is particularly applicable to lining materials, which are classified according to this characteristic.

surface vibrator A vibrator applied usually to the surface of a concrete mix immediately after placing to ensure correct consolidation. cf. **external vibrator** and **poker vibrator**.

surface water Rainwater from the ground surface, paved areas and roofs which is to be drained away.

surface water drain A drain which does not carry **soil** or **waste** drainage but merely carries **surface water**, otherwise known as storm water.

surface waterproofer A water repellent in the form of a liquid which, when applied to concrete, or brick or stone wall surfaces, discourages water penetration (except that of water under pressure). Surface waterproofers are often based on **silicone** resins and are not visible on the treated surface.

surround One material placed around another to provide decoration or protection.

survey An inspection of land or buildings to assess the condition, value, etc. This may be accompanied by the taking of measurements to allow a plan, etc. to be drawn. cf. **level survey**.

suspended ceiling A ceiling which is constructed below a floor or roof structure, leaving a gap above the ceiling in which **services** are often run.

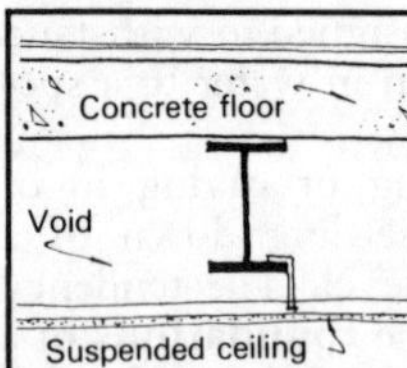

SUSPENDED CEILING

suspended floor A floor consisting of a series of beams or **joists** or of a reinforced concrete slab, intermittently supported or supported at the spanning element's extremities rather than continuously supported as in the case of a **solid floor** constructed next to earth.

suspended scaffold A **cradle** or **bracket scaffold**.

suspended shuttering **Formwork** which is not propped from below, but is carried on the supports for the floor which is being cast.

suspension 1. Very small particles of matter distributed throughout a liquid, rather than dissolved in the liquid as in the case of a solution. Many paints are suspensions. 2. An emulsion in which one liquid is distributed in another, as in an **emulsion paint**.

Sussex garden wall bond **Flemish garden wall bond**.

swage A tool for working hot or cold metal, consisting of two sections, male and female, one acting as a hammer, the other as a shaped anvil.

swage-setting A method of **setting** circular saws used for ripping in which the point of each tooth is spread to give a symmetrical, slightly fish-tailed section rather than the usual sideways set. Swage-set saws take a faster feed than other saws.

swan neck 1. A pipe in the form of an S-bend, particularly that leading from a **gutter** to a **rainwater pipe**. 2. A combination of **ramp** and **knee** to give a **handrail** a quick rise.

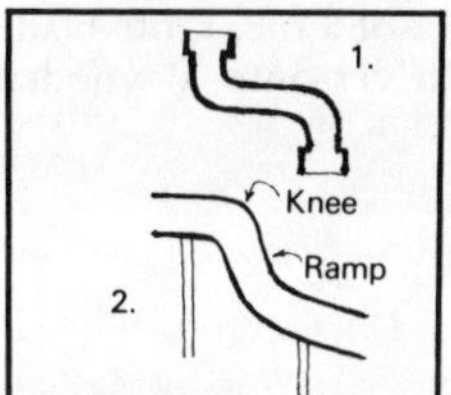

SWAN NECK

swan-neck chisel A long, curved **socket chisel** used to lever out the core of a mortise.

swatch A sample piece of a material such as a decorative laminate, veneer, paint colour, floor finish, etc. The term is often used to indicate a collection of samples fixed together either by a light chain or some other form of connector.

sweated joint (USA) A **capillary joint**.

sweating 1. The operation of soldering together two pieces of metal by 'tinning' their surfaces and then heating them whilst they are pressed into close contact, so that the solder flows and the surfaces are fused together. cf. **capillary joint**. 2. A term applied to a surface showing traces of moisture due to the formation of condensation or to water having come through a porous material of which the surface is a part.

sweating out The reverse of drying out, in which a plaster surface seems wet and soft after setting, as a result of contamination in the sand, an impervious backing or cold weather.

sweep tee A **tee** in which the branch is not perpendicular to the main run, but curves away from it.

swelling An increase in dimensions, caused by an increased **moisture content**.

swept valley A **valley** in a tile or slate roof using **tile-and-a half tiles** or slates cut into the angle between the roof surfaces in alternate courses, with a wedge shaped tile, or slate, on the other courses, straddling the change of direction. This valley gives continuous coursing of tiles over the **valley board** and avoids the use of a **valley gutter**.

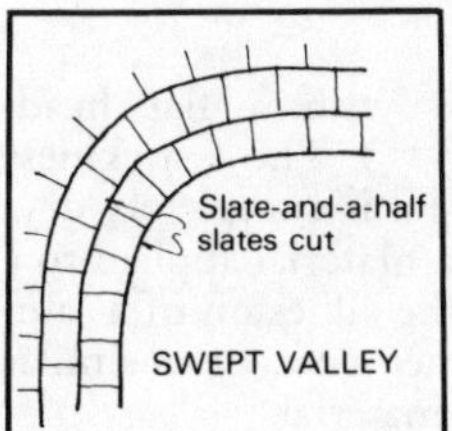

SWEPT VALLEY

SWG **Standard wire gauge**.

swing door A door operated by a spring hinge, such as a **floor spring**. A single swing door swings only one way and closes to normal **stops**; a double swing door swings in both directions and has no stops on its frame.

swinging post A post to which the gate is hinged.

switch-fuse See **fuse-switch**.

switchboard 1. A group of hand-operated electrical switches to control a series of fittings or circuits, face mounted together, with or without instrumentation. cf. **switchgear**. 2. A telephone subscriber's exchange.

switchgear A general term for electrical switching devices and their combination with associated control, measuring, protective and regulating equipment. When referring to a combination of control gear, this term is usually preferred to the term **switchboard** for larger installations.

switch socket outlet A **socket outlet** with a single pole switch.

synthetic resin A synthetically produced **resin**; originally a member of a group of synthetic substances which resembles and shares some properties of natural resins, but now used for materials which bear little resemblance to the natural resins. It is generally understood to mean a member of the heterogeneous group of compounds produced from simpler compounds by **condensation** and/or **polymerization**, such as amino or phenolic resins. Synthetic resins are used in the manufacture of **plastics**, **glues** and **paints**.

synthetic resin adhesive An adhesive based on synthetic resins of the amino-plastic (urea formaldehyde, melamine formaldehyde) or phenolic type (phenol formaldehyde, resorcinol formaldehyde) or a mixture of the two. They are immune to attack by moulds and bacteria and resistant, in varying degrees, to moisture.

synthetic stone (Scotland) **Cast stone**.

system building **Industrialized building**.

T

tack 1. A short nail with a flat head. 2. See **lead tack**. 3. The stickiness of a paint film before it is completely dry.

tack coat A coat of a material applied to a surface to improve the adhesion of a later treatment or a further coat of a similar material to the base material.

tacky A description of a paint film before it is completely dry.

tag A small strip of copper sheet folded several times and used to wedge the edge of a sheet of copper in a masonry or brick joint.

tail 1. The lower edge of a roofing **slate** or **tile**. 2. The built-in end of a precast concrete or stone step.

tail bay The end span of a timber floor or roof.

tail bolts Bolts used to fix the bottom ends of **asbestos cement** roof sheets.

tailing in or down The building in of the end of a member projecting from a wall, such as a **cantilever step**.

tailing iron A steel member built into a wall over the top of a **cantilever** member to assist in holding down the **tail** of the cantilever.

tail joist A joist resting on a **tail trimmer**.

tailpiece (USA) A **trimmed joist**.

tail trimmer A joist (referred to as a tail joist) can be carried on a tail trimmer running parallel to the wall and just clear of it when it is undesirable for the joist to be supported on the wall.

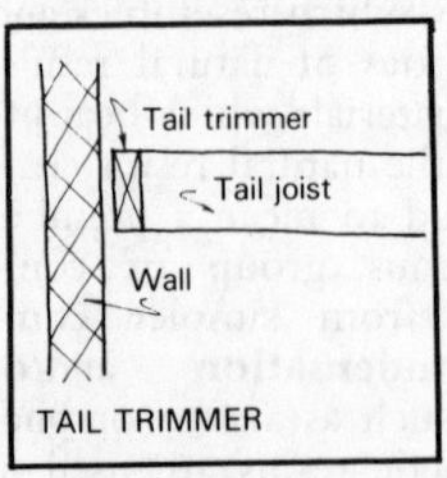

TAIL TRIMMER

taking off The first step in preparing a **Bill of Quantities**, in which the dimensions of materials required are measured from the drawings. Dimensions for each **item** are recorded systematically on dimension paper. The **squaring** of these dimensions is the next stage in the operation.

tally slates Slates sold by number rather than by weight. cf. **ton slates**.

tampin A **boxwood tampin**.

tanalized timber Wood impregnated with a **preservative**.

tang The pointed part of a file, knife blade or chisel which is driven into a wooden handle.

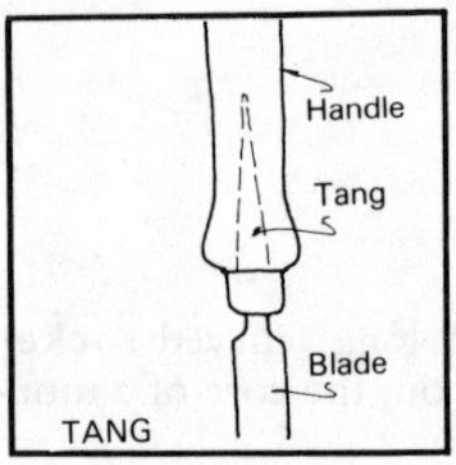

TANG

tangential shrinkage **Shrinkage** in timber which occurs parallel to the **growth rings**.

tank See **cistern** and **storage tank**.

tanking A waterproof membrane, usually of asphalt, butyl rubber or bitumen/polythene sheet suitably jointed, set on the outside of basement walls (and subsequently protected by an outside skin, often of brickwork) and within a basement floor under the **loading coat**.

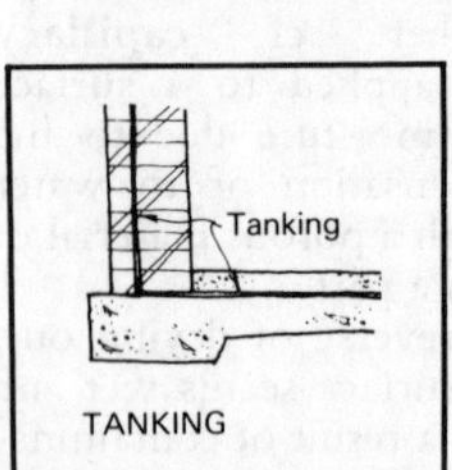

TANKING

tap 1. A screwed plug of hard steel used to cut internal threads. cf. **die**. 2. To form a thread in a piece of metal. 3. The flow control device on a water or gas outlet.

tape See **joint tape**.

tapered parapet gutter A **box gutter** behind a **parapet** which varies in width due to the fall in the gutter towards the outlet.

tapered-roll pantile A **pantile** with a roll which tapers from head to tail.

taper pipe An **increaser** or **reducer**.

taper thread A **screw thread** used on the ends of water and gas pipes to ensure a tight fit.

taping strip In **built-up roofing** a strip of felt which is stuck over joints in the **decking** prior to the laying of the first layer of felt.

tar A viscous black liquid with adhesive and waterproofing qualities, obtained from the distillation of various materials, including coal and wood. The source of the tar should normally be given; if not, it is usually assumed to be coal tar.

tarmacadam **Coated macadam** in which the binder is wholly or substantially **tar**.

tarpaulin A large, waterproof, canvas sheet used to provide temporary protection to building works and components on site; often nowadays replaced by sheets of heavy-gauge polythene.

tar paving The final surface of **tarmacadam** which is laid in one or two courses and used for areas of pedestrian or light vehicular traffic.

T-beam A beam in a reinforced concrete floor whose cross-section is in the shape of a T, *ie* part of the slab is considered as being the upper flange of the beam.

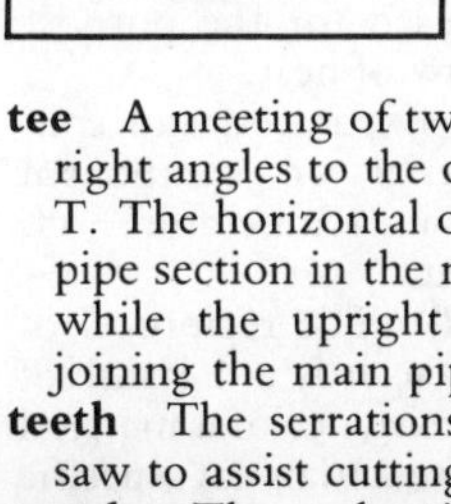

tee A meeting of two pipes, one usually at right angles to the other, in the shape of a T. The horizontal of the T represents one pipe section in the main **run** of pipework, while the upright represents a **branch** joining the main pipe run.

teeth The serrations along the blade of a saw to assist cutting.

tegula The under tile in **Italian** or **Spanish tiling**.

telescopic centering **Formwork** carried on rectangular steel bearers, made up in sections which fit into each other telescopically and can be adjusted to the span between bearing surfaces.

temper To toughen steels and non-ferrous metals by mechanical or **heat treatment**.

tempering 1. The treatment of steel in order to produce certain mechanical properties by heating it to some temperature below transformation range, holding it at that temperature for a time and then cooling it at a specific rate. 2. The mechanical treatment of wet clay or other material to improve its workability.

template 1. A full size pattern made in wood, metal or other suitable material to act as a gauge of the actual profile required when cutting or forming a material to shape. 2. A pad to carry a concentrated load.

temporary bench mark In the absence of an **Ordnance bench mark** in the proximity of a site, a temporary bench mark is established (on some permanent surface or object which is not going to be disturbed by the building works) to which all site levels, new or existing, can be related.

tender A price given by a contractor to undertake a building operation after studying the drawings, **specification** and (often) pricing the **Bill of Quantities**. The tender is usually given in competition with other contractors. An 'open' tender is one in which the contract is advertised, and any contractor wishing to tender may do so. A 'limited' tender is one in which a list of contractors is agreed and those on the list are invited to submit a tender.

tendering The process of preparing a **tender**.

tenon A rail, or other similar component, that is shaped at its end to reduce its area, so that it can enter a **mortise** formed in another component to which it is to be joined. The width of a tenon should be about four times its thickness.

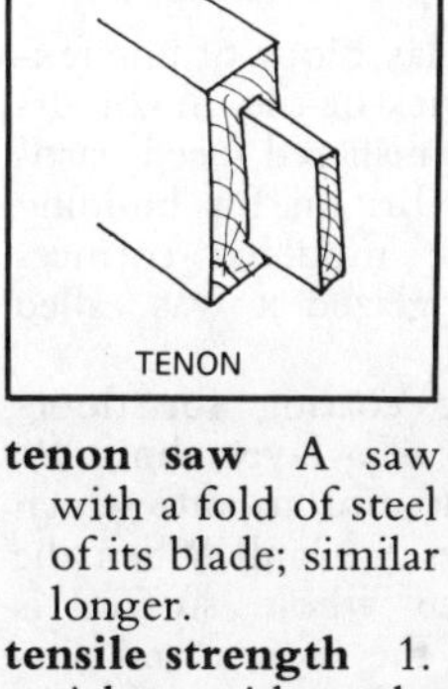

tenon saw A saw about 300 mm long with a fold of steel or brass over the back of its blade; similar to a **dovetail saw** but longer.

tensile strength 1. The ability of a material to withstand **tensile stress**. 2. The stress at which a material fails in tension.

tensile stress The result of the application on a component of a load which endeavours to elongate the component. cf. **compressive stress**.

tension Use **tensile stress**.

terminal 1. The connector on an item of electrical equipment to which an electrical wire is fixed. 2. The end of a piece of equipment such as a gas **flue** or **lightning conductor**.

termite An insect, belonging to the order of *Isoptera*, indigenous to tropical parts of the world and some temperate regions of the USA, which causes considerable damage to timber and other building materials. Because termites live in colonies, their attack can be so ferocious as to cause structural collapse in a relatively short time. Timber can be protected from termite attack by impregnation by an insecticide.

termite shield A metal overhanging lip at approximately **damp-proof course** level which prevents ground or subterranean **termites** from entering a building or its structure.

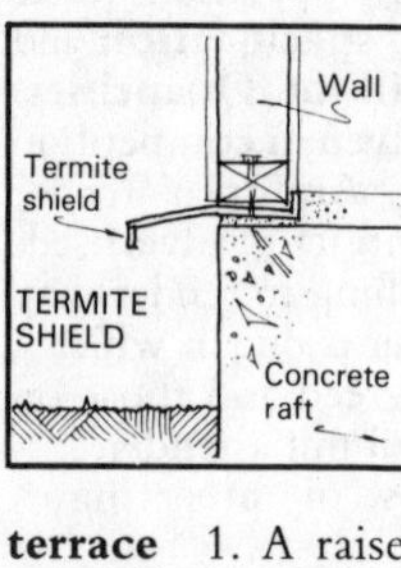

terrace 1. A raised platform with at least one side well above the surrounding ground level and protected by a **retaining wall** or earth bank. 2. A flat roof to which access is encouraged.

terrace house One of a row of three or more houses, having a **separating wall** on either side between it and its neighbours.

terra cotta A burnt clay block of fine texture, resembling a brick or tile, in colours from yellow to brownish-red, used particularly in Victorian Britain for building blocks, facing slabs, moulded cornices and the like. When glazed it was called **faience**.

terrazzo A finishing coating for floors and walls consisting of a layer about 19 mm thick of cement mortar into which multi-coloured stones are laid. When the cement has set, the whole surface is abraded to smooth the stones and improve their colour and give a smooth, easily cleaned durable surface. Today prefabricated terrazzo tiles are available which involve less site labour.

tessellated paving **Roman mosaic**.

tessera A small cube of marble, glass, stone, etc., used in **tessellated paving.**

textured brick A **rustic brick**.

textured finish 1. A roughened finish applied to a plaster or render coating by throwing plaster on to the surface (see **Tyrolean finish**), or otherwise working it. 2. A paint surface achieved by a sand or fine stone aggregate in the paint. 3. A finish achieved by the use of a paint with a consistency that will accept rough textured finishes from profiled rollers.

theodolite A telescopic instrument used in land surveying for measuring angles, in either a vertical or horizontal plane.

thermal capacity That property of a material or element of structure which expresses both its ability to store heat and the rate at which the temperature of the material or construction will alter with changes in the temperature of the adjacent air. Materials of high thermal capacity take longer to heat up and store heat longer than materials of low thermal capacity. Generally thermal capacity increases with density and mass.

thermal conductance (***C***) The **thermal transmittance** between inner and outer surfaces of a construction, depending on the thickness and the thermal properties of the materials making up the construction, but ignoring the resistances of the inner and outer surfaces. cf. **surface resistance.**

thermal conductivity (***K***) The quantity of heat in **steady state conditions** which is transmitted in unit time through unit area of unit thickness for unit temperature difference. It is a property of the material which is measured in W/m°C.

thermal insulation Material of low **thermal conductivity** used for the purpose of obstructing the flow of heat.

thermal movement Expansion and contraction of a material or component caused by changes in temperature. cf. **moisture movement**.

thermal resistance (***R***) The reciprocal of **thermal conductance**. It is a measure of the overall thermal resistance of a material or combination of materials of specific thickness to heat flow. The total thermal resistance of an element of structure, including the resistance of the inner and outer surfaces and of any enclosed cavities, is the reciprocal of the total **thermal transmittance** (*U* value). It is measured in m^2 °C/W.

thermal resistivity (*r*) That property of a material regardless of size or thickness which is the reciprocal of its **thermal conductivity** (m°C/W)

thermal transmittance (*U*) The quantity of heat that will flow through unit area in unit time per unit difference of temperature between the internal and external environments in **steady state conditions**. It is measured in W/m^2 °C and differs from **thermal conductance** only in that it includes inner and outer **surface resistances**. Standard *U* values are thermal transmittances given certain standard conditions such as exposure and moisture content of the building element.

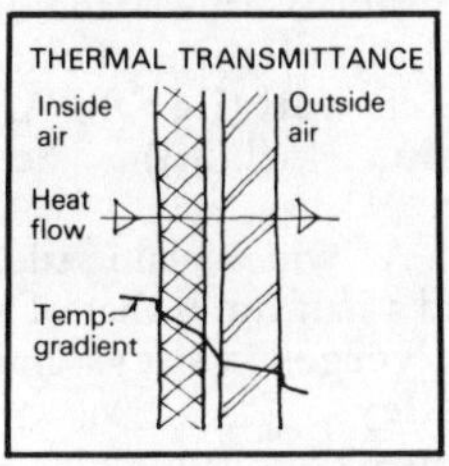

thermoplastic A description of a **synthetic resin** or other material that softens on the application of heat and hardens again on cooling. cf. **thermo-setting**.

thermoplastic tile A floor tile which is made from a **thermoplastic** resin with other additives, such as asphalt, asbestos fibre etc. It requires a solid, non-flexing **substrate**.

thermo-setting A description of a synthetic resin which can be used to form a plastic or adhesive and which, once formed, cannot be softened by heating; in fact a thermo-setting adhesive hardens on heating. In general, thermo-sets are more heat-stable and resistant to solvent action than **thermoplastics**.

thermostat An automatic device, often electrical, which is responsive to temperature changes and is used to maintain a constant temperature. This is usually done by a bi-metal strip which bends on heating or cooling and makes or breaks an electrical circuit.

thickening See **fattening**.

thicknessing machine A mechanical plane which reduces the thickness of a piece of wood which already may have had one face made true by a **surface planer**.

thimble A **sleeve piece**.

thinner A volatile liquid which lowers the viscosity of a **paint** or **varnish**, such as **white spirit** or **turpentine**.

thinning ratio The proportion of **thinner** used with a particular paint for a specific purpose.

thin-wall fixing A fastener which is designed to make a secure fixing into thin materials or thin-walled cellular materials. cf. **cavity fixing**.

thixotropic A full-bodied material which suffers a reduction in body when disturbed by shaking or stirring, but which readily returns to its original state when allowed to stand. This description is often applied to a paint which, although easy to brush out, tends not to drip and can therefore be applied thicker without danger of running or sagging.

thread A helical or spiral ridge formed on a cylinder or cone by cutting or casting. The shape and **pitch** of the thread will vary depending on the thread type, *ie* **Whitworth**, **Unified**, or **International Standards Organization (ISO) threads.**

three-coat work Plastering of a high quality in three coats (**render**, **floating** and **setting** coats respectively).

three-pin plug An electrical plug for insertion in a **socket outlet**, usually, nowadays in the UK, making a connection into a ring main. These plugs have rectangular pins and the plug head carries an interchangeable cartridge fuse up to 13A in capacity.

three-ply Consisting of three layers; a term frequently used to denote the most common form of **plywood** with a core and two outer **veneers**, or **built-up roofing** employing three layers of felt.

three-quarter bat A **brick** cut across its length to reduce it by one quarter. cf. **King closer**.

three-way strap A steel tee-plate with its three arms angled to fit the intersection of timber components, to which it is bolted or fixed with **coach screws** to increase the strength of the joint.

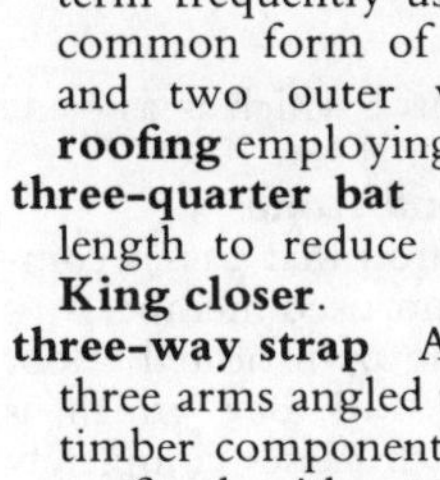

threshold A horizontal timber member at the foot of a door (usually an external door).

threshold of hearing The minimum level of sound of a particular frequency which excites the sensation of hearing. This level will differ with different people.

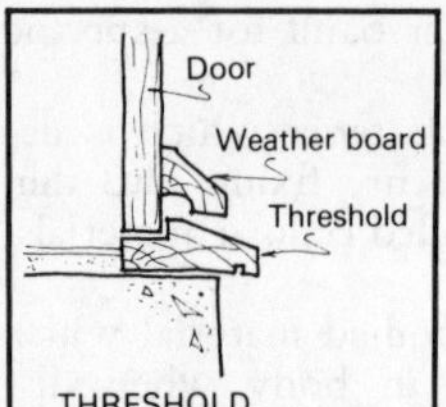

THRESHOLD

threshold of pain The level at which sound of a particular frequency will cause distress to a person hearing the sound. This level will differ with different people.
throating 1. The undercut profile of a **drip**. 2. A flue **gathering**. 3. The opening in a hand plane from which shavings appear.
through bonder A **bond stone**.
through-fixing A fixing that is achieved by the complete penetration of both the components which are being fixed together.

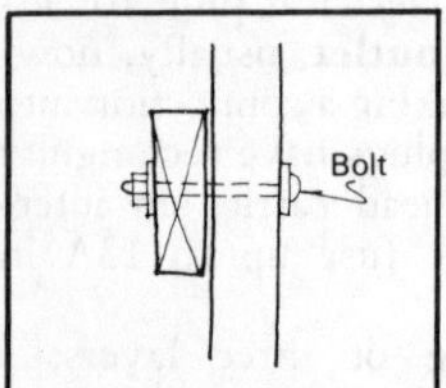

THROUGH-FIXING

through lintel A **lintel** which is as wide as the wall in which it is set.
through stone A **bond stone**.
through tenon A **tenon** that passes completely through the mortised member.
thumb latch An unsophisticated door latch, comprising a **fall bar** which is raised by a lever which passes completely through the door and is depressed by the thumb on one side of the door. A **pull** handle is fixed on the opposite side of the door from the fall bar.
thumb screw 1. A **wing nut**. 2. A device to lock a **sash** window, consisting of a long metal hand-operated screw which can be secured through both meeting rails.
tie (Scotland) A fixing **clip** for **flexible-metal roofing** sheets.
tie beam The horizontal and lowest member in a **roof truss** which ties the feet of the rafters together.
tier (USA) A leaf of brickwork half a brick thick.
tight A description of the dimension of a piece of material, which is **bare** or slightly undersized.
tight cesspool (USA) A cesspool that needs pumping out, *ie* by intention or otherwise it does not drain. cf. **cesspit**.
tight knot A knot that is firmly set in the surrounding wood; the opposite of a **loose knot**.
tight size In glazing, the actual dimension between glazing rebates. The **glazing size** is 3 mm less than this dimension, both horizontally and vertically.
tile 1. A roofing element made of burnt-clay, concrete, metal, or asbestos-cement in various shapes and sizes, all of which achieve weathertightness by overlapping. cf. **plain tile**, **single-lap tile**, **pantile**, **Italian tile**, **Spanish tile**. 2. A small element of floor or wall covering made of burnt-clay, concrete, **linoleum**, plastic, asbestos-cement etc. cf. **wall tile**. 3. An **agricultural drain**. 4. (USA) See **structural clay tile**.
tile-and-a-half tile A wide plain tile, with a width one and a half times that of a normal tile, used at **verges**, **valleys** and **swept** and **laced valleys**.
tile batten A square-sawn timber between 12 × 25 mm and 30 × 75 mm nailed horizontally over the **common rafters** (or **counter battens**) at spacing equal to the gauge of the slates or tiles and intended to receive the nail fixings of the slates or tiles.
tile creasing See **creasing**.
tiled valley A valley covered with purpose-made **valley tiles**.
tile fillet Cut tiles bedded in mortar and set at 45° between a roof and an abutting wall; used in place of a **flashing**.

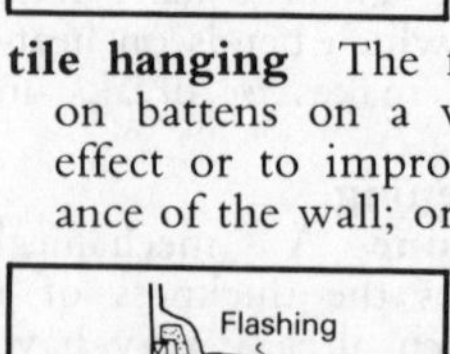

TILE FILLET

tile hanging The fixing of roofing tiles on battens on a wall face for aesthetic effect or to improve the weather resistance of the wall; or the tiles so hung.

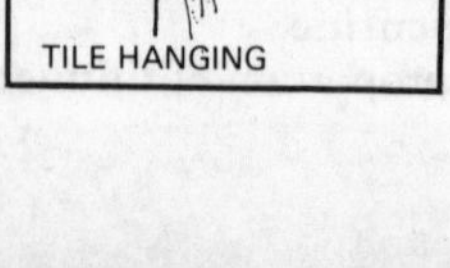

TILE HANGING

tile listing A **tile fillet**.

tile peg A large round-headed **clout nail** with a countersunk head for fixing roof tiles.

tiling batten A **tile batten**.

tilting fillet 1. A board of triangular cross-section nailed to the foot of **common rafters** or roof boarding under the **double eaves course** of tiles or slates to ensure that the **tails** of the lowest tiles bed tightly on each other. 2. A similar fillet on either side of an open **valley gutter** and along an abutment between a roof and a wall. 3. An **eaves fascia** projecting above the line of the top edge of the rafters which performs the same task as in 1 above.

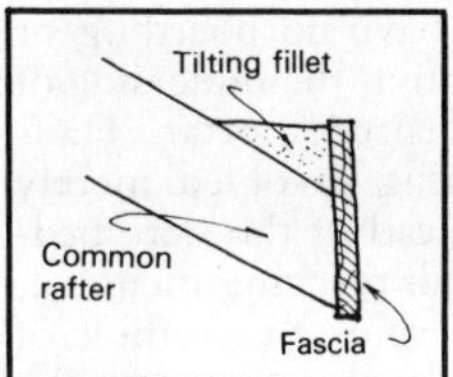

TILTING FILLET

timber brick A **fixing brick**.

timber connector See **connector**.

timber framed construction A building based on a loadbearing timber frame, lined internally and faced externally by a non-structural brick skin, **tile hanging**, **weather-boarding** etc. cf. **balloon frame** and **platform frame**.

timbering All temporary work in timber including **centering** for arches, **formwork** for concrete, and supports for excavation and **shoring**.

timber preservative See **preservative**.

tingle A strip of lead, copper or zinc, about 37 mm wide, used in **flexible-metal roofing** to fix down the sheets in such details as **hollow rolls** or seams; also used to fix glass in **patent glazing**.

tin saw A **saw** with which a bricklayer cuts bricks.

tin snips Strong scissors used to cut thin metal sheet.

tint A colour of paint made by mixing coloured pigment with **white pigments**.

tinters **Stainers**.

tinting A fine adjustment of the **colour** of a **paint**.

titanium white (TiO_2) An opaque **white pigment**.

toat The handle of a bench **plane**.

toe 1. The lower section of the **shutting stile** of a door. 2. The below-ground horizontal part of a **retaining wall**.

toe board On a **scaffold**, a vertical board set at the outside edge of a platform of **scaffold boards** to prevent tools and other objects from being accidentally pushed off the platform.

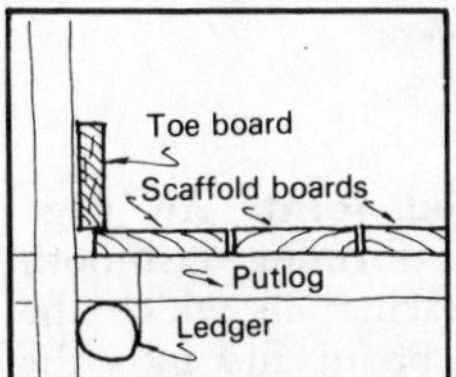

TOE BOARD

toe nailing **Skew nailing**.

toggle bolt A **cavity fixing** device which is designed to make a strong fixing to thin panels, such as plasterboard, or cellular composite material, operating by the opening of a part of the device after its insertion through a pre-drilled hole. On tightening, the expanded section is drawn against the rear surface of the panel.

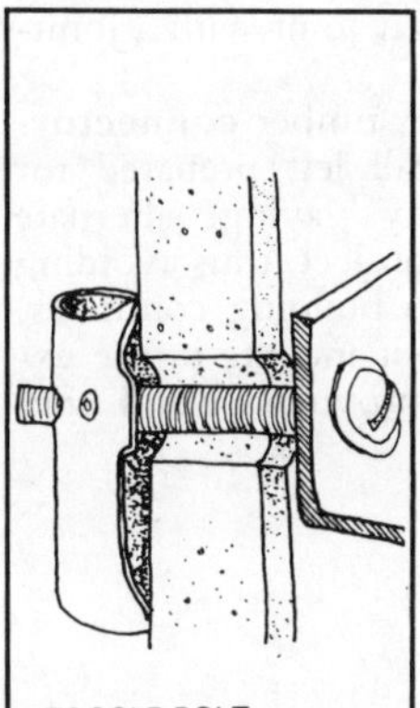
TOGGLE BOLT

tolerance The permissible amount by which the dimensions of a product may vary from the **work size** specified, usually stated as a plus or minus dimension (*eg* $\pm$ 3 mm).

tommy bar A loose bar inserted in a box spanner to aid turning.

toner A pure dye without any **extender**.

tongue A means of stiffening a joint, consisting of a long thin strip (usually of wood or metal) inserted in a groove or grooves at the interface of the joint. The tongue may be cut into one of the elements joined, as in a **tongued and grooved joint**, or may be a separate component (**cross tongue**).

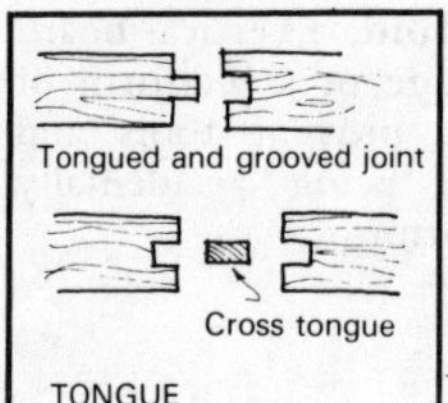

TONGUE

tongued and grooved joint An edge joint between boards forming a smooth wall, floor or roof facing, in which the **tongue** cut in one board fits into the groove cut in the adjacent board.
ton slates **Random slates** sold by weight, not by number.
tool A device for working material. A hand tool is operated by hand, as in the case of a hammer, spade, trowel, screwdriver etc. or is hand-held, like an electric screwdriver or drill. Machine tools are fixed devices, such as a **surfacer**, circular saw or lathe.
tooled surface A **batted surface**.
tooling 1. **Batting**. 2. (USA) Working the surface of a mortar joint with a jointing tool.
toothed connector A timber **connector**.
toothing A brick wall left prepared for future extension by laying alternate courses so that they project, thus avoiding a straight joint when building continues, or the need to cut out indents in the existing brickwork to provide a **bond** with the new.

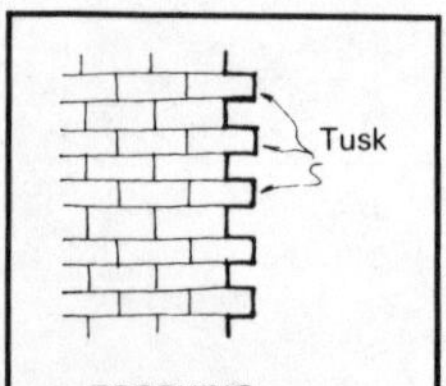

TOOTHING

top beam A **collar beam**.
top course tile A tile, shorter than normal, making up the top course, adjacent to the **ridge**, on a roof slope.
top-hung window An outward opening window, such as a **night vent**, hinged on its top edge and operated by a **casement stay**.

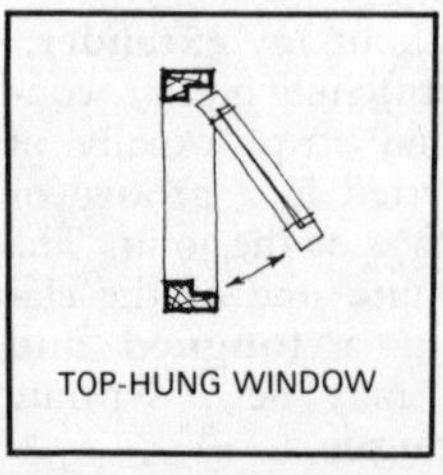
TOP-HUNG WINDOW

top lighting The lighting of an area from a high-level source, usually through the roof by means of **rooflights**, or from windows at clerestory level.
topping When sharpening a saw, topping is the first operation, in which the tips of all **teeth** are filed to a level. cf. **shaping**, **setting**, **sharpening**.
topping out A term used to indicate the completion of the construction of the building shell, after which internal fittings and finishes have to be completed.
top rail The top horizontal member of a frame or a panelled door.
top soil **Vegetable soil**.
torching The now almost obsolete practice, in roofs which have no boarding or **sarking felt**, of pointing the underside of slates or tiles with haired mortar. Half-torching or shouldering involved merely pointing where the head of the slate bedded to the **batten**. Full torching included, in addition, the plastering of the whole of the underside of the slates or tiles between the battens.
torsion Use **torsional stress**.
torsional stress The stress induced when a component is twisted about its major axis.
torus roll A lead-covered horizontal **roll** weatherproofing the intersection at the junction of the two slopes on the same side of a **mansard roof**.
touch dry The stage in the drying of a paint film in which, when touched with the fingers, no marks are made on the surface.
toughened glass Glass whose surface has been rapidly cooled from near softening point so that residual compressive stresses remain in the glass after cooling. These stresses increase the thermal and mechanical strength of the glass and it tends to shatter into smaller, less angular, pieces on breaking.
tough-rubber sheathing (TRS) A form of electrical cable insulation made from rubber.
tower bolt A large **barrel bolt**.
trade A building trade or craft. A **Bill of Quantities** groups all the items of work into the main trades whose work is required to complete the work. cf. **sequence of trades**.
transducer A device which transforms one type of energy into another, *eg* thermal or mechanical into hydraulic or electrical, thereby allowing a signal to control an operation.

transfer coating A method of coating a substrate by first forming a plastic coating on a carrier, then bringing the substrate and carried coating together and later separating the carrier, leaving the coating on the substrate.

transformation range That range of temperature within which a constitutional change occurs on heating or cooling in a material in a solid state.

transformer A static apparatus which, by electromagnetic induction, transforms alternating current at one voltage to a higher or lower voltage.

translucent glass A glass which transmits light diffusely, and through which vision varies from almost clear to almost obscure.

transmission factor A numerical factor which expresses, usually as a percentage, how much of the light incident on a substance passes through that substance.

transom 1. A horizontal member which separates the lights of a window. cf. **mullion**. 2. (USA) A **fanlight**.

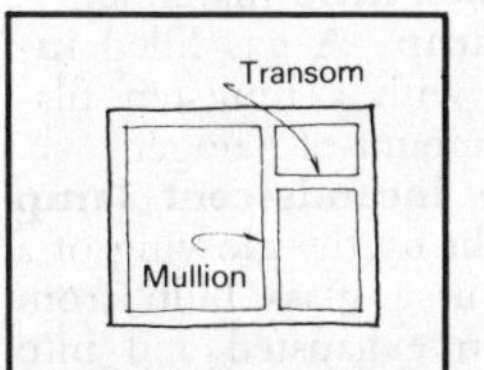

TRANSOM

transparent Permitting the passage of light without diffusion.

trap A means of retaining water in a pipe in order to avoid the passage of drain smells up the pipe, usually taking the form of a U-shaped bend or a **bottle trap**.

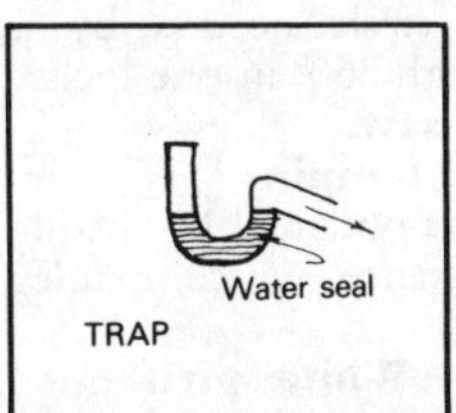

TRAP

trapped gully A **gully** containing a **trap**.

traverse A **dressing iron**.

tread The horizontal component of a **stair** on which one stands. cf. **rise.**

trenail A carpentry equivalent to a **dowel** in joinery – a hardwood pin, not to be confused with a **drawbore pin**, which fixes a **mortise and tenon joint.**

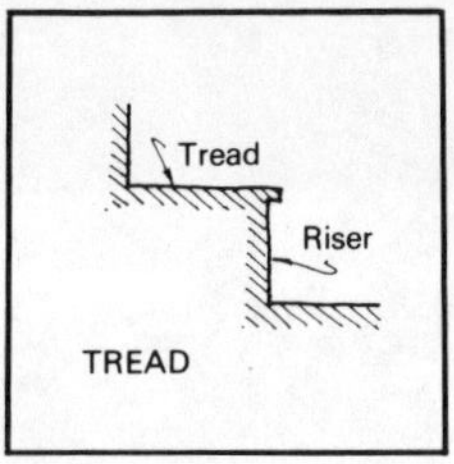

TREAD

trench 1. A long, narrow hole dug in the ground, as in foundation trench. 2. A long, narrow groove cut in a piece of timber; a housing for another component. cf. **housed joint**.

trestle A short support (used in pairs) for a low **scaffold**, similar to a broad pair of steps, used by plasterers and painters.

trial hole A hole dug on site to establish the nature of the **subsoil**; often part of a **site investigation**.

trim A minor element which covers the junction of two materials, such as an **architrave**, **skirting**, picture rail etc.

trimmed joist A **common joist** which is carried on a **trimmer joist** and is therefore shorter than the normal common joists.

trimmer 1. A **trimmer joist**. 2. (USA) A **trimming joist**.

trimmer arch A brick arch spanning between the chimney back and the **trimmer joist** and carrying a hearth.

trimmer joist A short joist on one side of an opening in a timber floor or roof, at right angles to the **common joists**, which carries the **trimmed joists**. The trimmer joist is carried on the trimming joists or a **trimming joist** and a wall.

trimming Framing an opening in a timber floor or roof to stiffen the aperture.

trimming joist A joist thicker than the **common joists** and parallel to them, to which the **trimmer joist** is fixed.

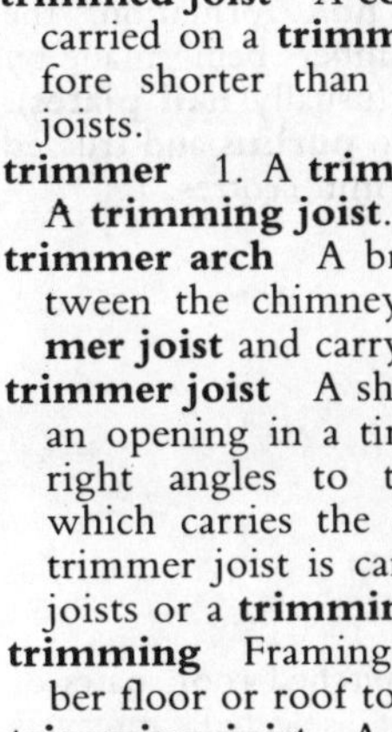

TRIMMING JOIST

trimming piece A **camber slip**.

trough gutter A **box gutter**.

trowel A tool with a steel blade and a wooden handle used by a bricklayer, mason or plasterer for speading mortar etc. cf. **float**.

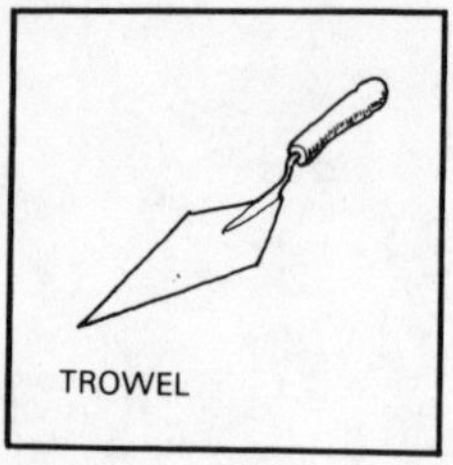

trowelled face A plaster or screed surface finished with a **trowel**.
trunking An enclosure made of metal or plastic in which service cables and pipes run, usually with a removable cover or access panels.
truss A frame designed to act as a beam. cf. **roof truss**.
trussed beam A beam in the form of a **truss**.
trussed purlin A **trussed beam** used as a **purlin**.
trussed rafter roof A light timber roof used in domestic work in which each pair of rafters is formed into a light truss, usually of **fan** or **fink** formation, the joints between the timbers being made by timber **connectors** (usually **nail plates**). This roof requires no **purlins** and trussed rafters are set at 600 mm centres.

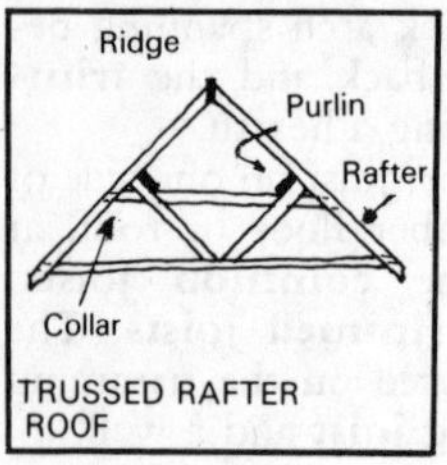

trussed rafters In a pitched roof, pairs of common rafters at selected intervals which are triangulated to support the **purlins**.
try plane A long bench plane over 500 mm long; often called a trying plane.
try square A tool for establishing the squareness of an angle or marking out a line at right angles to another face, consisting of a steel plate set in a timber block (often metal edged) so that the angle between the two is a true right angle.

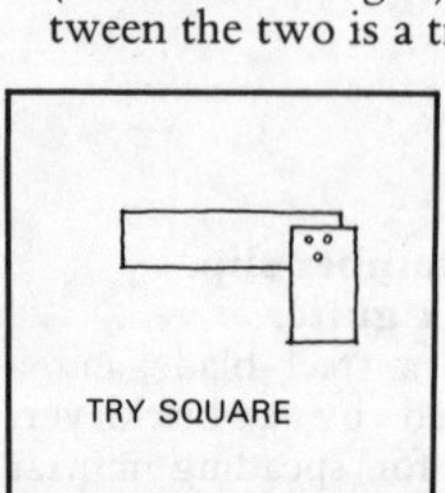

tubular saw A **hole saw**.
tubular scaffolding **Scaffold** made up of metal tubes, usually about 50 mm in diameter, with a range of connecting fittings.
tuck A groove formed in a horizontal mortar joint when tuck pointing old brickwork, the groove receiving a **lime putty** fillet which creates a strong horizontal line (often slightly projecting).
tuck pointing See **tuck**.

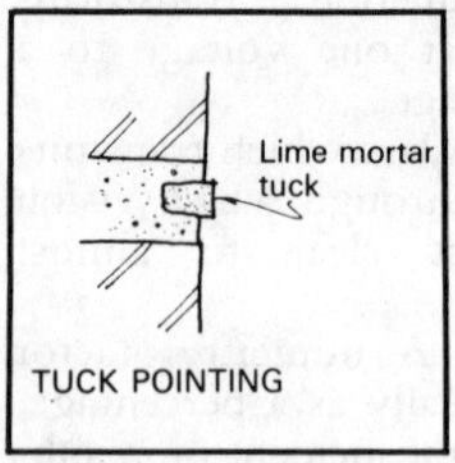

tumbler That part of a lock which restrains the bolt until the key is turned.
tumbler switch A normal, lever-operated, electrical switch.
tumbling bay A **back drop** manhole.
tungsten halogen lamp A gas filled **incandescent lamp** with a tungsten filament and a small amount of halogen.
tungsten lamp An **incandescent lamp** which produces light by the glowing of a tungsten filament in a glass bulb from which air has been exhausted and into which a controlled high purity mixture of argon and nitrogen has been introduced.
turn button An unsophisticated cupboard catch consisting of a piece of wood or metal, loosely connected by a screw through its middle so that, when fixed to a frame, it can be turned to prevent the door from opening.
turning Forming a cylindrical component on a **lathe**.
turning circle The circle needed by a vehicle to turn through 360° in one lock.
turning saw A **bow saw**.
turnpin A **boxwood tampin**.
turpentine A **solvent** obtained by distilling a resinous substance which exudes from pine trees.
turpentine substitute **White spirit**.
turret step A tread in a traditional stone **spiral stair**.
tusk A projecting walling element in **toothing**.
tusk nailing **Skew nailing**.
tusk tenon A **tenon** formed on the end of a **trimmer joist** in a now rarely used joint between a trimmer joist and a **trimming joist**. The tenon is about ⅙th of the depth of the trimmer joist and is

strengthened by a bevelled shoulder above and a short projection (the tusk) underneath, fitting into a suitably cut mortise in the other piece. The tenon projects through and beyond the trimming joist and the whole joint is brought up tight by driving a wooden wedge down through a hole formed in the tenon.

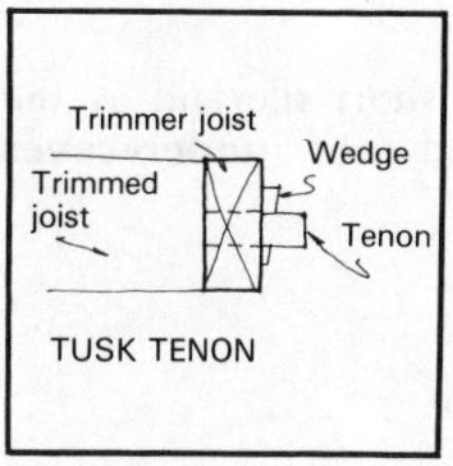

twin cable A cable comprising two conductors in a common insulating covering.
twin tenon See **double tenon**.
twist **Warp** in a spiral direction.
twist drill A hardened steel **bit** with helical cutting edges sloping at about 30° to the axis of the drill.
twisted fibres See **interlocking grain**.
twist gimlet A gimlet with a thread to dispose of wood cuttings, and a tapered shank.
two-coat work The application of a surfacing material in two coats, *eg* plaster, paint or asphalt.
two-handed saw A large hand saw operated by two men, working on opposite sides of the piece being cut.
two-part adhesive (paint, sealant etc.) A material which, in order to bring it into a workable state, needs the addition of a curing agent or **accelerator**. After the mixing of the material and the additive, its working life is limited.
two-pipe system A drainage system having the **soil** and **waste** systems in two separate pipes, the soil pipe conveying soil drainage direct to the drain, and the waste pipe conveying waste water to the drain through a **trapped gully**.
two-stage joint A joint, between external components of a building, which does not rely on only one method of weather protection. A **drained joint** is a two-stage joint.

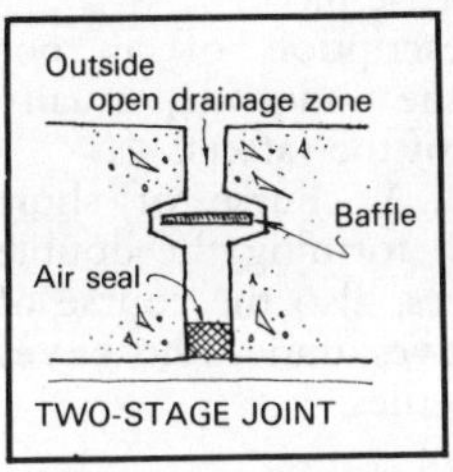

two-way reinforcement Reinforcing bars in a concrete slab, arranged in two series at right angles to each other so that the slab receives support on all four sides.
Tyrolean finish A spattered, rough, plaster finish achieved by plaster being thrown against a wall by a hand-operated machine.

U

U-gauge or U-tube gauge In an **air test** of drains or pipe work, a U-shaped glass tube half filled with water connected by a flexible tube to the system under test. Movement of the water indicates that the system is leaking.
ultimate bearing capacity The load at which the ground below a foundation fails in shear; usually determined by field load tests on small areas or strength tests on undisturbed samples.
ultimate load The load at which a structure or structural member fails.
ultimate tensile strength The maximum tensile load that a member can carry before failure, divided by the original cross-sectional area of the member before any distortion takes place.
ultra-violet radiation (UV) Radiation which is invisible to the human eye because it lies beyond the violet edge of the visible spectrum. It can be converted into visible light by certain chemicals. This is the basis of the fluorescent tube.
unbuttoning The demolition of steel framed buildings or structures by breaking off the rivet heads.
uncoursed A description of stone walling in which the stones are of considerable irregularity of shape, making their being laid to long horizontal bedding joints impossible; the term applies particularly to **random** or **snecked rubble**, although both can be coursed.
uncrushed gravel **Coarse aggregate** resulting from the natural disintegration of rock.
undercloak 1. That part of the lower

sheet of flexible metal roofing which is overlapped by the upper sheet at a **drip**, **roll**, **seam** or **welt**. 2. A course of tiles or slates on which the tiles or slates at a **verge** are bedded.

undercoat 1. The coat or coats of paint with good hiding power applied to a surface after priming, filling etc., or after the preparation of a previously painted surface and before the application of the finishing coat. 2. A coat of plaster under the **finishing-coat** of plaster.

undercuring Insufficient hardening of a glue as a result of too short a hardening period or too low a temperature.

under-cut tenon A **tenon** whose shoulder is cut off square so that its edges bear perfectly on the mortise piece.

under-drawn A description of a roof which is lined on the underside, usually following the pitch of the rafters.

under-eaves course A course of short plain tiles (or slates) forming the double thickness at the eaves; also the course of plain tiles at the eaves under the **eaves course** of single-lap tiles.

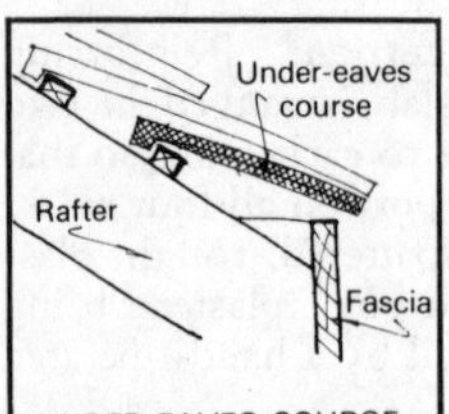

UNDER-EAVES COURSE

under-eaves tile A short tile in the **under-eaves course**.

underfloor heating A method of heating a building by burying heating elements in the screed of a concrete floor. These may be heated electrically or by hot water.

underlay 1. A layer of material used to isolate the roof covering from the substructure, such as the **sheathing felt** under asphalt roofing. 2. A waterproof membrane of plastic sheeting or waterproof paper between the sub-base and a concrete slab to deter water in the concrete from draining into the sub-base.

underpinning Support introduced under an existing building to prevent settlement during adjacent excavation or other building works.

under-purlin lining The internal lining of a sheeted roof in which the lining sheets are suspended under the roof **purlins**. Compare **over-purlin lining**.

underslating (or underlining) felt **Sarking felt**.

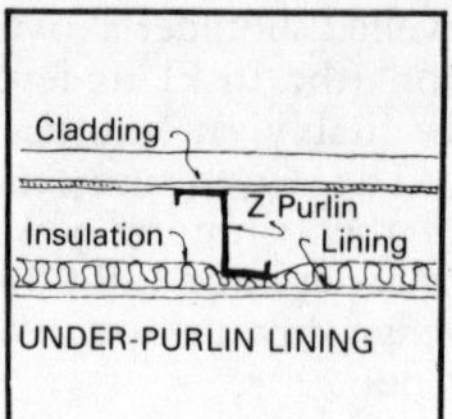

UNDER-PURLIN LINING

under-ridge tile A short tile laid as the top course of a tiled roof. **under-eaves tile**.

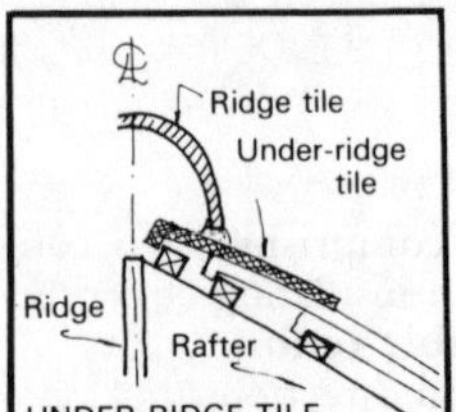

UNDER-RIDGE TILE

under tile A **tegula** in **Spanish** and **Italian tiles**.

undressed timber **Unwrought timber**.

uneven grain That grain in wood which shows considerable contrast between spring and summer growth.

unframed door A **batten door** or a **ledged and braced door**.

ungauged lime plaster A **lime plaster** made up of sand, lime and water only, without the addition of **Portland cement** or **gypsum plaster**.

unified thread A style of thread for a bolt or a **machine screw**, being either UNC (unified coarse) or UNF (unified fine); now largely superseded by ISO thread profiles.

uniformly distributed load (UDL) A load which is evenly spread over the length of a beam or the whole of the area of a structural slab. cf. **concentrated** or **point lead**.

union A threaded fitting for joining pipes.

union bend A bend with a union at one end.

unit heater A fixed space heater which transmits its heat by forced convection from a heating element enclosed in a sheet metal housing with air grilles towards the top and bottom, and incorporating a fan.

universal column or universal beam A hot rolled mild steel structural member in and I-shaped cross-section and in which each size of column or beam is made with a number of flange thicknesses to give a range of structural performances within the same overall size of section.

universal plane A hand plane with many interchangeable **cutting irons** to cut different mouldings, grooves, **tongues** etc.

unsound knot A knot that is softer than the wood around it.

untrimmed floor A floor carried on **common joists** only.

unwrought timber Timber which has been sawn, but not planed, and is therefore at a **nominal size** and not a **finished size**.

up-and-over door An **overhead door** operated as a single leaf.

UPEC classification A classification system for thin floor coverings, based on work done by the French Agrément Board, and relating to wear, indentation, behaviour in association with water and resistance to chemicals.

upside-down roof An **inverted roof**.

upstand 1. That part of a felt or **flexible metal** flashing or roof covering which is turned up against a vertical surface, and is then covered by a **counter flashing**. 2. A curb or similar vertical projection above a flat roof surface (*eg* around **rooflights**) against which the roofing is dressed up.

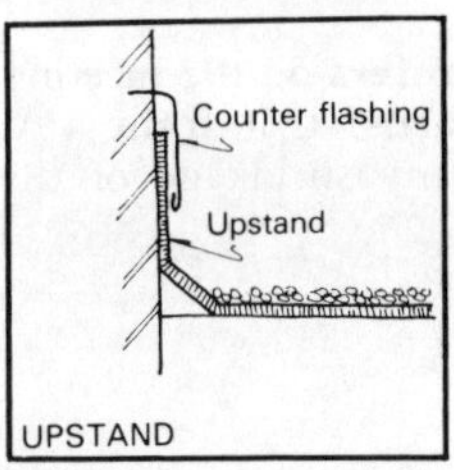

UPSTAND

upstand beam A beam, usually in a reinforced concrete floor or roof, which projects above the top of the slab as well as, or instead of, projecting below. The beam is monolithic with the slab.

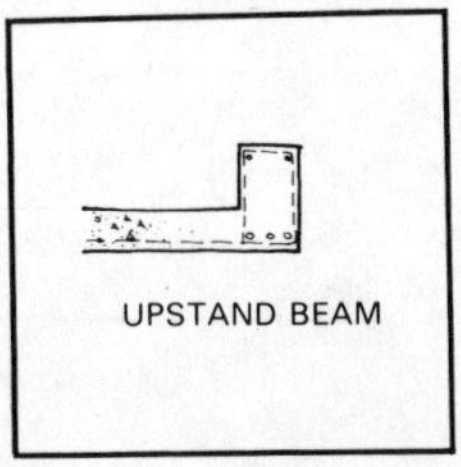
UPSTAND BEAM

uPVC Unplasticised **PVC**, used to form cold water, waste and overflow pipes, windows, etc.

urea-formaldehyde (UF) A **synthetic resin**, one of the thermo-setting group of amino-resins, used with an **accelerator** to manufacture a glue or foamed as an insulating material.

urea resin An amino-resin derived from urea.

urinal A sanitary appliance for the reception and flushing away of urine. It can be in the form of a straight slab, a series of stalls or bowls or a continuous trough and is either ceramic, of glazed fireclay, vitreous china, or stainless steel.

usable life **Pot life**.

U value A value, measured in watts per m^2 of structure per °C change in temperature, for the **thermal transmittance** through the structure from air to air on each side of the structure, and taking into consideration the thermal resistance of the external and internal surfaces as well as the thermal resistance of the materials of structure and any cavities in the structure.

V

vacuum forming The forming of a component by evacuating the space between the sheet **workpiece** and the die so that forming is effected by atmospheric pressure.

valley The intersection between two sloping pitched roof surfaces belonging to two abutting roofs, usually meeting at right angles. cf. **valley gutter**.

valley board A board used to support slates or tiles in a **laced** or **swept valley**, the board being nailed to the **valley rafter**.

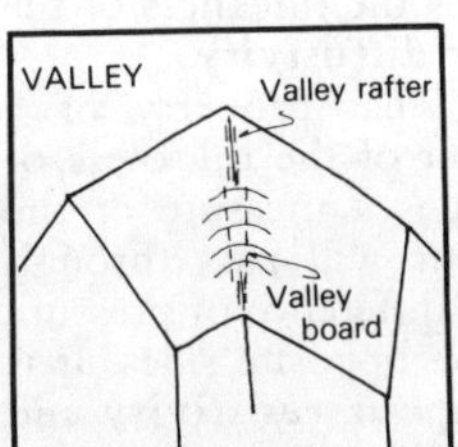

VALLEY

valley gutter A gutter on the line of a **valley**, lined with **flexible metal** or other waterproof material. cf. **secret gutter** and **box gutter**.

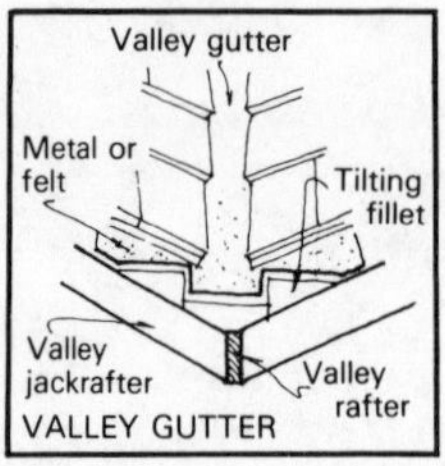

VALLEY GUTTER

valley jack (USA) A **jack rafter** connected to a **valley rafter**.

valley rafter The **rafter** on the line of the valley to which the **jack rafters** are connected and supporting the **valley board** or **valley gutter**.

valley shingle A **shingle** cut with its grain parallel to the valley and laid next to the **valley**.

valley tile A special concave tile shaped to form the valley waterproofing without the aid of a **valley gutter** or the lacing or sweeping of the tiles.

valve A device to regulate or completely shut off a flow.

vaporization The change of state from liquid to gas; also the extension of liquid into droplets in suspension to allow it to be finely sprayed.

vapour barrier An impermeable layer to prevent the penetration of water vapour from the interior of a building into the thickness of the structure, thereby avoiding **interstitial condensation**. cf. **vapour check**.

vapour check A material or part of a construction that offers a high resistance to the passage of water vapour. cf. **vapour barrier**.

vapour diffusance That property of a material which determines the rate at which water vapour passes through unit area of the material at a specific thickness under the influence of unit vapour pressure difference across the thickness of the material. cf. **vapour diffusivity**.

vapour diffusivity That property of a material (independent of the thickness of the material) which is a measure of the rate at which vapour will pass through the material when a difference of pressure exists between air on opposite sides. It is the reciprocal of **vapour resistivity** and is measured in gm/MN.

vapour permeance The rate of passage of water vapour through unit area of a material at unit difference of water vapour pressure between surfaces.

vapour pressure That part of the total pressure which is contributed by water vapour.

vapour resistance The overall resistance of a material or combination of materials of specific thickness to vapour diffusion in MN/g. Vapour resistance is used to express the resistance to vapour diffusion of thin membranes. That of other materials is their **vapour resistivity** multiplied by their thickness.

vapour resistivity That property of a material (independent of the thickness of the material) which is a measure of its resistance to vapour diffusion.

variation order A written instruction, usually issued by the architect, authorizing the contractor to vary the work from that described in the **contract documents**; such variation may involve an alteration in the contract value.

varnish Resin dissolved in spirit or oil and used as a finishing coat for painted surfaces. It sets to give a hard glossy protective coat.

vault 1. A masonry roof with an arched form and a curved **soffit**. cf. **barrel vault**. 2. A strong room, usually at basement level.

vee joint Small **chamfers** on the meeting edges of **matchboards**, that form a V shape and conceal any shrinkage of the boards.

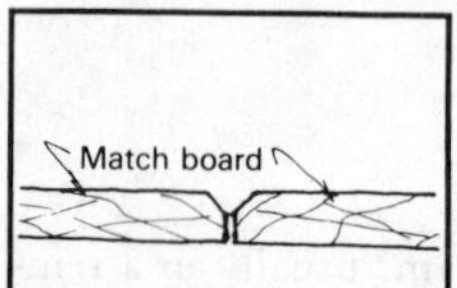

VEE JOINT

vegetable glue A glue made from vegetable ingredients; either a starch glue or protein glue.

vegetable soil The top layer of soil, above the top strata of subsoil, being the layer in which plant life grows. This layer of soil is always completely removed over the entire area of a building before building operations commence.

vehicle The liquid constituent of a paint, containing the **binder** and **thinner** but not the **pigment**.

veneer 1. A thin layer of wood used as a facing for another material, or for a less attractive timber; alternatively used in combination with other veneers to form a

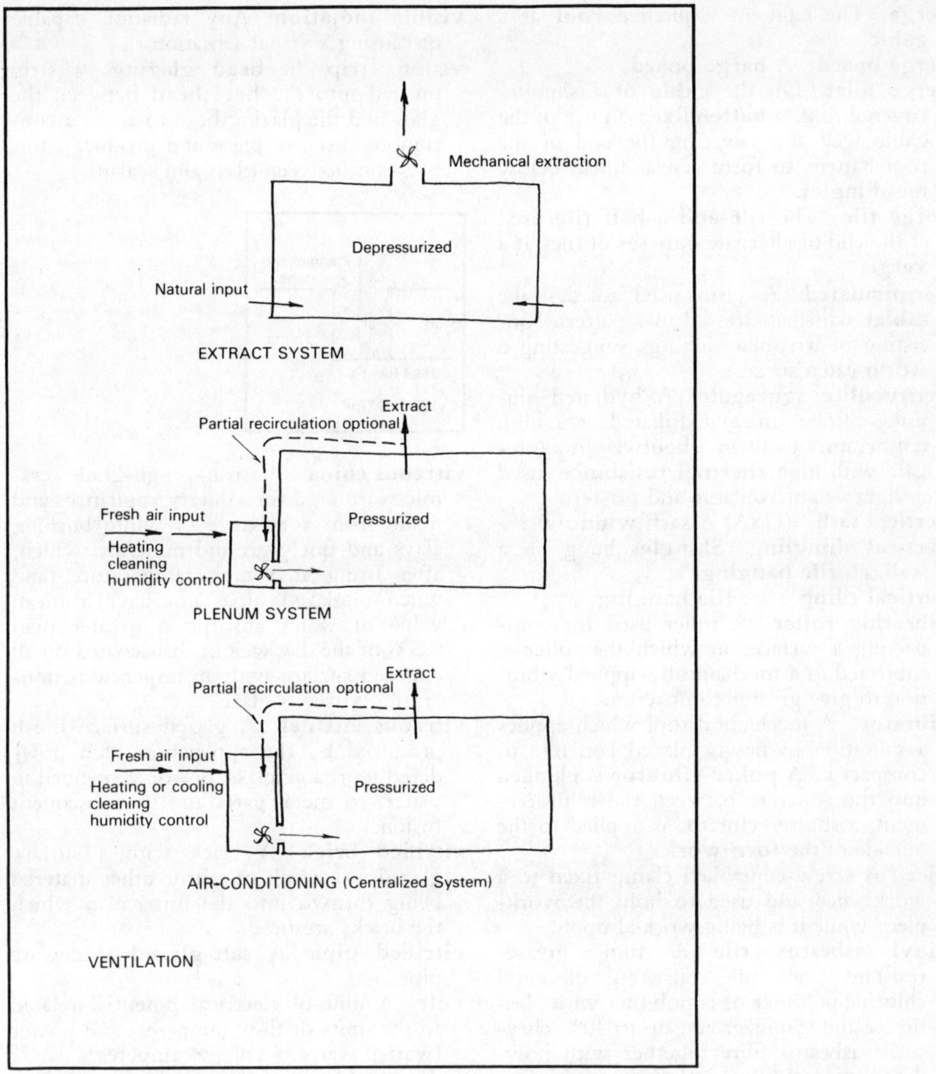

sheet material, such as **plywood** or **core-board**; the term is also used to describe a decorative **plastic laminate**. 2. (USA) A facing of brick, stone or other material on a wall of less attractive material.

veneered wall (USA) A **cavity wall**.

veneering The fixing of a decorative **veneer** on to a structural backing.

veneer tie (USA) A **wall tie**.

Venetian blind A window blind consisting of horizontal slats whose angle can be adjusted to exclude the sunshine. The slats can be raised to bunch at the window head or into a blind box.

vent An outlet to the outside air.

ventilated lobby A lobby which contains openable windows or permanent ventilation to the open air.

ventilating bead A **deep bead**.

ventilating brick An **air brick**.

ventilation The introduction of fresh air into an enclosed room, or the extraction of vitiated air from the room, either by windows or ventilators (**natural ventilation**) or by means of electrical fans (**mechanical ventilation**).

ventilation pipe or vent pipe or vent stack A vertical **soil pipe** whose upper end is open to the outside air to ventilate the drainage system and prevent the siphoning of the traps on the sanitary appliances.

ventilator A means of ventilating a room, ranging in size from an air brick to an industrial roof ventilator.

vent pipe or stack A **ventilation pipe**.

verge The edge of a pitched **roof** at a **gable**.
verge board A **barge board**.
verge fillet On the **gable** of a shingle-covered roof, a **batten** fixed on top of the gable wall and covering the end of the roof battens to form a neat finish below the **shingles**.
verge tile The **tile-and-a-half tile** used at the end of alternate **courses** of tiles at a **verge**.
vermiculated A term used to describe **ashlar** which is dressed in a pattern consisting of irregular sinkings suggesting a worm-eaten surface.
vermiculite aggregate A hydrated alumino-silicate (mica) exfoliated at a high temperature to form a lightweight aggregate with high **thermal resistance**; used in lightweight concrete and plaster.
vertical sash (USA) A **sash window**.
vertical shingling **Shingles** hung on a wall. cf. **tile hanging**.
vertical tiling See **tile hanging**.
vibrating roller A roller used for compacting a surface, in which the roller is subjected to a mechanically applied vibration to give greater compaction.
vibrator A mechanical tool which applies a vibration to newly placed concrete to compact it. A **poker vibrator** is plunged into the concrete between the reinforcement; a shutter vibrator is applied to the outside of the **formwork**.
vice A screw-controlled clamp fixed to a workbench and used to hold the workpiece while it is being worked upon.
vinyl asbestos tile A thin, grease-resistant floor tile consisting of vinyl chloride polymer or copolymer with plasticizer and stabilizer and up to 40% chrysotile asbestos fibre together with powdered mineral fillers and pigment.
vinyl resin A **synthetic resin** of the thermoplastic type obtained by the **polymerization** of **monomers** in the vinyl group.
viscosity The internal resistance to flow possessed by a liquid.
visible radiation Any radiation capable of causing a visual sensation.
vision strip In **bead glazing**, a strip pushed into the **heel bead** between the glass and the glazing bead to act as a continuous distance piece and produce compression between glass and sealant.

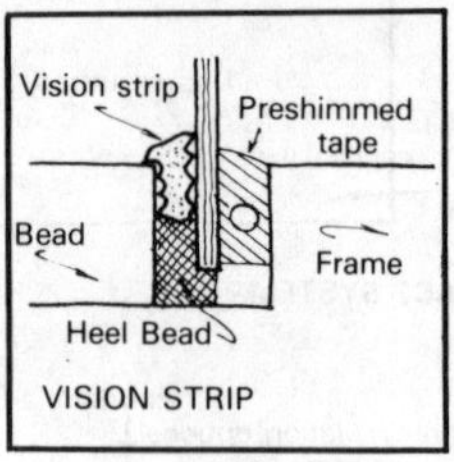

vitreous china A strong, high-grade ceramic ware used for sanitary appliances and made from a mixture of white burning clays and finely-ground minerals, which, after firing at a high temperature (and when unglazed) does not have a mean value of water absorption greater than 0.5% of the dry weight. It is coated on all exposed surface with an impervious non-crazing vitreous glaze.
vitreous enamel A glazed surface finish produced by the application of a powdered inorganic glass, dry or suspended in water, to metal parts and its subsequent fusion.
vitrified brick A brick with a surface glazed as a result of salt or other material being thrown into the furnace in which the bricks are fired.
vitrified pipe A **salt-glazed** stoneware pipe.
volt A unit of electrical potential related to the units of flow (amperes) and power (watts): watts = volts × amperes.
voltage Electrical potential expressed in volts.
volume yield The volume of **concrete** of a particular mix produced from unit weight of cement.
voussoir A wedge-shaped stone or brick in an **arch**.

W

waffle floor A flat slab reinforced concrete floor which is profiled on its underside by the use of a series of proprietary **forms** to reduce its weight.
waist The narrowest part of an object as in **waisted bolt** or the waist of a concrete stair – the dimension normal to the sloping underside of a flight from the internal

angle between the tread and the riser to the sloping face.

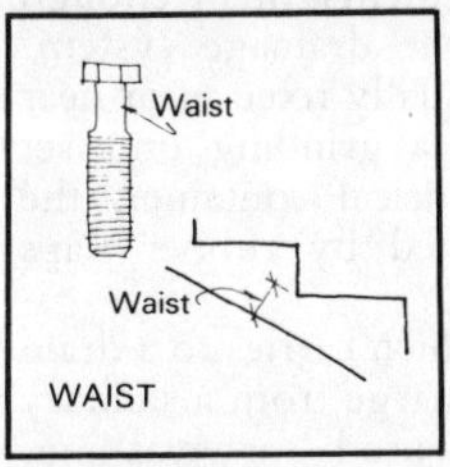

WAIST

waisted bolt A high strength bolt whose **shank** diameter is reduced below the root diameter of the thread, causing failure of the bolt to occur not as in a standard bolt (in the thread) but in the shank. The use of a special washer induces a more uniformly distributed load along the thread.

waling A horizontal member supporting **poling boards** in the **timbering** for an excavation.

walking line A line 450 mm from the centre line of the **handrail**, along which the **going** of **winders** in a stair is the same as that of the **fliers**.

walkway A permanent gangway or platform to give safe access along the length of a roof.

wall The vertical enclosing element of a structure, which may be either loadbearing (*ie* supporting the floor or the roof above) or non-loadbearing (*ie* an infill panel between structural columns.

wall anchor A steel strap which anchors a **common joist** into the brickwork which supports it and which ensures that the joist gives **lateral support** to the wall.

wallboard Boards manufactured as panels for surfacing walls, as opposed to insulating them, *eg* **gypsum plasterboard**.

wall column A structural column on the line of an external wall and built wholly or partially into the wall.

wall hanger A steel **stirrup strap** built into a wall and designed to support the end of a joist rather than building the joist into the wall.

wall hook A heavy spike or nail driven into a wall to carry a pipe or other member.

wall joint A joint in a wall parallel to the wall face.

wall panel A non-loadbearing walling element, often prefabricated (*eg* a precast concrete or timber wall panel), which is used to enclose the structure but not to support it. The wall panel is supported by the structural frame.

wallpaper Paper, usually printed with a decorative pattern, used for covering the

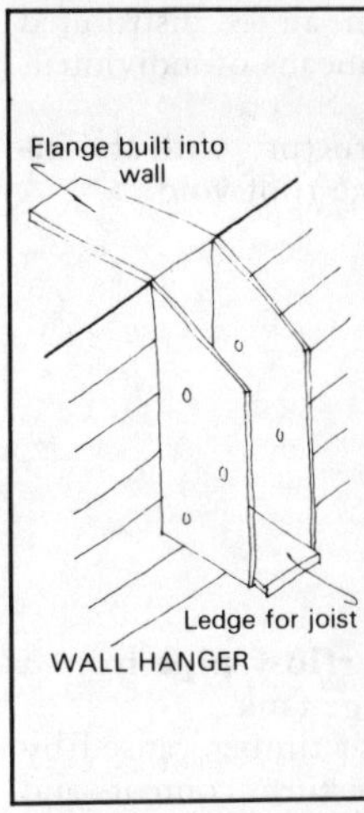

WALL HANGER

interior walls of buildings, either to give a decorative appearance or to cover up defective plasterwork and form a base for decoration. In the latter case it is known as **lining paper**.

wall piece A vertical member fixed against a wall and on which a **raking shore** bears. Also called a wall plate.

wall plate 1. A horizontal timber, set on the top of the wall, to which the roof joists or rafters are fixed. 2. In raking shoring, a vertical member on which the **raking shore** bears.

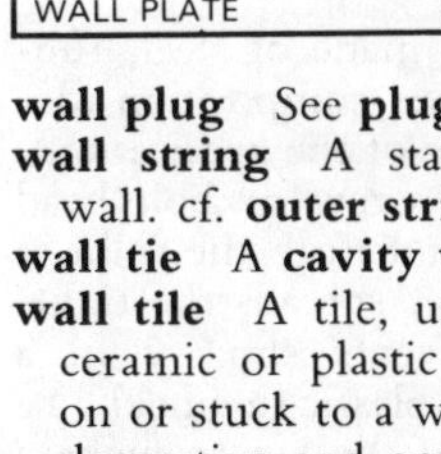

WALL PLATE

wall plug See **plug**.

wall string A stair **string** next to the wall. cf. **outer string**.

wall tie A **cavity wall tie**.

wall tile A tile, usually manufactured of ceramic or plastic material, which is set on or stuck to a wall to give it a smooth, decorative and generally impervious surface.

wane The original rounded sapwood surface, with or without bark, remaining on the edge of a square-sawn timber.

waney edged The description of the piece of timber having **wane** on one edge.

warm air heating A system of **central heating** in which air is heated and blown into the rooms by fans. Heating takes place either in a central heater unit, in which case the warm air is distributed through ducts, or by means of individual, low capacity heaters.

warm roof A roof structure with the insulating layer above the roof void.

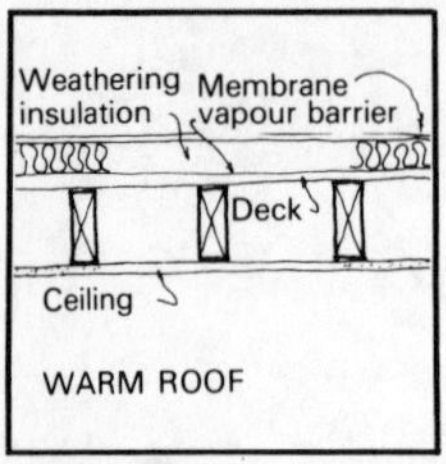

WARM ROOF

warning pipe An **overflow pipe** from a **cistern** or water storage tank.

warp Any distortion of timber caused by a change in the moisture content and often occurring during seasoning, *eg* **cup**, **bow** and **twist**.

wash (USA) A weathered slope on the upper surface of an element.

washability The ability of a paint finish (particularly a **water paint** finish) or other surface to withstand washing without damage.

washable distemper See **water paint**.

washbasin A sanitary appliance intended primarily for washing the hands, face etc. It is usually made of ceramic ware, but can be made of metal or plastic.

washboard (USA) A **skirting board**.

washboard grooves Grooves in the opposing faces of a **drained joint** which encourage water entering the joint to drain away from the interior of the joint.

wash-down closet A **water closet** in which the clearing of the pan is effected entirely by the flushing of clean water through the pan and not by suction. cf. **siphonic closet**.

washer 1. A flat ring made of steel, rubber, plastic or a fibrous composition (depending on the nature of the application). It is placed under a screw or bolt head and/or under the nut before the joint is tightened. The washer spreads the tightening load and prevents slip. 2. In a water tap, a rubber or plastic ring held by a nut to the **jumper** of the tap to make a watertight joint when the tap is turned off.

waste 1. An allowance made, in the measuring of the quantity of a material required for unusable material that will occur in the normal course of use; often taken as 10%. 2. Used water from washbasins, baths, sinks etc., but not including soil drainage from w.c.s, urinals, etc. 3. (USA) Building debris.

waste disposal unit An electrically operated mechanical device for reducing kitchen garbage into fragments small enough to be flushed into the drainage system. The unit, which is usually fixed in or near the sink, comprises a grinding unit set within a large cylindrical container, the orifice being protected by rubber flaps and a removable plug.

waste pipe A pipe which carries to a drain or **soil pipe** the discharge from a sanitary appliance which is used for washing, drinking or culinary purposes. The discharge passes through a **trap** to prevent drain smells from backing up the waste pipe.

water absorption The mass of water, expressed as a percentage of the mass of dry material, which is absorbed when the material is fully immersed in water for a specific time at room temperature.

water bar 1. A galvanized steel flat, bedded on edge in a groove in a concrete or stone sill. The flat either fits into a corresponding groove in a timber sill to form a barrier to water penetration through the joint, or alone performs a similar function at the foot of an external door. 2. A plastic, rubber or synthetic rubber strip set in construction joints and expansion joints of concrete to act as a barrier to the ingress of water.

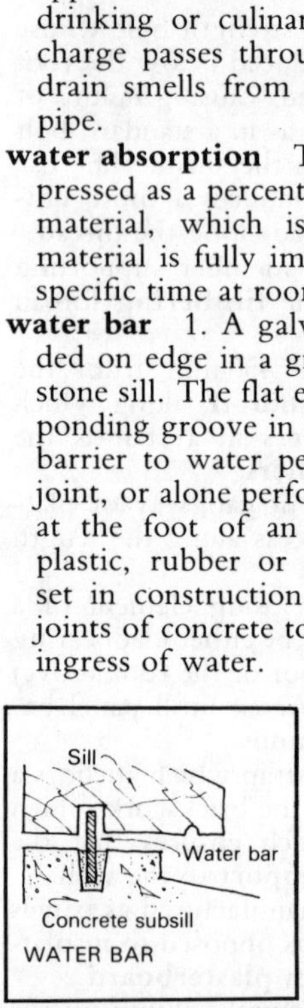

WATER BAR

water-bound macadam A material for road construction consisting of broken stone, slag or gravel interlocked and compacted with loam, sand and stone particles and water.

water/cement ratio The ratio between the total weight of water (including water absorbed by the aggregate) and the weight of cement in a mix.

water channel A **condensation groove**.

water check A wood **roll** or similar member projecting above the roof level at **verges** to prevent water from discharging over the roof edge.

water check groove A groove, such as a **throating**, to discourage the flow of water through a joint.

water-closet (w.c.) A sanitary appliance consisting of a pan for the reception and disposal of urine and faeces, usually manufactured in vitreous china, and fitted with a flushing arrangement from a **flushing cistern** to clean the pan and wash its contents to the drains. The flushing cistern may also be made of ceramic ware or plastic and may be integral with the pan or separate, joined by the **flush pipe**. cf. **siphonic closet**, **wash-down closet**, **squatting closet**.

water content The **moisture content**.

water gauge See **U-gauge**.

water joint A **saddle joint**.

water level A simple instrument used to set out levels on a site and consisting of two glass tubes connected by a rubber tube filled with water.

water paint Any paint in which the volatile part of the vehicle is wholly or mainly water; the paint therefore can be thinned with water. **Oil-bound water paint** and PVA **emulsion paint** have a **binder** which is, or becomes, insoluble in water. **Distemper** has a binder which is, and remains, soluble in water.

waterproof cement **Water-repellent cement.**

waterproofing The making of a surface or structure resistant to water penetration either by the application of a membrane, such as **asphalt**, **bitumen felt**, plastic, rubber, cement rendering etc., or by means of an integral treatment using a **water repellent** additive.

water repellent A material that, when applied to a mixture or surface, improves the resistance to moisture penetration; usually an integral treatment in the form of an additive to a mixture (concrete, rendering etc.) but the term is also used to describe a surface application.

water-repellent cement A **hydraulic cement** with a higher resistance to water penetration than ordinary **Portland cement**.

water retentivity That property of a **mortar** which encourages it not to give up water to bricks of high absorption, or, in the case of bricks of low absorption, does not allow its water to rise to the bonding surface. This characteristic aids the formation of a good bond.

water seal The water in a **trap**, which acts as a barrier to the passage of air through the trap.

water seasoning Seasoning of timber by first soaking the timber in water before air drying it.

water softener A piece of equipment that chemically treats water to remove the calcium and magnesium salts, thus reducing the hardness of the water, which would otherwise cause **furring** in hot water pipes and boilers, etc. Types include **base exchange** softeners and **soda-lime process** softeners.

water spotting A defect in a paint film; pale spots which are caused by water drops on the surface of the paint. These spots may, or may not, be permanent.

water stain 1. The discoloration of a converted timber which sometimes occurs as a result of its having become wet. 2. Water-borne colouring matter which is applied to wood to improve the colouring of the grain.

water table 1. The level of the **ground water** on a site. 2. A projection at the base of a wall with an inclined upper surface, intended to deflect falling water away from the wall.

water test A **drain test** in which a length of drain is stoppered at the lower end and filled with water with a head of 600 to 2,100 mm. The level of the water must not fall during the test period (usually 1 hour).

water vapour diffusance See **vapour diffusance**.

water vapour permeance See **vapour permeance**.

watt A unit of power, 1 watt equalling 1 joule per second.

wattle fencing A fence made up of hurdles consisting of thin hazel rods woven between thicker hazel uprights. Hurdle heights are from 600 to 1,800 mm.

wavelength The distance between two wave fronts in which the phases differ by one complete period. It is equal to the phase velocity divided by the **frequency**.

wavy grain A curved grain of attractive appearance typical of birch, sycamore and mahogany.

wax polish A polish used mainly for interior timber surfaces to maintain a gloss and protect the surface against wear; based on various natural and synthetic resins.

WBP adhesive An adhesive or glue that is 'weather-proof and boil-proof'. It is highly resistant to weather, micro-organisms, cold and boiling water and dry heat. A typical member of this category is **resorcinol formaldehyde resin** adhesive.

w.c. pan A pan, usually of vitreous china or stainless steel, for the reception of body waste products, forming part of a **water closet**.

wearing course The upper surface layer of a roadway which directly supports the traffic.

weather The **lap** of one shingle over the next shingle but one below it in shingle roofing.

weather bar 1. A **water bar**. 2. A term sometimes used to describe propriet-ary metal or wooden rain excluding devices for windows or doors.

weather-board 1. A moulding, housed into the bottom rail of a door, which throws the water which has run down the face of the door clear of the **threshold**. 2. A board in **weather-boarding**.

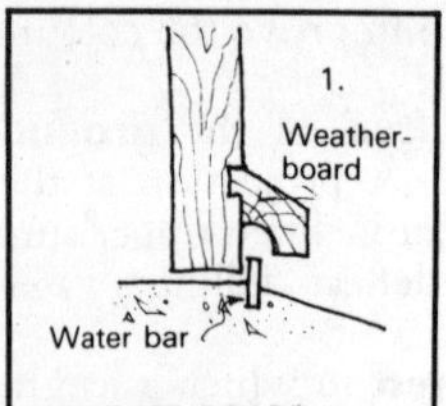

WEATHER-BOARD

weather-boarding An external cladding consisting of horizontal boards nailed to the outside of the building, each overlapping the one beneath, with or without a rebate in the upper board to receive the lower one. **Clapboard** has no such rebate; **shiplap boarding** does.

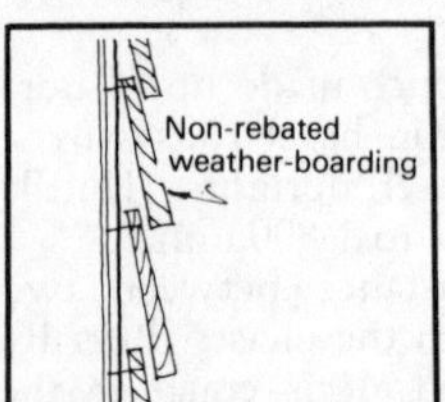

WEATHER-BOARDING

weather check A **drip** or **throating** or sometimes a **rebate**.

weathered Shaped so as to throw off water. cf. **weathering**.

weathered pointing A **weather-struck joint**.

weather fillet A **cement fillet**.

weathering 1. A slight slope given to the upper surface of a feature to throw off the water. 2. A change in colour or texture of a building material after exposure to the sun, rain and wind. 3. The break-up experienced by some untreated woods after prolonged exposure to the rain and sun; not to be confused with **decay**.

weathering steel A steel which has the property of forming a patina of fine and closely adhering rust under the action of the weather. This patina, once formed, inhibits further corrosion.

weather joint A **weather-struck joint**.

weather moulding 1. See **weather-board**. 2. A stone **drip** or **string course**.

weather shingling **Vertical shingling**.

weather slating **Slate hanging**.

weather strip A strip of metal, rubber or plastic etc. fixed in the rebate of a door or window to discourage the passage of draughts or water through the joint. A strip of nylon pile may also be used for this purpose.

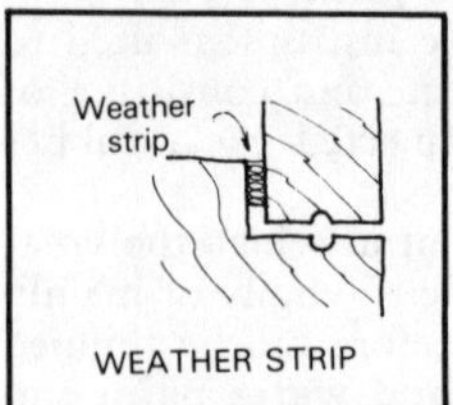

WEATHER STRIP

weather-struck joint A mortar **joint** smoothed by a trowel so that the upper edge of the joint is inset and the bottom edge is flush with the brickwork; the profile serving to lead water out of the joint.

weather tiling **Tile hanging**.

weaving The practice, at the junction of two shingle-covered faces at a ridge, hip or corner of two walls of setting the shingles so that the two faces lap each other alternately.

web The vertical part of a steel **universal beam**, **RSJ**, channel or **cold-rolled section** which separates the two **flanges**.

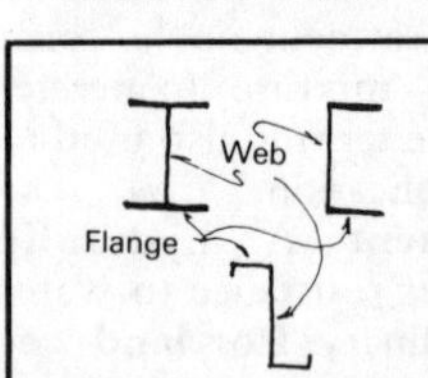

WEB

wedge A tapered piece of wood or steel used in joints to tighten one element against another. cf. **folding wedge**.

wedge coping A **feather-edged coping**.

wedged tenon A **stub tenon** fitted into a stopped or **blind mortise** of a slightly dovetailed shape. The tenon has one or more **wedges** inserted into sawcuts in its end before it is inserted into the mortise so that when it is driven home, the tenon will be forced open to fit the mortise.

weep hole A small aperture or pipe through a **retaining wall** or the outer leaf of a cavity wall to prevent the accumulation of **ground water** behind the wall, or water in the cavity above a **cavity tray**.

weight box The space in a **cased frame** of a sash window in which the **sash weights** travel.

weld A joint (or the action of making such as joint) between pieces of metal at faces rendered plastic or liquid by heat, or by pressure, or by both heat and pressure. A filler metal whose melting temperature is of the same order as that of the metal to be jointed may also be used.

welded joint A joint made by welding. cf. **weld**.

well 1. The horizontal distance between **flights** of a **stair**. 2. An open space passing through one or more floors, *eg* a **lift well** or a **light well**.

Welsh arch A small opening in brickwork, less than 300 mm wide, spanned by a stretcher (cut into a wedge shape) resting between two corbelled bricks with matching cut ends. A similar opening in stonework is also referred to as a Welsh arch.

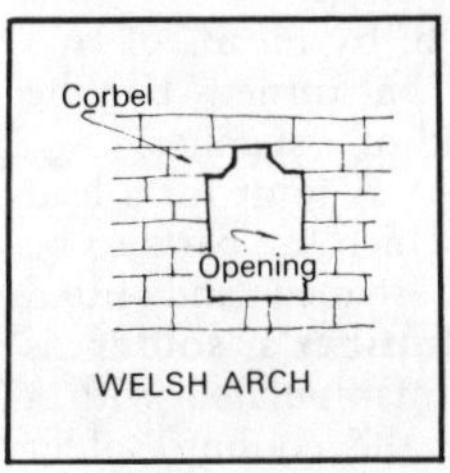

WELSH ARCH

welt A **seam** in **flexible-metal roofing** in which the edges of the metal sheets are folded together and dressed down flat. A single fold is called a single welt and a double fold a double welt.

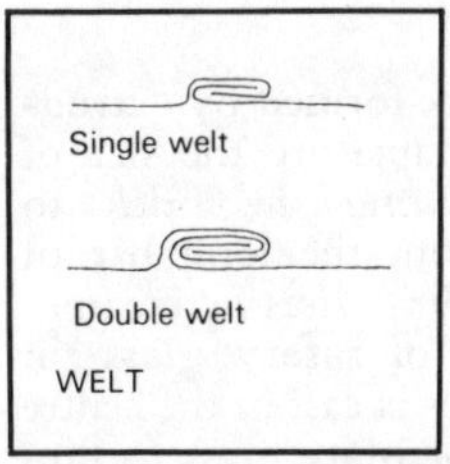

WELT

welted drip At the **eaves** or **verge** of a roof covered with **roofing felt**, the detail at the edge of the felt where it is turned down to form a drip and is then folded back and continuously sealed to the roof.

welted nosing In **flexible-metal roofing**, a junction between a horizontal and a vertical sheet in which a **welt** is formed at the top of the vertical sheet and dressed down on to the vertical surface.

welting strip A continuous strip of **flexible metal** secured along one edge to the structure, the other edge being folded to engage with the lower edge of a vertical covering sheet to retain it in position.

Westmorland slates Thick (6–15 mm) heavy **random slates** with a rough texture and rough edges and a predominantly grey/green colour; quarried in the English Lake District.

wet and dry bulb hygrometer An instrument comprising two similar thermometers, one with its bulb dry and exposed to the atmosphere, the other with its bulb covered with wet muslin, cotton or other absorbent wick. The latter thermometer will register a lower temperature than the former, due to evaporation of the water from the covering of the bulb, unless the air is saturated. It is used to determine the **relative humidity** of the air.

wet heating system A **central heating** system which is operated by means of hot water in pipes and radiators.

wet-on-wet Painting using special paints that can be applied one coat on another before the first coat is dry.

wet rot (***Coniophora cerebella***) A decay of timber caused by a fungus which flourishes in alternating wet and dry conditions. *Coniophora cerebella* is the commonest form of wet rot, and is not to be confused with **dry rot** (*Merulius lacrymans*).

wetting agent A substance that reduces the surface tension of a liquid, thus causing it to spread more readily on a solid surface.

wheeling step (Scotland) A **winder**.

whetstone A hard stone used to sharpen cutting tools by grinding.

white cement A Portland cement made from specially selected ingredients free from iron and other contamination, to which white pigment is often added.

white coat A plaster **finishing coat**.

white lead An opaque white pigment based on lead carbonate ($2PbCO_3.Pb(OH)_2$) which, because of its poisonous nature, is now less used in the manufacture of paint **undercoats** than previously.

white lead putty A weather resistant, good quality putty used to fill narrow gaps in woodwork, etc.

white lime **High calcium lime**.

white pigments The most common white pigments used in paint manufacture are: **zinc oxide, antimony oxide,** basic lead sulphate, **leaded zinc oxide**, **titanium white**, **white lead** and **whiting**.

white spirit A solvent composed entirely of petroleum products, used as a thinner for **oil paints** and **varnishes**; often called turpentine substitute.
whitewash **Limewash**.
whiting A cheap white pigment made from crushed chalk, also used as an **extender** and in the manufacture of **distempers** and **glazier's putty**.
Whitworth screw thread A British screw thread; now largely superseded by the ISO thread profile.
whole-brick wall A one brick thick wall.
wicket gate A small door, for the use of personnel, formed in a large industrial door or exterior gate; often referred to simply as a personnel door.
wide-ringed timber Coarse grained timber in which the **annual rings** are widely spaced, indicating quick growth. In **softwood** it usually indicates a less strong timber, but this is not as frequently true in **hardwood**.
Winchester cutting The two tiles at the ends of each course of **tile hanging** in a **gable**, next to the **verge**, which are both cut so as to allow one nail hole each.
wind or winding A form of warping of converted timber in which the timber twists about its longer cross-sectional axis throughout the length of the piece. cf. **warp**.
winder A tread at the change of direction of a **stair**, or wedge shape on plan.

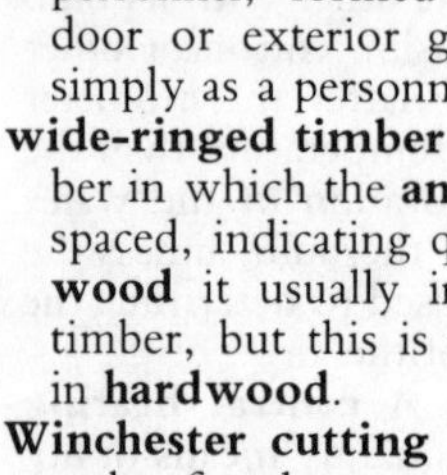

wind load The load produced by the wind pressure, which is a function of the wind velocity; it is usually, for design purposes, assumed to act normal to the building surface.
window A glazed opening in a wall, as opposed to a **rooflight**. A window may be openable to give ventilation (an opening light) or be non-opening (a **dead light**). Opening lights may be side hung (**casement**), vertical sliding (**sash**), horizontal sliding, vertical or horizontal **pivot-hung**, **top-hung**, **projecting top-hung**, etc.
window bar A **glazing bar**.
window bead A **guard bead**.
window board A horizontal board at sill level fixed like a shelf on the inside of a window.

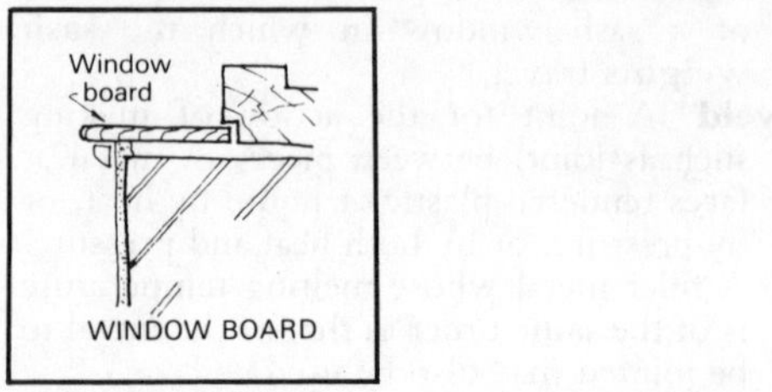

window frame That part of a window which surrounds the **dead lights** or the **casement window, sashes** or other **opening lights**.
window furniture The pieces of ironmongery attached to an **opening light** of a window to facilitate its opening and locking, *eg* **casement stay**, **sash fastener**, **sash lock** etc.
window lock A **sash fastener**.
window stile A **pulley stile**.
window stool (USA) A **window board**.
wind stop A **weather strip**.
wing nut A nut which, by means of two opposed wings can be turned by the fingers without the aid of a spanner.
wiped (soldered) joint A joint for a lead or lead alloy pipe in which the parts to be joined are prepared, shaped and fitted together. Molten **plumber's solder** is then poured on and manipulated with a pad of special cloth, the cooling solder being wiped around the pipe to give it the shape and size required for the strength of the joint.
wiping seal A draught seal on a sliding door or window in which the seal achieves its effect by distortion against the closing surface.
wire comb A **drag**.
wirecut brick A brick formed by extruding clay through an aperture the size of the **header** and cutting the brick to **stretcher** length, from the long bar of plastic clay, by a grid of wires in a frame.
wired glass A form of **safety glass** in which a mesh of wires is cast in the centre of a piece of **sheet** or **plate** glass to prevent the glass, on breaking, from falling apart.
wire gauge A method of specifying the diameter of wire by using a number which originally referred to the number of passes through decreasing diameter dies made by the wire during information. Many gauge types exist. In the UK, Standard Wire Gauge (SWG) has been most

common; it is now being replaced by metric diameters.

wire nail A nail made from round or elliptical wire, such as round-headed wire nails, **lost-head nails** or **panel pins**. There is a tendency for diameters still to be referred to in the UK by **wire gauge**, with metric equivalents.

wire scratcher A **devil float**.

withdrawal load The pull-out load that needs to be applied to a nailed or screwed connection to dislodge the fixing devices.

withe 1. One leaf of a **cavity wall**. 2. A **mid-feather** 1.

withy Flexible willow stick plaited together to form a cable which is used to tie down thatch.

wobble saw A **drunken saw**.

wood block flooring Quarter-sawn or flat-sawn blocks in widths of up to 90 mm, lengths of from 150–380 mm and thicknesses of from 19–38 mm nominal, with chamfered bottom edges to take excess adhesive in laying; laid on any solid sub-floor in **herring-bone pattern** or **basket weave** pattern.

wood brick A **fixing brick**.

wood chip wallpaper A wallpaper often used to cover cracked plasterwork. It provides a neutral background for decoration and also an irregular texture caused by chips or flakes of wood in the paper.

wood flour Fine sawdust, often used as an **extender** for glues.

wood mosaic Wood blocks, approximately 115 mm × 25 mm × 13 mm thick, arranged in groups to form approximately 115 mm squares in basket weave pattern. They are assembled on a backing sheet or on a removable upper sheet in 460 mm squares and are laid with bitumen adhesive.

wood preservative See **preservative**.

wood ray A **medullary ray**.

wood roll A round-topped piece of wood used to form the longitudinal junctions between sheets of metal in **flexible-metal roofing**. The wood roll is fixed to the decking and the sheets of metal are dressed over it, lapped and folded into a **welt**.

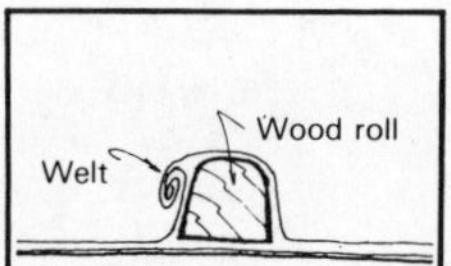

WOOD ROLL

woodscrew A screw with a drill thread for fixing into wood. cf. **machine screw**.

wood slip A **fixing fillet**.

woodwool nailing slab A woodwool **slab** with a timber fillet let into it along its centre line and flush with its upper surface; intended to receive nail fixings.

woodwool slab A slab, made up of long shavings of wood and cement, which has good thermal insulation properties combined with a degree of structural strength. Reinforced woodwool slabs have light metal channels let into their edges, the channels either being plain or having a tongue and a groove to interlock with the adjacent panels. The slabs are used as roof decking or as wall lining and can be plastered or spray coated.

woodworm A misnomer for the larvae of wood destroying insects, *eg* **common furniture beetle**, **death-watch beetle**, **longhorn beetle**, **powder post beetle** etc.

workability 1. A property of freshly mixed concrete, mortar etc. which determines the ease with which it can be manipulated and fully compacted. 2. Term used in grading types of timber to indicate their relative ease of working, from lignum vitae which is extremely difficult to work to spruce and poplar which are easy.

work edge (USA) The **face edge** of a piece of timber.

working The movement of timber as it swells and shrinks, reacting to changes in the **relative humidity** of its environment.

working drawing A drawing of a building or part of a building containing information, such as materials and dimensions, from which the building can be constructed. It can be drawn at various **scales** and consists of **cross-sections,** either horizontal or vertical, and **elevations** (cf **detail drawings**).

working edge The **face edge** of a piece of timber.

working life The **pot life** of a glue.

working load See **permissible working load**.

working plane A plane of reference used when establishing illumination levels, referring generally, but not invariably, to normal bench or desk height, or 850 mm above floor level.

working stress See **permissible working stress**.

working up The operation of **squaring** quantities and adding them up in the preparation of a **Bill of Quantities**.

workpiece The material being processed.
work size The size of component which is specified and to which it has to be manufactured. The actual size of the component should conform to this within specified permissible deviations or **tolerances**.
worm hole Damage to wood caused by wood destroying insects such as the **common furniture beetle**, **death-watch beetle**, **longhorn beetle**, **powder post beetle**.
wreath Part of a handrail in a **geometric stair**, which curves in both plan and elevation.
wreath piece That part of the **outer string** of a **geometric stair** which is below a **wreath**.
wrecking bar A **pinch bar**.
wrench A spanner, which is usually adjustable.
wrinkle A defect in veneering caused by a lack of glue in patches behind the **veneer**.
wrinkle finish See **ripple finish**.
wrot An abbreviation for wrought, as in **wrought timber**.
wrought iron An iron with a very low carbon content (0.02–0.03%), obtained by refining pig iron in a puddling furnace. It contains varying amounts of slag, some of which is expelled by compacting by hammering. Used for chains, hooks, bars, etc. and also for decorative iron-work.
wrought timber Worked timber which has been planed on one or more faces.
wye or Y A 45° branch pipe leading off a main drainage **run**.
wythe A **withe**.

X

Xestobium rufovillosum The **death-watch beetle**.
Xylenol resin A synthetic resin of the phenolic type manufactured from xylenol.

Y

yard gully A gully set in paved areas and intended to drain surface water from the paving; sometimes fitted with a bucket or grit basket. cf. **petrol intercepting trap**.

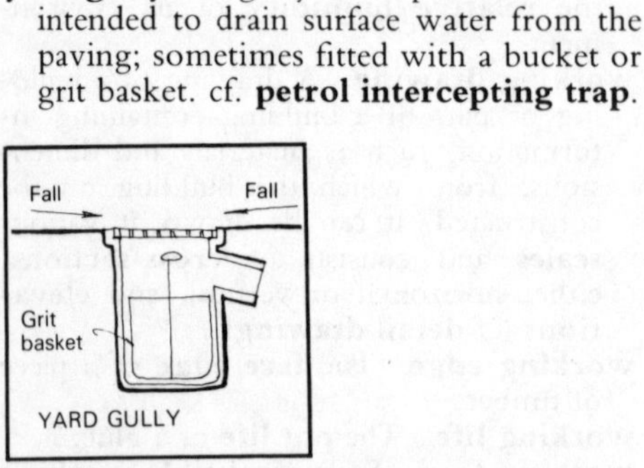

YARD GULLY

yard lumber (USA) **Lumber** graded in size, length and intended use.
year ring An **annual ring**.
yield point The **stress** at which the elongation of a material subjected to a tensile load begins to increase without further increase of the load.
yield stress The stress (load divided by the original area of the section in question) at which the component subjected to a tensile load begins to elongate without further increase of the load.
Yorkshire bond **Monk bond**.
yorky A slate having a curved cleavage.
Young's modulus The **modulus of elasticity**.
Y-type gasket A form of **structural glazing gasket** with a Y-shaped cross-section.

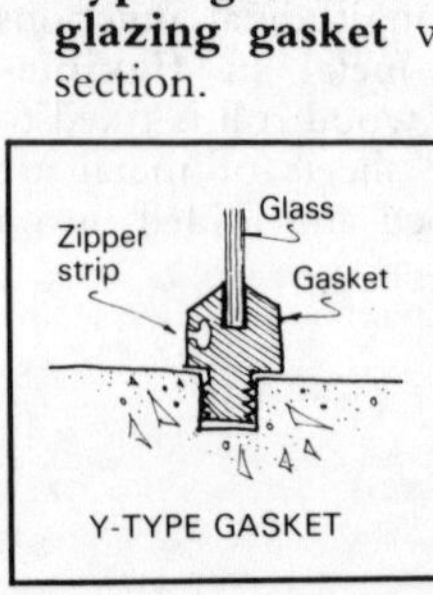

Y-TYPE GASKET

Z

zax A slater's tool with a blade like a butcher's chopper and with a point on its back which is used to punch holes in slates.

ZAX

Z corbel A **corbel plate** bent twice at right angles in the form of a Z.

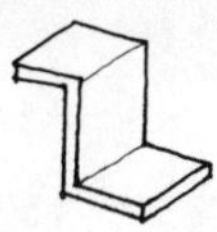

Z CORBEL

zed purlin A cold rolled steel beam in the shape of a 'Z', used as a **purlin** or **sheeting rail** in steel framed, sheet clad buildings.

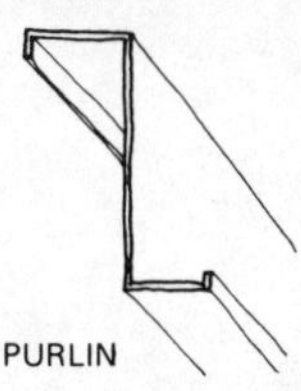

Z PURLIN

zeolite A mineral reagent used in the **base exchange** process to soften water.

zig-zag rule A metal or wooden rule with its sections pivoted together, not hinged as in a **fourfold rule**.

zinc A metal used in **flexible-metal roofing**, as a **flashing** material and as a coating in **galvanizing**.

zinc chromes Bright yellow **pigments**.

zinc dust Powdered zinc used in the manufacture of priming paints and in sherardizing.

zinc oxide A white **pigment**.

zipper strip A locking strip of tough synthetic rubber inserted into cavities in **structural glazing gaskets** of Y or H types after the positioning of the glass, thereby exerting compressive forces on the glass.

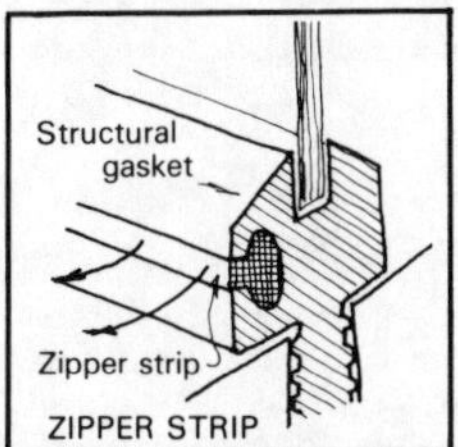

ZIPPER STRIP

zone In **dimensional co-ordination**, a space between two **reference planes** (horizontal or vertical), the space being provided to contain a component or group of components, which may or may not completely fill the space.

zoning The restricting by the Planning Authority of development in certain areas of land to buildings of a particular type, height or usage.